Dealing with Dragons, Bears, and Some Nice People Too

 ADST-DACOR DIPLOMATS AND DIPLOMACY SERIES
Series Editor MARGERY BOICHEL THOMPSON

Since 1776, extraordinary men and women have represented the United States abroad under widely varying circumstances. What they did and how and why they did it remain little known to their compatriots. In 1995, the Association for Diplomatic Studies and Training (ADST) and DACOR, an Organization of Foreign Affairs Professionals, created the Diplomats and Diplomacy book series to increase public knowledge and appreciation of the professionalism of American diplomats and their involvement in world history. This is the 76th volume in the series. During LYNN PASCOE's forty years as a U.S. diplomat and five years as U.N. under-secretary-general for political affairs, he was intimately involved with most of the great foreign policy issues of his time: relations with China, the end of the Cold War with the Soviet Union, humanitarian disasters in Asia, and the role of international organizations in peacekeeping and humanitarian efforts.

RELATED SERIES TITLES

NANCY BERNKOPF TUCKER, ed., *China Confidential: American Diplomats and Sino-American Relations, 1945–1996*
HENRY CLARKE, *A New Embassy along an Ancient Route in Uzbekistan*
HERMAN J. COHEN, *Intervening in Africa: Superpower Peacemaking in a Troubled Continent*
TED CRAIG, *Pakistan and American Diplomacy: Insights from 9/11 to the Afghanistan Endgame*
CHARLES T. CROSS, *Born a Foreigner: A Memoir of the American Presence in Asia*
ROBERT E. GRIBBIN, *In the Aftermath of Genocide: The U.S. Role in Rwanda*
BRANDON GROVE, *Behind Embassy Walls: The Life and Times of an American Diplomat*
PARKER T. HART, *Saudi Arabia and the United States: Birth of a Security Partnership*
DEANE R. HINTON, *Economic Diplomat: A Life in the Foreign Service of the United States*
CAMERON R. HUME, *Mission to Algiers: Diplomacy by Engagement*
KEMPTON JENKINS, *Cold War Saga*
CHARLES STUART KENNEDY, *The American Consul*
TERRY MCNAMARA, with Adrian Hill, *Escape with Honor: My Last Hours in Vietnam*
WILLIAM B. MILAM, *Bangladesh and Pakistan: Flirting with Failure in South Asia*
ARMIN MEYER, *Quiet Diplomacy: From Cairo to Tokyo in the Twilight of Imperialism*
KEITH W. MINES, *Why Nation Building Matters: Political Consolidation, Building Security Forces, and Economic Development in Failed and Fragile States*
RUFUS C. PHILLIPS III, *Stabilizing Fragile States: Why It Matters and What to Do about It*

For a complete list of series titles, visit <adst.org/publications>.

Dealing with Dragons, Bears, and Some Nice People Too

A Diplomatic Chronicle

B. LYNN PASCOE

AN ADST-DACOR DIPLOMATS AND DIPLOMACY BOOK

Washington, DC

Copyright © 2024 by B. Lynn Pascoe

New Academia Publishing/VELLUM Books, 2024

The opinions and characterizations in this book are those of the author and do not necessarily reflect official positions of the United States Government, the Association for Diplomatic Studies and Training, or DACOR.

All rights reserved. No part of this book may be reproduced or transmitted in any form or by any means, electronic or mechanical, including photocopying, recording, or by any information storage and retrieval system.

Printed in the United States of America

Library of Congress Control Number: 2024921542
ISBN 979-8-9900542-5-7 paperback (alk. paper)
ISBN 979-8-9900542-6-4 hardcover

 An imprint of New Academia Publishing

 New Academia Publishing
4401-A Connecticut Ave. NW, #236, Washington DC 20008
info@newacademia.com - www.newacademia.com

To my wife Diane who has been a wonderful partner
all along our journey

Contents

List of Illustrations	ix
PART I: IN THE FOREIGN SERVICE	1
Introduction	3
1 Getting There	9
2 A Junior Diplomat in Bangkok	15
3 Watching China from Washington	25
4 China in Turmoil	33
5 Carter's Washington and the Establishment of Formal Diplomatic Relations with China	65
6 Superpowers in Deep Crisis	85
7 Gorbachev and a New Era of Cooperation	127
8 China after Tiananmen	149
9 A Brief Return to Washington	187
10 Taiwan, China's First Democracy	201
11 Where is Nagorno-Karabakh?	245
12 Ambassador to Malaysia	253
13 Central Asia after 9/11	271
14 The South Caucasus and Eastern Mediterranean	293
15 "Help Indonesia Succeed"—The Tsunami	217
16 "Help Indonesia Succeed"—From Counterterroris to Public Health	343
PHOTO GALLERY	359

PART II: AT THE UNITED NATIONS   371

17 A New Challenge at the UN   373
18 Applying the New Approach to Africa   391
19 Georgia, Kyrgyzstan, and Cyprus   429
20 Promoting Democracy in Asia and Central America   447
21 The Middle East and the Arab Spring   473
22 Some Closing Thoughts   507

Index   516

Illustrations

Illustrations appear in the Photo Gallery that begins on page 359

1. The Pascoe family at the Great Wall, 1974
2. Lynn Pascoe at his desk at the U.S. Liaison Office in Peking, 1974
3. Lynn Pascoe and Barbara Bush with a Chinese official, 1975
4. Diane Pascoe and the girls always drew a crowd, Shanghai, 1975
5. American Staff at USLO under George H. W. Bush, 1975
6. Sending off Deng Xiaoping after his historic visit, 1979
7. Assisting Shultz at the Moscow Summit, 1988
8. After Taiwan President Lee's goodbye game of golf, 1996
9. July 4 ceremony in Malaysia, 2000
10. A view of the devastation in Banda Aceh, 2004
11. Loading a C-130 for Aceh relief with USAID chief Bill Frej, 2005
12. Former Presidents Bush and Clinton talk with President Yudhoyono before Aceh trip, 2005
13. Filling water bottles on the USS *Lincoln* for Aceh relief, 2005
14. USNS *Mercy* replaces USS *Lincoln* off Aceh, 2005
15. A grateful woman from Aceh, 2005
16. Diane and Lynn distributing aid after Yogyakarta earthquake, with Bill Frej, 2006
17. Briefing the Security Council, 2007
18. Discussing the Mideast with the Secretary-General and others, 2007
19. Arriving for talks at Somalia's Presidential Palace, 2010
20. President Barak Obama briefing the Security Council, 2009

Part I
In the Foreign Service

Introduction

Diane and I stood on the Aceh beach staring at the empty slabs of tiled concrete. Weeks before, houses had stood there, full of families with children laughing and parents enjoying the pleasures of a quiet Sunday morning. Then the gigantic killer tsunami swept them and more than 170,000 other Indonesians to their deaths. To our left, on higher ground, there remained a seemingly endless pile of debris, made up of pieces of those houses, children's toys, cooking utensils, palm trees, and even a cargo vessel that had ended up hundreds of yards inland. Standing there in the eerie quiet, my wife and I could only imagine what this village would have been like on the morning just before the wave hit. The stench of death was now gone, not like on my earlier trips, but those empty slabs and piles of everyday items stood as terrible reminders of the devastating human toll the tsunami took on Boxing Day of 2004.

As we rode back to Jakarta in the embassy's small two-engine plane, tossing violently in an electrical storm, my one consolation was knowing that the United States was doing all it could to help Indonesia and the people of Aceh get through this terrible tragedy. It was my responsibility, as ambassador, to make this happen. I had coordinated with the U.S. Pacific commander for an aircraft carrier, the USS *Abraham Lincoln*, and some sister ships to be deployed just offshore. Helicopter crews from the ships had flown thousands of missions, bringing fresh water to the isolated and desperate survivors and transporting the critically injured to the makeshift trauma center set up by our military and embassy doctors. The embassy had sent convoys of relief supplies by road, where possible, and provided medical help as soon as word of the disaster reached Jakarta. The U.S. Navy and Marines had begun their life-saving mission six days after the tsunami occurred. Several top U.S. officials had visited to provide resources and encouragement. Money was by now flowing to the relief efforts in large amounts—especially from Americans, who gave over $1.5 billion in public and private assistance; and we had helped the Indonesian government set up an agency that was using this money to rebuild Aceh effectively and without corruption. I was proud that U.S. government efforts had saved thousands of lives through this humanitarian effort. I also knew we were carrying out Secretary Colin Powell's simple instruction to me as he swore me in as ambassador: "Help Indonesia succeed."

Seventeen years earlier, my job had been to help another secretary of state, George Shultz, carry out the historic discussions with the Soviets that effectively brought an end to the Cold War. Shultz played the critical role in bringing President Ronald Reagan and General Secretary Mikhail Gorbachev to agree on vital issues involving nuclear weapons and global hotspots through his extensive negotiations with Soviet foreign minister Eduard Shevardnadze. They would meet in Moscow and Washington, building the trust and developing the compromises that changed the world's most fraught relationship. I had been part of the effort to get us to this point, first as deputy director of the Soviet desk during the "Evil Empire" period and then as deputy of Shultz's State Department Secretariat. During Shultz's meetings, his advisors normally worked into the wee hours of the morning, analyzing the Soviet comments and hashing out suggested points for him to use in his meetings the next day. My job was to ensure that Shultz's instructions were carried out, that he had full understanding of the views of his (often contentious) delegation, and that he had the information he needed at breakfast to review for the day's upcoming negotiations. It usually meant on the Moscow trips that we would work until two or three in the morning, catch an hour or so of sleep, shower, and be at Shultz's room by 6:00 a.m. This was Shultz's show; he and his top advisors deserve full credit for the breakthrough. For all of us who had a part to play in these events, there was a feeling of enormous satisfaction at being there as history was being made.

Earlier, in the mid-seventies I stood reading a wall poster near

Peking's Forbidden City under the watchful eye of the Chinese police. As one of the U.S. Liaison Office's two political officers, I needed to understand the meaning of the hundreds of Chinese political posters pasted up on walls that often included obscure historical references as part of the ongoing fight among opposing factions to control China's future. Mao was dying, and more traditional elements of the leadership, headed by Chou En-lai and Teng Hsiao-ping, had only a tenuous grip on power. The radicals in the Communist Party, led by Mao's wife Chiang Ching, were responsible for the massive destruction wrought by China's Cultural Revolution, and they were fighting hard to regain control. My job was to make sense of what was going on in China to a skeptical audience in Washington that wanted to preserve its opening to China and hoped the political infighting in Peking would simply go away.

Diane remained in Hong Kong for a couple of months with our daughters so that Kim could finish the school year. But she soon left behind the comforts of Hong Kong to make a home in the desperately poor and inhospitable Chinese capital. She found herself not only making all our bread, baby food, and meals, but also working part-time at the understaffed Liaison Office. Our family made the best of the experience, enjoying simple pleasures and sightseeing where we could. At work, I was having the time of my life in every political officer's dream job, keeping Washington informed of events in one of the world's most important capitals.

Some thirty-three years later, riding through the streets of Mogadishu in a South African armored personnel carrier wearing a helmet and flak jacket, I looked out on destroyed buildings as far as the eye could see. The devastated capital of Somalia had little in common with its past as a pleasant city perched above the Indian Ocean, where colorful villas provided homes for the rich. After its civil war and the continuing conflicts of the early nineties, Somalia had become the world's premier failed state, best known in the West for the U.S.-led UN force's failure to keep the peace. The nadir of that effort, depicted in the film *Black Hawk Down*, was a disaster that Washington tried to block from its collective mind. I was here, on the only road controlled by the ragtag African Union force that kept the beleaguered Somalia government in power, in my role as the United Nations under-secretary-general for political affairs.

Frustrated by the unwillingness of the world's leaders to even talk to him about Somalia, Secretary-General Ban Ki-moon gave me an instruction that sounded remarkably similar to Secretary Powell's before I went to Indonesia: "Figure out some way to fix Somalia."

Over time, we managed to get a reasonable government in place. The African forces gained control of most of Somalia's territory, the rampant sea piracy was virtually wiped out, and Somalia emerged with a commodity that had been in short supply for decades: hope. No one would call Somalia a garden spot today. Its government still does not function well, and the rebel groups continue to carry out terrorist actions. But we did prove that the United Nations can make a major difference even in the most unlikely places. Secretary-General Ban also instructed me to completely remake the UN's political department so it could help resolve impossible conflicts like the one in Somalia. We made considerable progress and found ourselves involved in conflicts in many parts of the world. While well outside my past experience, my five plus years at the UN proved to be an exciting and exhausting "retirement" job.

Usually when people hear the term "diplomacy," they think of earnest diplomats sitting around a large table in some ornate hall hashing out the terms of an agreement on some pressing international issue. The word may also evoke the image of elegantly dressed people dancing in a chandeliered ballroom or exchanging pleasantries at a reception. But the reality of life as an American diplomat is quite different. The world in which we work to advance the interests of the United States is constantly changing, and the need to understand the challenges we face to protect the interests of the American people are always pressing. There is also great satisfaction at being part of that passionately patriotic and devoted group of American diplomats, the men and women of the U.S. Foreign Service, who work each day around the world—often in some of its least appealing places—to protect and advance the interests of the people of the United States.

Diane and I faced the challenges of the Foreign Service together, but our family experiences would make an entirely separate book. In these pages, I've decided to stick for the most part to the job itself and the issues my colleagues and I faced. I make no claim for the results as a broad review of U.S. foreign policy or of the

Foreign Service experience as a whole. What follows is the story of one diplomat's experience, a kid from a small Missouri town on the Mississippi River who, blessed with a wonderful wife and family, was privileged to play his part in a collective effort to make the world a better and safer place.

1
Getting There

A Mark Twain Childhood

My childhood was fairly typical for a kid growing up in a small Midwestern town. La Grange, Missouri, a collection of some twelve hundred souls on the Mississippi River north of Mark Twain's hometown of Hannibal, had seen better days. The great humorist has been quoted as saying: "If you want to know about my childhood, read Tom Sawyer and Huckleberry Finn." Socially and psychologically, the area had changed very little by the time I grew up there a hundred years later. It was a simple life. My father owned a small furniture store that just managed to keep food on the table. Running the business by himself meant that he worked at the store all day, six days a week. With Sunday church attendance mandatory, family recreational activities were infrequent, but we did enjoy our annual family camping trips to one of the state parks. Naturally, I had to earn my own spending money, which I did by cutting lawns, helping my father in the store, "bucking bales" on nearby farms, and working as rough labor on road construction projects. My mother and I also worked together as custodians of our church. Like Twain's characters, life seemed totally normal to those of us living it. Money was tight, but I made enough to cover the limited opportunities to spend it.

My two brothers and I were blessed with caring and loving, if strict, parents, and my mother put me through the usual paces of childhood, including daily piano practice. My dad was the disciplinarian, a lifelong Marine, quite religious, and intensely patriotic. He expected his sons to be self-reliant and to get the college education he lacked. My doting maternal grandparents also occupied a key place in my childhood. My grandmother was always there with a hug and a smile. My grandfather loved to tinker, and his junk-filled garage was a young boy's delight. We made great contraptions, like a motorized kid's car and a pedal boat (it sank on first launch, so we rebuilt it) from scraps of metal retrieved from a junk yard.

My friends and I spent a lot of time in the summer swimming in nearby lakes and ponds or fishing in the Mississippi. As was typical of the time, I worked my way up through the Boy Scouts, looked forward to the usual Halloween pranks with a gang of boys (we never managed to push over the town's one remaining outhouse), and occasionally downed a can of Pabst Blue Ribbon after a scout meeting when we could talk one of the local winos into buying it for us. Overall, it was an ordinary small-town boy's existence.

The town's school was weak academically, but the teachers wanted to make sure we learned the basics. Good grades came easily, but I would invariably get marked down for being too talkative or unruly. At one point a teacher, fed up with my inability to keep quiet, made me stay after school and talk continuously for an hour and a half, probably useful training for a future diplomat. The town had a tiny library, but as a young boy I read all of its adventure stories and spent a fair amount of time thumbing the set of encyclopedias my father had purchased in the hope of furthering our education.

By junior high school, we had a few young teachers—mostly students or recent graduates who would work for the meager pay—who lit a fire about the possibilities of the outside world. One college student, Bob Gray, an academic star at the nearby Culver-Stockton College, taught math during my sophomore and junior years. Bob became a mentor (and a lifelong friend) who arranged for me to enroll in Culver as a part-time student. I did my freshman college work during my junior and senior years in high school. It was great fun and intellectually stimulating to study there and attend college events. But the most interesting and rewarding experience at the time was the pursuit of an intelligent and extraordinarily pretty girl named Diane Wolfmeyer from the town of Keokuk, Iowa, thirty-five miles upriver from La Grange. We had a great time attending events at three schools, and I confess I pursued her relentlessly.

On graduating from high school in 1961, I went off to join Bob at the University of Kansas (KU) to study mathematics. That fall I moved to a fraternity house (I had joined at Culver), an experience that made me a devoted fan of the movie *Animal House*. Fraternity life turned out not to be my cup of tea. I found it hard to keep up both the social schedule and the grades I had come to expect of myself. More to the point, I was desperately lovesick for Diane, then a freshman at the University of Iowa. As the year went on, I also became less enamored with mathematics and began wondering what I should do with my life. My mind was made up one Friday after a teacher spent the entire hour proving some advanced theorem and announced we would finish the proof on Monday. I just sat there, stunned. No way would I spend the rest of my life teaching math. By this time KU had done its job broadening my horizons, and I had developed a strong interest in politics and foreign affairs.

In September 1962 Diane and I married (the smartest decision I ever made, despite our youth) and headed back to Kansas. (Diane interrupted her education for a year to earn enough money for us to survive.)

Education of a China Hand

In this post-Sputnik era, the National Defense Education Act (NDEA) had authorized serious federal money to fund studies of foreign affairs and foreign languages, including a new Chinese studies program at Kansas. While finishing up my math courses, I soon found myself engrossed in studying Chinese and world affairs. I remember telling Diane during a college performance of *Paint Your Wagon* (probably while they were singing "I Was Born under a Wanderin' Star") that I had seen posters about the Foreign Service that sounded very interesting. Diane, as usual, thought I was in my dream mode (neither of us had any idea what the Foreign Service was about), but she was always willing to humor my whims. The whole concept sounded intriguing to a small-town kid from Missouri.

A leader of KU's China program, Bob Burton, suggested I consider attending graduate school at Columbia and sent a letter of introduction to his old friend Doak Barnett, who headed the program there. Barnett set up an interview at Columbia, which turned out to be in the week of President Kennedy's assassination. Given our tight resources and Diane's preparations for some pre-Thanksgiving exams, we decided that I would take the bus by myself to New York. Somewhere along the highway late in the evening, I heard a fellow passenger say that KU classes were canceled for the week. As it did not occur to me that campuses across the country including Columbia would also close, I called Diane at the next stop to ask if she would like to go to New York with me. She agreed, drove our beat-up old Plymouth across half of Missouri in the middle of the night, and we headed off to New York as only two totally clueless college kids would do.

Of course, when we showed up at Columbia at the appointed time for the interview, the gates were locked tight. I did manage to call the professor I had been scheduled to meet. He clearly had considerable experience with crazy college students and graciously agreed to come in from New Jersey to do the interview. Fortunately, he recommended that I be admitted to the master's program. After I graduated from KU in June, we returned to Keokuk for the summer. Diane worked in a factory making rubber gaskets for automobile doors and I worked as a rough laborer in a steel mill where my father-in-law had been employed for years. Staying with Diane's parents, we earned enough money for Columbia's tuition and some of our living expenses in New York.

The two years at Columbia were wonderful ones for us. Diane again supported us, working in a medical laboratory the first year and studying cancer research at Sloan-Kettering on a stipend the second. By then, I also had a small stipend as Doak Barnett's research assistant. We led the lives of typical college students, studying hard but trying to absorb as much as we could of the big city we came to love. With China courses from Doak Barnett, Don Zagoria, Edmund Clubb, and Martin Wilbur and Soviet-related classes from Zbigniew Brzezinski and Marshall Shulman, plus other political science and language courses, Columbia provided a great learning experience that later proved invaluable in trying to understand the world's events.

The growing anti-Vietnam War fervor among students at the

time made joining the government something akin to aiding the enemy. Nevertheless, I took the Foreign Service Examination in 1965, passed the written and failed the oral part. My oral test got off to a bad start when my interviewer asked a question about art history and various genres of painting. As a Midwestern math major from a small town in Missouri, I probably could not have defined the word genre, much less compared various artists or sound intelligent about the nuances of art history. The panel suggested I come back and try again the next year. Naturally I read up a bit on art history, but mercifully, the second panel asked me a general question about the Johnson administration's foreign policy and the Vietnam War. They may have known about a letter several of my fellow graduate students and I had published in the *New York Times* warning that U.S. escalation might bring China into the war; or it may just have been their standard opening question, given that the issue was so topical. Whatever it was, the question allowed me to talk at considerable length on a subject that I knew, or could pretend to know, something about. This time they put me on the Foreign Service roster.

With the Vietnam War heating up and growing draft calls, I had other exam obligations in New York, including military physicals at the Battery and an unforgettable trip to a Harlem police station—complete with shattered glass, smashed walls, and unsavory-looking characters—to be fingerprinted for a background check. We made our first trip to Washington in this period for interviews with both NSA (which, of course, liked my combination of math and Chinese training) and the CIA. Both offered me considerably more money than the State Department Foreign Service Officer's starting salary of just under $7,500 a year; but I was put off by the polygraph test, the generally secretive atmosphere, and the stigma of intelligence work. We chose to stick with the Foreign Service.

After two years at Columbia and with my master's coursework complete, Diane and I departed for Taiwan for more Chinese study at the Stanford Center in Taipei (paid for by the Ford Foundation and an NDEA Fellowship). We took a bus trip across the United States with a stop to see our parents in Iowa and Missouri and an interview with my draft board to see if they would allow me to leave the country. With a father deeply proud of his World War II service as a Marine, a young Marine lieutenant uncle killed leading his men in battle on Okinawa, and an older brother in the Army, I certainly had no problem doing my duty if the draft board called. The board decided, however, that since I was the only one from northeastern Missouri studying Chinese, I should finish the training, and they could then review my fate a year later after we returned to the United States.

Language training in Taiwan was fantastic—the teachers were among the best in the world. As we learned the language, we began to become familiar with Chinese culture and absorb the surrounding atmosphere. Whenever we could, we would go out on our bicycle—Diane riding side saddle Chinese style on the back rack—to explore the city and savor Taiwan's superb cuisine. I also developed a sense of the incredible pressure Taiwan's school system put on its students. In our Japanese-style duplex, the neighbors' twelve-year-old daughter did her homework on the other side of the wall, reciting out loud in the traditional Chinese fashion. I considered myself a serious student, but she was always at her studies before I began in the evening and was still going strong when I went to bed around midnight.

We had an interesting entrée into Taiwan's society when Diane was recruited by the Taipei Medical College to improve the quality of their cancer research program. The school was getting bizarre results from its examinations of cancer specimens, and one of Diane's mentors at Sloan-Kettering recommended her as an expert on the subject. In fact, she knew more about how to identify various forms of cancer cells than anyone on the island at that time, and they arranged to pay her as an assistant professor. As the medical school was run and almost entirely staffed by Taiwanese, we gained the friendship and heard the candid views of the people, under heavy pressure by the Chiang Kai-shek regime that had dominated the island after retreating from mainland China in 1949.

2
A Junior Diplomat in Bangkok

Our Foreign Service adventure began in August 1967. Before departing Taipei, I got my first taste of the bureaucracy's wartime mindset. At my last interview at the Embassy in Taipei, the security officer pulled out the letter we had sent to the *New York Times* and asked me about my political views. I responded indignantly and felt sufficiently feisty to tell the guy I didn't think what I said when I was in graduate school had any bearing whatsoever on whether or not I would make a good Foreign Service Officer. He harrumphed, but that ended the issue. In Washington, I was amused (and relieved) that one of our first introductions was to the credit union. We needed it because we had no money for rent or food, and my first Foreign Service check only appeared in our bank account some six weeks or so after arriving in Washington. The introductory A-100 class provided a nice way to meet colleagues in those days, but imparted little information about the career on which we were about to embark.

When assignments time came in October, most of the single men found themselves headed to Vietnam for the U.S. civilian advisory effort known as CORDS. We were assigned to nearby Bangkok. Before we left the country, I had to again appear before my draft board in Missouri. They decided I should go to Bangkok as a diplomat rather than to Vietnam as a soldier. Diane and I headed off to start our new career—but with one more little adventure before we arrived in Bangkok. When we were students in Taiwan, we had visited Hong Kong, and we decided to stop over again for a couple of days on our way to Bangkok. Short of cash, we stayed with our newly minted diplomatic passports in the same crummy hotel we had been to the year before. A fire broke out in one of the nearby rooms, but Diane, pregnant and suffering a terrific case of morning sickness, had no intention of getting out of bed. I listened to her moans and watched the fire, trying to figure out how to get out of the firetrap if it spread in our direction. Fortunately, it didn't. Chungking Mansions still stands on Nathan Road in Kowloon a half century later, looking as derelict as ever.

While Bangkok offered very little opportunity to use our newly acquired Chinese (other than ordering Chinese food in restaurants) and the State Department chose not to train us in Thai, Thailand turned out to be a fascinating assignment and a good introduction to life in the Foreign Service. Assigned to what was supposed to be a rotational post, I did six months of consular work and then was "stuck" in the plum junior officer job in the Political-Military Section for the rest of the tour because Washington ended the rotational tours. When we arrived, as the lowest ranking officer in the embassy, I was put "in charge" of the embassy warehouse over the Christmas break. I had no clue what my duties entailed other than being there to watch over things. My mischievous local staff decided to break in this young green American by taking him to an open-air restaurant famous for its deep-fried sparrows. Thanking my stars for our student experience in Taiwan, I dug right in, apparently passing their initiation.

The Consular Section in Bangkok reflected the chaotic atmosphere in those Vietnam War days. Naïve young soldiers would bring in their new brides only to discover they were a decade older than themselves and had been working as prostitutes for years. It was always sad to see the faces of these guys when you had to tell them that someone in Washington had looked at their application and concluded that their precious little child had been conceived two months before the two lovers had met and was therefore not a U.S. citizen. Ladies of the night would flash their wares to the young male consular officers to try to improve their chances of getting a visa, and the American contracting companies seemed to have attracted every scam artist in America to the boundless funds produced by the American war effort.

Down through the years, I have been enormously impressed with the quality and dedication of most members of the Foreign

Service and find them truly among the elite of our nation. But a big embassy like Bangkok in wartime attracted some less-desirable types. After coming in one morning feeling proud and happy to be serving my country and my fellow Americans, I was advised by a middle-grade boss who obviously was going nowhere in his career that I should bring in an extra suit jacket to put on the back of my chair. I could then take as long a break as I wanted since my colleagues would assume I was in the bathroom or conferring with a colleague. I was crushed by the stupidity and crudeness of this "advice." In general, though, I came away from the experience with great respect for our consular colleagues. There is nothing like a few weeks at the visa window to give deep insights into the creative capacity of many men and women to lie with a perfectly straight face. Once while providing consular services, I had to adjudicate between a ship's captain and one of his crew. Both knew all the legal loopholes involved; I didn't have a clue what I was talking about beyond what I had read in the regulations. I guess the manual and I made the right decision because they went their merry way, apparently satisfied.

I spent the next eighteen months in the embassy's Political-Military (Pol-Mil) Section. With 47,000 U.S. military personnel inserted into a country proud of its ability to fend off colonial and neocolonial pressures by manipulating foreigners; with massive military supply lines and incessant bombing of neighboring countries (Vietnam, Laos, and, as it turned out, Cambodia); with no Status of Forces Agreement (SOFA) to provide protection for our troops; and with a military-run government that (aside from the king) had only marginal legitimacy with its people—frictions between the Thai people and their American guests popped up everywhere. Our job was to somehow make this all better and allow the military to prosecute the war while keeping the Thai mollified and still friendly once the war was over, a challenging task to say the least. The Pol-Mil Section was mostly a six and a half day a week job, with Sunday afternoons and some U.S. holidays off. I once made the mistake of suggesting to our boss that we might have the next day's staff meeting a bit later since it was a major Thai holiday. He looked at me and growled: "Those aren't real holidays," and the meeting began as usual at 8am.

I had two primary responsibilities in Pol-Mil. The first was to assist a very able Air Force colonel and lawyer (who later became the Air Force judge advocate general) assigned to the embassy staff to negotiate a Status of Forces Agreement between the United States and Thailand. As often happens, we had put our forces on the ground to get on with the war without delay and then began demanding that the Thai sign an agreement with us along the lines of the SOFAs we had with Japan, Korea, and Europe to keep our forces from being subject to capricious local law enforcement. The Thai cherished their refusal to sign unequal treaties with colonial powers in the nineteenth and twentieth centuries and were not about to agree at this late date to formally give up jurisdiction over foreigners in the country. But being Thai, they would never put it that way. Instead, we endured endless hours of polite and circular discussions that went nowhere. The discussions continued for years after I left.

I quickly learned from the experience that negotiations are not always about finding agreement. In this case, the U.S. military took consolation in knowing that they had one of their top men trying to get an agreement; the Pentagon and State Department made themselves feel better by periodically demanding that we get the Thai to agree to a deal immediately; the Thai Foreign Ministry polished their skills in leading us on and never flatly saying they would not sign while upholding their right to apply their laws to our people, although never actually exercising the power except in the most egregious cases; and the U.S. continued to prosecute the war as it saw fit with little interference from the Thai. It all worked, although not without considerable friction.

It was a proud moment the day I accompanied my boss for my first diplomatic negotiation. We went to the Foreign Ministry to talk with the foreign minister's chief assistant, a brilliant young Thai diplomat named Birabhongsi, who later became a popular Thai ambassador to the United States. The discussions began along the usual lines—earnest explanations of our talking points about the value of a SOFA, possible compromise language for the text, and great protestations from Bira about their goodwill and hopes to find common ground but without any give whatsoever in the Thai position. About halfway through the conversation I reached for a sweet, knocking over my glass of sparkling water and dousing all the important papers on the table. My embarrassment was acute. It was definitely not a great way to start a diplomatic career. Needless to say, for the next forty-five years I carefully noted where the drinks were placed during such meetings.

My second responsibility in Pol-Mil was as nebulous as the overall aims of the section—to improve relations between our soldiers on the bases and the people surrounding them in the countryside. This included everything from encouraging the military to carry out more civic action programs in their environs, finding ways to minimize the disruption of 24/7 bombing raids on the airbase neighbors, trying (in vain) to get the military to control the massive prostitution industry around its bases, working with contractors whose mandate was to indoctrinate our troops to be sensitive to local customs and norms, and trying to get the PX and Commissary systems to adopt policies to minimize leakage to the black market (another total failure, since promotions in the system were based on increased sales volumes and anything damaged—like a scratch—was considered fair game to sell on the local economy).

I logged many miles on C-130 shuttles, going from base to base trying to make some impact. The only real thing that helped was the Thai capacity to take the inconveniences of the foreign "occupation" in stride, maintaining their famous hospitality and making billions of dollars in the process. (As I read the headlines from Iraq and Afghanistan, it reminded me how little the United States had learned in the past half century about managing its military campaigns abroad and the massive dislocations that go with the billions of dollars that flow through the Pentagon budget. The contracting system doesn't appear to have improved. Grand plans are laid out that are never fulfilled, and our civilian interests and structures are overwhelmed by the immense funds allocated to the military.)

One of my "responsibilities" bordered on farce. My superior told me when I arrived in the political-military section that I was the embassy person responsible for something called "Tommy's Tours." It didn't take me long to figure out that I would have nothing to do on that topic unless something went terribly wrong. Tommy's Tours was the R&R program in Thailand for U.S. forces fighting in Vietnam. After the horrors of combat (or maybe a less dangerous job) in Vietnam, large groups of U.S. military personnel would come to Thailand for five days of heavy drinking, whoring, doing drugs, and practically anything else they could think of before returning to the possibility of being injured or killed in the war zones of Vietnam. Tommy was the former chief of staff of the Burmese Air Force, and his partner was the (very active) Thai deputy chief of staff.

The program was totally corrupt but highly effective in delivering on its promise of troop recreation in Thailand. As far as we at the embassy knew, almost all American servicemen got back on the plane at the appointed times. No reports were filed about any of the numerous abuses, murders, and property destruction that undoubtedly occurred (families were paid off for silence), and brawls were handled quietly as routine parts of the enterprise. To this day, a part of me marvels at how well the whole thing worked from an American point of view; but one definitely had to leave all scruples at the door when dealing with this huge and incredibly lucrative enterprise. As for my "responsibilities," I was never quite sure whether my boss had been kidding or signaling that I would be the embassy fall guy if something went wrong.

I have always seen the Vietnam War as the low point for the U.S. government's internal integrity, although Iraq came in a close second. Even a Missouri skeptic like me continued to be surprised by the capacity of ranking American officials to lie to each other and themselves, keeping up pretenses even when the entire effort was going terribly wrong.

One example struck me as particularly shocking. When the United States and Thailand discussed the basing of U.S. bombers in Thailand to pursue the war against Vietnam, the American side formally agreed that the warplanes would not bomb targets in Cambodia. Responsibility fell on the American ambassador to ensure that the U.S. honored its commitment. The coordinates for each day's bombing raids out of Thailand would be sent to the embassy's Pol-Mil Section to be reviewed. Our section vetted the targets each day to be sure they did not include Cambodian territory. If any coordinates were found to be inside Cambodia, permission was refused. The embassy would then be sent new coordinates for that day's bombing runs. This was a serious effort on our part, carried out at an extremely high level of classification and tightly controlled. At first the violations were essentially spillover raids along the Vietnamese-Cambodian border; but after Nixon ordered the secret bombing of Cambodia in March 1969 the "mistakes" became more frequent. A few years later when the bombing became public, it was clear the whole process was a sham. Despite the agreement with the Thai, the embassy was being fed bogus coordinates; and the U.S. ambassador as well as the secretaries of State and Defense were kept in the dark. Even at that highest level of secrecy, we were lying to ourselves.

Our ambassador, Leonard Unger, and his wife, Anne, set a high standard that impressed young people like Diane and me. In the late sixties, white gloves and turned up calling cards were still required for the "ladies." My section head's wife once suggested that the wives help clean the ambassador's residence before an event. The wives explained to her that this was not in their job descriptions, fully confident that Anne would have been horrified to see her junior colleagues doing chores that a very large house staff was perfectly capable of managing.

A scientist by training, Anne Unger was famous in the Foreign Service for an incident that showed her confidence and grit. Once, when she was seated beside the arrogant Thai foreign minister, Thanat Khoman, at an official function, Thanat began to berate her for something that President Johnson had done a day or two before. Mrs. Unger rose from her seat, smiled politely, told the foreign minister that her husband, not she, was paid to hear such complaints, and walked off.

Throughout our tour, I was impressed by the way the ambassador, his DCM, and other leaders of the embassy kept the large and chaotic operation together. They dealt with the Thai with style and managed quite well the never-ending onslaught of arrogance from Washington, particularly from DOD civilians, who assumed they were in charge of the entire world.

I was also impressed by the critical role a strong ambassador could play by another incident that occurred before we arrived in Bangkok. When Lyndon Johnson visited Bangkok in the summer of 1966, Ambassador Graham Martin and the Secret Service backed by Secretary Dean Rusk engaged in a major argument over protection of the president. The Secret Service, as usual, flew an armored limousine in for the president to use. However, one symbolic event of the formal welcoming ceremony at the palace required the president to ride a few blocks with the god-like king of Thailand in his gold Rolls-Royce. Martin argued that not only would the president's use of his own limo be a great insult to the Thai, but that the seat next to the king was the safest place in Thailand, given the reverence shown him by the Thai public. The Secret Service, four years after Kennedy's assassination, saw this as a red line that could not be crossed, and they intended to put the upstart ambassador in his place.

The argument continued even as the president and Secretary Rusk were flying to Thailand. Rusk cabled Martin saying that, as secretary of state, he ordered Martin to tell the Thais that the president would ride in his own limousine; the king could accompany him or ride separately. Martin responded to Rusk that the ambassador, not the secretary of state, was the president's personal representative on the ground in Thailand; and since he was responsible to make the final call, the president would ride with the king. In the end, a smiling President Johnson rode with King Bhumibol in the Rolls-Royce, beginning a visit that all sides considered a great success. The story sent a strong message to a new twenty-five-year-old Foreign Service Officer that it was his responsibility to do what was in the best interests of the United States, no matter what the bureaucracy demanded. Only a direct order from the president could have swayed Martin.

Toward the end of our Thailand tour, Diane, our young daughter, and I were sent to Chiang Mai to help while the consul-general was away on home leave. An idyllic town in those days (although quite tough under the surface), I felt we should have been paying the U.S. government to be assigned there rather than drawing a salary. To be sure, the place had its drug traffickers, and events in Laos and to the north in China were of keen importance to the United States. Still, when we strolled past quiet shops and listened to the silversmiths hammering away on bowls and plates, Chiang Mai allowed us to be transported back to a simpler past and to forget the tensions of the world and the bustle we had left behind in Bangkok.

Our small wooden house looked out onto fields with water buffalo slowly chewing their cuds in the hot fall sun. Chiang Mai belonged to the old Foreign Service and a world soon to be gone forever.

Even with all the pressures of the war, the Thai managed to keep their sense of humor. The *Bangkok Post* ran an entire series on a laborer's efforts to sell "bullet-repelling amulets" for a thousand baht ($18) apiece. He claimed to have given one to a U.S. military officer to send to President Johnson. The paper challenged him to demonstrate its power by having a marksman shoot at a duck wearing one at a public event. On the appointed day, the unfortunate duck and three chickens became in the newspaper's words "the deadest ducks you ever saw," despite wearing the charms. The scammer then explained to anyone who would listen that the tests failed because the demonstration took place near a spirit house.

We also had our humorous moments. I enjoyed the formal warning sent out by the defense attaché for U.S. aircraft to avoid the airspace above the area of the annual elephant roundup to avoid a stampede. And a parting ditty I read at our departure dinner noted that only in Thailand could military statistics record 1006 cases of venereal disease for each 1000 men stationed at a U.S Special Forces base.

Thailand was a great first assignment. Political-military work on the edges of the wars in Vietnam and Laos presented daily challenges. Sitting through military briefings on the massive but ultimately ineffective bombing efforts to close the Ho Chi Minh Trail provided strategic lessons equal to the best War College lectures. Diane and I found Thailand as fascinating as Taiwan and would have liked more time to explore the country and meet its people. Unfortunately, my long hours and a newborn made that impossible. We did leave satisfied that we had done our small part in promoting U.S. interests on the leading issue of our time. Best of all, we were taking with us back to the States our one-and-a-half-year-old daughter Kim.

3
Watching China from Washington

We left Bangkok in November 1969 for me to take up an assignment in the State Department's Bureau of Intelligence and Research (INR). Normally considered a posting out of the mainstream, INR turned out to be an exciting place to work, with the right topic at the right time.

Trying to Fathom Chinese and U.S. Policies

My job was to analyze Chinese foreign policy (especially toward the United States and the Soviet Union) for U.S. policy makers at a time when the PRC was moving to reinvigorate its foreign policy. The worst of the Cultural Revolution was over, and China's leaders wanted to enlist U.S. support in its dangerous confrontation with the Soviet Union. No one in the West knew where Peking's new approach might be headed.

[In this text, I have used the Chinese spellings that were standard at the time. The PRC changed from traditional spellings/Wage-Giles to Pinyin in their English publications on January 1, 1979. Peking became Beijing; Nanking became Nanjing; Canton, Guangzhou; Soochow, Suzhou; Mao Tse-tung, Mao Zedong; Chou En-lai, Zhou Enlai; Teng Hsiao-ping, Deng Xiaoping; Chiang Ching, Jiang Ching, and so forth. I use the traditional spellings through 1978 and then switch to Pinyin spelling from 1979 on.]

China policy remained highly politicized in the United States, as it had been since the Communists took over in 1949—but the top levels of government, from the president on down, needed a better understanding of Chinese intentions and actions to formulate a response.

I was extremely fortunate to work for two of the country's top China specialists, Nicholas Platt and William Gleysteen, both endowed with incredibly good common sense, deep expertise on China, and long experience in dealing with the U.S. bureaucracy. Although the boss of INR at the time, Ray Cline (who once headed CIA operations in Taiwan against the mainland), strongly disagreed with Nixon's approach to Peking and probably with most of our analysis, his deputy, Evelyn Colbert, protected our efforts from political taint and gave us free rein to write and publish our views. We worked hard to understand what was going on, and our analyses received wide coverage, including at the White House. We may have contributed in a small way to the changes taking place in the U.S.-China relationship during that period. Chinese policy makers were driven not by a newfound love of the United States, but by the deterioration of the country's ties with the Soviet Union. The deep antagonism between the two Communist giants boiled over in July 1969 into military clashes on Chen Pao/Damansky Island in the Amur River. An on-and-off series of Sino-Soviet discussions began later in the year, but they stalled after the Chinese demanded a withdrawal of Soviet forces to behind the border line set in the 1689 Treaty of Nerchinsk rather than the line established in two treaties from the 1860s, which the Chinese viewed as unequal and imposed by Imperial Russia. Polemics between the two countries had become quite shrill by the time I started in INR. Analyzing the ups and down of the Sino-Soviet relationship had not only become far more interesting, but also was now of critical importance to the United States.

Richard Nixon came to the presidency in January 1969 determined to chart a new course for the U.S. relationship with China. The Chinese wanted to break out of their international isolation and, given the hostilities with the Soviets, had every reason to view some accommodation with the Americans as a vital necessity. An effort to restart the Warsaw Talks (the one formal channel of communication between the U.S. and the PRC) early in Nixon's term fell victim to bilateral frictions following the defection of a Chinese diplomat. However, shortly after the July battles between Chinese and Soviet forces on the Amur River, the United States renewed its efforts and made the first in a series of unilateral gestures to relax long-standing trade and travel restrictions. In July 1969 Secretary of State William Rogers publicly urged the Chinese to make reciprocal gestures and renewed the U.S. offer to talk. In early December (just as I was settling into INR), the American ambassador in Warsaw, Walter Stoessel, chased down the Chinese chargé after a diplomatic reception to put forward the president's proposal for a resumption of the discussions. The United States backed its proposal with two new gestures: a U.S. announcement of the end of U.S. naval patrols in the Taiwan Strait and additional exceptions to the trade embargo on China.

Two positive, substantive meetings took place in Warsaw on January 20 and February 20, 1970, and I wrote analyses based on the transcripts of both sessions. The key topics were Taiwan and an American proposal to send a presidential envoy to China for high-level talks on bilateral issues. After my second paper was circulated, an NSC China specialist called me to say that Kissinger had found my analyses quite useful (probably more flattery than truth) and asked (in the usual brazen style that the Kissinger NSC used to undermine the State Department) if I would send such pieces directly to him, since "they took too long" to arrive through the formal process. I, of course, bit on the flattery and agreed, although it ended up that there were no further meetings. The Chinese called off the third session in retaliation for the American incursion into Cambodia. Mao unleashed one of his toughest diatribes against the United States for the incursion (charmingly entitled "People of the World Unite and Defeat the U.S. Aggressors and Their Running Dogs"), but by July the Chinese sent their own signal looking for better relations by releasing some American citizens who had languished in Chinese jails for years.

Nixon believed the State Department had been dragging its feet on the envoy idea and distrusted its tendency to keep U.S. allies informed. He put Kissinger in charge of China policy and excluded the State Department. The president and Kissinger kept up the courtship of China, sending messages through the Pakistanis, Romanians, and French, but the Chinese moved cautiously. Pakistani president Yahya Khan passed a message directly to Chou in early

December 1970, saying the United States was ready to send an envoy to discuss all issues and suggested it would be willing to reduce its military forces on Taiwan. Chou responded positively, and the two sides began making preparations for a secret Kissinger trip, to be followed by Nixon's own visit to China. In INR, we were not privy to the details of any of these discussions but managed to keep somewhat informed through contacts with the Romanians and Pakistanis. In any event, we knew the pace of U.S.-Chinese relations had picked up by reading Chinese statements on the United States.

The Chinese made a dramatic move to signal change by inviting a U.S. ping-pong team to visit China in April 1971. Probably one of the better analytical pieces I wrote in this period—but also the most useless—discussed the intense Chinese desire for an American official to go to China. After initial clearance delays (undoubtedly because of the policy implications and the likelihood that the State Department would be cut out), we finally got the piece published and sent to San Clemente for Kissinger and the president to discuss when they met following Kissinger's return from a trip to India and Pakistan. The next day, July 15, the president made his dramatic announcement that Kissinger had just completed a secret trip to Peking and that he was preparing the way for his own visit. What I had picked up from reading the Chinese press was not an expression of a hope for the future, as I had thought, but a reflection of what was in progress, as the Chinese sought to give its own elite an inkling of what was going on. While the people at the White House probably had a good laugh at my expense, some at the top of the State Department concluded, wrongly, that we in INR knew more about Kissinger's efforts than they did. When a journalist called me that evening to ask about my reaction to the trip and whether I had known about it in advance, I replied truthfully: "No, I was as surprised as everyone else." In any event, U.S.-Chinese relations had been put on a dramatic new course, with very little input from the State Department.

During my time in INR, I wrote a large number of papers covering Chinese diplomatic initiatives, the running dispute with the Soviet Union, Chinese policy toward Taiwan, and the PRC's approach to Southeast Asia, Japan, and North Korea. The papers discussed Chinese efforts to reemerge as a major world power and their quest for the China seat at the United Nations. What could have been a sleepy assignment had, by the luck of timing, become a fascinating job. It was also a huge learning experience. While my academic background on China was valuable, it took some effort to turn my wordy academic writing style into the State Department's "just the facts and a short analysis" approach.

One hallmark of the Nixon era was the production of policy documents called National Security Study Memoranda (NSSMs) to help the system come to some consensus on new directions for policy and perhaps to provide a few new ideas or at least a framework for carrying out White House decisions. (Most people believe that Kissinger designed the NSSMs as make-work for the bureaucracy, while the White House focused on policy.) My contribution from INR was to be the State Department's representative on the group drafting the Intelligence Annex of the China paper on the intelligence and defense programs developed over the years (primarily in Taiwan) against the PRC. It was obvious to me that most of the programs had long since outlived their usefulness and that they would have to be phased out as part of the changing U.S.-Chinese relationship. The meetings of the group, which stretched out for most of a year, were chaired by a crusty, senior general clearly used to getting his way. The intelligence agencies were represented by people a decade or two my senior. As we went through the long list of programs, I had my first real taste of interagency debate and the lengths to which agencies will go to protect their programs.

One fight I remember well was over removal of the army's 500th MI (military intelligence) unit from Taiwan. When I told the CIA representative in the corridor that I had seen no useful information from them in a year and a half, she readily agreed that the program was worthless. But inside the room, the game was different. The Defense Intelligence Agency (DIA) representative argued forcefully for the critical importance of the program to U.S. security and received support from all the other agencies present, including the CIA woman who had just called them worthless. The CIA obviously expected the DIA to support their own pet projects in return. I challenged DIA to tell us what the unit had contributed to our knowledge of China. After several sessions, the DIA finally came up with the argument that it was critical to have the 500th MI on Taiwan as training for future missions. I responded that this was not acceptable, given the new realities of U.S. relations with China. The obviously angry chairman then pronounced that the room would take a vote on whether the 500th MI should stay or go, and of course I refused, since it was everyone else against me (the only 27-year-old in the room).

The last meeting of the group I attended occurred shortly after the president's July 15 announcement. The chairman surprised me by opening with an apology: "You were right all along." We then quickly redrafted several of the papers to make the Intelligence Annex conform to the changed world. Programs were reduced over the next few months and eventually terminated completely after the United States lowered its presence in Taiwan. Some were undoubtedly projects that Ray Cline had set up during his time as CIA spymaster in Taiwan that were managed from the same building that later became the home of our Taiwan pseudo-embassy, the American Institute in Taiwan.

A Low-Level Staffer in an Ignored Bureau

Shortly after the Kissinger trip to Peking, I moved to one of the junior officer staff assistant positions in the East Asian and Pacific Affairs Bureau (EAP). The move involved a classic FSO mind shift from involvement (if limited) in policy issues to concentrating on getting paperwork through the system on time, helping to ensure the bureau performed well, and keeping the bosses happy. Personally, it worked for us as a bridge assignment, so Diane could finish her bachelor's degree, which had been interrupted by our marriage and time in Taiwan and Bangkok. Nevertheless, the erratic hours, with a wife in college and a darling daughter that needed her dad to put her to bed, plus the lack of intellectual challenge made it by far my least favorite time in the Foreign Service.

The East Asian and Pacific Affairs Bureau under Marshall Green and indeed Secretary of State Rogers were shut out of the two key issues of interest to the United States in the region—China policy and Vietnam—both closely held by Kissinger and the NSC. Bill Sullivan nominally served as a deputy to Green, but he was Kissinger's

NSC assistant for Indochina. Green usually remained in the dark. Sullivan, a highly capable and brash operative, had his own small and extremely talented staff that worked with little connection to the rest of us. (During my time in Bangkok, we referred to Sullivan, then ambassador to Laos, as Field Marshall Sullivan, because he ran the shadow war there.) Green himself, beyond being one of State's top Asian specialists, was a much sought-after speaker. His hilarious puns would keep the audience in stitches, and they always went away satisfied they had heard a great speech. When I edited his speeches for publication, however, they came off as rather thin, because I had to cut out the puns, which comprised the first half of his remarks.

While it can be boring work, serving as a staff assistant is a good way to learn how to operate in the State Department, even in a bureau then playing a weak policy role. You are both the enforcer and breaker of the rules issued by the department, whether by harassing secretaries in those precomputer, carbon-copy days to produce letter-perfect documents for the White House or by making and distributing copies of highly restricted cables to relevant offices so the bureau could function. On several occasions I trudged up to the Secretariat (S/S), which manages the department's paper flow and policy recommendations for the secretary of state, to be reprimanded for making unapproved copies of sensitive documents that had somehow made their way back up to the Secretariat. The deputy executive secretary, who carried out this charade (everyone knew perfectly well that this was common practice throughout the building), seemed to take a perverse pleasure in berating junior officers for breaking the rules. I doubt he ever said anything to the assistant secretary or his deputies, who gave us our instructions. When I was a deputy executive secretary fifteen years later, I never called anyone to the office to put them through this show, which we all knew was a sham.

4
China in Turmoil

A few days after Diane obtained her BS degree from George Washington University in August 1972, we left Washington for the State Department's Chinese Language School in Taichung, Taiwan. It was an intense and extremely useful year, the teachers were excellent, and Diane and I enjoyed returning to Taiwan. Our daughter Kim attended a Chinese preschool, leaving her dad envious at the speed a four-year-old can pick up a foreign language. The opening of the U.S. Liaison Office (USLO) in Peking in June 1973 interrupted our plan to spend more time at the school. Hong Kong needed a replacement political officer, and they wanted us there as quickly as possible. Our daughter Gwen arrived on the scene in late July, and we boarded a plane to our next assignment the day she and Diane left the hospital. (I'm sure State's medical people—and probably the airlines—would frown on that these days. I've kidded Gwen who later became a Foreign Service Officer herself that she was born to travel.)

Watching from Hong Kong

Hong Kong was a great place to live in those days—it became Diane's second favorite city after New York—and a plum assignment for a budding China hand. Nixon's historic visit to China in February 1972 culminated in the Shanghai Communiqué, which provided the underpinning for a new U.S.-Chinese relationship. An agreement to set up liaison offices in Washington and Peking reached on Kissinger's fifth visit in February 1973 brought the relationship to a new level. Clearly, the Hong Kong Consulate-General would play second fiddle to the newly opened United States Liaison Office (USLO) in Peking, but our much larger staff and minimal duties other than China-watching meant we would have the lead in the day-to-day analysis of what was going on in China.

I soon realized that Jay Taylor, my new boss, had written most of what could be said about China's foreign policy before I arrived. *[After his retirement, Jay wrote the definitive biographies in English on Chiang Kai-Shek and his son Chiang Ching-kuo.]* Events in China and Washington, however, conspired once again to provide the challenge and make the job highly rewarding. In the relatively calm period of Chinese politics following Marshall Lin Piao's coup attempt and death in an airplane crash in September 1971, Chou En-lai with Mao's agreement had taken the first steps to dramatically alter the course of U.S.-Chinese relations and rebuild the government that had been largely dismantled during the Cultural Revolution. He brought back proven managers like Teng Hsiao-ping, who had been shunted aside years earlier, and paved the way for a new Communist Party Congress in September 1973 to formally set China on a more moderate course.

Outwardly, Chinese politics appeared fairly stable when we arrived in Hong Kong. The Party Congress outcome appeared to represent a balance in the leadership between the leftist Cultural Revolution leaders (Chiang Ching, Chang Chun-chiao, Yao Wen-yuan, and Wang Hung-wen) and Chou, Teng, and the moderates. On the bilateral front, things seemed on a steady upward path with the triumphant tour of the Philadelphia Orchestra the next month and other exchanges going well. Then trouble began to surface everywhere. Kissinger's sixth trip in November made no progress amid considerable Chinese questioning of the significance of political events in the United States (Ford had just replaced the disgraced Agnew as vice president, and the Watergate crisis was developing rapidly). The Party Congress supported the leftist-led "Anti-Lin Piao, Anti-Confucius" movement that looked more and more like an effort to undermine moderate elements in the Chinese leadership. The fight over education reforms (whether to keep the destructive educational policies of the Cultural Revolution or return to a more standard educational system) became another staple of media debate. Presumably, the Chinese leadership knew that Chou had been diagnosed with incurable cancer about this time and was now vulnerable. With Mao's health also failing, the struggle for the future of China was at hand.

The consulate-general's political section followed these signs closely, trying to understand their implications for Washington. By January 1974, attacks on Western music and a two-year- old Italian documentary clearly ratcheted up the campaign, and our section (led by the excellent head of the China Internal unit, Sherrod McCall) and most other leading China watchers in Hong Kong had become convinced that another full-blown Chinese political struggle was underway. The leftist, anti-Chou forces became more and more brazen as they mounted their attacks from their base in Shanghai. Despite Chiang Ching's close involvement in the Philadelphia Orchestra visit, one notable commentary critiqued Respighi's "Pines of Rome," a piece the orchestra had played, suggesting that the real target was Chou En-lai and his opening to the West.

The leftists used their new Shanghai magazine *Studies and Criticism* to launch indirect allegorical attacks on Chou, Teng, and their allies. In February I drafted a cable on an article in the magazine that criticized China's famous scholar Hu Shih for going to the pier in Shanghai in the twenties to meet the well-known U.S. educator John Dewey. I pointed out that a sophisticated Chinese reader would see the article as a scarcely veiled attack on Chou En-lai, who had greeted Nixon at the airport in Peking a year and a half earlier, as well as a critique of his policy of rapprochement with the United States. (Revelations following Mao's death and the fall of the leftists in 1976 confirmed this analysis.)

The U.S. Liaison Office (USLO) and some Washington analysts did not agree with our conclusions. They tried to explain away the allegories or suggest that they were primarily directed against the Soviets. USLO sought to assure Washington that Chou remained firmly in charge and the U.S.-Chinese rapprochement remained secure. Kissinger blew up when American newspapers carried stories from Hong Kong similar to our reporting. (Indeed, the *New York Times* carried a somewhat more cautious version of the "Studies and Criticism" piece I had reported on.) With Watergate pressing down on Nixon and Vietnam not going well, Kissinger did not want to hear that the crown jewel of his foreign-policy—the

China opening—might be on shaky ground. As the *New York Times* reported, Kissinger essentially put out an order for us to shut up and not talk to the press. He really wanted us to quit questioning the longevity of his China policy, but of course his complaints did not change our analytical reporting.

Regardless of how we puzzled through the clues of Chinese internal politics, the crisis was real and U.S.-Chinese relations were on hold. For the next three years Kissinger's public stance on China reminded me of the *Wizard of Oz* movie. In my mind, I could see the flashing lights and the wizard shouting into his microphone, as he tried to keep up the illusion that all was well. But political upheavals in both Peking and Washington meant there would be no further forward movement in the relationship for six more years.

The U.S. Liaison Office (USLO) Peking

As we comfortably settled into Hong Kong, the State Department decided to reassign me to Peking. Nick Platt, my mentor in INR and one of our finest officers, had been chosen to lead the political section when USLO was established. The other FSO in the section, Don Anderson, another superb officer, had interpreted at the Warsaw Talks three years earlier. Regrettably, the Chinese demanded Nick leave after his involvement in a deadly traffic accident. Despite it not being his fault, the Chinese logic, which we would see repeated in other cases, held that if an incident occurred involving a foreigner, the foreigner was inevitably at fault, since it would not have taken place if that person had not been in the country! Washington then made Don head of the political section and reassigned me to his former number two position. (James Lilley, the declared CIA station chief who later became my boss as ambassador, was the third person in the section.)

Suddenly, I found myself headed for Peking to one of the best jobs a young political officer could hope to have in the Foreign Service. It would have been an exciting assignment in any event, but this period of great uncertainty about China's future and the implications for the U.S.-China relationship made it particularly intriguing. Our comfortable life in Hong Kong would be replaced with one full of challenges, both professional and in day-to-day living. With the shortage of housing for USLO personnel in Peking, we decided Diane would remain in Hong Kong a few months longer so our older daughter could finish kindergarten. (Kim then spent her first and second grades at the USLO school in Peking, which had six kids in grades 1-8 and met in an enclosed balcony outside the DCM's apartment.)

As soon as the bureaucratic procedures were finished and visas obtained in early April, I headed off to China. Diane saw me off on this new adventure at the old Kowloon train station, and an hour later I arrived at the border at Lo Wu. In those days, all passengers were required to walk across a bridge to the Chinese village of Shenzhen, where after a long wait for the border guards to go through your bags and provide an undistinguished lunch of fried rice, you could continue on your way to Canton. With the extraordinary development of Shenzhen in recent years (it is now almost twice the size of Hong Kong), it is amusing to recall that in the seventies there was nothing to do in this sleepy backwater while the Chinese security people rifled through your bags but to watch water buffalo contentedly grazing in a nearby field.

During our time, USLO Peking had twenty-eight American employees, including six security watch-standers, working in a small compound that had clearly been well-wired by the Chinese in anticipation of the arrival of the Americans. My job description focused on what we could gather on the internal and external situation of China, but my duties also included liaison with the press, protocol, book buying (a serious pursuit for Americans in China in those days), and like all others in the mission, escorting visitors and doing whatever else was needed to make the office function. Incidentally, the Chinese are world champions at protocol, and the lessons I learned proved to be useful in later years. Diane worked part-time as a receptionist at the office. The Chinese staff (kept apart from sensitive areas) included some highly qualified people who in addition to keeping tabs on us were expected to learn how to interact with foreigners and improve their English. (I later worked with a Chinese ambassador at the UN who cut his teeth as a local staff member at the American Embassy in the early eighties.) They of course did not dare give us any real information on what was going on, but they provided useful help on sticky translations or in setting up appointments and arranging visits.

USLO's chief, David K. E. Bruce, wanted a small, compact mission. Despite constant pressure from Washington agencies, he only allowed the addition of an agricultural attaché and a secretary. Bruce also felt it important to keep a relatively low profile and announced early on that we would not attend state banquets or similar events that were not strictly bilateral. He did not attend normal diplomatic receptions, but the rest of us did go when we thought it useful. (The Chinese, always sticklers for protocol, would have seated Bruce below the Palestine Liberation Organization at state occasions because of our less than full diplomatic status.) Missing such events somewhat reduced our reporting capabilities, but it also insulated us from some crushingly boring events. One state dinner we unfortunately missed honored North Korean dictator Kim Il-sung. The reportedly grand but staid affair proceeded normally until one of the main courses appeared on the tables: a Chinese and Korean favorite—dog meat. The choice offended the Arab and other Muslim guests in attendance and revolted the Europeans, but the Chinese and Korean attendees reportedly devoured the dish with gusto.

David Bruce had been chosen as the first USLO chief by President Nixon to demonstrate the importance of the new opening to China. A Virginia patrician, a one-tour Foreign Service Officer who married a Mellon and then set up the Mellon-endowed National Gallery of Art, an OSS officer in World War II, U.S. ambassador to France, Germany, England, and NATO, Bruce also led the Paris Peace Talks with the Vietnamese. His second wife Evangeline had lived in China as a child when her father served as a counselor in the American Legation in Peking. She married her OSS boss (Bruce) and became the toast of Europe and Washington, one of the better-known society hostesses of her time.

Given the turmoil in Chinese politics and the decidedly ungenteel life at USLO, the posting turned out to be an obvious disappointment for both of them. The contrasts with the salons of Europe and the Washington social life they had enjoyed could not have been greater. Mrs. Bruce spent most of her time away from China, and her husband, a man of exceptional ability for whom I had a lot of respect, was far more comfortable in Europe than in the rough and tumble world of mid-seventies China. Presumably, Bruce had expected to carry on erudite conversations with Chou En-lai about the state of the world and our bilateral ties; instead he soon found himself talking not to the foreign minister but to an often-unpleasant assistant secretary equivalent. Bruce had only signed on to the job for a year, and it was obvious during the five months I worked for him that he could not wait to leave. In a calmer period, the Bruces might have been a reasonable selection for Peking and his talents used more fully, but they were out of place in the chaos and brutality of China in 1973–74.

Our small Marine Guard contingent originally assigned to USLO to provide internal security for the mission proved to be a particular irritant for the Chinese xenophobes. When they hoisted the American flag over the Liaison Office building in June 1973, Western commentators noted the strong symbolism of their return. The U.S. Marines had played a key role in defending the Legation Quarter during the Boxer Rebellion in 1900 (immortalized in Charlton Heston's *55 Days in Peking*) and then, up through the 1930s, they carried out patrols in Peking to protect Americans living there. The Communists considered the Boxers national heroes and had long stoked bad feelings against the "foreign devils," especially the Americans.

The Foreign Ministry was under pressure to look for opportunities to get rid of the Marines, an assignment Bruce's primary contact relished. The Chinese protested such normal activities as wearing uniforms in the office (USLO then agreed the Marines would stand guard in mufti); jogging in public parks with "Marines" on their sweatshirts; the noise coming from their popular small bar for foreigners; and the usual inscription on their Marine birthday cake. Finally, in April the Chinese "asked" that the Marines be removed for their many supposed "infractions" and on the grounds that they were the only "recognizable foreign military unit" in China. Soon after I arrived, I watched an infuriated David Bruce dictate a cable to Washington over the latest Chinese insult, with the reluctant recommendation to replace the Marines with civilian guards. They were withdrawn in May and early June. It was a victory for the leftists and some of their nastier supporters in the Foreign Ministry, and a clear marker that the high promise accompanying the initial establishment of the Liaison Offices had stalled.

In response to Evangeline Bruce's repeated requests to visit the old American Legation building just off Tiananmen Square where her father had worked, the Chinese hosted the Bruces and some other USLO personnel including Diane and me to their departure banquet in the building, which had been turned into a guest house. Anything having to do with the old Legation Quarter was a touchy subject in the political struggles of the 1970s. Indeed, the name bestowed on the main street of the Legation Quarter during the Cultural Revolution was "Anti-Imperialism Street." The old U.S. legation building symbolized the "imperialist" past, and the Marine barracks still stood on the grounds. Bruce, I'm sure, savored the irony of sitting in the shadow of that history. He was still angry over the treatment of the Marines.

The Chinese Succession Struggle

By the time I arrived in Peking, the "Anti-Lin Piao, Anti-Confucius" movement had deteriorated into a brawl between party factions, with attacks on party and enterprise leaders at many levels carried out openly through "Big Character Posters" pasted up in prominent places in Peking and other major cities. For a junior political officer, the posters provided a rare front seat to observe events in China. I immediately hit the streets to try to decipher the battle behind the posters and try to describe their meaning to Washington. Among other challenges, I had to learn quickly how to read Chinese handwriting, which had unfortunately been a course I missed when we cut short our time in Taiwan.

Jim Lilley made a deal with a foreign journalist for us to provide him film and develop pictures he took of the posters, thereby providing us with copies to forward to Hong Kong and Washington. This meant that I wrote cables on the posters and their implications based on my reading of them, and photos were sent to native Chinese speakers working for us in Hong Kong who would assist officers at the Consulate to do their own analysis. Needless to say,

I lived in considerable dread that I would get the analysis completely wrong and be embarrassed a few weeks later when Hong Kong sent in a corrective cable. Fortunately, the close attention Anderson and USLO's deputy John Holdridge paid to my reporting helped keep me from any major disasters.

For the next two and a half years, the political struggle ebbed and flowed. By the time I arrived, Chou began to miss most of the meetings he would normally have had with foreigners, although he occasionally met with visitors in the hospital. Teng Hsiao-ping took over the bulk of Chou's duties, both in dealing with foreigners and in running the government. The pragmatic Teng (short, blunt-spoken, and as tough as nails) had been one of the prime victims of the leftists during the Cultural Revolution, criticized particularly for his 1962 aphorism "It doesn't matter if the cat is black or white so long as it catches mice." But his banishment had not broken his spirit nor dampened his view that China needed stability to move forward. He had the support of many party and government officials who shared his moderate views. The military leadership, in particular, trusted Teng as they moved out of positions of power they had assumed when called on to keep the country from self-destruction during the early years of the Cultural Revolution. The Shanghai leftists, later labeled the "Gang of Four," controlled cultural issues, the press, and the propaganda apparatus. Mao, now in his dotage, played a limited role; both factions used his (sometime edited) words and grumblings to back their own positions. In this fluid situation, I once joked to a fellow diplomat who was trying to make sense of it all that you could only do your best; if you didn't get it right this week, in a month or two when the tide turned, people would call your earlier reporting prescient.

An Impoverished Country

Underlying the struggle was the obvious fact that twenty-five years of Communist rule had done little to raise the average Chinese from a life of deep poverty. Mao's foolish economic ideas and political campaigns had undermined the efforts of Chou, (former president) Liu Shao-chi, Teng Hsiao-ping, and other leaders to build a modern

China along the state-centric model of the Soviet Union. Millions of people died from Mao's lunatic ideas, which led to widespread starvation and the violent political campaigns of the sixties. As in Europe, the Communist system and Mao's political interference had robbed the people of the incentive to work hard other than for self-preservation. We commented that Chinese people worked extremely diligently everywhere in the world but in China. Despite the raptures of some wide-eyed foreign promoters, China was a dysfunctional society, and its people were dirt poor. Teng wanted to change that, but the leftists seemed satisfied to mouth praise for Mao's failed approach; their focus was on political power.

Peking and the surrounding countryside combined widespread poverty with a faded past grandeur. The party leadership and state cadre lived fairly well, but life for the average Chinese meant a continuous struggle, especially in the harsh winter when only the most basic food and necessities were available. Electricity was so scarce that drivers needed to be careful at night to avoid running over groups of Chinese men in the middle of major highways playing cards under streetlights. People cooked their meager meals on open charcoal burners on the sidewalks across the street from where the elite ate their elaborate meals in the walled Chong Nan Hai compound. Pollution left a pall over every Chinese city, but Peking was particularly bad during the cold and damp winters, with the air heavy with industrial pollution and charcoal smoke. In the spring, sandstorms that rivaled Cairo's were frequent. Most of the trees in the region—even in the cities—had been cut down during the period of starvation following the Great Leap Forward.

A major world capital in a country famous for its food, Peking by the end of the Cultural Revolution had only seven or eight restaurants (under the protection of patrons in the leadership) where foreigners would venture out to enjoy a formal traditional dinner. Sightseeing included a poorly rehabilitated Summer Palace, the mostly ruined Ming Tombs, and some restored attractions such as the Forbidden City and the Temple of Heaven. Our family enjoyed excursions to all of the available sites, especially picnics in the secluded tomb area. Bicycles and buses formed the primary modes of transportation, with automobiles reserved for the chauffeured elite and the foreigners. (I'm sure I wasn't the only person in the city who envied the head of the Chinese Medical Association's car, a powder blue 1957 Chevy that appeared to be in mint condition.) There were only three traffic lights along the entire main thoroughfare that ran past Tiananmen, and they were controlled by policemen at the intersections. Neither we nor the Chinese elite had to worry about stopping, though, since the policeman on duty switched them to green when a car, truck, or bus came near. The same thoroughfare sported Peking's only two neon signs, which translated as "Peking Station" (for the main train station) and "Long Live Mao Tse-tung."

In 1974 it was striking to consider how much better people lived in Taipei or in colonial Hong Kong than in the capital of the empire, Peking. Foreigners had privileged medical facilities (at the Rockefeller-built Peking Medical Union Hospital), but we were kept in the dark about an encephalitis outbreak in the city until one diplomat's child died of the disease. Plus, the government had closed down all but a few state-owned shops. You could get a lesson in petty bureaucratic tyranny by visiting the clothing shop that had only unisex Mao suits in blue, green, or black and watching the disdain with which the clerks treated hapless customers who had scraped together enough for a new outfit.

With places to buy things so limited in central Peking, Diane put together a guidebook for USLO numbering less than a dozen pages that showed where you could buy socks, nails, or other items for daily living. We had an apartment directly across from the entrance to the Friendship Store, which catered to foreigners only. If they happened to get in strawberries or some other delicacy, we could go down the five sets of stairs and hurry across the street to buy the item before it ran out. The heavy cream made great ice cream, but you had to know that fresh supplies came on Tuesday, or your ice cream had a distinctly sour taste. Diane had to bake our own bread and make baby food for Gwen. We once brought back a sack of small grapefruit from a trip to Hong Kong, giving one to each member of the staff as a small treat. They acted like we had brought back gold bars. While watching and reporting on Chinese politics was exciting, daily life in Peking could be a real challenge, even for the privileged.

Reading Tea Leaves

Figuring out what was going on in China required some guesswork but mostly painstaking attempts to piece together the meaning of the Orwellian language and historical allusions in the newspapers and posters that harked back a couple of millennia, a few hundred years, or maybe only a few years. What was the real issue behind the newspaper articles on the 81 B.C. "Salt and Iron Debate"? Or did the eighty-one additional chapters of the historical novel *All Men Are Brothers* (*Shui Hu Chuan*), now out of print, really say what the propagandists were claiming? No Chinese inside the country with some idea what was going on would be so bold as to provide a foreigner an honest explanation; it was simply too dangerous and they themselves may have had only their own reading of events and the regime's propaganda as a guide. The cloistered leadership had no interest in enlightening lower-ranking personnel, and the price of political missteps had been demonstrated all too clearly only a few years before during the Cultural Revolution.

Beyond the official propaganda, we had to rely on our reading of the posters, what we could piece together from diplomats or others who had a least some access to influential Chinese, and what we could see or pick up ourselves. We were only allowed to go to ten open cities outside a twenty-mile radius of Peking and the Great Wall and Ming Tombs; even there, permission would sometimes be denied. We would try to accompany U.S. visitors whenever possible to be helpful to them, to observe new cities, and to listen to the discussions for ourselves. We also tried to debrief any visitors willing to share their views. Personal travel with my family always required a notebook and camera close by to help remember posters and political tidbits from places we were allowed to visit. On one trip to Nanking two beefy Public Security officials tried to block my efforts to read posters, leading to a cat-and-mouse game until I was satisfied I understood the main points. I felt fortunate that I was never manhandled like some of my colleagues for straying across the poorly defined red lines of the permissible.

I also haunted the few Peking bookstores, in my book-buying hat for the Library of Congress and other Washington agencies, looking for the latest twists in the political winds or securing a recently republished classic that may have gone through some judicious editing to fit the current propaganda line. And we would occasionally get a stray piece of internal material that had been left on a park bench or brought in by someone needing to do business with USLO. When rumors flew in foreign media that Mao had died or some other dramatic event—often floated first on the Chicago commodities exchange, which was extremely sensitive to Chinese grain purchases—my CIA colleague and I would drive around the capital looking for any signs that key ministries or places like the Great Hall of the People had unusual activity. The much-vaunted American intelligence operation was in high gear around the world trying to get a clearer picture of events in China, and our consulate-general in Hong Kong had long been developing its sources. But closer analysis of the political situation in China often rested on the mundane and meager information we gleaned in Peking.

Since the Chinese did not confide in foreign diplomats—with some exceptions made for the Pakistanis, Romanians, and Albanians—the diplomatic community was reduced to talking to one another and trading bits of information, some of which was valuable and some merely useless gossip. Overall, the diplomats in Peking in those days were an impressive group. Leading world capitals sent diplomats of exceptionally high quality who spoke Chinese, creating a close-knit diplomatic community among us that led to many long-term friendships.

George and Barbara Bush at USLO

George and Barbara Bush, who arrived in Peking in late September 1974, proved to be very different leaders than the Bruces. While also part of the U.S. eastern elite, Bush had honed his skills in the Texas oilfields and the rough and tumble of Texas and national politics, including the worst days of Watergate. The Bushes were, in the best sense, politicians to the core. George Bush had been a congressman, ambassador to the UN, chairman of the Republican Party, and later CIA chief, vice president, and president of the United States.

Both Bushes were optimistic, great at people skills, and driven by a sense of duty. They acted as if there was no place on earth they would rather be than Peking. In fact, Nixon had chosen Gerald Ford rather than Bush to be his vice president after Agnew's resignation, and Ford in turn had picked Nelson Rockefeller rather than Bush as his VP. Ford offered Bush Peking rather than a coveted cabinet post where he would have been better placed to play the high-stakes politicking game in Washington. Kissinger knew full well little would happen in the bilateral relationship during Bush's tenure and told him he would be bored to death in the job. But the Bushes' upbeat approach allowed them to lead USLO effectively for fourteen months and helped keep relations with China on an even keel, despite the turmoil in internal Chinese politics. Even the Chinese public developed an affection for them, as their outreach efforts and bicycle excursions around Peking became famous. They both were always engaged, down to earth, and approachable to a staff under intense pressure.

Bush's sense of duty impressed me when I went to his residence to brief him on some issue one Sunday morning in early November 1975. He had just agreed to Ford's request that he take over the troubled CIA as part of Ford's reshuffling of the national security apparatus. Bush had hoped to become Ford's running mate in the summer and had been penciled in for commerce secretary as a possible steppingstone to the vice presidency, but at the last moment he was offered instead the poison pill of the CIA, which was under heavy scrutiny for its excesses. (Rumor in Washington had it that Chief of Staff Donald Rumsfeld engineered the appointment to sideline his rival.) Bush's private explanation to me was classic: "Lynn, when the president asks you to do something, you do it." A few weeks later, a CIA officer asked me what it was like to work for Bush. I told him that everyone in the agency from the lowest parking attendant would think that George Bush cared about him or her personally and how well he or she did their job. In later years when I ran into the Bushes in various settings, the conversation would essentially pick up where we had left off years earlier.

By the time of the Bushes' arrival, Teng and the moderates in China were getting the Anti-Lin Piao, Anti-Confucius campaign under control. China's propagandists emphasized political stability and unity as well as the country's economic development, and Teng returned to the Politburo. At the same time, however, events in the United States made the chances for bilateral progress slim. In August 1974, Nixon became the first U.S. president to resign (the news rated page 6 in *People's Daily*), and Gerald Ford assumed the presidency. We followed the news on short-wave radio and by reading the occasional piece on politics that the Chinese chose to reprint for foreigners. (Though we would devour our *New York Times* when it arrived in the mail, it was usually six-to-eight-weeks late.) Most of our time in this period was spent organizing visits of Americans to China and reporting on Teng's consolidation of power.

Henry Kissinger visited China again during Thanksgiving in 1974 (Bush proclaimed that Thanksgiving would be celebrated the Sunday before). The Chinese were clearly less impressed with U.S. power than they had been during his earlier visits. (Kissinger told reporters the Chinese saw us as a "wounded tiger.") The Chinese gave him a frosty welcome—no meeting with Mao and an earful on the Russians —but did agree to have President Ford visit Peking in 1975.

We were all aware of stories about Kissinger's treatment of subordinates, but I was surprised to find it so starkly on display when I met him for the first time during the visit. As the USLO officer responsible for herding the press contingent that accompanied Kissinger, we found ourselves alone together for a few minutes in a briefing room waiting for the group to arrive. Attempting to be courteous, I walked over to the great man to introduce myself as the member of USLO designated to handle the press. Kissinger did not respond, except to glare at me and make it perfectly clear that he was too busy to take notice of a junior officer.

A couple of years later, when I worked for the deputy secretary of state and needed to pass an urgent message while he was in a meeting with Secretary Kissinger, I received the same contemptuous look, which clearly meant that lesser beings (i.e., staffers like me) should not interrupt his meetings. Not surprisingly, when I was chargé in Beijing in 1989 and he needed information on what was happening in China, I suddenly was treated as a valued friend. He certainly would not have remembered his rude encounters with an insignificant young FSO years earlier.

The Chinese treated Kissinger to a side trip during his visit to Soochow, the ancient city near Shanghai famous for its silks and beautiful women. There was an argument over what airplane Kissinger would use to go there. The U.S. said that he needed his U.S. Air Force plane to stay in touch with the outside world. Chinese officials, presumably for security concerns, insisted he take a Chinese aircraft but agreed his plane could be flown to Shanghai to shorten his onward journey home. Kissinger and his entourage traveled on one of China's new Trident aircraft, and the Chinese agreed to provide a direct communications link to his plane in Shanghai.

The drive through Soochow to the guesthouse was surreal. We rode along mostly empty streets except for some prosperous-looking pedestrians (presumably government officials) walking on the sidewalks trying to "look normal"; the townspeople were kept behind barricades on side streets a block or two away. The contrast between the newly scrubbed walls and vacant streets and the vibrant city filled with Anti-Lin Piao, Anti-Confucius posters I had observed a week earlier along this same road when visiting with U.S. college presidents struck me as both absurd and a bit sad.

When we arrived at the guesthouse, some of Kissinger's staff and I went into an adjoining room to check out the communications line the Chinese had promised. To our surprise, a young female PLA soldier stood there with a World War I–style crank field phone. She cranked and cranked, connecting with at least half a dozen bases around China but never with Kissinger's plane some fifty miles away at Shanghai's airport. Then someone in our party suggested we use the international satellite system the United States had given China at the time of the Nixon visit to call the White House switchboard. It literally took a few seconds to get the White House Situation Room.

Asked about issues that could involve the secretary of state or the national security advisor (Kissinger held both positions at that point), the duty officer said: "Are you serious? It's Thanksgiving eve." The deputy S/S then threw up his hands and said: "To hell with it. We'll tell Henry everything is OK so he can go out and enjoy his sightseeing." That evening when we were seeing the group off at the Shanghai airport, the USAF crew told us that the PLA had indeed shown up with a field phone just like the one we had seen, but the crew would not let it on the plane for security reasons and kept it on the stairway outside the plane with the door closed to ward off the cold. The crew certainly could not have heard anything, even if the woman in Shanghai called the right number. Given the cold bleak day, the contrived atmosphere, and the sterile sights, I had no doubt Kissinger was relieved to end the Soochow trip and fly back to Washington in the comfort of his own airplane.

Another Kissinger story on the trip provided a telling reminder of the dangers of getting the cultural nuances right in translations. As a language student, I learned early on that using Chinese idioms (sometimes called "four-character phrases" or "Confucian sayings") is a dangerous thing unless you have a very firm grasp of the language. At a banquet in Peking, Kissinger decided to impress his audience with a Chinese saying at the start of his banquet speech. He predictably mangled the sounds, but when the Foreign Ministry's U.S.-born interpreter Nancy Tang gamely translated his words into understandable Mandarin, our Chinese hosts appeared surprised and gave each other knowing looks. I asked the Foreign Ministry official next to me about the reaction. He laughed and said that, while the sentiments were fine, they were words that a host would say to a guest, not vice versa. The phrase had apparently been given to Kissinger by a member of his entourage who had left China as a child. I vowed to myself once again that I would never use these phrases in my own Chinese speeches.

After much infighting, the Chinese leadership finally convened the National People's Congress in January 1975. Despite ardent efforts by the leftists (most specifically Chiang Ching) seeking government positions to consolidate their power, Teng won out and Chou came out of the hospital long enough to give the meeting's main speech. Teng became chief of staff of the PLA and began preparing for a trip to Paris amid considerable speculation that he might also go to the United States. Over the next few months, many officials who had been purged during the Cultural Revolution were rehabilitated and brought back to positions of responsibility. Teng and his supporters used Mao's earlier call for stability and unity as the rationale for their actions.

Everybody Wants to Visit

In the seventies, China was the place for Americans to visit. It was exotic, it had been closed to most Americans, including scholars, for almost a quarter of a century, and it was the ideal place for celebrities and politicians to "discover" and get extensive press coverage. The groups ranged from cultural and scientific delegations to serious academic and press specialists on China to a cross-section of Americans of all stripes. Some were sponsored by the U.S. government, some by reputable NGOs, and others through private connections with the Chinese.

Given the early involvement of the table tennis team, the U.S. sponsored several sports groups as a form of soft power that hopefully would not ruffle too many feathers in the touchy atmosphere in China. Nevertheless, we had several confrontations with the Chinese over the makeup of the visiting American groups. Chinese security personnel would comb through old files to weed out people they had pegged (usually falsely) as spies in the forties or who had written articles in the press they didn't like. Each rejection would create a major back and forth as we sought to facilitate the visits. We accompanied as many of the visitors as our small staff could manage (sometimes augmented from Hong Kong) to provide assistance and keep them out of trouble.

Congressional delegations came in a steady stream, as both the Americans and the Chinese tried to ensure the atmosphere in Washington was supportive of the new relationship. Many delegations were first-rate, with members seriously interested in fathoming the complexities of China. Others were merely embarrassing, like the House Speaker and his bevy of young female aides. But all contributed to strengthening understanding to at least some degree.

One of the more amusing incidents occurred at the end of 1975 during a visit of U.S. congresswomen that included such luminaries as Millicent Fenwick, Bella Abzug, Pat Schroeder, Margaret Heckler, Patsy Mink, and Gladys Spellman. During the meeting with Teng (it turned out to be his last for a couple of years with visiting Americans), the Chinese experimented with a new clip-on microphone. I noticed that, as a concession to the American women, the usual brass spittoon always at Teng's side was absent that day. About halfway through the session, Teng excused himself and went to a back room, where he proceeded to deliver himself of a classic Chinese spitting session designed to clear out the throat and nasal passages. I had seen Teng go through this procedure many times, but he outdid himself this time. Unfortunately, the microphone was still on, presenting his visitors a dramatic hot mic experience. When he finished, Teng returned calmly to his seat to continue the conversation. Everyone in the room kept their composure (though I amused myself thinking what must be going through the minds of the guests); but I have no doubt the memory of the event lingered with each of the congresswomen for the rest of their days.

The visit of a delegation of U.S. university presidents—including the presidents of Harvard, UCLA, Stanford, and Jay Rockefeller, then president of West Virginia University—proved to be particularly revealing. It may also have been the most depressing visit several of them had ever undertaken. Our visit to Peking University, the pinnacle of China's educational establishment, located on a campus built with Rockefeller Foundation money, disclosed an academic wasteland well below the group's already low expectations. The Cultural Revolution's "worker-peasant-soldier" students were totally out of their depth, and most of the professional staff had been sent to rural communes to shovel manure for their supposed sins. Our hosts took us to the library stacks, where we saw an America section consisting of row upon row of empty shelves, with one small group of books that mostly featured the works of Mark Twain. (I wryly commented to one of the presidents that at least for a kid from Mark Twain country they had managed to get one thing right.) Many of these people, who had dedicated their lives to education, had tears in their eyes as they looked at the travesty that had replaced this world-renowned educational institution.

We next went to Shenyang, the bleak Manchurian industrial city under the control of Mao's nephew and prominent leftist, Mao Yuan-hsin. After freezing in the guest house (the decrepit heating system had been turned on only after we arrived to save fuel), we were honored with a demonstration on a much colder, windblown hillside of China's great discovery that men could work on high-tension lines with their bare hands without being killed. We were then dispatched to see another campus (Shenyang University) that was by then a university in name and buildings only. Treated to an English class demonstration, I flipped through their propaganda/textbook discussing in simple English the evils of capitalism. It included a diatribe against John D. Rockefeller. Totally fed up with the whole Chinese charade by this point, I couldn't resist announcing in Chinese how fortunate we were to have Rockefeller's grandson with us that day and pointed him out to the group. The Chinese officials and the students looked as if they had seen the devil incarnate when they realized they had been exposed to an offspring of one of the world's worst capitalist devils. Our group had a chuckle when I later confessed what I had done.

The impressions that the visitors took home from these early visits varied greatly. The college presidents were stunned and depressed. Others left with an improved understanding of the complexities of modern China and the challenges it faced. I remember an excellent piece in the *New York Times* by my old mentor, Doak Barnett, trying to calm the euphoria by noting that China had obvious warts along with positive features. Many visitors, however, were eager to be impressed by the "new China" and swallowed any propaganda the Chinese dished out for them hook, line, and sinker. Even some serious academics and journalists bought into what we dubbed the "Shirley MacLaine syndrome" of wonderment and whitewashing of China. One of my favorite repeated stories from Americans referred to the perceived honesty of the Chinese people. Guests marveled that they could leave valuables in their hotel rooms without fear of them being stolen, and even trash discarded in the wastebaskets was returned. I commented to one such infatuated American that it was pretty easy to understand this honesty when the alternative was to be sent back to an impoverished village or to a labor camp. This was true, of course, but I doubt he believed me.

The Chinese Cultural Catastrophe

China was a cultural wasteland in the seventies. Mao had unleashed the Cultural Revolution in 1966 to unseat his enemies and to eradicate things he viewed as unhealthy in traditional Chinese culture.

Youthful Red Guards waving Mao's Little Red Book of quotations were encouraged to smash everything educated Chinese held sacred; monuments were defaced or destroyed, books burned, and irreplaceable artifacts smashed. The Chinese educational system was destroyed, and the "revolutionary" adaptations trivialized many of its great cultural traditions.

Eight years after the sad destruction of China's proud cultural tradition began, we still had to endure many hours of "entertainment"—bright-eyed and rouged kids singing paeans to Mao; bad music and dancing to honor the workers, peasants, and soldiers; acrobatic groups; and, by far the worst, Chiang Ching's "Revolutionary Operas." In these excruciatingly boring shows, any actor wearing a necktie was labeled a foreign imperialist (yes, the diplomats and visitors were the only ones in the audience in suits and ties) or KMT counterrevolutionary. The plots and music were childish, and the outcome was never in doubt. (Teng reportedly walked out of one performance and never attended a second one. Those of us in the diplomatic corps sincerely wished we had the same option.) It was no wonder that Western orchestras were such a hit with the Chinese audiences or that, when the lights dimmed at our July 4 film showings, the Chinese would start quietly tapping their feet to American musicals like *Hello, Dolly* and *That's Entertainment*.

The Philadelphia Orchestra's tour to Peking and Shanghai in September 1973 was the most notable cultural exchange after the 1972 visit of the U.S. ping-pong team. It signaled the triumphant return to China of Western music, banned during the Cultural Revolution. Promoted by Chiang Ching as well as by more traditional cultural actors, the orchestra arrived just after the September Party Congress had put the stamp of approval on China's more moderate course. Chiang attended a concert in Peking, dictated some of the music played (including Beethoven's Sixth Symphony and "Home on the Range"), and appeared to bask in this tribute to her role as cultural tsar. Four months later, however, the political tides had turned, and attacks on the orchestra's program became part of the leftist onslaught led by Chiang on the moderates.

Another exchange highlight not criticized was the Chinese Archeology Exhibition sent out to various European countries and later, after extensive negotiations in Peking, to Washington, Kansas

City, and San Francisco. I probably had more meetings with the Chinese on this exhibit than on any other topic, but the results were worth it. Diane and I saw the exhibit at the National Gallery in Washington and were as wowed by its quality and presentation as were the thousands of others who saw it. It glorified a China that had been under severe attack at home for almost a decade. The high point for me took place when the pieces returned to Peking, and I had the opportunity to see the curators lovingly open the boxes and sense their joy at having their precious objects back home. (The United States had guaranteed the safe return of the objects, and two Smithsonian curators and I were designated as observers during the handover back to the Chinese.) Instead of the usual propagandists spouting arid speeches about China's culture, these men, all older specialists, knew their business and treated each object with reverence.

Seeing people so devoted to China's rich traditional culture, which had been scorned and destroyed on the streets and in the media for years, was a truly moving experience. When I asked one of the men about recent discoveries, including the fabulous terracotta army just discovered in Xian, he looked at me conspiratorially and said that Chinese archeologists knew the location of many treasures still hidden in the ground but added, "We're not going to open up these sites until we're sure these fools won't destroy them." It may have been my most genuine conversation with a Chinese official during those twenty-seven months in China. The Chinese frequently complained about the looting of their art objects by Westerners or the trove of ancient treasures the Nationalists had taken with them to Taiwan; but these professionals were quite aware of the wanton destruction of priceless art objects by the Cultural Revolution's Red Guards and the extensive government sales in Hong Kong markets of exquisite stolen art (often grabbed by Red Guards during their home invasions). True to my interlocutor's statement, hundreds of archeological sites were "newly discovered" later in the decade after the political tides had turned.

Typhoons, Oil, and Milton's Demise

Given the political atmospherics in Peking and China's general self-isolation from international issues, our sporadic business with the Foreign Ministry dealt mostly with routine démarches on mundane issues and visitors' arrangements. One topic that generated more than usual interest was a U.S.-Philippine proposal to seed Pacific typhoons to see if their direction or intensity could be modified. The United States had put considerable effort and money into Project Stormfury, seeding Atlantic hurricanes in the 1960s and early '70s, with mixed results. As support for the project in the Atlantic waned, with its relatively small number of suitable hurricanes, project managers with the strong backing of the Philippines, which often bore the brunt of Pacific typhoons, decided to move the project to the Pacific. But first, they needed to get the agreement of the countries that might be affected. The project would have been tricky to sell in any case (Mexico had long been a skeptic of the Caribbean experiments), but it became particularly difficult after press reports claimed the U.S. military had been seeding clouds over North Vietnam in an attempt to flood its agricultural dikes.

In July 1974, I went to the Foreign Ministry's Americas Division to pitch the project, armed with the Chinese equivalents of the technical terms in the démarche that I had carefully looked up the night before. It was an interesting discussion between people (including me) who clearly did not know what they were talking about. The Chinese response was appropriately noncommittal. The Philippines kept pressing for the project, aided by intense lobbying by William Sullivan, now the U.S. ambassador in Manila. To their credit, Chinese representatives at international meetings engaged in technical discussions that showed some interest, while insisting the project could not go forward without the agreement of all countries concerned. In the end, both the Japanese and Chinese responded with a firm "no" and the United States abandoned the effort. The Chinese remained interested, however, and used cloud seeding and other weather modification techniques over the years far more aggressively than did the U.S.

The United States' 1971 return of Diaoyu/Senkaku islands in the East China Sea to Japan as part of the reversion of Okinawa set off a loud outcry from the Chinese government about its sovereignty claims in the East China Sea. They also soon resurrected the "Nine Dash Line" from a 1947 Nationalist government map that laid claim to most of the South China Sea. In January 1974, they deployed forces to take over the Paracel Islands from a weakened South Vietnam no longer backed by U.S. forces. When Teng returned to power, he turned down the volume on Chinese territorial sea claims, only to have Xi Jinping revive the claims with a vengeance in the next century.

At the time, Chinese and foreign companies were excited by the underwater oil prospects, and the CIA and other analysts began talking up China as a major oil exporter. But after a visit to the famed Taching oil field in Manchuria, former oilman George Bush was unconvinced. He told us that the Chinese were using crude methods that hastened the depletion of their fields. The offshore oil test wells also generally disappointed. The CIA reversed its forecasts soon after Bush arrived as director. As he had foreseen, China became a major oil importer—not an exporter—in the nineties.

When China gave two pandas to the United States as part of the Nixon visit, the U.S. reciprocated with two musk oxen (Milton and Matilda) from Alaska. There is no doubt that the U.S. got the better end of this deal. While a fierce competition developed among American zoos to get the loveable and photogenic pandas, the musk ox is an ungainly and, at mating times, a particularly smelly animal with little attraction for the average zoo visitor. Despite their lack of appeal to either adults or children, the oxen naturally had to be a stop when Diane and I took the girls to the Peking Zoo early in 1975. We were surprised to see only one musk ox (it turned out to be Matilda) by itself off in the corner of a large, penned area. Our queries about her mate were met with the usual Chinese shrugs.

In mid-March, Smithsonian Secretary Dillon Ripley visited Peking and tried without success to pay a courtesy call on zoo officials (the pandas had, of course, ended up at his National Zoo). When he asked his escorts (at our suggestion) about Milton, they told him China had received only one ox. Three days later the Chinese came clean when a Foreign Ministry official informed us in a funereal tone that Milton had unfortunately died in February of reticulitis traumatica (hardware disease). It seems poor Milton had eaten some old nails that were undoubtedly left lying around in the notoriously dirty Peking zoo. Our government decided not to bother sending a replacement.

President Ford Visits, December 1975

While Teng and the moderates had done well at the January 1975 National People's Congress, their success unleased a counterattack from the radicals, who used their control of the propaganda apparatus to mount a new campaign, now mostly against Teng. Chiang Ching's sidekick Yao Wen-yuan penned a broadside warning against the "bourgeois elements" trying to seize power in China. While Teng seemed to be mostly getting his way in reorienting the government to concentrate on development and stability, it hardly felt like anything was finally settled in Peking.

The dying off of the Communist Party's old guard added to a general sense of unease (ironically, in Taiwan Chiang Kai-shek also died). Chou appeared only in his hospital bed, and Mao was obviously in terminal decline. A series of earthquakes in northern China with dire warnings of more dangerous ones to follow portended to superstitious Chinese that the "Mandate of Heaven" was passing from the current leadership to be followed by an inevitable period of chaos. It was also a bad time for American prestige in Asia, with the fall of Saigon and Phnom Penh in April. Nothing in the U.S.-Chinese relationship was moving forward except planning for the Ford visit, a prospect that engendered minimal enthusiasm on either side.

The leftist campaign burst out again in September 1975 with a major campaign involving Mao's favorite novel, *All Men Are Brothers*. The campaign, presumably sanctioned by Mao, sought to demonstrate how the leader of an outlaw band had capitulated to the imperial government rather than carry out a people's revolution. There could be little doubt that Chiang Ching and her group were going after Teng again; but, like all these campaigns, it was unclear how much traction it would get or if Mao (who was barely sentient at times) wanted to get rid of Teng or merely rein him in.

As this new campaign gained force, Kissinger arrived in Peking to settle the final details for the Ford visit with Teng. The tone was cool. The Chinese had fended off the usual horde of American officials who advance every presidential trip. A large team actually boarded as USAF aircraft in Washington prepared to go to China in early November; but they had to disembark, return to their offices, and endure two more weeks awaiting Chinese permission to arrive. The Secret Service was particularly incensed that they were blocked from doing their usual advance planning—and even after they arrived, Chinese security officials let them cool their heels in a hotel for another week before beginning serious discussions. The Chinese kept telling us they were perfectly capable of handling Ford's security while he was in China, and they were right.

After providing some input on the policy papers prepared in advance, my role during the visit was to help take care of the massive press corps that accompanied the Fords to Peking. I enjoyed meeting with and briefing such heavyweights of the U.S. press as John Chancellor, Ted Koppel, Dan Rather, Marvin Kalb, and others. They didn't expect much to happen on the trip (they were right), but it was a major media event that exposed most of them to China for the first time. As part of their coverage of the trip, Diane and I had an extended interview with ABC designed to show Americans something of the diplomatic life in China.

Gary Trudeau did some of the best journalistic work on the trip in his Doonesbury comic strips. I had never heard of Trudeau, but one of the journalists pointed him out as he walked around with the others. He stayed well back in the pack and did not ask any questions, but his eye for the foibles of China was right on target. One of his cartoons, published a few weeks after the visit, showed the character Duke as the newly arrived American ambassador at a standard Chinese banquet. As part of the conversation, he asks his Chinese counterpart about politics in China. The official tries to divert his guest by suggesting he try the food. When Duke persists, the official points to the vegetables, to which Duke responds: "Speaking of vegetables, how's the Chairman?" Most of the Western political officers in China had that cartoon on their walls for months afterward.

Another classic Trudeau cartoon strip had the drug-using Duke making a speech recommending the distribution of recreational drugs in China and blasting China's human rights record. As he continued his speech, the applause became louder. At the end of his speech, he turned to his Chinese interpreter Honey, patterned on Nancy Tang, to ask if she had perhaps taken some liberties in interpreting his speech. After conceding at first that she had maybe "softened a word here and there," she then confessed he had just made a speech in Chinese expressing his admiration for last year's ball-bearing output. Her verdict: "You were spellbinding, sir."

Nancy Tang was an excellent interpreter who had the substance down cold. She was also Mao's favorite interpreter at the time. After listening to the chairman's brief indecipherable mutterings, she would craft a polite and substantive response to a question. Trudeau got it just right. Visitors never knew for sure what was Mao and what was Nancy; she even took part as a transmission belt when the visitor spoke French or some other language. Nancy paid the price of operating at such rarified levels. She disappeared from her position in March 1976, presumably because Chiang Ching wanted to establish herself as the only person having direct access to Mao in the months before he died. Fifteen years later Nancy and I had a nice chat at a reception at our embassy, which she attended as a ranking official of the Railways Ministry, obviously rehabilitated but well out of the limelight.

We saw all the feuding leaders (except Mao and Chou) during the Ford visit as they turned out for the various formal occasions. One such standard affair was the huge group photo at the Great Hall of the People that featured the Fords, Teng, Chiang Ching, and the visiting Americans and Chinese hosts. Diane and I happened to be placed in the photo just a bit above Chiang Ching, and I amused myself at the devious thought of reaching down and helping myself to one strand of her hair for posterity (and the CIA files.). Fortunately, I suppressed the temptation, but having her DNA on file might have been an interesting intelligence coup.

A Year of Turmoil in China

In 1976 events in China took a dramatic turn. The hardships of the Cultural Revolution, while waning, were still evident in the regime's approach to education, political indoctrination, and repression, and stunted the country's economic growth. The most senior leaders left standing after years of purges were dying off one after the other, and any Chinese could see the deterioration in Mao's health. The battles in the leadership over who would take power when he died were evident to anyone interested in China's politics. For the average Chinese, powerful portents such as a continuing series of earthquakes and meteors entering the atmosphere signaled the end of the regime's mandate to rule. To counter these deeply held ancient beliefs, the regime engaged in extraordinary efforts to debunk them with scientific explanations, demonstrating to us observers the power of these conceptions among the populace. The portents were to prove true.

Chou En-lai's death on January 8, 1976, produced a huge outpouring of grief in China, from ranking officials to ordinary people. Several hundred thousand Chinese citizens lined the street in Peking to view Chou's funeral cortege. When I attended the public ceremony to pay respects four days later in the Forbidden City, the mourners were deeply distraught. These were not false signs of grievance. Tears, swollen eyes, and a sense of loss and desperation were widespread. Some of it probably reflected affection for Chou the person, but mostly it stemmed from the fear that they had lost their protector against the radicals in the upcoming chaos. The *People's Daily* had emphasized the leftist theme of "class struggle" in its New Year's editorial, several moderate earthquakes put people on edge, and rumors of a new political struggle ran rampant. The one consolation the elite had was the expectation that Teng, who had delivered the eulogy at Chou's funeral, would take over as premier, a job Chou had held for the entire period of Communist rule.

Then on February 7 came the shock. Security czar Hua Kuo-feng, not Teng, was appointed acting premier, presumably as a compromise, maybe as a stalking horse for the left, but certainly not the determined supporter of Chou's moderate policies that Teng would have been. The other shoe fell a few days later when a nasty poster campaign started at Peking University naming Teng as a "capitalist roader." *People's Daily* charged that "capitalist roaders within the Party" had distorted Mao's instructions, emphasizing stability and unity and economic growth and downplaying class struggle. When I went to the university to see the posters for myself, a small forest of them attacking Teng had been pasted up. However, one prominent poster, ostensibly criticizing Teng but clearly put up by a supporter of his policies, probably captured the view of the university elite far better than the rest of the propaganda barrage. It said something to the effect of, "Can you believe that this Teng Hsiao-ping believes that educational advancement should be based on merit, not politics? Can you believe he puts economic development ahead of class struggle?" etc.

In the midst of this chaotic political situation, former president and Mrs. Nixon returned to China as guests of the PRC government, arriving on a Chinese 707 with journalists in tow. Not only was the timing bad in China, but Nixon arrived just as Ford was engaged in a tough battle with Ronald Reagan in New Hampshire for the Republican presidential nomination. Ford was said to be livid about the timing. He did not need the American public reminded again of his pardon for Nixon. USLO, superbly led at the time by Harry Thayer after the Bushes had departed, walked a fine line between courteous treatment of a former president and angering the current one. The Chinese made no secret that they preferred Nixon over Ford, and they also wanted to use the visit to demonstrate that their new leadership was in control. Despite numerous awkward moments, Nixon understood USLO's dilemma and let us decide how deeply we should be involved.

A few photos of Hua and Nixon in *People's Daily* could hardly cover up the political crisis in China. Diane, the girls, and I were in Nanking in early April on the way to a brief vacation in Hong Kong when we saw a large group of demonstrators commemorating their hero, Chou En-lai, on the traditional Tomb Sweeping Day holiday. At the same time a massive demonstration of wreath laying took place in Peking's Tiananmen Square, with posters praising Chou and Teng and criticizing the current leftist leadership. Peking police efforts to clear the square on the night of April 4–5 resulted in pitched battles, with many people killed and injured. Over 4,000 demonstrators were said to have been arrested. The leftist leadership formally named Hua Kuo-feng premier and second in command to Mao and stripped Teng once again of his party and government posts. The battle lines had been drawn, and the leadership of a post-Mao China remained to be settled.

Although the Chinese polemics with the Soviets continued through the seventies, there had been no further clashes on the 1969 scale. Lin Piao had been denounced for supposedly plotting with the Soviets, and the up-and-down negotiations on the border went nowhere. In every conversation with American political figures, the Chinese leadership hyped the Soviet threat and tried without success to dissuade the United States from pursuing détente with Moscow. The Russians, for their part, accused the Chinese of creating a false threat to entice American support. The simmering conflict became a real concern to us in Peking when an unidentified man set off a large bomb at the front gate of the Soviet Embassy compound in late April 1976, killing several guards and barely missing a large group of Russian schoolchildren who had been in the area a few minutes before. The Chinese never gave the Soviets a satisfactory explanation for the bombing (they claimed everyone involved was killed by the bomb). Diplomats from other missions were left to wonder whether the bomber was anti-Soviet or anti-foreign, and if they faced a similar threat.

Our third USLO chief, Thomas Gates, arrived in May 1976. A former secretary of the Navy, secretary of defense, and Morgan Guarantee Trust chairman, Gates meant well but seemed out of his depth dealing with the kaleidoscopic changes engulfing China. We had the opportunity to view China's new premier Hua Kuo-feng up close when Gates paid an initial courtesy call on him in June to deliver a letter of introduction from President Ford and discuss future relations. None of us in attendance were impressed. Hua's stock statements and wooden demeanor hardly looked like a man who could lead a country as big and complex as China. Hua gave the impression that he had gotten his position by not offending anyone. As things evolved over the next year, it was clear that much of the Chinese leadership shared our negative assessment.

Peking had been an exciting assignment, but our two years were up in the summer of 1976. Diane and I had hoped to leave Peking in June for a trip with the girls via the Trans-Siberian Railroad to Europe, but a debate in Washington over my next assignment led to a delay in my transfer orders. Finally, Diane and the girls went home on our credit card (an adventure in itself, as Northwest went on strike and stranded them in Tokyo); and I was asked to delay my departure until after USLO's Fourth of July Bicentennial celebration. With orders finally in hand, I left a few days after the Fourth on an Air Iran flight to Japan—one of only two international flights a week to Tokyo—and then home. It looked to me as if I was probably one of two paying passengers on the virtually empty Boeing 707.

Shortly after I left Peking, the portents of impending doom were realized. A massive earthquake on July 28, 1976, at Tangshan, just over a hundred miles from Peking, killed hundreds of thousands of people, destroyed the city, shut down transportation over much of north China, and left most residents of Peking sleeping on city streets to protect against falling debris from aftershocks. Families of diplomats were sent to neighboring countries or home. We were lucky to be safe in Washington and were not surprised when our household effects arrived many months late due to Chinese port closings. It was a terrible time for the Chinese trying to cope with the disaster and tough on diplomats and their families stuck in Peking. Mao's health deteriorated rapidly during the summer of 1976, and he died on September 9. A month later the "Gang of Four" were arrested and charged with various crimes. Hua Kuo-feng, backed by Mao's dictum—"With you in charge, I'm at ease."—hoped to set the future course of China; no one expected him to succeed. Over the next couple of years, he would be pushed off the stage by Teng, who accomplished another of his famous comebacks.

5
Carter's Washington and the Establishment of Formal Diplomatic Relations with China

Working for the Deputy Secretary

Orders finally came through assigning me as a special assistant to Deputy Secretary of State Charles Robinson. The office naturally demanded that I report immediately, leaving Diane and me about a week to look for a house in Washington and get settled with the girls. We soon found a place in Alexandria, Virginia, that was an easy commute to the State Department. It became our Washington area home for the next thirty-five years.

Despite the Bicentennial, mid-1976 was not a happy time in Washington or the State Department. Ford had just managed to edge out Reagan for the Republican nomination, Kissinger's reputation had plummeted, and U.S. foreign policy seemed to be in disarray. Kissinger clearly did not see my boss, the deputy secretary, as a partner in the formulation of policy. Chuck Robinson was an intelligent and decent man who could have played an important role if allowed. It hurt to see him lurk outside Kissinger's office hoping to be allowed into the "presence" for a few minutes to raise some issue of importance. After Ford lost the election to Carter, the administration went into the "lame duck" mode. We kept the papers moving as needed, but there was little of substance to do except await the new team, while watching events like the drama unfolding in China from afar.

The Carter administration came into office vowing major changes in the "failed" Kissinger foreign policy. On the Seventh Floor (where the secretary and top department officials work) most staffers who had served the previous administration found themselves looking for new jobs. But for some reason, perhaps because I had only been there a few months, I was kept on by the incoming group. My new boss, Warren Christopher, was a splendid person, an extremely capable, if low-key, lawyer. Suddenly, the State Department had a new vitality and a desire to make long-overdue policy changes in a more open, collaborative approach.

The new administration's top priorities were arms control, human rights, Korea, the Middle East, and a Panama Canal Treaty. China, in a period of leadership turmoil, was lower on the list. Besides managing the flow of policy papers, my usual responsibility, I also tried to help the new deputy secretary and his staff get settled into the department's routine and fend off a deluge of would-be office seekers. It's a tradition as old as the Republic itself that hordes descend on Washington seeking positions in a new administration, but I had never seen the process up close. A staggering number of Christopher's "close friends" and Democratic activists felt they were qualified for senior jobs in the State Department after eight years of Republican rule. I churned out hundreds of polite "thanks, but..." letters, which Christopher dutifully signed as either "Warren" or "Chris," depending on his relationship to the disappointed petitioners. I also met with people he could not fit into his schedule.

Carter Presses on Human Rights

President Carter came into office vowing to promote human rights and democracy as central elements of U.S. foreign policy. He had campaigned on a promise to infuse a higher morality into foreign relations and emphasized a "clear-cut preference for societies which share with us an abiding respect for individual human rights" in his inaugural address. The policy provided a stark contrast to Kissinger's realistic (critics would say cynical) approach; but it also played to Americans' long-standing sense of exceptionalism and their need to improve the world in which we lived. The promotion of human rights was a popular policy that fit with Americans' idealistic strain in dealing with the reality of a difficult, or even brutish, world society. The administration spoke out early against human rights violations in the Soviet Union, Czechoslovakia, and

Uganda and sanctioned Argentina, Ethiopia, and Uruguay for the treatment of their people. Although Secretary of State Cyrus Vance sought to temper the new emphasis on human rights somewhat by saying the United States would not comment on every issue or use "strident and polemical" language, I strongly doubted that the president agreed.

Christopher headed the interagency human rights working group that formulated the details of the president's human rights policies and led the effort to carry them out. He brought a young lawyer with no foreign affairs experience onto the staff to draft the new policy. I had several problems with parts of the draft that seemed unrealistic and argued it would weaken the system of alliances that we had built over several decades to counter Soviet and Chinese influence. My complaints were passed off by the drafters as reflecting a Foreign Service officer's affection for past policies, but to his credit Christopher listened carefully to my concerns.

The administration brought Patricia "Patt" Derian, a prominent Mississippi human rights activist and deputy director of the Carter-Mondale campaign, into the department to implement the new policy. It was obvious from the first day she came in to be "interviewed" by Christopher that *battles royal* lay ahead in the department. Patt had strong views and never shied away from a fight. I often disagreed with her on policy (although as the deputy secretary's representative I had to stay neutral in the department), but I had to admire her tenacity and willingness to take on all comers.

Patt could afford to be both tenacious and pugnacious because the president strongly agreed with her. Beyond direct discussions with the president by the secretary and deputy secretary, the Seventh Floor's main vehicle for informal interaction with the president was the "Night Notes" sent to the White House each evening by the secretary or the acting secretary. We took the preparation of these brief summaries very seriously, and the president obviously read them with care. In the early days of the administration, when the subject was human rights, the notes would invariably come back with annotations in Carter's careful handwriting, offering encouragement (or demands) to keep up or increase the heat on some government and signed by his definitive "J.C." There could be no doubt that the president was committed and determined to carry his policy through. However, making foreign policy through an overly simplistic human rights optic soon caused a major revolt in the department.

While many people in those early days felt too intimidated to state their opposition openly, it fell to those of us on Christopher's staff to keep him informed of the strong opposition that was brewing. Richard Holbrooke, the assistant secretary for East Asian Affairs and a person not easily intimidated, spoke up early on the need to make changes in the policy. The president's (and Patt's) approach threatened to completely undo our system of alliances in Asia with its criticism of Korea, the Philippines, and Thailand, at a time when we needed to rebuild our reputation after Vietnam and dampen speculation that we were withdrawing from the region. Kissinger and Nixon's new opening to China would also obviously be at risk if the sole criterion of American engagement depended on how a government treated its people. With Dick Holbrooke speaking out, others in the department came forward with their complaints. Christopher had the unenviable task of serving as the lawyerly dispute resolver, a task that occasionally meant he had to modify what he knew were the president's instincts.

The president's fervor clearly subsided after the shah of Iran visited Washington in November 1977 and he and Mrs. Carter spent New Year's Eve in Teheran. It seemed to me the human rights policy had lost its glitter during the New Year's Eve banquet in Iran. But in fairness, it was the realities of the world that made the president bend in his approach. The exhortations in the Night Notes dropped off, and Carter appeared to be backing away from one of his signature policies. Again, Christopher stepped into the breach. Now, instead of softening the president's approach, he found himself pressing the human rights agenda to preserve the administration's reputation. It was a thankless task, but none of us ever heard a word of complaint from Christopher.

Questionable New Approaches

While people in the State Department could understand (and mostly support) a nuanced policy of promoting human rights as an integral part of American foreign policy, another signature Carter program from the campaign seemed to make no sense whatsoever to the hard-nosed professionals in State and Defense. Carter had become convinced that U.S. ground troops in South Korea were nothing more than a trip wire to ensure that the United States would be involved if the North should invade again. On top of that, South Korea's Park Chung-hee regime was a classic case of a U.S. ally being a notorious human rights violator. People who had been dealing with the Korean problem for years readily conceded Park's authoritarian ways; but at the same time Kim Il-sung, North Korea's leader, was a far worse tyrant and universally seen as dangerous and unpredictable. Kim had attacked the south in 1950 when Dean Acheson left Korea out of the U.S. defense perimeter, and it seemed foolhardy in the extreme to tempt him again only two years after the fall of Saigon.

Carter nevertheless pressed on. On a visit to Japan only weeks into the administration, Vice President Mondale affirmed that the United States intended to withdraw ground troops from the peninsula, leaving its airpower to help the South Koreans. The withdrawal, Carter specified, would take place over four or five years. The reaction among Koreans, Japanese, and members of Congress was one of horror. Holbrooke and the U.S. military worked tirelessly to get the policy reversed. Finally, the administration delayed and then shelved the withdrawal, but the controversy made Carter's initiatives appear naïve and the administration divided.

The Conventional Arms Talks (CAT), carried out under the president's instructions by Leslie Gelb of State's Political-Military Bureau, were another ill-fated effort on which we had some impact. This initiative derived from Carter's view that one way to make the world a safer place would be to cut the level of arms available worldwide. In May 1977, Carter had announced that he planned to reduce the export of weapons unilaterally. For such a reduction to have an impact, the United States and the Soviet Union would have to agree, since these two countries provided the bulk of weapons sales—38 and 34 percent respectively, by one estimate. The always skeptical Europeans were content to stand aside and hold our coats, since they did not expect anything to come from the talks.

I remember going to Christopher after reading the U.S. policy decision on the issue to complain about its assertion that the sale of U.S. weapons abroad would be an "exceptional instrument" of U.S. policy. The implementation of such a policy, I argued, would destroy our alliances, since our friends relied on us for the weaponry, and would weaken our defense industries, because of falling sales. The whole concept seemed poorly thought out and should, I thought, be reconsidered. Christopher looked at me calmly and pointed out that the president had signed it. It was already U.S. policy.

I wasn't the only one who figured out that blanket limits on our arms sales could wreck U.S. alliances. The Soviets, not surprisingly, gradually changed their initial opposition—and by March 1978 had agreed to form a working group to study the problem, positioning themselves to demand that the U.S. make serious cutbacks of weapons sales to its allies. The Pentagon and Zbigniew Brzezinski's National Security Council (NSC) were working overtime to scuttle the negotiations. In December 1978, five months after I left the deputy secretary's office, the whole effort collapsed at a meeting in Mexico City. Gelb received instructions to walk out if the Soviets raised arms curbs in the Persian Gulf, China, or Korea. He argued to get the instructions changed but failed, and the Soviets did indeed raise cuts to those areas. The CAT discussions were a radical idea that may have had some intellectual validity; but they were doomed to failure from the start when confronted with global realities and the power balance the United States had created over decades. Gelb left the administration soon afterward.

Carter had some major foreign policy successes—the Panama Canal Treaty, SALT II, the Camp David Accords, China normalization, and the restoration of an ideological edge, namely human rights, which was critical for the American public's support of its government's foreign policy. But he got precious little public credit for them. Instead, the general view of the administration put the emphasis on failures (Brzezinski-Vance competition, the Iranian revolution and 444-day hostage crisis, the Soviet invasion of Afghanistan, high energy prices, and so on) and on a general sense of disarray and incompetence that led to his defeat for a second term in 1980 by Ronald Reagan.

Sadly, the flaws were visible from the early days when I was in the deputy secretary's office. Carter himself lacked real experience with foreign policy and insisted on policies he had formulated in the campaign that simply could not work. Even with good ideas like injecting human rights into the equation, he pushed the concepts well beyond a reasonable point and with a stubbornness that refused to take the downsides into account. One reporter noted that Carter's micromanagement style left him "doing good things badly." The excessive fixation on Kissinger and his legacy in the early days also weakened clearheaded analysis of new policy formulations. It almost seemed as if the department had to do the opposite of anything that Kissinger had done, a dubious proposition at best and a sure way to unsettle allies and confuse friend and foe alike. The Kissinger NSC model also poisoned the Brzezinski-Vance relationship, sowing the seeds of the policy failures that later dogged the administration.

Normalization of Relations with the PRC

As I was finishing up my time on the deputy secretary's staff and planning a one-year Congressional Fellowship, Dick Holbrooke asked me to move instead to the China desk as the chief political officer. Fresh from accompanying Brzezinski to China, Dick asserted this would be the year that the United States and the PRC normalized diplomatic relations, and he needed my help with the drafting of U.S. negotiating positions. The offer was impossible to turn down, even though it promised a hectic year rather than a nice relaxed one learning how Congress works. We agreed it would be a one-year assignment, because I was lined up to take Russian and go to Moscow in 1980.

Much had changed in China in the two years since we left Peking. As expected, Hua proved to be a weak leader. China under his leadership seemed to be flailing, Teng resumed his position as vice premier in July 1977, and the Gang of Four were formally expelled from the party. From then on, Mao's pet leftist policies (worker-peasant-soldier students, youth to the countryside, autarkic economic policies) began to fall by the wayside to be replaced by college exams, the return of purged leaders, and an emphasis on science and economic development. In December 1978 Teng's role as China's leader and his moderate "Reform and Opening Up" approach were enshrined as national policy. Modernizing China's industry, agriculture, national defense, science & technology, "seeking truth from facts," and making China "a modern, powerful socialist country" were the new themes. The past was heavily criticized, and twenty-nine years after the establishment of Communist rule China finally embarked on a firm path of modernization. Although Teng was without doubt the most powerful man in China, he retained his modest title of vice premier.

Given China's internal situation, the political cost of cutting U.S. ties with Taiwan, and the pressure of other foreign policy issues, it was hardly surprising that China policy had not been at the top of the new Carter administration's priorities. The Chinese made conciliatory noises about solving the "Taiwan issue" through negotiations but also made clear that their position had not changed from the line laid down with Nixon and Kissinger—namely, how China would liberate Taiwan was a domestic affair and not negotiable with the United States. China sought to pressure the administration by reminding it that both Nixon and Ford had promised to normalize relations in their "second terms."

Secretary of State Vance made his first visit to China in August 1977, for what was labeled in the U.S. as "exploratory talks." Teng, who had just returned to the Politburo, served as the Americans' primary host once again, and Vance stated publicly that the United States wanted to move to full diplomatic relations. But neither side really offered anything new, both were distracted by other issues, and the trip produced no results. When Vance returned home, Carter proclaimed that normalization "is undoubtedly going to be well into the future" and talked of it as an "ultimate goal." After somewhat more positive remarks on the trip by a White House staffer claiming progress, Teng chose to correct the record by calling the trip a "setback" for relations between the two countries.

As the Chinese internal situation stabilized and the administration became more firmly established, Carter decided to send Brzezinski, an advocate for moving forward quickly on normalization, for another high-level discussion with China in May 1978. Vance objected to the trip, as his attention remained focused on getting a SALT II agreement with the Soviets. Vance's concerns about Brzezinski playing the "China card" on the trip were justified. The national security advisor took a strongly anti-Soviet line with Chinese leaders and clowned around in front of reporters on a trip to the Great Wall, challenging his host in front of the press that "the last one to the top had to oppose the Soviets in Ethiopia." Brzezinski briefed the Chinese on the state of talks with the Soviets and announced that the United States had made up its mind to move to full diplomatic relations with China. It was shortly after the delegation returned to Washington that Holbrooke asked me to change my plans for the next year.

The Brzezinski trip inaugurated a series of tightly held negotiations to finally establish normal diplomatic ties between the two governments. President Carter instructed Brzezinski and Vance to manage these negotiations together with Leonard Woodcock, head of the U.S. Liaison Office in Beijing, supported by their close assistants, Mike Oksenberg at the NSC, Dick Holbrooke at State, and Stapleton Roy, Woodcock's DCM in Beijing. Presumably, Vance kept his deputy Warren Christopher in the loop and also involved the department's legal advisor. But the secretary of state needed to be able to say they had kept the promise to the president to hold the negotiations close.

Holbrooke turned to Harry Thayer, the China Desk chief, for help; and he in return involved his deputy, Don Anderson, and me. This gave Holbrooke the support staff he wanted, but neither Anderson nor I was ever present during Thayer's discussions with Holbrooke or Holbrooke's meetings with Vance on the China negotiations. We saw and commented on most of the drafts up until the last month, when the circle of people involved was tightened even more. At one point, Holbrooke chided Thayer that a draft (which I had prepared) was too neat. Without the usual typing mistakes, people up the line would suspect (correctly) that there were others in the loop.

On December 15, 1978, President Carter read a joint communiqué to a surprised world announcing that the United States and the People's Republic of China would establish diplomatic relations on January 1, 1979, and the United States would "maintain cultural, commercial and other unofficial relations with the people of Taiwan." He announced that Teng Hsiao-ping would visit the United States at the end of January to "strengthen and expedite the benefits of this new relationship." Diplomatic relations would be broken with Taipei, the defense treaty ended, and all U.S. troops withdrawn in four months, but the United States would continue to provide arms to Taiwan. The press and indeed the Congress and the U.S. bureaucracy had been kept in the dark on the negotiations, and some reacted strongly against the announcement. I found it somewhat galling that I was later criticized in at least one serious publication for not having kept Congress fully informed about the negotiations, even though I was supposed to know nothing about them.

The U.S. press was later briefed (presumably by Brzezinski) that detailed instructions were sent to Woodcock for the negotiating sessions he carried out over the previous six months. President Carter had been personally involved in approving all of the instructions, which were sent through White House, not State Department, communications channels. The United States had informed the Chinese that it would continue commercial and cultural ties with Taiwan, wanted a peaceful settlement of the issue, and would continue to sell arms to Taiwan after normalization with Peking. In classic U.S.-Chinese ambiguity, we said the United States would continue arms sales and wanted a peaceful settlement, while the Chinese formally objected but agreed to normalization. At the State Department, we had made our modest contributions to the process, but President Carter, Brzezinski, Woodcock, and Teng deserve the credit for making normalization happen.

The Deng Visit

The December 15, 1978, announcement started a frenzied process to complete the details of the normalization process, prepare for the visit of Deng Xiaoping (Teng Hsiao-ping) to the United States and set up the new relationship with Taiwan.

[As noted earlier, the Chinese changed to the Pinyin system of romanization on January 1, 1979, and I will follow that practice.]

Normalization of relations with China added to the already highly charged political atmosphere in Washington. Carter clearly needed a successful Deng visit to buttress his political position on normalization, and the new ties with Taiwan had to be set up with the same finesse as full ties with Beijing (Peking). Politics were also churning in China. Deng's development strategy had just been adopted, but he needed a dramatic trip to convince his rivals and the Chinese people that his policy of openness to the West was the right one and that China could play on the same field as the world's most advanced country.

Famous for his pragmatism, Deng had concluded that the path out of poverty for China lay in adopting the openness and export-promotion policies that Japan, Taiwan, South Korea, and Singapore had used to modernize. When it came to politics, Deng was no liberal reformer, but he concluded that China could undergo a rapid economic transformation with the Communist party keeping tight control of the politics. The trip to the United States provided an unparalleled opportunity for him to demonstrate the possibilities of this openness policy for the Chinese people.

When we were in China in the seventies and nineties, it was quite common for the Chinese to refer to their aspiration to achieve China's "rightful role" in the world. As I tried to explain to our American visitors, for the country whose GDP had been the highest in the world only a hundred years earlier and probably for a millennium before that, most Chinese believed their rightful place was "number one." Mao's policies had kept them from fulfilling that destiny. Deng was determined to reverse those policies and use his trip to the United States to make his point.

To manage this extraordinary task, the State Department set up a small working group of officers under EAP deputy assistant secretary Roger Sullivan. My boss on the China Desk, Harry Thayer, acted as deputy and effectively managed the process. Other members included Harvey Feldman, who led the approach to Taiwan, and a selection of officers pulled together for their expertise and capacity for work, rather than their formal positions in the bureaucracy. My job was initially something like a chief of staff to Thayer, but it soon evolved into managing the details of the Deng visit, ensuring that it not only went well but that it also sent the right messages to both the Chinese and American people. Others prepared the background papers and talking points, as well as setting up the structure for the new relationship with Taiwan. From December 15 to February 5, when Deng departed the United States, my only day off with my family was Christmas. The hours, as one would expect, were brutal, but the China Working Group was the place to be in the State Department for those fifty-plus days.

The focus of our trip planning was to get the new relationship between China and the United States off to a good start. Predictably, Carter's decision to establish relations with Beijing and break formal ties with Taiwan evoked a strong attack from conservative Republicans (and some Democrats), especially over the question of the defense of Taiwan against a Chinese military attack. For his part, Deng needed to bolster his openness strategy by showing that cooperation with the outside world was possible and could have great benefits. Unlike the usual public relations visit, Deng wanted to see and to show to the Chinese people the world's top technology, which the Chinese coveted for themselves, and to make clear that the path to progress for China was through cooperation with its former chief enemy, the world's most advanced country. Both countries wanted to establish the new U.S.-Chinese relationship as a reality of the international order (in our case, without overly ruffling the feathers of the Soviet Union, with which we were trying to reach a new accord on the control of strategic weapons).

Given the mostly congruent aims of the two sides for the trip, our task (and that of the Chinese advance team that arrived in Washington on January 12) was to put together an itinerary with appropriate events to accomplish these basic goals. This resulted in a jam-packed schedule, heavy on commerce, scientific achievement, and public displays of cooperation, with an emphasis on the future potential for increased trade between the two countries. The trip achieved these goals and then some.

For the first couple of days after Deng's arrival on the afternoon of Sunday, January 28, 1979, the events mostly followed standard American state visit protocol (which was unusual, since although clearly in charge of China, Deng was formally only a vice premier.) The positive tone for the visit began in the welcoming ceremony on the White House lawn, followed by the usual discussion between the visitor, the president, and their entourages, lunch at the State Department, a State Dinner at the White House (the year's most sought-after invitation), and a gala at the Kennedy Center to entertain the guests and show off American culture (the second-most sought-after ticket, even though the show was described by attendees as something of a mishmash that had to be put together on extremely short notice.)

Diane and I watched the first of many protests against Deng's visit from our spot on the White House lawn at the welcoming ceremony. Two American Maoists who had obtained press credentials shouted insults at Deng during his speech for drifting away from Maoist principles. They were quickly hauled away by the Secret Service, but that evening a hundred or so Maoists took part in a demonstration that turned violent and resulted in dozens of arrests.

Brzezinski breached protocol by hosting Deng to an informal dinner at his house on Sunday night just after his arrival in the United States The dinner seemed primarily designed to demonstrate Brzezinski's importance in the Washington pecking order. It also deprived Deng of the chance to go to bed early after the long flight from China to prepare for the hectic schedule during the remainder of his trip.

The most sensitive political events took place the next day on the Hill, as Deng met with members of the House of Representatives and lunched with some eighty-five senators. Deng's straightforward approach and his adroitness in handling the Taiwan issue defused a considerable part of the anger of the congressmen and senators over the "abandonment of Taiwan." Deng said the Chinese were in no hurry for reunification but needed to retain the possibility of using force to maintain its negotiating position with Taiwan. His soothing performance helped ease the way for the president in later negotiations with Congress on the Taiwan Relations Act and gained essential support for the president's China policy.

For that evening, the Chinese embassy had organized an event (rather foolishly we thought) for seven hundred people from pro-Chinese leftist groups to dine with Deng. We were concerned that the dinner would cut out many far more important centrist groups that had labored hard to improve relations and could also sour the atmosphere by making the visit seem like an issue dividing the American left and right. We worked with the more prominent organizations that had promoted relations with China to set up a complementary reception and have Deng attend both.

White House staffers vetoed my first suggestion, that we use an auditorium, because they wanted a larger event and feared Deng would give a stemwinding, anti-Soviet speech that would only rile Moscow. Instead, they argued for a venue where speechmaking could be kept to a minimum and U.S. participants would have some chance to mingle with Deng. The White House soon came up with a reception in the newly opened East Wing of the National Gallery of Art, which had been designed by the famous Chinese-American architect I.M. Pei. Receptions in museums were fairly common, the Pei connection seemed right, and the Chinese by then had told me that Deng was not planning to make a formal speech. We worked hard to produce an event that would set the right tone, and it certainly looked good when we did the preliminary walk-throughs. A platform had been set up for Deng to make his expected short remarks of greeting and then take a short tour of the museum to allow some circulation among the guests.

Despite our planning, the venue and the event proved to be a disaster. As the large number of guests began to pack the building and gather around the scattered tables, the gorgeous setting soon became as noisy as a bazaar, and the tiered seating made it hard to meet other guests or be seen by your peers. Even informal conversations with nearby guests were difficult. Deng did, in fact, come armed with a tough anti-Soviet, anti-Vietnam diatribe, which he proceeded to deliver as soon as he arrived. No one in the audience that evening could hear very clearly because of the bad sound system and acoustics; but the thrust of the speech was obvious to us all. I later learned that some Chinese blamed me for the venue and the sound system, reasoning that I had done it on purpose to ensure that Deng's speech would not be heard. (I was hardly that clever.) Deng left immediately after his speech (probably unhappy, but maybe just tired), passing up the scheduled tour of the new building, with its Sino-American connotations, and the opportunity to rub shoulders with some of the guests. Many of the guests also left unhappy; they had hoped to get a chance to see the honored guest up close or, at least, be able to hear his speech. After the reception I trudged slowly across the Mall to my car, blaming myself for the disaster and regretting that I had not fought harder for a more appropriate venue.

Fortunately, the trip turned upbeat the next day, with the signing of several agreements on scientific and cultural exchange, consular issues, space-based technology, physics, education, and agriculture. Deng then embarked on his tour of the United States, beginning in President Carter's home state of Georgia. Deng had lunch with the Chamber of Commerce (1,400 attended, with another 1,200 on the waiting list), laid a wreath at Martin Luther King's grave, and toured the Ford Motor Co. plant. As in other stops, there were many pro-and anti-Deng demonstrators. But strangely, the preponderance of demonstrators in most places (like the two on the White House grounds) tended to be members of the Revolutionary Communist Party and other Maoist groups rather than supporters of Taiwan. I was particularly amused by the chatting among several ranking Chinese officials in an elevator as they looked at the demonstrators' flags. One pointed out a distinct flag, only to be told by his colleague that it must belong to a Taiwan independence group. I couldn't resist breaking into their conversation to point out that in fact the flag was the "Stars and Bars" of the American Confederacy from our own Civil War.

Next, the stop in Houston turned out to be a highlight of the trip. The Texas establishment's initial political reception of Deng was decidedly cool. Opposition to the treatment of Taiwan remained high, and even Texas Democratic senator Lloyd Bentsen felt it politic to stay away from the welcoming ceremony. Deng's charm and the lure of large business deals, however, quickly turned the tide. Deng himself seemed to blossom as a tourist when he visited the Johnson Space Center and took a ride in the simulator designed for the space shuttle program. (He asked for and got a second landing.) Deng was selling his vision for China to his home audience, and pictures of him in the simulator flooded the Chinese propaganda network at home.

The biggest scheduling gamble of the trip turned into a public relations triumph. With some trepidation, we treated Deng and his entourage to a dude rodeo in Simonton for Texas barbecue and some typical Texas entertainment. Donning cowboy hats, watching bull riding and other events, and observing the clichés of the American West turned out to be great fun for the Chinese delegation. When offered a ride around the ring in a horse-drawn stagecoach, Deng acted as if he had worked as an American politician for his entire life, waving his cowboy hat and reacting to the cheers of the audience. For the Texans, in particular, and for the Americans, in general, Deng's behavior struck just the right note. For the Chinese home audience who watched it all on television, the event was a sensation, showing Deng not as the usual stiff Chinese politician but as a global figure who could play to the Americans as well as he played to his people at home. No one had ever seen a Chinese Communist leader enjoying himself like this, much less doing it on American soil. It portrayed a very different future relationship with the Americans, who suddenly seemed far more human than most Chinese would have expected after thirty long years of heavy anti-American propaganda.

Several months later, Diane and I were with a United Nations group in a rural area of western Sichuan where Americans had not been seen in three decades. The village propaganda board contained a large display of pictures of Deng's trip, including several from the rodeo. In one of them, I could be seen in the bleachers several rows behind Deng. When I pointed this out, I became instantly popular in this out-of-the way agriculture station. It brought home again the trip's enormous impact on the Chinese public.

In Houston, Deng and his wife also met with George and Barbara Bush, the only Republican presidential candidate willing to be seen associating himself with Carter's China policy. The two couples had last seen each other during the 1975 Ford visit to Beijing. I hadn't seen the Bushes either since they left Beijing, and it was a delight to talk old times before the Dengs arrived.

During his last stop in Seattle, an obviously exhausted Deng had the usual political and press meetings followed by a trip to the Boeing 747 plant (keeping the emphasis on trade potential) and dinner at a local steakhouse. Don Anderson had told me that the State Department China desk's response to inquiries about what to feed the delegation noted that most Chinese preferred small amounts of meat with vegetables. By Seattle Deng had had his fill of minced veal; he wanted a real American steak and ate it with relish. The next day (February 5) a tired Deng departed for home, presumably elated that he had accomplished his goals, but undoubtedly calculating the next steps in his campaign to transform China and the timing of his planned invasion of Vietnam. The U.S. side, from the president on down, breathed a sigh of relief that the trip had gone so well. But the hard work to build a long, effective relationship between the two countries that seemed destined to lead the world of the future had just begun.

Revising the U.S.-Taiwan Relationship

Recognition of the PRC as the government of China rather than Taiwan meant the United States had to quickly construct a new relationship with Taiwan. Obviously, the U.S. Liaison Office would be transformed into the U.S. Embassy in China, but Deng had emphasized to Vance in 1977 that they would not accept a formal "liaison office" in Taiwan like USLO. The establishment of diplomatic relations between Japan and China in 1972 provided the United States and China with a precedent for setting up an "unofficial" office in Taiwan that would allow the United States to maintain "commercial and cultural" relations with the island. The Japanese had been able to do this fairly easily, but they were not the defenders of Taiwan, nor did they have the serious legal hurdles faced by the United States.

The administration sent Congress a bare-bones draft to authorize such an office after the December 15 announcement, but Congress insisted on a much more political document that provided assurances to the people of Taiwan that we were not abandoning them. Intensive negotiations followed in Washington, especially over efforts by Senate Republicans to link Taiwan's security to that of the United States and, essentially, to provide for the continuation of the U.S. Mutual Security Treaty with Taiwan under a different name. In the end, the administration's view prevailed. Both the House and Senate settled on a statement that an attack on Taiwan would be "of grave concern" to the people of the United States. After a series of close votes setting up the American Institute in Taiwan (AIT), the Taiwan Relations Act passed, China protested as expected, and the deal was done.

Normally, when a government is recognized as a country's government, it automatically receives the property that was held by its predecessor. Taiwan immediately sought to protect its property. This included the ten-acre "Twin Oaks" estate, one of the most valuable privately owned residences in Washington, which they sold to a friendly group of Americans for ten dollars. I remember well the first call after the normalization announcement in December by the head of the Chinese Liaison Office, Chai Tze-min, on Deputy Secretary Christopher. I drafted a briefing paper for Christopher saying the ambassador probably wanted to exchange congratulations on normalizing relations and discuss the modalities of the upcoming Deng visit. Christopher must have thought his old special assistant had lost it when Chai came in, guns blazing, to demand that the United States hand over all of Taiwan's property immediately. There were no congratulatory comments, just a tough demand for the property. To be sure, Chai did not have the smooth diplomatic style of his predecessors; but this was over the top and a striking example of Chinese negotiating style when they thought they had the advantage.

After conferring with State's Legal Office, I informed the Chinese that property issues in the United States ultimately had to be decided by the courts (especially since the Taiwan government had "sold" the property to a private entity), and that they needed to engage a good law firm immediately to support their case. The State Department would provide an opinion that property should go to the duly recognized government, and they would presumably win their case. The Chinese refused to take our advice. Instead, over the next couple of months they repeatedly demanded that we just hand over the property. Ultimately, the matter was settled in the Taiwan Relations Act, which gave the property to Taiwan. The Chinese had played it badly and were too late to make their claim. Today, the head of Taiwan's Washington office continues to entertain at the splendid Twin Oaks estate, which they quickly reclaimed after the Taiwan Relations Act was signed.

Although I had given up my year as a Congressional Fellow to be part of the normalization process, I actually spent an enormous amount of time over the year dealing with members of Congress and their staffs. Many in Congress wanted to see Deng's new, post-Mao China for themselves. If a country is fashionable (for positive or negative reasons) on the Hill, this means a heavy load of briefings and trip planning for any State Department desk officer. After normalization on January 1, 1979, the rush from the Hill to China was unstoppable and the demand for papers and oral briefings almost endless. Over the Easter break, five separate congressional delegations, with sixty-five members of Congress, their wives, and staffs, visited China. All had to be briefed on the situation in China and U.S. policy and have their particular demands catered to.

True to Deng's hints in Washington, Chinese troops invaded Vietnam days after his U.S. trip ended. The ostensible reason for the invasion was to "teach the Vietnamese a lesson" for their invasion of Cambodia, siding with the Soviets in their dispute with the Chinese, and expelling hundreds of thousands of Chinese living in Vietnam. The Chinese withdrew two months later, having proved little except that the battle-hardened Vietnamese, with their American equipment acquired from the South Vietnamese forces, could hold their own quite well against the ill-equipped and overly politicized Chinese forces. Stories leaked out that the Chinese troops were communicating with semaphore flags and other outdated means during the fight, a rumor that certainly resonated with me; I had seen the Chinese military's communication equipment in action in Soochow during Kissinger's visit five years earlier. It was a major wake-up call for the Chinese military and the beginning of a long-running internal Chinese debate over military modernization. For the Vietnamese, it reminded them that their close friend and partner in the war against the Americans was the same old bullying China that had stolen the Paracel Islands less than a decade before.

6
Superpowers in Deep Crisis

In the fall of 1979, Diane and I began the nine-month Russian course at the Foreign Service Institute (FSI) in preparation for our assignment to Moscow. Unfortunately, the program's heads decided to experiment with a new approach that proved to be agony for us students and even worse for the teachers. The course turned out to be a huge disappointment after the superb Chinese training program we had had both as students and at the State Department school in Taichung. I managed to get by in Moscow, but even reading the predictable propaganda in the Soviet press took considerably longer than it should have.

Daily one-on-one encounters with the teachers (some of whom had arrived quite recently from the Soviet Union) did, however, provide a small window into the Russian view of the world. I remember one discussion in which my teacher called the Central Asians worthless freeloaders and other names too choice to put on paper and asserted that they were a huge drag on the "cultured" core of European Russia. I thought of this conversation a dozen years later as the Russian leadership let the outer parts of the empire that had been acquired over centuries at great cost go without complaint and with the obvious consent of the Russian populace. Later, of course, Putin and the empire-gatherers went to great lengths to try to get them back. Another teacher gave me a sense of the intense animosity felt by many Ukrainians toward their Russian brethren. Those conversations were helpful in making sense of later developments.

While we were trying to learn Russian at FSI, relations between the United States and the Soviet Union went into a nosedive. The high hopes of June 1979, when SALT II was signed, soon gave way to the steady deterioration of relations in the fall (by contrast, U.S.-China ties were improving rapidly.) The Iran hostage crisis beginning in November added to the tensions, and then the Soviet invasion of Afghanistan two days after Christmas 1979 ensured we were in for years of confrontation. The United States reacted to the invasion with anger and resolve. President Carter announced a series of sanctions on the Soviet Union in January that included an embargo on the sale of agricultural products, a cutoff in high technology sales, severe curtailment of Soviet fishing privileges in U.S. waters, a delay in opening consulates, and the deferral of new cultural and economic changes. (A colleague on the Soviet desk who developed the list in less than an hour told me his instructions were to draw up a list of possible sanctions from which the White House could choose. Surprisingly, the administration chose everything on the list.) Carter also warned that continuation of the invasion could threaten U.S. participation in the Moscow Olympics set for the summer. When it became obvious the Soviets would not withdraw, Carter called for a boycott of the 1980 Moscow Summer Olympics. Spurred on by the U.S. example and our strong lobbying around the world, almost half of the planned participants boycotted the games.

Moscow

We arrived in Moscow to begin our tour in this poisonous atmosphere in July 1980, a couple of weeks before the Olympics were to open. It was a cold, wet summer, and we worried about our girls being warm enough at the embassy dacha camp outside Moscow. (The girls' main memory of the summer was the prevalent leeches along the river where they swam.) Suddenly, shortly before the Olympics began, the air over Moscow cleared, and the sun shone brilliantly for the duration of the games. Then, right on schedule after the final ceremony, the weather reverted to wet and nasty. The Soviet press later described the major rainmaking project during the Olympics that drenched the Moscow environs but created a donut hole of clear skies over the city for the event. The Chinese have frequently used the same technique to modify the weather when they host major international events.

The weather seemed to be something of a portent for our two years in Moscow. The embassy's political counselor, Sherrod McCall (who had done such extraordinary analytical work in Hong Kong), asked me to fill the Asia slot in the Political Section's External Unit. Most of my attention in the first six months focused on Afghanistan and China. I soon learned that the Foreign Ministry's Afghanistan experts were pessimistic about the prospects for the Soviet invasion. Stories had begun to circulate in Moscow about sealed caskets returning from Afghanistan containing horribly maimed bodies, and the attempts to hide the heavy causalities suffered by Soviet troops became more and more frantic. The ministry specialists fretted about the sustainability of the Soviet effort.

A few months after our arrival, a frightened Soviet Army private forced his way into the U.S. Embassy in Kabul and sought asylum. In a remarkable State Department lapse for a country in which the Soviet Union was calling the shots, our embassy there had no one on its staff who spoke Russian. They could not communicate in any detail with the intruder. I was called into the Embassy to read a cable asking for help and went over to Spaso House (the ambassador's residence) to see McCall, who was attending a black-tie dinner hosted by the ambassador. Decidedly underdressed in my casual attire, I stood in the fringes of the dining hall and waved frantically at Sherrod to get his attention. After a short discussion out of sight of the other guests, the ambassador agreed that one of our best Russian speakers could go to Kabul to help out. In the end, with clear communications reestablished, the private decided to accept Soviet promises of demobilization and forgiveness and returned home.

I suspect few people in Washington were paying much attention to our cables from Moscow in this period. Carter lost the 1980 election because of his foreign policy "failures" and domestic difficulties. The group that President Reagan brought into his cabinet were not interested in improving relations with the Soviets. Caspar Weinberger at DOD, William Casey at CIA, and Richard Allen at the NSC, supported by people such as Richard Perle and Richard Pipes, were all known to take a hardline view of Soviet motives and intentions. They saw little good coming from discussion with the Soviets on any topic. Secretary of State Alexander Haig also used tough rhetoric on the Soviets, but he soon found himself in shouting matches with others, as they outflanked him on the right. Reagan himself was known for his disdain for the Russians and gave no indication in his first two years that he was willing to take a more accommodating approach.

Our embassy in Moscow was going through a troubled time. The ambassador, IBM's Thomas Watson, who had arrived in Moscow just before the Soviet invasion of Afghanistan provided a lesson about the dangers in the American spoils system of appointing amateur ambassadors to important posts. A friend of Secretary Vance, Watson had no diplomatic experience and had supposedly been picked to promote trade between the two countries. Unfortunately, he was completely out of his depth in running Embassy Moscow during a crisis. He decamped just before Reagan was inaugurated, taking with him his able DCM Mark Garrison to open a Russian studies center at Brown University.

McCall then took charge of the embassy until the department dispatched Jack Matlock, ambassador-designate to Czechoslovakia and former Embassy Moscow DCM, to act as chargé until a new ambassador could be named. McCall served as Matlock's acting deputy, my immediate boss, Ed Djerejian, took over as political counselor, and I ran the external unit, my main beat now switching from Asia to U.S.-Soviet relations. Matlock immediately reestablished a sense of professionalism at the top of the embassy, as we tried to serve as a bridge between Washington and Moscow and to explain what was going on in each capital to the other.

Leonid Brezhnev was clearly near the end of his tenure as general secretary. Each time he appeared on television to give the standard long and boring speech he looked as though he might die on the spot or have to be carried offstage in midsentence. You could almost hear a sigh of relief across Moscow when, toward the end of our tour, Brezhnev just read the first few sentences of his speech, with a television announcer doing the rest. The Russians were deeply embarrassed by his frailty and growing senility, which made endless material for their famous political jokes.

One story that made the rounds—which several Russian friends swore was true—had Brezhnev starting a meeting with Indira Gandhi by saying, "It is a pleasure to welcome Margaret Thatcher here today." His staff whispered in his ear that it was Indira Gandhi, and Brezhnev started over, again welcoming her as Margaret Thatcher. When his assistant again prompted him, Brezhnev burst out: "I know it's Indira Gandhi, but my paper says it's Margaret Thatcher!"

Even if the United States had been anxious to move forward on bilateral ties at the time (which it wasn't), there was no way any dramatic policy changes could have been made by the Soviet side. This would be true in Moscow for most of Reagan's first term. (Incidentally, the most popular reporting from the embassy at the time was its monthly wrap-up of recently heard Russian political jokes.)

Washington's tough line toward Moscow had little real effect, since the sanctions and limited contact had become a fact of life from the last year of the Carter administration. There was no danger of Embassy Moscow taking a soft line. Dealing with Soviet bureaucrats up close while serving in the embassy or the consulates did little to endear the Soviet system to Americans. Some of our people had a deep appreciation of Russian culture and sympathy for the plight of the Russian people, but I never heard anyone say a good word about the Soviet government or its leadership.

China remained a raw wound for the Soviets. One afternoon in early fall I attended an open Znaniye (Knowledge) lecture given by a leading Soviet China expert, Oleg Rakhmanin. The crowd had been warmed up with footage of Soviet students being roughed up as they departed China by train in 1966 at the start of the Cultural Revolution. Rakhmanin's speech was a recital of Chinese perfidy and hostility toward Russia and the Soviet Union. In describing future Chinese plans, Rakhmanin flashed on the screen a graphic that would have warmed the heart of any Pentagon briefer: Superimposed on a map of China and the Soviet Far East was a huge red arrow showing Chinese military forces sweeping northeast to take over territory from Khabarovsk through the Maritime Provinces, including Vladivostok—land Beijing argued Russia had stolen as part of the unequal 1858 Treaty of Aigun. The audience was duly impressed. For me, the lecture provided a vivid illustration of the primordial Russian concern for its Far East, which lurked under the surface even as the Chinese and Russians later moved to a friendlier relationship.

One real disconnect the embassy had with Washington involved Soviet policy toward Central America. The Reagan administration came in greatly exercised over the possibilities of a communist takeover of Central America—"It's closer to Texas than Texas is to Washington."—and hyped both the Soviet and Cuban roles. Our colleagues in Central America bought into this narrative and regularly sent cables that should have been entitled, "The Russians Are Coming! The Russians Are Coming!" We had no doubt that the Russians were happy to make us squirm by stirring things up in Central America, especially after U.S. aid to the anti-Soviet forces in Afghanistan began to bite; but there was no way Central America was a high priority for Moscow's feeble leadership, given its overreach in Afghanistan. We said this on several occasions to Washington, but it had no effect because it did not fit the administration's political narrative.

Poland was another issue of great concern during a good part of our time in Moscow. From its birth in August 1980, the Solidarity Movement led by Lech Walesa pressed the Communist government in Warsaw to meets its demands for economic benefits, human rights, and increased democracy. The other East European Communist regimes became increasingly concerned with this threat to their own hold on power and pressed Moscow to intervene, as it had done earlier in Hungary and Czechoslovakia. The Carter administration had voiced strong concern that the Soviets might do just that. We thought that the Soviets were unlikely to intervene short of a threat that the Communist government would be overthrown. When General Wojciech Jaruzelski took over as Polish prime minister in February 1981, the Reagan administration seemed to relax somewhat about the chance of a Soviet invasion. Tensions continued, however, as Solidarity pressed its demands, with considerable international support. In December 1981, Jaruzelski declared martial law and arrested Walesa and thousands of others, effectively suppressing the movement temporarily without a Soviet invasion.

We also attempted to give Washington a sense of what was going on in the Soviet leadership, but we had little to work with.

Moscow's press and leaders' speeches revealed almost nothing. The only Russians willing to have a serious conversation about politics were the dissident "refuseniks," who had their own agendas and little real access to what was going on. With the end of the Brezhnev era at hand, all my instincts, honed from the raucous atmosphere in Chinese politics of the seventies, pointed to a leadership jockeying for power. But the evidence was thin. American Sovietologists trained in the Brezhnev period had a bias toward believing that any changes were likely to be marginal and that the system itself would endure. I disagreed but had no way to prove it.

Our diplomatic colleagues did little better in finding out what was going on in the country. And given the pervasive Soviet security apparatus, they were often reluctant to endanger their few contacts by passing on information to us. Even our colleagues in other sections of the embassy seemed reluctant to tell us what they heard from their contacts. I remember being particularly perturbed when one senior colleague mentioned in a staff meeting that he had spent the evening drinking and talking with security chief Yuri Andropov's son. Since the elder Andropov was a major contender to succeed Brezhnev, I tried to get some useful information about what the son had said about the political scene or other Soviet leaders. Regrettably, it had not occurred to this seasoned diplomat to steer the conversation to Kremlin politics. I could only throw up my hands in exasperation that such a rare opportunity had been missed.

Matlock asked me to accompany him as notetaker on his first Moscow call on Deputy Foreign Minister Georgy Korniyenko. This was going to be a challenge, since Jack was well known as the best Russian speaker in the U.S. Foreign Service (he had taught Russian before joining) and had a reputation for being somewhat pedantic about it. My Russian—to put it mildly —still needed a lot of work. As expected, the entire conversation took place in rapid fire Russian, with Korniyenko complaining about Washington's tough line on Afghanistan and SALT II and Matlock forcefully defending the new administration. The meeting was long and animated. Riding back in the car and mulling over the conversation, I wondered how much of the conversation I had captured in my notes and how many nuances I had missed. I drafted the cable and handed it over to Matlock, fearing that he would point out that I had missed grammatical points that completely changed the meaning of the discussion or that he would feel the need to completely redraft the cable. I did, however, understand the old axiom that one should not look bad in his own cable, especially with the new lineup in Washington eagerly looking to see if he had been tough enough, so the cable fully reflected the fact that Matlock had held his own and then some. Matlock seemed happy to send the cable with only a couple of slight factual changes.

Life in Moscow was harsh, more so than it had been in China five years earlier, but far less than it would become for our colleagues a few years later. Living conditions were bad, contacts hard to get, movements outside the Embassy closely monitored, and a constant possibility of physical violence lurking. The Russians were standoffish, the KGB wanted you to think they were everywhere (and they probably were, when it came to us), the winters were dark and incredibly cold, food was limited, and travel was difficult. It was not a cheerful time for either Russians or foreign diplomats.

The KGB kept the atmosphere intentionally oppressive. One time when I called Diane at home from the ambassador's residence, I heard seven clicks as different tape recorders came on to immortalize our conversation about what time I would be home for dinner. One American businessman liked to relate that shortly after being notified by phone that the new company calendars had arrived, his Russian assistant informed him that the monitoring people upstairs had asked if they could have one. He agreed but said the guy would have to come to the office in person to get it. Shortly thereafter a man arrived, and the calendar was duly handed over to effusive thanks. After that exchange his minder regularly opened his window on the next floor up to wave at the businessman when he came to work.

Our officers designated to deal with dissidents had the best opportunity to use and improve their Russian language skills; but they were usually forced to drink far more vodka than was healthy in the course of their work, and several were seriously roughed up on the streets after leaving late-night meetings. The assailants would invariably be big men with good haircuts, wearing heavy coats, and acting drunk. The tipoff that they were all KGB agents came from their hard-to-find, high-quality leather shoes, which were not available to the normal Muscovite.

One colleague who had served in Moscow in the 1960s and '70s and again in the '80s on temporary duty had what he called his bread, sausage, and caviar index to the quality of life in Moscow. In the sixties, he said, Russian bread was excellent, many varieties of sausage were available in Moscow, and caviar was served freely from a container on the top of the market counter. In the seventies, the bread was only OK, the varieties of sausage more limited, and the caviar kept hidden under the counter but still available for a price. In the eighties, the bread was hard and barely edible, the stores had only one variety of tasteless sausage, and the only source of caviar was the black market.

We could explore Moscow and the surrounding area relatively freely despite the surveillance, but the grim tourist accommodations hardly made travel around the Soviet Union a treat for the family. Even in Leningrad (St. Petersburg), which had a few modern hotels, American embassy personnel were forced to stay in a third-rate hotel that had obviously been well-wired for sound many years before. Because of this and the need for a regular return to a sane environment, we chose to take our vacations out of the country in Scandinavia and Western Europe. As it turned out, our daughter Kim saw more of the Soviet Union on school trips (to Samarkand, the Baltics, and more) than Diane and I did.

By the summer of 1981, Arthur Hartman had arrived as ambassador, with Warren Zimmerman as his DCM. Both were pros in every sense of the word (Hartman had just come from a tour as ambassador to Paris), and the embassy settled into a normal routine. But our minimal interaction with Russians continued. My formal discussions at the Foreign Ministry largely consisted of trading complaints about the other side's actions, and then releasing the texts to the public. By the time we left Moscow in the summer of 1982, very little had changed. Brezhnev was getting weaker with every appearance, but guessing where the succession competition stood was just that, a guess. Neither the sclerotic Soviet leadership nor the anti-Soviet administration in Washington had much interest in improving relations, despite the critical need for stability between two superpowers armed to the teeth with nuclear weapons. U.S.-Soviet bilateral relations remained on hold.

Reagan and Shultz Take a New Approach to the "Evil Empire"

After Moscow, I spent a particularly enlightening year at the National War College in Washington. The professors were excellent, my military colleagues (colonels or lieutenant colonels and their Navy and civilian counterparts on the way up) were bright and wanted to learn, and the school's measured pace provided a chance to read extensively about grand strategy and planning. I particularly enjoyed the spirited give and take with the other students, as well as the opportunity to have some relaxed time in the United States with our family. Learning lessons from the Vietnam fiasco was the main topic on people's minds; out of the War College in this period emerged the strategy variously called the Weinberger or Powell Doctrine. This fairly conservative concept called for exhausting political, economic, and diplomatic means before engaging in military action. It also emphasized the importance of a clear understanding of our interests and objectives and insisted on a hard-boiled look at our capabilities and their costs. Finally, any military action required solid support from the American people, and when it was chosen, overwhelming force should be employed to attain the objective in the shortest time. Each time you say or write the doctrine, it sounds like common sense, but the combination has been rare in the application of American military power.

In July 1983, I returned to the State Department to take up my duties as deputy director of the Soviet desk. As any worker in a bureaucracy understands, the deputy is assigned all the unpleasant tasks of the office—in this case, personnel, on-time production of talking points and background papers, security, counterintelligence, and so on. I was extremely fortunate to work for Thomas Simons, a thoughtful, strategically oriented officer who was responsible for formulating and putting on paper almost all the main elements of the Reagan administration's policy toward the Soviet Union in the George Shultz era. Tom would close his door and spend hours (occasionally days) producing the approaches that the secretary would eventually take to the president. He left me with wide latitude to manage the day-to-day work of the desk and to take the lead in ensuring that we implemented the policy decisions of the secretary and president.

When I arrived, the desk had been quietly working on a new approach to dealing with the post-Brezhnev leadership in Moscow. George Shultz replaced Al Haig as secretary of state in July 1982. He and Nancy Reagan convinced the president that the administration needed to change its shrill approach toward Moscow, both to win the 1984 election and to build his long-term legacy. The change in tone first appeared in Reagan's January 1983 State of the Union address, when he replaced the anti-Soviet bombast with a new theme of working together to find solutions to common problems. Brezhnev had died in November, and the president (and Shultz) wanted to reach out to his successor, Andropov, to encourage changes in Soviet behavior.

During an informal February 1983 dinner arranged by Mrs. Reagan that included only the Reagans and the Shultzes, the president and his secretary of state discussed a new approach to the Soviet Union at length. Shultz arranged for the president to have a secret meeting with the longtime Soviet ambassador, Anatoly Dobrynin. The president outlined to Dobrynin his desire to move forward. Regular meetings then began between Shultz and Dobrynin to start repairing the bilateral relationship. Despite this opening, Reagan made a speech to Protestant leaders in Orlando on March 8 calling the Soviet Union an "evil empire" and "the focus of evil in the modern world." The speech had obviously not been cleared by Shultz nor had Reagan probably given its implications any thought, since it was in line with his earlier statements. The Russians lashed out in response, and the Europeans cringed at this return to the earlier rhetoric of the administration. Reagan never used the terms again.

Twenty days later Reagan announced his plans for the Strategic Defense Initiative (SDI), an approach designed to destroy missiles in space before they could reach their target. This concept amounted to a reversal of the long-standing strategy of Mutual Assured Destruction, which had governed the U.S.-Soviet competition on nuclear weapons. And theoretically, if it worked, SDI could negate the Soviet Union's nuclear arsenal and allow the United States to consider a first- strike capability. The Soviets reacted badly to this Reagan dream, and undermining it became their number one arms control priority. (SDI was immediately dubbed "Star Wars" by the press, and, like the "evil empire," owed its popular name to George Lucas's famous film series.)

George Shultz, Tom Simons, and others, however, were not to be deterred by one hardline White House speechwriter. They wanted to engage the Soviets seriously on arms control—SDI or not—to help stabilize the volatile superpower relationship. A few days later, Shultz sent a note to the president (drafted by Tom) laying out a four-part agenda for initiating broad talks with the Soviets. The agenda (human rights, arms control, regional issues, and bilateral matters) had something for everyone and carefully allowed for progress (or no progress) in any category, with no conditionality linking them. It also proposed an eventual summit, as the Soviets had been suggesting and Reagan clearly desired. The president approved the Shultz approach in March 1983, the same month as the "evil empire" speech and the SDI announcement.

Shultz went public with this agenda in a statement (cleared by Reagan) to the Senate Foreign Relations Committee in mid-June that was a masterpiece of Tom's "sheep in wolf's clothing" approach. Much of the language was tough enough that the *Washington Post* headlined its story "Shultz Outlines Policy of Opposing Soviets." In fact, it was an extensive statement of the new policy, namely, that the United States would be engaging the Soviets across the board. (The *New York Times* story entitled "Shultz Testifies Rifts with Soviet Are Not Inevitable" was more positive and more accurate.) Not only was Shultz's rhetoric tougher than the policy he outlined; it also used the debatable argument that the first years of the Reagan presidency (with its increased spending on the military and hardline rhetoric) had strengthened the United States sufficiently that it could now negotiate with the Soviets from a stronger position. The cast of hardline, anti-Soviet types spread across the U.S. administration had not changed, nor had their views softened; but Shultz and the president had effected a dramatic, fundamental change in U.S. policy toward the Soviet Union. The arrival of Jack Matlock at the NSC soon after (replacing the hardline Richard Pipes, who had adamantly opposed the Shultz proposals) added a critical ally in the White House for this new approach.

The Soviets, who were better clued in than the *Washington Post* because of the Shultz-Dobrynin discussions, then responded with a symbolic gesture to the president. In June 1978, seven members of two families of Siberian Pentecostals had rushed past Soviet guards to enter the American Embassy, beginning a saga that lasted almost five years. The embassy allowed them to stay and provided accommodations for them in the basement of the compound. It was not a comfortable existence for either side. The Pentecostals were not gracious guests—they complained regularly about their treatment by the embassy—and the Soviets were in no mood to allow them to leave the country. During our time in Moscow, two members of the group went on a hunger strike, with the condition of one of them becoming so serious the embassy had no choice but to take her to a hospital to save her life. President Reagan was deeply interested in the Pentecostals' fate, and he spent considerable time during his first meeting with Dobrynin pressing for their release. Following intense discussions between Shultz and Dobrynin in Washington and between Max Kampelman, U.S. ambassador to the Conference on Security and Cooperation in Europe, and a ranking KGB officer in Madrid, the Soviets agreed to their departure to Israel. It was an easy gesture for the Soviets. The woman who had been sent to the hospital a year earlier emigrated in April. The others then left the Embassy and departed the Soviet Union by July. For Shultz, it was an indication that a path to a new relationship was possible, if handled appropriately and without bombast.

When I arrived on the Soviet desk that summer, the groundwork had been laid to move forward, but the administration's tensions over Soviet policy were obvious for all to see. It seemed as if every day brought a new challenge. Under enormous pressure, Shultz carried on the fight with skill and perseverance. In August the NSC, under the notoriously hardline William Clark, tried to take control of U.S. policy toward Central America, the Mideast, and the Soviet Union away from the State Department. Shultz had to complain directly to the president and threaten to resign to maintain his power. For the rest of us down in the trenches, life was only slightly easier, as we found ourselves in a constant battle to carry out a new policy toward the Soviet Union that the president wanted but that most of his supporters throughout the national security apparatus hated. Worse, the president was disinclined to disown the naysayers or to force them to get on board his policy. We were thus in the position of pursuing a policy line approved by the president and driven by Shultz that had no buy-in from, and was often actively opposed by, much of the rest of the administration.

The four-point agenda—human rights, arms control, global issues, and bilateral issues—gave us a way to explore new avenues of cooperation to reduce tensions, lower the possibility of global conflict, and provide an umbrella under which we could manage the issues between us. It intentionally dropped the idea of linkage between different categories of issues that had been a feature of Kissinger's policy, supplemented by the Carter era approach on human rights and Afghanistan. To understand the challenges before us, we on the desk did a review of all areas where we interacted with the Soviets, including bilateral trade and programs that had been allowed to continue despite the sanctions. Startlingly, the entire sum of the U.S.-Soviet relationship filled less than one typewritten page. Containment, longstanding security-related strictures, and recent Soviet policies that provoked U.S. and Western sanction measures had reduced our interaction in most areas to virtually zero.

My tenure on the desk started improbably when Andy (Andrei) Berezhkov, the sixteen-year-old son of a ranking Soviet diplomat, left his Chevy Chase home one evening in mid-August and mailed letters to President Reagan and the *New York Times* saying he hated his country, loved the United States, and wanted to stay here. Andy had earlier lived with his parents in Washington and was now back in Washington on summer vacation and due to return with them in a few days to Moscow. (His father, Valentin Berezhkov, had interpreted for Stalin and Molotov and was a well-known fixture at Moscow's USA Institute.) Andy had returned to their house in the early morning hours after mailing his letters, but when the *New York Times* broke the story and the letter to the president was retrieved, the State Department demanded that he be interviewed before he left the country—since he was potentially seeking asylum. The Soviets argued forcefully that we could not interview the boy because he had diplomatic immunity and was under-aged. After eight days of high publicity and intense negotiations, a compromise allowed American officials to talk with Andy and the Russians to hold a press conference to tell their side of the story. In the end, he returned home with his parents. (Ten years later, when he seemed to be thriving in the new Russia and planning a move to join his family in California, Andy's business partner shot and killed him in Moscow.)

There were to be other, somewhat similar cases during my time on the desk. A Ukrainian boy, Walter Polovchek, fought a five-year battle in Chicago to stay in the United States after his parents returned to the Soviet Union. The case was resolved when he turned eighteen and thus could legally decide for himself where he wanted to live. A Soviet seaman twice jumped ship near New Orleans, proclaiming he wanted to stay in the United States, but in the end decided to return home. Finally, a Russian exchange physicist acted erratically and said he wanted to stay in the United States at the end of his tour. The Soviet embassy told us he had changed his mind and demanded that he be allowed to return to Moscow immediately. We finally resolved the issue after I asked the office of the secretary of the Health and Human Services for emergency help, and they arranged for the scientist to be interviewed by psychiatrists at St. Elizabeth's Hospital. He was judged sane and clear in his decision to return home.

The Destruction of KAL 007

On the evening of August 31 (twelve days after the Berezhkovs returned to Moscow), I received an urgent call from the State Department's Operations Center. "We need you to come in right away. We called Simons, who said he was drowsy from a sleeping pill and asked that we call you. There's a potentially serious problem with the Soviets and a missing airliner." Thus, for me, began the tragic saga of KAL 007, a South Korean airliner. I drove to the department to be briefed on what we knew at that point.

Scheduled to arrive in Seoul at 5pm Washington time, KAL 007 was now five hours overdue. Radar tracking from stations in Japan suggested that the plane had gone down near Sakhalin Island at 2:36 p.m. Washington time, but it was unclear whether it had crashed or landed safely. Korean Airlines first announced that the plane had landed and the passengers were safe, but we had no confirmation. The truth became clearer as the night wore on. It turned out that 269 passengers, including one of the most conservative members of the U.S. Congress (and head of the John Birch Society), Larry McDonald, died on the flight. The plane had indeed entered

Soviet airspace, and the intelligence community had indications that it had been shot down by the Soviets.

I briefed European Bureau Assistant Secretary Rick Burt and called in several more members of our staff as the situation became more ominous. Burt telephoned the Soviet chargé after midnight asking for immediate information about what had happened and the condition of the passengers. From the Ops Center we pressed for more intelligence information, monitored press reports from the area, and fielded a flood of calls, including many from frantic family members. Our task force tried to track down any information available amid the telephone calls and conflicting data that were coming in. Under Secretary of State for Political Affairs Lawrence Eagleburger arrived early the next morning, and I briefed him on everything we had learned overnight. Eagleburger listened to the grim report, told me to go home and get some sleep, and called the secretary. I briefed Simons when he came in, turned over responsibility, and went home. Eagleburger made some further calls to the intelligence agencies and gave a detailed brief to Secretary Shultz when he came in an hour later.

Shultz's instinct was to make known to the public what information we had as soon as possible. Transparency was critical to maintain credibility. We had, of course, been trying to keep people informed all evening, without divulging intelligence information. After discussing his plans with the president and considerable debate with the intelligence people about releasing their information, Shultz held a late morning press conference.

The Korean Airlines plane had strayed into Soviet airspace, he said, and the Soviets had tracked it for two and a half hours. Then, a Soviet pilot reported that, after visually sighting the aircraft, he had shot it down. The airplane disappeared from radar twelve minutes later, and the Soviets ordered ships to conduct search and rescue missions where the plane presumably went down. Shultz expressed revulsion over the attack and noted that we saw "no excuse whatsoever for this appalling act." The president, in California, denounced the "horrifying act of violence," demanded a full explanation, and cut short his Labor Day break to return to Washington.

We will never know who in the Soviet military hierarchy gave the definitive order to shoot down the plane or what was behind it, but there could be no doubt that Andropov badly mismanaged the Soviet response. According to credible reports from Moscow in the early nineties, Andropov overruled civilian advice from Vice Foreign Minister Korniyenko to come clean on what had happened and to apologize for the incident (as Yeltsin belatedly did nine years later). Instead Andropov adopted Defense Minister Ustinov's approach to stonewall and lie. (Andropov was not on vacation, as the Soviets reported, but in the hospital and probably gravely ill.) The coverup was a serious mistake made by a weak Soviet leadership. It earned international condemnation and almost derailed the effort by Reagan and Shultz to put bilateral relations on a more solid footing. The lying greatly compounded the problem for the Soviets and infuriated Reagan, Shultz, and most of the world.

After twenty-four hours of silence on the incident, TASS issued a lame statement that an unidentified plane had twice violated Soviet airspace, that it did not have its navigation lights on, nor did it respond to efforts by its pursuers to make contact. Then came the clincher (incredibly stupid, since Shultz had indicated hours earlier that we had the Soviet pilot's communications): "Fighters ... sent toward the intruder plane tried to give it assistance in directing it to the nearest airfield. But the intruder plane did not react to the signals and warnings ... and continued its flight in the direction of the Sea of Japan." The Soviet chargé came to the State Department to pass a similar message from Gromyko, adding that the plane may have crashed in the vicinity of Moneron Island near Sakhalin. I had been back at the Operations Center leading our team in a full crisis operation for some hours by then. We were appalled by the Soviet response to our request for information and issued a statement saying it was "totally inadequate."

Moscow continued to build on its story the next day. TASS called the flight a "pre-planned" espionage effort, blamed the United States for the incident, and claimed that warning shots had been fired but did not concede the obvious fact that they had shot down the plane. The Soviets started throwing out all kinds of red herrings to deflect criticism, including asking why the United States hadn't warned Moscow or the South Koreans that the plane was off course, suggesting CIA involvement in the flight, and passing off U.S. statements as an American smear campaign. The crisis brought out the very worst in a weak and defensive regime, and its disinformation effort was at full throttle. Shultz responded in a press conference by citing the facts as we knew them to refute the Soviet statement. He then condemned their refusal to admit that they had shot down the plane, adding that the "world is waiting for the Soviet Union to tell the truth."

But Shultz saw no reason to heed the calls of the hardliners in the administration and Congress to break off contacts with the Russians or add more sanctions. He saw President Reagan immediately on his return to Washington, and they agreed that the policy of looking for areas to cooperate with the Soviets—in place since the spring—remained fundamentally sound. In an NSC meeting on September 2, NSC chief Clark, Secretary of Defense Weinberger, White House chief of staff Donald Regan, and others argued for tough retaliatory measures. But the president remained steady and calm. He backed a planned Shultz-Gromyko meeting in Madrid and the return of the arms control negotiators to Europe and turned down calls for additional strong sanctions. Although Reagan's rhetoric was tough, he kept the U.S. actions against the Soviets limited, despite pressure from many of his closest aides and members of Congress. The sanctions imposed merely delayed a few items on the agenda and halted Aeroflot flights to the United States for a few months. (Gromyko had to skip the September UNGA meeting because he could not land in the United States.) Several other countries agreed with Shultz and their pilots' unions to enforce similar bans. In Europe, which was debating the deployment of Pershing-II missiles, Reagan won wide praise for his restraint in the crisis, while he was roundly criticized by his conservative supporters in the United States who wanted a complete trade embargo and a cut-off in dealings with Moscow.

Speculation began immediately over why the Korean plane was so far off track and what the Soviets might have been thinking when they shot it down. Casey added fuel to the fire when he told reporters that a U.S. RC-135 reconnaissance plane had been in the area, buttressing an argument by some that the Soviets may have mistaken the airliner for a spy plane. Once this hit the press, the Soviets had a field day, claiming it supported their case that the Korean plane was on a spy mission. (The RC-135 had been orbiting

1500 miles away and returned to its base an hour before the shootdown.) To refute several lies put out by the Soviets in their effort to deflect responsibility, the United States played an eleven-minute tape of the Soviet fighter pilot's comments before and just after downing the plane at an open meeting of the UN Security Council. The Soviets at that point (one week late) conceded that they had shot down the plane. In his Madrid meeting with Shultz, Gromyko again sought to blame the whole affair on the United States. Naturally, Shultz rejected his lies.

The U.S. and Japanese navies had begun an intensive search-and-rescue mission shortly after we knew the plane had been shot down to look for remains, debris, and the black boxes to explain why the plane had entered Soviet airspace. These efforts met considerable resistance from Soviet naval forces in the area, even though the U.S. and Japanese ships were operating in international waters. A decade later we learned that the Soviets had carried out a major ruse to keep international searchers away from the aircraft, which they had already found in shallow waters off Moneron Island. The Soviets retrieved the boxes, bodies, and remaining debris, but kept this information from the international community because, as the Soviet military told Andropov at the time, the information in the boxes supported the Americans' case. The U.S.-Japanese search went on for more than a month before being abandoned.

In the meantime, some debris and body parts from the aircraft had been recovered on the beaches of Japan's Hokkaido. The Soviets invited the Japanese and American governments to collect additional debris from the aircraft that they said had washed up on Sakhalin and Moneron Islands. The task fell to me to lead the U.S. delegation, which also included Denis Wilham, the FAA's senior representative for Asia, a Navy captain from the U.S. Pacific Fleet, and a UPI photographer. My Japanese counterpart was an old diplomatic colleague from Beijing, Minoru Tamba, accompanied by two other Japanese officials and a photographer. A representative of the International Civil Aviation Organization (ICAO) accompanied us but was not allowed to get off the boat.

On September 26, after a fifteen-hour trip from Hokkaido aboard a Japanese patrol boat, we arrived at the Sakhalin port of Nevelsk and were escorted to a dilapidated Soviet military building, which had a coat of bright blue paint so fresh it was still sticky to the touch. The chief of the border forces for Sakhalin made a presentation that went on for considerably longer than seemed necessary for a formal handover of the boxes. Japanese and American photographers were allowed in to record the occasion and then escorted to an adjoining room. While waiting in the next room, the UPI photographer produced one of my favorite photos. Noticing a crack in the wall to an adjoining room, he put his lens to up to the hole and took a picture of GRU (Soviet military intelligence) personnel recording the talks in the main meeting room. Somehow, juxtaposing the formal photos of our "negotiations" in the large room with one of earphone-clad GRU types huddled in the next room monitoring the talks seemed a perfect metaphor for our dealings with the Soviets in the eighties.

Despite the high publicity surrounding the trip and the formal atmosphere in that room on Sakhalin, the Soviets' handover of the five wooden boxes of personal effects and pieces of the aircraft honeycomb structure that day was a sad charade. There were no bodies, no black boxes, and a minimal number of personal items. I was quoted in the press on our return to Japan, casting doubt on the Soviet assertion that this was everything they had retrieved by commenting, "Do you believe in Santa Claus?" Tamba publicly doubted the items would prove useful to our investigation. For the families of those who lost their lives, the debris handed over was a huge disappointment and frankly cruel. Other than having a picture distributed worldwide of us looking at a piece of the aircraft wreckage, it is hard to know what either side gained from the entire effort.

The KAL 007 tragedy evoked an outpouring of conspiracy theories in the United States and elsewhere not seen since the Kennedy assassination. This partly resulted from the Soviet disinformation effort, which spewed out falsehoods in its attempt to deflect the obvious conclusion that the Soviet military had done something extraordinarily stupid. It also fed off U.S. government and private "experts" who were happy to substitute speculation for missing facts on why the plane had strayed into Soviet airspace and what the Soviet chain of command must have been thinking to shoot down a civilian aircraft. The theories were also a byproduct of the

Reagan administration's lack of credibility when discussing Soviet actions. The right's conspiracy theories tended to be driven by the death on the flight of Congressman McDonald and the near miss of others, including Senator Jesse Helms who was aboard 007's sister flight that took off fifteen minutes later.

These suspicions and the desire for sensationalism in the media bedeviled our "just the facts, ma'am" approach from the start. Our effort to stick to what we knew reflected our institutional bias and Shultz's natural style. But it was also essential for our survival, when every word was analyzed to find some mythical "State Department cover-up." We understood that our best defense was openness about what we knew and when we knew it, but our every move came under a suspicious microscope. Even our situation reports from that first night, retrieved under "Freedom of Information" requests, were scrutinized and distorted. While the conspiracy theorists were perhaps unavoidably out of control, it was disheartening to see establishment commentators like Tom Wicker of the *New York Times* keeping speculation alive through regular discussions of "unanswered questions."

To bolster the department's and the administration's credibility, I put one of our desk officers, Tom Maertens, full-time on the effort to track down far-fetched claims, refute them if possible, and dig up everything reliable we could find from U.S. government or other sources to respond. Maertens met with a wide range of researchers, wrote a number of op-ed pieces, and fired off letters to the editor to respond to newspaper stories across the country. We were open to talk to anyone who had questions, including the well-known investigative reporter, Seymour Hersh. Although Hersh assumed at first that there was a U.S. government conspiracy to cover up some nefarious scheme against the Soviets, he had the honesty to conclude in his 1986 book that there was no such conspiracy.

Hersh still got a few points wrong, such as suggesting that the Soviets did not know it was a civilian airliner—the pilot said he knew it was a Boeing but felt he had no choice but to carry out his orders to shoot it down. But overall, the Hersh book tamped down the conspiracy debate. The establishment press seemed to say: "If Sy Hersh couldn't find a conspiracy, there probably wasn't one." The documents released by Yeltsin in the early nineties vindicated our approach and should have put all these theories to rest. Indeed, Yeltsin cited KAL 007 as an example in a June 1992 address to the U.S. Congress, vowing, "There will be no more lies—ever." Later that year, he apologized to South Korea for shooting down the airliner and turned over data from the black boxes to both the South Koreans and ICAO. The facts did speak for themselves.

In a tragic coda to the whole affair, the U.S. Navy shot down an Iranian civilian airliner in the Persian Gulf during the last year of the Reagan administration, supposedly mistaking the Airbus for an F-4. It was an awful event and caused numerous comparisons with the KAL 007 tragedy; but at least the American military admitted its mistake, apologized for it, and paid compensation to the victims. If the Soviets had done the same thing, the shootdown of KAL 007 would have had much less impact on the U.S.-Soviet relationship and done far less harm to the Soviet image worldwide.

A Near Fiasco on a Small Island

Two months after the KAL tragedy, the administration's overblown anti-Communist rhetoric led to the invasion of the tiny Caribbean island of Grenada by U.S. Marines to overthrow a leftist government and expel its Cuban and Soviet advisers. It took a considerable stretch of the imagination to see events there as a serious threat to the United States. Even if one were to accept the basic rationale, it would seem that the way to counter it would have been a covert CIA operation rather than a military invasion. For the world, it looked like the worst kind of U.S. bullying against a small country near its shores. Despite considerable support among Grenada's neighbors for the U.S. action, it was just the kind of act we had long condemned the Soviets for undertaking. But even if this affair seemed somewhat comic, it turned out to have possible serious ramifications for U.S.-Soviet relations.

When the marines invaded, one of their first moves was to cordon off the Soviet Embassy, probably a violation of international law and certainly a frightening experience for the diplomats there. The Soviets denounced the invasion as "undisguised banditry" and asserted that a U.S. warplane had fired on the Embassy and injured a staff member—this despite our assurance on the first day of the invasion that we would protect their citizens and provide safe passage out of the country. Both the State Department and the U.S. military denied that the Embassy had been fired on, but we decided to send Steve Mann from our office to Grenada to deal directly with the U.S. military and explain to them the consequences for our people in Moscow if they did not observe international legal norms. He also needed to make contact with the Soviet embassy on the island. Its communications with the outside world had been cut off. To reestablish a minimal communications channel for them, Mann went to the Embassy, and I had the Soviet deputy chief of mission in Washington come to my office so they could talk over our phones in our presence.

Naturally, the Soviets were outraged and humiliated by this makeshift arrangement, but they knew there was no alternative and viewed us, at least, as interested in affording some protection for their people in Grenada. Nine days after the invasion, the forty-nine Soviets on the island went home via Mexico without any further major incidents. A disaster had been averted, but it had been a close-run thing. Apparently, no one had bothered to brief the U.S. invading force about the inviolability of diplomatic property or thought through how to deal with the Soviets and Cubans on the island once they had landed. Since the aim of the operation was to get the Soviets and the Cubans off the island, it was striking that planning on how to do it legally had been overlooked.

One thing we did not understand at the time was just how paranoid the Soviets had become about the Reagan administration. Most of the Soviet leadership seemed to have convinced themselves that KAL-007 had something to do with a CIA plot and that the primary aim of the administration's approach after the event was to humiliate them. Few seemed to understand that the real problem was their lying and attempt at a cover-up. The rancorous meeting between Shultz and Gromyko in Madrid a week after the KAL 007 shoot-down only strengthened that belief. Grenada suggested that the administration would use force if it chose with little regard for the views of others, and the original cavalier treatment of their embassy on the island suggested how little the United States cared about Soviet concerns.

At the same time, the United States continued on course to deploy cruise missiles in Europe, prompting a Soviet walk-out from the arms control talks in Geneva. All these issues we knew, but we did not know how weak the decision-making process in Moscow had become since Andropov—the man who was supposed to get the Soviet Union moving again after Brezhnev's death—lay dying in the hospital.

We were unaware how close this Russian paranoia brought the world to the brink of nuclear war during this time. In September a Soviet military officer responsible for monitoring early warnings had chosen to doubt the system's alert (a false warning, as it happened) that indicated the United States had launched missiles to attack the Soviet Union, thus avoiding a Soviet counterattack. Then in November the Soviet leadership badly overreacted to a NATO nuclear exercise, believing it to be a cover for an actual attack. The hopes in the summer for a change in the dangerous superpower confrontation seemed to have slipped away. Indeed, the situation had become more dangerous and the mutual recriminations more shrill than they had been for years.

Spies, Spies, Everywhere

The American press dubbed 1985 "The Year of the Spy," but all of the 1980s were years of the spies. The Soviets and Americans had been spying on each other for decades: the famous carved Seal of the United States hanging in Spaso House, presented by Russian schoolchildren in 1945 and discovered only in 1952 to contain a listening device to pick up conversations in the U.S. ambassador's residence; the Rosenbergs were executed in 1953 for providing nuclear secrets to the Soviets; the British code-breaking experts Burgess and McLean fled to Moscow in 1951; the shootdown of Gary Powers's U-2 flight in 1960. These had all been sensational news, but by the late sixties and early seventies, as détente became the main theme, fewer spy stories hit the press. The CIA had gone through a long demoralizing mole hunt for Soviet spies that ruined many careers, and the agency had come under an enormous cloud in the mid-seventies after a domestic spying scandal.

During the Carter administration, espionage issues with the Soviets again became a staple of the evening news. The Soviets tossed out an American embassy employee for spying in 1977, three Soviets were arrested in New York (two without diplomatic immunity were traded for Soviet dissidents), and a Soviet trade official was ousted from Washington. The State Department and our embassy in Moscow went public with complaints against the Russians for directing a dangerous level of microwaves against the Embassy that caused a potential health threat to our employees, and an embassy Seabee discovered a tunnel the Soviets had dug to put a cable in a chimney designed either as a listening device or power source for devices implanted in the Embassy. After the Soviet invasion of Afghanistan, things would only get worse.

Virtually everyone above my level in the department understood that this was a dirty, no-win business, so it naturally fell to the Soviet desk's deputy (me) to deal with counterintelligence (CI) issues unless they had to be escalated to the secretary or under secretary's attention. During my three years on the Soviet Desk, I never attended a meeting at the Senate Foreign Relations Committee, the State Department's normally closest contact in Congress, but I met on Soviet counterintelligence issues many times with senators and staff members at the Senate Select Committee on Intelligence and members of the President's Foreign Intelligence Advisory Board.

The divisions among Reagan's cabinet members on the Soviet Union were further inflamed in the counterintelligence areas by long-standing institutional rivalries. FBI director J. Edgar Hoover had tangled with the CIA's predecessor agency from the time it was created, and the feud between the two organizations had gone on for almost four decades by the time I arrived on the Soviet desk. Relations declined further after the decision by Carter's FBI appointee William Webster and Attorney General Griffin Bell to publicize stepped-up FBI efforts to counter Soviet espionage. They undertook a series of made-for-the-media arrests (often at the UN) of Soviet personnel caught spying. These actions by the FBI made life miserable for the CIA, whose personnel were then subjected to reciprocal treatment in Moscow and Leningrad. The State Department in the Carter era generally came down on the CIA's side, since it preferred to handle these events quietly in order not to sour the public atmosphere at a time the administration was negotiating the SALT II agreement. But by the eighties, relations between the CIA and the FBI (we studiously worked to have good ties with both) had become so bad that I would sometimes invite their representatives to meet in my office just so they would have a neutral ground to discuss burning issues.

Equally problematic from the State Department's point of view was the attitude of the National Security Agency (NSA) toward the State Department. I was never sure whether the hermetically sealed NSA simply misunderstood the open engagement imperatives crucial to diplomacy, or they genuinely believed that the State Department had an inexcusably lax approach to its own security, or they simply wanted to increase their bureaucratic power by taking over State Department communications. But there was no doubt the upper levels of the NSA had developed a deep antipathy toward the department and Embassy Moscow.

After the discovery of a KGB penetration in a friendly embassy, the NSA concluded that the Soviets must be running the same effort against Embassy Moscow and came up with a plan to carry out a secret investigation. A later self-congratulatory unclassified NSA review of the project (code-named "GUNMAN"), revealed that the NSA chief did not inform the State Department of his concerns "because relations were poor," nor did he tell the CIA, "which would mishandle the NSA plan." The GUNMAN project called for the removal and careful analysis in the United States of all the embassy's electronic equipment and its replacement with new equipment. The NSA informed their nominal boss, Defense Secretary Weinberger, and the president, and the president approved the NSA proposal. Shultz and, after considerable debate, Under Secretary Eagleburger were also told of the plan. Ambassador Hartman was informed by handwritten note only after the team arrived in Moscow. It took the team ten days on the ground to switch the equipment; the cover story for embassy personnel was that they were getting a communications upgrade.

The NSA search of the equipment required a meticulous effort to crack the Soviet technology. They found nothing in the communications equipment but eventually discovered highly sophisticated "bugs" in sixteen of the embassy's IBM Selectric II and III typewriters that transmitted to the Soviets what was being typed before it was encrypted. There were two types of "bugs"—the older ones ran on batteries and the newer model used A/C current. They could be turned on and off remotely to avoid detection by scanning equipment. The "bugs" had been installed when the Soviets managed to get the typewriters away from our diplomatic couriers for a few hours.

The typewriter that I used in Moscow from 1980 to 1982 was one of the compromised Selectrics, but it was unclear just when its battery died. The Soviets may or may not have had the privilege of reading my drafts even before they had been cleared by my bosses to send to Washington. There was no way to know just how much material was compromised from 1976 to 1984; but judging from the output of the political section during my time, I can honestly say that the damage would not have been earthshaking. The NSA coup was leaked to the press in March 1985, building their reputation and hurting that of the department and the embassy while adding to the overall clamor about espionage activity in the media. In the end, the State Department tightened up its procedures under its new Diplomatic Security Service, and the NSA did not achieve its goal of controlling State Department communications. During one of our meetings, the NSA head of security ranted to me that he "knew" that all of the State Department's communications equipment in Moscow (not just the sixteen typewriters) were bugged. I responded that as far as I knew, NSA had gone over all the equipment only a year before and asked him if they had found anything to support the accusation. He admitted that they had not and changed the subject.

With the general concern over Soviet spying and abuses by other countries gathering force, East German diplomats sought to purchase an apartment in Arlington directly overlooking offices of senior Pentagon officials. This was the last straw in a long series of property and other security incidents in the United States. At the same time, anger was mounting about the shabby treatment our diplomats often received abroad. Congress passed legislation creating the State Department Office of Foreign Missions (OFM) to put controls on foreign diplomats in the United States and force other countries to treat our diplomats as well (or nearly so) as the United

States treated their diplomats. The office regulated to some degree the property and movement of foreign diplomats from designated countries. For countries that behaved correctly, OFM was a major help in navigating the intricacies of the U.S. government system by consolidating the various rules and regulations. For those who had felt no compunction about using our open system to their advantage and had no incentive to treat our people well in their countries, OFM could be used as a valuable cudgel to bring them into line.

As the person who dealt with both espionage and lack of reciprocity issues involving the Soviet Union (and who had experienced quite similar Chinese practices), I strongly supported the new office and worked closely with it as it began to implement new policies. Some of my colleagues in the department had difficulty with OFM's overly zealous approach to its counterespionage responsibilities (it was headed by a hardline former FBI agent); but I saw it as a way to get some control over the actions of the Soviets and their allies in the United States and some justice for our colleagues suffering in the Soviet Union.

As the midlevel State Department representative on most of these Soviet-related espionage issues, I found myself chairing quite a few interagency meetings to develop a coordinated U.S. position. Often in these meetings, I had an uneasy feeling that perhaps half of the people in the room considered me (by dint of my employer) soft on the Soviets at the very least, and perhaps even willing to sell out the country at worst. I deeply resented this attitude from people (usually political appointees) who often struck me as ignorant, foolish, or both. Their attitude and body language were hard to take for someone who had spent years dealing with the Chinese and Soviets and had developed a deep dislike for their systems. But I worked hard to keep my cool.

One issue that became extremely controversial at this time involved the new U.S. Embassy building in Moscow. The need to construct new embassies had been a major topic of discussion since the 1930s. Stalin had forced the U.S. embassy to move to a large apartment building on Tchaikovsky Boulevard (built by German prisoners of war) shortly before he died in 1953 to get it away from the Kremlin. The place was a firetrap, totally unsuited for the heavy electrical and physical burdens we placed on it, and a disaster waiting to happen. An embassy fire in 1977 gutted several floors of the main working area and opened sensitive offices to Soviet snooping, but fortunately did not cause any injuries. The two countries finally agreed on an exchange of sites for new embassies in 1969. Despite some wild statements that the United States had settled on a bad site in a swamp, the Moscow property was both close to the ambassador's residence at Spaso House and across the street from the striking new Russian Parliament building.

Wrangling continued over the construction terms, with U.S. negotiators opposing the Soviet insistence that components of the embassy in Moscow be fabricated off-site. However, the Nixon White House (Kissinger) overruled our negotiators and accepted the Soviet position in order to have an accomplishment to show during Nixon's 1972 visit to Moscow. The European Bureau (EUR) was deeply concerned that the security of the building could easily be compromised and sent a memorandum to Secretary of State Rogers arguing against signing the agreement. Rogers and Kissinger went ahead anyway. Both later attempted to deny responsibility, but there was no question that the faulty deal was done on the direct orders of the White House against the objections of the professionals in the State Department. When an NSA representative at one of our interagency meetings a dozen years later charged that the department had caved in to the Soviets on the terms of construction, I showed them the EUR memo and told them to direct their anger at Kissinger.

Construction of the new building was well underway by the time we arrived in Moscow. I knew my colleague from language training, Ken Crosher, and his special team of Seabees were laboring hard to inspect the tons of material arriving at the site and keep tabs on the Russian workers in subzero temperatures during the long and dark Moscow winter. American security experts from the various involved agencies had expected the Soviets to bug the embassy and knew the building would require additional security measures, but, as usual, they underestimated the level of Soviet sophistication. A specially designed scanning machine, along with a larger security team, arrived in Moscow in 1982 to begin a serious analysis of the security aspects of the construction. The Soviets helped confirm our suspicions when their workers walked off the job for a time to protest the equipment's arrival (ostensibly because it used x-rays.) The scanning effort required slow and methodical work to cover the entire multistory structure. One day, a year or so after I had taken up my job in the department, Crosher walked into my office with the bad news: "Lynn, after a thorough review of the data from the new scanner, we've concluded the new embassy is completely infested with extraordinarily sophisticated listening devices. It will be difficult to fix." The State Department ordered Embassy Moscow to shut down the Soviet construction in August 1985, and Soviet workers were locked out from the site two days later.

The U.S. intelligence community still believed, however, that countermeasures could neutralize the Soviet bugging and briefed the Senate Intelligence Committee that the building could be fixed. However, the more they studied the Soviet construction, the more worried they became. The story of the bugged building became public knowledge in 1987 shortly after the Marine Security Guard scandal (discussed below.) Following a period dominated by the usual overheated recriminations over who was at fault, the debate settled into an argument about whether to tear down the building and start over or to knock off the top two floors and rebuild a secure part of the structure (the so-called "Top Hat" option). Both the Reagan and Bush administrations (strongly supported by the Senate) advocated tearing it down, but the House preference for the cheaper Top Hat option won out in the end. A deal with the new Yeltsin government allowed construction to begin with all-American crews. Reconstruction finally got underway in 1997, including the replacement of the building's red brick façade with a shiny white skin of American marble. The new Embassy was opened for business in the summer of 2002.

During my time on the desk a public debate raged over the flip side of the embassy issue— the Soviet construction of its facility in D.C. This too had a history. The Soviets first chose a site for their new building in Chevy Chase, Maryland, only to run into heavy opposition from the local residents. The U.S. government searched for another suitable site, and after a series of interagency discussions, settled on the land occupied by an old veterans' hospital at Mt. Alto near the National Cathedral. The possibility of using microwaves to spy on U.S. facilities (or on Soviet facilities in Moscow) apparently was not considered an issue by the intelligence agencies when they agreed to this site. When construction began in the early 1980s a few years later, the intelligence agencies had become acutely aware of the possibilities afforded the Soviets by having a high-rise built on one of the highest points in Washington and took their concerns to Congress and the media.

The Soviet construction at Mt. Alto occupied our agenda in several of the interagency meetings that I chaired as the public outcry grew. I could see the building above the Washington skyline every morning as I drove to work from Virginia as a reminder of the controversy. One morning John Scali of ABC called to interrogate me about how the people in the State Department could be so stupid as to allow the Soviets to build on such a prime espionage site. At an interagency meeting about the same time, the NSA representative berated me for the foolishness of this State Department action. Fortunately, I came prepared with a copy of the original interagency memorandum that included a signature of approval by the NSA representative as well as the rest of the intelligence community and noted that the site itself had been suggested by other agencies, not the State Department.

Predictably, when talking to Congress and their friends in the media, the intelligence agencies attempted to shift all the blame onto the State Department for a decision they had supported. A public outcry was inevitable. The atmosphere in this and similar meetings was nasty, but for me it was just another day in the weird conditions in which we were trying to do our work in the mid-eighties. Despite the press sensationalism and the constant criticism from Congress (including a Senate vote at one point to force the Soviets to move to a new site), the Soviets were eventually allowed to keep it. (It was completed in 1985, but they were not allowed to occupy their Chancery until just before a visit by President Yeltsin in 1994.) In a final irony, the press reported years later that the FBI had itself dug a surreptitious tunnel under the new Soviet Embassy, only to have it disclosed to them by Robert Hanssen, a Soviet mole in the FBI.

In mid-August 1985, the CIA briefed me on information they had that the Soviets were using an unusual chemical to track the contacts of American personnel (presumably officers they suspected to be spies) in Moscow. Any item or person who had had recent contact with Embassy personnel exposed to the chemical would reportedly fluoresce under appropriate lighting. Since little was known about the yellow chemical (a potential carcinogen called NPPD, soon dubbed "spy dust" by the press), we and the CIA felt we had no choice but to brief our personnel at Embassy Moscow, and the Leningrad consulate and to try to get the Soviets to stop using the powder. The death from leukemia of former ambassador Walter Stoessel revived the controversy over the health hazard posed by the Soviet bombardment of our embassy with microwaves. In the end, extensive reviews on the microwaves and analysis of the spy dust by an interagency group that included EPA and HHS determined that neither posed a serious health risk for our people. And, in response to our complaints and the bad press, the Soviets did stop using spy dust and turned down the microwaves; but the story of more Soviet perfidy against Americans in Moscow fed the narrative of the Evil Empire.

In American popular culture, a fascination with spies and spying had been stoked for years by the James Bond movies and the works of John le Carré, with le Carré introducing terms such as "mole" that the press and professional spy-catchers themselves adopted. In 1981 and 1982, two Soviets had been expelled for spying (including the general who headed their attaché office in Washington), and the next year three of our people were expelled from the Soviet Union. One of my tasks as deputy director was to call in a Soviet deputy chief of mission to inform him that one of his people had been caught spying and declared *persona non grata* by the United States (i.e., expelled). The explanations were usually accompanied by spy novel narratives about dead drops and clandestine meetings. I was fascinated that the Soviets only complained once that the FBI had fingered the wrong man. They argued he was a genuine diplomat who had picked the wrong time and place to go into the woods to relieve himself. Although my interlocutor put his best show of sincerity into the effort, I was fairly certain our information was more accurate. The Soviets were less careful about expulsions than we were, expelling people from both the State Department and the CIA in Moscow.

Perhaps because of their weak political leadership or the rise of their longtime leader Andropov to the post of general secretary in November 1982 the KGB approach to our people in Moscow became steadily nastier. The days of genteel spying and quiet expulsions were over. In the Soviet Union, the press kept up an almost daily drumbeat of propaganda on the supposed threat posed by American spies operating there. In addition to potentially dangerous practices like the use of spy dust, garbage was dumped into cars and some of our people were roughly handled. I tried to get the FBI to reciprocate a bit by roughing up a couple of KGB agents in the United States to help our CIA brethren, suggesting at one point that a burly officer might confront a rather slight KGB guy who we knew was stealing scientific microfiches from local libraries. The FBI, however, refused to help, on the grounds that "We have to be nice to these guys since we are trying to recruit them." Unspoken was their total lack of interest in helping the CIA.

Fortunately, the Prince George's County police came to my rescue. Russian diplomats, who were notorious for shoplifting at low-end stores, were caught in a county Walmart trying to sneak out some merchandise. The Prince George's police, whom the store had called, nabbed the group rather roughly. At the time of their arrest, the Russians held up their IDs yelling, "Diplomat, diplomat," to which the officer in charge responded, "I don't give a sh-- who you are, you're spending the night in jail." And they did.

When my usual Soviet counterpart came storming into my office the next day to protest the "outrageous" treatment of his people, I looked him in the eye and noted solemnly our great concern over the treatment of our diplomats in Moscow and Leningrad. Unsurprisingly, the treatment of our people showed some improvement almost overnight. I've always been grateful to the Prince George's police for making life a bit better for us in Moscow. Unfortunately, I could not thank them or encourage future breaches of diplomatic immunity. We certainly never told them of the Soviet complaint.

Paranoia within the administration, in Congress, and in the press over Soviet espionage grew worse and worse. In the U.S. government, the GUNMAN project, concerns about Mt. Alto, KAL 007, worry that our new Moscow Embassy could not be fixed, and a tendency of many to hype the Soviet threat in part to thwart State

Department "plots" to work out new agreements with Moscow combined to make our interagency meetings tense and unpleasant. In April 1984 a U.S. Navy intelligence officer in Tokyo was arrested for handing sensitive information to the Soviets, and in October a Navy analyst was arrested for selling a secret photo to a British magazine. The next day our government jailed an FBI agent for spying for the Soviets. He had been working in counterintelligence for years in San Diego. All these cases made sensational headlines in the United States, and stories continued for days and weeks, fed by leaked details and articles analyzing the motivations of the arrested Americans. An assistant attorney general noted in testimony that while there had been no U.S. prosecutions for espionage from 1966 to 1975, in the decade since there had been thirty-seven cases (twenty-seven of them Soviet-related). A tally by the Associated Press at the end of 1984 said nine Americans were awaiting trial on charges of spying for the Soviets and their East Bloc allies.

Then came 1985, "The Year of the Spy." In May, a former Navy chief warrant officer named John Walker, along with his brother (a former Navy lieutenant commander), his son (an active-duty Navy yeoman), and a close friend were arrested on a tip from Walker's ex-wife. It turned out he had been feeding information to the Soviets for money for eighteen years, and his arrest created another sensation. Media coverage carried details as breaking news for months, with publicity that some compared to the Rosenberg case in the fifties. Congress, of course, piled on, condemning the espionage.

Then, in early August, a senior KGB officer named Vitaly Yurchenko defected to the CIA in Italy. During his debriefing in Washington, Yurchenko revealed the names of two former American officials who had spied for the Soviets: Edward Lee Howard, who had been fired by the CIA in 1983, and Ronald Pelton, who had resigned from NSA in 1979 and lived in poverty in Maryland. Tipped off by the Russians, Howard made a dramatic escape from his house in Arizona and ended up in the Soviet Union. Pelton was soon arrested and tried for handing over NSA secrets to the Russians, again for money. The level of spy mania reached fever pitch in Washington. There was no question that Yurchenko had indeed fingered two traitors, but both were no longer of much value to the Russians. Then, after handing over his sensational information,

Yurchenko slipped away from his CIA handler at a Georgetown restaurant in early November and returned to the Soviet Union.

While the media and Congress were ventilating in public about the spy issues, with most of the focus on the Walkers, Howard, and Pelton, the American intelligence community itself was in a panic. Although not revealed at the time, virtually all the top CIA and FBI operations against the Soviets had apparently been shut down by the KGB in the space of a few months and their informants either jailed or executed. During the summer, the KGB chief in London, Oleg Gordievsky, a longtime highly valuable source for both the British and the Americans, defected publicly after having been called back to Moscow. Other top spies were nabbed, and their fates detailed by Soviet media. Suddenly, the U.S. espionage effort in Moscow had collapsed, only part of which could be blamed (with some stretch of the imagination) on the two men named by Yurchenko. The United States had built up these intelligence assets over time; their collapse deprived us of valuable insights into the critical changes then going on in the Soviet leadership.

It is hard to exaggerate the level of paranoia and anguish in Washington over Soviet spying and the West's vulnerability in the first months of Gorbachev's rise to power in Moscow and in the period leading up to the first Reagan-Gorbachev Summit (set for November 1985 in Geneva). All of the espionage issues seemed to be connected, while the ability of the agencies of the U.S. government to work together had reached rock bottom. Unusually, the situation became worse, not better, the more you knew.

Only years later, with the arrest of the moles Aldrich Ames (CIA) in 1994 and Robert Hanssen (FBI) in 2001 did the truth of what had happened in the summer and fall of 1985 emerge. Ames was the CIA's counterintelligence branch chief for the Soviet Union from September 1983 to September 1985 and first told the Soviets in April 1985 that he wanted to exchange information for money. He handed over the names of some agents and operations in the next couple of months and on June 13 provided the Soviets with copies of documents that reportedly identified at least ten top spies working for the CIA and FBI in the Soviet Union. Over time, he is reported to have disclosed more than one hundred operations to the Soviets, including virtually all operations against the Soviet

Union and several against Soviet bloc countries. For his treachery, the Soviets reportedly paid Ames $2.5 million, which he used to pay off debts and live the high life with his new Colombian wife. The Soviet leadership decided to quickly arrest and execute the most important people Ames had fingered (a few like Gordievsky escaped), but they had to somehow deflect attention away from their new golden source.

Enter Yurchenko, a "defector" designated to throw the United States off the scent of the moles, as bold an espionage effort as the engineering of the "megaphone" United States embassy building in Moscow. The Soviets threw away two sources no longer of any value to them, one of whom, Howard, plausibly could have divulged some of the compromised operations to get the spy-catchers in Washington away from Ames's scent. The CIA, desperate to explain their losses, fell for it hook, line, and sinker and put most of the blame for the disclosures on Howard, by then out of reach in Moscow. To make the irony even greater, Ames had been one of the top CIA de-briefers of Yurchenko.

There was a problem, however. Howard had been fired two years earlier and could have at most known of only half the operations at the time; and new operations begun after he left were compromised. Ames began Italian language training in September 1985 but continued to have close ties and access to his old office and kept feeding the Soviets bags of information. CIA counterintelligence investigators, after a couple years of fruitless effort, concluded that maybe their communications had been compromised, and the search for a mole faded away. They also kept under wraps just how bad the situation had become. Ames was finally caught only after being fingered by an FBI informant in 1993.

The FBI fared no better. After criticizing the CIA for years, it turned out that they too had a high-level Soviet mole. Their internal investigations flailed around with no results until, in 2001, some sixteen years later, a Russian source provided a scrap of a plastic bag from old Soviet files that had fingerprints on it. The prints belonged to Robert Hanssen, a twenty-five-year veteran FBI agent and top computer expert, who had been spying on and off for the Soviets for most of his career. He had revived his efforts in October 1985 at the height of the spy mania by handing over names that confirmed material Ames had sold the Russians a few months earlier and continued to betray FBI sources, methods, and operations for years afterward.

The bad blood between the FBI and the CIA had finally caught up with the two organizations as they tried to staunch their losses. But they failed to pool resources or combine their spy-catching operations. Each ran their own internally flawed investigations that seemed to go nowhere, and only began to cooperate seriously on counterespionage operations in the early 1990s. Meanwhile, as the Soviet Union was collapsing and the need for accurate information was acute at the highest levels of the U.S. government, the U.S. intelligence-gathering operation was on the ropes, providing little good information and some (planted) disinformation to the nation's leaders, as two of Moscow's top moles worked with impunity to sabotage American operations.

As the public clamor over Soviet espionage grew through the early eighties, the administration decided to "do something" and took up a longtime FBI proposal to reduce the number of Soviet officials in the United States and restrict their operational mobility. It had been obvious for years that the Soviets in the UN structure acted on orders from Moscow, in contravention to their international obligations. And the Soviet staff of their UN mission in New York, which was larger than that of the United States and Chinese combined, spent a considerable part of its time spying on the United States rather than devoting its efforts to UN business. Also involved in the debate was the perceived danger of spying by the Soviet employees at our embassy in Moscow and the consulate-general in Leningrad. Senator Patrick Leahy, chairman of the Senate Select Committee on Intelligence, had denounced the embassy as a "sieve," pointing out that half of its staff were Soviet nationals, ignoring the measures in place to keep them away from sensitive material. The 1985 Inman Report, which reviewed security issues at all U.S. missions abroad, advised Secretary Shultz to cut the Soviets on our staffs in Moscow and Leningrad; by mid-1985 plans were underway for a Soviet staff reduction.

On June 29 President Reagan in his weekly radio address called for a reduction in the size of the hostile intelligence threat in the United States, adding that 30–40 percent of the 2,500 Soviet officials in the country were known or suspected intelligence officers. He called for a balanced number of U.S. and Soviet officials in each other's country and better control over foreign intelligence agents working at the United Nations. In September the United States imposed a twenty-five-mile-radius travel restriction on UN officials from the Soviet Union and five other countries. It was also decided—although the announcement was delayed to March 1986—to cut the Soviet Mission at the United Nations from 275 to 170 by April 1988.

Another major spy brouhaha almost derailed the planned second U.S.-Soviet summit, to be held in October 1986 in Reykjavik, Iceland. In August the FBI, continuing to play its high-stakes game to demonstrate its prowess to the American people, arrested a Soviet spy named Gennadi Zakharov, working at the UN Secretariat. He was entrapped by the FBI after paying a "defense contractor" for information and jailed pending a court appearance. In retaliation, the KGB set up and then arrested longtime *US News & World Report* Moscow correspondent, Nick Daniloff, by handing him an envelope supposedly containing sensitive information. The Soviets then linked the two cases, noting that neither had diplomatic immunity. The United States refused to accept the linkage of the two cases and demanded Daniloff's release. Shultz expressed his outrage and emphasized that the United States would not release a spy for an innocent journalist. Reagan also demanded Daniloff's release, but the Soviets held the advantage, even when the Americans upped the ante by suggesting the upcoming Reykjavik Summit might be imperiled.

The Soviets formally charged Daniloff on September 8, 1986, and a grand jury indicted Zakharov the next day. After thirteen days of negotiation, the United States accepted a Soviet proposal to put each man in the custody of their ambassador pending their trials. American conservatives predictably condemned the administration for going back on its promise of "no trade." In mid-September the United States announced the decision to expel twenty-five intelligence operatives from the Soviet Mission in New York by October 1. With Soviet Foreign Minister Eduard Shevardnadze in New York and Washington for the UN General Assembly, Shultz engaged in intense negotiations on Daniloff. We provided talking points for the secretary, but Shultz, the old labor negotiator, went toe-to-toe with Shevardnadze to get Daniloff out.

Daniloff finally left Moscow September 29. Zakharov pled guilty on September 30 and returned to Moscow, after some last-minute obstruction by Department of Justice lawyers. And the Soviet dissident Yuri Orlov and his wife were allowed to leave Russia, as a sweetener for the United States. The two sides announced that Reagan and Gorbachev would meet in Reykjavik, Iceland, on October 11 and 12. It was hard to see much that was gained for either side in this standoff, but Shultz and Shevardnadze had established their reputations as tough negotiators. Shultz was furious that sloppy CIA spy craft in Moscow had helped set Daniloff up by using his name to establish contact with a possible source; but he could not blame them publicly. It is possible that the sloppiness was born of desperation, since the CIA sources had been decimated. What can be said for certain is that the FBI's sting operation against Zakharov had put an American correspondent in serious danger and almost brought down a planned summit between Reagan and Gorbachev.

After a post-Reykjavik round of expulsions that included Moscow's withdrawal of all Soviet employees from our missions, each side ended up with 251 diplomatic and administrative personnel assigned to their bilateral missions. The FBI and the State Department's congressional critics felt that they had won a great victory; but while these people continued their comfortable lives in Washington, their fellow Americans in Moscow and Leningrad suffered the consequences. The support staff for routine activities had disappeared. The embassy had no one to do the mundane tasks of translating administrative documents, cleaning, cooking, driving, or fixing the toilets. Life became truly difficult in do-it-yourself Moscow and Leningrad until the State Department managed to hire contract Americans to take over some of the maintenance work. Few people commented on the ridiculousness of the original argument of dangerous spying by the Soviet staff, as the Soviets themselves were happy to pull them out of the Embassy. They surely would not have done so if the employees had provided valuable intelligence. The climate in Washington was too overheated and the rhetoric too exaggerated to allow any rational discussion of the pros and cons of the mass expulsions.

Finally, one last episode in this entire counterintelligence drama (or perhaps farce would be a better word) summed up the surreal atmosphere that had been created in Washington—the Marine Guard scandal at Embassy Moscow. In late December 1986, an embassy Marine Security Guard, Sergeant Lonetree, who had left Moscow in March, confessed to having had sexual relations with a Russian female embassy employee and supplying the Russians with secret information. Then a second guard confessed that he and Lonetree had allowed Russian agents into sensitive areas of the Embassy. Washington counterintelligence officials assumed the worst, and the press and Congress went into a new phase of breathless spy sensationalism. The department reacted by replacing all the Marines in Moscow and Leningrad, closing down Moscow embassy communications, and again replacing the communications equipment. Then a third Marine was arrested, and two others placed under suspicion. The embassy's top security officer was recalled to Washington, two senators descended on Moscow to proclaim security at the embassy disastrously lax, and Art Hartman, who had endured six years of the upheavals and accusations, retired under criticism. Anti-spy hysteria had reached a new level.

But then it turned out most of the stories were wrong. After careful analysis and review, the case fell apart. Lonetree's amended story of handing over some documents and naming a few non-State personnel in Moscow and Vienna earned him a thirty-year sentence for espionage (he served nine years), but none of the rest of the story checked out. The second Marine had recanted his story within minutes after he gave it. The two had not been on duty together long enough to carry out the alleged plot. It became apparent that his Marine interrogators were eager to get evidence of a major espionage operation, regardless of the facts. In the end, no one other than Lonetree was convicted. And after extensive postconviction discussions with Lonetree and other Marines, investigators concluded that stories about Soviets gaining entry into the Embassy were the product of the overly zealous interrogators, with no evidence it ever happened. Gorbachev himself told Shultz on a trip at the time that there had been no Soviet penetration of the Embassy.

As I reflect on the espionage saga of the eighties with its charges and countercharges, bureaucratic brawls, lurid headlines, overblown rhetoric, executions and imprisonment of traitors, and the loss of so much "top secret" information, it's important to ask what it all added up to in the end. In some ways the fevered debates tell us more about ourselves and a self-induced hysteria than about the Soviet Union, which we already knew was a police state in decay with a security apparatus out of control. The real intelligence losses turned out not to be from "lax security" at Embassy Moscow, or its local Russian staff, or the bits of information acquired by the average Soviet spy in New York or Washington, or the site of the new Soviet embassy, or what Navy secrets the Walkers could dredge up, or even from the bugged embassy typewriters. Rather, the damage was done by two well-placed Russian spies —Ames and Hansen—who were willing to sell out their country for money. In an open society like ours, state secrets on the really big issues have a fairly short shelf life. It is the curse of foreign diplomats and spies in the United States that the real information about U.S. intentions comes from reading what our leaders say and what the *Washington Post* and *New York Times* report on the decision-making process. For their part, the Soviets learned the names of their own traitors, details about CIA and FBI operations, and some useful technical information. The penetrations and expulsions also limited information available to the United States during the critical period of transition in the Soviet Union. But truthfully, the sad series of events hardly proved a serious danger to the United States.

Apart from all the noise and gnashing of teeth about Soviet espionage in the 1980's, the undeniable fact is that the United States won the Cold War because the Soviet Union collapsed from its own inability to fulfill the needs of its people, not because of any espionage coups or Western radio broadcasts. Indeed, for those inclined to find high-priced intelligence material superior to the day-to-day diplomatic reporting, it is important to remember that during the time of the Soviet Union's collapse and the emergence of Russia and fourteen other smaller states, the United States had little information from its human intelligence operations and relied instead on embassy reporting and publicly available information. It's useful to ask ourselves if we would have acted much differently if by some stroke of luck CIA operatives had been given the record of each of the Politburo meetings in those critical years. The answer is: Probably not.

7
Gorbachev and a New Era of Cooperation

Fortunately, in contrast to the espionage mania dominating the press and panicking the intelligence community in the mid-eighties, there emerged an entirely different narrative, driven by Reagan and Shultz (backed by State Department planning and detailed work) and Gorbachev and Shevardnadze. With Gorbachev's rise to power in March 1985, Reagan finally had a new generation Soviet leader that he could talk to and who presented hope for an improvement in the U.S.-Soviet relationship. The feeble and unimaginative leadership of Andropov and Chernenko could not respond usefully to the initiatives that Reagan and Shultz had been putting forward for over two years. A cruel, but on-target Soviet joke captured the mood in Moscow about their leadership: As Ivan walked around one day in early 1985, he saw a friend standing in a line snaking around Red Square and said: "Comrade, what are doing in this long line?" His friend responded: "I'm waiting to buy a ticket to Chernenko's funeral." Ivan: "What a fool you are. I bought a season ticket years ago."

Gorbachev impressed Vice President Bush and Secretary Shultz when they met him at Chernenko's funeral, and their report fueled Reagan's desire for a summit with the new leader. But Gorbachev was fully occupied during his first months consolidating his internal powerbase and had little time to spend on U.S.-Soviet relations. As part of his government overhaul, he brought in the regional leader from Georgia, Eduard Shevardnadze, a fellow reformer, to replace the aging Gromyko as foreign minister in July. After it was decided that Reagan and Gorbachev would meet in Geneva November 19–20, 1985, Shultz and Shevardnadze (and we lower-level laborers) began an intense effort to make the summit a reality.

I represented EUR on the presummit advance trip to Geneva to work out detailed arrangements for the meeting, returning to Geneva in November as a low-level member of the delegation, to help ensure everything went as planned. Mark Palmer, the deputy assistant secretary, and Mark Parris, head of the Soviet desk, dealt with the substance of the visit, preparing talking points and taking notes in the meetings themselves while I worked the details. The president's handlers always tried to make Reagan's actions look spontaneous and relaxed, but he was probably the most scripted president the United States has ever seen. The old movie actor had his lines typed out on three-by-five cards and his movements were laid out in great detail. No doubt he engaged and forcefully argued points on issues he believed in, especially SDI, during his meetings with Gorbachev. But nothing outside the rooms (and remarkably little in them) was left to chance.

On the advance trip, our group looked over all the possible venues, including intruding on the wife of the Aga Khan in her villa, where the Reagans were to stay, and we planned scenarios for each event. My job was to keep a political eye on the planning to ensure the arrangements would promote the overall aims of the trip and avoid political missteps. During the meeting itself, commentators made much of the two leaders' taking a walk in the garden of one of the villas, suggesting the idea came spontaneously from Reagan when talking with Gorbachev. In fact, the walk had been thoroughly scoped out by the advance team, down to an improbable photo of the two presidents walking alone and talking together, even though they had no common language. We later learned from our interpreter that the first half of the walk had gone well (with interpretation, of course). But when Reagan ran out of talking points on his 3x5 cards, he began telling Gorbachev some of the old anti-Soviet jokes from his Hollywood days, referring, as he often did, to Nikolai (not Vladimir) Lenin. Gorbachev, who had looked forward with great anticipation to the private walk as a way of connecting with the American president was evidently frustrated and not amused by the jokes and tried repeatedly to correct Reagan's mistake on Lenin's name.

The summit had its tense moments, but the basic aim of the session was for the two leaders to take each other's measure. It succeeded well, resulting in an upbeat joint communiqué, promising summits in Washington and Moscow, with reassuring pictures of the smiling leaders that signaled a new era of détente. On the evening of his return to Washington, Reagan briefed a joint session of Congress on the meeting's success. From our perspective on the desk, the encounter had more than fulfilled its goal of heading the new relationship in the right direction, showing the world that a new, positive U.S.-Soviet interaction was possible. On substance, the four-point agenda was established as the framework for future negotiations.

The meeting between the two leaders did not, however, bring an immediate change in the bilateral arms control negotiations and other issues, which returned to their usual stale pattern. Major events were happening in Moscow, as Gorbachev and Shevardnadze revamped the Soviet Union's foreign policy ideology—replacing struggle against the West with cooperation—as well as implementing structural changes. A major cleaning out of Gromyko's people from the Foreign Ministry and embassies abroad created predictable reactions from the conservatives. Under fire at home for the lack of substantive progress in Geneva, Gorbachev was determined that the Washington and Moscow summits agreed in Geneva would produce substantial results, especially on arms control.

The arms control talks that had been restarted by Shultz and Gromyko in January 1985 made little progress despite the smiles in Geneva. Then in January 1986 Gorbachev proposed to Reagan that the two sides work on a phased program to eliminate all nuclear weapons worldwide by the year 2000. It contained many ideas the United States had promoted and caught the attention of the American arms control community. Reagan himself was particularly intrigued by the possibility of eliminating nuclear weapons. The United States reacted positively to Gorbachev's proposal. Over the next few months, the administration toyed with various counterproposals, including eliminating ballistic missiles. Another major internal wrangle arose over whether or not the United States would continue to abide by SALT II limits; the treaty had not been ratified by the United States following the Soviet invasion of Afghanistan, but its limits were being observed. Then Shevardnadze canceled a visit to the United States after the American bombing of Libya in April. The U.S. administration wanted to get on with the promised summits, but Gorbachev was extremely wary of being maneuvered into another summit without concrete results. And nothing substantial had been accomplished in the months following Geneva.

As I departed the Soviet desk after three hectic years, one of my most satisfying thoughts involved the excellent people I had worked with. Recruiting good people for the desk and for Embassy Moscow and the Consulate General in Leningrad was a normal responsibility of the deputy director. The desk had a reputation as the place to be in the 1980s for ambitious FSOs. As positions became available, I usually had twenty or more officers vying to fill each slot; and the challenge was picking the very best, not beating the bushes for capable candidates.

Because we had to engage the Soviets on issues around the world, we searched throughout the department to fill slots in Moscow and on the desk, recruiting some of the department's most talented officers, who could match their Soviet counterparts in region-specific knowledge. This had the added benefit that when these officers returned to their "home" bureaus, we had a cadre of people throughout the bureaucracy in Washington who were knowledgeable about, and not intimidated by, America's chief opponent. The system also meant that we had a superb group of officers at the ready when the Soviet Union broke up and we needed to get Russian-speaking ambassadors to the new countries immediately. If my count is correct, at least twenty-two of the FSOs I served with in Moscow or on the desk went on to become ambassadors, many to multiple ambassadorial postings.

Working for George Shultz

In the summer of 1986, my old boss Nick Platt recruited me to become one of the department's two deputy executive secretaries. The State Department under Shultz was almost unique in modern history for his placement of Foreign Service officers in high positions and the trust he put in them. On his immediate staff, Charles Hill, his executive assistant, served as his closest advisor, note-taker, and the ultimate inside operator. Nick Platt, as executive secretary of the department, took part in virtually all of Shultz's substantive discussions and served as his chief action officer to ensure that the department carried out his wishes. Nick's deputies, Kenneth Quinn (an old friend from the A-100 class) and I, formed the connection to the department, getting papers and ideas up from the bureaus, transmitting instructions downward, and ensuring that decisions were carried out. Nick, Ken, and I would meet four or five times a day to go through our notebooks with the checklists, information, and gossip necessary to ensure the secretary's close connection to his department.

My primary areas of responsibility were Europe, heavily focused on the negotiations with the Soviet Union, and Latin America, almost entirely Central America, with several other bureaus such as Policy Planning and International Organizations thrown in for good measure. We did not make grand policy in the Secretariat; our job was to ensure that the secretary and his top deputies were provided the policy and background papers, formal documents, and briefings they needed to carry out their responsibilities and to help focus their many meetings in pursuit of their goals. Then we were responsible to ensure that the department carried out their decisions.

Working for George Shultz was a great honor and privilege. I believe he was one of the best secretaries of state in the post–World War II era. Shultz had come to the State Department after Al Haig's firing in June 1982. U.S. foreign policy was in disarray, with Casey, Weinberger, and Clark off in their own versions of reality and Haig trying to counter them with tantrums, fights, and outsized reactions to perceived slights. Shultz had served in three cabinet-ranked positions during the Nixon administration, Labor, OMB, and Treasury; but he resigned in a disagreement with Nixon over using the IRS to target people seen as Nixon's enemies. He had the reputation of a traditional conservative, confident, optimistic, not prone to flare-ups, patient, and a man with rock-solid integrity. He worked the foreign policy issues for Reagan and traveled extensively to "tend the garden" (as he put it) in meetings with our allies as well as opponents. Uniquely for a secretary of state, he would spend two weeks in New York at the start of the UN's annual General Debate to meet with virtually every head of state and foreign minister who wanted to see him. His personal attention and devotion of time paid huge dividends, as his interlocutors, often leaders of quite small countries, returned home giving glowing reports of their unprecedented meetings with the U.S. secretary of state.

My first encounter with Shultz was as deputy on the Soviet desk when I briefed him on some long-forgotten topic. Shultz lived up to his reputation as a Buddha while I made my points, listening to what I had to say without comment or reaction. When I left his office, I felt my effort had been a total failure, and I was unsure whether he had even been listening. Two days later I accompanied a Soviet visitor to his office to discuss the topic of my briefing. To my astonishment, Shultz used every point I had made to him, weaving them into his own narrative to get what he wanted out of the meeting. From that moment on, I realized that I had better be absolutely sure of anything I told him, as his passive demeanor masked close attention to what I was saying and his assessment of its accuracy. As I later watched him in action many times, he seldom changed this Buddha style, although he could be charming and funny when the occasion called for it.

Behind the quiet exterior, Shultz was a determined and steady bureaucratic fighter, with a brilliant mind. Commentators noted that he had been a blocking tackle at Princeton and a determined Marine, and "he just keeps on coming." In his six and a half years as secretary, his adversaries repeatedly tried to gut his power or get him fired; but Reagan (and especially Nancy Reagan) came to his support time after time, because they trusted his judgment and integrity. One by one, Shultz's opponents found themselves outmaneuvered and left the administration. These included Bill Clark, Robert "Bud" McFarlane (a sometime Shultz ally), and John Poindexter at the NSC, Cap Weinberger at DOD, Bill Casey at CIA, Ed Meese at Justice, and Jeane Kirkpatrick at the UN. In the end he, not they, set the policy on arms control, relations with the Soviets, and other major foreign policy issues.

His battles against broadening the use of polygraphs at the State Department beyond espionage cases showed his devotion to principle—he saw the polygraph threat as a tool to intimidate

U.S. government employees rather than earn their trust—and to practicality—the tests could be easily beaten by trained personnel, as demonstrated by the American spies who routinely covered up their actions and by the CIA's Cuban network, who turned out to be double agents despite multiple polygraph sessions. I cheered for Shultz extra hard on this one, since I had found the polygraph test given me during my 1966 NSA job interview one of the most demeaning things I had ever done (for the record, I passed). Shultz believed in trust as the basis for managing people, since it inspired trust and loyalty in return. He had confidence in the people who worked for him (derided by conservatives as "Foreign Service elitists") and engendered strong staff loyalty in return. His insistence on appointing Foreign Service officers to key positions reinforced this loyalty in the building.

The Shultz-Shevardnadze relationship was a fascinating one. At the end of July 1985 Shultz came back quite impressed from his first meeting with Shevardnadze, whom Gorbachev had just named foreign minister. After two years of unpleasant meetings with Gromyko, Shultz quickly recognized that he now had as a counterpart an intelligent human being who was willing to explore with him ways to improve the superpower relationship. The secretary told us that, while Shevardnadze was relatively ignorant about the outside world (he had been the provincial leader of Georgia), he had a strong inquisitive intellect and would be a good interlocutor. Shultz, the old professor, took it upon himself to tutor Shevardnadze in global political and economic trends. When Shevardnadze first visited Washington a couple of months later, Shultz and his wife Obie invited Shevardnadze and his wife to their house for a steak dinner that Shultz cooked himself in the fireplace, with only interpreters present. The Shevardnadzes reciprocated in Moscow, and the quiet evenings for four became a fixture over the next four years. Shultz used these sessions to talk about economics, the state of the world, and global trends, tactfully educating his new friend on the world they both faced. Shultz would think carefully about what points he wanted to make during each evening, and Shevardnadze proved to be an eager and open-minded listener. (Shultz also buttonholed Gorbachev when he had a chance during breaks in Moscow to explain changes taking place in global communications and trade. Gorbachev was as appreciative of the discussions as Shevardnadze.) The Shultz-Shevardnadze relationship was key to the transformation of bilateral relations over the next few years.

Shultz made some critical institutional changes beyond his very real bonding with the department—which unfortunately was mostly dissipated by his successor Jim Baker's coterie of advisors, who did not trust the Foreign Service professionals and cut them off from the press and Congress. After the bombings in Beirut and the report of the Inman Commission, Shultz instituted a complete reworking of the department's approach to the security of our missions overseas. He also put U.S. diplomatic training on a solid, long-term basis by securing a new campus for the Foreign Service Institute in an Arlington facility vacated by the military, now appropriately named the George P. Shultz National Foreign Affairs Training Center.

Reykjavik

As August 1986 arrived with little progress in U.S.-Soviet relations in the nine months following the Geneva summit, Gorbachev again took the initiative by proposing that he and Reagan meet in London or Reykjavik for a preliminary session to break the arms control impasse and ensure the success of the Washington and Moscow summits. Reagan was willing; but since the offer arrived in the midst of the argument over the Daniloff detention, the United States would not agree to announce a new summit until Daniloff was allowed to leave the Soviet Union. In the end, the United States had ten days after the announcement to finalize plans for Reykjavik. We scrambled hard to get appropriate briefing material to the White House. It turned out that the Russians were planning to offer major concessions in return for an American agreement to restrict the development of Reagan's pet defensive arms control project, SDI, or Star Wars. What followed was the most dramatic and consequential meeting between the leaders of the two superpowers since World War II.

The story of the Reykjavik Summit has been told many times. Over two days, October 11–12, 1986, the two leaders came close to an agreement to work for the total elimination of nuclear weapons and ballistic missiles. Both passionately believed in the importance of the elimination of nuclear weapons—to the horror of their staffs, who could agree to reductions and controls but believed the weapons were critical to their and their allies' defense strategy, as well as validation of their superpower status. In the end, Gorbachev refused to agree to the grand scheme unless Reagan would consent to limiting his SDI program to the laboratory stage. The president said "No," and the meeting broke up seven hours late with no agreement. The basis had been laid, however, for several far-reaching agreements on the limiting of the two sides' nuclear weapons.

As usual, my job had been to ensure the briefing material was prepared and to help support the secretary in Reykjavik. But the actual discussion was very much a two-man show between the leaders, with Shultz and the arms controllers trying to come up with ways to support the president. When it was over on that cold, bleak night, Shultz and his team boarded his plane to Brussels to brief NATO and put the best face on a meeting that had almost left Europe exposed to the superior conventional forces of the Red Army. As an obviously exhausted Shultz met with us on the plane that evening, he tried to sort out the two days' events in his own mind and figure out how to present it to the Allies. Virtually all the staff members on the plane were relieved the meeting had failed: the military considered the president's position a disaster, the arms controllers felt it put the United States at a disadvantage vis-à-vis the Soviet Union, the Europeanists felt no nukes meant an abandonment of Europe, and the sole China-type on the plane (me) wondered if the leaders had given any thought about bringing the Chinese on board (of course not).

Relieved NATO leaders gave Shultz a warm reception. Shultz later maintained his support for Reagan efforts at Reykjavik, even though he earlier had tried several times to dissuade Reagan from his dream of a nonnuclear world. After his retirement, Shultz became a strong advocate of stepping up the pace to eliminate nuclear weapons. He led a group that included Henry Kissinger, William Perry, and Sam Nunn in writing a series of op-ed pieces advocating movement toward a nuclear-free world, and he organized a conference to this end on the twentieth anniversary of the Reykjavik Summit to promote this vision. I last chatted with Shultz in September 2009 at the UN, when the Security Council, chaired by President Obama, endorsed the vision of a world without nuclear weapons that his group had championed.

Travels with Shultz

When the secretary traveled, Nick Platt remained in Washington to keep the department running smoothly. It was the responsibility of one of his two deputies to ensure all aspects of the trip went well on the road. In my two years on the job, I accompanied Shultz on trips that included forty-seven country stops, each one involving long hours, great pressure, and tremendous satisfaction when things went well, as they usually did. Some notable exceptions included the time we arrived in Vienna and the secretary needed by noon a clean text of the speech he had edited on the plane that he was to give to the CSCE. It should have been easy to get the speech typed in an hour while Shultz caught some sleep; but the cleared embassy typists were unfamiliar with the new Wang computers in the office and the backup Secretariat printer that we carried with a small portable computer refused to work. With profuse apologies, I ended up handing an obviously annoyed Shultz the last page of his speech on the elevator ten minutes after he was scheduled to begin speaking. Years later, I mentioned the episode to a European diplomat. He responded: "I was in the audience that day in Vienna. All of us wondered why Shultz, who was always so punctual, showed up fifteen minutes late. We assumed there must be some great crisis." "No," I confessed, "it was my failure to get him the text of his speech on time."

The most memorable trips were the critical ones that the secretary made to Moscow for talks with Shevardnadze and Gorbachev. Shultz would take his entire team of arms controllers to meetings with the Soviets. Thus on each trip Shultz was accompanied by twenty-plus substantive advisors, with highly diverse views and much personal animosity among them. (Shultz would tell me with a twinkle in his eye to "just try to keep them happy so we can get some work done." I would grimace in return before saying I would do my best.) Shultz firmly believed in keeping people inside the tent so they could feel themselves part of the action and, equally important, not be back in Washington sniping during his arms deal negotiations. I knew he was right. We had to suck it up and make it work.

Shultz had an inner core of advisers that included Roz Ridgeway (backed by Tom Simons, now the deputy assistant secretary, and Mark Parris), Paul Nitze (backed by Jim Timbie), National Security Advisor Frank Carlucci or Colin Powell (backed by Jack Matlock), and, at times in the negotiations, Richard Perle from the Defense Department. We always produced two versions of the briefing books for the trips. One for the secretary and the core group and a "lite" version for the others that discussed his policy positions in more general terms. Shultz's negotiating team would consist of Carlucci or Powell, Nitze, Ridgeway, and Matlock, with Simons or Parris taking notes. He would return after each session to brief the larger group in a secure area (the bubble). I would attend the debriefings (but not the negotiating sessions) to find out what the secretary needed for the next day.

I first traveled to Moscow with Shultz in April 1987. It had been six months since the failed Reykjavik summit, and Washington was still in turmoil over the Iran-Contra affair. A whole new challenge had arisen from the Marine Guard scandal at Embassy Moscow, particularly with the second marine's testimony that he and Lonetree had allowed Russian intelligence agents to compromise the embassy's security. Embassy functions had been essentially closed down, with no electronic communications with Washington, and Weinberger and the head of NSA demanded that the president cancel Shultz's trip. Shultz argued that the trip should go on and the president agreed, but Weinberger did manage to get severe limits on Shultz's talking points. Seventy senators voted for a resolution opposing the Shultz trip to Moscow at the time.

Security on the trip and how to communicate with Washington became major problems. Given the NSA attacks on State communications, Shultz suggested, and it was agreed, during one of the White House discussions that a White House communications (WACA) van and State Department portable secure rooms (bubbles) be sent to the Embassy. He told me when he came back to the office that I had to make the new plan work and to get NSA's certification of the van. The only problem with this White House decision was that the WACA vans at the time had zero security protection against the kind of microwave intrusion that Moscow had long used against the Embassy. The temporary State Department security boxes provided far superior protection, but NSA had limited its own options by denigrating the department's security. There followed a frantic effort by the NSA staff to stuff a WACA Winnebago van with all sorts of countermeasures to support their boss's agreement to Shultz's proposal. In the end, NSA never certified the van (our security people measured it as about half as secure as a State Department box), but it was shipped to Moscow on an advance plane to be moved around in our residential parking area. Neither Shultz nor anyone else inquired further if it was secure or if NSA had given its final approval.

The cramped facilities in the secure boxes meant that the entire arms control crowd could not be briefed by Shultz at one time. This increased the pressure on him after an exhausting day of negotiations to do two briefings and led to childish disputes among the supposedly sophisticated advisors about who could go in first and who could stay. One evening after a particularly tough negotiating session, Shultz decided to take a few minutes with his close-in staff to gather his thoughts. During the discussion, one of the more difficult DOD members of the delegation started banging on the door of the secure box. When I opened it, he said: "Lynn, others of us want to be in the meeting." I responded: "F—off," and slammed the door. Shultz did not break his train of thought during the interruption, and the offending staffer later apologized to me for his behavior on the plane home. (Frank Carlucci fired him when he became secretary of defense in the fall.)

As it turned out, despite the naysayers and all the noise over security, the trip was a major success. Gorbachev delinked restrictions on SDI from an agreement on intermediate-range missiles in Europe and appeared eager to sign an agreed treaty on Intermediate-range Nuclear Forces (INF) in the Washington Summit planned for later in the year. Shultz needed to have detailed discussions with our NATO Allies (they agreed in June), and Gorbachev gave up his demand to retain SS-20 missiles in the Far East. Things were falling into place for final agreement on the long-sought INF treaty. When Shevardnadze visited Washington in September, the two foreign ministers announced they had an agreement in principle.

Shultz usually traveled with his team to Helsinki a day before flying on to Moscow to rest up from jet lag and to discuss strategy in the more secure environment there. The competitive atmosphere among the arms controllers sometimes reached ludicrous levels. On one trip, the advisors were so anxious to ensure that no one beat them to a planning meeting with Shultz that they all crowded into the one elevator at the State Guesthouse, causing the doors to wedge shut and trap them inside. Pat Kennedy, who ably and creatively handled administrative issues on the trips, and I had walked the one flight of stairs to avoid being trampled by the crowd. Since it was Sunday, there were no mechanics available, and Pat was soon down on the floor with a screwdriver trying to free the group. I couldn't resist telling them to stay calm; joking that we would let them out when they agreed on a reasonable arms control strategy for the secretary.

In October, when Shultz was in Helsinki preparing for his trip to wrap up the last details for the Washington summit, Moscow was enveloped in a deep fog expected to last for days, making a flight to Moscow impossible. The resourceful and always helpful Finns offered up their president's private train for the trip. We set up a small communications dish on the train, the party and accompanying press went to work on the ample stock of booze, and the overnight trip turned out to be a memorable one for the Shultz happy band of travelers. Touting its prowess in the hour of need, Finnish Railway ran a large ad in the local papers a few days later showing Secretary and Mrs. Shultz waving as they boarded the train with the text "When you really have to get there, take Finland Railways."

The jolly atmosphere and optimism evaporated the next day when movement to resolve the last details of the treaty ended. Gorbachev subjected Shultz to a tongue-lashing and appeared to reinstate SDI restrictions as a prerequisite for the treaty and the summit, leaving the Americans to wonder what had changed. It turned out later that Gorbachev had been severely attacked in a Central Committee meeting two days before by Boris Yeltsin, who charged that Gorbachev's domestic and foreign policies were both failing. Shultz had the unenviable task of trying to put the best face on the setback with the NATO allies and the media when he made his usual stop in Brussels. Three days later, the Soviets reversed themselves, and Shevardnadze came to Washington to set the summit dates and confirm that the treaty would be signed.

Summits in Washington and Moscow

Detailed planning for the Washington summit, now scheduled for December 8–10, 1987, began immediately after Shevardnadze returned to Moscow. At one of the usual daily meetings to hash out the schedule and sort out who was to do what to make it a success, the White House announced the signing of the INF Treaty would be at 1:45pm the first day of the visit. I immediately questioned the timing, noting that the summit would have heavy press coverage the first day with Gorbachev's arrival and the day's meetings and suggested instead that we save it for the second day, which looked to be rather thin on news. This was quickly shot down by the chief participant from the White House with the comment: "This has already been decided by the East Wing." I was genuinely puzzled about why Mrs. Reagan would decide on such an odd time for the trip's top substantive announcement. A year later former chief of staff Don Regan wrote in his memoirs that she had decided on the advice of her astrologer that the first day was the propitious time. The same astrologer had apparently been paid to set the time for a number of other White House events.

As I sat in the White House's East Room watching the well-organized signing ceremony (although Reagan did get under Gorbachev's skin quoting his favorite Russian proverb, "Trust, but verify"), I wondered to myself what we were going to do for an encore the second day. Sure enough, the news for that day was not about Reagan and his success but about Gorbachev's charm during his meetings in Washington and stopping his motorcade to press the flesh of ordinary Washingtonians.

Overall, however, the public goodwill and glittering events provided for a successful summit that sent the message to the world that U.S.-Soviet relations were finally on the right track. The dark pre-Gorbachev days had been replaced by the possibility of a new era of good feeling between the two superpowers. The discussions covered the entire range of issues on the four-part agenda. However, in what may well have been an early indication of the Alzheimer's disease that afflicted Reagan after he left office, Reagan reportedly performed disastrously in his meeting with Gorbachev following the signing ceremony, as the president meandered and told bad jokes in front of a large group of onlookers. Shultz had to take over the meeting and carry on the substantive conversation with Gorbachev. Six months later in Moscow, Reagan's every move and statement would be closely planned in advance and controlled by his handlers to be sure he did not repeat that performance.

There were two Shultz trips to Moscow and a Shevardnadze trip to the United States after the Washington Summit to prepare for the last summit that the two leaders had agreed to in their first meeting in Geneva, namely the Moscow Summit of May 29–June 2, 1988. Shultz and Shevardnadze had by now met some twenty-five times in various cities, with the four-part agenda and the structure of their meetings well established. The Soviet withdrawal from Afghanistan and their effort to get the United States to stop aiding the Mujahedeen had replaced arms control as their top issue, but both sides also focused on making this last summit the capstone of their three-year effort.

We had the usual fights with the White House over housing and access, but more seriously over the content of the speech Reagan was to make at Moscow State University as a centerpiece of the trip. (As part of the usual White House staff pettiness, they tried to put Shultz well away from the government Guest House in Helsinki, where Reagan was to stay to prepare for Moscow and where Shultz had stayed many times on his travels.) Tony Dolan and his band of right-wing warriors still controlled the White House speech-writing process, and Reagan's public speeches continued to be far tougher on the Soviets than his private utterances. Reagan's public tone usually drove Gorbachev to distraction, as the speeches tended to get far more attention in Moscow than in Washington. After a considerable struggle that included intervention by Shultz, the Moscow speech ended up a good one and was widely praised.

Neither side expected major results from the conversations on substance. Reagan had reached lame duck status at this point, and Gorbachev and his program were under strong pressure at home. It was a time for nice words, good press ops, and camaraderie. Reagan was programmed on 3x5 cards to the nth degree (take three steps forward, turn to your right, greet Mrs. XX and congratulate her on YY, then take four more steps forward, wave to the crowd, and so on). The old actor Reagan clicked in, and he carried out his role well, despite his slipping mental capabilities. The one near-disaster came when he agreed to a walk along Arbat Street that degenerated into a brawl between startled civilians and Soviet security personnel. Otherwise, even the weather cooperated, and the visit went very much as planned. When a journalist asked Reagan, who was obviously enjoying himself immensely, about the "evil empire," the president passed it off as "another time, another era." This visit was a fitting end to an era noted for the remarkable changes that had come about through the intense efforts of the American president, his secretary of state, the Soviet president, and his foreign minister.

The four-part agenda that Tom Simons had created in 1983 had by 1988 become the standard framework for discussions between the two superpowers. Originally created to demonstrate that we were pursuing all issues with the Soviets but would not to be held back by linkage among the various categories, it came to be a convenient framework and division of labor to make progress in the 1985–1988 period. The Soviets wanted to keep the emphasis on arms control, while the Americans were equally determined to keep the Soviets' feet to the fire on human rights (especially the right of Soviet Jews and dissidents to emigrate) and on Soviet behavior in third world trouble spots, especially Afghanistan and Central America.

Shultz and Reagan were keen on human rights issues from the start, and the Soviet treatment of the Pentecostals in 1983 suggested that progress could be made through steady effort. Internal U.S. political pressure—to facilitate Jewish emigration (the synagogue in my neighborhood had an enormous sign in the yard that read "FREE SOVIET JEWRY") and to help brave Soviet dissidents such as the famous nuclear scientist Andrei Sakharov—meant there had to be progress on human rights to maintain support for our other work with the Soviets. Similarly, despite heavy foot-dragging from much of the State Department for any discussions with the Soviets on "their" issues (Chet Crocker of the Africa Bureau was a notable exception), Shultz believed that regional discussions with the Soviets were key to lowering superpower competition in the Third World and reducing global conflict. Finally, we had a considerable range of strictly bilateral issues (from trade to consulates) that had been brought to a virtual halt by the earlier sanctions imposed because of Soviet actions. By 1988 we had made solid progress in all of these areas, and the future looked bright indeed.

Latin America

The part of my portfolio as deputy executive secretary that I knew least about was Latin America. Shultz inherited a policy toward Central America, driven largely by National Security Advisor William Clark and CIA chief Bill Casey, that consisted of equal parts of sounding the alarm about a possible Communist takeover and paying others (the Contras) to do the dirty work to ensure it did not happen. They considered negotiations to end the conflict as inherently bad, talking to adversaries appeasement, and any sense of policy nuance suspiciously weak. More than fed up, the Democrats in Congress actively opposed the administration's policy. By the time I arrived on his staff, Shultz had outlasted both Clark and Casey, and the Iran-Contra affair soon discredited much of the old policy. The conservatives, however, continued to blast Shultz's efforts to negotiate a solution, and the Democrats in Congress did not trust anything the administration said or did on Central America.

Undoubtedly, Shultz's most uncomfortable period as secretary of state arose during the aftermath of the Iran-Contra scandal. News of the NSC/CIA rogue operation to sell arms to Iran to free American hostages and use the proceeds to fund the Contras in Central America broke just three weeks after the Reykjavik summit. When proposals had surfaced earlier in the year for an approach to Iran on hostages held in Lebanon, Shultz (and Weinberger) had strongly opposed them. They were then essentially cut out of the loop. Reagan authorized the operation without either's consent, and the NSC and CIA went ahead in secret. When the affair became a public scandal, the White House tried to use Shultz's reputation for integrity to protect itself, but Shultz made it clear to investigators and congressional panels that he had opposed any such effort from the start. In this period, his relations became quite strained with Nancy Reagan, his strongest supporter, who appeared to feel that he was not sufficiently protecting the president. Shultz held his ground, however, and emerged as the one senior administration figure to come out of the affair with his reputation intact.

The only time I saw George Shultz display his temper was when he learned that our ambassador in Beirut, John Kelly, had been briefed on the Iranian arms-for-hostages deal four months earlier and had not informed him. (Kelly's predecessor, Reginald Bartholomew, kept Charlie Hill informed of what he heard from the NSC.) I knew John Kelly from my first tour in Thailand, when he headed our consulate in Songkhla, and worked with him when he was EUR deputy assistant secretary during my time on the Soviet Desk. Shultz's reaction to John's foolish mistake was what one would expect of a man who put great stock in trust and loyalty, who appreciated the Foreign Service for its competence and loyalty to him as secretary, and who felt deeply betrayed by someone he expected to act with the utmost professionalism. (Shultz had contempt for Casey's cooking the intelligence on the Soviet Union at CIA, but he was genuinely upset when Bob Gates, Casey's deputy, did the same thing, because he expected far more from professionals than he did from politicians.) Shultz publicly criticized Kelly in congressional testimony and tried to get him fired, but the White House protected him.

Shultz never had full control of our Latin American policy like he had with the Soviet Union. The White House did not agree with Shultz's approach to the region, and Assistant Secretary for Inter-American Affairs Elliott Abrams was in many respects a one-man band who dealt directly with the secretary and the White House on most issues. Shultz stuck with him throughout his tenure, despite efforts by Abrams at times to go behind his back to support the Contras and enormous pressure from Democrats in Congress to fire him. Four different lead negotiators on Central America resigned in frustration over policy differences in these years.

I had worked well with Elliot on the Soviet desk when he was assistant secretary for human rights; and while I did not agree with some of his policy views on Latin America—and certainly not with the pummeling we received from many of his conservative friends—I found him personable, smart, and capable. We worked closely together on Shultz's trips to the region. He was a creative thinker, an excellent drafter, and completely cooperative in making sure Shultz got the maximum possible results out of the trips. He ran afoul of Congress for evasive testimony on the Contras, was convicted on a misdemeanor charge, and later pardoned by President Bush. Later, from my post at the UN, I would work a bit with Elliot when he was overseeing Middle East policy from the NSC.

Ultimately, the tide moved in Shultz's direction toward a negotiated settlement in Central America; but when I left, with six months remaining in the Reagan administration, nothing had really been resolved. For Shultz, Central American policy was an endless slog, with irrational policies being pushed by all sides of the U.S. political spectrum. Unlike the dramatic policy changes toward the Soviet Union, there could be little psychic satisfaction for Shultz in the Central America battle. On my last trip with him, we traveled to four Central American countries in one day. (As usual, in El Salvador the trip from the airport had to be made by helicopter high over rebel-held mountains, with nothing but a seatbelt between us and a several thousand-foot drop.) Minutes before we landed back in Guatemala for the night, an obviously exhausted Shultz leaned over to me in the plane and asked what was on for the evening. I told him he had a meeting with Contra leaders. Shultz looked at me wearily, obviously not thrilled with his upcoming evening, and asked, "Who made this schedule for me?" I responded, "I'm afraid I did sir." As he shook his head in resignation, we both knew the real answer. I had, of course, formally produced the schedule, but he had agreed to it. In all the long days and nights in Moscow, I had never seen him look so weary.

More Training: The Senior Seminar

The 1980s had been a wild time in relations between the superpowers, and I had been involved in varying degrees with the dangers, the passions, and the successes. But by mid-1988, the Reagan administration had basically run its course, and Gorbachev's efforts to reform the Soviet Union were coming under major stress. The time had come in the normal course of Foreign Service assignments for me to move on to other areas and issues. Since our embassy in Moscow had suffered severe stress, the secretary decided with zero input from me that I should go to Moscow as deputy chief of mission when I left the Secretariat. Planning had advanced to the point that we were talking about placing Gwen, our younger daughter, in boarding school in Switzerland. But in the end, Jack Matlock, now U.S. ambassador in Moscow, assured Shultz that he had things under control and there was no need to go through the disruption of switching DCMs.

Diane and I breathed a huge sigh of relief. We would, of course, have gone as the secretary requested, but a return to Moscow was low on our wish list. Happily, I had been selected for the State Department's Senior Seminar and had a year to recharge my badly drained batteries, reconnect with my family, and learn more about managing the U.S. foreign policy process. The seminar year was a good chance to catch up, and the advice on running embassies abroad would prove invaluable in the years ahead.

In addition to teaching us the qualities needed in a top-notch ambassador, the seminar also aimed to connect those Foreign Service officers who may have spent most of their adult years abroad with the realities of the United States. We had talks with New York financiers and border patrol officers working on the Mexican border. We spent time learning about the complexities of government in Miami and Baltimore. Perhaps the most diverse trip we took went first to a dairy farm and small town in Minnesota, where we learned the issues of classic heartland America (not much of a surprise to a guy from small-town Missouri). After spending a day and a night on the farm, we took a bus to Detroit, where we heard from the (later indicted) mayor about the issues facing a broken city and then spent the night riding with Detroit's police patrols as they faced the typical turmoil of America's inner cities. It was an eye-opening experience for all of us and brought home the complexity of our vast country.

Outside the seminar, events in the two countries I had followed most closely were rapidly evolving. Reform under Gorbachev was stumbling along as he sought to transform the political system (in the process, terminally undermining Communist rule); but his efforts produced almost no progress on the economic side that would give the average citizen a stake in the new order. Yeltsin and others kept Gorbachev's policies under heavy attack. In one discussion in Shultz's office on the future of Gorbachev's Soviet Union someone asked the obvious question about why Gorbachev did not emulate Deng in China and put the emphasis on economic reforms that would improve the lives of the people and thus build a base for his political reforms.

The answer lay partly in the fact that Gorbachev remained first and foremost a political animal. (I heard him give a speech in Taipei a few years later when he discussed the period with hardly a mention of the economy.) But it was also because the Chinese responded enthusiastically to capitalist incentives, while the Russians did not.

A story circulating in Russia at the time made the point: A Chinese peasant stepped outside his hut one morning and saw his neighbor had a new cow. He immediately went inside to wake up the entire family and put them to work, day and night, to catch up with the neighbor. After a time, he had enough money to buy his own cow and thus save face. A Russian peasant woke up one morning to the same problem but came up with a different solution. He went inside to retrieve his gun, came out and shot his neighbor's new cow. The equilibrium was restored, but there was no increase at all in anyone's wealth. Unfortunately, the second solution (or a variation where political leaders stole the cow) seemed all too common as we later sought at the UN to resolve conflicts and promote development in troubled countries around the world.

8
China after Tiananmen

During the eighties when I had been working on U.S.-Soviet relations, China underwent an extraordinary transformation. The capitalist-inspired policies unveiled for the economy by Deng Xiaoping in the fall of 1978 produced rapid change by allowing Chinese ingenuity, hard work, and aggressiveness, so common among Chinese outside the country, to replace a plodding economy held back by the dead hand of Communist fantasies. After thirty years of Mao's disastrous misrule, China finally had embarked on the classic East Asian path to development. Crucial changes—such as easing the party's vise-like grip on the economy, providing farmers a fair price for their goods (which led to skyrocketing agricultural production), returning the schools to a merit-based system, and allowing market-driven allocation of housing—had begun to transform the country. Loosening the party's control over economic goods also inevitably meant providing a somewhat wider scope for voicing grievances and political opinions.

When arguing for his policy to send large numbers of Chinese students abroad, Deng had acknowledged that "some flies" (i.e., Western liberal ideas) would enter the open window; but even he was clearly surprised by the effect of "openness" and the "revolution of rising expectations" on Chinese intellectuals and students. While Deng believed firmly in the party maintaining strict political control, his closest assistants (Hu Yaobang, who became party secretary in 1980, and Zhao Ziyang, the premier) had more open attitudes toward political change as part of China's modernization. They argued that a freer political environment was critical for achieving China's goal of a return to the first ranks of world powers.

Several intellectuals (including the astrophysicist Fang Lizhi) pressed hard for fundamental political changes. The attractions of the outside world combined with disgust at China's widespread corruption and inequality of opportunity produced a strong outpouring of student support for change. Student demonstrations in 1985–86 caused Deng (and the old conservative leaders he tried to keep mollified) great concern. Deng himself became increasingly disenchanted with his protégé Hu Yaobang as Hu protected some outspoken intellectuals, replacing him with Zhao in January 1987, and promoting Li Peng, the darling of the conservatives, to the premiership.

Critical, unorthodox thinking in China during this period had reached a level not seen since the 1930s. Emblematic of this ferment was a six-part documentary, backed by Zhao, called *River Elegy*, which depicted Chinese culture as stagnant and in need of refreshment from the West through trade and exchanges. The part I liked best was the criticism of the destruction of the Chinese 3,500-ship fleet (the world's greatest at the time) in the late 1400s, just as the Europeans began to sail the globe, and instead spending available funds on static defense by reconstructing the Great Wall that provided no protection from later Western incursions. Unleashing Chinese entrepreneurial instincts accompanied by some economic missteps produced high inflation (25 percent in 1989) and growing economic hardship, which eroded support for Deng's and Zhao's economic reforms and strengthened the conservatives.

By early 1989 the power struggle in China had become obvious to foreign observers. In March that year, Li Peng felt sufficiently emboldened to call for more central planning and to criticize Zhao's (and Deng's) policies publicly. China's economic disruptions and the demands by intellectuals and students for political change deeply split the party leadership, with Zhao openly sympathizing with the reformers and Li and the conservatives arguing things had already gone too far. The population sensed the weakening of the Communist party's grip on power and hoped to right long-suppressed grievances.

George H. W. Bush, freshly inaugurated as president, seized on the opportunity provided by the funeral of Japanese emperor Hirohito to make an early side trip to China in February 1989 to renew personal ties with the leadership and to ensure the warming Soviet-Chinese relationship would not weaken China's cooperation with the United States (A Gorbachev trip to China planned for June—the first of a Soviet top leader for thirty years—was expected to normalize relations between the two former enemies.) The U.S. understood there were serious tensions in the Chinese leadership, but clearly underestimated the impact U.S. actions could have on them. In January, Fang Lizhi (followed by a sizeable number of intellectuals) had publicly called for the release of all Chinese political prisoners, making him Deng's public enemy number one. When the embassy (with no Washington objection) included Fang on the guest list for the American reception during Bush's visit, the Chinese complained bitterly and then blocked Fang and his wife from attending. In conversations during Bush's visit, Chinese leaders objected strongly to U.S. pressure on human rights, even though Bush had not raised the subject. The combative Chinese tone in the meetings and the treatment of the Fangs overshadowed the entire trip. It was not an auspicious beginning for relations with "China's old friend." As usual, the American side (and the commentators) failed to place sufficient blame for the unexpected tensions on Chinese leadership struggles, instead questioning the embassy's handling of the affair.

The trip's failure added urgency to the need for Bush to put his own representative in as ambassador to China. James Lilley was the obvious choice. He had been the declared CIA representative in China during Bush's time as head of the Liaison Office, worked with him when he ran the CIA, set up the Bushes' trip to Tibet in 1977, and campaigned hard for him in the 1980 Republican primary. During the Reagan years (when Bush was vice president), Lilley had served as the director of the American Institute in Taiwan and as U.S. ambassador to the Republic of Korea. He and I had worked well together at USLO, and when he began reading in at the State Department in the spring of 1989 while awaiting Senate confirmation, I told him I would be interested in being his deputy chief of mission. Jim did a quick vetting around the department and then chose me for the job.

Lilley had an interesting biography. Born and raised in China, where his father worked for Standard Oil, he left in 1940 at the age of twelve when the deteriorating situation under Japanese occupation forced the evacuation of American dependents. He returned to the States, attended Exeter like his older brothers, did a tour in the army, and followed his brothers to Yale. Recruited, like many of his Yale classmates, into the fledgling CIA, Jim participated in operations against the Chinese Communists from bases in Taiwan, Hong Kong, and South Korea, and was later deputy of the large-scale, if theoretically covert, CIA-led war in Laos. Following his tour at USLO, Jim's career was closely tied to Bush's political fortunes. Inside the State Department Lilley had a controversial reputation because of his disdainful attitude toward the organization (he always preferred CIA or military operations to diplomacy and loved to take jabs at the State Department) and his strong sympathies for Taiwan; but I always found him a clear-headed, thoughtful, and serious steward of the U.S.-China relationship.

Like me and virtually everyone else from USLO who had seen China up close in the seventies, Jim Lilley was unsentimental about the Communist regime and viewed with disgust the tragedies it had imposed on the Chinese people. He could sound quite hardline toward China when talking to a conservative audience, but his policy instincts were mostly moderate and practical. I found him to be an excellent boss. One thing he and I agreed on emphatically was that straight talk with the Chinese was essential for both clarity and respect. The fawning, "me Tarzan, you Jane" approach (practiced for some odd reason by many Westerners), intended to flatter the Chinese, only made the foreigner more vulnerable to Chinese manipulation. The Chinese are masters at statecraft (they have taken a systematic approach for over 2500 years) and second to none in playing the relationship game.

The Tiananmen Massacre

When the relatively liberal Hu Yaobang died on April 15, 1989, with the fiftieth anniversary of the iconic May 4, 1919, student uprising approaching, Chinese students took to the streets in the heart of Beijing to air their grievances over official corruption and to press for greater political openness and economic opportunity. The party leadership was deeply divided on how to handle the protests and their indecisive half-steps only emboldened the students. Workers joined in, and the people of Beijing treated the cream of their youth demonstrating in Tiananmen Square as heroes. Lilley arrived in China on May 2, when the demonstrations were at their height; as he rode through the streets in his official car with its American flags flying, the crowds treated him like a celebrity. While the sentiments in the embassy (and on the streets of Beijing) clearly favored the students and their demands, embassy reporting by the end of May warned that the regime was likely to take extreme measures to suppress the dissent. Unfortunately, the United States could do little other than try to persuade the leadership not to use force. Two weeks after Lilley's arrival, the moderates and Zhao lost the fight. The leadership, with Deng the deciding factor, adopted the view that the students were "counterrevolutionaries," backed by the U.S. to change China, and that the fate of the Communist regime itself hung in the balance.

On June 4, the Chinese army carried out a brutal assault on the student-occupied Tiananmen Square and the streets leading to it. Armored personnel carriers rolled over tents and students, and machine gun fire raked the demonstrators indiscriminately. The horrified population of Beijing, after some heroic resistance, found itself occupied by its own army. A few days later elements of the army turned their fire on the diplomatic housing area where many Americans lived, forcing the evacuation of all embassy and consulate dependents from China. (A major disaster was averted only because the embassy had been alerted to leave the compound that day, and Chinese nannies protected several children who remained behind.) The embassy's investigation of the incident concluded it was a "premeditated attack" targeting U.S. living quarters, with the firing coming mostly from an apartment across the street, not from soldiers in the street.

CNN and other international news media broadcast the Tiananmen massacre to the world live, creating a firestorm of revulsion in Washington and across the country. The American public reacted with horror and deep disappointment that China's path to liberalization had failed. And its view of China's leaders turned negative to a level not seen since the nineteen fifties. Congress, controlled by Democrats but bipartisan on China, reflected this mood and demanded that the Chinese leadership be punished.

Several factors accounted for the intensity of this American reaction. First was the shock of the brutality involved in sending in troops to kill idealistic students who merely demanded a greater say in their future and repair of the Communist regime's worst features. The students clearly had the overwhelming support of the people of Beijing, who put their own lives on the line against the troops. There was no doubt that the softer line advocated by Zhao Ziyang and others could have led to compromises that would have benefited the whole of Chinese society; but the regime showed its barbaric side and chose to cow the population with overwhelming force.

There were deeper emotions in the American reaction. The modernization of China had been a major U.S. project for a hundred fifty years. It had been carried out by deeply committed American missionaries, educators, and businessmen, and the importance of the cause was deeply embedded in the U.S. psyche. For their part, China's modernizers had looked to the United States as the only real model to revive their vast country and to return it to greatness. America had been deeply disappointed once before when the Communists took over China in 1949 and sought to eradicate U.S. influence, which led to America's "Who lost China?" trauma of the fifties. After the Nixon visit, the sympathetic U.S. view of China had revived, and great hopes were created by Deng's emphasis on development through the eighties. Americans eagerly welcomed Chinese students, visited China in ever-growing numbers, and sought to assist the modernization effort by providing expertise and money. Trade between the two countries was rising rapidly. America's China project again appeared to be alive and well. Its seeming death at Tiananmen was a deep shock.

A third element in the U.S. reaction involved the rapidly declining Soviet threat. While many of us argued China's long-term geopolitical importance was growing as it developed economically, the immediate anti-Soviet rationale for being (sometimes overly) solicitous toward China had evaporated and with it the need to overlook China's many blemishes. At first, with the people most enthusiastic about China turning against Beijing, only the geopolitical types led by President Bush, who saw China's imminent rise to big-power status, pushed for a limited response to the Chinese leadership's bloody actions. Within a year, powerful U.S. business interests (aircraft, agriculture, importers, and others) who wanted to protect their investment and a potential huge market from being destroyed joined him in opposing major sanctions.

As I watched events unfolding in Beijing on CNN that June, I had no doubt my leisurely Senior Seminar days were over. I dropped the rest of the program (to some complaints from its organizers) and pitched in on the China desk to do what I could to help deal with the aftermath of the tragedy. It had been thirteen years since my family and I left China, and I had hoped to get up to speed on events in the country and brush up my now somewhat rusty Chinese. Not surprisingly, Lilley asked me to wrap up affairs at home as quickly as possible and get to China to help. Because of the evacuation order neither Diane nor Gwen could accompany me to Beijing, but fortunately Gwen had plans to spend the summer on an American Field Service program in France and was enrolled in Northfield–Mt. Hermon school for her last two years of high school. Diane opted to go to Hong Kong, a city she knew well and loved from fifteen years earlier, and from where she could join me in Beijing on short notice once the evacuation order was lifted. A friend from USLO days offered to share her Consulate apartment, an offer Diane gratefully accepted.

A Grim Beijing

When I arrived on July 12, Beijing was a city under military occupation. The population was cowed and sullen, afraid to associate with foreigners, especially Americans, armed military guards were everywhere, and many buildings along the main Changan Avenue had been riddled with bullets. The glass façade on the newly constructed World Trade Center was shattered by machine gun fire. Broken windows along the main thoroughfares provided haunting testimony to the chaos of a month earlier. Among the populace, the hopes and euphoria of the eighties had disappeared, making China once again the downtrodden and xenophobic country we had left in 1976. The conservatives, now clearly in the ascendency, redoubled their efforts to arrest leaders of the demonstrations (although they had trouble rounding up many protestors because of their widespread support among the population), creating a sense of fear throughout the city and surrounding countryside. Increasingly, they blamed the crisis of the spring on the "peaceful evolution" policies of the United States, often resorting to anti-U.S. rhetoric that had been largely absent since the early Kissinger and Nixon visits.

Immediately after the June 4 crackdown, Fang Lizhi and his wife Li Shuxian requested our protection. They were allowed to stay in the Embassy on instructions from Washington and became our ghost guests for over a year. Only a small number of people were allowed access to the Fangs (who were housed in one room behind the medical unit in the same compound as the ambassador) to ensure their safety. We were worried that the Chinese, who had issued a warrant for their arrest, might attempt to seize them by force, and restricted access to keep the Chinese unsure where they were staying. The medical unit provided some cover (the embassy nurse took care of their food and daily needs), and Jim and Sally, Diane and I, and a few other people paid them occasional visits, but their security was our most pressing concern. Fortunately, in contrast to the difficult Pentecostals that Embassy Moscow had sheltered for several years, the sophisticated and cultured Fangs proved to be model guests. Fang kept busy with his world-class work on astrophysics, publishing several scientific articles (we brought in materials by diplomatic pouch), and writing memoirs that were later published as *The Most Wanted Man in China: My Journey from Scientist to Enemy of the State*. Ms. Li, a scientist in her own right, also managed to stay occupied. The two were unfailingly polite, careful not to make demands, and patient under the most trying conditions.

Chinese officials constantly demanded privately and publicly that we turn over Fang and Li to the authorities. Early efforts to negotiate their departure from China met with no success. Aside from the heavy pressure the Chinese put on the embassy for harboring China's best-known dissidents, their presence provided some amusing moments, including an off-the-charts embassy Halloween party. In the days before the party (on October 28, 1989), some journalists had joked among themselves that the Americans planned to sneak the Fangs out of the country in Halloween costumes (one attributed the joke's origin to Jim Lilley, although I never confirmed that story.) The Chinese took their "intelligence coup" seriously.

On the night of the party, I was called by our security officer to come immediately to deal with a dangerous situation at the Embassy. (The ambassador was at a Chinese banquet with former President Nixon and showed up well after the party was underway.) When I arrived, hundreds of Chinese security officers filled the surrounding streets, blocking the Embassy's entrance so they could inspect our staff's cars as they entered the compound. I ordered our security people to open the Embassy gate and stood at the entrance motioning for our cars to enter the compound without stopping. When a senior Chinese security officer tried to again block the driveway so they could resume their visual searches for the Fangs, I told him in my coarsest Chinese to get out of the way or I would have someone run over him. He moved.

Everyone arrived safely in their costumes, and the excitement made the party a great success. I returned to the gate at the end of the party to ensure our people could leave without being hassled. A member of the attaché's office had come in a full gorilla suit, which he proceeded to wear home. He said Chinese security personnel followed him to the door of his apartment to be sure Fang was not in the costume. Naturally, the attaché did not take off his disguise until his door was closed. It turned out that a Foreign Ministry official had warned the ambassador against trying to sneak Fang out under the cover of the party (which, of course, we had no intention of doing.) Lilley laughed off the idea as absurd, but the events of the evening showed how "spooked" the Chinese were by our party.

After Tiananmen, conservative leaders operating through Li Peng carried out a policy of internal repression and economic belt-tightening, combined with an effort to distance China from the United States and the West. The emphasis on central control of the economy and state-owned enterprises did cut the rate of inflation, but it also caused a serious drop in output and increased hardship for the average Chinese. Deng, who had retired from all his formal positions by November, dutifully pushed reform in his rare public appearances. Now in his mid-eighties he was treated by the others for two and a half years after the Tiananmen massacre more as an old relative in his dotage than as the paramount leader of China. But the population remembered a different, hopeful China that had existed only months earlier, and resentment of the leadership was widespread. The economic reforms of the eighties had introduced a new dynamic in the society between the rising economic and societal forces—which produced jobs and opportunities—and the state enterprises and old social forms of the past, which didn't. Sharp disagreements among the leaders over the path to future Chinese prosperity continued, and Deng, down but not out, remained determined to revive the reform banner he had long championed.

Premier Li Peng could have served as the perfect model for the "colorless bureaucrat" label. In the numerous times I sat in on meetings with him, I found him to be a dour, unpleasant man, mostly tied to his talking points but always ready to refute any criticisms made by his American interlocutors. He cultivated the old communist guard and took advantage of his past ties to Chou En-lai and his wife Deng Yingchao, who was still alive and influential. He obviously had enough bureaucratic savvy to maintain his position, but no one would accuse him of any original thinking. He strongly preferred a traditional socialist economy based on state enterprises, the system he had come up through and knew well.

The successor Deng chose to lead the party after Zhao, Jiang Zemin, also seemed to be something of a lightweight, whose main ambition was to maintain himself in the new role thrust upon him. (He succeeded, staying in power until 2002 and exerting his influence on personnel issues even longer.) Jiang had little to show for his leadership in Shanghai (locals called him a "potted flower"), with the mayor Zhu Rongji doing the heavy lifting. Deng brought Jiang from Shanghai when Zhao was sacked days after June 4, appointed him as general secretary of the Party, blessed him as the "core" of the leadership (third in line after Mao and Deng), and finally turned over his military hat to him in November. In Shanghai, Jiang had talked a strong reformist line. In Beijing, he quickly switched to become a "me too" supporter of austerity and central control.

During the ambassador's first meeting with the new general

secretary, Jiang tried to impress us with his English, his recitation of part of the Gettysburg Address, and a long, simplistic discussion of transistors. We came out of the meeting literally shaking our heads. I thought the performance was worse than Hua Kuo-feng's debut with us in 1976. This ability to hide his real views, in addition to presumably impressing some Chinese as urbane and worldly, was what got him the job in the first place. Others in the Chinese elite passed him off as a "weathervane"—pointing in whatever direction the wind was blowing.

Increased security, rounding up people who might threaten the regime, and tamping down any free thoughts drove the political agenda of the leaders. Conservative, anti-Deng elements controlled the propaganda apparatus, even going so far as to question if Zhao's (meaning Deng's) policies should be "surnamed" capitalist or socialist. In what for me was a perfect illustration of how out of touch the party leadership was with the concerns of youth in urban areas, the propagandists launched a Maoist-style mass campaign to reprise the "Study from Lei Feng" movement. The campaign reeked of the sixties and early seventies, and while it might have seemed normal to people who had missed China's eighties reform or to some nostalgic oldsters in China, I doubt it engendered enthusiasm from any city kid over the age of five (who might be wearing rouge so they could have the privilege of performing in an inane Lei Feng propaganda skit.) The campaign's probable main effect on college students was to increase the applications for study abroad.

Policy and dealing with Chinese absurdities aside, a fair amount of my time for the first few months in Beijing had to be devoted to getting the embassy back in shape to carry out its basic functions. My first effort was to get the dependents back to China to restore some sense of normalcy to our staff. (Families transferring over the summer needed to pack out their household items as well.) We finally succeeded in getting the department's agreement on August 9, and it was wonderful to welcome Diane back to Beijing two days later. But it was only the first step in getting the embassy back on its feet.

Many of our people had acted heroically in reporting on the massacre and evacuating Americans out of harm's way after it happened. Remarkably, only two Americans were injured in the chaos, but one embassy reporting officer saw a Chinese student gunned down right next to him in the square. Overall, the psychic toll on the embassy was great. The excitement of April and May had turned into the oppressive atmosphere of June, July, and August, and many of our people felt the loss of hope for China's future personally. They especially regretted losing the Chinese friends and contacts they had made in the earlier, more permissive era.

While trying to keep up with events in China, embassy management had been neglected. The embassy had received a devastating report on its operations from State Department inspectors in the spring. The pressures from above and sometimes irrational demands had led to festering rivalries that left some embassy sections barely speaking to each other. It was obvious that some of the section chiefs were trying to build morale among their subordinates by denigrating colleagues in other sections. The loss of previous Chinese sources also meant that embassy reporting had deteriorated at a time when it was critical for Washington to have our best guess as to what was going on in the Chinese leadership. Finally, a bout of congressional austerity left the State Department and Embassy Beijing basically broke. In China, this resulted in our cutting personnel, reducing hours for our locally hired Americans, restricting travel necessary for effective reporting on this huge country, and putting off any purchases that were not absolutely essential. For two years running I had to send messages begging the department for money at the end of the fiscal year so we could pay the embassy's utility bills.

It was my responsibility as deputy chief of mission to deal with the low morale and get the embassy running effectively as soon as possible. I took a direct approach to the intersectional rivalry. Calling each section chief into my office separately, I told them the bickering had to stop immediately or I would note it in their efficiency report in the spring, a sure block to any hope of future advancement. I knew the ambassador would back me, and they knew it too. The nastiness quickly subsided. We worked to bring the four consulates-general (Shanghai, Guangzhou, Chengdu, and Shenyang) more closely into sync with Beijing on reporting and managed to get Guangzhou and Chengdu into new facilities over the next couple of years, despite Chinese obstructionism.

Diane was my strongest and not-so-secret weapon for improving post morale, as she was in subsequent postings in Taipei, Kuala Lumpur, and Jakarta. Working in the embassy consular section as an American local-hire employee, she had a keen sense of the concerns of embassy people and was more creative than I in figuring out how to resolve them. Diane also had a clear eye for physical improvements that could be made for relatively small amounts of money and provided a sympathetic ear for complaints that people were unwilling to make directly to me. We began an effort (followed in our later posts) to host dinners at our house that eventually covered all the American staff and their spouses and mixed people from throughout the embassy to increase the sense of belonging to a common effort. Marine guards, communicators, reporting, consular and commercial officers, and section chiefs plus their spouses would get together informally for an evening at our place, an ongoing commitment by Diane and her house crew that paid big dividends for the morale of our staff.

With our Chinese contacts after the Tiananmen massacre few and far between at all levels, we worked hard to explore new possibilities. We encouraged reporting officers to get out of the office to do what they could to begin rebuilding contacts despite the obvious difficulties. At higher levels, we accompanied delegations and traveled as much as possible. All of us worked on broadening our contacts at the various ministries, including regular informal lunches with officials and attendance at as many receptions as possible (I once did four diplomatic receptions in one evening.)

As an illustration of our desperate effort for more contacts, the ambassador stepped in my door one day and said, "You play bridge, don't you, Lynn?" I responded that I had learned a bit from my mom and played some a decade earlier at language school in Taichung. He said, "Great, you're the designated embassy bridge player." As everyone knew, bridge was Deng Xiaoping's favorite relaxation; and there was naturally a well-organized senior group of bridge players that usually gathered in the Great Hall of the People. The Bangladesh ambassador, a regular player, had asked the ambassador to join. Obviously, I was being designated in his place. (The other ordained sport, tennis, a favorite of NPC chairman Wan Li, was more to Lilley's liking.) I actually played bridge at the Great

Hall and at a few hotels with the group over the next couple of years; but as a way to make contacts it was basically a bust. Needless to say, I never played with Deng, and when other top leaders took part, they sat in virtual silence. I did play cards a few times with a friend from the American Chamber of Commerce and the minister of foreign trade that produced some interesting insights.

Even though our access to Chinese officials and ordinary people was greatly constricted, embassy reporting to Washington soon became first-rate again, often relying on the kind of China-watching techniques we had depended on fifteen years earlier that had fallen into disuse in the openness of the eighties. In another throwback to our earlier posting, diplomats in Beijing were again forced to talk more with each other as they tried to decipher the ups and downs of Chinese politics, since most of their Chinese contacts had gone on radio silence for self-preservation.

I talked regularly with a wide range of foreign diplomats to get a better understanding of China's internal and external issues, paying particular attention to the Russian DCM Vitaly Vorobiev, a sophisticated and knowledgeable observer of the Chinese scene. The Americans and Russians had had a long dialogue about China that extended back decades; but the rapid changes in Moscow and East Europe made the discussions particularly valuable for understanding the dynamics of the Chinese-Russian relationship. As their interaction moved from enmity to normalcy to the sale of sophisticated Russian weapons and technology, many on the Soviet side wondered if the strapped Soviet defense industry was not selling China the Leninist rope to hang themselves.

Tentative Steps to Repair Cooperation

The Chinese scene was tough during those first several months we were in Beijing. Tension hung over the city like its infamous pollution. Boycotted by Western embassies in Beijing, the PRC's fiftieth anniversary on October 1, 1989, felt more like a wake than a celebration. As a matter of self-protection, Chinese acted as distant in relations with foreigners as they had in the seventies. Of more immediate concern, some of our people (especially Asian-American staff members and spouses) were regularly hassled when they entered our compound. The young, poorly disciplined soldiers who surrounded our facilities carried automatic weapons, which they occasionally pointed at our children for amusement. Relations with all the Western diplomats in Beijing were bad, but the Chinese seemed especially determined to make Lilley and the embassy pay for supporting the students and protecting Fang.

In late October, former President Nixon visited Beijing as part of a U.S. effort to improve relations. Nixon met with virtually the entire leadership and spoke directly with them about American concerns both in private and in public, which they tolerated because of his special status. Among other gestures, he suggested that a Washington trip for General Secretary Jiang Zemin might be possible if the Fangs were allowed to leave China. Nixon had been at a Chinese banquet (along with the ambassador) when the Halloween Party drama played out. Three nights later, Li Peng hosted a smaller dinner for him that included Foreign Minister Qian Qichen, Vice Foreign Minister Liu Huaqiu, President Nixon, Mike Oksenberg (who accompanied Nixon), and me (as chargè, since Jim had departed for the States.).

I had briefed Nixon on the security problems at our Embassy, and during the dinner, I raised the subject of the dangerous actions of the soldiers surrounding our perimeter walls. Li (known in the Western press as the "Butcher of Beijing") became red in the face at the temerity of this lowly chargè raising such a provocative issue with the second most powerful person in China, and he launched into a heated rebuttal. Not missing a beat, Nixon put up his hand to cut Li off and said, "Mr. Premier, I don't know all the facts on this issue, but I'm going to the embassy tomorrow to see Lynn and his people, and I don't like to see a lot of guns. I sure hope the weapons are gone by then."

Miraculously, the troops with their automatic weapons withdrew overnight and were replaced by the usual People's Armed Police guards with their pistols. When Nixon met the American embassy staff and their spouses the next day at the Embassy, I gave him full credit for getting the troops removed. The embassy staffers and their spouses broke out in enthusiastic applause, giving the former president what I suspect was the warmest and most heartfelt welcome he had received since his disgrace and resignation fifteen years before. Nixon relished the moment and delivered an encouraging speech to the group. In my subsequent meetings with Li Peng, Li never failed to give me a harsh stare when we shook hands just to let me know he had not forgotten my impudence at the dinner.

At the White House President Bush and his NSC Adviser Brent Scowcroft were determined not to lose the China relationship in the wake of Tiananmen. But the shock of the regime's brutality would not go away, and the pressures from the Congress and the American public to punish the regime became more intense. Bush had immediately deplored the attack on the square, issued an executive order to allow Chinese students who wished to stay in the United States after their visas expired to do so, stopped arms sales and military visits, and declared there would be no more "business as usual." He then sent Scowcroft and Deputy Secretary Larry Eagleburger secretly to Beijing to emphasize his hope for continuity and to try to get the leadership to allow the Fangs to leave China. Little came from the trip except, I suspect, a Chinese feeling that the Americans were desperate to maintain good relations. The Nixon visit in October was immediately followed by a visit by Henry Kissinger, again offering to serve as a channel to restore relations and discussing tradeoffs for a resolution of the bilateral tensions.

These efforts did not produce any immediate results and pressures in the U.S. continued to rise. Congress voted overwhelmingly for a bill that would allow the forty thousand Chinese students in the U.S. to remain and gave them four years to decide whether to alter their visa status or apply for permanent residency. (Most of the students had exchange visas which would have required them to return to China for two years before they could apply for a new visa.) President Bush vetoed the legislation as an infringement on presidential powers but issued an executive order that provided essentially the same protections. As chargè, I was called into the Foreign Ministry by Vice Foreign Minister Liu Huaqiu, who delivered himself of a predictably tough protest about the new rules. Liu threatened to drastically cut the number of students going to the United States. (In fact, while there was some decrease in officially sponsored students, this was an empty threat.

The State Department estimated in 1991 that there were 70,000 Chinese students in the U.S., including the sons and daughters of much of the Chinese elite.) Two weeks later, I had to go back to the Foreign Ministry to get another dose of China's "utmost indignation" about the new rules.

Bush decided to send Scowcroft and Eagleburger on a second visit to Beijing on December 9–10 in an attempt to work out a path forward. Preparations again were kept secret, and Lilley had to rush back to China to participate in some of the meetings. In the meantime, as chargè, I accompanied Scowcroft and Eagleburger to the welcoming banquet. As Scowcroft rose to give his toast, the Chinese brought in a photographer to record the occasion and released the photos to the press. News of the visit sent shock waves across Washington and the foreign policy community. Major U.S. papers front-paged the photo of Scowcroft toasting the Chinese foreign minister (with me beside him raising my glass) the next morning and, citing some overly polite excerpts from Scowcroft's toast, blasted the administration for "kowtowing" to the "Butchers of Beijing."

In ten hours of meetings, Scowcroft discussed a set of tradeoffs, including freedom for the Fangs, lifting of martial law, release of Tiananmen prisoners, and a halt in Chinese missile sales to the Mideast in exchange for the resumption of World Bank loans, dropping the ban on Chinese launches of U.S. communications satellites, and some lifting of sanctions. After the meetings, the administration was coy about what had been discussed, but the reaction in Washington to the trip was overwhelmingly negative. It appeared to many to be a complete betrayal by the administration of its own restrictions on contacts (news of the earlier July trip also leaked to the press at this time.)

Over the next few weeks the two sides implemented most of the agreed upon steps (although the administration did not get the expected release of the Fangs), and the bilateral atmosphere in Beijing became somewhat better. But even this improvement in the tone was brief. Soon the barrage of criticism of the United States in the Chinese media returned, leaving the overall impact of the Scowcroft visit on the relationship minimal. In January 1990, after an intense lobbying effort, the Bush administration managed to sustain the president's veto of the student bill by a slim margin in the Senate. His efforts received very little acknowledgement from the Chinese, and the atmosphere in Washington did not improve, even though the administration tried to get some mileage out of the few agreements reached. By late February and early March, administration officials were venting their frustrations over the lack of cooperation from the Chinese and the general failure to improve the situation after months of trying. Once again, everything seemed to be on hold between the United States and China.

The Collapse of Communism in Europe

The failure of the Scowcroft mission to turn things around actually had little to do with Bush's actions or events in Washington; it had everything to do with Chinese leadership insecurities and infighting. The focus of the leaders after Tiananmen had turned to their own self-preservation. By December events in Europe, not relations with the United States dominated their attention. The international Communist system was collapsing in front of their eyes.

During the eighties, Deng had moved to reposition China between the U.S. and the Soviet Union. He reformulated Chinese demands on Moscow, dropping the "unequal treaties" argument and instead calling for the withdrawal of Soviet troops from Mongolia and the Chinese border, withdrawal from Afghanistan, and Soviet pressure on the Vietnamese to withdraw from Cambodia, a Chinese ally. The Soviets were interested, but given the leadership turmoil in Moscow during the first half of the eighties, nothing came of the preliminary discussions (much as the Reagan-Shultz efforts to improve ties with the Russians had not achieved anything useful in this period.)

When Gorbachev took over, however, he adopted a more positive line, and formal discussions began in 1987. (Gorbachev was already committed to a withdrawal from Afghanistan and was happy to reduce his forces on the Chinese border.) By 1987, Deng's "demands" had become fairly low-cost items to exchange for a new relationship with China, and Gorbachev pushed hard for change over the opposition of the Russian old guard. His May 15–18, 1989, visit to Beijing and Shanghai had been planned to mark the full normalization of relations between the two Communist giants. In the event, the visit was almost completely overshadowed by the student occupation of Tiananmen Square. But the final communiqué did say the two sides would settle the border, "relying on the treaties of the present Sino-Soviet border," and reduce military forces on the border to a minimum. (Detailed border treaties were signed in the next few years and other outstanding issues resolved by 2008.)

Despite his critical role in normalizing the Sino-Soviet relationship, Chinese leaders had no confidence in Gorbachev's leadership of the Soviet Union nor his approach to internal reform. His praise for the students occupying the Tiananmen Square during the ill-timed May trip did not impress the conservatives in control in Beijing.

More startling than Gorbachev's statements and the deterioration of the political scene in Moscow was the actual collapse of Communism in the Soviet Union's East European satellites. Hungary began dismantling its fortified border with Austria in early May 1989, Solidarity candidates won the Polish election the day Chinese troops stormed into Tiananmen Square, and they took over the Polish government (ending Communist rule) in August. The Russians made it clear they would not interfere or use force to maintain their East European empire. In October, East Germans began fleeing west in large numbers through Hungary and Czechoslovakia, and the Berlin Wall was destroyed on November 9. Communist governments teetered on the brink throughout Eastern Europe by December.

Then came the biggest jolt of all to the Chinese leadership, or so it seemed to those of us in Beijing observing the Chinese reaction: the overthrow and execution (on December 25) of Romania's president, Nicolae Ceaușescu, and his wife. You could almost feel a collective shudder go through the Chinese leadership with the grim death of their best friend in Europe, a fate many of them felt they had barely avoided six months earlier. These events produced an almost primordial fear in the Chinese leadership, which hurriedly convened a series of internal meetings to assess the fallout for China. They agreed on tightened security measures and increased indoctrination for the police and military. Chinese leaders were in no mood to make nice with the Americans during the West's victory celebration over Communism.

As the Eastern European countries moved out of the Soviet orbit, the fallout in Beijing's diplomatic community was notable. Some of the most talented diplomats in Beijing came from these countries; many spoke superb Chinese and were accomplished students of Chinese history. The Polish China expert who had helped us decipher the esoteric debates in the seventies, Zdzislaw Goralczyk, now was my counterpart as the number two in the Polish embassy. He had no difficulties in the transition to the new democratic government and later became the Polish ambassador to China. However, his East German counterpart, a brilliant linguist (fluent in five languages) and an acute political observer, fell victim to the dismissal of all East German diplomats after unification. While I understood the questioning of his loyalty to the new Germany or his security ties to Moscow, the West Germans had no diplomats with anything comparable to his expertise on the Chinese scene. The careers of other East European diplomats hung in the balance for months as they waited to see if they would still have jobs after vetting by their new governments.

The transition also affected our plans for building a new embassy in Beijing. Most East European diplomats worked in large "friendship" embassies built by the Chinese, which far exceeded their actual needs in China. The country next in line to get a new facility was Bulgaria, a neighbor to our hand-me-down buildings in the diplomatic quarter that had earlier been Pakistani and Romanian embassies before they moved to grander surroundings. We and the Chinese had planned for the U.S. to build a new embassy already designed by I. M. Pei on these three parcels of land. After the fall of Communism, the Bulgarians decided to stay put, placing our hopes for a new embassy near the center of town on hold. We later built farther out on a parcel of land that had been planned for staff housing.

Quiet Discussions to Stabilize Ties

As the pall descended again over U.S.-Chinese relations and the limits on high-profile visits became obvious, we tried a quieter approach to stabilize ties with the Chinese. I invited the director of the America desk, Zhang Yijun, and his deputy, Yang Jiechi, to an informal lunch for a quiet discussion of where relations were heading. Over the next two and half years we had almost two dozen such lunches, usually one a month, hosted alternatively by Zhang and by me. The embassy's talented political counselor, Don Keyser, joined me in these informal "no polemics" sessions. In marked contrast to his boss, the bombastic and difficult assistant minister, Liu Huaqiu, who served as the ambassador's chief contact, Zhang was a calm professional who genuinely wanted to find ways to get the relationship with the United States back on track. Zhang's approach quickly won our respect. Yang Jiechi had gained a lifelong connection with George Bush, who called him "Tiger" Yang when he served as interpreter during the Bushes' 1977 trip to Tibet. Young, ambitious, and bright, Yang later moved rapidly up a bureaucratic ladder that included three tours in the Washington (the last as ambassador, from 2001 to 2005), minister of foreign affairs from 2007 to 2013, and then chief foreign affairs advisor to the Chinese president and member of the elite Politburo of the Chinese Communist Party until the end of 2022.

In these lunches, we discussed all of the issues between the two countries, looking for ways to either resolve problems or to keep the situation from getting worse. For suspended programs like the Fulbright exchanges and Peace Corps volunteers to China, programs we all knew were in the interests of both countries, we worked to shape the talking points on both sides in the formal sessions. Bilateral issues, human rights, trade, investments, and global issues—nothing was off the table. Both sides recognized the discussions were informal and preliminary. Nevertheless, the "informal" nature of the talks did not mean we were not regularly passing messages to each other, with us reporting back to Washington or them briefing senior policy makers in Beijing. Both sides understood that this channel provided an opportunity for normal diplomatic interchange to promote our goals and ease frictions. We managed to fix a sticky Foreign Military Sales issue in the talks, get the Fulbright exchanges back on track, and keep the Peace Corps and International Visitors programs on the agenda for later reinstatement. We also worked to clarify many of the contentious issues between us and suggest ways forward to ameliorate or resolve them. Both sides found the lunches valuable. We were able to avoid unnecessary conflicts with this example of quiet diplomacy, engaging in the kind of contact at the core of our profession.

Human rights were, of course, near the top of the public agenda in post-Tiananmen China. In February 1990, the State Department's release of its annual report on human rights caused something of a sensation in Washington because of its candid review of China's miserable record the year before. It became public at the time when the administration was trying to get traction in Washington to implement the results of the Scowcroft-Eagleburger trip. When we began working on the report at the embassy in the fall of 1989, I told the ambassador that my goal was an honest, straightforward report on events for the year. He agreed. Fang Lizhi was correct when he complained that the U.S. had for years followed a "double standard" on human rights issues, criticizing the Soviet Union much more harshly than China.

In the fraught political atmosphere in Washington our report this time had to get the facts right to maintain the credibility of our overall China policy. I told the drafting officers that they had to have at least two good sources for any specifics in the report and that the narrative had to be totally honest without shading one way or the other. I personally read over the draft we sent to Washington several times to ensure the accuracy of the details and its overall tone. No one in Washington wanted to be accused of soft-pedaling the Chinese record, and our draft went through the State Department and NSC with almost no changes.

Our efforts were rewarded by the reaction in the United States. The *New York Times,* which had been harshly critical of the administration's China policy, called it the most meticulous, thorough, and authoritative assessment of human rights in China by any Government or private agency and quoted extensively from the text. Anthony Lewis, in a column entitled "The Power of Truth," echoed that assessment, adding somewhat gratuitously that it was in "striking contrast" to the comments of President Bush as he sought to protect his policy against Congress. The report played a significant role in reestablishing the U.S. government's credibility on events in China, especially since it was reported that the White House had cleared the document and chosen to make no changes. Beijing, predictably, did not like it. The Foreign Ministry said it had "flagrantly vilified Chinese leaders" and "slandered the Chinese government on a number of other issues that are purely China's internal affairs." Given the various reactions, I assumed that we had gotten the analysis just about right. Our reports on events in 1990 and 1991 were equally straightforward and unvarnished.

Cooperation against narcotics smuggling had become one area of considerable value to both sides. The Golden Triangle in Southeast Asia constituted the primary source of heroin in the U.S. at the time, and the main route of most of the heroin that flowed from northern Burma, across Yunnan province in south China, to Hong Kong, and then to the United States. Shutting down that route was a high priority for the U.S., and because some drugs are always sold locally as they are transported through a region, the Chinese found themselves with a growing drug problem in the south, something they had not seen since the Communists used draconian measures to suppress illegal narcotics in the early fifties. In March 1988 after police in Shanghai and San Francisco arrested a group of smugglers who had shipped seven pounds of heroin (worth $1 million) to the United States in condoms in the bellies of dead goldfish that were mixed in with a live goldfish shipment, the Chinese agreed to allow a man they had arrested go to San Francisco to testify as the chief prosecution witness. Once in the U.S., instead of repeating his story against the main defendant, the witness told the court he had been beaten, shocked with a cattle prod, and threatened by Chinese police to get him to testify. He then asked for asylum in the U.S. based on the threat to his life if he returned to China.

The case caused a furor in Beijing. The Chinese police and court system had been under heavy criticism both at home and abroad for the crackdown on the Tiananmen demonstrators and the later executions or long prison sentences, and now the Americans were reneging on their promises to return a criminal to China and bashing them once again with new complaints. The U.S. attorney's office came under heavy criticism for its handling of the case ("covering up torture"), and the man was allowed to stay in the U.S. On his release from detention, he returned to his old habits of dealing drugs and was found stabbed to death a few years later in New York. Unfortunately, despite my repeated efforts to get things back on track, Chinese officials refused to have any serious cooperation with the DEA for a decade.

China Works to Rebuild Its Image

By the spring of 1990, the Chinese started a campaign to revive their international standing, with visits by leaders and promises of increased trade opportunities. They called the policy "Nei Jin, Wai Song" (Tight Internally, Relaxed Internationally.) The process was hampered by China's unwillingness to concede that their actions were the cause of their problems or to take serious steps internally to ease the pressure on the students who had led the demonstrations. They nevertheless made some progress with European countries, Southeast Asia, and Japan. Li Peng made a highly touted visit to Indonesia, Singapore, and Thailand in August that established ties with Indonesia and Singapore and put relations with Southeast Asia back on an even keel.

In the fall China successfully hosted the Asian Games, an event that also helped refurbish China's reputation in Asia. The Chinese sports machine swept the medals in the games, and the leadership went to great lengths to portray a sense of grandeur and normalcy in Beijing for the thousands of guests (and the Olympics Committee considering China's bid for the Olympics). Most remarkably for those of us living there, the Chinese eliminated the chronic pollution in Beijing during the games by closing thousands of factories operating inside the city and for miles around and severely limiting the number of cars and trucks allowed in the city. (A few weeks earlier I had counted six distinct colors of smoke in the heavy pollution from an upper window of the World Trade Center.) All through the games the city's atmosphere was pristine, with a bright blue sky that must have reminded old-timers of their pre-Communist city and left some wondering why the government did not think it necessary to permanently reduce the pollution for the people of Beijing.

Better relations with Asia and Europe were important, but the big prize for China was to find a way to get back on track with the United States without giving in to U.S. demands for improvements in Chinese actions on human rights, trade, and sensitive arms exports. After a rough spring that reflected frustrations on both sides, President Bush announced in late May that he would renew China's Most Favored Nation (normal trade relations) status. There was a collective sigh of relief in Beijing (Li Peng welcomed the announcement publicly and called it a "wise" move), and days later Liu Huaqiu indicated to the ambassador that the Chinese were willing to talk seriously about allowing the Fangs to go abroad.

After intense negotiations carried out by Ambassador Lilley, which led to some appropriately fuzzy wording on the Fangs' lack of support for the Chinese constitution and allusions to their health, enough face was saved all around for them to leave on June 25, 1990. After a brief sojourn in Britain (again to save Chinese face), they moved to Tucson, Arizona, where he continued his professional work at the University of Arizona until his death in 2012. Later that year, Congress made a strong push to attach conditions on the granting of MFN privileges, but the effort fell flat when the Senate allowed the deadline to pass without a vote.

Iraq's invasion of Kuwait on August 2 played a major role in calming the U.S.-Chinese relationship. Suddenly, the United States needed Chinese support in the UN Security Council, and the Chinese were quick to make the most of their opportunity to accommodate the U.S. on an issue that cost them nothing. They quickly supported an effort by navies of other countries to enforce a UN-mandated weapons blockade and stopped their own deliveries to Saddam. As U.S. secretary of state Baker sought international support to forcibly oust the Iraqis from Kuwait, he offered Foreign Minister Qian Qichen a Washington trip. The Chinese then indicated they would not block the effort at the UN. As chargé at the embassy during the negotiations leading up to the Security Council vote, I was busy making démarches to the Chinese and reporting their views to Washington.

Baker attempted a last-minute effort to get the Chinese to vote "yes" at the Security Council (rather than abstain) by backing away from a promised Qian meeting in Washington, but the Chinese made it clear they expected Baker to hold to his promise of meetings in Washington with Baker and with the president. In the end Baker (not so gracefully) caved. Qian abstained on the November Security Council vote to support the "use of all necessary means" to force the Iraqis to withdraw and was received in Washington. The Washington talks with Qian were fairly stiff, but they broke the barrier on high-level meetings. When the United States pressed on human rights, the Chinese chose a ploy that later became a pattern for managing the U.S. and Europe on human rights, letting the State Department assistant secretary for human rights visit Beijing for talks. In his mid-December visit, Assistant Secretary Richard Schifter pressed for the release of 150 political prisoners and publicly expressed optimism that the Chinese would become more flexible on the issue. Unsurprisingly, the Chinese did nothing to follow up; in fact they used the focus of international attention on Iraq as an opportunity to step up trials and harshly sentence people involved in the Tiananmen demonstrations.

The swift American victory in Iraq shook the Chinese military to its core, as leaders watched the high-tech U.S. military render the level of armaments available to the PLA totally obsolete. The television coverage led to a complete rethink in the Chinese military and an emphasis on rapid modernization.

At the embassy, we had something else to worry about when the U.S.-led attack began. Washington informed us the same day that the Iraqi regime had dispatched a hit squad to Beijing working under the Iraqi DCM (and intelligence chief) to assassinate Ambassador Lilley, a well-known friend of President Bush and a soft target in low-threat Beijing. (I knew the Iraqi DCM from diplomatic gatherings. He had last served in Washington and was outwardly very friendly to our staff, who lived in the same housing compound, swapping videos with them to show his children.) Jim informed the Chinese immediately, and Washington sent a personal bodyguard. While the threat of an attack against the Embassy or the main entrance to the Residence seemed low, the ambassador's car at the time was not armored and it would have been relatively easy to enter the compound by scaling a neighboring wall down the street from where Lilley lived. The Chinese moved quickly to neutralize the hit squad. To ensure the Iraqis did not use local assets, they also organized a tour in South China for foreign students in Beijing and made sure all students from the Middle East were on it. With the quick success of the military operation in Kuwait and the Chinese countermeasures, the threat disappeared.

All the contentious issues—human rights, including Chinese actions in Tibet, China's soaring trade surplus and illegal trade practices, prison labor exports, and the export of sensitive weapons and nuclear technology to Pakistan and the Middle East—were at the fore as Washington geared up for another fight in June 1991 over MFN for China. Former president Jimmy Carter and his wife Rosalynn visited China in April to promote improved prosthetic devices for China's disabled and to talk frankly with the Chinese leadership. He saw top leaders, except for Deng, and pressed them publicly and privately on an amnesty for political prisoners and improved bilateral relations. He was treated courteously but did not appear to make any impression on his Chinese interlocutors. A May visit by Bob Kimmitt, the State Department's under secretary for political affairs (the highest U.S. government official to visit in the year and a half since the Scowcroft trip) also made no progress that could be used to defend renewing MFN.

President Bush, often referred to as the government's desk officer for China, preempted the MFN debate a few days later by saying he would renew MFN for China despite its record on human rights. Bush explained that he had no desire to isolate China and appreciated its help on Iraq. His comments caused another firestorm in Congress, where a consensus was developing to grant China MFN status (a result of increased lobbying by U.S. business interests) but conditioning further extensions on improvements in China's record on human rights. The Senate, however, did not have sufficient votes to override a presidential veto.

Jim and Sally Lilley departed Beijing in May 1991 leaving me in charge for the next three months until his successor, Stapleton Roy, arrived. Although the Lilleys had planned to leave around that time for months, he was careful to avoid spreading the word around the diplomatic community to avoid the inevitable barrage of good-bye parties, a "health hazard" for any ranking diplomat.

Jim told me he had learned his lesson in Seoul, where the parties on their departure had totally exhausted them both.

Stapleton Roy, a fluent Chinese speaker and one of the State Department's most capable senior diplomats, arrived in August to take over as ambassador. Stape, who was also born in China and spent his early years there, had been deeply involved in the normalization negotiations during his time as deputy in USLO and knew the China brief and the Washington bureaucratic structure cold. He also proved to be a superb boss.

By this time congressional visitors had returned to the China circuit. Despite the American public's disdain for congressional travel, I always considered it a critical part of their job to be informed on foreign issues and appreciated the opportunity to bring them up to date on problems we faced. My enthusiasm for such travel was tempered somewhat when, during their Beijing press conference, Congressmen Frank Wolf and Chris Smith waved socks they had been given at a prison camp as evidence of prison labor exports to the United States or when Nancy Pelosi and others unfurled a black banner in Tiananmen Square that said, "To those who died for democracy in China." Both stunts undoubtedly had some resonance with constituents at home, but they did nothing to help the situation in China. A major part of our effort was to explain our nuanced, and often not popular, approach to China to members of Congress, staffers, newsmen, businessmen, academics, and general visitors to China. Eventually it paid off in increased understanding of the administration's approach.

By the summer of 1991, we not only had the regular lunches with Zhang Yijun and Yang Jiechi covering the full range of bilateral issues, but I had also developed normal working relations with the heads of the various departments in the Chinese Foreign Ministry. In addition, to formal calls in the office, I would invite them to lunch (at our apartment to save money) for more informal discussions. One of the major issues was Cambodia and working out an arrangement through the UN to resolve the war. Another perennial topic was North Korea (one Chinese official joked to me that the Koreans were so difficult, perhaps we should just trade allies and try again. I responded equally tongue in cheek that only they had the expertise and patience necessary to deal with the North;

we preferred to be allied to the democratic and prosperous South.) Disputes in the South China Sea over the Spratly Islands and in the East China Sea over the Senkaku/Diaoyu islands were a constant headache for us, as our close allies in the region jousted with the Chinese over territorial claims that could affect freedom of navigation (for both civilian shipping and military vessels) in areas of vital interest to the United States.

Negotiations between China and Britain over Hong Kong were also a matter of major interest as the colony moved to Chinese control in 1997. Chinese repression in both Tibet and Xinjiang arose periodically, while Iraq had been a major topic of discussion with Chinese officials responsible for the United Nations and Iraq. Given the level of public noise in the relationship and the suspicions about each other in both capitals, I felt we were doing a reasonably good job day to day making sure the priority business of the United States was carried out.

Secretary of State Jim Baker had a strained relationship with the Chinese. The small group around him considered the China issue a political tar baby (and therefore a loser in their effort to position him for the presidency in 1996). He knew his boss George Bush would make the final decisions on China, and his encounters with the Chinese foreign minister, particularly after Tiananmen, had been difficult and usually unrewarding. Baker was happy to cede the China portfolio to the White House and delegate responsibility in the State Department to his deputy, Larry Eagleburger. Baker had famously overflown China in 1990 and 1991 on trips to newly democratic Mongolia (where he had planned a hunt for an argali sheep until State Department people pointed out it was an endangered species), which the Chinese took as a slight. Pressed by the Chinese and by Bush, Baker finally agreed to visit Beijing in November 1991 after the APEC meeting in Seoul. In announcing the trip, he pointed to the "very real problems" in the relationship and the press quoted one of his aides as calling the trip "risky." The clear message was: "Don't expect much."

The embassy welcomed the visit as a chance to gain greater cooperation from the Chinese and to promote U.S. aims. As DCM I was in overall charge of arrangements for the trip (I had been on the other side dozens of times when I worked for Shultz). It was a remarkably tense visit, as Baker and his staff, who reflected their boss's nervousness, made it clear they didn't want to be there. (I couldn't help thinking of the old W.C. Fields epithet for his tombstone: "I'd rather be in Philadelphia.") And I was personally disgusted with the way the State Department staffers treated our embassy people, since I knew they did not have to act so boorishly to make the trip go smoothly.

Baker sparred with his Chinese interlocutors for three days on human rights, arms control, and trade. His meeting with Li Peng was particularly brutal, as the premier poured out his anger against the U.S. on Baker. The final wrap-up session with Qian on Sunday had been planned for a couple of hours in the morning, but it dragged on until 5:30 in the afternoon, hours after the scheduled departure, as Baker tried to wring out some positive result he could claim for the trip. The Chinese gave a bit on proliferation issues but little else. When they agreed to have Dick Schifter engage in talks on human rights (selling this ploy for the second of what was to be multiple times over the years), I whispered to Dick to be prepared, because I had dealt repeatedly with the person they named and had gotten nowhere at all. Having been in China the year before, Dick knew what he was in for. In his memoirs, Qian proclaimed the meeting a success for the Chinese (they had managed to get the secretary of state to visit and gave him virtually nothing), Bush proclaimed the trip "worthwhile," and Baker tried to put the best public face on it while making clear his disappointment in private.

Events in Moscow Again Haunt Beijing

Visits to Moscow by Li Peng in April 1990 and Jiang Zemin in May 1991 provided the opportunity for the signing of an agreement on the eastern portion of the border and for the two sides to exchange friendly words (although Li Peng made it clear publicly that there was no room in China for Gorbachev's political reforms). In reality, Chinese leaders continued to be quite wary as events unfolded in Moscow. They were pleased at first when reactionary elements in the Soviet leadership mounted a coup attempt against Gorbachev in August 1991 but then changed tack when it failed, contrasting it with their "correct" handling of events in Tiananmen. They were aghast at the demise of the Soviet Communist party and the breaking away of parts of the Soviet Union to declare themselves independent countries.

The collapse of the Soviet and Russian empire carried potentially enormous implications for Taiwan, Tibet, Xinjiang, and the integrity of China (or, as some would put it, the Chinese empire). When Gorbachev resigned on Christmas Day 1991, four days after the effective dissolution of the Soviet Union, Chinese media blamed Gorbachev's policies of "new thinking, glasnost, political pluralism, and U.S. efforts at "peaceful evolution." They again proclaimed the correctness of their own repressive approach and predictably tightened up internal security.

Deng Upends the Conservative Drift

China's approach to its economy remained focused on retrenchment, even though the people's hardships kept mounting. In January 1991, the chief conservative propagandist attacked Deng's economic policies quite directly, even making a reference to "capitalist roaders," the epithet hurled at Deng during the Cultural Revolution. In a major speech in March Li Peng pushed for further tightening of controls and slowing of reform. But while weakened, Deng was not finished. The first hint of change came in April 1991when Zhu Rongji was brought from Shanghai to replace a central planner as vice premier. Zhu was the man who put Shanghai back on the road to greatness. (He also was the first ranking Chinese to visit the U.S. after Tiananmen to try to improve ties.)

A true visionary and extraordinarily effective administrator, Zhu had managed the 1989 demonstrations in Shanghai without resorting to violence, laid out plans for modernizing China's premier city, and developed the enormous Pudong project (the area east of the Huangpu River), while preserving the former French Concession and the west side of the Bund to protect the city's distinctive cosmopolitan flavor. When our family first visited Shanghai in the early seventies, it was a city in a time warp, looking like a 1930s movie set, boarded up due to hard times. By the early nineties, under Zhu's leadership, the city was regaining its bustle and swagger, with large-scale mockups to show visitors the grandiose plans for future development. We weren't the only visitors skeptical that the grand buildings shown in the models would actually be built just across the river in place of the ramshackle apartments and decrepit warehouses. But many of Zhu's plans for Shanghai were completed within five years; and Shanghai was returning to its brash, confident self, retaking its place among the world's greatest cities. Zhu was a welcome addition to the Beijing scene, but he, like Deng, had trouble getting enough traction for reform in a city where policy was controlled by the old guard, carried out by Li, and overseen theoretically by a hapless Jiang.

In a classic Chinese maneuver to attack his enemies from an outside base, the 87-year-old Deng, who had been out of sight for most of 1990 and 1991, traveled to south China with his daughter and son in January 1992. His destination was to the greatest beneficiaries of his openness policies, the Special Economic Zones in Shenzhen and Zhuhai and booming Shanghai. During his tour, Deng made speeches praising the accomplishments of economic reforms and attacking opponents who had been in charge post-Tiananmen by name. The press in Hong Kong quoted extensively from his speeches, but the central press did not get on board until late February. Deng had said that reform and opening up should borrow useful things of capitalism and blasted the favorite conservative bugaboo "peaceful evolution" as something not worth worrying about. He proclaimed that "leftism remains the main dangerous tendency inside the CPC." He argued that promoting reform and economic development was the only way the Chinese Communist Party could avoid the Soviet party's fate.

Deng had a reason to make this final drive to change policy. Not only was he getting increasingly feeble, but the 14th Party Congress set for late 1992 would determine the party's leadership and direction for the future. He had tried to turn the tide during a 1991 Chinese New Year trip to Shanghai, ordering the publication of a series of pro-reform articles in the local *Jiefang Ribao*, but the effort didn't succeed, and Li Peng criticized the articles. During the 1992 trip, Deng summoned Jiang and other leaders to Shanghai to demand they adopt his approach. The conservatives eventually buckled, and Deng's speeches were widely circulated in party circles, causing a sensation throughout China. Although the conservatives fought several rear-guard actions, they had lost the battle, and the Jiang-Li leadership fell into line to support economic reform. Deng had restored China to the course that was to make it one of the world's two economic superpowers.

Since the normalization of relations in 1979, U.S. policy toward China had been to allow and even encourage (as we had for more than 150 years) the country's return to a prosperous and modern global player. There would be no policy of containment as was applied toward the Soviet Union. (Indeed, we had been granting Most Favored Nation—the tariff rates between almost all countries of the world—to China and refusing it to Russia for more than a decade.) The two caveats to this policy were that we expected China in return to play by the international rules that we had painstakingly put in place since World War II and to remain friendly toward the United States. Chinese actions at Tiananmen and the American reaction, as well as rising Chinese nationalism and the collapse of the common Soviet enemy put a severe strain on the "friendly" part of the relationship. This was compounded by a large dollop of arrogance, suspicion, and misreading of intentions on both sides. The relationship became much more transactional, making the U.S. more insistent that a rising China had to play by the international rules. The Chinese, for their part, were determined to reach their goal of "China's rightful place in the world" (namely, No. 1) by whatever means necessary and were happy to apply the post–World War II "made in America" rules when it benefitted them but to evade the rules when it didn't.

Economic Agreements Apply Only When in China's Interest

This reality was especially evident on economic issues. Even though relations between the United States and China on the political level could be described as rocky at best, trade between the two countries was booming. U.S. companies had come down with the old China-market contagion very badly, and it often seemed to us in Beijing that no amount of business failures (and there were many involving U.S. companies in the eighties and nineties) could calm it. Large American manufacturing and agricultural exporters were doing well in China, smaller ones faring rather poorly, but the real story involved U.S. importers (Walmart, et al.) seeking cheap merchandise from capable Chinese exporters who relied on their business acumen, a seemingly endless supply of low-priced labor, and government support. Chinese exports to the United States exploded even at a time of conservative economic policies. There was a conscious Chinese effort to dampen down imports at a time when exports to the U.S. were rising rapidly. The U.S. trade deficit with China ballooned, making it second only to Japan.

At the embassy, we had a very active policy pursued by the ambassador, our economic, commercial, and agricultural sections, and me to promote U.S. exports and deal with the increasing frictions in our trading relationship. We would regularly brief the American Chamber of Commerce members and individual businessmen on trends and events in China as well as changes in U.S. policy; we would help them make contacts, hold trade shows, and participate in contract signings and office openings whenever asked by an American company. I attended (and spoke at) dozens of these events. One I remember well was a large gathering for a major Oracle event in China. The speakers were televised on large screens, and it all looked very high tech; but someone had forgotten to adjust the spotlights so the person on the podium could see his or her notes. As I started to give my formal ten-minute speech, I realized there was no way I could face the camera and read the Chinese text before me. There was no choice. I turned sideways to use the spotlight to read my text, giving the audience a profile view of me and presumably a view of the text for the entire speech.

As the trade deficit grew and the U.S. efforts to reduce it proved ineffective (including by Congress, which could not muster the votes to override the president's annual MFN renewal because of U.S. business lobbying), complaints about China's unfair trading practices became a major staple of discussion in Washington. Like China's political repression and biased trials, China's trade practices were indeed unfair. Unlike before Tiananmen when the U.S. looked the other way on some violations, the Bush administration was the first of many to try to level the playing field. The Chinese used many questionable incentives to make their products competitive for export and applied its laws and innumerable subterfuges to suppress imports. Chinese copyright piracy and the reverse-engineering of foreign products were legendary. At one point, almost all of the software in government and private computers in China had been illegally copied, and foreign designs were routinely used in Chinese products without payment. It was said that one of the ten original Boeing 707s purchased after the Nixon trip had been taken apart and analyzed piece by piece so the Chinese could replicate the technology to build their own aircraft industry. This approach never changed. The Russians became so fed up with Chinese reverse-engineering of their military equipment that they sometimes refused to sell top-of-the-line equipment even when relations were friendly.

Many American companies were squeezed out of China by outright fraud. The Chinese wanted to get into the General Agreement on Tariffs and Trade (replaced in 1995 by the World Trade Organization) even as their trade practices became less compatible with the organization's rules, in part because Taiwan seemed likely to get in. When the United States imposed limits on Chinese exports, notably on textiles, Chinese companies circumvented the rules by attaching another country's label and falsifying invoices. The U.S. had encountered many similar problems earlier with Japan, Taiwan, and Korea, but the size of the China market and manufacturing base increased the stakes severalfold.

Carla Hills, the U.S. trade representative, took a no-nonsense approach to the various Chinese trade transgressions and sent her representatives (usually led by Joe Massey) to engage in a series of tough negotiations. In the end, and after intense pressure from the American side to take steps to reduce China's exports, Beijing signed agreements or took internal measures designed to deal with the American complaints. But as with all such agreements, the signing ceremony was only the first step toward achieving the desired result, and implementation was far more problematic. The American problem was that the next administration never followed up with sanctions for China's breaking past agreements.

The Chinese were usually not very subtle in their actions, though there were some humorous moments. During one banquet for Massey at the end of a difficult negotiating session, Chinese waiters brought to the table a dish specially prepared for the occasion. It consisted of a pile of yellow rice with a great many small, dried scorpions scattered on it. It took a major effort on my part not to break out in an uproarious laugh. There was no doubt the Chinese meant to imply we were the scorpions, although the record suggests it should have applied to their side. (As an aside, dried scorpions don't taste like chicken; they taste like dried scorpions.)

By the time Diane and I left in the summer of 1992, daily life in Beijing had pretty much settled into the new normal. While security remained heavy, it did not overly interfere with our activities, and life for the average citizen in Beijing and the large numbers of foreigners had improved dramatically from the seventies. The changes in the daily lives of the local population as the economy grew bore striking similarities to what we had observed in Taiwan twenty-five years earlier. As an example, when the first McDonald's restaurant opened on Wangfujing across from the Beijing Hotel earlier that year, nearby restaurants suddenly underwent facelifts and cleaned up their acts to compete. As Beijing's youth flocked to this new hamburger Mecca, which was not only exotic but clean and cheerful, restaurant renovations soon spread to other parts of the city. Similarly, by 1992 Beijing hosted a sizeable number of world-class hotels with foreign chefs helping their local staff learn (or with Chinese food, relearn) how to cook and handle foods at world standards. Shoppers were out in force, buying from shops filled with items made in Chinese factories for export. The days of Mao suits in a choice of three colors were long gone.

A few months after we returned to Washington from China, I tried to sum up my conclusions in a speech to the National War College. Given the steady 10–11 percent GNP growth in its export-led economy, China was likely to become the world's second largest economy in a couple of decades. Our trade with East Asia was 50 percent greater than with Europe and three times that of Latin America, and China would benefit from our engagement. The security situation in the region appeared to be relatively stable, but I told the group that old points of contention such as Taiwan and territorial sea issues lurked just under the surface, and other countries in the region harbored deep concerns about China's rapid rise. Despite its booming economy, China's politics were in flux. Deng was feeble, the leadership had trouble dealing with the transformation of domestic attitudes caused by rapid growth. Ideology was dead and the party's legitimacy in question. I warned that authoritarianism was very much alive and the pull of national unity strong, but I rashly (and wrongly) suggested there was still a reasonable chance for an Asian-style evolutionary change toward a more democratic order.

As I laid out the challenges for the United States, I told my listeners we needed to create a new world order that took account of the rise of China. We had to consider the implications of a wealthy and nationalistic China that was creating a modern navy (just at the time we were withdrawing from our Philippine bases) and selling missiles and other military equipment in extremely sensitive regions of the world. The issue of trade was critical and of key importance to the U.S. role in East Asia in the twenty-first century. We needed to find ways to get China to play by international rules and to ensure we were ready to compete effectively with the Japanese and others for the growing Chinese market. In the talk, I touched on human rights, narcotics trafficking, illegal immigration, and Hong Kong. I also mentioned China's approach to Taiwan, but perhaps was too optimistic about its patience, giving my audience no hint of the difficult days that lay ahead.

9
A Brief Return to Washington

Diane and I had been planning for some time to go to the States to visit our families before proceeding to my next assignment as DCM in Bangkok. I had received orders in December and begun Thai lessons with a tutor in February. We were looking forward to returning to the unique country we had left twenty-three years before. As part of my reeducation in things Thai, I had taken a trip to the southern Chinese town of Xishuangbanna to get a look at Chinese interaction with their Thai, Lao, and Burmese neighbors. The trip was fascinating culturally. The region looked physically little different from villages on the other side of the border dominated by the same tribal groups. Once inside one of the smoky roundhouses, my first impression was that the chaos in China in the intervening years had changed tribal culture relatively little.

Once again, things did not work out quite as planned. While the State Department bureaucracy continued to send cables to make arrangements for us in Bangkok, Assistant Secretary for East Asian Affairs Bill Clark had different plans. He called just before we left Beijing to ask me to come to Washington to be his principal deputy responsible for China, Taiwan, Mongolia, and Korea. I was happy to accept. While China, Taiwan, and Mongolia were a normal grouping, the addition of Korea (on which I had zero expertise) was a surprise. Clark, a specialist on both Japan and Korea, wanted to shake up thinking on Korea in the Department and gave other responsibilities to the Japan deputy. Our household effects were re-routed to Washington, Diane and I moved back into our house in Alexandria (our daughters were now both in college), and I reported for duty in the East Asian and Pacific Affairs Bureau (EAP) in early August.

Taiwan Arms Sales

The first interagency meeting I attended in my new job involved the sale of F-16s to Taiwan, always a major sticking point in the U.S. relationship with the PRC. In Kissinger's, Nixon's, and Ford's discussions with the Chinese, Beijing had pressed for the U.S. to cut off all arms sales to Taiwan as part of the normalization of relations. During the Carter administration, this had again been a deeply contentious issue in the negotiations on the establishment of diplomatic relations. Agreement was reached only after Deng dropped the demand that the U.S. end arms sales to Taiwan. However, in a classic demonstration of Chinese diplomacy, Beijing tried to renegotiate the deal soon after full relations were established on January 1, 1979.

The Reagan administration's initial approach on Taiwan added fuel to the fire. Reagan had promised much stronger support for Taiwan, and the island's friends in the administration began an immediate effort to secure upgraded arms from the United States. Reagan had said during the campaign that Taiwan was a country and that the U.S. should recognize it and sell it whatever arms it needed. (He sent his running mate George Bush to Beijing during the campaign to reassure the Chinese.) Soon after Reagan became president, Beijing again demanded that the U.S. cut off all arms sales to Taiwan, threatening to downgrade the bilateral relationship and worrying Secretary of State Al Haig that he might lose the "China card" against the Soviets. The Chinese threat was a standard Chinese ploy to create an artificial crisis to get a "resolution" that was more favorable to their interests. The puzzling thing is that a conservative administration fell for the Chinese ploy.

When the Defense Intelligence Agency (DIA) concluded in a 1981 study that Taiwan had adequate defenses against China's aging MiG-21 fleet, the State Department eagerly informed the Chinese there would be no upgrade in weapons sales to Taiwan, and then suggested talks on a 3rd Sino-U.S. Communiqué to regulate arms sales. (I could never understand the logic of the U.S. proposing these talks, in effect giving the Chinese an opening to renegotiate the terms of normalization.) Haig had already offered up a statement that there would be "no increase in quantity or quality of what we sold to Taiwan" and said he expected a "tapering off" as time went on. In the August 17, 1982, communiqué (signed ironically after Haig was fired), the U.S. said it "did not seek to carry out a long-term policy of arms sales to Taiwan," such sales would "not exceed, either in qualitative or quantitative terms" those of recent years, and it would "reduce gradually its sales of arms to Taiwan." The administration then separately reassured Taiwan that it had no plans to seek a revision of the Taiwan Relations Act, to press Taiwan to negotiate with Beijing, or to engage in consultations with Beijing on arms sales to Taiwan. The agreement and side assurances appeared to me at the time as unnecessary, clumsy, and unfulfillable, satisfying no one. For good measure, it also enraged Reagan's political base.

A decade later, in the summer of 1992, the situation had changed dramatically, and flaws in the 1982 communiqué were clear to anyone who chose to look at it objectively. Chinese military modernization, including the purchase of surface-to-air missiles, advanced submarines, and SU-27 fighters from Russia, had changed the balance across the strait. A new DIA report reversed the earlier conclusion on Taiwan defense preparedness. Even though the old (pro-Taiwan) China lobby was dying out, the contrast between Taiwan's democratization process (emphasized by Taiwan's still potent public affairs effort) and the nasty authoritarianism in post-Tiananmen China made assistance to Taiwan a popular issue among Democrats as well as Republicans. With Bush now fighting for a second term, he could not afford to lose his home state of Texas in the upcoming presidential election. On July 30 he told newspapers in Texas (where General Dynamics, the maker of the F-16, had announced layoffs of 5,800 workers due to slow sales) that he was considering selling Taiwan 150 F-16s.

On my second or third day on the job I walked into the interagency meeting carrying State Department talking points that said the F-16 sale would violate the August 17 Communiqué and anger the Chinese. I didn't agree and was not about to press the point. It was clear to me that the sale should go through to preserve the military balance in the strait, and after three years of listening to Chinese bombast, I was not overly worried about their reaction. Jim Lilley represented the Defense Department in the meeting and pushed for the sale. Bush, who had undoubtedly already made his decision, announced his approval at the General Dynamics plant on September 2. He explained his action to the Chinese as a political necessity (they still hoped he would beat Clinton, who had denounced Bush for "coddling dictators from Baghdad to Beijing.")

I suggested that the administration send an envoy to Beijing so they could have someone to beat up on, thus saving face and getting their complaints out of their system. I'm not sure my boss Bill Clark ever totally forgave me when he was picked to make the trip and had to listen stoically as the Chinese "refuted the unjustifiable explanations of the U.S. side." The efforts by Bush and the State Department worked. For all the huffing and puffing, Beijing in effect shrugged off the sale. They similarly ignored the visit of U.S. Trade Representative Carla Hills to Taiwan that fall, the highest American official to visit Taiwan since January 1979.

Given the decline in purchases of arms internationally following the end of the Cold War, the French and others decided to test the water on arms sales to Taiwan. In late 1991 the French sold six Lafayette class frigates worth a total of $2 billion to Taiwan and closed a deal for sixty Mirage fighters worth $3.8 billion a couple of months after the U.S. F-16 announcement. In contrast to their lack of action on the F-16 sale, the Chinese retaliated against the French by closing the French Consulate in Guangzhou, hoping to discourage other countries from following the French lead.

New Players

Dramatic changes occurred in both China and the United States in the fall of 1992. Deng's southern trip in early 1992 succeeded brilliantly in changing the course of Chinese economic development; but to cement his success, Deng needed to put reformists in key positions in China and shore up Jiang Zemin's shaky leadership. Key reformers like Zhu Rongji were promoted and many of the old conservative leaders replaced. In the spring Jiang was formally named president of the PRC. Deng had done everything he could to set Jiang on the road to becoming China's third core leader, but Jiang never attained the power that Mao or Deng had in their heydays, and his weaknesses had serious consequences.

Meanwhile in the U.S., China policy continued to be a major issue in the presidential campaign, with Bush vetoing human rights conditions on MFN for China (U.S. business leaders had by now become fully engaged and strongly supported the effort to sustain Bush's veto), while Clinton vowed he would be much tougher on the Chinese and demand changes in their behavior. The Chinese, to help Bush, not only downplayed the F-16 sale but also signed a major trade deal with the U.S. designed to repair many of the unfair Chinese practices of the past. In the end Clinton won, and the ever-practical Chinese started to court the new administration. They now had to deal with Winston Lord, who replaced Bill Clark as assistant secretary for East Asian and Pacific Affairs. Lord was Jim Lilley's predecessor as U.S. ambassador to China and a determined advocate of conditioning MFN on China's human rights practices. Nevertheless, the new administration agreed to grant MFN in the summer of 1993 but with conditions.

Abortion and Immigration

When we were in China in the seventies, the Chinese touted their effort to control the country's high population growth, enforced by the regime's usual crude methods. Visits to villages or city health facilities often included a briefing on steps underway to limit the population. To say they were intrusive is an understatement. I recall a village health office with a chart on the wall of all women in the village of child-bearing age, with dates indicating when each would be allowed to have a child (no more than one or two) so that the village's overall total of births would be in accordance with the regional plan. In addition to the propaganda and social pressure to encourage women to keep to these schedules, it was apparent to visitors that tougher measures, including abortions, would be used when contraceptives failed or were not used. It was all part of a totalitarian system that told people when they could get married, where they could live, what work they could do, and so forth.

Pressures by antiabortion activists in the United States led to a decision by the Reagan administration and Congress to suspend funding the UN Population Fund, which provided some assistance to Chinese family planning efforts (but not to forced sterilizations and abortions). In 1979, China tightened its population policy considerably under the "one child" rubric.

From the seventies on, a growing number of Chinese illegal immigrants flowed into the United States by way of Latin America or by ship off the U.S. coast. The well-organized operation mostly smuggled in people from Fujian Province who paid up to $30,000 for the voyage. One particular case involved 525 Chinese illegals on a Chinese ship that we intercepted. After several days of hectic work, I managed to coordinate with the immigration authorities and the Chinese to get them all back to China.

It did not take long for the alien smugglers and their lawyers to come up with the idea of tying these mostly young men leaving China to the abortion debate. They argued that the young men were fleeing the persecution imposed by the "one child" policy. At the end of the Reagan administration, Attorney General Edwin Meese issued a memorandum saying that "a well-founded fear of persecution" (language from the immigration law) could reasonably be found for people fleeing China because of the one-child policy. Immigration officials reportedly buried the memo, with no follow-up. The battle waged throughout the Bush administration, but the antiabortion advocates did manage to get a temporary order in place that supported asylum requests based on the Chinese policy.

Just ten days before the end of the Bush administration, I was called over to the White House for a meeting on Chinese immigration, accompanied by a bright young State Department lawyer. We entered a room full of people that included many standing along the walls. Most of these people were staunch antiabortion conservatives who obviously hoped for a major antiabortion victory. My opposite number that day turned out to be the INS general counsel Grover Rees III. The convener of the meeting asked for Rees to start. He outlined the evils of the Chinese "one-child" policy and argued that it made sense to grant asylum to anyone who might be affected by the policy. Then it was my turn to give the State Department's view.

I made the obvious points that we were talking mainly about young men who had likely never kissed a woman and were from an area in Fujian province notorious for smuggling aliens into the

United States. Their aim was simply to "get rich," as local legend had it that anyone could do in the U.S. It was a real stretch to tie them to the "one-child" policy. I spent a bit of time on the long tradition of human smuggling from South China. In conclusion, I suggested that if the advocates were thinking about proposing legislation at this late date, perhaps we should give it an honest name like "The Fujian Alien Smugglers' Relief Act." A gasp went around the room, and I thought I might be tarred and feathered on the spot. The convener hurriedly suggested that the State Department and INS get together to work out a compromise and adjourned the meeting.

I designated my legal colleague to represent the State Department in talks with Rees. As we walked out the door, he asked me for instructions. I said: "Stall, make up conditions he won't accept." A few days later, our lawyer somewhat sheepishly called me to say Rees had accepted all his ploys. I told him to think up some new ones. In the end, the ten days elapsed, and the Clinton administration began, with no action being taken. I have no doubt the career INS people were pleased with the outcome, but the puzzle to me was how the people proposing a permanent rule thought it could survive the Clinton administration. Perhaps they just wanted to show their supporters that they had accomplished something that sounded like it would endure. (A dozen years later the Bush II administration appointed Rees ambassador to East Timor while I was ambassador to Indonesia. We worked well together and never mentioned our little confrontation at the White House.)

Korea

My responsibilities in the East Asian Bureau also included the Koreas, Mongolia, Hong Kong, and Taiwan. Early on Beijing and Seoul established diplomatic relations. The South Koreans wanted to develop their ties with Beijing to promote their strategic interest vis-à-vis the North and to establish a foothold in the rapidly growing Chinese economy. Seoul's break with Taipei had all the hallmarks of a bad divorce, with genuine bitterness in Taiwan as it lost its last major Asian supporter. In November, Boris Yeltsin visited Seoul to tie up loose ends on the KAL-007 shootdown (he had released transcripts and internal memoranda in October) and to put their bilateral relations on a solid footing. Then, in December, the South held their most democratic election to date, bringing the opposition leader Kim Young Sam to power. The South Koreans were on a roll. Our bilateral relations were also excellent. My main contact at the Korean embassy at this time was its extremely capable deputy chief of mission, Ban Ki-moon, who fifteen years later would be my boss at the UN.

While South Korea prospered, the North under Kim Il-Sung was flailing. Kim could only watch as China moved toward closer relations with his archenemy in the South, and Yeltsin formally ended all support for the North Korean regime during his visit to Seoul. As the elder Kim's health began to fail (he died in July 1994), his son Kim Jong-Il asserted increased day-to-day control over military matters. IAEA inspectors, operating under the rules of the Nuclear Non-Proliferation Treaty (NPT) to verify Pyongyang's adherence to its May 1992 declarations, carried out a series of inspections through the summer and fall that suggested the North's nuclear weapons program might be considerably more advanced than it had declared. The IAEA demanded to look at two more sites, the North Koreans refused, and in March 1993 Pyongyang announced it would withdraw from the NPT. As I left the bureau in early April, the IAEA requested sanctions against North Korea.

Mongolia Freezing

America's first resident ambassador to Mongolia, Joseph Lake, and his wife Jody were old friends of Diane's and mine, and Embassy Beijing had done everything it could to help make their pioneering effort a bit easier. For example, we sent four officers to Ulan Bator on the once-a-week flight on a day's notice to provide support for Baker's 1991 visit. Life was difficult for diplomats there—in the mid-seventies I had seen European diplomats straggle down from Ulan Bator to Beijing for R&R and supplies acting as if they were in Heaven— and the Lakes and their new embassy needed a lot of help. Things went from difficult to near the breaking point after the country, which was heavily dependent on Soviet aid, found itself left adrift following the collapse of the Soviet Union. In December 1992 the city's central heating system virtually collapsed during the brutal Mongolian winter. The country lacked basic material, such as spare parts for trucks, coal mining equipment, blasting caps and explosives needed to mine the coal, and the wherewithal to repair their heating equipment. USAID sent in some engineers to see if we could help. Meanwhile, Joe sent daily cables informing us it was 48ºF in his office one day, then 47ºF the next, then 46ºF, and so on down. We worked hard to get action in Washington with the critical help of Secretary Eagleburger. (Secretary Baker had left State to try to rescue Bush's floundering reelection campaign.) In the end, the United States sent an entire military cargo plane to Ulan Bator filled with Soviet parts and supplies that matched the city's heating equipment. The system was soon restored, and the city survived the winter.

A Review of Taiwan Policy

I had heard complaints while in Beijing about the petty problems suffered by our people assigned to the American Institute on Taiwan (AIT). Taiwan officials also chafed at the many indignities we put them through to demonstrate our "unofficial" relationship. After three years in Beijing, I knew that Chinese officials couldn't care less about who signed the paycheck of AIT employees or other administrative trivia that so bedeviled AIT (unless, of course, we made a big deal of it.) They had their fig leaf of the "unofficial" Institute rather than an "official" Liaison Office and that was what they deemed important.

This elaborate (and sometimes ridiculous) charade had a history. When Secretary Vance proposed to Deng Xiaoping in 1977 that the U.S. formally recognize the PRC and set up a liaison office in Taipei, Deng had pulled out the record of conversations with Gerald Ford, where Ford had promised there would be no official U.S. representation on Taiwan. After the failure of the Vance trip, the head of the desk dealing with Taiwan, Harvey Feldman, was tasked to develop in total secrecy an "unofficial" office structure for future relations with Taiwan (he was later allowed to work on the problem with the Department's top lawyer.) Harvey used the Japanese office on Taiwan as his model and built the structure of a separate nonprofit corporation that would be staffed by Foreign Service and other governmental officials who had temporarily "separated" from the government. The 1979 Taiwan Relations Act laid out the "dos and don'ts" in considerable and confusing detail.

David Dean retired from the State Department to head the organization's Washington office and engaged in heroic battles with the Department's administrative structure and lawyers to somehow make the unwieldy concept function. Despite his efforts, the problems created for our staff by this "fig leaf" were quite serious. A dozen years later people were still having their careers harmed by not getting credit for their work in Taipei or being forgotten at promotion time. During my in-briefing on AIT, I decided to try to turn this jumble of demoralizing rules into something friendlier to our people and more effective as an organization. Most changes could be made with little public notice, and China—which had just absorbed the F-16 sale—had far bigger issues to be concerned about.

I worked with Joe Borich and Dave Keegan on the Taiwan desk to launch an in-depth review of what could be done with AIT and our Taiwan friends without endangering the basic deal with Beijing or revising the Taiwan Relations Act (TRA). None of us had in mind any wholesale revision of the basics of the U.S.-Chinese relationship; but with Taiwan pressing for a higher international profile, I thought it should be feasible to get them more access to nonpolitical international organizations such as WHO and ICAO.

And there was no reason to continue inflicting pain on our people or insults to Taiwan on what would be minor issues for Beijing or, if handled low-key, not even noticed. As an example of the latter, I could never understand why the TRA did not specify that USG personnel would be "seconded" to AIT rather than "separated" (which the lawyers and State admin people had turned into "resignation"). It seemed to me we could at least save a lot of anguish by putting the "resignations" in a drawer, ignoring them, and tearing them up when people returned to their normal jobs. I also found humiliating and needless the restrictions on Taiwan officials visiting the State Department or AIT people going to the Foreign Ministry or Presidential Palace in Taipei (there had been a big fight on this issue early in the Reagan administration). In drafting the new approach, the Taiwan desk did an excellent job figuring out how to make the Taiwan construct more rational for everyone involved. Unfortunately, the Taiwan Policy Review was later badly handled by the bureau. It became highly controversial and ended up with no improvement in the conditions of service for our people stationed in Taiwan.

Between Jobs

With the changeover to the Clinton administration, I assumed that Winston Lord would want Peter Tomsen (his DCM in Beijing and my predecessor there) as his senior deputy and China person, and I was right. Peter and I had been friends for twenty-five years (we were junior officers together in Bangkok), and I had good relations with Lord. Even though I was quite happy with my job, there were no hard feelings, and I was determined to make the transition as smooth as possible. I stayed on as deputy assistant secretary until early April 1993 to ensure the new team was settled in, and then found myself without a job.

Strobe Talbott, the well-known former *Time* correspondent and Soviet specialist (and college friend of President Clinton), had been named to the new position of Special Adviser on the New Independent States (an assistant secretary–equivalent position responsible for Russia and the twelve new states on its periphery), and he asked me to become his deputy. With the rapid and critical changes taking place in the former Soviet Union, this was a key job and an exciting prospect. I accompanied Strobe on some of his early calls as we were setting up the new office. But Lord and Tomsen had a different idea. They wanted me to be the director of AIT in Taipei. When I told Strobe of the offer, which I intended to turn down, he strongly encouraged me to take the ambassadorial-level job. So instead of transitioning again to Russia and its neighbors, Diane and I found ourselves heading back to East Asia after only a year in Washington.

Since the incumbent director in Taipei was not due to leave until the summer, the department asked me to act as the executive secretary of a temporary panel Secretary Christopher set up to study the embassy response to the tragic events in El Salvador in the 1980s. (The fact that I had only been to the country once, when I worked for George Shultz, may have been my main qualification for the job.) El Salvador, one of the smallest countries in Latin America, became a huge issue in the early days of the Reagan administration, as right-wing death squads carried out nasty assassinations to stamp out a leftist guerrilla movement. The Reagan administration had considered the threat of communism in Central America to be a major danger to the United States and gave full support to its conservative governments. Critics in the U.S. media, human rights organizations, and Democrats in Congress believed the administration had given some of the region's most unsavory characters a pass and made a mockery of the U.S. human rights policy.

The accusations of administration complicity in the killings, cover-ups in the media, and lying to Congress had roiled political debate in Washington throughout the eighties. In the first few months of the Clinton administration, the El Salvador Truth Commission created by the peace process in the country issued a report that sought to get to the truth of what had happened there. Following the report's release there was a clamor among congressional Democrats for the State Department (which they thought had been complicit in encouraging human rights violations) to review its own record. Secretary Christopher asked two senior former ambassadors, George Vest and Richard Murphy, along with two distinguished professors to form a panel to review the records of the embassy and the department. Being obviously available at the time, I was asked to do the actual research and writing along with two young Foreign Service officers who also happened to be between assignments.

Over the next three months, we read through the mountain of cables, memoranda, speeches, and congressional testimony, assembling a digestible amount for the panel's review, convened dozens of panel interviews, and held a public hearing with testimony from twenty-five witnesses. We then drafted the final report, which concluded that the embassy reporting had been solid on human rights and its personnel had consistently attempted to improve the overall human rights situation. It did, however, fault early statements by department leaders in Washington that conveyed a sense of callousness toward Salvadoran human rights.

Some critics predictably denounced our report as a "whitewash." But after the bulk of the documents were released in the following months, media reports agreed with our conclusions. What I got out of the job was the chance to observe up close the way several of our ambassadors led their embassies and dealt with local officials, Washington, and the public during a crisis. (The young Tom Pickering stood out on all counts.) For me, these three months of looking at our ambassadors in action was worth years of Senior Seminar training. For the country, our work may have had some effect in reducing the controversies around U.S. policy toward Central America.

10
Taiwan: China's First Democracy

With the publication of the El Salvador report on July 15, 1993, we headed back to Taipei to take up my first chief of mission duties as director of the American Institute on Taiwan. It is a testimony to Diane's commitment and managerial abilities that we could change our plans once again on such short notice. But both of us had fond memories of our two times as students in Taiwan in the mid-sixties and early seventies, and we looked forward to returning, this time as the American pseudo-ambassador. (I found it amusing that this was my second tour in greater China to be posted to a sham embassy with an unusual name, USLO and AIT.) Before leaving Washington, I met with a group of Taiwan reporters, recounting stories from our student days on the island and the kindnesses we had received at that time. I told them about the China Airlines official who loaned us airline tickets for a flight from Hualien to Taipei when our bus route home was blocked by floods. It turned out the man now lived in Hawaii, saw the interview, and sent me a nice note of congratulations. The interview apparently set the right tone in Taipei for our next three years.

Upon arrival in Taipei, we were taken to a pleasant old house high up on Yangmingshan (Yangming Mountain) overlooking Taipei, where previous AIT directors had lived. The house had a history. The story goes that it had been built in the early fifties by one of Chiang Kai-shek's senior generals, who made the mistake of inviting Chiang over for dinner. When the austere generalissimo saw the house, he is supposed to have said "No general of mine should live in a place like this," causing the general to move out post haste. The Taiwan military (which, had paid for the place out of public funds) was at the time looking for an appropriate house for the American admiral who headed the Taiwan Defense Command and offered it to him. When the U.S. military left and AIT was set up, the AIT director took over the house. It was by no means palatial and needed serious repairs (Taiwan's frequent typhoons always left us mopping up copious amounts of water, the noise from our ancient military generator riled the neighborhood during electricity outages, and I expected the pool to empty over the mountain during every earthquake); but it had a superb view when pollution levels allowed, and the price was right, since the U.S. paid no rent.

The "Golden Age" of Taiwan

Taiwan had changed fundamentally from the quiet little dictatorship in the early stages of economic development, when we studied Chinese there twenty-seven years before. By the early nineties, Taiwan had become an economic powerhouse, the thirteenth largest trading nation in the world and the fifth largest trading partner of the United States. Its people enjoyed a per capita income level of $8,000 (twenty times that of mainland China), virtually no unemployment, and a growing consumer society looking to buy the finer things of life, including a car, a nice home, and imported luxuries. The government had announced a plan a few years before to finally upgrade Taiwan's neglected infrastructure with a $300 billion program to build roads, railways, subways, schools, and more.

Under U.S. pressure to open its economy (a necessity well understood by the island's economic elite), the island shed its old image as the world's greatest copyright pirate (a title rapidly assumed by the mainland) and sought to take its place as a responsible member of the world economy. During the discussions with the U.S. over the terms of its entry into GATT (later the World Trade Organization), Taiwan negotiators reportedly listened to their American counterparts demanding "this, this, and this" and responded: "Oh, no. You want us to do this, this, this, and this and this. That's terrible." The shocked Americans soon understood that President Lee and his people knew full well that they had many internal inefficiencies that were a legacy of Japanese times, and the way to handle the changes politically was to blame the Americans for making demands. The end result was Taiwan's entry into GATT with a streamlined economy well suited to compete in world markets.

The political transformation of Taiwan was even more dramatic. Taiwan's best-known social critic and democracy advocate Bo Yang (with nine years in prison for his efforts) called the period a "golden age" for Taiwan. He noted correctly that the people were developing the first true democracy China had seen in its several-thousand–year history. The speed of the change made it even more dramatic. Chiang Kai-shek's son, Chiang Ching-kuo, who took over as the island's leader when the elder Chiang died, had concluded by the mid-eighties that the time had come to begin loosening the KMT (Kuomintang, or Nationalist Party), mainlander-led authoritarian regime. In 1984 he named as his vice president a Taiwanese, Lee Teng-hui, a Cornell-trained PhD, formerly the minister responsible for agriculture, mayor of Taipei, and governor of Taiwan. When Chiang Ching-kuo died in January 1988, Vice President Lee succeeded him as president over the strong opposition of Madame Chiang Kai-shek and other conservative party leaders.

Lee began to cautiously loosen the KMT's grip, allowing the opposition Democratic People's Party (DPP) to participate openly in elections in 1989 (it won 35 percent of the seats). Years of U.S. programs to promote democracy through the Asia Foundation and other organizations inevitably associated us with the democratic trends, so much so that some in the KMT held the U.S. responsible for creating the DPP. The next year, by outmaneuvering old guard opposition Lee was elected president in his own right by the National Assembly, most of whose members had themselves been last elected forty years earlier on the mainland. Large-scale student demonstrations at the time demanded the direct election of the president, and Lee agreed with them. In his May 1990 inaugural address, he made clear that he would speed up the democratic transformation. Lee further announced that he would remove the arbitrary powers associated with the "Communist rebellion" declaration and reversed Taiwan's longtime policy of having no dealings with the mainland, calling instead for a cross-strait dialogue.

In December 1991, the DPP pressed hard during parliamentary elections for a declaration of Taiwan's independence (raising concerns and threats from Beijing), but the 31 percent of the vote they received made it clear this was a bridge too far for the average Taiwan voter. The aged National Assembly members were eased out by the end of the month, but Lee chose a conservative mainland general, Hau Pei-tsun, as his prime minister for political balance. When Hau resigned two years later in January 1993, it was clear to all that Lee and his Taiwanese compatriots had taken full control of their island for the first time in history. Mainlanders who wished to play political roles had to compete for the majority's support. Bo was right. The unthinkable had happened in a Chinese society; thousands of years of authoritarianism had been discarded in Taiwan and replaced by a democratic government responsive to the will of the twenty million people on the island.

With the economic and political transformation of Taiwan, suddenly this traditional backwater region became the envy of educated youth all over China. Deng Xiaoping lumped Taiwan with Singapore, Japan, and South Korea as models to study for economic development. (Indeed, if it had not been for Mao's outrageous economic policies, mainland China would probably have looked fairly similar to Taiwan economically instead of being fifteen to twenty years behind.) Noting that all Chinese since time immemorial had been taught that the choice was between an authoritarian regime and "chaos," I once asked President Lee how he managed to stay the course during the tense confrontations and demonstrations of the early nineties. He told me that as a PhD candidate at Cornell during the American tumult of 1968, he assumed that the U.S. government would collapse, but instead saw how the American democratic system took the tensions in stride. This experience convinced him that democracy was the path for any government that wanted long-term stability and that desired to genuinely reflect the will of its people. He later reiterated this point publicly in his 1995 Cornell speech.

Lee and his government reached out to Beijing during this period, responding in part to the desire of Taiwan businessmen to move some of their low-tech (or dirty) manufacturing plants to low-wage China and to ensure that they got their share of the expanding China market. Despite concern in Beijing over the DPP's independence demands and the tug of Taiwan's new culture on mainland youth, lowering tensions with Taiwan also met the needs of the beleaguered Communist government. While they would have clearly preferred for the KMT old guard to remain in control (and were always suspicious of the Taiwanese Lee Teng-hui), they were powerless to affect the outcome of Taiwan's democratization process. Representatives of Beijing and Taipei met in Singapore in April 1993, three months before we arrived in Taiwan, to work out details of the growing interactions between Taiwan and the mainland. They agreed to step up exchanges across the strait, to increase cooperation in areas of mutual interest such as fighting crime, and to accept each other's official documents. The most important outcome of the meeting was to establish formal (if ostensibly "unofficial") organizations on each side to carry out regular consultations.

Decades later arguments continue over whether the two sides also reached a "consensus" at the meeting that there was one China, with each side having its own definition of what that meant. (The term "consensus" was invented by a Taiwan participant several years later to rein in DPP talk of independence for the island.) While both sides undoubtedly expressed their support for "one China" in the session, during my time in Taiwan I never heard of any agreement on a "consensus" along the lines later suggested. There was certainly an agreement to focus on practical issues, leaving larger political problems for the future. The Chinese side had pressed hard for direct air and shipping links across the strait, but Taiwan wanted to move more deliberately, fearing the island could easily be overwhelmed by the billion people on the mainland.

When we arrived in Taipei in July 1993, the trend lines all looked positive for the island. The drastically altered situation on Taiwan made it evident that the United States would have to change its defensive (and somewhat negative) approach to dealing with the people and government there if we were to retain our influence and secure our share of Taiwan's bustling trade. These changes formed the basis for our Taiwan policy review that I had initiated in Washington. To meet the trade challenges others posed, we would obviously have to be much more proactive in the trade and public diplomacy areas.

Another critical task was to help nudge Taiwan's democracy along a path to ensure it was firmly entrenched while avoiding conflict with Beijing. This would inevitably be tricky, as the self-confidence (some would say hubris) of the Taiwan side contrasted with the weak and unpredictable leadership in Beijing.

Finally, on a more mundane, but important level, I arrived just after the department's inspectors had issued a highly negative report on AIT, essentially arguing that it had used its unique status to play fast and loose with the State Department's financial and other regulations. They left no doubt that in the future AIT had to be run like a normal embassy in every way possible.

Taiwan held high hopes for the Clinton administration. Unlike President Bush who had a long-standing relationship with Beijing, Clinton had never been to the mainland but had visited Taiwan four times as governor of Arkansas. Clinton's tough rhetoric against the Bush China policy and his emphasis on human rights and democracy fit well with Taiwan's new reality. But the Clinton administration's early attention was focused on crises elsewhere in the world. When it turned to China, its problem was to square the campaign rhetoric and congressional criticism of China with the reality of China's growing economic prowess and its ties to the U.S. business community. Winston Lord's East Asian Bureau took the lead on the day-to-day dealings with China, and he and my successor, Peter Tomsen, did not want to be distracted by problems with Taiwan. The upside of this focus was that it gave me a fairly free hand to act within the obvious policy constraints.

I was not particularly concerned about adopting a higher profile in Taipei. After dealing with the Chinese bureaucracy over the last four years on a range of topics, including Taiwan, I felt I had a pretty good idea of what pushed their hot buttons and what did not. For example, my predecessor at AIT had been adamant in trying to control how he was referred to in public and in the press. During our first big introductory dinner in Taipei, the American Chamber of Commerce host pleaded with me to ignore it if one of the Taiwan guests referred to me as "ambassador." Apparently, at a similar occasion three years earlier, my predecessor had started his speech with a ten-minute lecture on why he should be called "director," not "ambassador," after a speaker had referred to him as ambassador. Needless to say, the comments had a dampening effect on the entire evening and left the cream of Taiwan's business elite feeling insulted. Our host did not have to worry about me starting off like that. People in Beijing knew that I understood the rules and would not urge people to call me "ambassador." But it was ridiculous and insulting to try to police the media to ensure they got my title right every time.

I was convinced, as I had been when initiating the Taiwan policy review, that Beijing's focus was on the major issues—notably, the meaning of Taiwan's democratization for cross-strait relations and whether the Americans would stick to the normalization deal to discourage Taiwan's independence. Beijing usually seemed less obsessed with the trivia of U.S. representation in Taiwan than were many of my own colleagues in Washington. With the right presentation, and with quiet implementation, we could do many things more sensibly. During the next three years when my name was in Taiwan's press on most days, the PRC only complained once about my public posture (when I called on President Lee in his offices, under instruction, as part of the Taiwan Policy Review.) For people on Taiwan, however, the public attention from the chief U.S. representative was both flattering and reassuring, and contributed significantly to advancing our interests on the island and to managing the tough times ahead.

All of the major China stories during our first year in Taiwan dealt with problems between the United States and China. Taiwan stayed below the radar except for references to its economic successes or high praise for its demonstrated democratic progress. By 1993, elections in Taiwan were free and mostly fair, although vote-buying and fraud had built a strong tradition in local elections and occurred in higher-level elections as well. The DPP consistently polled about 35 percent of the vote. If the KMT stayed united, it won; but if an election featured a close contest between the KMT and a breakaway rival, the DPP could win.

With its economy booming and its social changes breathtaking, Taiwan nonetheless retained its core social values remarkably well. Sometimes it clung to its traditions too well. American-trained educators on Taiwan desperately tried to move away from the test-driven, tutor-ridden madness that robbed Taiwan's children of their childhood (like the young girl who had studied out loud on the other side of my wall twenty-four years earlier). One retired

University of Illinois professor who returned to Taipei to become the minister of education liked to tell parents: "I know you want your kids to graduate from Harvard, MIT, or Yale, but my three kids did that without working late every night. They played sports on weekends and had plenty of time for trips to the zoo, picnics, and the like. We don't have to destroy our kids to be sure they excel in life." He was fired in less than a year—he obviously did not understand the importance of children studying seven days a week from morning to night in order to get ahead. The "student hell" in Taiwan continued. The mania also bled over to the Taipei American School, where Taiwanese parents' drive and the high capabilities of children out of the Taiwan system provided fearsome competition for students moving from the U.S. or from more relaxed American or International schools abroad.

Unsurprisingly, the contrast in the contacts Diane and I had with the people of Taiwan and the people of China could not have been more extreme. In Taipei, we entertained and went to peoples' homes or to restaurants for dinner with a sizeable slice of Taiwan's elite. Golf games were full of uproarious laughter, especially if I happened to be presented the "Longest Day" trophy after the match. Although my picture appeared regularly in the papers, the threat level against Diane and me as the ranking Americans remained incredibly low. Diane had bought a Mercury Capri convertible as our private car before we went to Taipei, and we drove all over the northern part of the island with the top down when the weather permitted. One Sunday, as we stopped at a red light in the middle of Taipei, a black Mercedes with dark-tinted glass pulled up beside us. The rear window opened and the (rather sinister) Taiwan security chief smiled and waved. "Hi, Lynn," he said, "You made my day. I know I'm doing my job well if the American ambassador (that forbidden word again) can drive around in a convertible with the top down." Taiwan was the most open and friendly place we ever served. The society had changed in many ways, but it was still the same friendly atmosphere we had first encountered as students.

At its core Taiwan was deeply pro-American, and part of my job was to keep it that way. In addition to the crucial U.S. role in Taiwan's security and economic development, the social ties were also strong. A dramatic number of Taiwan's elite had attended universities in the United States. In Lee's cabinet in 1989, nine of fourteen cabinet appointees (plus Lee himself) had doctorates from U.S. universities, and the number stayed approximately the same throughout our time there. For several years in the early nineties, Taiwan had the largest number of foreign students in the U.S. (their numbers were later passed by China). Diane and I went to numerous meetings of alumni associations of American universities, the prestige of which often defined the status of their former students in Taiwan society. Needless to say, the American universities tried to keep close tabs on their well-to-do Taiwan alumni. At first, we had only a general guess at the number of American citizens on the island, because many families had a U.S.-citizen or Green Card holder as a safety net, in case things went wrong with the mainland. A couple of years later, we had a much better idea of the true number.

We found our residence a good place to entertain. The cook and staff were good, and Diane worked hard to make the place attractive and ensure the staff performed up to high international standards. On our first Thanksgiving, we invited the president, prime minister, foreign minister, and their wives to a small dinner, comfortable that all of them would have memories of Thanksgiving feasts from their times in the U.S. Diane worked closely with the cook to prepare her traditional feast of turkey, dressing, cranberry sauce, and the works as well as pumpkin and pecan pie. We did what we could to ensure the house and setting were at their best. Although it was still fairly warm on Thanksgiving Day, I wanted to use the fireplace to give the occasion more of a cozy wintry feel. The staff assured me it worked well. We cranked up the air conditioning to its coolest setting and by a half-hour before our guests were to arrive, everything seemed in perfect order. I then suggested they start the fire so it could be burning nicely by the time the guests arrived.

Disaster struck. Suddenly, smoke poured into the sitting room and throughout the house. Diane rushed in horrified, our houseboy looked on helplessly, and I made a mad effort to get the fireplace to begin to draw properly. It soon began working, but the house now smelled like it had been on fire. With fifteen minutes to go, we opened all the windows and started all available fans. With five minutes to go, we closed things up and hoped for the best. When our guests walked in the front door precisely on time, we looked like we had been calmly waiting for them, although the house still had a distinct smell of smoke. The president was the first to comment, "Oh, you even have a fire for us"; and the dinner with great food and good conversation was sufficiently successful that the Lees came again the next year (with no fire in the fireplace).

Given the time it took to drive up the mountain from central Taipei, we converted a small house downtown (also provided to us free of charge) into a place where we (usually me) could quietly hold business lunches. Again, Diane took on the redecorating to make the old place look presentable, and the cook and staff soon became quite adept at bringing food and utensils down from the mountain for the lunches. The venue worked well as a place to reach out to Taiwan's society. One memorable lunch featured Mstislav Rostropovich and a few members of Taiwan's cultural elite. "Slava" entertained Diane, me, and our guests for a couple of hours with his stories, charming everyone around the table and underscoring to the people present that we believed Taiwan had "arrived" on the world cultural scene.

Promoting American business abroad is a basic responsibility of any U.S. ambassador, and in Taipei it became a vital part of AIT's activities. Taiwan's rapidly growing wealth and active role in the world economy (combined with uncertainty on the mainland) attracted our foreign competitors to the island, a place they had earlier been happy to ignore. All the other "nonofficial" pseudo-embassies were basically staffed with people to promote trade, not manage political relationships, and they were aggressively pursuing Taiwan's business as it spent heavily to upgrade its infrastructure. AIT needed a much higher profile to compete. I was not about to let the U.S. lose out after we had been Taiwan's sole serious backer for forty-plus years.

AIT's commercial office (led by the formidable Ying Price), agricultural office, and military staff (all retired) formed a superb team. We would have blowout "America Weeks" promoting U.S. products and numerous agricultural shows. (I was once set up for a photo op by my staff acting like I was reeling in a large frozen fish; the picture of my antics appeared in virtually every newspaper on the island.) I gave speeches promoting U.S. products at scores of company openings and other events, always being sure I had Chinese and English versions ready, since such events in Taiwan could be in either language or mixed.

One thing seemed constant: the newspapers usually showed me smiling or occasionally (as with the frozen fish) looking downright silly. I once asked a good Taiwan friend about this coverage, saying there was no way I could be only smiling at these events. He replied that the pictures in the paper and on television served a clear purpose in Taiwan. For the local audience, seeing the American representative smiling or even clowning around was deeply reassuring. Not only did it show respect for Taiwan's people and their accomplishments; it also told them that the island's security remained solid despite the increasingly hostile statements coming from Beijing. I was mostly trying to sell U.S. products at these trade events, but I also heeded his advice when the security situation later became more precarious.

Business was good for our companies as we pressed Taiwan to open its markets and ensure a level playing field. One success we had—assisting Westinghouse win the contract for Taiwan's fourth nuclear power reactor—illustrated how we could help. When Westinghouse told us the specifications for the plant had been written (presumably after a sizeable bribe) by its Japanese competitor to ensure it would get the contract, AIT exposed the effort as fraud and pressed for more neutral specifications and fair consideration of the Westinghouse bid. We managed to turn the negotiations around and secure one of the island's largest contracts for an American company.

Interestingly, one of our best talking points at the time was the American Foreign Corrupt Practices Act (FCPA) that had been passed after a Lockheed scandal in Japan in the 1970s. The Act, which remained controversial, with some arguing it put American companies at a disadvantage in winning contracts, had the opposite effect in Taiwan. The government was working to put its history of sleazy practices behind it and wanted to bring its companies' actions up to the top international standards. This high-minded purpose was reinforced when the Taiwan Navy officer responsible for the purchase of French frigates—and undoubtedly for spreading around the bribe money that accompanied it—was found face down in the water at an ocean beach, obviously murdered by someone unhappy with his share or desperate to shut him up. Buying military equipment through the Pentagon's Foreign Military Sales program might be tedious, but no one could accuse you of being bribed, since the documents were available for all to see. Similarly, because of the FCPA, buying American greatly reduced the chances of flawed deals or the defective materials that often accompanied contracts facilitated by bribes.

Perhaps nothing better illustrated the changes going on in Taiwan than the growing movement to improve Taiwan's environment. When we were on the island in the sixties and early seventies, Taiwan's society had the usual Chinese approach to the environment: clean your house and compound every day, then sweep the trash out the front door and dump it on the street, maybe near a garbage can, maybe not. On a grander scale, Taiwan's industrialists had carried out a similar approach in their business decisions, resulting by the early nineties in bad air, polluted water, and damaged agriculture. A favorite excuse for Taipei's foul air was to blame its location in a bowl-shaped valley, not Taiwan's polluting companies. In the "old days," we saw Taiwan's fertile fields littered with plastic bags and trash that had been dumped along the roads with little consideration for their negative impact on Taiwan's agricultural economy. People had little incentive to ensure they had a clean environment in which to live and work, and I was not aware of any nongovernmental organizations interested in the environment. (Those NGOs that did exist under Chiang Kai-shek's rule tended to be in the areas long promoted by American missionaries and educators—women and children's welfare, health, and education.) But a rising environmental movement in the eighties had been closely tied to the island's democratization, with some of the opposition leaders cutting their political teeth arguing for improvements in the environment.

We were determined to promote this trend as a valuable good in itself but also understood that it was an area where American expertise could be quite helpful, and profitable. I remember being on a television panel one evening with Taiwan officials and the Taipei representative of U.S. Waste Management, often stretching my Chinese vocabulary to its limits, since I would have had trouble following some of the technical commentary even in English. I also found myself regularly at the starting point of the large number of fund-raising races for environmental causes, calculating early on that it was far easier to give a speech urging the runners on than trying to keep up with them on the ups and downs of Taiwan's mountains. By the time we left Taipei, I marveled at how far this society had advanced in using nongovernmental organizations and other civil society groups to better their own lives. Unlike across the strait, the people on Taiwan had learned to voluntarily join with others to improve their living conditions, and their government encouraged them to do so. Remarkably, because of the island's tight environmental controls, when we visited Taipei two decades later the air and streets in Taipei sparkled.

Having derived extraordinarily little benefit for U.S. interests from my bridge playing in Beijing, I now found myself among some of the world's most avid golfers. In my interview before arriving in Taipei, I had said that I did not play golf, a statement that I soon found was like waving a red flag in front of a bull. (I did not add, fortunately, that I thought golf wasted too much time.)

Soon after our arrival in Taiwan, local business leaders pressed me to learn to play, noting it was essential that I play at least one round with the president. Reluctantly, I realized that golf had to be part of my outreach to the Taiwan elite. Thereafter, every Saturday morning at daybreak when the weather was decent, I would be out on the golf course with my coach trying to learn the basics. (The timing had a second benefit, because I felt that, barring an emergency, my staff should not work the State Department's usual Saturday mornings. It was more important that they have time off to be with their families or to explore the island. I told them if they came into the office on Saturday to impress me, they were wasting their time because I wouldn't be there.) Predictably, given my poor track record as an athlete and the fact that every time I went to the driving range to practice people would come up to me asking, "Aren't you Bei Lin?" (my Chinese name), ensuring the ball would veer off wildly, my golf game remained mediocre at best.

However, unlike the Beijing bridge table, the golf course was an excellent place to make contacts and hear the political views or business plans of Taiwan's movers and shakers. I became a member of one group that brought together some of the most articulate and forward-thinking people on the island. One businessman (whose drives occasionally appeared to go deep into the woods only to be miraculously discovered by the caddies just at the edge of the fairway) described to me in detail the factors he considered in deciding where to build his next overseas plant (including wages, bribes to local officials, work ethic, and the legal structure). He had chosen Vietnam, where "they work like Chinese, but at lower wages, and are twenty years behind on the size of bribes demanded." He liked to manufacture his products in the U.S. but always had to weigh the higher wages there against the bribes demanded in Asia.

Fred Chien, Taiwan's highly capable foreign minister, would ask me to play golf when he had something particularly important or sensitive to pass on. He obviously knew the golf cart offered the most secure environment for a conversation, and I was always eager to hear what he had to say. After three years of losing games (even with the maximum handicap), laughing off my high scores, making many friends, and learning a great deal about Taiwan, the big day finally came for me to play with President Lee and his top cabinet officials. It was rainy and cold, but in Taiwan that only meant we put on our plastic rainwear and slogged out onto the course. Lee and his colleagues were excellent players (he never was far above par), while I felt I had a good day when I broke 100. The rain grew heavier, the mud thicker, and the scores higher, before the president mercifully stopped the game well before the 18th hole, and we headed for the showers. The rest of the evening consisted of a delightful dinner and an interesting conversation, a far cry from perhaps the least enjoyable game of golf I ever played.

Tensions Rise across the Strait

Despite the 1993 meeting in Singapore and a series of cross-strait sessions that dealt with other issues such as hijacking, illegal immigration, and increased economic interaction between the two sides, Beijing never really trusted Lee Teng-hui. Chinese leaders were frightened both by Taiwan's democratic example in the post-Tiananmen era, which contrasted with their own harsh governing methods, and by the DPP's open advocacy of independence. Given the leadership competition in Beijing, efforts to move Taiwan along a more independent path were anathema to the leadership, and "softness" on the Taiwan issue was a sure ticket to oblivion.

Lee, however, wanted to carve out more international space for Taiwan (without advocating independence) to get his people the international recognition they deserved for their accomplishments. He also tended to shoot from the hip (and to be overly candid) in his public comments. And he had no intention of fitting into the box he felt China and the U.S. had made for him and his people. He adopted the approach that there existed one China, but with two governments, and this reality should be recognized by the international community, including at the United Nations. (The two Koreas entered the UN on similar terms in 1991.) At times, it also sounded like he was continuing his internal political battles with the mainlanders on Taiwan in his assertions of the Taiwanese identity.

Perhaps Lee's most egregious heresy from Beijing's point of view were his frequent statements of admiration for Japan. Unlike people from other former Japanese colonies, Taiwanese in general had a positive view of the Japanese. Lee's generation had been the beneficiaries of Japan's rule in Taiwan, coming up through the Japanese educational system and often serving in the Japanese colonial regime and army. Educated Taiwanese Lee's age spoke far better Japanese than they did Mandarin (which became the language of Taiwan's education system only in 1947); and in the nineties, they would usually speak Japanese or Taiwanese—a southern Fujian dialect—rather than Mandarin among themselves on social occasions. One of Lee's comments to a Japanese magazine that he "felt more Japanese than Chinese" (undoubtedly true, but indiscreet) produced howls of condemnation from Beijing for weeks. It also played into the Chinese government's effort to whip up anti-Japanese sentiment as part of an effort to boost its own popularity.

By the nineties all Taiwan politicians (whether of mainland or Taiwan heritage) felt it essential to stress that the people on Taiwan (including second and third generation mainlanders) were different from the mainland. They wore their democracy and freedoms as a badge to prove their uniqueness. For Beijing, however, recovery of

Taiwan remained an integral part of its propaganda and nationalistic rationale for communist rule. The PRC has never been willing to concede Taiwan's historically distant relationship to the mainland, its backwardness when it was handed over to Japan as a war prize in 1894, and its emergence into the modern era as a Japanese colony. Nor did it acknowledge that the bad treatment by the KMT when the island returned to China after World War II and during forty years of authoritarianism under an exile mainland elite left little enthusiasm in Taiwan for reattachment to the "motherland."

As time went on, Beijing began to label Lee a "splittist" who wanted to separate Taiwan from the mainland. Ominously, they backed up their rhetoric by moving missiles to Fujian just across the strait from Taiwan and conducting military exercises designed to warn Lee and his associates to back off. They proclaimed they would use force if Taiwan declared independence. While I had a good relationship with Lee, I had virtually no success in getting him to tone down his rhetoric. He was not about to take advice on handling the mainland from someone twenty years his junior, even if that person represented the island's sole protection from invasion. In his view, the cross-strait issue was an argument among Chinese, or Chinese and Taiwanese, and a foreigner's opinion was worth little.

With Deng becoming weaker, tensions in the Beijing leadership grew throughout 1994 and 1995. As Jiang Zemin ("the "weathervane") tried hard to shore up his leadership, he came to rely more and more on the PLA for support, and their advice emphasized a military rather than a diplomatic end to Beijing's "Taiwan problem." With Deng virtually out of the picture, there was no one to prop Jiang up, or to search for novel solutions to their "problem," or to negotiate acceptable adjustments with Lee. Jiang, himself, certainly did not have sufficient internal standing to come to a basic understanding with Lee. After an August 1994 agreement on a landmark antihijacking deal and the return to the mainland of Chinese illegal immigrants in Taiwan, the cross-strait dialogue lost its effectiveness as a buffer to ease problems in the relationship, and the PRC suspended meetings after Lee's U.S. visit the following year.

Beijing was especially rattled by Lee's "flexible diplomacy," an effort to break Taiwan out of its isolation by using its riches to entice small countries to recognize it or by exploiting the attraction of business deals to get major countries to upgrade their "unofficial" relations with the island. An international aid fund started in October 1988 with $1 billion successfully encouraged several small countries to establish formal ties, and a cultural exchange effort put Taiwan on the map of many countries where its imprint had previously been negligible. Beijing complained about Taiwan using "silver bullets" to enhance its international status, but the PRC soon followed suit, causing some countries in Africa to switch their allegiance back and forth, depending upon which side of the strait was offering the bigger aid project.

Beijing's complaints did not deter Lee. He stepped up efforts to gain international recognition, membership in the United Nations and its agencies, and wider ties with countries like the United States who could help it win more space from Beijing. A high point in this effort was his successful "vacation diplomacy" over Chinese New Year in 1994. Ostensibly on vacation, Lee traveled to Indonesia, Thailand, and the Philippines and met with the country's leaders or other high-ranking officials. The PRC protested these actions vigorously, canceled visits of its own leaders to countries Lee had visited, and made it clear it would not tolerate future meetings at the presidential level. In May, Lee traveled to Central America and then to South Africa for Nelson Mandela's inauguration. He had no luck, however, wrangling an invitation for himself to the Seattle APEC meeting in November 1993 (his economic chief went instead), and the Japanese canceled an invitation to the Asian Games in Hiroshima the next fall after a Chinese protest.

America's Struggling China Policy

As the deadline for the 1993 MFN decision on China approached, the Clinton administration faced a major dilemma. Clinton had campaigned on the Democratic demand that China be punished for Tiananmen by taking away its most favored nation privileges unless it made major improvements in its human rights record, and the new assistant secretary, Winston Lord, had been one of the leading Republicans pressing this case. By this time, however, four years had passed since Tiananmen. While taking away that status would have been feasible (and almost happened) in the early years of the Bush administration, by 1993 China's booming economy had become more closely entwined with that of the United States through investments, purchases, and sales. The China trade was simply too big to lose. U.S. businessmen lobbied the Clinton administration (and Congress) hard to continue China's trade status unchanged.

The administration took the easy way out—approving China's MFN in 1993 but vowing it would be taken away in 1994 if things did not improve. (The Democrats in Congress had been pushing this "conditional" approach to the MFN issue since Tiananmen.) What must have seemed to be a clever compromise at the time proved to be a disaster the next year when the decision whether or not to renew arose again. China had done nothing in the meantime to help its cause. China's divided leadership had no one of sufficient stature to offer concessions to the Americans, so they simply called the administration's bluff. An April 1994 trip to Beijing by Secretary of State Warren Christopher to wring out some justification for continuing MFN turned into an American embarrassment when the Chinese stonewalled. In the end, the administration gave up, basically severing the link between MFN and human rights, and justified its approach with words that sounded very similar to those of the Bush administration.

The Clinton administration never made a serious effort to change its ad hoc approach into a coherent China policy. The real U.S.-China relationship was undergoing a major transformation while U.S. policy remained stuck in old arguments. As the bilateral trade grew exponentially, the traditional dream of an unlimited China market for U.S. goods had been replaced by American companies deciding that products sold to the Americans and around the world could be made more cheaply and of a comparable quality in China rather than in the U.S. Ross Perot was wrong about NAFTA producing a "great whooshing sound" as companies crossed the border south to Mexico. The "great whooshing sound" was actually made by American companies moving production to China. By the end of Clinton's first term, the U.S. trade deficit with China had surpassed that with Japan, and the gap was growing quickly. The administration had no effective strategy to deal with this threat to American manufacturing, and indeed there may have been no way to stop it under a liberal trading regime. But there was no doubt about what was going on. Some American sectors (airplanes, agriculture, later automobiles, and other sectors) did manage large sales to China, but lower-tech manufacturing in the U.S. suffered an egregious decline. To its credit, the administration tried to take an aggressive approach on specific trade issues (especially intellectual property piracy and restrictions on access to China's market), but the Chinese usually found ways to ignore the agreements they signed soon after the ink had dried.

The administration's political agenda with China emphasized improving the PRC's human rights, halting Chinese nuclear and missile proliferation to sensitive countries, and securing Chinese help with North Korea. The Chinese government, with Li Peng still premier, had no intention of improving its human rights record, especially after it succeeded in calling the administration's MFN bluff. They did the usual minimum on North Korea, and although they did eventually modify some of their sales of destabilizing weapons abroad, the real military story was the steady growth in the PRC's capability, fed by the sense of PLA inferiority after the Gulf War. During his August 1994 visit to China, Commerce Secretary Ron Brown apparently hardly mentioned human rights issues, thus ending any pretense that human rights would continue to dominate the relationship. The Republican takeover of Congress that November reduced the Clinton administration's room for maneuver even further.

As for Taiwan, Washington seemed happy for me to promote trade and democracy there and to try to keep Taiwan's leadership focused on the importance of cross-strait harmony. They did not want to have Taiwan complications enter into the picture as U.S. relations with Beijing seemed to careen from crisis to crisis. I had no indication that Taiwan figured prominently in any of Washington's China policy discussions, except for being mentioned as a nuisance and distraction. This was short-sighted. Taiwan would not remain quiet, and mishandling Lee and his people's aspirations caused the trilateral relationship to blow up in our faces.

Taiwan had long relied on its Republican backers in Congress, who were provided free trips to Taiwan for "consultations" (a few of whom were infamous in the Foreign Service for never quite making it to any formal discussions). By the nineties, Democrats, impressed with Taiwan's democratic progress and fed up with Beijing, joined in the free trips. Over congressional breaks, it was not unusual for us to be juggling three or four congressional delegations at once, along with a separate group or two of staffers. All were wined and dined appropriately and given meetings with the president or ranking Taiwan leaders. I found these trips valuable as a way to explain our Taiwan and China policies to influential Americans, and it helped us to keep up to date on the Taiwan leadership's thinking. In addition to members of Congress, Taiwan invited other current or former U.S. officials (and state governors) to hear their case. At the time, Taiwan was considered to have the second (after Israel) most effective foreign public relations effort in Washington. To give its people a sense of international importance, Taiwan organizations also paid high-powered speakers from the international lecture circuit, including George Bush, Margaret Thatcher, and Mikhail Gorbachev, to give lectures in Taipei in exchange for hefty fees.

Upgrading AIT's Office

As part of emphasizing the "unofficial" nature of the U.S. presence, the embassy building in Taipei had been closed in 1979 (it was abandoned and in shambles by the nineties), and the staff moved into the old CIA compound on Hsinyi Road, where Ray Cline and Jim Lilley had both worked in the fifties mounting clandestine operations against the mainland. When we were students in Taipei, the military base that had at that time been across the street seemed fairly far out of town, but now it had become a park, and AIT was very much inside the city. Since it was deemed to be "temporary accommodations," little effort had gone into upgrading the building in the fourteen years it had been the State Department's responsibility or, for that matter, in the forty years since it had been built. It had the drab wainscoting, tiled floors, and ugly décor of the early fifties, reminding me of the Harlem police station where I had been fingerprinted for my Foreign Service application. Given the dramatic economic development going on in Taipei, it must have been one of the more depressing office spaces in the city. Diane, with her practiced eye for work environments, was appalled at first look. Part of the problem could be laid to poor management and maintenance, but it was also indicative of Washington's treating AIT like an orphan and a State Department that was starved for basic funding.

Fortunately, my predecessor Stan Brooks and his staff had pushed through an innovative idea with Washington to use AIT's unique status to double the cost of obtaining a U.S. visa in order to help fund our operations. The increased cost did not deter the newly affluent people of Taiwan from seeking a visa; but using visa fees to fund operations somehow seemed unclean to many in the State Department. In Washington, I praised AIT's approach as a way to help solve the department's acute financial difficulties. (I plagiarized the old Maoist slogan of "In agriculture, learn from Tachai," suggesting it should be "In visa fees, learn from Taipei.") It soon dawned on the State Department and Congress that we were on to something at AIT, and now the department's entire visa-issuing process is self-sustaining. By the time of our arrival in Taipei, AIT was beginning to accumulate sufficient funds to undertake a serious upgrade of its facilities.

We discovered that our administrative people were surprisingly reluctant to make changes, so Diane and I found ourselves selecting paint colors, designing small alterations, and choosing the carpet samples. One argument the staff made was that the carts used to move materials would destroy carpets. I countered that every new hotel and office in Taipei had carpeted floors without a problem, and perhaps we needed to upgrade our carts. As if to prove the naysayers' point, one of our local staff crashed his cart into a pristine wall within a week after the project was finished. I had it repaired immediately, and it never happened again. When we were leaving, several members of our local staff thanked us profusely for the upgrades, saying it made them proud to come to work in a more modern environment.

One morning as we arrived at the office, Diane looked up at the roof of the building and asked me if all of the ugly aerials, including a rusty old tower, were really necessary. I gathered appropriate members of my staff later in the day to ask which of the aerials they actually used. It turned out that only two modest aerials still functioned. All the rest were the accumulated junk from past spy or communications operations. Within a few days the old aerials were gone, making our compound a much more respectable presence for its upscale neighbors. I also thought it foolish that no U.S. flags were in evidence in the office (hotels and even banks proudly hung the American flag in Taipei), and we soon had flags in my office, the front foyer, and the travel (consular) section. I chose not to push my luck with Washington by putting up a flagpole and flag outside like a traditional embassy or consulate, but I cheered when one of my successors, Steve Young, took that step a few years later without significant blowback.

Just as we were getting our old fifties military-style building in better shape, several DPP members of the Taipei City Council began to argue that we should be forced to vacate the site entirely. After all, we were occupying valuable space in downtown Taipei rent-free and the building hardly lived up to the city's new image or, for that matter, the prestige of the island's greatest friend and protector, the United States. Taipei wanted to regularize its land-ownership rules as part of its modernization and to return land confiscated by the Nationalists (like the site occupied by AIT) to its rightful owners. We were willing, of course, to pay a reasonable rent, but the actual ownership of the land was quite complex. The issue became a political football when the DPP candidate, Chen Shui-bian, won a three-way race to become mayor of Taipei.

When I called on Chen in January 1995 to congratulate him on his victory, we began with the usual polite chit-chat in front of the cameras. Our agreement had been that the media would then leave so we could carry on a substantive conversation. Instead, more cameras and reporters came into the room, and Chen turned to me and said, "And now about your AIT building," making the case that we were occupying the property without a legal basis and were not even paying rent. Fortunately, I had gone over my talking points in Chinese just before the meeting (Chen spoke very little English). I turned to the camera, explained our strong support for Taiwan, emphasized our willingness to pay a reasonable rent for a multiyear lease, and related how a provision of the Taiwan Relations Act had protected Taiwan's real estate in the United States, including one of the most valuable residential properties in the city of Washington. A couple of weeks later, we received a call saying the mayor wanted to visit me at AIT. He arrived at the office without his usual press contingent, which we kept outside the compound, and indicated within minutes that he was ready to deal. We haggled a bit for propriety's sake and then struck a deal on a long-term lease that would give us time to build the new and more appropriate facility we had long discussed. (The new facility opened twenty-three years later.)

One morning in mid-April 1995, I was sitting at my desk when my deputy broke in to announce that one of our junior officers, Kirby Simon, had died in his government-provided apartment the night before. There was no foul play. Unfortunately, the personable, generous young man Diane worked with in the Consular Section had died of carbon monoxide poisoning from a defective hot water heater. Kirby, who suffered from asthma, apparently sealed his apartment, ran the heater (which had originally been outside the apartment) for a long soaking bath, and was overcome by the killer fumes. Well-liked by all, the 33-year-old first-tour consular officer's death was a huge tragedy for AIT. His parents set up the J. Kirby Simon Foreign Service Trust (run on a voluntary basis by his former colleagues) that twenty years later had handed out over $1.5 million dollars in small grants to support voluntary projects carried out by the Foreign Service community overseas.

A Snub and Its Consequences

After the initial successes of his "vacation diplomacy," President Lee decided to further push the envelope in May 1994 by traveling to Costa Rica and Nicaragua and asked for a rest stop and a day of golf at a Taiwan businessman's resort in Hawaii. I told Washington that I thought this unofficial stop could be managed with Beijing by ensuring there were no press conferences or meetings with U.S. officials. Traveling to Central America by way of Hawaii was an obvious route, but there could be no doubt that Lee wanted to promote his flexible diplomacy agenda by saying he had been to the U.S. The PRC ambassador in Washington protested to Win Lord, demanding that Lee not be allowed to make the stop. Focusing on Beijing's complaint and Christopher's recent bad meeting in Beijing rather than weighing the consequences of rejecting the thin-skinned Lee's request or the dangers of handing leverage on Taiwan issues to the PRC by accepting their complaint as valid, the department decided against the rest stop. Instead, it determined that Lee's plane would only be allowed to refuel on the military side of the Honolulu airport, and Lee could only deplane to the military VIP lounge. When a Taiwan aide reported to him on the austerity of the facility, Lee voiced his outrage at the treatment to Nat Bellocchi (the AIT Washington chairman who was there to greet him) and refused to get off the plane.

After Lee returned to Taipei, Fred Chien called me over to his house to vent their obvious anger about Lee's treatment and loss of face. Chien emphasized that we had insulted a good friend, asking why the State Department didn't have the guts to stand up to PRC complaints. Fred could be a tough interlocutor even under pleasanter circumstances, but he outdid any of my previous opposite numbers in Beijing and Moscow in the vitriol he spewed out on this occasion. Even filtering out the hyperbole, Lee obviously had ordered him to be sure we understood the extent of his anger. My political chief, Doug Spelman, took down Fred's words in detail, and I instructed him to prepare the cable as nearly verbatim as possible, so Washington (which had ignored our suggestions on how to treat Lee) could understand the problem their actions had created. Even though I agreed with some of Fred's complaints, I defended Washington's position in the meeting. It seemed to me that the episode had been amateurishly handled by the department from the first.

A further factor in Fred's anger was that he probably understood at that point that he had lost control of Taiwan's policy toward the United States. Frustrated at Washington's inaction, President Lee turned away from his foreign minister's cautious advice and asked his old friend, the head of the wealthy KMT business empire, Liu Tai-ying, to take a more aggressive approach toward the United States. Liu hired the Washington lobbying firm Cassidy

& Associates to take Taiwan's case to Congress and the media in order to circumvent and counteract what Lee saw as the State Department's kowtowing to Beijing. It seems unlikely that State and the East Asian Bureau understood the challenge. In the end, they were overwhelmed by it.

Taiwan had always had traditional close ties to the Republican establishment and a heavy lobbying presence in Washington (although the $4.5 million Cassidy deal was seen as extravagant by observers, even by Washington standards). But now Taiwan had a new narrative as a plucky, democratic, and rich but mistreated friend that contrasted sharply with Beijing's abysmal human rights record and trade practices. Taiwan's investment in hosting American legislators and their staff, and Cassidy's reach with both Republicans and Democrats in Congress proved to be a far greater threat to the traditional China policy than the administration had realized. The story of Lee's "shabby" treatment in Honolulu by the State Department provided the icing on the cake.

Congress pressed EAP to conclude the Taiwan Policy Review that had apparently been repeatedly promised after my departure but never delivered. Our original idea had been to meet some of Taiwan's aspirations, ease some of our own burdens without changing the basics of our policy, and implement as much as we could under the radar to avoid tempting the PRC into exaggerated complaints. Instead, what Washington decided to do proved to be disastrous on all sides. The presidential policy decisions (released over the 1994 Labor Day weekend) did little to mollify Taiwan, nothing to help AIT's internal problems, and yet elicited a huge howl from Beijing.

After one and half years of work, the U.S. government had decided only that Taiwan could change the name of its U.S. offices from the nonsensical name they had been saddled with in 1979 (The Coordinating Council for North American Affairs) to a somewhat better one (The Taipei Economic and Cultural Office—TECRO); AIT officials in Taiwan could go to all government offices on the island; and TECRO personnel were welcome everywhere in Washington except the White House, the NSC, the State Department, and the Pentagon (some lawyer must have suggested this one to keep up the "nonpolitical" pretense). Transits by Taiwan leaders through the United States would now be allowed, but not visits. The policy also said we would support Taiwan's membership in organizations that were not restricted to governments (thereby saying we wouldn't help with any of their UN efforts, including with specialized agencies, no matter how vital or nonpolitical they were). There was nothing to remove those of us in the trenches from all of the silly restrictions that would have been easy to eliminate. Worse, now on the back foot with Congress, the administration felt a need to puff up these steps as major changes (which they obviously were not), ensuring that the PRC would turn up maximum fire in protesting them.

To demonstrate the "importance" of these changes (i.e., make a show for Congress), I received instructions to call on President Lee and other ranking officials in their offices to explain the new policy. I made the calls the next day. The Taiwan papers and the international press played up my formal calls on the president, prime minister, and foreign minister, and the Chinese denounced them. In truth, very little had really changed except that some in Beijing probably believed their own propaganda line that the U.S. had taken steps "to split off" Taiwan from China. For his part, Fred Chien called the changes "not enough," a sentiment echoed by their now growing ranks of supporters in Congress. Needless to say, I was deeply disappointed to see our earlier innocuous initiative turned into a debacle.

Knowing full well that the AIT director's call on President Lee in his office and a new name for Taiwan's offices in the U.S. were hardly earthshaking changes in U.S. policy (and being reassured of this many times by the department and Embassy Beijing and by the recent Ron Brown visit), Chinese officials did not dwell long on the changes. They also limited themselves to a pro forma protest when Transportation Secretary Federico Peña visited Taiwan (making him the second visiting U.S. cabinet member since 1979). The Chinese had more pressing issues with the U.S., the mainland's trade continued to expand with Taiwan, and cross-strait talks reached modest results, despite Beijing's frustration with Lee's public rhetoric and flexible diplomacy. Jiang Zemin was far more focused on trying to get an exchange of summits with President Clinton to boost his shaky internal prestige.

In January 1995 Jiang issued an eight-point proposal for

resolving issues with Taiwan that fell flat on the island. Lee's response three months later merely showed the gulf between the two sides. In essence, Beijing wanted Taiwan to agree to an eventual Hong Kong–style autonomous entity as part of the PRC. But Taiwan insisted that China had two sovereign governments, which should be recognized internationally—like the two Koreas— and negotiate a mutually agreed basis for unification sometime in the future. Lee repeatedly stated publicly and privately that he only sought a higher international profile for Taiwan, not independence or permanent separation from the mainland, and that unification remained his long-term goal. Privately, Taiwan's leaders were clear that the only possibility of unification was after a democratic regime emerged on the mainland that could negotiate a reasonable compact with Taiwan (and Tibet and Xinjiang) on a unified Chinese state, not a likely prospect after Tiananmen.

Meanwhile, Lee and Liu Tai-ying's next effort with the U.S. (which we at AIT only learned of months later from newspaper articles) was to arrange a donation of $2.5 million to Cornell University, ostensibly from alumni in Taiwan, to endow a Lee Teng-hui chair at the university. Cornell then issued an invitation to Lee to speak to an alumni gathering as part of its graduation ceremonies in June 1995. Over the next few months, Cassidy & Associates pulled out all the stops to make it happen. The East Asian Bureau was out of its league, and my efforts in Taipei to get Lee to back off from the Cornell trip failed completely. In May, Congress passed a nonbinding resolution urging President Clinton to allow a Lee visit, with a vote more like one in Beijing or Moscow than in Washington (396-0 in the House and 97-1 in the Senate).

Since the whole Cornell trip was an obvious ploy on Lee's part, I thought President Clinton would block it despite the support for the trip in Congress and the equally enthusiastic press, both of which had received copies of Cassidy's talking points. I was wrong. Clinton decided two weeks after the congressional vote not to emulate George Bush's all-out effort with Congress to save MFN; Clinton instead ordered that Lee be issued a visa to go to Cornell. In place of a quiet day of golf in Hawaii, Lee now had a forum in New York state for a major speech. I'm not sure whether Fred Chien or I was more stunned. Stape Roy, still our ambassador in Beijing, had the unpleasant task of trying to explain the inexplicable to the apoplectic Chinese.

Lee's June 9 speech in Cornell turned out to be fairly standard stuff—reminisces of his time at the school, expressions of gratitude to the United States, and a description of Taiwan's remarkable political and economic progress. A couple of weeks after the event, when I was in Washington for consultations, Lord showed his continuing frustration at the turn of events as he upbraided me for Lee's speech being "political." I could only respond with, "What did people expect after granting him a visa?" Several of Taiwan's congressional supporters flew to Ithaca to bask in the occasion. I'm sure the Cassidy people popped champagne corks after their victories (and enjoyed Taiwan's continuation of the lucrative contract for the next several years), but we were left trying to clean up the mess. It was a striking example of why Congress should keep some distance from the day-to-day foreign policy issues. Their meddling led directly to the most dangerous U.S.-China crisis in decades.

The Chinese protested strongly, withdrew their ambassador in Washington, put acceptance of the new U.S. ambassador–designate on hold, and announced a series of military exercises off Taiwan that were to continue well into the next spring. They also began to press for a reaffirmation of the U.S. "one-China" policy and assurance that there would be no further such visits. To add to the tensions, they arrested the anti-prison labor activist Harry Wu, a U.S. citizen, on espionage charges and refused our embassy consular access.

In Washington on consultations, I learned of a strong push from the East Asian Bureau and the Policy Planning Staff as well as at the NSC to undertake a fourth round of negotiations to conclude a new U.S.-China communiqué to mollify Beijing. The idea struck me as totally daft. The Third Communiqué of 1982, limiting arms sales to Taiwan, had committed us to an arms reduction that we could not fulfill without abandoning our promise to ensure Taiwan had sufficient arms to defend itself. The Chinese would use new talks as leverage to further limit Taiwan's future path, an outcome that would be foolish in strategic terms and disastrous politically in the United States. We would essentially be rewarding Taiwan's new democracy by agreeing with Beijing to further limit its future horizons (more than we had done nine months before by saying we would not support Taiwan's efforts to get into UN specialized agencies or other intergovernmental bodies.)

When I paid a call on Under Secretary for Political Affairs Peter Tarnoff, the Chinese ambassador Li Daoyu was going out the door. I voiced my objections to Peter against starting new communiqué talks, but he remained unconvinced. He reiterated what Li had told him about the possibility of dire consequences if the United States did not engage in these new talks.

I said, "Peter, the Chinese have been making similar threats about Taiwan for years."

He responded, "But Lynn, they really mean it this time!" I threw up my hands and, following the meeting, asked to see Secretary Christopher to discuss the plans for new talks.

Christopher greeted me warmly. We talked about our families, to the surprise of the Policy Planning chief sitting in the meeting, who apparently did not know I had worked for Christopher in the Carter administration. I went through my rationale on why new discussions on a communiqué with Beijing were such a bad idea. He didn't respond immediately, but in a meeting that afternoon to decide the issue (I was not invited), the secretary apparently listened as others made the case for starting negotiations on a Fourth Communiqué, and then vetoed the talks.

Shortly after the Cornell visit the PLA fired a round of missiles off Taiwan (continuing Beijing's preference for a military approach rather than diplomacy.) The U.S. did not react to the missiles (although it presumably came up during discussions with the Chinese), nor had it complained as China broke a tacit agreement not to deploy its short-range missiles to Fujian, which placed them within easy range of Taiwan. This set of missile tests may also have been intended to bolster the effort by some KMT conservatives to keep Lee from running in Taiwan's first direct democratic presidential election to be held the following March. If so, they had the opposite effect and quickly boosted Lee's popularity in Taiwan polls. The missile tests caused concern in Taiwan, but no panic. AIT worked hard to ensure the leadership did not overreact, and the atmosphere remained calm. The Chinese canceled a scheduled cross-strait meeting, while Lee made soothing calls for a return to dialogue.

The administration moved ahead to try to restore better relations with Beijing, beginning with a Christopher meeting with Foreign Minister Qian at an ASEAN gathering in early August 1995. I received instructions to tell Taiwan's leaders after the meeting that Christopher had not given in to the Chinese demand that Lee not be allowed to visit the U.S. again and that, despite the "rumors," there would be no negotiations on a "fourth communiqué." While there was some improvement in the tone of U.S.-Chinese private discussions, PRC propaganda continued to accuse the U.S. of trying to tear Taiwan away from the mainland and to weaken China economically, politically, and militarily. (Since American consumers were financing the country's 10 percent growth rate, the economic charge was particularly ludicrous.) An authoritative Chinse editorial pronounced U.S.-China relations to be at their lowest level since the establishment of diplomatic relations.

Another major setback for U.S. policy at this time was the departure of Stapleton Roy from Beijing to take up his new posting as ambassador to Indonesia. Stape's wisdom and steady hand in managing the relationship from Beijing for four years was sorely missed in the next few months as tensions mounted, and his successor (former senator James Sasser) was delayed first by Beijing and then by Jesse Helms in one of the senator's capricious efforts to manage the State Department.

By the time Under Secretary Tarnoff arrived for discussions in Beijing in August, the missile tests had been halted and Wu released. The U.S. had some cards of its own to play, including again dangling the possibility of a Jiang-Clinton Washington summit and holding back on a decision on whether Hillary Clinton would attend the UN women's conference scheduled the next month outside Beijing. The Chinese returned their ambassador to Washington and granted agrèment for Sasser. Nothing fundamental was resolved, but the conflicts had been papered over for the time being. The stock markets in Taiwan recovered, and life on the island returned to normal. But Lee's Cornell appearance and Beijing's reaction upset the delicate balance we had maintained for two decades in the triangular relationship. Lee's ego and popularity, not Taiwan's security, were the main beneficiary of the whole Cornell gambit. U.S. credibility for managing this sensitive issue was the main loss. A few months later fallout from the trip produced the most dangerous confrontation between the U.S. and Chinese militaries since the Korean War.

A New Taiwan Strait Crisis

While U.S.-China relations began to ease (even after Hillary Clinton's tough speech at the Beijing women's conference), tensions between the mainland and Taiwan only increased. Lee kept explaining to anyone who would listen (including me) that he only wanted greater international recognition and space for the island (which was true, at least at that point). But Beijing continued to proclaim ever more loudly that his real aim was independence and vowed to use all means, including force, if necessary, to stop the effort.

The attitude of most people on Taiwan remained quite understandable: If the island had been located near Hawaii, they would have voted overwhelmingly for independence; but they are practical people and well aware Taiwan is only ninety miles off the China coast. Most understood the need to maintain the fiction (and perhaps the reality under the right conditions) of eventual unification with the mainland.

It was the power struggle in Beijing, not Taiwan's democracy nor Lee's ultimate intentions, that drove confrontation. The leadership took a hard line not only against Taiwan but also against the British over Hong Kong, against Tibet, and against its own dissidents. The military (and its spokesmen) decried Taiwan's purported move toward independence almost every day, provoking the weak civilian leadership to embrace their views.

While the Cornell trip was grandstanding on Lee's part (aided by congressional fecklessness on the American side), it need not have been the earthshaking event the Chinese leadership made it out to be. Taiwan's geographic reality had not changed, its deep economic ties to the mainland were growing by the day, and repeated elections over several years showed no great desire by the people on Taiwan to buy the DPP's dream of independence. Wiser heads in Beijing would have understood Taiwan's mainlander-oriented New Party had no chance of coming to power, and a smarter policy would have dictated the need to reach an accommodation with Lee and his KMT. But the Chinese military exploited the Taiwan issue to bolster its claim for greater resources (the Soviet threat was now almost nonexistent) and to advance its political role in the struggles going on in Beijing with Deng's incapacitation. Longer term, it served the military's interests to portray the United States as a growing enemy bent on containing China and fostering an independent Taiwan.

Jiang Zemin attempted to bolster his internal position by repeating the PLA's tough rhetoric while craving the prestige that would come with being treated to full honors of a state visit to Washington. The administration eventually offered an "official working visit"—a summit without the bells and whistles—in connection with Jiang's planned October visit to New York for the UN's fiftieth anniversary. But Jiang held out for a full state visit. In the end, the two sides held a two-hour meeting in New York that produced statements about wanting to work together more closely on various issues of common interest, but little concrete progress. A meeting in New York certainly caused less domestic grief for the administration, particularly since Jiang clearly had nothing to offer, even if he had been given the full protocol treatment in Washington.

In the December 1995 Taiwan legislative elections, the breakaway (from the KMT) New Party won twenty-one seats (getting most of the 15 percent mainlander voters). The DPP added to its seats, but the KMT kept control. Lee remained far ahead in the polls for the March 1996 presidential election. Despite the fact that the PRC's intimidation campaign against him had helped rather than weakening Lee, Beijing decided to double down. Chinese military authorities warned their U.S. counterparts about their war preparations against Taiwan as part of the effort to intimidate Lee and to get the U.S. to pressure him. In response a U.S. aircraft carrier passed through the Taiwan Strait (the first such transit since 1979); and in early January Secretary of Defense William Perry publicly expressed his concern over the Chinese campaign. Li Peng added pressure in late January by saying that after Hong Kong and Macao reverted to China in 1997 and 1999, reunification of Taiwan would be a top priority for the PRC.

Tensions continued to increase, with widespread speculation in the press about a possible Chinese invasion of the island. I thought the Chinese actions were a calculated effort to scare Taiwan's voters, weaken the island's march to full democracy, and perhaps rein in Lee if he did win the election. Few military experts believed the Chinese had the capability to actually invade and occupy the island, but they could undoubtedly make life miserable for its people.

As tensions mounted, the pressure on us at AIT grew exponentially. Thousands of people visited our consular section to update U.S. passports for themselves or their American-born children, to apply for visas, or to ensure their paperwork was in order (or perhaps taxes paid) so they would have a clear escape route if a Chinese invasion became imminent. AIT personnel, including spouses teaching at the Taipei American School, were watched closely to see if they were preparing to leave. I appeared regularly at public functions to reassure the people of our sympathetic stance and support. I also asked AIT staff to stick closely to their daily routines and avoid any speculation that might spark panic in the population. As the Taiwanese assumed the Americans had inside information, we were under close observation to see if we planned an early escape. There was little doubt that missteps on our part could have had serious consequences.

On March 5 (eighteen days before the election), the Chinese announced a plan to test missiles off Keelung (Taipei's port) and Kaohsiung (Taiwan's second largest city and southern port), effectively bracketing the island to demonstrate they could hit anywhere on it and close off its international commerce. They fired the missiles three days later. The Chinese official responsible for Taiwan said the tests were designed to show the world that the island was "still part of China" and that Beijing had "the determination and capability to safeguard our sovereignty and territorial integrity." He said the PRC still wanted a peaceful settlement of the issue but added, "We would not hesitate to use all means, including military means, to achieve reunification of the motherland." Any sense of subtlety in the Chinese position had disappeared. This was a direct military threat against Taiwan, justified as a response to Lee's "flexible diplomacy" but more a reaction to Taiwan's vibrant democracy and a direct challenge to the United States as Taiwan's lone military supporter.

The morning after the missiles splashed into the ocean, I made a point of going to my normal Saturday golf practice to show that AIT was not spooked by the Chinese threats. Word went around quickly that Pascoe and AIT remained calm. Lee and other Taiwan leaders urged the public to stay firm in the face of Chinese bullying and efforts to disrupt the election. In fact, the people on Taiwan, while deeply concerned, put on an amazingly stoic public face. The stock market went down at first and there was a run on some basic necessities (the usual response of people in Taiwan in the face of an approaching typhoon) but no widespread panic. And the politicians continued their campaigns in the face of the PRC provocations. The Beijing leadership had not caused the chaos it undoubtedly hoped for and expected. Lee was right; democracy proved to be an effective stabilizer.

On Sunday, the Pentagon announced that the U.S. had ordered the aircraft carrier *Independence* to sail to a position off the Taiwan Strait. Christopher followed up by denouncing Chinese actions as "reckless" and warned of "really grave consequences" if Beijing continued to threaten Taiwan. He also announced that a second battle group led by the *Nimitz* had been ordered to sail from the Persian Gulf to the Taiwan area.

By this time, the international press had descended on Taiwan in droves, and I was busy backgrounding reporters on events and the U.S. response. With the *Independence* in place the U.S. Navy implemented a strategy that would have made the ancient Chinese strategist Sun Tzu proud: they invited a large group of journalists (international and local) to board the *Independence* for a demonstration of U.S. military might. CNN carried hours of coverage of warplanes roaring off the carrier, described the power of accompanying U.S. ships that bristled with the most advanced equipment and missiles, and interviewed no-nonsense American military personnel ready for action if necessary. It was a raw demonstration of U.S. power designed to show the world that the big guy had arrived in the neighborhood to deal with the local bully. Sun Tzu would have been thrilled that not a shot was fired. Morale in Taiwan skyrocketed as people stayed glued to their televisions.

Beijing got the point. The Chinese hastily informed American officials that China had no intention of invading Taiwan, and while they continued their exercises along with a fair amount of huffing and puffing, their effort had failed. The PLA had been bested at its own game. (Chinese military leaders admitted as much later, vowing they would not lose face to the Americans in a similar fashion again.)

The Taiwan presidential elections went forward on March 23 in a festive manner, with a huge voter turnout and massive international press coverage. Reporters who had come to the island to report on the expected war instead found themselves lauding Taiwan for the first ever direct election of a Chinese leader. Lee won 54 percent of the vote in a four-man race that saw the DPP candidate getting only 21 percent and the China-friendly New Party again getting 15 percent. PRC propagandists now tried to spin Lee's victory as a vote against independence and a victory for their intimidation efforts, citing the DPP's vote.

In a classic abrupt reversal, the PRC offered conciliatory gestures to Taiwan and (temporarily) dropped their anti-Lee rhetoric. Chinese readers must have had a severe case of whiplash from these propaganda shifts. China called off its exercises and the U.S. began withdrawing its ships. The crisis was over. Lee had won by a larger than expected margin, the people of Taiwan had shown their grit and support for democracy, and the PLA intimidation effort mostly succeeded in further undermining China's global reputation. The Clinton administration had earlier stumbled badly in its China policy; but when the chips were down, it came through with a demonstration of power that reaffirmed the U.S. role as the guarantor of East Asia's security.

The last three months of Diane's and my time in Taiwan were blissfully quiet. Lee used his inaugural address on May 20 to announce his readiness to travel to Beijing for high-level talks. The Chinese turned down the proposal, even though they had seemed open to such a meeting in the immediate aftermath of Lee's election. Among other issues, Beijing appeared quite worried that Lee might take up Jesse Helms's invitation to visit the U.S. once again, but Lee understood that the U.S. Congress might be less enthusiastic than it had been the year before, given the consequences of that trip. I praised Lee's outreach to Beijing and gave full U.S. backing for any effort to east tensions in one of my final speeches in Taipei.

We hoped productive cross-strait talks could be resumed, and I knew that the Lee administration had earlier decided to accept PRC proposals for direct air and sea links between the mainland and Taiwan. (It finally happened a decade after initially planned.) A successful visit to Beijing by National Security Advisor Tony Lake appeared to have laid the basis for improved ties in Clinton's second term. Much work remained to be done, but when we left Taiwan at the end of June, the triangular relationship appeared to be back on the right track.

Jim Wood, the Clinton Funding Scandal, and AIT's "Missing $5.3 million"

One area where I failed miserably during my time at AIT was in reforming the organization's unwieldy management structure and eliminate the petty annoyances that were part of everyone's life at AIT. David Dean had worked his way through an incredible number of bureaucratic obstacles to set up the unique AIT operation after normalization of relations with Beijing; but, inevitably, the new system's flaws became more and more apparent as time passed. The evolution of AIT in Taipei toward a more normal diplomatic post and the East Asian and Pacific Bureau's determination to treat AIT's director as a normal chief of mission kept the AIT "chairman" in Washington and his staff well removed from any policy tasks and increasingly focused on routine administrative issues (setting up meetings, handling funds flowing into the organization, signing contracts others had negotiated, and the like). Policy was made in EAP and higher up in the State Department and executed through the director in Taipei.

Unfortunately, AIT Washington's greatest weakness was where it should have been strongest—namely, in its administrative staff—and this had serious repercussions for us in Taipei. While the substantive side of the department and other agencies seemed to have few problems dealing with AIT's ambiguous role, the administrative side of the department still tied itself up in knots on issues involving AIT, just as it had a dozen years earlier when Dean set up the structure. People did not want to cross any ill-defined AIT

Taiwan: China's First Democracy   237

red lines, but they had no template to follow. They viewed AIT personnel and funding issues as complicated and best ignored. Given the obvious problems and the strong demand of the State Department inspectors to regularize procedures, I tried without success for three years to get the EAP's administrative people to take more responsibility for AIT. In the end, no one in the department would engage on AIT administrative reform, and problems were dumped on AIT Washington's administrative officer, who proved incapable of handling them.

AIT Washington's problems eventually led to a serious, self-inflicted crisis for the organization and the State Department. When I was in Washington on consultations in June 1995, the department's under secretary for management, Dick Moose (a former FSO and member of Clinton's Arkansas mafia), informed me that despite intense opposition from EAP, President Clinton would be appointing Jim Wood to the AIT chairman's position. Wood, a DC lawyer originally from Arkansas, had worked for some time in the early eighties for State's Office of Foreign Missions and later at the New York Stock Exchange. At Moose's request I met with Wood in the department's cafeteria. I explained how AIT worked and the importance of close coordination with the department and conformity to its regulations. Wood expressed surprise at my description of the limited role of the AIT Washington office, saying he believed AIT was meant to play a more independent role; he also made no effort to hide his anger at the department's strong opposition to his appointment. In our discussion, Wood talked up his relationship with President Clinton, but he came off to me as "the last Arkansan left standing" (desperately seeking a patronage job from his Arkansas buddies.) I left the session under-impressed and concerned about what his appointment meant for the future.

By December when I was in the department for consultations, Wood had received his security clearance and appointment to the job, despite Win Lord's continuing opposition and the resignation of two of the three board members of AIT who refused to be part of appointing Wood. By this time, Wood had been telling anyone who would listen that his reading of the Taiwan Relations Act made clear that AIT should act independently (in direct contradiction to the fact that it had been specifically established as a facade to continue our ties to Taiwan under State Department direction). He also expressed his bitterness toward Lord and EAP.

At the time of Wood's appointment, Acting Secretary Strobe Talbott sent him a letter (drafted by State's lawyers and EAP) making clear that AIT must follow the direction of the secretary of state in conducting relations with Taiwan and would receive its instructions from the EAP assistant secretary. The letter stated that the AIT director in Taiwan, "similar to a chief of mission," had responsibility for all overseas operations of AIT and worked under the policy guidance and supervision of the EAP assistant secretary. AIT Washington's job (again under direction of the EAP assistant secretary) was to meet, host, and accompany important Taiwan visitors, arrange and attend meetings as appropriate, sign documents, coordinate military sales, monitor financing, prepare budgets, and support AIT/Taiwan. Then came the punch line: "It is especially important that you coordinate closely with the department in fulfilling the responsibilities you will undertake." Getting the respective roles of EAP, AIT/Taipei, and AIT/Washington down in black and white was progress, but the instruction proved to have little effect on Wood. Before I went back to Taipei, Wood and I had another amicable discussion of our duties, but he left no doubt that he disagreed with his instructions. He still believed AIT should play an independent role and not be subject to the policy directives of the department.

Given Wood's penchant for asserting AIT's separate legal status and his inflated view of AIT Washington's importance, I instructed my financial people in Taipei to speed up our effort to ensure all our finances were in order and to get any excess money into the fund we had established to pay for the planned new AIT building in Taipei. The 1993 inspection report had been quite critical of AIT's multiple bank accounts and demanded a consolidation with clear records. (We deposited our visa fees with the department's regional financial office in Bangkok, and in accordance with normal department practice, spent those funds first before dipping into our U.S. dollar–appropriated funds.) When my administrative people tried to move a $5 million surplus to the building fund in 1994, AIT Washington scuttled the effort and months later said simply that the money was unavailable. Our staff tried to sort out the differences, concluding that the money must still be at the U.S. Treasury awaiting withdrawal. In March 1996, the AIT Board mandated a thorough audit to pin down exactly what money was where. I strongly supported this effort and welcomed the auditors to Taipei, learning only months later (well after we had left Taipei) that the AIT Washington administrative officer had directed the auditors to find out what AIT Taipei had done with the "missing $5.3 million." Needless to say, they found nothing useful in Taipei, because we had never seen the money.

Wood visited Taipei three times while I was director: for two weeks in February 1996 for orientation, a trip with the AIT Board, and as part of the U.S. delegation (headed by Vernon Jordan and Senator Jay Rockefeller) for the inauguration of President Lee in May. We usually saw very little of him during the visits except when our people accompanied him to formal government discussions. His meetings with some of the island's wealthier people aroused our curiosity and concern, but neither he nor his contacts would brief us on the discussions. At Lee's inauguration, I saw him with John Huang, a former deputy assistant secretary of commerce who I had worked with to promote trade with Taiwan, and with other Americans I didn't recognize.

After Lee's inauguration, I received a call from Taiwan's foreign minister, Fred Chien, essentially ordering me to play golf on Saturday. In the quiet of the golf cart, Chien unloaded. He told me that Wood had been using his visits to solicit campaign funds from Taiwan for the Clinton reelection effort and to persuade them to switch the lucrative Cassidy public relations contract (with the KMT, not the government) to a man named Paul Berry, who attended the inauguration with Wood. Chien said they knew well that U.S. law forbade campaign funds from non-American entities, since the Taiwan government had been badly embarrassed in 1992 when their representative in Honolulu hosted a fundraiser for Clinton. (Later newspaper accounts suggested that Liu Tai-ying, who had paid for the Cassidy contract out of KMT business funds, was less careful on funds for the Clinton campaign and may have offered to give $15 million before Chien and the president intervened to stop it.) Suddenly, Wood's earlier comments to me that Taiwan needed to quit supporting the Republicans and instead support their real friends, the Democrats, now made sense. I reported back to EAP by phone immediately after the golf game ended. Taiwan officials also informed the NSC and others in Washington, leading the Department of Justice to initiate an investigation into Wood's actions.

I left Taiwan a month later and heard nothing further about this issue until U.S. newspapers broke the story in late October that John Huang had led an effort to solicit money for the Clinton campaign from wealthy Asian donors. The articles usually carried a paragraph or more on Jim Wood's involvement. In early November, the FBI interviewed me about Wood's activities, and I told them what little I knew. The story continued for some time after the November election, but Wood's involvement seemed to fade because, as usual, he had apparently been inept in actually securing any money. (John Huang reached a plea bargain deal in 1999 giving him a year on probation for soliciting illegal foreign funds for the Democratic National Committee.)

As disgust in the department over Wood's antics grew, Secretary Christopher gave Wood the option of resigning or being fired. On Christopher's last day in office (January 19, 1997), Wood tried to hide out to avoid either happening; but he was finally forced to submit his resignation letter late in the afternoon to avoid being fired. Predictably, Wood did not go quietly. On February 23, 1997, he lashed out in a press conference, proclaiming his innocence and accusing AIT Taipei of fraud, corruption, and other alleged misdeeds he claimed he had tried to root out. The department spokesman refuted his statements point by point the next day. The media soon concluded Wood's allegations were phony, and Congress, which demanded it receive all relevant documents, was satisfied that AIT Taipei and the department had acted properly.

When the AIT Washington administrative officer resigned shortly after Wood's departure, the "missing $5.3million" miraculously appeared exactly where we had told them to look a year and a half earlier—it had never been withdrawn from AIT's account at the Treasury Department. Barbara Schrage, an old friend who as AIT Washington's deputy kept the organization together during Wood's disastrous tenure, called me with the news as soon as the money was discovered. Wood later sued the department for wrongful termination and damage to his reputation, but the court threw out his case. Subsequently, Wood filed a separate False Claims suit against AIT, which was thrown out on appeal. The ruling provided an excellent recounting of AIT's historical role and its legal status as an "instrumentality of the United States." [*See U.S. Court of Appeals for the D.C. Circuit. James C. Wood, Jr., Ex Rel. United States of America v. the American Institute in Taiwan, et al., Appellees, 286 F.3d 526 (D.C. Cir. 2002).*] The damage done to our "fig leaf" AIT operation by an unqualified political appointee had by now become sufficiently clear to the administration that it named an experienced China specialist as his successor.

Another Brief Break

Our departure from Taiwan in the summer of 1996 turned out to be as problematic as the moves from Beijing and EAP. In early June Under Secretary Tarnoff and Deputy Secretary Talbott asked me to go to Bosnia as deputy to Dick Klar, the newly named U.S. reconstruction czar for that benighted country. It was hardly a choice assignment. I would be separated from Diane for an indefinite period, and apparently my main function would be to keep an eye on Klar, who was known as a rich, take-no-prisoners San Francisco builder. Klar's style may have been what was needed to jump-start the effort to rebuild Bosnia, but serving as a buffer between him and the Europeans and other international aid donors as well as the Bosnians was not going to be a picnic.

After being formally assigned to the position, Diane and I split our shipment to separate things I would need in Sarajevo. Diane would go alone to the U.S. and get our house in Alexandria (which we had rented out) back in order. Then, during our final departure banquet in Taipei, I was pulled away from the head table to take a phone call from Talbott. Apparently Klar realized that the department leadership wanted me to keep an eye on him, and he responded by refusing to have any career official as his deputy. I breathed a huge sigh of relief and told Strobe I greatly appreciated his call. When I returned to my seat to tell Diane and Fred Chien what the deputy secretary had said, they both responded with huge smiles. Diane's relief at not returning to Washington alone was understandable; Fred explained that he had a flashback to the U.S. announcement breaking relations in December 1978 and feared this might again be some kind of bad news. Diane and I happily got on the plane a couple of days later and flew back to Washington.

Now in Washington (summer 1996) with no onward assignment, Lord asked me to write a paper on China policy that would serve as an introduction for people new to the China portfolio (especially political ambassadors). He also asked if I would like to do the annual three-month detail to the U.S. Mission to the United Nations, lobbying Asian ambassadors to support U.S. positions on issues before the General Assembly. Both jobs were very appealing. The New York position not only put us in a city we both loved; it also gave me the opportunity to learn something of the ways of the UN and to get to know a group of top-level Asian diplomats. Some people in the State Department thought a tour in Taipei would somehow tarnish one's reputation in Beijing, but Chinese colleagues now at the UN greeted me like an old friend and asked me about my "last tour" in Taipei. (So much for those who had argued against taking a high profile in Taipei.)

I worked on the China paper (inevitably dubbed by colleagues as a "Dummy's Guide to China Policy") through the fall and turned it in to Lord in early January. Intended to be readable and to the point, the forty-page essay gave an overview of the history of U.S.-Chinese relations, discussed some major issues in the relationship, looked at the tactics and perspectives of Chinese negotiators (including their skewed antiforeign take on the country's modern history), and tips on how to negotiate with the Chinese. I tried to explain, among other things, how the Chinese prepared for a negotiation and sized up their opponent. I included the truism that signing an agreement with the Chinese was only a first step. They would continue to implement what they considered the beneficial parts of the agreement and ignore what we wanted unless pressed with serious consequences for not following through. With some updating on China's new superpower status, the piece remains valid a quarter of a century later. However, I doubt that over four or five people ever read it. Given the track record of our later dealings with the Chinese, its recommendations obviously had no effect on U.S. policymakers.

I was also tasked to do a "Terms of Reference" paper for the planned Four-Party talks with the North Koreans (a subject I was far less familiar with), which I later learned was part of an EAP project to get me up to speed on the subject if the president signed off on a plan to name a Special Negotiator for North Korea. Again, I dodged a bullet when the position was not established.

11
Where Is Nagorno-Karabakh?

The aborted Bosnia assignment knocked me out of the running for other jobs when we returned to Washington, but I wasn't complaining about having some time to settle back into our house and spend a few leisurely months at the UN. The allegations of Jim Wood and his administrative officer about financial problems at AIT Taipei probably also played a role in the delay, especially since it would put a shadow on anything that involved Senate confirmation. After Wood left and his accusations were disproved, that problem went away. Strobe Talbott (now Deputy Secretary) called me to his office early in the year to offer me the job as Special Negotiator for Nagorno-Karabakh (N-K), a place I had barely heard of and could not have located on a map.

The breakup of the Soviet Union unleashed numerous ethnic conflicts in the newly independent countries, starting with the fight between Armenia and Azerbaijan over Nagorno-Karabakh, a region with a mixture of Armenians (the majority) and Azerbaijanis that Stalin had included as part of Azerbaijan. In 1988 (three years before independence), the Armenians began to push hard to get Nagorno-Karabakh incorporated into Armenia. Moscow refused and temporarily jailed the petitioners. The Armenian efforts soon led to nasty pogroms in Azerbaijan against Armenians, who fled. (Azerbaijan's capital, Baku, had been the sophisticated, leading city of the South Caucasus region and had a large Armenian population at the time.) When Azerbaijanis were similarly targeted in Armenia, they too began to flee in large numbers.

Gorbachev's government sent in a military force to preserve order, but they only further inflamed the situation. Some of the

Russian troops began to fight as mercenaries for either side and distributed sizeable quantities of weapons in exchange for cash. After the breakup of the Soviet Union in 1991, the two newly independent states engaged in open warfare. The Armenian/Karabakhi army emerged victorious, and in May 1994 the Russians brokered a ceasefire agreement that brought fighting to a halt and left Armenian/Karabakhi forces in control of Nagorno-Karabakh and seven surrounding (indisputably Azerbaijani, but now largely depopulated) provinces. By 1997, the Organization for Security and Co-operation in Europe (OSCE) Minsk Group, composed of three co-chairs (Russia, the United States, and France) and seven supporting countries (Belorussia, Denmark, Finland, Germany, Italy, Sweden, and Turkey) had assumed responsibility for settling the conflict.

Talbott was the Minsk Group's U.S. co-chair and by the time of my appointment had become fully engaged in seeking a solution. After receiving Senate confirmation (it was an ambassadorial posting), I replaced Joe Pressel as Strobe's deputy and became the U.S. representative to the Minsk Group.

Our interests in settling this distant conflict were quite straightforward. As I told the Senate, "We want to promote the resolution of conflicts that hold back social and economic progress, help them develop their economies and democratize their societies, and support the kind of regional cooperation that will give them the strength to counter 'divide and rule' tactics of players of the 'Great Game' that have plagued them for centuries." The issue also had political significance in the U.S. due to the intense concern of the one million or so Armenian-Americans and their powerful lobby, as well as our strategic stake in the region's rich oil potential.

Joe's and my superb deputy, Philip Remler, produced a negotiating paper (labeled the "step-by-step" approach) that formed the basis of the Minsk Group's efforts. Basically, the paper put the focus on resolving immediate security and humanitarian concerns and left the ultimate status of Nagorno-Karabakh to future negotiations.

[Remler's 2016 IPI paper "Chained to the Caucasus" is the definitive description of international efforts to resolve the Nagorno-Karabakh conflict.]

Over the next few months, Remler, Michael Keays, and I made six trips to the region and an equal number to Moscow, Paris, Vienna, Copenhagen, and Warsaw for consultations and negotiations.

In addition to the many hours of negotiations, the trips themselves were fascinating. Both Yerevan and Baku had air links to the outside world, but no commercial flights existed between the two countries. We flew on OSCE-chartered planes, usually Azerbaijani commercial aircraft, but made a couple of trips on UN-chartered planes with Swiss crews. The first time we used a UN plane, we sat on the Baku airport tarmac for two hours as Remler and his Russian counterpart sought to convince airport personnel that the UN plane would not pay a bribe to be allowed to take off. The fact that we had just been in a meeting with President Aliyev apparently did not persuade them sufficiently to forgo their usual reimbursement. A direct presidential order finally convinced them to let our plane go. (As a symbol of the level of corruption in the region, the new Baku airport terminal remained half completed at the time because the official in charge had stolen a large part of the construction money.)

Helicopter rides over the mountains to Nagorno-Karabakh were always nerve-wracking. The old Soviet MI-8s in the Armenian Air Force barely cleared the passes and presumably had no capability to deal with night or fog-enshrouded flights. Our Karabakhi hosts kept looking out their windows when we were in the N-K capital, Stepanakert, to be sure we took off for the return to Yerevan before any storms came through, a matter of real concern since twenty ranking Russian and Armenian officials had been killed a few years earlier when their helicopter slammed into a fog-enshrouded mountain on a similar peace mission. On one of our trips, a young girl hitched a ride on our helicopter. When we landed in Stepanakert, she immediately jumped off, knelt down on the ground, and began crossing herself. I could only think: "My sentiments exactly, kid."

When Strobe and French deputy foreign minister Jacques Blot joined us on a trip to Stepanakert in early June 1997, there was serious concern in Washington over the safety of this helicopter ride. Commerce Secretary Ron Brown had been killed a year earlier in a USAF crash in Croatia, and no one wanted to take chances with the deputy secretary of state's safety. After considerable back and forth with our defense attaché in Embassy Yerevan, the Armenians assured us they would use the presidential helicopter to carry the high-level guests to N-K. As we walked across the tarmac, my heart sank. Standing there waiting for us to board were the same old MI-8s that had become the stuff of our nightmares. Strobe, the former foreign correspondent, calmly climbed aboard, and we were on our way. (The French diplomat seemed considerably more dubious.)

The trip and meetings (other than the usual negative reactions on substance by the Karabakhis) went smoothly, including a visit to the formerly Azerbaijani mountain town of Shusha. (Leaving Shusha was like taking a tourist helicopter over the Grand Canyon, the ground literally dropped out from under you, going from a few feet to over a mile off the ground in seconds.)

On the flight back, Strobe used his excellent Russian to strike up a conversation with the pilot: "So, this is the president's helicopter, right?"

The quick response: "Oh, no. He has a good helicopter, but it is under repair today, and so we're using this old one." We all had a good chuckle.

A few weeks later, the Armenians did, in fact, provide us with the presidential helicopter for a trip to N-K when the fog was particularly bad. When we reported to Strobe on the results of our trip, I presented him with a photo of our group in front of the real "Presidential helicopter." He tacked the photo on his bulletin board, and I'm sure retold the story many times during the rest of his tenure at the department.

The negotiations with the Armenian president Ter-Petroysian and Azerbaijan's president Aliyev on our proposal were detailed and tough, but both wanted to cut a deal, and Philip Remler's draft was right on target. Azerbaijan would not agree to Karabakh leaders taking direct part in the talks, although we included them by traveling to Stepanakert for talks during each round.

(In the discussions, our French colleague Georges Vaugier spoke in French, I spoke in English, and Yuri Yukalov in Russian. In Armenia, Ter-Petroysian spoke in Armenian or Russian, but he also understood French well. Vice Minister Oskanian spoke Armenian and English, but limited Russian; Presidential Adviser Liberidian spoke Armenian, English, and French; Vaugier and I understood

Russian better than we spoke it. We kept the interpreters busy, and I found myself following my colleague Vaugier's comments in the Russian interpretation, since I don't speak French. In Azerbaijan and Nagorno-Karabakh, it was less complicated. Aliyev and the N-K leader spoke Russian, and our French and English comments were translated into Russian.)

After incorporating their changes, we had the agreement of both presidents by September 1997 and hoped to sign a document to lock it in at the annual OSCE meeting in December. In essence it called for Armenian/Karabakhi forces to withdraw from for all the occupied territories except Nagorno-Karabakh and Lachin (which included the corridor connecting Nagorno-Karabakh and Armenia proper); OSCE peacekeepers would deploy to ensure the peace; refugees could return to their homes in these areas; and the blockades would be raised. The final status of Nagorno-Karabakh would be subject to some sort of future popular referendum.

The Armenians would get recognition of the status quo in Nagorno-Karabakh, with its connections to Armenia and the lifting of the Azerbaijani (and, more importantly, the Turkish) blockades. Azerbaijan would get its provinces back, resolve its refugee problem, and nominally keep N-K as part of Azerbaijan for an undetermined length of time. Neither side would achieve the maximum goals it had failed to get on the battlefield, but it was a deal the international community (including the Russians) could accept. And it would provide the basis for a new era of cooperation and economic development in the South Caucasus region. As a further sweetener, there were discussions about the planned oil pipeline from Baku to Turkey possibly passing through Armenia. I went to Geneva for discussions with the UN's humanitarian chief, Sergio de Mello, to develop a plan for the return of refugees, including a major demining effort throughout the affected region.

Our plans for a December signing still faced two serious obstacles. Ter-Petroysian did not have the agreement of Nagorno-Karabakh leaders, and neither side had prepared its peoples for the necessary compromises. Ter-Petroysian understood it was essential for Armenia to develop its sluggish economy to ensure its long-term independence and stability. Removing the blockade by Turkey and Azerbaijan that cut off the country from its natural trading partners was key to his plan. A longtime champion of the Karabakhi cause, he was confident they would agree that the OSCE plan ensured that Nagorno-Karabakh would become a part of Armenia in the future. It turned out, however, that Karabakh officials (backed by the Armenian military) declined to agree to any plan that left the final status of their region up in the air. They argued Armenia had won the war and Azerbaijan must formally accept Nagorno-Karabakh's independence or incorporation into Armenia before it could get its other territories back. The Armenian president had also undermined his own popularity (and legitimacy as president) by rigging his 1996 reelection and suppressing opposition protests. To shore up his support after the election, he had brought in the clever and focused leader of Nagorno-Karabakh, Robert Kocharian, as his prime minister, a move that proved his undoing.

Neither Aliyev nor Ter-Petroysian had adequately prepared his own people to accept a compromise agreement. The Azerbaijanis tried to begin this effort through calculated leaks of the substance of the negotiations during the summer, but the leaks only made it more difficult for the Armenian side. While Aliyev had a tight grip on power in Azerbaijan and could weather the inevitable grumbling, Ter-Petroysian proved unable to manage the fallout in Armenia. N-K leaders led by Prime Minister Kocharian took their case to supporters in Armenia and the international Armenian diaspora over the summer and fall, turning opinion in these groups against the proposed settlement.

In early November during a visit by Stephen Sestanovich (who was now the State Department official responsible for countries of the former Soviet Union), Steve asked Ter-Petroysian how he planned to ensure the Armenian people's support for the deal. The president proudly announced that he had issued that very day a written statement explaining the agreement. The Americans in the room looked at each other stunned; at that moment, it seemed certain our efforts would not succeed. Predictably, Ter-Petroysian's enemies brushed off his explanation as traitorous. His statement failed to turn Armenian public opinion in favor of the deal, and his most powerful supporters deserted him. The December OSCE meeting turned out to be a pro forma discussion of the Nagorno-Karabakh issue rather than the victory celebration we had hoped for.

Three months later Ter-Petroysian resigned the presidency under threat of being removed by force. Kocharian won the election to replace him and promptly denounced the agreement. When our group traveled to Yerevan to talk with the new president, Kocharian left no doubt that the step-by-step approach was dead. He argued that the Karabakh side had been ignored during the negotiations (despite our repeated visits to Stepanakert) and that they could not agree to any deal that left open the possibility that the region might return to Azerbaijan's rule. We made one final trip to the region in our Minsk Group capacity in June 1988, which merely confirmed Kocharian's lack of interest in moving along the path that we had charted.

All of us involved were disappointed with this outcome including, I think, the Russian negotiators, although the role (or roles) the Russians were playing always remained somewhat obscure. My Russian counterparts, Yuri Yukalov and Vladimir Lozinsky, were friendly enough and acted collegially, unlike their predecessor, who had wanted to keep other mediators out of the game. Yeltsin had made a notable effort with the Armenian and Azerbaijani presidents in the spring to uphold the ceasefire, end inflammatory propaganda, and work toward an agreement. He also supported the extra muscle that U.S. participation could bring to the process. And at the G-8 meeting in Denver in June 1997, Presidents Clinton, Yeltsin, and Chirac made a strong show of unity by issuing a joint statement on the conflict.

But Russian foreign policy was far from unified; the security services had their own policy toward the former Soviet republics, which was to bring them back under Mother Russia's control. While Russian mediators worked closely with us using common talking points, we were never sure what the Russian intelligence and military personnel might be saying to their counterparts behind our backs. We suspected the Soviet security services were egging on the tough line of Karabakh and anti–Ter-Petroysian Armenians against a peace deal

With the failure of our efforts, it was clearly time for Remler and me to move on to other issues and turn the Nagorno-Karabakh negotiations over to others. There were two later times when it appeared a negotiated settlement might have been possible. In 1999,

Kocharian and Aliyev met four times to work out a land swap deal in great secrecy. Both the Minsk Group negotiators and their own foreign ministers were apparently kept in the dark. The effort collapsed after a group of gunmen stormed the Armenian Parliament in October, killed the Armenian prime minister and six other officials, and held forty parliamentarians hostage. During his time as president of Russia, Dmitry Medvedev made a determined effort to resolve the Nagorno-Karabakh issue, hosting some eleven meetings between Azerbaijani president Ilham Aliyev and Armenian president Serzh Sargsyan. But he had no more success on Karabakh than earlier efforts had and gave up when he felt the two sides were merely stringing him along.

Then, in September 2020 Azerbaijan's forces initiated a new war and this time won. Russia mediated a settlement in November that left Azerbaijan in control of those of its districts that had been occupied by Armenia. But its peacekeepers failed to halt further Azerbaijani advances. Three years later Azerbaijan took over all of Nagorno-Karabakh, and most of its Armenian citizens fled to Armenia. A quarter century of negotiations had failed, and those Armenian hardliners both in Armenia and abroad who opposed the solutions the world community had offered saw their worst fears come true.

12
Ambassador to Malaysia

I received a call in March 1988 from the director general of the Foreign Service, Edward "Skip" Gnehm, asking if I would be interested in going to Malaysia as ambassador. He said the department's leadership was looking for someone to take on the rocky relationship with Malaysian prime minister Mahathir bin Mohamad; my time dealing with the Chinese and Russians apparently served as my main qualification for the job. After clearing the offer with Diane, I agreed, and became the department's nominee. The White House informally agreed to the appointment, and the paperwork went quickly, as I had just been through the confirmation process a year earlier for the Nagorno-Karabakh position.

I turned my attention to learning about Malaysia and the Asian economic crisis gripping the country. The picture was not a pretty one. Malaysia's 73-year-old Prime Minister Mahathir was a brilliant, hard-driving leader who had taken on the role of CEO of his country of twenty million Malay, Chinese, and Indian people. In a couple of decades he had transformed it from a plantation-based agricultural exporter to a major manufacturing nation that played a key role in the East Asian electronics export chain. Arrogant, conspiratorial, authoritarian, and prone to monumental projects, Mahathir had reason to be confident in his successes. Unfortunately, he also had a huge chip on his shoulder against his real and supposed enemies.

Seventeen months earlier, in January 1997, everything had seemed to be going right for Malaysia and for the prime minister. During a visit to Silicon Valley, Mahathir was feted by the giants of the American technology miracle. He asked them to invest even more in Malaysia to help build a replica of their California success in his small country. After a decade of 8 percent economic growth, Malaysians' standard of living had soared. Mahathir's eye-catching development projects, paid for by oil revenue from its efficient national oil company Petronas, were well on the way to completion. To explain his success (and justify his authoritarian style of rule) Mahathir had taken up the slogan first put forward by Singapore's Lee Kuan Yew, touting "Asian values" (including hard work, education, and collectivism) as being superior to the West's liberalism and human rights.

Then, Mahathir's cozy world fell apart. On July 2, 1997, the Thai government devalued the baht, shining a spotlight on the volatile combination of corruption, cronyism, and bad loans embedded in much of the Asian economic miracle. China's rise added to the problem since it drew in many of the low-wage export jobs that had fueled the early success of the Asian tigers. Suddenly, the economies of all these countries came under the international microscope in a stress test of their economies and their currencies. Malaysia was in a much stronger position than Thailand, Indonesia, Hong Kong, or South Korea, all of whom had massive international debts. But Mahathir gave in to his paranoia and frustrations, taking the setbacks personally. Always a petulant critic of the West, he now unleashed a bitter attack on the international financial system, which had provided the infrastructure that allowed him to create modern Malaysia.

He lashed out at "foreign conspiracies" that were in his view responsible for undermining Malaysia and other Asian countries, putting the blame for the crisis on foreign and internal currency speculators, especially his old bête noire, George Soros. (Soros, famous for bringing down the overvalued British pound in 1992, had earned Mahathir's enmity when the Malaysian PM authorized his Finance Ministry to speculate with the country's currency reserves in support of the pound, losing the bet and most of Malaysia's currency reserves to Soros.) Mahathir now found currency trading to be "unnecessary, unproductive, and immoral." He even blamed the crisis on what he called an international Jewish conspiracy designed to thwart Muslim progress. For good measure, he denigrated the "Universal Declaration of Human Rights" as oppressive and condemned the West as racist.

His deputy Anwar's effort to appease the international financial community with a softer tone could not repair the damage. Seeing the formerly rational, if acerbic, Mahathir come unglued unnerved the international financial community and drove the country's currency, the ringgit, and the Malaysian stock market into a massive fall. In the annual meeting of ASEAN in Kuala Lumpur (KL) in late July 1997, Secretary of State Madeleine Albright mocked Mahathir's fantasies in her widely publicized "Don't Cry for Me ASE-ANIES" skit, singing, "Called George Soros. Talked market forces. Hatched a conspiracy. The rest is history." Meanwhile, the Malaysian economy continued to tank and interim attempts to stop the decline failed.

By December 1997, Mahathir and Anwar threw in the towel. As Thailand, Indonesia, and South Korea agreed to tough IMF austerity measures in exchange for large loans, Malaysia instituted its own set of austerity measures and controls that mirrored the IMF approach, while denouncing the IMF as part of the conspiracy. The effort provided some stability, but its main consequence was to squeeze any remaining dynamism out of the economy. Growth dropped from the 8 percent of past years to a negative 2.8 percent in the first quarter of 1998 and a negative 6.8 percent in the second quarter, with a 22 percent decline in construction. By then, the ringgit had lost 40 percent of its value and the Malaysian stock market had declined 75 percent in dollar terms. Mahathir's instinctive but foolish bravado and the IMF-type program both seemed to produce nothing but disastrous results.

In Washington in the summer of 1998, as I was reading up on events, the situation looked dire indeed, and prominent American economists were questioning the entire Treasury/IMF approach to the crisis. Adding to the deep concern in Washington, the Russian economy was in freefall. Mahathir had had enough. He reduced Anwar's role in economic decision making—Anwar had supported the IMF approach—and moved to stimulate the economy and cut the high prime interest rate. On September 1 Mahathir imposed currency controls and fixed the exchange rate of the ringgit to the dollar. There was a predictable storm of protest in the international press and among many prominent economists. But when I was making the rounds prior to going to Kuala Lumpur, I asked Under

Secretary of the Treasury Tim Geithner what I should say about Mahathir's "unorthodox" approach. He gave me some excellent, if surprising, advice (which certainly rang true from my reading about the crisis): "Don't say anything if you can get by with it. We don't really know what caused this mess, and we're not sure what the best approach is to fix it. Mahathir's way may turn out to be as good as any other."

A Delayed Arrival

Meanwhile, an odd game played out in Washington over the summer, raising doubts about whether I would be formally nominated by the president and confirmed by the Senate to go to Malaysia. The nomination process for my appointment had mysteriously slowed. My friend Dick Hecklinger, picked for ambassador to Thailand at the same meeting at which I had been chosen for Malaysia, had been announced by the White House on June 25, but my nomination remained in limbo. Then in late July I saw a copy of a nasty, totally inaccurate memo that accused me of various financial irregularities at AIT, echoing Wood's accusations of eighteen months before, including the "missing $5.3 million." The charges were easily refuted since they had already been debunked by the department. Then I heard that the White House had instructed State Department security people to thoroughly investigate other details of my time in Taipei, including going over all official entertainment vouchers. The security people were appalled at having to spend valuable time reviewing whether we had accurately counted each egg served to official guests when there was no evidence of wrongdoing. Fortunately, Diane and my superb office assistant, Kathy Gaseor, had kept meticulous records of our extensive entertaining in Taipei. The review turned up nothing, but the White House continued to stall on the announcement.

As I stopped by to talk to the director general one afternoon, I was surprised to see the former AIT Washington administrative officer who had given us so much grief in Taipei and lost her position over mishandling of the $5.3 million issue and other lapses. It turned out she worked part-time in the office and had learned of my pending nomination to KL. Apparently, she had written the memo charging me with all sorts of misdeeds and had worked with Jim Wood to get an old friend in the White House counsel's office to block my assignment. Even though we now knew what was going on (and she quickly had to look for another job), Wood's White House contacts continued to drag out the process. Finally, under a deadline from the Senate Foreign Relations Committee, Secretary Albright called the White House counsel and demanded they quit stalling and announce my nomination so the Senate could consider me for confirmation. The announcement was made that same day, September 9, and the Senate confirmation hearing went forward without any problem.

Anwar's Downfall

With my appointment already delayed, my predecessor, John Malott (who had been held up by Senator Helms in 1995) asked to stay in Kuala Lumpur until Christmas in order to host a planned visit by President Clinton to the November APEC summit to be held in KL. This was fine with me since it gave me more time to study and consult on this small, but complex country, learn a bit more Bahasa, do a formal swearing-in, and enjoy Christmas with our family. But, in yet another example of the vagaries of the State Department assignment process, the delay also meant I was available when the department's pick for ambassador to Pakistan came under heavy criticism in the Senate, and they needed a quick replacement who could be easily confirmed. I was asked and, of course, agreed to be considered, but suggested their other available candidate, Bill Milam, a South Asia specialist, was far better qualified than someone who had only spent one week in the country on a War College trip. Common sense prevailed, he got the job, and we were again on track to go to Malaysia.

In the meantime, U.S.-Malaysian relations took a dramatic downturn, ensuring that we would arrive to an extremely frigid reception. Just before my confirmation hearing, Mahathir had imposed currency controls and fired his deputy, Anwar Ibrahim. Outside observers initially tied Mahathir's actions to a dispute over policies to manage the economic crisis, but Malaysians knew better. This was an existential political brawl between the country's two most experienced political fighters for control of the future of Malaysia.

Anwar was (and is) an ambitious and gifted politician. First emerging on the Malaysian scene as a firebrand Muslim youth leader, he surprised his supporters by joining UMNO, the government party, rather than the opposition Islamic party PAS, reportedly because he calculated that UMNO was a far better vehicle for his ambitions. Mahathir, who had become the head of the party and prime minister a year earlier, recognized Anwar's skills and his appeal to Islamic and youth constituencies, where Mahathir's own following remained weak. Anwar became a minister a year later, rising to become finance minister in 1981 and deputy prime minister in 1983.

Anwar's charming personality, free market leanings, espousal of liberal political views, and administrative and rhetorical skills made him a darling of the international media and the global political elite. The contrast between the urbane and reasonable Anwar and Mahathir's arrogance and acerbic personality fed the narrative that Anwar was the new type of liberal Muslim leader so desperately sought by the West to deal with the global rise of fundamentalist Islam. *Time* magazine's Asia edition put him on its cover in October 1997 with the heading "Anwar and the Future of Asia." The *New York Times* called him "a standard-bearer for a new and more liberal generation of Asian leaders." Washington and the American Embassy in Kuala Lumpur agreed with this appraisal. On the other hand, many members of the Malaysian elite and minority groups in Malaysia were far less enamored with Anwar, distrusting his ambition and Islamist roots, and more comfortable with the Mahathir-led status quo.

Tensions between the two men boiled over in June 1998 when a prominent Anwar supporter decried nepotism and cronyism in the ruling party and government and emphasized the need to clean up corruption. Mahathir quickly turned the tables on his attackers, cut Anwar out of a decision-making role in the economy, and dismissed some of his prominent supporters. At the same time, an explosive book appeared in KL accusing Anwar of various crimes and sexual improprieties.

Anwar was fired on September 2. His supporters took to the streets to call for his reinstatement and Mahathir's overthrow. Anwar addressed several of these rallies, which included thousands of protestors, stoking feelings of resentment and demanding that Mahathir and his cronies resign. Calling itself *"reformasi"* (after the successful Indonesian model that forced President Suharto's resignation), the movement drew heavily from Anwar's traditional youth and Islamic constituencies. But it also revealed deep strains in Malaysian society brought on by the country's closed political leadership, widespread corruption, and the economic downturn.

Mahathir remained in firm control and ruthlessly used his domination of the political scene, police, courts, and press to destroy his rival. Anwar was arrested and beaten by the police, along with a number of his supporters. (The timing could not have been worse, since a large number of foreigners, including Queen Elizabeth II, were in town for the Commonwealth Games.) The Malaysian press carried lurid stories about Anwar's sex life and his supposed crimes against the state. In the West, particularly in Washington, these events seemed to mean not only the loss of a friend, but also a reversal of history and a defeat for future democratic forces. Anwar was again on the cover of the Asian edition of *Time*, this time with the caption "Malaysia Without Anwar".

Anwar's trial on sodomy charges began in early November with high drama and a fair amount of farce, just two weeks before Malaysia hosted the APEC summit that was to include President Clinton and other world leaders. Anwar showed up in court with a black eye, which only added to the sense that he was being treated unfairly and being tried on trumped-up charges. In the end, Vice President Gore attended the meeting in President Clinton's place, and Secretary Albright met with Anwar's wife to show U.S. support. In his speech to the formal banquet that included other APEC leaders, Mahathir, and several members of the Malaysian elite, the vice president praised *reformasi* and "the brave people of Malaysia" who had demonstrated for Anwar. He and most of his delegation then left the room. Mahathir and the Malaysians, along with quite a few others at the dinner, considered Gore's comments a crude insult. Gore's departure before dinner ended (although the hosts had been informed he would leave early) only added to the sense of a deep breach of diplomatic protocol and offense against Asians' sense of courtesy. Mahathir's firebrand trade minister Rafida called the performance a "disgusting, rude intervention into our local affairs" and chided Gore's "bad manners." The mild-mannered Foreign Minister Badawi charged that it was a "gross interference in the internal affairs of the country" and "abhorrent" for the U.S. to incite lawlessness by people trying to overthrow the government. Mahathir fumed but said little publicly.

Gore and his entourage defended the speech, cheered on by American editorial writers. But most of the other APEC participants appeared perturbed that the Americans had turned a major economic meeting into a political brawl at a time of regional economic distress. Some Malaysian observers thought the remarks probably hurt the *reformasi* cause by allowing Mahathir to portray the movement as a tool of outsiders whom he had been blaming all along for the economic crisis.

I happened to be in Silicon Valley consulting with high-tech firms when several American businessmen returned from the meeting. These normally Democratic supporters expressed anger at Gore and unloaded their frustration on me. They thought it foolish to offend the Malaysians in such a public way and expected it to hurt their own operations in Malaysia. Rafida told the press that several Americans had apologized for Gore's performance; and judging by what I heard in California, I don't doubt it.

Focusing on U.S. Interests

As Diane and I arrived in Kuala Lumpur in January 1999, I couldn't help comparing the atmosphere with the tensions in Moscow after the Soviet invasion of Afghanistan and the boycott of the Moscow Olympics or in Beijing after the Tiananmen massacre. But our underlying relationship with Malaysia had a much stronger basis than with the two Communist governments, and we both needed to preserve and build on that base despite the very public displays of animosity.

My formal instructions from President Clinton included the usual charge to promote American prosperity, American security, and human rights and democracy. The informal instructions from Washington, however, were clear: do what you can to turn down the noise and get things back to fundamentals with Malaysia. Policy makers in Washington by now understood that their preferred leader Anwar had lost a power struggle, and we would have to continue to deal with Mahathir despite his off-putting style. And, whatever its leader's faults, Malaysia was still a multicultural society with a moderate Muslim majority that functioned much better than many other multiethnic countries. Its fundamentally British-style political and legal structures, however flawed, remained in place. Its moderate internal and external policies generally supported U.S. goals. It had just been elected to the UN Security Council and could prove to be valuable in the growing global struggle with Islamic extremist organizations. Malaysia continued to be a major U.S. trading partner. U.S. companies, Malaysia's top investors, valued its key role in the Asian electronics industry, with its efficient companies and commitment to protect trade secrets. Malaysia also remained the chief protector of the Malacca Strait, a critical link in the global economic infrastructure.

Despite the personal spats, my instructions were to get things back to "Malaysian normal," cooperating with Malaysia where possible and trying to encourage improvement in some of the policies and areas we considered flawed, including democracy and human rights. In addition, I intended to try to restore a dignified image of the United States as a friendly superpower and avoid the temptation to sink into useless acrimonious exchanges with Mahathir.

The U.S. Foreign Service prides itself on providing Washington with accurate reporting on the situation abroad whatever political winds are blowing at home, and I was determined that Embassy KL would keep up this tradition. We tried to describe events accurately even if it did not fit into the Washington perception of Malaysia, including predicting (accurately) that Anwar's movement would do poorly in the November 1999 polls. We took all the necessary steps to promote democracy and human rights, such as calling on all opposition figures with flags flying and reaching out to civil society, but Washington trusted us to find a balance that allowed promotion of U.S. interests across the board.

In my Senate testimony, my swearing-in speech, and brief

remarks on arrival in KL, I emphasized the broad range of positive economic and security ties between our two countries, the critical need for close cooperation in pursuit of common goals, and the promise of future cooperation, while noting our differences and calling for an end to Malaysia's anti-U.S. rhetoric. I emphasized that the United States hoped for Malaysia's political and economic progress and harbored no hidden agenda in its relations with Malaysia. Asked the inevitable question on our arrival in KL if my approach on the Anwar issue would be the same as my predecessor's, I avoided substantive comment, noting that we had just arrived and needed time to better understand the situation in Malaysia. Our support for democracy and a fair trial for Anwar were, of course, staples of my speeches, and I made an early, well-publicized call on Anwar's wife to demonstrate our support for democracy and justice. But U.S. interests in Malaysia were wide-ranging, and our other interests could not be held captive to Anwar's fate

Efforts to Bridge the Gap

For the first month and a half after our arrival, Diane and I were restricted by the dictates of protocol to deal only with the American community and the Foreign Ministry until we had formally presented credentials to the king. Malaysia has a rotating kingship in which each of the seven regional hereditary sultans acts as head of state for a term of five years. Although Mahathir had eliminated the royals' political power, the king, the sultans, and their elaborate ceremonies served as important symbols of Malay domination of the country. Pictures of Diane and me dressed for royal occasions show me togged out in a morning coat and her in a very proper hat and gloves. (I couldn't help thinking we looked more like the emperor and empress of Japan than representatives of the American government.) I had hoped to call on each of the sultans in their domains, but the elaborate protocol of such visits (planned a month or so in advance with the potential for great offense if it was necessary to cancel) made visits to some of them impractical.

Over the next months and years, Diane and I worked hard to connect with Malaysians by an intensive effort to reach out to them. We attended or hosted hundreds of events, using our charming residence and excellent cook to connect with Malaysians of all religions and political stripes. (Given the Muslim strictures against pork and Indian avoidance of beef, we served so much chicken that I swore off eating it for several months after we returned to Washington.) Diane is a superb hostess and organizer, and she worked at our outreach effort with great energy. She orchestrated three glittering Fourth of July receptions at our residence, complete with exotic tenting, the enthusiastic participation of chefs and staff from all American-branded hotels in the city, and, of course, formal ceremonies that included our resplendent Marine Guards. These affairs (paid for by donations, not the American taxpayer, and organized using the free labor of Diane and others) were a highlight of the KL social scene and well attended. (Fortunately, the often-stormy July weather cooperated each time, although one year the clouds burst just as we were escorting our last guests to their car.) Small lunches (often one-on-one) at our residence provided the best way to learn what was really going on among the Malaysian elite, to promote U.S. interests on a wide range of issues, and to inform visiting Americans of the realities of the country as we saw them.

While I worked the political, business, and sometimes cultural side, Diane took an active part in reaching out to the extremely influential women of Malaysia. The social scene was highly organized; the young queen wed to the septuagenarian king enjoyed the social whirl with foreigners; and Diane found herself running booths at bazaars, attending lavish luncheons, concerts, and other social events to show the flag and reinforce the fundamentally friendly (if sometime volatile) relationship. While these efforts form a key part of the diplomatic life in most countries, they were particularly critical in a small country that bristled all too easily at superpower arrogance, and where our leaders had engaged in harsh exchanges. Diane's willingness to volunteer her time and expertise played a critical role in helping promote U.S. goals.

A Recovering Malaysian Economy

When we arrived, we could see evidence everywhere of the Malaysian economy's disastrous previous year and a half. Half-finished buildings and idle cranes dotted the downtown areas; new buildings sat empty after companies went bankrupt or downsized. The only exceptions were the government-sponsored megaprojects. The newly completed KL airport vied with Hong Kong's to be Asia's most modern aviation facility; the Petronas Twin Towers, then the world's tallest buildings, proudly dominated the KL landscape even though virtually empty; and construction continued on Petrajaya, the new administrative center, and Cyberjaya, the new high-tech city, both strategically located between Kuala Lumpur and the airport. By the spring of 1999, the economy as a whole was on the upswing—Mahathir and his supporters credited his unorthodox approach, although countries that followed the IMF austerity formula were growing at about the same pace—and large investment inflows soon resumed. By the end of our tour in Malaysia in the summer of 2001 most of the cranes were back in service, with the shell buildings completed or under construction and economic growth back on track.

Promoting U.S. business, as in Taipei, was again a major responsibility of the embassy. I made speech after speech extolling the benefits of close cooperation in high-tech ventures, the bright future for e-business, the advantages of American universities, and the value for both countries of close Malaysian-U.S. cooperation on trade and investment issues. The extensive manufacturing ties between Malaysia and the United States had been in place for decades, and the economic crisis proved to be little more than a blip in continued heavy U.S. investment in the electronics sector. But the bad political blood between Mahathir and American leaders meant that the Malaysians needed considerable reassurance on the political side about the future of those ties. I also sought in my speeches and conversations to push forward a dialogue on trends in the global economy and their meaning for our two countries. With the potential of e-commerce just beginning to take shape and the influence of the internet expanding by the day, Malaysia sought to stay ahead of the trend, relying on the U.S. to help point the way. Several of Malaysia's "smart" innovations in areas like highway tolling and identity cards were well ahead of the norm in the United States.

The tendency by many Malaysians to mimic European rhetoric on the import and use of GMO products occupied more of my time than it should have. As a boy growing up in Missouri farming country, I saw new crop strains being tested in fields all the time. It was frustrating to note how easily intelligent people who had never seen a wheatfield replayed the unscientific objections to genetically modified grains. I took it as a personal challenge to deflect Malaysian objections and protect U.S. grain exports, but the overheated news stories flowing in from Europe proved to be a major challenge.

The Malaysians for their part expressed anger over a growing U.S. movement against the use of latex medical gloves. While not denying that latex allergies could be a problem, they believed much of the U.S. concern was being stoked by the synthetic glove industry to undermine a major Malaysian export. Similarly, they felt the U.S. overplayed health concerns about palm oil, another important Malaysian export, undermining its sale to the U.S. and the rest of the world. I had many tough discussions with Malaysian ministers on all of these issues, but I tried hard to stick to the science, listening carefully to their concerns while pressing them on restrictions on GMO products.

The U.S. government took seriously the possibility that the rollover of computer systems at the turn of the millennium on January 1, 2000, might have serious consequences for businesses and global infrastructure. The possible danger that computers programmed with the year given in two rather than four digits might read the date as 1900 rather than 2000 and thus malfunction with drastic consequences—the so-called Y2K bug—led the U.S. to issue global warnings. As part of our outreach on the new internet economy, we put out press statements and held numerous discussions to ensure the highly computerized Malaysian economy would not itself suffer major harm or export problems to the U.S. or other countries. Our seminars in the spring of 1999 were "standing room only," as Malaysian and U.S. businessmen sought the latest USG assessment of the potential danger and suggestions for countermeasures. In the end, the Y2K problem turned out to be mostly a nonevent, but efforts years later by hackers to disrupt major infrastructure systems demonstrated that the underlying concern was real.

In Kuala Lumpur, the Y2K issue also provided the theme for the Sean Connery–Catherine Zeta-Jones movie *Entrapment*, released in April 1999 and set in Malaysia. The film presented a stunning portrayal of the Twin Towers and KL's modernity, but Mahathir, always on the lookout for perceived slights from foreigners, chose to blast the film as part an international plot to denigrate Malaysia because it showed some footage of a traditional Malacca canal in Kuala Lumpur (clearly meant to signal to the audience that they were in Asia). It was again a striking example of Mahathir letting his paranoia get the best of what should have been a nice bit of free publicity and branding for Malaysia.

A Tragic Terrorism Miss

Malaysia had the misfortune to become a significant footnote in the 9/11 disaster. By 1998, according to the Report of the 9/11 Commission, Al-Qaeda had established a link with the Southeast Asian terrorist organization Jemaah Islamiyah (JI). The danger of this connection became evident in the ensuing years. To encourage tourism, Malaysia had a relaxed visa regime that allowed visa-free entry to almost all of the countries in the Mideast. This ease of entry, along with a belief among the Jihadists that the new airport had lax security, despite U.S. help to improve it, plus the Al-Qaeda-JI tie made Malaysia a convenient connecting point for regional and global terrorist actions.

In early January 2000, I was informed that the U.S. had learned (through NSA intercepts, according to the Commission Report) of a meeting of Al-Qaeda terrorists underway in Kuala Lumpur. I suggested we ask the Malaysian police to arrest them under their Internal Security Act, which allowed for preventive detention for up to two years (we had never liked the law, but I felt this case merited it.) I was told that Washington's instructions were only to keep an eye on the terrorists so they could find out what they were up to. I frankly thought the Malaysian police had adequate means to extract information on their intentions, but this was not an argument I could win with Washington. A few days later, three of the men flew to Bangkok, where the CIA promptly lost track of them. Two of them then flew on to Los Angeles on January 15 and entered on legitimate visas. Neither the State Department nor the FBI had been notified about the potential danger they posed.

Tragically, these two men led the group of hijackers on American Airlines 77 that flew into the Pentagon on 9/11. Among those killed was our neighbor (and the mother of our daughter Gwen's close friend) Norma Steuerle, as she began a trip to visit her daughter, then a Navy doctor in Japan. The 9/11 Commission Report bemoaned the fact that the two terrorists had not been picked up in the United States, interrogated, and had their connections investigated. The report concluded that "the simple fact [was] their detention could have derailed the [9/11] plan." They could equally well have been detained and interrogated in KL twenty-one months earlier and sitting in a Malaysian jail on 9/11.

Increasing Religious Conservatism

Many longtime observers of the Malaysian scene commented to me about the increased influence of conservative Islam in the country in the eighties and nineties. Saudi contributions of mosques and religious teachers—a policy Anwar's detractors blamed on him—had been a key factor. But a growing disenchantment with the urban elite, UMNO's crony politics, and the continued lag in the standard of living of poor provincial Malays, despite the laws biased in their favor, contributed to this trend.

Two attacks in April and July 2000 heightened concerns about religious extremism. Militant Muslim separatists from the Philippines kidnapped twenty-one foreigners on the popular diving island of Sipidan. (An American couple avoided being taken captive by refusing to board their boats.) We facilitated cooperation between the Philippine and Malaysian authorities on the Sipidan incident, since we had excellent contacts with both sides on counterterrorism operations. Then twenty-nine members of a Malaysian Islamic group looted weapons from army camps in Perak state.

The arms seizures involved a level of violence not seen in Malaysia since the end of the Communist insurgency.

The country's sharia courts, which had jurisdiction in marital matters, became increasingly assertive, and women were pressed more and more to wear the hijab in public. In reaction to changing public opinion, Malaysian royalty and political leaders at cocktail parties had become adept at sensing when a camera came into range and hiding their drinks. Large receptions would have nonalcoholic punches out in front for the cameras, with most guests hanging around in a back area where the champagne, wine, and liquor flowed freely. The government did eventually regain control of the mosques and calmed the content of the sermons. The rise of conservative Islam, however, made it hard for UMNO to ignore the religious pressures or to win elections without resorting to measures that further undermined the party's legitimacy.

We worked hard at the embassy to reach out to all Malaysians and to develop an understanding of the growing importance of conservative Islam. We also tried to start a dialogue inside the U.S. government to better understand this trend and to develop a policy to deal with it. At the time (pre-9/11), our efforts stirred little interest, and only our embassy in Pakistan joined the discussion. As it turned out, the political counselor there, Dick Hoagland, later worked for me as director of the Caucasus and Central Asia Office in EUR, where we continued to work on this project in the more understanding post-9/11 environment.

Piracy in the Malacca Strait

The Malacca Strait has been a key passage for world trade for centuries, and piracy has long been an endemic problem. During our time in Kuala Lumpur, piracy in the strait reached a new high with the audacious and vicious kidnapping of ships, cargo, and crews. The Acehnese insurgency across the strait in Indonesia created a chaotic atmosphere, with limited Indonesian control, and piracy provided a major money-making opportunity for the rebels. We worked closely with the Malaysians and their neighbors to find a way to deal with this menace to international commerce, providing training and state-of-the-art radar and other equipment to their police and military. But as would prove to be the case with the Somali piracy crisis a decade later, the problem was essentially lawlessness on shore, not something that could be solved by sea patrols or better technology, and it mostly went away when the Indonesian government and the Acehnese reached a peace agreement in 2006.

A New Start with Bush

I maintained a high public profile in KL, making speech after speech that emphasized our close ties, promoted U.S. political and economic interests, and pushed against the frequent anti-US rhetoric of Mahathir and others. Over time, I felt that our efforts were making progress. Serious bilateral business was moving forward with a minimum of friction. Malaysia proved a prudent and moderate member of the UN Security Council, where we frequently sought their help on key issues.

George W. Bush's election over Al Gore in 2000 was a dream come true for Mahathir. The prime minister not only pronounced himself happy that his old nemesis Gore had lost; he also declared that "Bush's victory will restore good ties between the two countries." Three months after the inauguration, Mahathir called me in for a formal meeting. He usually did not "waste time" on meetings with ambassadors assigned to KL, so the invitation to his office was meant as a clear signal of his desire for better relations. I had talked with Mahathir many times in informal settings or when accompanying others in meetings with him, but this was our first, and only, formal session. Mahathir wanted to underline his desire for good relations with the new administration. It was an occasion for happy talk and a positive atmosphere badly missing when we arrived in Kuala Lumpur. I was to visit the prime minister's office fairly frequently in subsequent months as he sought to ingratiate himself with every ranking American delegation that came through the city.

We left KL in August 2001 satisfied with the state of U.S.-Malaysian relations. The country's politics remained badly tarnished by Mahathir's ruthless treatment of Anwar, but the prime minister was headed toward retirement, and his more personable successor, Abdullah Badawi, was firmly in place. (Mahathir would later turn on Badawi and his successor as inadequate to lead Malaysia.) The economy was back on track, with U.S. investment growing, and Malaysia seemed to be holding its own against the rising Chinese giant by emphasizing its protection of trade secrets and its record of reliability. Our bilateral cooperation in areas of common interest was the best it had been in years.

Mahathir clearly hoped for a formal visit to Washington to refurbish his reputation at home and internationally. After the 9/11 tragedy the United States was looking for allies around the world, especially countries with moderate Muslim leaders. Mahathir's stock went up in Washington, and he received his coveted visit to Washington in 2002. When I saw him in Washington during the events in his honor, this complicated and difficult man was all smiles.

13
Central Asia after 9/11

A World Turned Upside Down

With our tour in Malaysia coming to an end, Beth Jones, the new assistant secretary for European Affairs, offered me a job as her deputy for Greece, Turkey, Cyprus, the South Caucasus (Georgia, Armenia, and Azerbaijan), and Central Asia. It certainly was not the most glamorous position in the EUR front office, but I was reasonably familiar with the Caucasus from the Nagorno-Karabakh job, always wanted to spend some time in Central Asia, and did not think someone from the so-called vodka-drinking part of EUR, namely, Eastern Europe and the Soviet Union, could pass up being responsible for EUR's part of the Eastern Mediterranean. When I showed up for work in early September 2001, I looked forward to a pleasant, if quiet, assignment and to learning more about these interesting countries.

A week later we were in our office waiting for the morning staff meeting when the television flashed dramatic pictures of an airliner crashing into one of New York City's World Trade Center towers (our family had stayed in the hotel there on several trips to the city). We assumed it was a terrible accident, felt stunned by the tragedy, but headed on into our 9:00 a.m. meeting. Minutes later we were called back out to watch in horror as the TV replayed coverage of a second plane crashing into the other tower. The United States had been attacked for the first time since Pearl Harbor. As we attempted to make some sense of the very sketchy information available, a third plane crashed into the Pentagon. Instructions went out immediately to evacuate the State Department; after locking up classified files, we headed down the stairs. Those with cars in the basement were told to leave for home immediately, while others gathered outside the building. As I headed out on what was normally a fifteen-minute drive, sirens wailed incessantly, and smoke billowed out of the Pentagon across the Potomac. It took two hours to get home to Alexandria.

Diane and Gwen had driven to Chicago over the weekend to celebrate the christening of Kim's son, our first grandchild. They were headed back to Washington on the Indiana Turnpike when they heard the news. In that mostly pre-cellphone world, they pulled into the next rest stop to call me, but they couldn't get through. They decided to keep driving toward Washington following the news on the radio. I spent most of that day reaching out through Washington's overloaded phone system, on both my official cellphone and home landline, to each of the embassies under my responsibility to check on their well-being, inform them we were OK, and provide them initial guidance, with the promise they would have more formal instructions as soon as we could get back in the office. Between the calls, I spent some time trying to think what the new world meant for our relations with Central Asia and how we were going to be able to reorder our priorities toward the region. (Diane and Gwen arrived safely late that evening.)

Central Asia Takes Center Stage

I went to work the next morning to help deal with a world turned upside down. The "backwater" Central Asian states had become the frontline in our plans to eliminate the Al-Qaeda threat and overthrow its supporters in Afghanistan. We needed their help, and we needed it fast. When the Taliban refused to turn over the perpetrators of the attack, a U.S. invasion was inevitable.

Our policy toward Central Asia after the collapse of the Soviet Union had been quite straightforward: improve the political and economic lot of their peoples, establish a solid connection with their governments, and support their newly won independence. Strobe Talbott laid out this strategy in a 1997 speech that emphasized the United States had no interest in a new "Great Game." We wanted to help the countries of Central Asia consolidate the freedom they had gained in 1991, develop into viable twenty-first-century nations, and live at peace with themselves and each other. We emphasized economic and political reform, helping the countries abandon statist policies for the free market and develop democracy, with its stress on rule of law, civilian control of the military, and respect for human rights.

By 2001 the United States had put a reasonable amount of money into these efforts, especially in the development of a civil society that could provide political backing for reform. We also encouraged the construction of oil and gas pipelines that would give the resource-rich countries control over the marketing of their own fuel, freeing them of the Soviet-era distribution system and helping diversify the global energy market. And we participated in military cooperation with the region through NATO's Partnership for Peace, to give the Central Asians sufficient support to avoid their being preyed on by their powerful neighbors. It was a well-thought-out but modest agenda, reflecting the limited importance of these new countries to perceived U.S. national interests.

The Central Asian leaders themselves had not been enthusiastic about the breakup of the Soviet Union. Suddenly, the large subsidies from Moscow ended, and the Russian market for their products (such as oil and cotton) was imperiled. The old Soviet divide-and-rule approach toward drawing republic boundaries had left major ethnic issues in most of the new states, which hindered the development of a sense of national pride or cohesion. By 2001 none of the Central Asian states had regained their Soviet-era GDP level. They were poorly governed, and a rise in radical Islamic agitation and terrorism mentored by the Taliban regime in Afghanistan made all their governments vulnerable. Moscow was too preoccupied with its own internal issues to provide much economic or security help, and China was still a minor player in the region.

Our first task on September 12 was to revise this minimal U.S. policy framework to meet the challenges of the new era. Now we were going to fight a war in the region and needed allies. The possibility that one of the Central Asian states could emerge as a breeding ground like Afghanistan for terrorist attacks against the United States had become a real threat. We had a draft of a new Central

Asia policy on the secretary's desk a few days later, which was then adopted by the interagency group I chaired to ensure a common U.S. government approach. We also needed to get an embassy back up and running immediately in Tajikistan, a country now critical to the war effort in Afghanistan. That embassy had been closed for security reasons three years earlier.

Our new Central Asia policy was also quite straightforward: The region's well-being and cooperation had now become critical issues for the United States We needed these countries' help with overflight rights, bases for our aircraft and operations against Al-Qaeda and the Taliban, and fuel and other supplies for the upcoming war. Helping the governments in the region become more effective and supported by their people no longer was a post-Soviet democracy project, but an urgent necessity, as we sought to isolate the terrorists.

We understood that carrying out political and economic reforms to ensure long-term prosperity and stability would be a difficult struggle. My first background note for the policy draft said in its first sentence that the states were weak, poorly led, and impoverished. Their elites, all products of the Soviet system, still operated in their post-Soviet bubble, unimaginative and fixed on the need to keep control. They were deeply dependent on traditional clan politics and a corrupt distribution of wealth that made reforms extremely difficult. The Uzbeks, Kyrgyz, and Tajik leaders had done a poor job in countering radical Islam. The Al-Qaeda–linked Islamic Movement of Uzbekistan (IMU) and the radical Hizbut-Tahrir group had been growing in strength in the Ferghana Valley region of all three countries. Countries and regimes frozen in the Soviet past would probably require a generation for significant change to occur. We had to build cooperation in weeks. Achieving the aims of our new policy would take significant increases in aid, patience, and all the diplomatic skill and leveraged cooperation we could muster.

The first priority was to get permission for overflights and bases needed to carry out our military strategy in Afghanistan. It would take close cooperation with the Pentagon and the U.S. Central Command to make this happen. It was critical that U.S. civilian and military efforts be well coordinated and mutually reinforcing. Much of the work of putting together an antiterrorist military coalition initially fell by default to Defense Secretary Donald Rumsfeld and the Pentagon, with the State Department playing a supporting role.

Moscow, at first, reacted negatively to U.S. plans to operate out of Central Asia and station forces in the region, but Uzbekistan ignored the Russian complaints and offered help days after the 9/11 attack. It soon agreed to the use of its Karshi-Khanabad base (called "K-2" by the Americans) as a staging area for U.S. support operations (including search-and-rescue missions). U.S. Special Forces had been training Uzbek military personnel and providing some equipment to support its fight against the IMU for a couple of years, and our understanding explicitly included helping Uzbekistan deal with the IMU and with any blowback from our operations in Afghanistan. The U.S. bombing campaign on terrorist targets in Afghanistan began on October 7, less than a month after the attack on the World Trade Center.

Tajikistan initially had been more hesitant in the face of Russian opposition; but when Putin withdrew his objection to the U.S. presence, Tajikistan also offered its bases on the Afghan border. CIA and Special Forces operatives began using them within days. All of the Central Asian countries opened their airspace to U.S. military aircraft. After a quick survey of airstrips in the region, the Pentagon chose Manas in Kyrgyzstan for its air operations. The civilian airfield served the Kyrgyz capital Bishkek, but it had been built by the Soviets to handle large bombers. Within weeks of the 9/11 attack, the U.S. had the military cooperation it needed in Central Asia to carry out the Afghan war.

The rapid success of the U.S. attack in Afghanistan has been described many times. CIA and U.S. Special Forces units, operating out of Central Asian bases and building on earlier CIA contacts, moved quickly to direct U.S. firepower on enemy targets in support of the advance of the Northern Alliance, which did the bulk of the fighting, and other warlord armies. Within a couple of months, the U.S.-led coalition had overwhelmed the Taliban and driven Al-Qaeda leaders out of the country. In our daily State Department meetings on the war, I argued for a significant American military footprint on the ground to ensure that we could help determine the future course of a civilian government and reduce factional feuding.

U.S. military commanders, who like me had been convinced in the post-Vietnam debates that gaining solid control of the military situation was a prerequisite for constructing a viable civilian government that could stand on its own, made the same point.

Rumsfeld, however, was not buying that line from his staff, and the State Department did not press the case. He believed in a "light footprint" on the ground that let others do most of the fighting. He delighted in ignoring the post-Vietnam wisdom that by now was known as the "Powell Doctrine," in honor of his rival at the State Department, and he saw Afghanistan as something of a distraction from his effort to tie Saddam Hussein to the 9/11 attack and oust him from Iraq.

Rumsfeld's approach, which may have looked good in the short term, failed miserably over time. The United States was never able to control the situation on the ground in Afghanistan. The leadership of both Al-Qaeda and the Taliban slipped through our hands. Our failure to establish effective central control over regional warlords meant that any new Afghan government would be in a constant struggle to establish its authority across the country. The end result of the Rumsfeld approach in Afghanistan was the longest war the United States has ever fought, a huge drain on resources and social cohesion in our own country, and the Taliban back in power.

The leaders of Central Asia well understood the danger presented by Taliban support for terrorist operations, and they backed the U.S. approach in order to eradicate the danger to their own countries. They had little interest in carrying out anything more than minimal internal reforms. Concepts like democracy and human rights had no historical roots in the region nor were they something the Soviet-style leaders would readily accept. Most of the leaders simply did not see it worth the risk to rely on winning public support rather than repressing dissent.

I made my first trip to the region in early November. (Several legs of the trip were on CIA "special flights" in the company of big, tough, tight-lipped Americans in camouflage uniforms, obviously headed to or from the war zone.) My task was to ensure that our broad, long-term policy could be pursued hand in hand with, and not be overwhelmed by, our military strategy. Secretary of State

Colin Powell visited the region in early December, with a similar message, promoting our overall relationships and urging the region's leaders to make the reforms necessary to ensure the survival of their states over the long run. Most leaders Powell talked to paid at least lip service to reform. But Uzbek President Islam Karimov dodged and weaved in their discussion like an old prizefighter, sticking closely to his plan on military cooperation while promising nothing tangible on reform. I was reminded of painful conversations with Chinese and Soviet leaders on similar subjects from a decade or two earlier.

Sadly, patience is not an American virtue when it comes to regime reform, democracy, and human rights. Intellectually, Americans interested in U.S. foreign relations understand that it takes a generation or two for countries without a democratic tradition to succeed in making the transition to democracy (as in Taiwan and South Korea); but the American press, NGOs, and political leaders chose to focus on the failings of our new partners in Central Asia from day one and demanded immediate change. The Central Asians did not get a honeymoon period or any "benefit of the doubt" for their cooperation. A *New York Times* editorial three weeks after 9/11 warned against the danger of Washington's being pulled "ever closer to tyrants and satraps in Central Asia," including "some of the world's worst violators of human rights," where "mistreatment of Muslims is especially brutal," News stories reporting the cooperation of Uzbekistan and others in the war effort inevitably carried a few paragraphs bemoaning their bad human rights situation. Appreciative references to the help we received from the Central Asians were normally accompanied by several sentences reminding the reader that they were really nasty guys. This narrative was not wrong, just arrogant, naïve, and in its demand for immediate changes totally at variance with historical experience, yet it set the tone in Washington for our dealings with the region.

I testified before various congressional committees, briefed numerous groups with an interest in the area, and made speeches defending our strategy to help these countries with political and economic reform at the same time we cooperated militarily. The Uzbeks and others did, in fact, take some steps in response to our pressure, but not enough to overcome the well-established negative American narrative. Following a standard playbook, it was far easier for critics to complain about the regimes and the administration's "coddling" of them than to attempt to do anything serious to help change these societies. Some of my congressional inquisitors seemed to truly believe we should not be dealing with these regimes at all, but most appeared to understand we had no choice. My testimony merely provided them a foil to burnish their human rights credentials.

Another sign of the unpopularity of our Central Asian partners in official Washington could be seen at diplomatic functions. When ministerial-level Central Asian officials came to town, I would regularly be the ranking U.S. government official at these events. Occasionally, Secretary Rumsfeld would drop by, but not higher-level officials from the State Department or the White House.

If we were to have any chance of helping put these countries on a more solid path, our new policy needed to be adequately funded. But the negative narrative meant money for a substantial program that might push these countries more rapidly toward reform never got off the ground. Washington simply had no appetite to engage in a program approaching the scale of our activities in Afghanistan or Pakistan. Indeed, it became increasingly clear over the next couple of years that the U.S. was prepared to pay just enough—through the Pentagon and in modest AID increases—to keep their cooperation and the bases but remained totally uninterested in authorizing the resources necessary to make a real long-term difference in these countries. Washington went into its standard, if unappealing, pattern when dealing with an issue like reform in Central Asia: political leaders (and officials like me) made nice-sounding speeches encouraging reform, the press heavily criticized the regimes for falling short, and the budget people and Congress looked the other way when it came to civilian programs significant enough to accomplish reforms.

Uzbekistan: Help, But No Reform

Uzbekistan, whose 25 million people made up 45 percent of the region's population, was usually the main focus of criticism. The country had a long tradition as an Islamic cultural center, enjoyed relatively strong social cohesion, and appeared poised to lead the region when the Soviet Union collapsed. However, former Soviet Politburo member Islam Karimov's leadership looked inward, mired in old-think, and was hobbled by endemic corruption. Despite the country's promise, Uzbekistan's GDP had not grown in the ten years of independence, and political repression had worsened. Karimov's harsh efforts to suppress the Islamic Movement of Uzbekistan terrorists seemed to merely make them stronger. Many times when dealing with leaders in the region, I would think back to Mahathir and Malaysia. Mahathir, for all his problems, understood what it took to modernize a backward state and had the vision and determination to carry it out. I kept thinking of the possibilities in Central Asia, if only the leadership there had a quarter of his drive and vision.

Karimov did, however, understand the opportunity offered by closer cooperation with the United States. His decision to help the U.S. war effort played a critical role in the early victories in Afghanistan. In return for this cooperation, he expected us to support Uzbek independence, provide substantial monetary assistance, and enhance counterterrorism ties. At the same time, he was determined not to undertake real economic or political reforms that would undermine his own power or that of his cronies, despite the demands of the United States. He would make some gestures on occasion to mollify his critics at home and abroad, but he clearly had no intention to take the kind of steps that we considered important to the future of Uzbekistan and Central Asia. This, and the intense criticism by human rights advocates, ensured that the U.S.-Uzbek relationship would remain transactional at best, with little chance that it would become close.

There was never any doubt that Uzbekistan's human rights record was abysmal. Thousands of political prisoners languished in its jails, often with little evidence that they posed a real threat to the regime. Stories abounded about the continuing torture and abominable conditions in the prisons. In one case that occurred just before 9/11, a man who was said to have radical connections had his fingernails pulled out before being tossed alive into a vat of boiling water to die. The British ambassador became sufficiently disturbed over these events to denounce the Uzbek government's actions loudly and publicly without regard to his instructions from London, eventually leading to his recall. Meanwhile, the regime's educated and cultured front men would try to convince us that political and economic reforms were just around the corner.

As if the regular run of skullduggery and torture was not enough to sully Uzbekistan's international reputation, I found myself regularly démarched by the Uzbek ambassador and foreign minister on the troubles of the president's daughter Gulnara Karimova and her divorce. The glamorous and talented Gulnara had married an Afghan-American businessman in 1991 and moved with him to New Jersey. A month or so before I arrived in EUR, she had defied court orders by taking the children (along with nannies and bodyguards) back to Uzbekistan while divorce proceedings were underway. In a replay of the Chinese effort to get us to solve their Twin Oaks property problem two decades earlier, the Uzbeks refused to listen to my explanation that the U.S. government had no control over what a judge would decide in a divorce case. They needed to get a good lawyer rather than ask us to intervene. Eventually Gulnara did get a lawyer and custody of the children. However, she was later arrested in Uzbekistan in connection with several high-profile corruption cases.

Four months after Powell's December 2001 trip, Karimov was rewarded for his cooperation against Al-Qaeda and the Taliban with a White House visit, a normal expression of appreciation for an ally but an abomination for American and Uzbek human rights groups. We worked out an agreement with his foreign ministry that outlined steps to be taken in the areas of human rights, security cooperation, economic reforms, civil society, law enforcement cooperation, and freedom of expression and the media. Congress then tied our aid to Uzbekistan to making progress in the agreed areas. Although the Uzbek government initially took some positive steps, the pace of reform soon petered out, and Uzbekistan returned to business as usual.

In early 2004 we warned their government that $18 million in U.S. civilian aid could be in jeopardy because of the lack of progress on reform. A major terrorism outbreak in Tashkent in late March evoked very little sympathy in the United States. The *New York*

Times story on events there included a statement from the International Crisis Group that terrorism should not excuse the country's human rights record and also claimed, once again, that the U.S. government had given Karimov and his government a "free ride." An editorial on the attack spent its time not on sympathy for those killed but on the iniquities of the regime. As I left EUR that summer, the Bush administration ended the aid, because it could not certify that the Uzbeks were making 'substantial and continuing' progress on human rights as demanded in the legislation.

Ten months later, the Uzbek government responded to a major prison break and large demonstrations in the Fergana Valley city of Andijon by killing hundreds of people in the city square in cold blood. The massacre sparked widespread outrage in the United States and Europe. In retaliation, Karimov ordered the United States to leave K-2, and the era of U.S.-Uzbek cooperation (and our ability to help shape the country's future) was over by November 2005.

Human rights critics of our Central Asia policy would argue that we never had a chance to transform Uzbekistan under Karimov, and they are right given the minimal commitment of U.S. money and the short time involved. But the home-front assault on our efforts from the beginning meant we never had the support to mount a sustainable program that could have had a major impact on the post-Karimov era. We should have done more to help shape the country's future when we had the opportunity.

Kyrgyzstan Provides an Airbase

Kyrgyzstan, a country of 4.5 million people, provided a refreshing contrast to its autocratic neighbors in the 1990s. Askar Akayev. a noted physics and mathematics professor in Leningrad, became the country's first president. He set out to reform the country's political and economic systems, encouraging free enterprise and a broad and vibrant civil society. The West saw the country as a shining example of democratic progress in Central Asia. Akayev and his wife were cultured and charming people. Our meetings were always cordial, and Diane and I thoroughly enjoyed their company when we hosted them at the Kennedy Center performance during a Washington visit.

People in Kyrgyzstan could openly debate their future, the economy, and the country's political leaders without the same sense of fear as in other Central Asian countries. At the American University of Central Asia in Bishkek (funded by the Soros foundation, the U.S. government, and others) I met with a group of impressive students from across the region who challenged me in an open debate, an experience I found both exciting and highly reassuring for the future of Central Asia.

By the 2000s Akayev's reputation had been tarnished. The economy of this extremely poor country had not grown despite his support for free enterprise, and corruption (especially among his relatives) had become a major problem. Many observers saw Akayev as a weak leader, easily swayed by others and without a strong vision of where the country should be headed. Hemmed in by geography and troubled neighbors, he had few successes to show by the 2000 election. To compensate, he and his colleagues blatantly manipulated the results, his main rival languished imprisoned on flimsy charges, and the formerly vibrant press was cowed into submission.

In our conversations, I always found Akayev happy to engage. He said all the right things about promoting democracy and human rights and the development of the Kyrgyz economy. But the gap between his rhetoric and his actions steadily grew. Protests against him gathered strength across the country. Compared to the terrible human rights situation in Uzbekistan and elsewhere, Kyrgyzstan was still an island of civility, but the trajectory was downward and Akayev's domestic popularity had long since peaked.

The agreement to allow the Americans and NATO (primarily France) to use Manas fundamentally changed the U.S.-Kyrgyz dynamic. By Christmas 2001, Manas was functioning as a logistics base for troops and supplies headed for Afghanistan, with as many as two thousand foreigners on the ground. F-18s and French Mirages flew daily sorties against targets in Afghanistan. As the Americans replaced their tents with permanent structures and the base became an essential part of the U.S. and NATO war effort, it appeared to Moscow that the Americans were in for the long haul.

The Russians became alarmed at this growing U.S. military presence on the soil of their former empire and demanded that it too be allowed to station forces in Kyrgyzstan. Russia then deployed forces to Kant airfield, forty miles from Manas, and also sought to fan discontent among the local population against the Manas base.

While the U.S. spent hundreds of millions of dollars to build and operate out of the airbase, with an estimated $50–$60 million a year going to the Kyrgyz economy, much of that money unfortunately went to Akayev's family or others in the elite. (The largest amount was spent on fuel from companies owned by family members.) Relatively little of the new wealth actually trickled down to the country's citizens. Formal U.S. aid also increased, but too little of it demonstrably improved the lives of Kyrgyzstan's people. As a result, the Manas base never gained much public Kyrgyz support. The Russians kept up pressure on the Kyrgyz government to close it.

The corruption of Akayev's family, his efforts to retain power, and the continued deep poverty of Kyrgyzstan's south caught up with the president in the March 2005 parliamentary election nine months after I left EUR. International observers agreed with local opposition leaders that the vote had been rigged. Demonstrations in the south protesting the election snowballed, and the government soon lost all three major southern cities to the opposition. Demonstrators in Bishkek entered the Presidential Palace as the police looked on, forcing Akayev and his family to flee the country (via the Russian airbase), and the former professor returned to his academic roots in St. Petersburg. His opponent, Kurmanbek Bakiyev, was appointed prime minister and later elected president.

Unfortunately for the people of Kyrgyzstan, very little changed. Corruption flourished (only the beneficiaries had changed), and public anger at the government quickly returned. Bakiyev then began looking for ways to use funds generated by the Manas base for his own interests, despite intense Russian pressure to close it. Over the next several years the Kyrgyz and Americans wrangled over the amounts the U.S. had to pay, and the Russians maintained their heavy pressure on Bakiyev to close the base. Eventually, after the base had lost much of its value to the U.S., the Kyrgyz bowed to Russian demands and closed it in mid-2014.

During the time I had responsibility for U.S. policy toward Kyrgyzstan, we tried to reinforce the better instincts of the Akayev government and encourage him to return to his earlier reformist policies. Unfortunately, it did not work. As his popularity declined, the very civil society we had helped develop brought him down. Bakiyev proved to be even less able to govern this small country with its rampant corruption and overbearing neighbors, and political reform became an even more distant hope.

Tajikistan

Tajikistan's bases also played a key part in the war effort. This impoverished, but beautiful country defined mostly by the incredible Pamir mountain range, had suffered a ten-year civil war after independence, fueled by clan rivalries, religious extremists, and Russian and Iranian rivalries. Over 80 percent of its population lived in poverty. Its president, Emomali Rahmonov (he later changed his name to Rahmon as part of a de-Russification program), managed a state farm in the Soviet days and emerged as leader of the country in the early years of the civil war. Like Uzbekistan and Kyrgyzstan, Tajikistan had endured several years of attacks by IMU terrorists based in Afghanistan. Rahmonov was anxious to use the opportunity provided by U.S. involvement to resolve his security problems and obtain leverage against his enemies to advance his and his country's prospects.

After 9/11, the Pentagon seriously considered using an airbase in Tajikistan in addition to Manas to fly aircraft in and out of Afghanistan. Rahmonov wanted a greater U.S. presence, and one of the bases would have been an acceptable alternative for the U.S. Air Force. Given the fragility of the political situation in all of these states, it made sense to hedge our bets with a Tajik base as an alternative to Manas. But in the end, Rumsfeld decided on what I assume was financial grounds to settle on Manas as the major airbase. When the war proved to be much longer than Rumsfeld had estimated and we lost K-2 in Uzbekistan, we found ourselves in a weak negotiating position on Manas. Once again, trying to do Afghanistan on the cheap had long-term costs that we kept paying years later.

Rahmonov, like most of his colleagues, ruled through a sham democracy but allowed some room for civil society to grow and tolerated a weak opposition. Radical Islamic groups and disaffected clans posed the real threat to his government, thus giving us some space to try to build a viable polity in Tajikistan that would ensure the country's long-term stability and independence. Never a part of the Moscow power structure, the Tajik president chafed at continuing Russian pressure on him and on the Tajik economy, the continued presence of Russian border troops on Tajik soil, the vulnerability presented by the million or so Tajiks working in Russia, and Russian ownership of Tajikistan's one real industry, a huge aluminum combine that relied on the available cheap hydropower.

In every conversation I had with him, Rahmonov would include a long riff on his problems with the Russians. He was a delightful and passionate interlocutor, totally unlike the reserved Chinese and Russian diplomats I had dealt with for years. Most of his complaints against Moscow were valid; to get their way in a vulnerable country, the Russians used bribes, a disinformation campaign in the independent press (often accusing us of nefarious plans), and open threats.

Rahmonov's other major foreign problem (as if the Russians and Afghanistan weren't enough) was Uzbekistan. Tajikistan's mountains provided much of the water Uzbekistan used (and wasted) to grow cotton for export. The Tajiks wanted to build a gigantic dam to generate electricity for export to Afghanistan and Pakistan, a project the Uzbeks were determined to stop or delay. Soviet leaders had designated a sizeable number of ethnic (Persian-speaking) Tajik areas (including the cities of Samarkand and Bukhara) as parts of Uzbekistan when Tajikistan became its own republic, ensuring Tajiks' irredentist feelings. To top it off, Karimov and Rahmonov could not stand each other, and the Uzbek leader turned a blockade of Tajikistan on and off at will. Trying to get the Uzbeks to back off their pressure on Tajikistan became a staple of my conversations in Tashkent. Over time, as a counter to Karimov and Moscow, Rahmonov turned increasingly to China and Iran to promote the country's development and trade.

Besides providing assistance to help improve the daily lives of ordinary people, most U.S. aid to Tajikistan went to bolstering Tajik antiterrorism and antinarcotics efforts. Helping the Central Asian countries stem the flow of drugs from Afghanistan to and through their countries was an element in all of our aid programs, and Tajikistan had been doing a particularly good job. On one of my trips to the capital city, Dushanbe, I visited a women's textile cooperative supported by USAID that sought to provide a livelihood for women working in a village outside the city. (All the able-bodied men in the village worked abroad and came back once a year to visit their families.) My gift for the occasion, a cow, seemed totally inadequate, given the scale of the problems faced by these women, but it was received with obvious appreciation.

On a larger scale that we hoped would be more broadly effective, I worked hard with the Pentagon to get funding to build a $37 million bridge to Afghanistan at Nizhniy Pyanj, which had the potential to greatly increase the trade between northern Afghanistan and Tajikistan. The Army Corps of Engineers did excellent work getting this bridge built in the face of obstacles in both countries. It opened with considerable fanfare in 2007.

Turkmenistan under Turkmenbashi

The strangest country in the Central Asian group was Turkmenistan. Ruled by another former Soviet Politburo member, Saparmurat Niyazov, the country had the sixth largest gas reserves in the world, but its people were also one of the poorest. Niyazov, who styled himself Turkmenbashi (leader of the Turkmen), had absorbed the worst traits of Soviet governance and applied them to his small country of five million people. For the first eighteen years of independence, Turkmen gas and oil depended almost entirely on Russian pipelines to move them to the outside world; and the Russians ensured the price they paid was well below what they received when they exported it. While the income was impressive for a small country, it went into vanity projects for Niyazov, a heavy secret police security apparat, and the bank accounts of Niyazov and his cronies in Europe.

Niyazov used the bulk of Turkmenistan's wealth to contract with French and Turkish companies to turn the capital, Ashgabat, into a white marble Turkman version of Disneyland, without the entertainment or the smiles. Social programs to help the people were always starved for funds, and the lot of the average Turkman seemed to deteriorate steadily, with well over half the potential work force unemployed. Unlike the rest of Central Asia, tight restrictions on travel abroad limited the opportunity to find work in Russia or other nearby countries.

Niyazov had sought to break the country's deep ties to Moscow by expelling Russian residents, discarding old textbooks, and discouraging use of the Russian language. He substituted instead a cult of personality; his name and likeness appeared everywhere. He closed hospitals outside the capital and turned the education system from the Soviet period into a farce. There was no independence movement, no wave of liberalism, no flush of global activity in Niyazov's Turkmenistan, just a retrograde Communist country without a Communist party. Our programs since independence had been designed to help at least some of the people get a taste of the modern world, with the usual training programs, political and human rights events, and Peace Corps volunteers. The relatively small number of Turkmenistan's people I came into contact with struck me as quite personable and eager to be part of the world community, but the regime severely limited the scope of U.S. programs. I had great admiration for the staff in the embassy and for our aid workers and Peace Corps Volunteers, who all worked hard to assist the people in this incredibly difficult environment.

Most of my conversations in Turkmenistan were with Niyazov's foreign minister, Rashid Meredov, who always took copious notes and promised results, few of which ever panned out. Niyazov wanted no part of formally joining our effort in Afghanistan, but he did grant the U.S. overflight rights and cooperated with United Nations humanitarian flights to Afghanistan. We also had fairly robust antinarcotics and antiterrorism efforts on the Turkman-Afghan border.

During a 2004 visit to Ashgabat, I had a surprisingly positive conversation with Niyazov that spanned cooperation on Afghanistan, human rights, release of prisoners, and a proposed Trans-Caspian Pipeline. He even proposed a "divert agreement" that would allow U.S. warplanes in distress to land at a base in Mary. In the end, nothing came of the suggestion, as the Russians and Iranians pushed back on the proposal and Niyazov later withdrew the offer.

Russia opposed new pipelines, as it sought to maintain its monopoly on Turkman gas. But two years later, Niyazov signed a deal with the Chinese that led to a route for his gas through Uzbekistan and Kazakhstan into China. While the deal initially provided Turkmenistan some badly need leverage against the Russians, it eventually led to almost total dependence on the Chinese market on terms that would later become known as a "debt trap," with much of the gas revenue paying off the loan for the construction of the pipeline.

Kazakhstan Takes the Lead

Even though Uzbekistan would have been voted the most likely to succeed when the Central Asian states gained their independence, Kazakhstan soon outclassed its southern neighbor. With a land area twice the size of the four other Central Asian states combined, stretching from China to the Caspian Sea, Kazakhstan was blessed with great oil potential. Its impressive leader, Nursultan Nazarbayev, successfully managed the art of balancing the interests of his highly diverse population and those of foreign powers.

Kazakhstan had been the dumping ground for many of Stalin's victims—individuals and whole ethnic groups—and the site for Khrushchev's Virgin Lands scheme. At independence, the country had a Russian population, about 40 percent, that roughly equaled its Kazakh population. Nazarbayev, like his former Politburo colleague Karimov, was no democrat. He suppressed dissent when it raised its head, but he did it with a lighter touch that did not create the international outcry that Karimov's methods produced. Nazarbayev promoted the Kazakh language and ethnic Kazakhs but without alienating the Russian population, which eventually dwindled to about 15 percent of Kazakhstan's population. He also was careful to cooperate closely with the Chinese, especially on economic and transportation issues, despite concern that the Chinese might covet Kazakhstan's vast, fertile, and sparsely populated lands.

Exportable oil, however, soon became Kazakhstan's primary

ace in the hole. Nazarbayev partnered with Mobil in the large Tengiz field in the Caspian Sea and sponsored a pipeline through Russian territory to the Black Sea, which opened in 2001. At about the same time, the vast Kashgan deposit—the largest oil find in thirty years—was discovered in the Caspian, ensuring there would be a steady money stream for the country well into the future.

Corruption remained a serious issue in Kazakhstan, as in all of Central Asia (and Russia); but Nazarbayev kept the kleptocracy (including his own) in check so that it did not destroy the growing economy. He built an entirely new capital, Astana, in the frigid northern plain to ensure that Russia could not lop off a sizeable portion of the country where ethnic Russians predominated. Like Turkmenistan, Kazakh oil and gas pipelines to China would eventually make China Kazakhstan's largest export market.

Nazarbayev gave the United States overflight rights for the war in Afghanistan early on and cooperated closely, but he had less to fear from Islamic radicals than other countries in the region. Despite his government's authoritarianism, its relatively moderate internal policies shielded it from much of the criticism aimed at other countries in Central Asia. Indeed, Nazarbayev used the country's ethnic and religious diversity to good effect in promoting the country's image.

Russia, China, and U.S. Indifference

Soon after my arrival in EUR, a lively debate in our front office meetings centered on what Vladimir Putin was up to. President Bush had famously assured the world that he had looked into Putin's eyes and gotten "a sense of his soul." Putin had agreed to cooperate with the U.S. on Afghanistan soon after 9/11, and Russia entered into a new partnership with NATO. His efforts to stabilize the Russian government made it seem to many people that the stage was set for a new era of good feelings between Russia and the United States. But that is not how it looked from my perspective. My discussions with Russian officials and Central Asian and South Caucasus leaders left no doubt that a primary goal of Putin and his old KGB cronies was to regather the lost lands and rebuild the

Russian Empire rather than become best friends with the United States and Europe.

When Putin bemoaned the dissolution of the Soviet Union a few years later, no one who dealt with the Russians in what they possessively called their "Near Abroad" could have been surprised. I'm not sure what Bush saw in the former KGB agent's eyes, but Putin's support for the initial U.S. actions to defeat Al-Qaeda should hardly have been surprising. Neither he nor the Central Asians could rid the area of the Taliban and Al-Qaeda on their own; he may even have taken some pleasure at the real possibility that the U.S. could be dragged into the Afghanistan quagmire that had helped destroy the Soviet Union a decade earlier. But the Russians had a genuine fear that the U.S might establish major influence in what they considered their sphere of influence. Within months, after the initial American successes, Moscow began to pressure the Central Asians to limit the U.S. role. The propaganda effort against the U.S. (often via widely watched Russian-language television) grew in intensity, as did direct pressures on their leaders.

The Russians need not have been concerned about Central Asia. Neither Powell nor Bush ever considered the region of sufficient importance to mount a major effort to develop a long-term U.S. role. They were happy to leave the heavy lifting to Vice President Cheney, Secretary Rumsfeld, and lower Pentagon and State Department officials to maintain support for the war for the limited time they thought it would be needed. Powell's visit in December 2001 was his only trip to the region. Policy toward Central Asia was driven at the top levels by the war in Afghanistan, with little attention to a long-term strategy to deal with Western interests in the heart of Asia or Chinese and Russian efforts to dominate the area. The primary aim of President Bush and his advisers was to end the lingering war that Rumsfeld's light footprint had created and to get American soldiers back to safer soil. Our attempts to get some attention paid to a longer-range U.S. strategy that would help shape a future Central Asia more in our interest were simply ignored. The drumbeat of criticism in the press and Congress of the Central Asian leaders on human rights grounds, the blowup with Uzbekistan over events in Andijon, and the movement of American logistics support inside Afghanistan sealed the fate of our involvement. The collapse of our political and military position became inevitable as we dialed the U.S. role back to the limited engagement Strobe Talbott laid out in 1997.

The high hopes held by many of the Central Asians that the U.S. would become a counterweight to Russia were eventually transferred to China, which was just becoming active in the region during my time in EUR. It is always useful to remember that Central Asians would probably speak Chinese today if a Tang Dynasty army had not lost the Battle of Talas (in 751AD), in today's Kyrgyzstan, to an army of the Abbasid Caliphate. As the Tang general prepared a counterattack, the An Lushan Rebellion broke out in China's capital Changan, and their armies in the West were called back to quell the rebellion. A millennium and a quarter later, the Chinese were back wielding checkbooks rather than swords.

The Chinese-constructed pipelines that gave them a major portion of Kazakh oil and most of Turkmenistan's gas made a major contribution to our efforts to diversify the world energy market, but it also greatly increased the Chinese economic and political stake in Central Asia. The Belt and Road initiative announced by Xi Jinping in Astana in 2013 left no doubt that the Chinese intended to become the dominant economic power in Central Asia. They also used the Shanghai Cooperation Organization (SCO), which included Russia, China, Uzbekistan, Kazakhstan, Tajikistan, and Kyrgyzstan, when it was established in 2001 as an important tool for increased political and security influence in the area. China provided the bulk of the funding and drive for this organization. Russia acquiesced in China's role but kept up its own effort to stay in the political/security lead (especially as the U.S. role diminished after 2005), while ceding economic and infrastructure leadership to the Chinese. Karimov pushed for the U.S. to join the SCO as an observer in its early days, but when I raised this idea with Secretary Powell's staff, they turned it down flat. The secretary did not like to travel, and they had no interest in putting something like the annual SCO summit on his schedule.

A year or so after I left EUR, responsibility for Central Asia in the State Department was moved on instruction from the White House from the European to the South Asia Bureau, an action that may have made geographical sense but ignored the last couple hundred years of history and effectively removed it from the State Department's Russia/China strategic calculus. Again, with the U.S. never willing to commit to a long-range approach to Central Asia or ascribe a strategic interest beyond prosecution of the war in Afghanistan, we could do little to help these countries build prosperous, democratic societies or avoid becoming pawns of their neighbors.

14
The South Caucasus and Eastern Mediterranean

Georgia Moves Westward

The second region under my responsibility, the South Caucasus (Georgia, Armenia, and Azerbaijan) was driven by a dynamic not tied to Afghanistan. But the competition with Russia was more direct. No country of the former Soviet Union felt greater heat from Russia during the early 2000s than Georgia.

Georgia had a glorious tradition as an independent country, including a golden period in the twelfth and thirteenth centuries and another three years of independence between the collapse of Tsarist Russia and the invasion of the Red Army. However, like the other small kingdoms in the region, it had been buffeted for centuries by competition between the Persian, Ottoman, and Russian empires before being incorporated into the Russian Empire in the early 1800s. During the Soviet period, Georgians from Stalin to Shevardnadze had played important roles in the Soviet Union; but unlike the Central Asians, the Georgians wanted to get out from under Russia's control. They agitated for independence as soon as the Soviet Union began to weaken, and Georgia was one of the first to attain it.

Its president Eduard Shevardnadze was a hero in the eyes of many in the West for the key role he had played in ending the Cold War and rebuilding the new world order. He had stood up to the generals and security people who had profited from the Soviet system (and particularly from the war in Afghanistan). I saw him in action many times after he became Gorbachev's foreign minister. He was gracious, highly intelligent, and sincerely interested in resolving the many outstanding issues between our two countries. He became a highly respected counterpart to both secretaries Shultz and Baker. But many in Russia (especially KGB types like Putin) hated him for his role in the collapse of the Soviet Union and its East European dependencies. When Putin came to power in 1999, Shevardnadze immediately understood the Russian leader's primary foreign policy goal was to regather the lost empire and regularly warned U.S. officials and the press of Putin's true aims.

In Georgia Shevardnadze's legacy as the Communist Party leader who took on Georgia's massive corruption made him popular enough to become the country's leader again. His people elected him president in 1995 with 70 percent of the vote. Georgians also saw him as having the international prestige necessary to lead them toward an independent future tied to Europe and NATO rather than to the smothering embrace of Russia. When I saw him in 1998 (in my Nagorno-Karabakh and Regional Conflicts hat), Shevardnadze projected optimism and self-confidence despite having survived a third Russia-backed assassination attempt only four months earlier. He and his colleagues had made considerable progress by that time in transforming Georgia's laws, unifying the Georgian state (minus Abkhazia and South Ossetia), and orienting the dreams of the population toward the West.

Unfortunately, by the time I returned to the region in 2001, Shevardnadze's fortunes had taken a dramatic turn for the worse. Despite support from the West and his reputation for toughness, Shevardnadze proved to be an ineffective president who seemed unable to control fractious Georgian politics, grow the economy, or even keep a lid on the corruption of his own family. His popularity took a further hit during the badly flawed election in 2000 that he claimed gave him 80 percent of the vote (unbiased polls suggested he should have received about 50 percent.) When I began dealing with him in my new role, he remained friendly but seemed to have run out of ideas and enthusiasm. His public support was plummeting.

The Georgian economy, long a bright spot in the Soviet Union, had begun to seriously deteriorate in the 1980s. After a war in the early nineties with the country's separatist region Abkhazia (a vacation spot for the KGB and others in the Soviet elite), the Georgian economy was in disastrous shape. It continued to stagnate during Shevardnadze's presidency. A trip to the region by car from Yerevan to Tbilisi offered a pleasurable mountain ride through Armenia on decent roads, but the Georgia portion proved a disastrous mix of potholes and broken pavement lined by sad impoverished towns. With corruption rampant, the economy stagnant, and salaries and pensions unpaid, Georgia was ripe for political upheaval.

Georgians had readily embraced the idea of a vibrant civil society, which had originally provided strong support for Shevardnadze. But the newly vocal groups and young political stars eventually broke with him out of disgust over the lack of economic progress and the widespread corruption. We had helped Georgia develop some of the most forward-looking administrative, legal, and economic laws of any country in the region; but despite the formal structures, the normal administrative channels simply did not function well. Bribes were demanded for the most basic services, and poorly paid police would repeatedly stop drivers for money to pay "fines" for imagined offenses. As I met with a wide variety of Georgians during my visits, I could feel the intensity of the frustration with the seeming hopelessness of the Shevardnadze administration. Predictably, Shevardnadze and his people had begun to manipulate election results to stay in power, despite our best efforts to help them pursue steady democratic progress in the country.

The Russians tried to make matters worse and destabilize the government of a man they despised. They cut gas supplies during the coldest winter months; they instituted a visa regime to inconvenience and manipulate the well over 10 percent of Georgia's 4.5 million people who survived by working in Russia; they encouraged the separatists in Abkhazia, South Ossetia, and Adjara; they refused to carry out their promise to withdraw from military bases in Georgia; and they threatened to invade the Pankisi Gorge area of Georgia on the grounds that Chechen rebels were using it as a staging area to carry on their war with Moscow. The Russians also coordinated their efforts with anti-Shevardnadze forces in Georgia who hoped to gain power.

During my first two years as a deputy in EUR, I spent considerable time dealing with Georgian problems. We repeatedly went toe-to-toe with the Russians on their harassment of Tbilisi. Our aid programs sought to help deal with repeated economic crises and strengthen the government—a particular imperative was to reform the tax system so the government could be properly funded. The critical U.S. military effort to train and equip Georgian armed forces later included the creation of a Georgian Coast Guard to patrol its Black Sea border. We used it to introduce a novel program that cut to the heart of Georgia's corrupt system of government payments. Instead of handing out cash payments for the troops to senior officers, who always took their cuts, we did it the American way—by directly depositing the soldiers' pay into new individual bank accounts and issuing them bank cards to access their accounts. Getting their full pay produced strong loyalty in troops who were now able to support their families adequately. The concept was eventually adopted across the government payroll, a huge blow to endemic government corruption.

Throughout this period, Georgia proved a strong friend of the West, sending forces to help in the Iraq War and cooperating with the United States on a broad range of international issues. Shevardnadze also tried to appease Moscow, even though the war across the border in Chechnya made this extremely difficult. We encouraged Shevardnadze and his ministers to maintain positive relations with Moscow despite the provocations. We also pressed Putin and others in Russia hard to ease up on Georgia and give the country a chance. In congressional testimony I warned the Russians about their intemperate language and threats to intervene on Georgian territory.

When I stopped in Tbilisi on one of my regular trips to the region in May 2003, internal tensions were running high. I talked with a wide range of Georgian politicians, emphasizing that the November 2003 parliamentary elections would be an important test for the country's democracy, in essence, a dry run for the presidential election planned two years later to choose a successor to Shevardnadze, who was term-limited by the constitution. Over the next few months we focused hard on trying to ensure an honest election that would begin to revitalize the country, an effort that included visits to Tbilisi by long-time Shevardnadze supporters James Baker and Strobe Talbott.

But it was not to be. Our ambassador, Richard Miles, described the November election as a "mess." Other international observers agreed. As vote tabulations dragged on, the top opposition leaders, Mikhail Saakashvili, Nino Burjanadze, and Zurab Zhvania denounced the election. Saakashvili and Zhvania urged their supporters to take to the streets and called for Shevardnadze's resignation.

Massive demonstrations against election fraud and blatantly false preliminary results from the autonomous Ajara region brought tensions to a head just as I visited Tbilisi again on November 18–19. I talked at length with Shevardnadze and the three opposition leaders, as well as all the other major parties, urging them to resolve their issues peacefully before the situation spiraled out of their control. Publicly, I made it clear that we were pressing both sides to compromise on a path out of the mess, but emphasized this was a Georgian problem that they had to resolve themselves. As I headed for the airport, Saakashvili called to say they had proposed a compromise to resolve the issue with Shevardnadze but that the president had refused to consider it. When the government released blatantly false results on November 20, the State Department denounced the election as a "massive vote fraud" and expressed deep disappointment with the election and the Georgian leadership.

When Shevardnadze attempted to open the new (fraudulently elected) Parliament on November 22, Saakashvili and his supporters stormed into the building carrying red roses. Shevardnadze fled with his security detail, and Nino Burjanadze announced she would be acting president in accordance with the constitution, pending a new election. Shevardnadze called both Putin and Secretary Powell for support. Powell did not suggest Shevardnadze resign, but he certainly did not give the kind of backing the president had expected. He also talked with both UN secretary-general Kofi Annan and Russian foreign minister Igor Ivanov on a joint strategy to resolve the issue peacefully. Ivanov flew immediately to Tblisi to negotiate with the parties, emphasizing the importance of a peaceful settlement. With the clear lack of support from Washington and Moscow and his disinclination (and that of his security forces) to use force, Shevardnadze resigned on November 23, ending twelve years as Georgia's president. The "Rose Revolution" had succeeded with no causalities. The White House deputy press secretary the next day voiced support for the opposition's actions "to restore the integrity of Georgian democracy." New elections were set for January 25, 2004.

Following a post-Thanksgiving trip with Secretary Powell to an OSCE Ministerial in Maastricht, The Netherlands, I headed back to Georgia with a delegation that included representatives from DOD, Treasury, and the Justice Department to determine Georgian needs for the election and for carrying out the reforms planned by the new leaders. Our group met with counterparts in the Georgian government as well as its new leadership. At a press conference as we were leaving, I announced the U.S. would give Georgia $5 million in emergency assistance plus $2 million for a winter heat program and would continue to support the troop training. I made it clear that the $5 million would go to priorities set by the Georgians themselves.

As usual I met with leaders across the political spectrum, but the saddest session by far was with Shevardnadze. He still could not fully comprehend why he had been ousted or how badly living conditions had deteriorated for the average Georgian during the last few years of his presidency. He told me that he had made a mistake in not going out in the countryside to campaign before the November election, clearly not appreciating the futility of such an effort when his support in the polls hovered around 5 percent. No doubt he felt betrayed by his friends in the United States and said as much publicly, even though we praised him and his accomplishments extensively after his fall and encouraged the new leaders to treat him with dignity in retirement. They did. And he was allowed to spend the next decade until his death living in the presidential mansion.

We had long supported the Georgian demand that the Russians leave their bases in Georgia. Moscow had agreed in 1999 to vacate the last two bases in Georgia proper; but then the Russians began dragging their feet on implementation. We backed the Georgian demand under both Shevardnadze and Saakashvili for a quick implementation of the agreement. I had made this a major issue in press conferences in Tbilisi during my stops there. Following visits by President Bush to the two countries in 2005, they finally reached an agreement. The Russians were out by late 2007, but they continued to station troops in Abkhazia and South Ossetia, the two breakaway regions Moscow had backed since the early 1990s.

Unlike the problems we had with Congress in getting money for Central Asian countries, American legislative leaders were eager to support Georgia and its new leadership. Senators McCain, McConnell, and Leahy argued in a letter to Secretary Powell that a "significant infusion of U.S. assistance to the Georgian government would serve American interests." Given this kind of backing, we were able to find additional funds for Georgia. I informed the Georgians in a mid-December teleconference that we would increase our emergency assistance by $14 million to cover unpaid government salaries and pensions, emphasizing to them that they would have to pick up these responsibilities in the future by raising the necessary revenue themselves.

Saakashvili won a crushing victory in the free and fair January election. His inauguration attracted high-profile guests, including both Secretary Powell and Foreign Minister Ivanov. The new Georgian leaders demonstrated their ambitions by hoisting the EU flag along with a new Georgian flag and playing the EU anthem "Ode to Joy" during the ceremony. His speech clearly placed Georgia in Europe (as well as at a crossroads of civilizations), promised to root out corruption, and pledged good relations with all friendly states. The United States and Powell took pride of place, but Saakashvili held out an olive branch to the Russians as well, asking for friendship and cooperation.

Burjanadze stayed on as leader of the Parliament, and Zhvania became prime minister, where he acted as a calm influence on the younger and more impetuous president. The ministers were young and strongly reformist. (Tragically, Zhvania died a year later of what was officially said to be carbon monoxide poisoning, but which sparked numerous conspiracy theories. His moderating influence, which I observed on several occasions, was to be sorely missed.) The new government set to work with solid backing from the West to transform Georgia. Its impressive successes predictably stirred up a strong reaction, egged on by Russian propaganda, from people who had benefited from the old corrupt system.

I traveled to Georgia again in January (my third visit in three months) to check in just before Saakashvili's inauguration, to finalize our assistance agreements, and to ensure that planning was well underway to give the new government a firm basis as it set out on its critical reform path. Publicly, I gave strong backing to Saakashvili and the new government, emphasized the need to get corruption under control, and pressed for normal Georgian-Russian relations, while once again calling on the Russians to vacate the bases and offering assistance on the costs of resettling the Russian servicemen. I underlined the importance of the Georgians' getting their own house in order. A month later in Brussels I encouraged the European Union to keep the Georgians' feet to the fire on reform, to press the Russians to treat Georgia as an independent country, and to increase assistance to the Saakashvili government.

One major piece of unfinished business for the new government was dealing with Aslan Abashidze, the pro-Russian leader in Ajara who had made a major effort to increase his power in the November parliamentary election. After an obviously fraudulent vote, Ambassador Miles and I flew to Adjara to convince Abashidze to back off and allow the election to proceed in his region. He allowed the vote but continued to oppose the government in Tbilisi. Soon after his election Saakashvili moved to bring the region under control. He tried to travel to Ajara himself to bolster Georgian nationalist elements but was stopped at the border. He then closed the region's border with Turkey, shut down its port, blocked road and rail access to the rest of Georgia, and froze its leaders' assets. After a huge anti-Abashidze demonstration in Ajara in early May and the intervention once again of Russian Foreign Minister Ivanov, Abashidze resigned and fled to Moscow. Saakashvili's confrontation tactics had proved successful in bringing a troublesome region under central control.

The "Rose Revolution" was hailed in the West as a great victory for democracy, but it sent shock waves through the capitals of other states that had been part of the Soviet Union. When Ukrainians revolted against a rigged election in November, it was labeled the "Orange Revolution," and Akayev's overthrow in Kyrgyzstan in April 2005 was labeled the "Tulip Revolution." Putin reportedly told Burjanadze that other leaders in the region were "sh---ing in their pants" over events in Tbilisi.

The desire to join NATO and the European Union grew exponentially throughout the region. In March 2004 Bulgaria, Estonia,

Latvia, Lithuania, Romania, Slovakia, and Slovenia entered NATO. Poland, the Czech Republic, and Hungary had been admitted in 1999. Then in May the three Baltic States, Hungary, Poland, the Czech Republic, Slovakia, and Slovenia entered the EU along with Malta and Cyprus. Georgia's inclusion in the expansion of European institutions looked like an achievable goal.

There is no doubt that Putin saw the Rose and Orange Revolutions as a Western plot to pull countries he considered part of Russia's sphere of influence to the West, like the incorporation of former Warsaw Bloc countries into the EU and NATO. In most of the Central Asian and neighboring Caucasus countries, the governments moved to restrict activities of U.S.-supported NGOs like those that had help stoke events in Georgia out of fear that they might see their own "color revolution."

Armenia: Stuck in Conflict

Armenia is a small country overwhelmed by its history. With a continuous identity dating to the sixth century BC, it was the first state to adopt Christianity as its religion (in 301AD) and boasts of the world's oldest cathedral, dating from the same period. Over the next millennium and a half, it too was buffeted between the Persian, Ottoman, and Russian empires, ending up in the early 1800s with western Armenia part of the Ottoman Empire and the eastern part integrated into the Russian Empire. The "Young Turks" who controlled Turkey after the overthrow of the Ottoman Empire during World War I accused the Armenians of being a Russian fifth column and carried out a terrible massacre that killed or drove out most of them from Turkey. Estimates are that between one and one and a half million Armenians died during what became known as the Armenian Genocide. The refugees and their descendants created a virulently anti-Turk diaspora. It is estimated that some eight million ethnic Armenians lived in other countries, primarily Russia, the U.S., and France, and only two–three million lived in Armenia.

Like Georgia, Armenia had another short period of independence in the aftermath of the Tsarist regime's collapse during World War I. It was retaken by the Red Army and made a part of the Soviet Union in 1922. In September 1991, with the impending disintegration of the Soviet Union, Armenia declared its independence. A terrible earthquake in 1988 and the war with Azerbaijan over Nagorno-Karabakh had left Armenia's economy in disastrous shape. The country's marketable natural resources are limited, and Russian investment dried up, while its borders with natural trading partners Azerbaijan and Turkey were closed.

The continuing talks on Nagorno-Karabakh were going nowhere in the early 2000s. I discussed the issue with President Robert Kocharian on several occasions, but our conversations primarily dealt with the war on terror and bilateral issues, including efforts to promote Armenia's democratic development and struggling economy. Our aid program and Peace Corps remained focused on providing hope to the country's poor but intelligent and energetic people.

We had generally good cooperation with few bilateral disputes with Armenia, but one provided a good illustration of how the U.S. can tie itself into knots by pursing conflicting policies. Armenia's nuclear power plant, similar to the Ukrainian Chernobyl plant that blew up in 1986, had been closed after the 1988 earthquake. It reopened in 1995 with some revamping (mostly on American advice) and provided almost half of Armenia's electricity. Despite the repairs, European and American scientists believed it to be a disaster waiting to happen, and the Europeans offered to pay for its dismantlement. Armenia wanted to replace it with a pipeline to gas fields in northern Iran, a proposal that conflicted with our sanctions on Iran. We found ourselves opposing both the power plant and the pipeline, with no solution to suggest. The Armenians predictably ignored our advice.

Armenians felt the tug of Europe and the West as much as their neighbors in Georgia—there were many more ethnic Armenians than Georgians living in Europe—but the isolation resulting from the Nagorno-Karabakh conflict made it essential to keep good relations with Russia to protect their security and trade. The Russians kept their military base at Gyumri and provided equipment for the Armenian military. The West, including NATO, offered Armenia increased economic and security cooperation; but when the Russians felt the Armenians were going too far, they would pull the chain on Armenia's leaders to keep the country solidly in their camp.

Among the regular visitors to my office were Armenian-Americans pressing for us to do more for Armenia. Their lobby was one of the most potent political forces in Washington, and it was my job in the State Department to always hear them out and be helpful when we could, in the overall context of our ties to the region. The Armenian diaspora also provided a vital source of humanitarian and developmental aid to people inside Armenia as well as a powerful magnet for the country's continued depopulation.

The diaspora in the U.S. exerted heavy pressure on the Congress and the administration to grant official U.S. recognition of the genocide and condemnation of the Turks. I felt that the unwillingness of the Turkish government to recognize the tragedy that occurred almost a century earlier was foolish and self-defeating. But its adamant refusal to take responsibility put the administration between a major NATO ally that was moving to liberalize its policies and a small country that, while friendly, remained close to Russia. We attempted to maintain a balance (as between Azerbaijan and Armenia) that served U.S. interests, but our approach sometimes led to tortured semantics. The diaspora took a considerably tougher approach than the Armenian government, which was trying to reach an accommodation with Turkey to liberate its economy. Unfortunately, the diaspora's "all-or-nothing" approach toward a Karabakh settlement with Azerbaijan ended up with Armenia's people being the ultimate losers. The country's talented citizens continued to leave their country for greener pastures.

Azerbaijan

Azerbaijan did not have the ancient tradition of Georgia or Armenia as an independent thriving kingdom. It had been known in history for its oil, even getting a reference from Marco Polo. Under the Russian Empire, its oil industry underwent considerable development, and the Swedish Nobel family turned it into a modern, productive industry in the early twentieth century. Baku became the region's leading city at the time, with impressive buildings and a lively cosmopolitan culture paid for by its oil wealth. The Clinton administration saw the potential for additional oil for Europe not dependent on the Russians or the Middle East and strongly backed the development of a new pipeline from Baku through Georgia to Turkey. Oil began to flow through the Baku-Tbilisi-Ceyhan (BTC) pipeline in 2006, ensuring Azerbaijan would not be dependent on Russian goodwill to get its oil to the market.

Former Soviet Politburo member Heydar Aliyev ruled the country as his own fiefdom, giving little room for the opposition. In many ways, Aliyev was an enlightened despot who, like Nazarbayev in Kazakhstan, used oil wealth and the independence it provided to advance his country's interests. But the level of corruption (as our N-K negotiating group had witnessed at the Baku airport) put a severe drag on the economy. Little money went to help the desperately poor countryside or the refugees from the Nagorno-Karabakh war still living in inadequate encampments.

Aliyev loved to tell stories about his time as a Soviet Politburo member. He once described the concern he and his wife had about Brezhnev's last visit to Baku in 1982. His wife had berated him for inviting the obviously declining leader to visit Baku, not because Aliyev was required to waste money building a new palace for Brezhnev's two-day stay but out of fear that they would both be arrested if Brezhnev died in Baku. When the Aliyevs returned from the airport after putting Brezhnev on the plane, the relieved couple went downstairs to the bar in their mansion to break out their very best bottle of champagne. Less than two months later, Brezhnev died safely back in Moscow.

Heydar Aliyev himself died in a U.S. hospital in December 2003. His son Ilham was duly elected to succeed him, in the usual murky election process. Once in power, Ilham updated some of his father's policies, but his approach, including suppression of the opposition and a balanced foreign policy, remained the same. Our efforts to encourage governmental reforms in Baku or movement on the Nagorno-Karabakh issue produced very little success. Azerbaijan did, however, offer strong and continuing assistance on oil pipelines and the war on terror. The Aliyevs cooperated in supporting the Afghanistan war effort, including reliable logistical flows, worked to eradicate terrorism in their region, and helped block movements of weapons of mass destruction from a turbulent Russia to Iran.

I always found Azeri officials somewhat distant in our

conversations, and they clearly bridled at our efforts to soften their treatment of the opposition. Nevertheless, they valued our cooperation and technical help. Baku's dealings with Russia mirrored in many ways its Kazakh neighbor across the Caspian, staying wary, maintaining its room for maneuver, and avoiding antagonizing its powerful neighbor. Its relations with Iran (where there are twice as many ethnic Azeris as in Azerbaijan) remained fairly distant, but again Baku went to considerable lengths not to provoke its southern neighbor.

Turkey under Erdogan

The Eastern Mediterranean was also changing. During the first fifteen months of my time as EUR deputy assistant secretary, the most important country in my portfolio, Turkey, was in turmoil. The old regime collapsed under a major economic crisis, and its traditional politicians failed to offer a way forward that appealed to most Turks. The election on November 3, 2002, saw a dramatic shift in Turkish politics, with all the traditional political leaders ousted from Parliament. The new Islamic-oriented AKP (Peace and Justice Party), led by the charismatic former mayor of Istanbul Recip Tayyip Erdogan, won over two-thirds of the seats.

Erdogan had been jailed for four months in 1999 for "inciting violence." He was banned from political office and could not actually take over as prime minister until March 2003, so the cofounder of the AKP, Abdullah Gul, occupied the position on an interim basis. The challenges Erdogan and Gul faced were enormous. The Turkish state structure and economy needed to be rebuilt, Turkey's opportunity to begin formal negotiations to join the EU had reached a crucial stage, the Americans demanded Turkey's support for its war plans on neighboring Iraq, and the fraught situation in Cyprus was coming to a head.

Erdogan, by far the most popular politician in Turkey, made his reputation as the capable and moderate mayor of Istanbul. The United States invited him to Washington a month after the election, and President Bush met with him at the White House—technically a "drop by" during his call on National Security Council chief Condoleezza Rice, since Erdogan held no official position. His meetings in Washington were a major success for both sides. The U.S. welcomed this impressive, moderate politician in charge of a key NATO ally and appreciated his assurances of continuing close relations with the United States. During those meetings I first met his foreign policy advisor, Ahmet Davitoglu, a highly capable academic/politician who formulated the country's new diplomatic outreach to Turkey's neighbors and the world. The trip proved to be a great start with the new Turkey.

Fallout from Iraq. At the time of the Turkish election, President Bush and his top advisers were focused on ousting Saddam Hussein from power in Iraq. U.S. military planners calculated that an effective invasion would require a northern front mounted through Turkey to complement the main force entering the country from Kuwait.

While Turkey's cooperation was seen in Washington as key to the success of the Iraq invasion, the Turks themselves were deeply skeptical. From their point of view, Saddam provided no threat; the real threat to their interests was the possibility of Iraq coming apart after Saddam's overthrow, thus giving the Iraqi Kurds the opportunity to create a state of their own. Kurds comprise 15–20 percent of Turkey's population, and the government had sought for years to suppress its own Kurdish independence movement, the PKK. They saw an independent Iraqi Kurdistan as a direct threat to Turkey.

The Turks also believed their cooperation in the first Iraq War had led to huge economic losses, promises of U.S. aid that did not arrive, and encouragement of Kurdish independence resulting from the No-Fly zone in northern Iraq. With Turkey's economy in freefall, another U.S. invasion of Iraq had disaster written all over it. At the same time, Turkish leaders were proud of their long cooperation with the United States, including the deployment of troops to Afghanistan and their active role in NATO. The military especially did not want to jeopardize those ties.

Erdogan, Gul, and the AKP had been opposed to a U.S. invasion of Iraq when they were in the opposition; but once responsible for Turkey's future, Erdogan came to believe that it was important to cooperate with Turkey's long-time strategic partner and to be in

Iraq in the war's aftermath to help shape its future. The U.S had undertaken a major campaign to garner support at the UN for an invasion and to bring its NATO allies on board. With the forward deployment of U.S. logistics for an invasion well underway, the U.S. pressed Turkey's new political leaders and the military to support a northern front. U.S. war plans now included staging up to 62,000 ground troops through Turkey, a Turkish military deployment to northern Iraq of up to 10,000 troops to ensure stability in the area (Ankara saw it as a check on Kurdish ambitions), and a major U.S. economic aid package for Turkey. The invitation to Erdogan to visit Washington was part of this effort.

In the ongoing negotiations, the Turks overplayed their hand by demanding a much larger aid package as part of the deal, and they dragged out negotiations for a U.S. survey team to assess logistical issues concerning the movement of U.S. forces through Turkey. Despite U.S. pressure, the date kept slipping for Parliamentary approval of the deployment of U.S. forces on Turkish soil and Turkish soldiers to Iraq. Gul, as prime minister at this point, tried to organize a meeting of Middle East countries to press for a peaceful resolution of the conflict and privately indicated he opposed a U.S. deployment through Turkey, a stance in sync with Turkish public opinion.

With tempers frayed, deadlines passing, a U.S. invasion certain, and its supply ships poised just off Turkey's coast, the AKP finally put the question to a Parliamentary vote on March 1, 2003. To the astonishment of the government, which had a large majority in Parliament, the resolution lost by three votes. Erdogan was humiliated, U.S. leaders were furious (especially in the Pentagon, where many felt they had been double-crossed by the Turkish military), and the invasion of Iraq went ahead without a northern front. Thirty-some ships loaded with logistics for the war remained stranded in the Mediterranean, and the American troops that were to use the equipment cooled their heels in Texas. U.S. plans for major Turkish cooperation in the war collapsed, and the bilateral warmth of December had been replaced in March by frigid relations and heavy mutual recriminations.

The Turks' worst fears were realized when the U.S. military— left without its own invasion force or the support of a coordinated

Turkish military effort—had to rely on help from their only local ally, the Kurdish Peshmerga, to gain control of the north. Although the Turkish Parliament had authorized the deployment of Turkish military forces to northern Iraq, the U.S. made a determined effort to keep the Turks out. The Peshmerga advance to replace the collapsing Iraqi army was a nightmare come true for the Turkish military, a nightmare made worse by the fact it was self-inflicted.

Secretary Powell made a quick trip to Ankara on April 2 to soothe bruised feelings and dissuade the Turkish military from invading northern Iraq on its own. He succeeded by confirming to the government that the U.S. would not let the Kurds take the cities of Kirkuk and Mosul or control the Iraqi oil fields in the area. He also offered $1billion in aid to replace some of the package the Turks had forfeited with the March 1 vote. The Turks agreed to the shipment of nonlethal supplies through Turkey to U.S. forces in Iraq. Despite Powell's promise, however, Peshmerga forces entered Kirkuk ten days later, an action the Turks had said was a red line that would trigger a Turkish invasion. In the end, the Turks swallowed their pride and did not intervene.

When I went to Ankara in mid-May to assess the state of relations and press for more cooperation, I made it quite clear that disappointment with Turkey's handling of our requests on Iraq remained quite high in Washington. We had welcomed the November election results, fully supported Turkey's EU accession efforts with our friends in Europe, and gone to great lengths to satisfy their concerns on Iraq. We had every expectation, based on the assurances that we had been given, that Turkey would support us on Iraq, and U.S. disappointment was real. I noted that Secretary Powell's visit made clear that we wanted to rebuild the relationship with Turkey, but that it would have to be based on concrete actions taken by the Turkish side. Turkish officials told me they also wanted to improve relations and get past current tensions, but they offered very little in concrete steps that would help get things back on track.

On July 4, trust between the two countries received another major blow when U.S. army troops captured a group of Turkish Special Forces in Sulaymaniyah, in Kurdish Iraq, that was reportedly planning to carry out the assassination of the newly elected Kurdish governor of Kirkuk. The treatment of the Turkish troops, including pictures of them hooded and shackled by their American allies, caused a sensation in Turkey, and officials threatened to close American access to Incirlik Air Base. After frantic telephone calls between Erdogan and Vice President Cheney and between Powell and Gul, the soldiers were released; but Turkish pride had again been seriously damaged and goodwill toward the U.S. undermined. In Ankara the incident was seen as proof once again that the U.S. was colluding with the Iraqi Kurds at Turkey's expense.

The shortage of troops on the ground led to disastrous consequences, particularly in the so-called Sunni Triangle north of Baghdad. The absence of the northern front meant that U.S. and Turkish troops were not available to suppress the pockets of resistance at an early stage and maintain the delicate strategic balance in the region. My colleagues and I were shocked when the supplies in the Mediterranean were just left there after the war started, but it fit in with Rumsfeld's delusion that fewer troops could do the job. It also meant, of course, that U.S. troops needed to rely more on their Kurdish allies in the north. The Turks looked on with deep concern about the growing role of the Kurds and the hollowness of U.S. protestations that we could deal with their concerns about the PKK and Kurdish demands for autonomy. The bombing of the UN office in Iraq on August 13, 2003, demonstrated the failure to pacify even Baghdad, much less the volatile north.

As Rumsfeld's minimalist approach proved inadequate, Bush requested help from other countries. The Turks were receptive but tied their response to having the U.S. take action against the PKK, which was thought to still have around 4,000 fighters in Iraq. To deal with their demand, I led an interagency group to Ankara that held seven hours of discussions in September to try to reassure the Turks that we were listening to their (almost constant) demands about eliminating the PKK terrorist threat from Iraq and would develop an action plan to accomplish this end. The talks were tough, but we and the Turks agreed on a way forward to deal with the PKK. Overall, the Turks seemed somewhat assured of our seriousness in dealing with their primary concern. Our approach was heavy on repatriation and political pressure and light on military action against the PKK, but the Turks chose to take our statements as a firm commitment to deal more aggressively with their primary security issue.

In early October, the Turkish Parliament overwhelmingly agreed to send "peacekeepers" to help the Americans in Iraq. But again, hopes of cooperation between Turkey and the U.S. failed to materialize. Contrary to assurances given to the U.S. authorities in Iraq, the Iraq Governing Council condemned the deployment of Turkish troops, embarrassing Erdogan, who had used considerable leverage to ensure a positive Parliamentary vote. A month later, Ankara and Washington agreed to drop the whole idea. I went back to Ankara soon after that, again trying to smooth over bruised feelings. Ever-skeptical Turkish officials noted our promises of action against the PKK but pressed for details on implementation. We made clear the U.S. could not contemplate a military campaign against the PKK in the near future.

Both sides had a keen interest in patching up the relationship. When Erdogan came to Washington on an official trip in late January 2004 to show that relations between the two allies were back on track, the Kurdish issue remained very much on the agenda. He pressed for assurances that Iraq would remain a unified state and that the oil revenues controlled by the Kurds would go to the central Iraqi state. Bush reaffirmed that the United States wanted Iraq to be "a democratic state that is territorially intact," and Powell said the country's resources should belong to "all the Iraqi people." But the Turks not surprisingly remained unsure the U.S. would live up to its promises.

A Key Moment with the EU. The Erdogan government came to power at a critical historical moment for Turkey: Would the country's destiny be as part of the European Union? Or would it remain a bridge between East and West, with its primary identity centered on its Ottoman heritage? Turkey had been reaching out to Europe since the days of Ataturk and had applied to join the European Union's predecessor, the European Economic Union, in 1987. The EU confirmed Turkey's path to Europe in 1989 but deferred consideration of its membership then and again in 1997. As Turkey's relations with Greece dramatically improved and with the EU's effort to expand to eastern European countries well underway, the EU agreed to make Turkey a candidate for membership in December 1999. The Turkish government began taking steps to modernize the country's laws and improve its treatment of its Kurds to conform to EU demands. As the United States had been a strong supporter of European integration as a fundamental strategic goal since the 1950s, often more so than the individual European countries, bringing Turkey into that enterprise was part of our long-term effort.

In December 2002 in Copenhagen a critical meeting of the EU took place that would decide whether to begin formal negotiations on Turkish accession. It was a key moment for Turkey's future and that of the entire Western alliance. The U.S. pulled out all the stops to support Turkey's effort, and the new AKP leadership committed to make the internal reforms necessary to conform to EU membership. The UK and several other EU countries backed Turkey, but Germany and France opposed moving forward. Public opinion in these two countries seemed concerned about allowing a large Muslim country into the European club, and their leaders—who were at loggerheads with Washington over Iraq—bridled at the U.S. pressure. Some suggested our motive in supporting Turkey was to get its help on Iraq. Sadly, Europeans punted again, putting off talks on Turkey for three years as they moved to bring ten other new members (including divided Cyprus) into the EU.

Turkey accepted the decision and worked hard to meet EU demands. In conversations that I and other members of the administration had with the Turks or the Europeans, we pressed for progress on both sides. Formal negotiations did begin in October 2005, but critical momentum had been lost. In the end, disputes over Cyprus, qualms in Europe (perhaps fed by Russian disinformation), and Erdogan's drift to authoritarianism effectively put the entire project on hold. It was a major loss for the West and for the Turkish people, who saw their chance for a modern democratic country anchored in Europe turn inward, authoritarian, and increasingly isolated.

A Lost Chance with Armenia. Despite being one of the first countries to recognize the independence of its much smaller neighbor, Armenia, the Nagorno-Karabakh War ended with Turkey backing its ethnic kin in Azerbaijan and closing the border with Armenia. The Armenians for their part, and especially among the diaspora, harbored deep feelings of historical injustice against the Turks for the genocide and expulsion of Armenians from Turkey. To find a way out of the impasse, we supported a Track II (nongovernmental) effort called the Turkish-Armenian Reconciliation Commission (TARC), led by David Phillips, deputy director of the Center for Preventive Action at the Council on Foreign Relations, to find a way around the historical deadlock on the genocide issue and to develop productive contacts between the two sides.

[Phillips's book Unsilencing the Past *gives the definitive review of TARC's three years in existence.]*

Phillips was indefatigable in getting prominent Armenians and Turks to work together, despite opposition to the process from many in the diaspora and the Turkish establishment. Ultimately, TARC commissioned an impartial study by the International Center for Transitional Justice, which concluded that Turkish actions fit the definition of a genocide but that the Genocide Convention could not be used retroactively to support claims for compensation or territorial adjustments. The discussions, despite many ups and downs, led to increased contacts between the two sides. We also encouraged quiet government-to-government talks on opening the border, and Turkish commentators began to gingerly discuss the events of 1915-16.

Swiss mediators took up the issue a few years later, and Turkish president Gul visited Armenia for a football match in a major gesture of goodwill in September 2008. A year later the two sides and the Swiss announced an agreement between Turkey and Armenia to normalize relations and open the border. Unfortunately, the agreement died under withering criticism from Azerbaijan and the Armenian diaspora.

By the time I left EUR in 2004, Erdogan had a firm grip on power, the country had its negotiating date with the EU, and the economy was on its best footing in years. Under pressure from the EU (which we supported), Turkey was becoming a model of moderation and democracy among its neighbors. Relations between Turkey and the United States had been righted after Turkey's failure to support the U.S. in Iraq, but tensions remained over U.S. reluctance to confront the PKK. The accession talks with the EU were going to be difficult, as the Europeans struggled to bring new members up to its standards; and several of its major members remained skeptical of bringing such a large Islamic country into the European fold. But, in general, the trends were positive. Turkey was heading in a direction that the United States welcomed and applauded.

Cyprus Fails to Unify

One issue still unresolved for the Turkish government, intertwined closely with its pursuit of EU membership, was the effort to end the division of Cyprus—hardly a front-burner issue for the United States. But the U.S. had been deeply involved since the 1960s in the effort to avoid a military conflict between two crucial NATO allies, Greece and Turkey, which separately supported the two communities on the island.

Strategically nestled in the Eastern Mediterranean just forty-seven miles off the Turkish coast, Cyprus was ruled at various times by the Byzantine Empire, the British, the French, the Venetians, the Ottomans, and again by the British after the Ottoman collapse. Growing sentiment on the island for *enosis*—union with Greece, promoted heavily by the Greek Orthodox Church—became a major problem for the British. Turkey had a strong strategic interest in ensuring that the island not become part of a hostile country. The Turkish Cypriot population (20 percent) and Turkey both supported continued British control. In the 1950s, agitation for independence, led by Archbishop Makarios, and intense terrorist activities put heavy pressure on the British to find a way to leave. In 1959 the foreign ministers of Greece and Turkey agreed on a constitutional framework for an independent Cyprus, with British military bases remaining on the island, and in August 1960 Cyprus became an independent country.

Makarios and his supporters sought to undermine Turkish Cypriot privileges from the first, and fighting between the two communities broke out three years later. In March 1964 the UN sent a peacekeeping force to the island and established a Special Mediator to try to resolve the dispute. President Johnson twice managed to forestall a Turkish invasion. In 1967 his envoy Cyrus Vance achieved a compromise that led to a withdrawal of most Greek troops and a limit of 650 soldiers each from Greece and Turkey to help keep order on the island. In the summer of 1968 serious discussions between Glafcos Clerides, leader of the South's parliament, and Turkish leader Rauf Denktash under the sponsorship of the UN mediator began making headway toward a deal.

Then in August 1974 the Greek junta ousted Makarios and called for the island's union with Greece. This time Washington's diplomacy failed. The crisis occurred during the Nixon impeachment drama (Nixon resigned just over two weeks later), and Kissinger, who was indisputably in charge of foreign affairs and supported the junta, had failed to avoid a conflict. The Turks invaded on July 20, 1974, enlarging the area they controlled after the ceasefire to just under 40 percent of the island. In time, almost all Turkish Cypriots on the island moved to the Turkish-controlled area, and Greek Cypriots moved to the other side of the dividing line patrolled by UN peacekeepers. The UN produced numerous plans and resolutions over the next quarter of a century, but the status quo remained with 25,000–30,000 Turkish troops on the island, UN peacekeepers on the Green Line separating the two sides, and talks locked in their own set of arcane arguments. The two communities went about their daily lives with relatively little interchange.

By the time I arrived in the European Bureau in August 2001, hope was again in the air that a Cyprus solution might be possible. Cyprus had entered negotiations with the European Union as part of a large expansion that would include much of the former East Europe and, it was hoped, eventual membership for Turkey. The aging Clerides, who had been negotiating on the Cyprus issue for over thirty years, was now president of (Greek) Cyprus and wanted to leave a united Cyprus as his legacy. He knew every detail of the issue and was one of the few people in Cyprus capable of coming up with the kind of compromises that were needed to pull off an agreement. His frenemy Denktash continued to be obstinate, wanting to preserve the status quo of two separate governments.

The United Nations was making a renewed push to take advantage of the EU deadlines. U.S. policy was driven by our highly capable envoy for the talks, Thomas Weston, with my boss Beth Jones and I weighing in as needed.

[Tom's oral history interview for the ADST <https://adst.org/OH%20TOCs/Weston,%20Thomas%20G.toc.pdf> provides the best inside review of the talks during this period.]

With Clerides eager for a settlement (and providing the needed critical compromises), EU pressure for Cyprus to enter as a unified country, and the rapidly changing political situation in Turkey, the time was right for the UN mediator to put forward a comprehensive agreement (the Annan Plan) in November 2002, just after the Turkish election. When I visited Nicosia at the time, I found Clerides, the Communist Party (AKEL) leader Christofias, and the UN mediator de Soto all quite optimistic that a deal could be made. Denktash was predictably negative.

The UN (strongly backed by the U.S.) hoped to use the critical Copenhagen meeting to force a breakthrough on Cyprus. Unfortunately, Turkey's new government, for all its pro-settlement rhetoric, found it had little leverage on Denktash, who relied on the support of the Turkish military and foreign policy establishment, not the AKP government. Denktash did not even bother to go to Copenhagen to participate in the discussions. The agreement to bring Cyprus into the EU (as a result of intense Greek pressure), with or without the north, meant that the European Union lost its leverage to move the Greek Cypriots toward a settlement. As with the failure of the EU to open accession negotiations with the Turks at the meeting, we were also disappointed that our best card to get a Cyprus settlement had been squandered.

Then the Annan Plan lost its critical supporter (and virtual author) two months later when Clerides was badly beaten in a presidential election by conservative leader Tassos Papadopoulos. As the clock continued ticking toward the deadline for Cyprus's entry into the EU on May 1, 2004, and with strong backing by Greece and Turkey (and the U.S. and the EU), Annan negotiated a deal with the two leaders in New York in January 2004 for a last effort to get a settlement. Intense discussions by the two sides, including between the leaders and Annan in Switzerland, failed to complete the plan, and, as had been agreed, the UN filled in the missing portions. The final plan was voted on by the two sides in referenda on April 24, 2004. Both Papadopoulos and Denktash denounced the final version of the plan. Sixty-five percent of the Turkish Cypriot voters supported it, but seventy-five percent of the Greek Cypriots voted against it.

Cyprus entered the EU with the Turkish Cypriots effectively excluded, and the most promising opportunity in forty years to settle the "Cyprus problem" was lost. As a full-fledged member of the EU, Cyprus then used its new power in Brussels to block any efforts to give further concessions to the Turkish Cypriot north and further complicated Turkey's own accession negotiations. U.S. efforts, as well as those of the UN, the EU, and Turkey, had once again failed to bridge the deep divide on the island.

15
"Help Indonesia Succeed": The Tsunami

In the fall of 2004, Diane and I returned to Asia after my confirmation as ambassador to Indonesia. I was not an expert on the country, although I had followed events there fairly closely when serving as ambassador in neighboring Malaysia. Reading in to my new assignment, I could not help but be struck by the awesome challenges facing the world's fourth most populous nation (and its largest Muslim-majority country) as it struggled with making the transition from autocracy to democracy. Not well understood in the United States, Indonesia found itself at the center of the key ideological struggle of the time—the competition between democracies and militant Islam. As heads of the dominant power in Southeast Asia, Indonesian leaders aspired to a greater international role, one that could be critical in the face of China's rapid rise. In short, the direction Indonesia took internally and in the world would be of great consequence to Asia and to the United States.

Indonesia's path to democracy following President Suharto's fall from power in 1998 had been a rocky one. First came a year's transition under Suharto's vice president, B. J. Habibie. Then came the well-meaning but largely ineffective presidency of Gus Dur, who, under pressure, handed over power to Vice President Megawati, the daughter of Sukarno, Indonesia's first president. Megawati also proved an indifferent leader during a period of continuing crisis. The Indonesian Army (TNI), which had been all-powerful under Suharto, nursed its grievances after its nasty withdrawal from East Timor in 1999, having unleashed local militias to carry out a month of murder and destruction after the East Timorese voted for independence. On top of this, the transition from autocracy and the security state to a new democratic polity opened the way for an outbreak of ethnic and religious tensions and terrorism. Al-Qaeda–affiliated Jemaah Islamiyah leaders returned to Indonesia, employing terrorist tactics in an attempt to achieve their radical aim of establishing a caliphate. The first of numerous church bombings took place on Christmas Eve 2000, and the first Bali bombing occurred in October 2002, killing 202 people, 80 percent of them foreigners.

Ironically, as Indonesia worked to put a modern democracy in place, relations with the United State declined dramatically. U.S. sanctions imposed on the Indonesian military after its actions in East Timor stirred up nationalist anticolonial rhetoric reminiscent of the Sukarno era. Then, across the Islamic world America's reputation declined as it carried out its "War on Terror" following the 9/11 attack. The reaction in Indonesia to the American invasions of Afghanistan and Iraq, fanned by new press and intellectual freedoms, was almost totally negative. With Islamic fundamentalism and the accompanying terrorism carried out in its name on the upswing in Indonesia, public opinion widely viewed U.S. actions as anti-Islamic. In front of the Embassy, anti-U.S. demonstrations became a daily fact of life. In the U.S., press coverage portrayed a floundering Indonesia beset by terrorism, a weak government, and economic disaster.

In 2004 the first direct election of a president in Indonesia gave Susilo Bambang Yudhoyono, a retired army general, a victory over President Megawati, with 60 percent of the vote. SBY, as he is called in Indonesia, had a reputation as a moderate, politically astute army general who managed to escape criticism for the suppression carried out by Suharto in his final days or blame for the East Timor fiasco. He campaigned on a platform of economic development, social cohesion in a multicultural society, and rebuilding Indonesia's badly tarnished international reputation. Washington viewed Yudhoyono's victory as a major turning point and wanted to help him transition the country into a thriving democratic member of global society that could serve as a model not only to Asia but to the Islamic world generally. But it was unclear whether the country could, in fact, make the transition, given the tensions it faced or if SBY would be able to deal with the vast array of problems he confronted.

Again, I faced a delay of several months after my selection as ambassador, while our embassy pressed Megawati to sign the *agrément* documents acceding to my assignment and forwarding it to the legislature. Deep in an election campaign, the president had other more pressing priorities than signing a routine document agreeing to the next American ambassador. The process upset Washington's preferred timetable of having Diane and me there in early fall for the transition to the new administration. When the *agrément* request was finally approved, it was unlikely I could officially present my credentials before SBY's October 20 inauguration, so my predecessor stayed on to attend the ceremony. We arrived in Jakarta three days later.

Indonesia faced enormous problems when SBY took over. Its economy remained sluggish, and power in the country was shifting from its former concentration in the hands of the ineffective Jakarta bureaucracy to democratically elected regional and local authorities. Domestic terrorism was on the rise, corruption was rampant, and Indonesia's international standing was low. Once touted as the "next Asian tiger," the country's economic recovery from the Asian economic crisis remained far behind others in the region. Indonesia lacked a serious economic strategy, and corruption among the elite drained the economy of its vitality. In the face of these difficulties, the instruction Secretary Colin Powell had given me when he swore me in as ambassador was succinct and to the point: "Help Indonesia succeed."

The Tsunami in Aceh

I presented my credentials to SBY in early December and began the usual diplomatic calls on Indonesia's leaders, reaching out to the press and parliament, and attending with Diane a round of holiday functions. These normal diplomatic niceties came to an abrupt halt on the morning of December 26, 2004, when an earthquake measuring 9.1 on the Richter scale triggered a massive tsunami that ravaged Aceh Province on the northern tip of the Indonesian island of Sumatra. Suddenly, the new government and its friends faced a disaster of truly Biblical proportions. News of the tsunami and its resulting destruction first filtered to us in Jakarta from television reports describing the devastation on Thailand's resort island of Phuket. Little was known at first about Aceh, a closed military area due to the government's thirty-year effort to suppress an insurgency led by the Free Aceh Movement (the GAM).

As reports began to trickle in, President Yudhoyono cut short his Christmas visit to Christian communities in West Papua, in Indonesia's far east, and flew to Aceh, the country's westernmost point, to comfort the stricken people there and assess the damage. The tsunami had cut off virtually all the region's limited communications with the outside and severed the main road along the island's west coast. The first real news of the extent of Aceh's tragedy came from the president and the journalists accompanying him as they visited the region. The initial reports talked of a few hundred casualties, but that number quickly rose to thousands and tens of thousands in the following days, to an eventual estimate of some 170,000 people killed. News clips from the Yudhoyono visit began to shed light on the enormity of the tragedy.

SBY ordered the TNI to cease offensive military operations against the insurgents and to concentrate on rescue work. When he returned to Jakarta, the Indonesian government assessed the scope of the disaster and decided to seek foreign assistance. Vice President Kalla assembled the diplomatic corps and international organizations the next morning to request help. These critical early decisions by the Yudhoyono government were by no means a given—the TNI had pretty much done what it wanted after the fall of Suharto, and the decision to seek foreign assistance could easily have gone the other way, given Indonesian paranoia about foreign intervention and the steady diet of antiforeign rhetoric since Sukarno's day. But the decisions showed the new government's confidence and the necessity of immediate aid for the survivors. The decisions also demonstrated a level of practicality and decisiveness that had been sorely lacking in Indonesia.

The tsunami first and foremost was an enormous human tragedy. On my first trip to the region with Secretary Powell ten days after it occurred, we observed the damage from a helicopter. The coast of Aceh was stripped bare by the force of the water to a line 25-to-30 feet high on the surrounding bluffs. Palm trees lay on the ground as if felled by a giant scythe. Other trees were completely uprooted and washed to the bluff line or back out to sea. The few left standing had been completely stripped of their leaves. The most haunting picture was of the tiled concrete slab floors that were all that remained of houses in the city of Banda Aceh and the coastal villages, where people had been living up to the minute they and their homes were swept away by the killer wave. Enormous piles of debris from houses, trees, vehicles, and, for a while, human bodies and pet carcasses lined the cliffs and higher ground. Everyday household effects that had been part of the people's normal lives, from cooking utensils to children's toys, stood out in the rubble. During those first few weeks the stench of death was everywhere.

On my numerous visits over the next several months, I could never get over the sense of sadness for the terrible loss of lives. Along what had been Aceh's main transportation artery you could only travel as far as a ship sitting on dry land well away from the beach where it had been left by the great wave. In Banda Aceh itself, the haunting decorated concrete floor slabs stretched for miles; and a barge hurled in by the force of the wave sat in the middle of a neighborhood almost a mile from the shoreline. The stories of the survivors we talked with were truly heart-wrenching. Often only one or two people would be left from an entire family. People told horrible stories of holding on to their children, trying to protect them, only to have them torn from their hands by the strong currents. Tragically, many people were said to have run out to pick up fish as the waters receded in front of the tsunami, leaving them no chance of survival when the waters roared back minutes later. The people of Aceh have for centuries been the most conservative religious Muslims in Indonesia. Nothing, however, could have prepared them for nature's wrath that day.

American Assistance

At the time of Vice President Kalla's briefing, the extent of the devastation was only beginning to be understood. However, I had already authorized that the $100,000 in the ambassador's contingency fund be allotted immediately to the Indonesian Red Cross, which had access to the area. We worked with them to organize a truck convoy of relief supplies to go to Aceh from Medan, the largest city in Sumatra and the site of a small, but active U.S. consulate. Since we had no presence in Aceh because of its closed status, we wanted to provide funds to people who were already active on the ground, basically the Indonesian Red Cross and a small Save the Children operation. Although our first attempt to send in a truck convoy from Medan was turned back by GAM insurgents, it did make it the second day and regularly thereafter. We quickly hired eighty trucks for a month to form these convoys, organized by our consulate in Medan to provide desperately needed food, water, and medicines to be delivered by aid groups operating in Aceh.

With such a huge need, we had to get immediate funding for the relief effort. The embassy placed a hold on any contracts that had not been signed in our ongoing, quite sizeable AID program to Indonesia so the money could be used for tsunami relief. This meant we had some $63 million in cash ready and available to use for critical operations in the first weeks. Washington backed our approach, promising that replenishment funds would be put in a supplemental appropriations bill to fund U.S. government contributions for the tsunami. (President Bush announced early on that the United States would spend $350 million on tsunami relief and reconstruction in all the affected countries, an amount later increased to $950 million.) We were thus able to get money to aid groups on the ground right away while other governments and organizations were still talking about what they intended to do in the future. In the end, the U.S. government contribution for relief and reconstruction in Indonesia amounted to $401 million on the civilian side, over $100 million from our military budget, and the American public contributed well over $1 billion.

Vice President Kalla's briefing was a straightforward plea from the heart for foreign help in Indonesia's time of need. When he'd finished, I approached him privately to offer condolences and asked what they needed most from the United States. "Helicopters," he said. "We can't get to the areas, the roads have been cut, and without helicopters we can do nothing for the people." When I returned to the Embassy, I immediately called Adm. Thomas Fargo, commander of the United States Pacific Command in Honolulu, and asked if they could help. Fargo told me that he had ordered the aircraft carrier *Abraham Lincoln*, which happened to be in Hong Kong transiting from the Indian Ocean to its home base in San Diego, to immediately depart for Southeast Asia. He was not sure how the carrier and accompanying ships could be of use, but he wanted to be in position to act quickly if the governments in the area requested our help. I asked him how many helicopters were on an aircraft carrier. When he said seventeen, I said that was exactly what Indonesia had just requested and asked him to send the carrier directly to Aceh. He was not sure what Washington would decide (especially given the press attention to Thailand and not Indonesia); but we agreed to go through our separate channels to Washington to see if the carrier could get orders to go directly to Aceh.

When I approached the Indonesian government on the possibility of having a U.S. aircraft carrier off its coast, President Yudhoyono made another critical decision, formally requesting the carrier and agreeing that our personnel and equipment could operate in the sensitive Aceh region. (We later negotiated a temporary, unprecedented Status of Forces Agreement to protect our military personnel as they carried out their work.)

Relations between the U.S. military and the Indonesian military had a checkered history. During the first twenty-five years of the Suharto era (1966–1998) relations had been close, and SBY was a proud graduate of the Ft. Leavenworth U.S. Command and General Staff College. Many of the other top TNI leaders had been similarly trained in the U.S., and the TNI's equipment was mostly American. However, after a massacre at Santa Cruz in East Timor in 1991, Congress ended the military training. Restrictions grew on equipment sales in the nineties, as the Suharto regime adopted increasingly harsh actions in its effort to control East Timor, and they were cut off completely after the TNI-backed rampage in East Timor in 1999 following the vote for independence. An attempt to restart cooperation with the TNI to encourage the development of Indonesian democracy and counter international terrorism had been blocked by the Senate in 2002 after Indonesian soldiers were suspected of involvement in the killing of two American teachers and an Indonesian colleague at Timika, West Papua.

When the tsunami occurred, only eight of Indonesia's twenty-five C-130s and a few of its American-made helicopters were operational. To say that the military leadership was suspicious and resentful of the United States would be an understatement. The ill feelings were most pronounced among lower-ranking officers, who had had little contact with the U.S. because of the training cut-off. In short, the Indonesian leadership's decisions in those first hours after the tsunami, particularly in relationship to the United States, were gutsy, harbingers of a new relationship, and obviously driven by the desperate situation in Aceh.

When the *Abraham Lincoln,* under the command of Adm. Doug Crowder, and the *Bonhomme Richard* entered the Strait of Malacca on the east coast of Sumatra on New Year's Eve, I gave Crowder a call to welcome the task force and brief him on the current situation. I explained Indonesian sensitivities, particularly those of the Indonesian military. I specifically asked that they not fly high-performance planes off the carrier over Aceh or over Indonesian waters because of the resentments over the military embargo. He understood, saying this was a mission for his helicopters and the crew's medical personnel. Crowder sent a party to Medan to start coordinating plans with the TNI, the Indonesian civilian leadership, and our staff on the ground, while the carrier sailed on to Aceh at the north of the island. Doug and I stayed in close touch throughout his mission, talking on the phone daily. I found him an excellent partner who immediately understood what it would take to succeed in this unique effort. In the end, I felt that this operation brought out the very best in all sides and provided an excellent example of how the U.S. military and civilian structures can work together for the common good.

By the time of the *Lincoln*'s arrival in Indonesian waters, the U.S. had managed to send a few C-130s loaded with relief supplies from Utapao, Thailand, via Medan to the airport in Banda Aceh. We had also dispatched several truck convoys overland from Medan. The embassy's attaché plane had flown reconnaissance missions with ranking TNI officials along the coast of Aceh so the Indonesians and we could have a better sense of the scope of the problem. We had three doctors from our Naval Medical Research Unit (NAMRU) attached to the embassy working in the stricken city of Meulaboh to help the rescue efforts. Singaporean and Australian military assistance personnel had arrived a couple of days earlier and were providing critical help, but the bulk of the efforts fell on the Indonesian Red Cross and the TNI before the *Lincoln* arrived. Over this first week, we had expended some $5.6 million in emergency AID assistance for use and distribution by the Indonesians, Save the Children, and the International Organization on Migration.

At noon on New Year's Day, a Saturday, the *Abraham Lincoln* was in place off Aceh and began flying helicopter rescue missions along the coast. The embassy worked closely with the American Chamber of Commerce, American church groups (notably the Mormons), and NGOs to assemble a large collection of relief supplies for the first USAF C-130 flights from Jakarta to Aceh. I took a group of embassy volunteers with me to the airport to help load the C-130s. To allay suspicions about U.S. military involvement, I held a press conference (expertly organized by the embassy Public Affairs Officer Charles Silver) to explain to the Indonesian public what we were doing. I discussed the contribution we were making, emphasized the leading role of the Indonesian government and the fact that our efforts were in support of them, and noted that we would continue to help only as long as we were needed. The press conference received massive coverage inside Indonesia and internationally, and a picture of USAID chief Bill Frey and me loading a sack of rice onto a C-130 was carried in almost all of the Indonesian newspapers. It was obviously my responsibility to carry the public messaging on the U.S. aid effort, and this press conference was followed by others at regular intervals.

In Aceh, the *Lincoln*'s helicopters quickly became the critical element in getting the desperately needed water and food to the stricken survivors and bringing back people who needed emergency medical treatment. Adm. Crowder's medical people immediately set up tents in Banda Aceh to treat patients (our embassy medical staff flew up to help), and the rescue effort was in full swing by nightfall. The embassy also had a civilian/military group on the ground to coordinate the effort with the Indonesians.

Crowder told me the story of one of his young pilots that demonstrated the close cooperation, individual initiative, and basic good sense that characterized the entire operation. The pilot, who flew some of the first helicopter missions, reported to the admiral that he was not sure he had done the right thing when one of the embassy people (a young public affairs officer) asked him if he could take a correspondent and his cameraman on board one of the first flights. It turned out that his passenger was Mike Chinoy of CNN, whose initial coverage gave a horrified global audience its first clear look at the extent of the tragedy in Aceh. Those of us involved in the effort will never forget the footage of desperate villagers running to the arriving U.S. military helicopter for help. It was one of the more dramatic pictures of the whole operation and clearly demonstrated the role of the American military in saving lives and helping the people of Indonesia. There is no way anyone could have come up with a PR plan that would have been comparable to the decision of these two young Americans to give Mike and his cameraman the chance to report directly to the world what was happening along the Aceh coast. The embassy/military cooperation continued along the same vein throughout the U.S. military's efforts in Indonesia.

By the time the international conference on Aceh opened in Jakarta on January 6, 2005, with Secretary Powell in attendance, the U.S. military and civilian efforts had become quite impressive. The combined U.S.-Indonesian actions were functioning smoothly, although there was some grumbling by the TNI about the rescue of GAM members along with ordinary Aceh villagers. We had made it clear from the first that the operation would help everyone in need, regardless of their politics.

Cooperation between the American civilian and military assistance efforts was virtually seamless. For example, when LTG Robert Blackman, the overall U.S. military commander of the tsunami rescue effort, came to Jakarta two days after the *Abraham Lincoln* arrived in Aceh, we discussed various aspects of the mission and how to get the coordination right. When my AID chief Bill Frey mentioned how critical safe drinking water was to avoid an almost universally predicted outbreak of cholera, we all lamented that bottled water took an enormous amount of weight and space on the C-130s. Blackman noted that an aircraft carrier could produce a vast amount of clean water if we could figure out a way to get it to the people. Bill responded that USAID would buy as many plastic water containers as could be found in Jakarta and put them on the C-130 flights going from Jakarta that afternoon. Blackman imme-

"Help Indonesia Succeed": The Tsunami 327

diately notified the *Lincoln* to be prepared to fill the water containers that night. Ingenious members of the ship's maintenance crew gathered every water faucet and small piece of pipe they could get their hands on from the *Lincoln* and its sister ships. By evening they had jerry-rigged a system that could fill 750 five-gallon jugs an hour. Officers and enlisted men and women whose jobs normally were to fly airplanes, repair them, or carry out other tasks on the carrier found themselves squatting down in the heat on the flight deck until late in the evening filling water containers the embassy had sent from Jakarta so they could be on the helicopters for delivery the next morning. Over the next few days and weeks as this process became routine, the critical water problem was solved, and the predicted cholera epidemic was avoided.

A rather more negative example also demonstrated our close military-civilian cooperation at the top. My attachés, who were monitoring the military effort and had people at the airport in Medan to help coordinate the massive international presence there, informed me that a U.S. Special Forces unit had showed up without prior coordination. Because of the airport capacity problems at Medan and Banda Aceh, I had used my authority to control the presence of official Americans in the country to demand that all U.S. personnel be cleared by the embassy in advance and that no U.S. government planes (military or civilian) come to Indonesia without a full load of relief supplies. When I asked what the Special Forces unit was doing there, I was told they said they were assessing the situation. I ordered their immediate departure and had the complete backing of the Pacific command and General Blackman. The unit left the next day, and we had no further problems of military units showing up without permission.

It was disconcerting to see how assistance organizations felt they could waste precious days by sending in people to do an assessment, write a report, and then decide what might be needed to help. I made it clear that this was absurd, given the circumstances. If it wasn't obvious to everyone what the immediate needs were, they were in the wrong business. All USG planes that landed in one of the precious slots had to be delivering relief supplies, not just a bunch of assessors with their laptops. This caused great anguish in AID Washington in particular, but there was no reason they couldn't put some people on an airplane filled with relief supplies to assess what the next steps needed to be. Washington swallowed hard, but our logic carried the day. (Incidentally, we maintained this stance with other visitors: Secretary Powell's aircraft carried relief supplies, and Deputy Secretary Paul Wolfowitz came in a loaded C-5A.)

As with the separate assessment teams, we also succeeded in fending off efforts at "disaster sightseeing" in these first weeks. The ranking American visitors who did come were extraordinarily helpful in offering our sympathies to the Indonesian people and in providing publicity on the scope of the tragedy for the U.S. and international community and the need for assistance. The day before the January 6 conference Secretary Powell had visited Aceh along with Florida governor Jeb Bush and the heads of FEMA and USAID. The devastation that we and the accompanying journalists saw that day helped convey to the American people the extent of the tragedy in very human terms.

Powell's plane took off immediately from the airport in Banda Aceh after delivering its passengers, because there was no room to park the plane amid the supplies being landed and transferred to trucks. The Banda Aceh and Medan airports were overwhelmed. A relief flight had earlier clipped a water buffalo on landing, leaving the plane in the middle of the runway and blocking all air traffic for half a day. While Banda Aceh had barely any usable apron space, the airport in Medan had aircraft from around the world lined up on the edges of the runway with huge stacks of relief supplies covered in plastic spread around the apron. Many of those supplies went to Aceh along the twelve-hour land route in trucks we had rented at the start of the relief effort.

Ten days after Powell and Jeb Bush came to Jakarta and Aceh, Deputy Defense Secretary Wolfowitz arrived to review our military's activities, congratulate our troops on their work, and reach out to the TNI. He was accompanied by Admiral Fargo, whose superb cooperation from the first days of the mission had ensured its success. Wolfowitz had been ambassador to Indonesia two decades earlier and retained a strong interest in the country. (I suspect he had signed off on the *Lincoln* deployment to Aceh.) The shipboard schedule of their January 16 visit to the carrier may have been

"Help Indonesia Succeed": The Tsunami 329

unique in the annals of the U.S. Navy. Instead of the normal formalities on the flight deck of the carrier, with demonstrations of the prowess of the jets and their pilots front and center, Wolfowitz and Fargo met down in the belly of the ship with the less glamorous crews of the helicopter contingent, who were, without doubt, the heroes of the day. They got the special treatment they deserved. As one of the admirals present said to me, it was a first time ever that a high-ranking official from Washington came to an aircraft carrier specifically to praise the men and women who flew its helicopters.

During his visit, Wolfowitz also worked to repair ties to the Indonesian military, which were now being restored at the working level by the close cooperation and growing mutual respect between the two militaries in Aceh. Later that month, the U.S. announced that $1 million in C-130 parts and technical help had been approved for Indonesia. The parts and technicians arrived soon thereafter, as the U.S. worked with the TNI to get the aircraft up and running so they could manage the relief work and reconstruction efforts after U.S. planes had departed.

The impact of the helicopters from the *Lincoln*, the equipment and personnel from other U.S. ships involved such as the *Bonhomme Richard,* and the medical people on the ground is hard to exaggerate. During my frequent trips to Aceh, I was struck by the dedication and efficiency of our service people. There was no evidence of an overbearing American military role, only enthusiastic American young people trying in every way they could to help a desperate population. What happened on the ground the first few weeks of 2005 was an incredible demonstration of the good that the United States can do with its wealth and power to help people in truly desperate straits. It also provided invaluable help to the new government of Indonesia by demonstrating that it and its friends were doing everything possible to help the people. The appreciation of the Indonesian public was genuine, and our assistance will be long remembered.

The *Abraham Lincoln* departed the Aceh coast on February 4, its crew having been delayed for a month in getting back to their families in California but all extremely proud of the work they had done to save lives and help the people of Aceh. They had flown over 2800 relief missions, treated some 2200 medical patients, and delivered

4000 tons of relief supplies. Speaking to the men and women of the task force on the deck of the *Abraham Lincoln* that day, Admiral Crowder and I expressed our great pride in the work they had done. The Indonesians, led by the minister in charge of recovery and the chief of staff of the Indonesian military, were also there to convey the profound gratitude of the Indonesian government and people for their effort.

At the same time the *Abraham Lincoln* headed off to California, the USNS *Mercy* arrived. I have a wonderful picture on my study wall of the two ships sailing together with the scarred cliffs of Aceh in the distant background: The warship representing the immediate relief work the U.S. had provided and the *Mercy* representing a longer-term commitment to helping the people of Aceh and Indonesia. The *Mercy* was also the product of a new kind of U.S. civilian-military cooperation. Kept ready to sail but basically an anachronism in a modern military, the *Mercy* was one of two large hospital ships maintained by the U.S. Navy, one on the East Coast and one on the West Coast. When the tsunami occurred, the Navy leadership at the Pentagon came up with the idea of sending the *Mercy* to the region staffed by civilian medical personnel. The chief of naval operations contacted Jon Howe, head of Project Hope, which had operated a decommissioned hospital ship, the *Hope*, from 1958 to 1974. Howe reacted enthusiastically and soon had 4000 volunteers from medical facilities across the U.S. who wanted to take part. In the end, 217 civilians from 55 facilities in 36 states were chosen and joined the ship when it reached Singapore.

The *Mercy* itself sailed from the West Coast only eleven days after the tsunami. By the time it arrived in Aceh on February 4, it obviously could not provide immediate assistance for the survivors; but it embarked on a major effort to deal with lingering medical problems from the tsunami and give badly needed medical services in general to the stricken region. For a critical period, it provided highly valuable medical help to the traumatized people. The volunteers on the *Mercy* came to their job with the same enthusiasm and dedication to accomplishment as the sailors and airmen on the *Abraham Lincoln* and the *Bonhomme Richard*. For the Acehenese it was a strong symbol that the world was not abandoning them when the *Abraham Lincoln* sailed away.

The *Mercy* left the Aceh region six weeks later for a tour of the South Pacific to continue its medical assistance to other countries in serious need of help. (This continued the earlier tradition of the *Hope*. When Diane and I were in West Timor a few months later, a local leader proudly showed us a picture on his wall of the *Hope* visiting the region in 1960.)

As the *Mercy* carried out its work in East Timor on March 28, a magnitude 8.7 earthquake occurred (along the same fault line off West Sumatra) near the island of Nias, causing major devastation. Again, emergency medical help was desperately needed in this relatively isolated region. I called Admiral Gary Roughhead, the number two at the Pacific Command (and later chief of naval operations), to see if the *Mercy* could be sent back up the coast from East Timor to help. He agreed on the spot and sent orders to the ship to get underway that evening. We informed Washington through our separate channels, but it was unlikely anyone would object to a second deployment of the *Mercy* to Indonesia. The ship indeed got underway that evening. Despite its age, the captain ordered the proverbial "full speed ahead." One of the ship's officers told me later he had never heard a ship creak and groan like that old vessel did as it sped to Nias. It arrived five days later, and its volunteer personnel immediately began to take care of the wounded, repair limbs, and manage longer-term health issues.

During a visit a few days later to Nias, I talked with the people on the ship that I had seen off from Aceh only weeks earlier. They were again working hard to help Indonesians in acute distress, both on the ship and on land, and assisting Indonesian authorities (with help also from USAID) to get the city's only hospital running again. I looked in at a makeshift dental clinic set up in a mostly undamaged school building. With a line of patients snaking down the street, the *Mercy*'s dental staff busily provided much needed dental care, using normal wood office chairs and desks rather than fancy dental facilities.

We gave other help in this emergency, including immediately flying Indonesian regional authorities to the scene in our attaché plane and providing relief funds, in addition to the *Mercy*'s visit. The Indonesian government was now better organized to move quickly, and the UN sent teams to Nias from Aceh to help.

We tried to nudge the international organizations to be more active. When one of our embassy medical people at Nias told me the UN relief people were being overly bureaucratic in distributing food supplies, I called the UN's Food and Agriculture Organization representative on the scene to ask why the distribution was so slow. He said something about being sure the food went to people who were really qualified. I blew a cork. I told him the United States was paying for the food; they should stack it in the street and let anyone who needed food pick up a bag without questions. If anyone in his chain of command complained, he should tell them to call me. I would be happy to take the blame. Suddenly, the food magically became available, the crisis was solved, and I never heard any more about it.

As a way to demonstrate the American commitment to help and to encourage contributions from average Americans, the White House sent former presidents George H. W. Bush and Bill Clinton on a February trip to the areas affected by the tsunami. The two former presidents had had a frosty relationship ever since Clinton's defeat of Bush in 1992; but traveling together on this humanitarian mission, they bonded in a way only two people who have carried such a heavy responsibility can. When they alighted from their USAF plane in Medan for a meeting with SBY, I was struck by the frailty of both men. The elder Bush was showing his eighty-one years after a trip halfway around the world, with a whirlwind stop in Thailand, and Clinton, who had undergone a quadruple bypass surgery four months earlier, looked haggard and a shadow of his former hearty self. SBY was obviously touched that these two most prominent Americans (neither obviously in good health) would make such a hard trip to help his country, and the warmth of their meeting was striking. As we flew to Aceh, the two former presidents swapped stories; and my old USLO boss Bush couldn't resist telling a few on me from our days together in China.

On arrival in Aceh, the two men slipped easily into political mode as they visited the affected areas, viewing the devastation by helicopter and consoling victims on the ground as the press cameras rolled. Later in the afternoon, we helicoptered to the USS *Bonhomme Richard* to meet with the men and women who had spent almost two months helping Aceh. The scene verged on the chaotic.

The young Marines and sailors all wanted pictures to send home, jostling the two presidents for individual and group shots. Despite the grueling day, Bush and Clinton were in their element, obviously relishing the opportunity to relive their former lives. After a while, I took the Indonesian foreign minister accompanying us into an air-conditioned meeting room to escape the oppressive tropical heat. Half an hour later, an obviously exhausted Bush came in to rest. Then, forty-five minutes later a sweat-drenched Clinton came in for a breather. I was desperately hoping the day would not end with one of our former presidents experiencing a medical emergency.

When we headed back to the helicopters, the requests for "one more photo" came again. The former presidents' political adrenaline kicked in, and suddenly the two men who had looked totally exhausted minutes before were all smiles once again. That night back in our Jakarta residence (after another harrowing ride in the embassy's small attaché plane through heavy thunderstorms), feeling totally spent after a long day, I watched the two former presidents being interviewed on CNN in Sri Lanka (their next stop). They were dressed in suits and ties, looking like they had just spent a normal day at the office. Diane and I were amazed at their energy and composure. Seeing how political adrenaline had carried these two pros through such a brutal day in terrible heat gave me a much better understanding of the rush politicians get from ceremonial duties and adoring crowds. Clinton remained involved in Aceh issues as a UN representative, helping to rein in various groups to ensure they were working for the common good of the tsunami victims.

As I reflect on the U.S. effort to help Indonesia and the people of Aceh in the wake of the tsunami, I'm deeply proud and impressed by the American sense of compassion and the willingness of millions of Americans to contribute their hard work and their money to help the people there. This is especially true for the thousands of Americans engaged directly in the relief effort. People worked until they were exhausted, and they did it without seeking praise or monetary benefit. Americans wanted to fix the problems to the extent they could, avoid pontification about their efforts, and then leave before they had worn out their welcome.

The people of Aceh and Indonesia expressed their appreciation for the American support—from formal speeches to the grateful look in the eyes of the tsunami survivors to the public opinion polls that showed respect for Americans skyrocketing. Indonesians had seen the best side of America and this, the most populous predominantly Islamic country in the world, now rated Americans in polls as a friendly country, with the highest percentages of any Islamic-majority countries in the post-9/11 world. The people also gained a great deal of confidence in their democratic government, knowing it had been right to work closely with its friends to meet Indonesia's greatest humanitarian challenge.

A Massive NGO Effort

The tragedy produced by the tsunami brought an unprecedented outpouring of support to Indonesia from the international community. Overall, $8.5 billion was reportedly promised from governments and private donations to help the people of Aceh and rebuild their region. Most of it was actually delivered to help alleviate the suffering and rebuild the affected areas. Americans were particularly generous in their support. The Indonesian government and the international humanitarian community sought to come to grips with the enormity of the destruction and to use well this unprecedented outpouring of money entrusted to it.

The government of Indonesia had, as noted, opened the door to international help in the most politically sensitive part of its territory; and through that door poured a truly disparate group of people, most with only the purest humanitarian motives, though some a bit less so. At one point, the press reported that 124 foreign NGOs were working in Aceh. The traditional humanitarian groups found themselves facing massive demands and at times had trouble setting priorities. Some succumbed to the traditional temptation of using the tragedy to raise funds (a normal step for them that proved quite unnecessary with the tsunami); but more often they had plenty of money but no experience dealing with a tragedy of such enormity.

I found the self-promotion of some of the groups hard to take.

I was particularly irritated for the first couple of weeks with the UN's operation, which seemed more interested in talking and taking credit for others' actions than in getting on the ground and helping to manage the effort. The Indonesian government desperately wanted the UN to ride herd on the flood of NGOs that came to Aceh and to coordinate the overall operation, but that turned out to be beyond the UN's capability. (Later, as under-secretary-general at the UN, I had several discussions with my humanitarian colleagues about the need to do better in the future, and I believe they learned from the Aceh experience.)

The larger NGOs flooded in and did good work. But the huge sums of money and obvious need tempted them to get into areas beyond their expertise. Over time this caused some serious problems when groups such as Oxfam and Save the Children threw up substandard houses, many of which turned out to be uninhabitable. The government turned down a plan by the UN High Commissioner for Refugees to build 35,000 houses in Aceh (for which UNHCR had already solicited $40 million in contributions), turning the task over instead to the government's own reconstruction organization, which did an excellent job.

As in any emergency, raw materials and honest builders were in short supply, while scam artists thrived. Several groups came to Aceh fired up to do good but with no idea of how to go about it or any ability to do so. And, most sensitively, some American fundamentalist Christian groups showed up to take advantage of what they saw as an opportunity to convert souls. Needless to say, Christian proselytizing in this conservative Islamic stronghold proved to be one of the most delicate issues we and the government had to deal with. Established religious charities and local Indonesian Christian groups were appalled at this behavior and did what they could to minimize the damage.

After a few weeks the Indonesian government moved to register the various humanitarian groups so they could keep some track of what the groups were doing. They also set time limits on how long the foreigners could stay and criteria to ensure that the groups stuck to only providing emergency assistance. These actions were both rational on their merits and an effort by the government to deal with the xenophobia in the Indonesian body politic about foreigners running all over Aceh. When I was asked about this at one of my press conferences right after the announcement of the new rules, I came down hard on the government's side, noting that it obviously had a right to say what groups could be in the country, to set permissible rules on their behavior, and to determine how long they could stay. I also made clear that the U.S. government had no intention of keeping American military forces there longer than needed. When Vice President Kalla said foreign military forces would be out before March 27, some in Congress took offense at the idea that Indonesia would limit our stay. I said publicly that we supported the government's deadline, which promptly killed the story. (We were actually planning to be out much earlier.)

Despite a few scandals and some frictions with the Indonesian government and local officials, the humanitarian community deserves enormous credit for the lives they saved in Aceh, for the provision of food and medical help, and for the construction of schools and housing. The assistance provided by many governments and individuals around the world constituted an incredible statement of the international community's concern for the people of Indonesia. The UN effort on the ground also hit its stride after a few weeks and helped with overall coordination. And not least, the humanitarian community should be given credit for some hard-hitting post-facto analyses of what had initially gone wrong in carrying out the effort in Aceh, to ensure that the same mistakes did not recur in future crises.

The Indonesian Government Steps Up

The key to the successful post-tsunami effort was the response of the Government of Indonesia. The Yudhoyono government had been in office just over two months when the tsunami occurred. The Indonesian bureaucracy had a well-deserved reputation for incompetence and corruption; and some of the new cabinet members brought in for reasons of political balance had checkered reputations. SBY himself was known for his honesty and made the fight against corruption a key part of his political platform. But any effort to clean up the bloated and ineffective bureaucracy would take a long time, and he had a reputation for putting off tough decisions. When the tsunami struck, however, he took charge from the first day. He made repeated trips to the region to show support and brought a reluctant TNI to heel, pivoting from suppressing insurgents to providing relief, rescuing victims, and burying the dead, and forced it to accept foreign help. The TNI received relatively little international praise for its humanitarian efforts in Aceh because of its infamous reputation; in fact, it did a credible job of helping the population after the tsunami and proved tolerant of extensive international involvement in the relief and reconstruction effort. It later also acquiesced in the Aceh peace settlement.

For coordinating the overall Indonesian government response, SBY relied heavily on Vice President Yusuf Kalla, a tough, deal-making politico who headed Golkar (Suharto's old party), and some of his star cabinet ministers, such as Sri Mulyani Indrawati, to manage the crisis. U.S.-educated Sri Mulyani had been SBY's choice to run the Finance Ministry, but her appointment to this powerful position ran into strong opposition because of her reputation for incorruptibility and her previous job as IMF executive director for Southeast Asia. (In the late 1990s, well before her time there, the IMF had established a reputation as the enemy when the Indonesian economy collapsed while carrying out IMF demands. An infamous photo of IMF director Michel Camdessus standing with his arms folded watching over Suharto as he signed a humiliating deal with the IMF was sometimes compared with the picture of MacArthur towering over Emperor Hirohito when they met after Japan's defeat.) Sri Mulyani received the consolation prize of director of the National Development Planning Agency (BAPPENAS), a position that, fortunately in the tsunami's aftermath, was responsible for developing a blueprint for the reconstruction of Aceh.

Naturally, all of the government agencies wanted a share of the big pot of money coming in from governments and private donors overseas after the tsunami. Sri Mulyani quickly lived up to her reputation as smart and tough, totally focused on what was good for her country. I lobbied quite hard for the establishment of a separate independent Indonesian government organization. And when the overall plan was presented on April 18, 2005, it contained the key element of setting up an independent body, the Agency for the

Rehabilitation and Reconstruction of Aceh (BRR), SBY appointed Kuntoro Mangkusubroto, a Stanford-trained professor and former minister of mines and energy known to be capable and incorruptible, to head the agency. The organization, its powers, and its leadership were all fought over furiously to the very last moment. I argued both in public and in private that the establishment of an independent, clean, and effective organization to manage the reconstruction effort was critical, because any evidence that the outpouring of aid was being wasted would have been devastating for Indonesia's reputation. In the end, full credit should go to SBY, who demanded that the BRR be strong and independent, and to Sri Mulanyi's ability to make it happen.

The BRR, a later UN study noted, had "enormous power to cut through red tape and make decisions quickly." All rebuilding and development programs had to be vetted and approved by BRR, with enforcement of strict application procedures and required benchmarks. Programs had to clearly spell out how the World Bank–monitored funds were spent and by whom, in an effort to combat the corruption that often follows disasters. Every agency had to submit information on proposed projects, including funding sources, location, budget, and performance indicators, before being given approval to work on tsunami recovery in Indonesia. All reconstruction projects were required to meet new codes designed to make buildings more resilient to the forces of nature, especially earthquakes and tsunamis but also hurricanes.

The BRR structure was conceived as a way around the cumbersome Indonesian bureaucracy. Under Kuntoro it soon established itself as the single most effective governmental organization in Indonesia. Kuntoro picked deputies who were clean and competent, often Indonesian executives from international accounting firms. The McKinsey consulting firm provided gratis its top Indonesian expert, Adam Schwartz, author of one of the basic books on Indonesia, to serve as an advisor.

The BRR had the task of working in a region that had endured an unimaginable tragedy and that was profoundly resentful of Jakarta after years of war. Naturally, everyone had urgent and quite reasonable demands that could not quickly be met. Equally problematic were the constant frictions with the bureaucracy in Jakarta, which Kalla or the president often had to settle. The organization set out to methodically define the most critical problems of the reconstruction effort and to work out solutions. It had a lean structure and top-of-the-line technology to ensure up-to-date monitoring and feedback, and it was well financed, thanks to international generosity.

To get the BRR up and running, we needed to help them get money fast and to ensure that they, not corrupt government departments, received the bulk of international governmental financing, so that the money could be used effectively. Most governments and international organizations that pledged large sums for reconstruction assistance did not actually deliver any money on the ground until the fall of 2005. Some were reluctant to put it through this new organization. Indeed, several of my colleagues seemed to prefer using their old contacts. I made the argument more than once to my fellow ambassadors that none of the money given to the old (corrupt) agencies might ever be spent in Aceh, and certainly not soon enough to be useful. The Indonesian parliament also acted relatively slowly in getting funds to the BRR.

We used funds from the unobligated AID money, which could be disbursed immediately, supplemented by contingency funds from Washington, to help the Indonesians get the BRR to up and running. The World Bank's country director, Andrew Steer, proved extraordinarily supportive in this effort. Steer took charge of an international multi-donor assistance fund that brought in hundreds of millions of euros from European governments and put most of that money into BRR programs. He and his people monitored the funds closely and gave the BRR credibility with the international community.

When the BRR closed up shop after four years' work in April 2009, it had succeeded far beyond the hopes of those of us who helped set it up. It had overseen the construction of 140,000 homes, 1,700 schools, almost 1,000 government buildings, airports, and seaports, and 2,300 miles of roads. It had trained an entire new leadership group of teachers and administrators for the province and then smoothly turned over its functions to the GAM-led government elected by the people of Aceh.

The BRR that Kuntoro and his colleagues built proved to be

not only the cleanest organization in Indonesia but also its most effective. It maneuvered through endless negotiations with the Indonesian bureaucracy, international governments, NGOs, and local politicians to provide the rebuilt Aceh promised by President Yudhoyono and the international community. International studies of the relief and reconstruction effort in Aceh all praised the organization's accomplishments, usually noting the irony that an Indonesian government organization had proved more successful than the much-ballyhooed international NGOs and the United Nations. The UN and other studies cited the BRR as a model for global disaster efforts. The World Bank dubbed the Indonesian approach a "highly successful reconstruction effort," calling Aceh "a transformed place, the result of a lot of money, good organization, and hard work." Before the tsunami, such praise for an Indonesian government organization would have been unthinkable.

The major project the U.S. government undertook in Aceh involved the long-term reconstruction of the key west coast highway from Banda Aceh to Meulaboh. This $250 million project was a complex operation, given the physical destruction, the tangled mess of land ownership resulting from the loss of public records, and a range of local problems, from decimated local governments to inconveniently located cemeteries. Seven years later, the U.S. and Indonesia dedicated the highway built to American standards along a route likely to survive any future tsunamis. We knew at the time that the task would be a tough one. But the end product was worth it, and its construction a tribute to American persistence and engineering.

In my public comments (and in our private actions), I had consistently emphasized that Aceh reconstruction was an Indonesian effort and that we and the international community played supporting roles. We did everything possible to ensure that the arguments of our detractors—that we were "taking over" or that we had ulterior motives for our assistance—were demonstrated to be false. In the end, our decision to put the full weight of the U.S. government behind the BRR paid large dividends. We rebuilt our bilateral relationship with Indonesia and strengthened the positive elements in the Indonesian government, thereby helping prove that a democratic government could respond effectively to the needs of its people without enriching a few unscrupulous officials. The tsunami was a huge human tragedy, with the deaths of an estimated 170,000 people, and could have been a total disaster for the new and inexperienced government. But as the immediate relief efforts turned to long-term reconstruction, I was satisfied that we had carried out Secretary Powell's injunction—"Help Indonesia Succeed."

Peace in Aceh

SBY and Kalla made the peaceful resolution of the Aceh conflict a key campaign promise and began looking for a resolution as soon as they took over the government. A first meeting between the government and GAM, the separatist Free Aceh Movement, was being set up in Finland with the country's former president, Martti Ahtisaari, as mediator when the tsunami struck. After five rounds of tough negotiations, the two sides reached an agreement in August 2005 that called for an amnesty and reintegration of GAM fighters into society, decommissioning GAM weapons, withdrawal of Indonesian troops and police beyond what would be needed for normal defense of Indonesia, a monitoring mechanism for implementation led by the EU and ASEAN, and a path to allow GAM to form a political party and compete in local elections. Implementation on the ground was skillfully handled under the EU's leadership, and Kalla and SBY brought along Indonesia's parliament and military to carry out the agreement.

The relatively smooth implementation of the agreement resulted in a GAM-led government in Aceh that played a critical role in the reconstruction effort. It also strengthened democratic governance on the ground, maintained the territorial integrity of the Indonesian state without additional bloodshed, and stood as a major political win for the SBY government. The government and mediators kept us informed on the progress throughout this effort. But except for some seed money to keep the process moving and training for police and other officials after the agreement had been made, we were not involved. Full credit for reaching the peace went to the government, Ahtisaari and his team, and GAM leaders. Not coincidentally, piracy in the Malacca Strait soon became yesterday's news.

16
"Help Indonesia Succeed": From Counterterrorism to Public Health

Countering the Terrorist Threat

A successful response to the tsunami tragedy was critical to SBY's and democracy's credibility in Indonesia, and I felt we had provided extensive and effective support when it was desperately needed. But domestic terrorism posed an even greater threat to Indonesia's democratic future. The danger was real and immediate when we arrived in 2004. A suicide bomber drove a panel truck of explosives into the gate of the Australian Embassy only six weeks before SBY's inauguration, killing nine people and injuring more than one hundred fifty others. Like dozens of other bombings in Indonesia that had killed hundreds of Indonesians and foreigners since the fall of Suharto, it was the work of one of the world's deadliest terror groups, the Jemaah Islamiyah (JI). Founded in 1992 as an offshoot of the Darul Islam network that had for decades fought the Indonesian authorities with a goal of turning Indonesia into an Islamic state, JI's ultimate goal was the establishment of an Islamic caliphate spanning the southern Philippines, Malaysia, Singapore, Indonesia, and southern Thailand. JI's leaders, including its "spiritual" leader, Abu Bakar Ba'asyir, or ABB. returned to Indonesia from exile after Suharto's fall in 1998. The organization then pulled off a series of bombings that included an attack on the Philippine ambassador's residence in August 2000; Christmas Eve bombings of several churches that same year; major attacks in Bali in 2002 and 2005; and bombings of the Marriott hotel in Jakarta in August 2003 and 2009, as well as the September 2004 Australian Embassy bombing.

JI's ties to Al-Qaeda dated to the war in Afghanistan, when the first Indonesians went to Afghanistan to fight in the mid-eighties. Other Indonesians developed links to the Moro Islamic Liberation Front (MILF) and the Abu Sayyaf Groups (ASG) in the Philippines in the mid-1990s. The terrorists rapidly expanded their reach in the more permissive atmosphere in Indonesia after the fall of Suharto's autocracy. In this they were abetted by a poorly informed public that was in denial over the nature of the problem, hypersensitive to Western criticism, and inclined to side with any activity or organization labeled "Islamic." The terrorists received extensive training and ideological support from international terrorist groups as well as funding from the Persian Gulf states.

Terrorism had to be tackled quickly and ultimately rooted out for the new democratic system in Indonesia to thrive and prosper. Given the U.S. Congress's restrictions on help for the Indonesian military after the East Timor debacle and in response to the critical need to counter the terrorist upsurge, most of our assistance to Indonesia's security sector went to support the police (INP) particularly its units that dealt directly with counterterror operations. We also provided assistance to improve the judicial system.

We urged the government to move forcefully to eliminate the terrorists through arrests, trials, and isolation from the public at large; to build the capacity of the Indonesian police, intelligence agencies, and if possible the military to apprehend the terrorists; to cooperate closely in the area of intelligence sharing; to improve the ability of the judicial system to keep the terrorists behind bars; to encourage regional cooperation; and to provide assistance where possible to counter the rising Islamic radicalism that fed the terrorist networks. It seemed obvious that if we could not succeed in this modern, pluralistic Islamic-majority country, we had little chance of success in more radicalized Muslim societies.

At the same time, we needed to upgrade the protection of our own facilities and those of other Americans in Indonesia. We worried a lot about (and worked hard to improve) the security of the International School of Jakarta, American-branded hotels, and other American facilities that were potential terrorist targets. The U.S. Embassy remained, as usual, at the top of the terrorists' list, as well as the magnet for mass demonstrations at regular intervals. (I repeatedly made the point publicly that we had no problem with the demonstrations so long as they were peaceful.) At one point in 2005 we closed the Embassy for a short time after a detailed diagram of the property, including the location of my office, was published on the internet. The posting included the helpful suggestion that the best way to attack the Embassy would be to launch a rocket-propelled grenade at my office. (The embassy's windows facing the main street had been covered with ugly steel plates to mitigate the danger of a possible car bomb, but they probably would not have stopped an RPG.)

For much of our time in Indonesia, we knew from our sources that the terrorists considered me their number one target for assassination, even ahead of SBY, and they strove actively to carry it out. Diane seemed less than amused when our little outings to a nearby mall to shop or get a meal took place in the bubble created by my eight-member security guard detachment. For several months when the threat reached its peak, Diane had a policewoman accompanying her for protection. Needless to say, we enjoyed our freedom and anonymity when we were out of Indonesia for a few days of rest.

The U.S. strategy to help Indonesia eradicate the terrorists and strengthen moderate forces in Indonesia fit closely with SBY's own approach. He pressed the system hard to reduce the threat and appointed dedicated and noncorrupt officials to lead the battle. Our own contribution included strong support for "Team Bomb" and "Detachment 88," the core of the Indonesian counterterrorism strike force. We provided training, logistical support, and intelligence to enhance their effectiveness. The U.S. Department of Justice played a critical role along with the Australian National Police in helping turn the police, the corrupt and perennial stepchild of the TNI before 1999, into a reforming, competent, and modern police force. U.S. programs dealt with everything from basic management skills to human rights training for patrolmen. (I remember watching a new training film with the leadership of the police in which a policeman's clubbing of a peaceful demonstrator elicited a groan throughout the audience. The film made the point emphatically that the offending officer had to be disciplined.)

One of the most difficult tasks in dealing with the police

involved reforming the heavily armed Mobile Brigade (aptly abbreviated as Brimob in Indonesian)—an essential element of the police force, given the unsettled conditions in Indonesia, but with a bad record of human rights violations. In the regular takedowns of terrorist cells, its personnel took the lead in the raids and suffered the consequences. In 2003, Congress had barred the State Department from using its security funds to train Brimob. I tried, without success, to get a cooperative training program for Brimob underway with the Italians or the French, who had excellent democratic gendarme forces. Unfortunately, they did not have the money to do it themselves, and we could not fund it because of the congressional ban. We had good success in vetting the counterterrorism (and counternarcotics) forces with the Indonesians, but a broader effort to weed out bad actors in Brimob that would meet congressional funding mandates proved a major challenge. In the end, we recommended that carefully structured training be given to some elements of Brimob, using DOD funds to enhance the counterterrorism program and limit human rights violations.

With an ambivalent public instinctively inclined to support Islamist actions against Western interference, the Indonesian government always felt it necessary to carefully calibrate its antiterrorist actions to retain popular support. In my public statements, I emphasized the international cooperation among people of all religious faiths to curb the terrorist menace. At one point, the British and Australian ambassadors and I met jointly with the Indonesian parliament on the global effort, hoping to allay the concerns of its more skeptical members. Terrorism was a sensitive subject, and we had to be careful not to provoke an anti-American backlash that would have weakened the entire effort.

Years of autocracy had left Indonesia with a deeply corrupt judicial and penal system. President Yudhoyono told his attorney general to clean up his notorious department and made the eradication of corruption a basic goal. Though we provided the attorney general's office with training and other resources to help in this task, changing a culture where bribes and connections usually win out over the rule of law is a generational project. The prosecutors became quite adept at trying terrorism cases where the stakes and publicity were high. But judges were slow to hand down appropriately lengthy sentences, often giving terrorists who had murdered many people just a few years in jail, with terms that were routinely reduced by holiday amnesties. In addition, Indonesian jails were notoriously lax about security, allowing senior JI leaders to continue to lead operations from prison. Over time, the control over inmates improved as people throughout the system came to realize the importance of ending the terrorist threat.

While terror cases were prosecuted, the courts continued to be mostly ineffective in seriously attacking the endemic corruption. High-priced defense lawyers and bribes often trumped the good intentions of the attorney general's office. And the courts usually proved unable to deal with wrongdoing by high-level officials.

A particularly egregious case involved the poisoning of one of Indonesia's leading human rights activists, Munir Said Thalib, in September 2004. Thalib was given a drink laced with arsenic on an Amsterdam-bound flight on Garuda, Indonesia's state airline. The police had clear evidence that Munir had been poisoned by an off-duty Garuda pilot, assisted by two members of the flight crew, at the behest of the chief of Indonesian intelligence and his deputy. We pressed hard for years to get the Indonesians to bring the perpetrators to justice, including an offer of forensic help from the FBI. Eventually, the pilot was tried and convicted, the deputy intelligence chief was brought to trial but let off, and the former intelligence chief who was behind the murder was never prosecuted.

One area where the Indonesians had more success than most other governments was in using soft tactics to gain the confidence of captured terrorists, then turning them and thereby gaining critical intelligence, while warning others away from answering the terrorist siren call. While some other countries such as Saudi Arabia carried out (often ineffective) brainwashing efforts, the Indonesians often managed to use moderate Islamic arguments to persuade captured terrorists to accept the error of their ways. The Indonesian police had a right to be proud of this effort, which remained one of their top methods to develop information and neutralize further threats. But the U.S. government was not flexible enough to provide any meaningful support, such as removing reformed offenders from terrorist lists as an incentive to others.

We worked to ensure that the counterterrorist campaign in Indonesia stayed closely integrated with global counterterrorism efforts. Many of the Indonesian terrorist leaders learned their trade in Afghanistan and initially received the bulk of their funding from the Gulf States. The two top terrorist operatives in Indonesia were Malaysians who had earlier been driven out of their home country. Most of the Indonesian terror groups trained their people in the Southern Philippines, moving back and forth between the two countries with ease.

SBY asked me to help on regional coordination, since we had good counterterrorism cooperation with each of Indonesia's neighbors. We developed regional counterterrorism plans with neighboring U.S. embassies, including hosting a meeting of my colleagues with the State Department's chief counterterrorism officer to encourage greater local cooperation. We also worked to shut off financial support for terrorism from the Gulf. Over time, the outside financing dried up, and JI and other terrorist groups in Indonesia had to rely on their own limited resources.

By 2007 when we left Jakarta, the Indonesians were making genuine gains in bringing terrorism under control. The JI spiritual leader, Abu Bakar Ba'aysir, was back in jail, one of the top two operatives had been killed in a shootout in November 2005 (the other was killed in 2008), and their level of support in the Indonesian population had steadily dwindled. Hundreds of terrorists had been arrested and jailed, regional cooperation had improved, and foreign funding greatly decreased. The weakest areas continued to be internal Indonesian government coordination, Indonesia's capacity to control its sprawling archipelagic borders, and the judicial system. But the determination of SBY and his government to eliminate the terrorists, the greatly improved police capabilities, and an improving justice system had reduced a dangerous threat to Indonesian democracy to a manageable level.

Working with the Indonesian Military

The brutal actions of the TNI and their militias in East Timor had ended the traditionally close relationship between the U.S. military and the TNI. With Senator Patrick Leahy and his aide, Tim Rieser, in the lead, by 2000 Congress had imposed a virtual embargo on dealing with the Indonesian military and instituted strict vetting rules to ensure against interaction with TNI personnel involved in the atrocities. The 9/11 attacks the following year, however, made it obvious that we needed to reengage with the TNI if the country was to become an effective partner in the War on Terror, act as a counterbalance to growing Chinese ambitions in the region, and manage its own humanitarian disasters. Then the August 2002 killing of two American teachers and the wounding of eight others outside the Papuan town of Timika near the American-owned Freeport mine derailed this reengagement effort. Suspicions of TNI involvement in the teachers' killing contained in the initial police report, the fact that the attackers were dressed in military uniforms, and the TNI's lack of cooperation early in the investigation convinced Congress (again spurred by Leahy) to add a restriction against training and normalizing the relationship until the TNI fully cooperated on the Timika case.

Indonesia's new democratic leaders understood that the TNI had to be brought under control and subordinated to the civilian government for Indonesia to become a modern democratic state. As part of the process, parliament passed laws in 2002 and 2004 that banned the military's role in politics, provided broad powers to the civilian minister of defense, mandated an end to TNI business enterprises, and subordinated the military to the president and the minister of defense. The intent was to end the Indonesian military's political role. As President Megawati's coordinating minister for security affairs, SBY had been deeply involved in this process. Indeed, while still in uniform in 1998, he had been a key player in TNI-generated reforms that gave up the "dual function" role that legitimized the military's political activity under Suharto. The military had been slowly withdrawing from their positions in the parliament (they were all out by 2004) and turned over all police functions to the National Police. President Yudhoyono discussed military reform in most of our conversations and with almost every visiting American official.

Powell, Wolfowitz, and Powell's successor as secretary of state, Condoleezza Rice, all worked to reengage with the TNI. Leahy and

Rieser complained, not surprisingly, about these efforts. At about this time, I called on Rieser in his office to discuss resumption of our cooperation with the TNI. After I made my initial pitch, with Rieser slouching in his chair and looking bored, he responded, in an obvious putdown, that if that was all I had to say then there was nothing more to discuss. I said "OK" and got up to leave. At that point, Rieser became civil and asked me to sit back down. We then had a reasonable conversation, although neither of us changed our views.

When SBY visited Washington in July 2005, he and President Bush agreed that normal military-to-military contacts were in the interests of both sides. I met with SBY soon after his return to discuss how to implement this commitment. I made the case to Washington that we needed the full package of assistance to the TNI (including Foreign Military Sales) if we were to be effective in helping the government reform its military. In October the State Department announced that the United States was completely ending the Indonesian arms embargo. Secretary Rice stated the case simply: "A reformed and effective Indonesian military is in the interest of everyone in the region." And she began referring to a "strategic relationship" between the two countries.

The primary excuse for continuing the embargo after 2002 had been the suspicion of local TNI involvement in the Timika murders. Patsy Spier, the wife of one of the victims and herself wounded in the incident, was an effective advocate for justice in the case. She did an excellent job of keeping Washington's feet to the fire and met twice with President Yudhoyono himself to ensure justice was done for her late husband. I, along with other members of the embassy, met with her regularly and did everything we could to help. After an exhaustive investigation, FBI agents concluded that Anthonius Wamang, a man with ties to the Papuan independence movement, was the gunman, not the TNI, and that he carried out the attack with several other Papuan civilians. They found no evidence of TNI involvement. The perpetrators were later arrested and tried for the crime, with Wamang receiving a life sentence for the murders.

With little direct external threat except terrorism and border protection, the military played a critical role helping the Indonesian state manage the never-ending series of humanitarian crises produced by Indonesia's position in the Pacific Ring of Fire. The U.S. military and the TNI had learned to work together in the Aceh humanitarian effort, and cooperation on disaster relief made a natural fit.

A second area where the TNI had experience and potential involved UN peacekeeping. SBY was proud of his record as a UN peacekeeper in Bosnia. A revived TNI role in peacekeeping would keep its troops employed, provide a major boost to morale, and give the forces experience in real world operations. SBY volunteered a sizable contingent to Lebanon following the Israeli-Hezbollah confrontation in the summer of 2006; and after overcoming some early misgivings by the Israelis, an Indonesian component to the peacekeeping force was approved. (I visited them a few years later as UN under-secretary-general and found that they had an excellent reputation among their UN colleagues.) Indonesia continues to be an important contributor to UN peacekeeping missions.

Strengthening Indonesia's Democracy

As we sought to help Indonesia resolve its many problems, we were acutely aware that the ultimate goal was a democratic, prosperous, and forward-looking Indonesia, managing its own affairs and serving as a model of a large developing country with a population that is 87 percent Islamic. It seemed obvious that if Indonesia became a modern democracy based on the principles of tolerance, rule of law, and peaceful exchange of ideas, extremists and terrorists would lose their relevance and popular support. Fortunately, this vision was shared by President Yudhoyono, his supporters, and most of Indonesia's elite.

The United States had been helping Indonesia build such a society for some time, with an emphasis on education, public health, rule of law, civil society, emergency preparedness, and democratic structures and norms. We encouraged Indonesians to study in the United States and began laying the groundwork to reestablish the Peace Corps in Indonesia to increase contacts and promote English proficiency. Indonesia's vibrant civil society played a key role in the transition to democracy. We had long-standing ties with Indonesia's two most important Islamic social organizations, Nahdlatul Ulama (or NU, established in 1926) and Muhammadiyah (established in 1912). While they differ somewhat in ideology and their social base, both are highly effective social organizations active in education, medicine, and the provision of aid and support to their 100 million members. We worked closely with these organizations for years, directly through AID and indirectly through the Asia Foundation, supporting programs to promote social welfare and modern democratic concepts. Both were strong moderating forces in Indonesian society and strong supporters of democracy.

But expanding support for democracy and improving the image of the U.S. were not all smooth sailing. While the Indonesian public perception of the U.S. rose dramatically following our assistance to Aceh, radical Islamic anti-American forces remained strong in Indonesia. They were tuned in to global issues and used any anti-Islamic incidents as ammunition against the U.S. and the West. Ironically, as support for terrorism waned in Indonesia, sympathy for Islamic radicalism in general seemed to grow. Moderate Muslim leaders and educators expressed to us their concerns that the radicals were finding a growing receptivity on university campuses.

To help deal with this trend, we put together a detailed package of public affairs activities that included increased interaction with the press and opinion leaders, greater support to the government's programs, backing for moderate publications (to counter the stacks of hardline material available, thanks to Gulf money), and a major increase in exchanges. Unfortunately, Washington, which was spending billions of dollars on the wars in Afghanistan and Iraq, could not come up with a few tens of millions of dollars for the peaceful struggle in Indonesia.

Democracy and religious tolerance (the latter a centuries-old tradition in Java and most of the rest of modern Indonesia) were making headway in Indonesia, but they were doing so in the face of strong headwinds. SBY's government took considerable criticism from many in Indonesia and abroad for not doing more to shut down the radicals. But while I often thought his approach was overly cautious, I was not so foolish as to believe we had a better feel for what was possible in the country than the president and his advisors. For a country that less than a decade earlier had been in the tight grip of authoritarian control and endured a bumpy transition, Indonesia was doing a truly impressive job of consolidating its democratic future.

Continuing Crises

Violent acts of nature created the Indonesian archipelago's 17,000 islands, and disasters were a part of Indonesia's daily existence. The Aceh earthquake (one of the biggest ever at 9.1 on the Richter scale) and tsunami were the product of the fault line between the Indo-Australian and Eurasian plates that grind together far under the Indian Ocean off the west coast of Sumatra. The tsunami was followed by the Nias earthquake. And in May 2006, a large earthquake struck a densely populated area southwest of Yogyakarta, a major center of Javanese culture and tourism, again along the fault line. An estimated 6,200 people died, with perhaps 50,000 others injured. The Indonesian government, NGOs, and the embassy moved quickly to help. USAID allotted $2.5 million in emergency aid, most of which went to the Indonesian Red Cross and other NGOs active in the area. By the next day we had people on the ground (including embassy and NAMRU doctors) to give aid, help get a mobile hospital in place, and pay to bring in ambulances from other cities in the region. Four days after the earthquake, a U.S. Marine field hospital, staffed by approximately one hundred Marines from Okinawa, was taking care of patients, and our AID people helped solve an acute water shortage.

When Diane and I visited the stricken area, we met with SBY, the Sultan of Yogyakarta, and our people involved in the rescue work. The effort was on a far more manageable scale than Aceh, the relief better organized, and the embassy's disaster team well practiced. Again, our help to Indonesia in a time of need drew wide publicity and appreciation from the Indonesians. Some scientists expressed fear that the earthquake might induce a major eruption of the nearby Mt. Merapi volcano, which had been rumbling and spewing lava and ash for weeks before the earthquake. Nature's power was again on display, as Diane and I watched the belching volcano from our aircraft on the return to Jakarta. Fortunately, the earthquake seemed to have little effect on the volcano's own timetable.

Avian Influenza

As if dealing with terrorism, natural disasters, and the struggles of democratic governance were not challenge enough, Indonesia found itself at the epicenter of a potentially devastating global epidemic of avian influenza (aka bird flu). A particularly dangerous strain (H5N1) had first appeared in China in 1987 and spread slowly throughout Southeast Asia and worldwide. In Indonesia, the first cases of this new strain were discovered in chicken flocks in 2003. The disease spread quickly, and by 2005 it had become widespread among both commercial and domestic chickens. Human cases began to mount. The death rate among infected humans in Indonesia was high (around 75–80 percent), and the world health community viewed Indonesia as "ground zero" for a possible global pandemic.

With a health system in decline due to governmental decentralization, as well as insufficient funding and ineffective coordination in the Indonesian bureaucracy, managing the bird flu crisis presented a daunting challenge. The Ministry of Health was weak and poorly led, but the Agriculture Ministry, one of Indonesia's most hidebound bureaucracies, proved even worse, incapable of coping with the root of the problem—backyard chickens—in any meaningful way.

The most immediate and practical assistance the U.S. provided came from the Naval Medical Research Unit (NAMRU-2), located at the Indonesian Ministry of Health's National Institute of Health. Established by the U.S. Navy toward the end of World War II to study the effect of tropical diseases on the U.S. military and develop counters to them, NAMRU-2 moved to Jakarta in 1990. It had a remarkable record of success through the years in working on diseases, including malaria, dengue fever, and cholera, and its expertise proved invaluable when Indonesia became the focus of world attention on avian influenza. The U.S. Navy doctors and researchers and local medical personnel assigned to the unit (18 Americans and 145 Indonesians) were extraordinarily talented and dedicated people. For years, the unit had worked closely with the Indonesian Ministry of Health, and when bird flu came to Indonesia, it was natural that they cooperated from the first to help analyze samples of the virus as it developed.

They had the best analytical lab in the country for this kind of work. Their teams went to local sites where outbreaks were reported and helped bring samples to Jakarta, where they analyzed them and shared all the details of their work with their Indonesian colleagues and with the CDC in Atlanta. The close collaborative relationship gave the Indonesians real-time and highly accurate information on the development of the disease. The unit was well integrated into the embassy family and served as a bridge between the Indonesians and the CDC in Atlanta.

The strangest and ultimately most destructive player in the Indonesian avian influenza saga was SBY's first-term minister of health, Siti Fedilah Supari, a cardiology specialist with a research background and a growing political appetite. SBY had chosen her at the last minute to balance out his cabinet with another female and a member of one of Indonesia's opposition parties. In my initial meeting with the minister, she praised NAMRU and its leader, who was part of my team in the meeting, noted the organization's work on avian influenza, and supported a new agreement on NAMRU's status. I left the meeting expecting her to be a strong partner on health issues.

However, in the months that followed, with the growing pressure in Indonesia to do something dramatic as deaths mounted, it became clear that she and some members of her staff harbored deep resentments against NAMRU and its expertise and needed a foreign scapegoat to explain their lapses in controlling the disease. She turned to classic populist rhetoric to use the crisis to promote her political ambitions. When a major Australian pharmaceutical company announced it was patenting a new flu vaccine derived from an H5N1 sample that Indonesia had shared under standard practice with the World Health Organization, Minister Supari decided (or was convinced by some of her colleagues) that the World Health Organization's approach was unfair. (Under the global rules in place since the 1920s, countries agreed to share samples of new strains of flu within twenty-four hours, which were then provided to pharmaceutical companies to develop vaccines to counter them.) She proclaimed that the system disadvantaged Indonesia and other developing countries, who had to pay the drug companies for the vaccines, a mantra with considerable appeal to the xenophobia that always lurked just under the surface of the Indonesian psyche.

NAMRU researchers began to feel a chill from their Indonesian colleagues, and we and other international donors were bombarded with requests to build a high-security laboratory for Indonesia so it could carry out much of the reference work itself. The U.S had no problem with the concept of a top-security Indonesian lab. Both NAMRU and USAID tried to assist, and the Japanese also promised major funding to upgrade Indonesian laboratories to the required levels. But the complaints and accusations about NAMRU's supposed sins became louder and louder.

In August 2006, Minister Supari announced that Indonesia would not send further samples to the WHO reference lab in Hong Kong, saying Indonesian labs and NAMRU could do the task themselves and called for agreements to ensure that companies did not benefit from samples that were provided for research. By late 2006, the minister began arguing that the flu viruses were the intellectual property of the Indonesian government, and Indonesian rights had to be protected. She demanded that NAMRU and Indonesian health organizations stop sending samples abroad until these agreements were in place. The World Health Organization and other international health officials were horrified. The world faced a potentially catastrophic pandemic, and its member at ground zero of the threat was flouting a process that had been in place since the Spanish flu pandemic to protect the health of the global community.

This issue was just heating up when we left Indonesia in early 2007, but the fight became stranger and stranger in the following months and years. Supari's statements became increasingly shrill. She published a book accusing the USG and NAMRU of using Indonesian avian influenza samples to develop biological weapons (which U.S. Defense Secretary Gates publicly put down as "nutty"), accused NAMRU of spying, and called the avian influenza threat a divine intervention. The minister made common cause with SBY's political opponents, including some of the most radical Islamic groups, to undermine his efforts to bolster Indonesia's international reputation. Efforts to negotiate a new NAMRU agreement stalled as the atmosphere became more and more charged. Even the Foreign Ministry (clearly feeling the heat generated by Supari and her supporters) began to voice objections, and Indonesian supporters of NAMRU were attacked as being too close to the Americans. Typically, SBY said all the right things in meetings with me and other American officials, but he was obviously unwilling to take on his health minister directly.

An agreement was never reached, and NAMRU-2 withdrew three years after we left Indonesia. By that time, Supari herself had come under considerable criticism for her extreme views, but it was too late to save NAMRU, and the collective health of Indonesians was the loser. U.S. cooperation with Indonesia on health issues continued, but our best asset had been destroyed. Fortunately, Indonesia and the entire world got lucky as the threat of an avian flu pandemic receded.

***

In the late fall of 2006 as we passed the two-year mark in Indonesia, Diane and I began looking forward to completing our tour the following summer and retiring from the Foreign Service after forty extraordinarily satisfying years. Given all the crises in Jakarta, I felt we had made good progress in carrying out Secretary Powell's instruction to help Indonesia succeed. Problems still abounded, but the SBY administration was doing a reasonable job in dealing with them. I would have preferred a more aggressive implementation of governance reforms and a more forceful approach to dealing with the religious bullies and extremists, but I knew the president well enough to understand that he would not give up his cautious style. His procrastination would later become a serious issue as problems festered that could have been resolved with more forceful leadership. But his success in dealing with crises, reducing corruption, building the economy, promoting democratic governance, and repairing Indonesia's international image during these first two years had made an excellent beginning in consolidating Indonesia's democratic future.

The U.S.-Indonesian relationship had also been restored. Our poll approval ratings were high, working relations with the government were close—SBY and Mrs. Yudhoyono made the unusual gesture of personally attending all our Fourth of July celebrations. Washington now viewed Jakarta as a close friend and ally, with numerous meetings of our two presidents and successful visits to Indonesia by President Bush, Secretaries Powell and Rice, and others.

Photo Gallery

1. The Pascoe family at the Great Wall, 1974. Author's collection.

2. Lynn Pascoe at his desk at the
U.S. Liaison Office in Peking, 1974. Author's collection.

3. Lynn Pascoe and Barbara Bush with a Chinese official
at USLO, 1975. Author's collection.

4. Diane Pascoe and the girls always drew a crowd, Shanghai, 1975. Author's collection.

5. American Staff at USLO under George H. W. Bush, 1975. Author's collection.

363

6. Sending off Deng Xiaoping (shaking hands with Lynn Pascoe) after his historic US visit, 1979. White House Photo.

7. Assisting Secretary of State George Shultz at the Moscow Summit, 1988. State Department Photo.

8. After Taiwan president Lee's goodbye game of golf, Taipei, 1996. Taiwan Presidential Office.

9. Typical July 4 Ceremony in Malaysia, 2000. US Embassy Photo.

10. A view of the tsunami devastation in Banda Aceh, Indonesia, 2004. Author's collection.

11. Ambassador Pascoe loading Aceh relief supplies on a USAF C-130 with USAID mission director Bill Frej, 2005. US Embassy Photo.

12. Former presidents George H. W. Bush and Bill Clinton talk with Indonesian president Susilo Bambang Yudhoyono (at right) before visit to Aceh; Lynn Pascoe (at left) and Indonesian presidential assistant Dino Djalal (2nd from right), 2005.
Indonesian government photo.

13. Crew on aircraft carrier USS *Abraham Lincoln* filling water bottles for Aceh relief, 2005. US Navy Photo.

14. *USNS Mercy* arrives as *USS Abraham Lincoln* departs Aceh, 2005. U.S. Navy Photo.

15. A grateful woman from Aceh expresses her view on U.S. assistance, 2005. Author's collection.

16. Diane and Lynn Pascoe distributing aid after Yogyakarta earthquake, with USAID mission director Bill Frej, 2006. US Embassy Photo.

17. One of Under-Secretary-General Lynn Pascoe's regular briefings of the UN Security Council, 2007. UN Photo.

18. Discussing the Mideast with UN Secretary-General Ban Ki-moon, Chef de Cabinet Vijay Nambiar, and Special Mid-East Coordinator Michael Williams (clockwise from upper left: Ban, Nambiar, Pascoe, Williams), 2007. UN Photo

19. Under-Secretary-General Pascoe arriving for talks at Somalia's Presidential Palace, 2010. UN Photo.

20. President Barak Obama briefing the UN Security Council with Under-Secretary-General Pascoe in his usual chair. Other officials include UN Secretary-General Ban Ki-moon; Secretary of State Hillary Clinton and U.S. Permanent Representative to the UN Susan Rice (behind Pascoe); and UN Chef de Cabinet Vijay Nambiar and UN Disarmament Representative Sergio Duarte (behind Obama), 2009. UN Photo.

Part II
At the United Nations

17
A New Challenge at the United Nations

I had turned down the possibility of another ambassadorship and planned to retire the next summer after forty amazing years in the Foreign Service. Diane and I were just beginning to discuss where we wanted to live and what kind of post–Foreign Service work might be appealing. Then in November, I received a call from Under Secretary Nicholas Burns, who said Secretary Condoleezza Rice had worked out an agreement with the incoming UN secretary-general, Ban Ki-moon, for an American to be named to the post of under-secretary-general for political affairs. She knew about my retirement plans and wondered if I would be interested in being one of the U.S. candidates. Rice, President Bush, and the U.S. permanent representative to the UN, John Bolton, had apparently pressed hard for the United States to get either the head of the Peacekeeping Department (DPKO) or the Political Department (DPA). They preferred Peacekeeping, which was more glamorous and cost the U.S. much more money; but Ban considered that too much of a reach, because the U.S. had not contributed troops to UN peacekeeping since the fiasco in Somalia a dozen years earlier.

When I heard the news in October that Ban had been elected UN secretary-general, I was delighted to see an old colleague achieve such a high honor. I had a great deal of respect for him and thought he would do an excellent job at the United Nations. After our brief time working together in the early nineties, Ban had moved on to become the South Korean national security adviser and foreign minister before winning the race to lead the UN. We had not seen each other in over a decade.

I knew little about what the UN political job entailed (or how the UN worked in general for that matter) and assumed Rice would pick someone with UN experience or perhaps a political choice outside the Foreign Service. But the opportunity to continue working as a diplomat, to live in New York, and to work with Ban made the offer a tempting one. Despite my low expectations, I agreed to have my name put in the mix. It turned out that when I was proposed to Ban, he accepted the suggestion right away, presumably happy that the United States had offered up a professional diplomat he knew rather than a conservative ideologue in the Bolton mode.

Ban's Vision for the UN's Political Role

I called on Ban at his apartment in New York on New Year's Day 2007, ostensibly for a job interview but in reality to discuss his plans for the Political Department and the role he expected me to play. Ban made it quite clear he intended to carry out a major overhaul of the UN system. Having served at the South Korean mission as a young diplomat and as chief of staff for the Korean General Assembly president, Ban knew a great deal about the UN and how it did and did not work. The U.S. talked a lot about "UN Reform" but had failed to make much headway during the many years an American headed the UN's Department of Management. Most U.S. efforts had focused on cutting costs rather than changing the system. Ban, on the other hand, was committed to carry out a major overhaul to make the UN more effective.

The new secretary-general was particularly focused on the role he wanted the UN to play in carrying out its principal responsibility of promoting international peace and security. He expected the Department of Political Affairs to lead the effort. Ban pointed to the last American to manage the UN political affairs, the legendary Ralph Bunche, who had worked to resolve conflicts from the Arab-Israeli war to the Congo. Ban believed that the peaceful settlement of disputes as laid out in Chapter VI of the UN Charter had to be restored for the organization to live up to its lofty aspirations. Over the years, financial and other resources had gone to peacekeeping, humanitarian actions, and establishing international norms, while the department responsible for preventing conflict languished, starved for both funds and attention.

Advocates for UN reform had complained for some time that this core political responsibility of the United Nations had been largely ignored. These concerns formed the basis for the 2005 UN World Summit's emphasis on increased UN attention to preventive diplomacy and mediation. The global leaders called for a "culture of prevention" and strengthening the capacity of the UN to implement "effective means for the prevention and removal of threats to peace." Ban strongly embraced this approach, but he also knew that the statements by themselves (a UN specialty) could not produce results. He laid out for me in our New York meeting his determination to put the settlement of disputes and the political department back at the center of the UN's work.

The push to upgrade the Political Department was also driven by the exponential increase in peacekeeping costs and a growing appetite for more flexible (and much cheaper) political missions (called Special Political Missions, or SPMs) to manage world hotspots. The appeal of these missions had led to a major expansion in their use by the Security Council, but inflexible funding mechanisms and DPA's managerial weakness hindered the effort. Indeed, when a large UN political mission was set up in Afghanistan in 2002, it was placed under DPKO rather than DPA because of the latter's inferior management and logistical capabilities. As Ban analyzed the problem, the entire structure needed radical transformation to enable the UN to fulfill its responsibility as stated in the Charter.

Ban described his conclusions and my marching orders on that New Year's Day in the Waldorf Astoria. After some initial pleasantries and a renewal of our previous ties, he shared with me his concern that peacekeeping had been pampered during Kofi Annan's ten years as secretary-general (Annan had previously run DPKO). It had become self-satisfied, arrogant, bloated, and too focused on its own self-promotion. And the Security Council had become too inclined to think of peacekeeping as a solution to every problem when early and effective political action would have been a more sensible and less expensive approach. Even with the interest in political missions growing, the bias toward peacekeeping had led to an explosive expansion of DPKO's responsibilities, huge costs, and an overextended administrative structure. These costs were exhausting the generosity of member states and diverting money away from other critical UN functions. Ban's solution to the problem was to split off a logistics department from DPKO to support both peacekeeping and political missions. Fixing the support problem would allow DPA to develop an aggressive and capable political operation without duplicating DPKO's expensive support base.

He laid out what he saw as my task in taking over the Political Department. He wanted a complete remake of the department and its mission. His vision would require a fast-moving, highly professional, activist DPA focused on resolving conflicts where possible and finding ways to ease tensions where solutions remained beyond reach. He had no illusions about the difficulties of this task, understanding that the UN dealt mainly with issues that the big powers wanted to avoid. We had little chance of playing a major role in conflicts that directly involved the five Permanent Members of the Security Council or major regional players other than by providing a buffer (political or peacekeeping) that allowed a semblance of peace or the maintenance of the status quo. But there was a great deal the UN could do to resolve conflicts that did not rise to that level, and the UN had not been doing it.

The UN secretary-general had always played a key role in trying to calm and resolve international disputes. With a steady flow of meetings with presidents, prime ministers, foreign ministers, and others, a heavy load of travel to global hot spots, and numerous telephone conversations, the secretary-general was called upon to use his persuasive powers and the authority inherent in his position to engage his "good offices" to lessen or resolve conflicts. Kofi Annan and all of his predecessors had done this. But Ban wanted a hard-charging, competent Political Department to support him in these activities and to share the responsibility by operating on its own. He expected me to create such a department, with its fingers on the pulse of international conflicts, focused on getting results, less bound to its desks in New York, closer to conflicts, and oriented toward engaging quickly on problems before they developed into full-blown crises. Ban understood that the resource-poor, unfocused DPA as it existed when he came into office was not up to the task;

but he was determined to ensure that it soon would be. He told me to make strengthening the department my most urgent task. The details and their implementation were up to me.

The United States and others had urged Ban to carry out a clean sweep of senior officials at the UN to remove much of the deadwood at the top and to bring in people dedicated to improving the UN's functions and effectiveness. This fit Ban's own plans and his determination to undertake a wholesale shakeup of the organization. He told all his new appointees that they would be limited to one-year renewable contracts, which he expected would last for no more than five years. This approach caused considerable grumbling among some officials who had become permanent fixtures in New York and from some countries who occupied a disproportionate share of the top jobs. But the new secretary-general was determined to get into place quickly reliable people who shared his vision. Doubters soon learned that perseverance was one of Ban's outstanding characteristics. The self-effacing and modest man also had another motivation. He couldn't stand the many self-important (but mostly ineffective) prima donnas in high UN posts who had come to view the organization as their own little club; and he did not want to waste his time dealing with their personal vanities and outsized egos rather than tackling the global challenges he faced.

Not surprisingly, word of my pending appointment leaked to the press shortly after our meeting. There was considerable speculation at the UN and in the press that I must be an anti-UN conservative. The Canadian head of the disarmament department proclaimed she wouldn't work for an "American neocon," a label that would have surprised both the neocons and my colleagues in the State Department. However, a conservative ideological assault on the UN was clearly not what Secretary Rice and the president had in mind. By appointing a career diplomat without political baggage, they obviously hoped to strengthen Ban's hand as he sought to reform the United Nations structure that the Americans and many others had talked about for years. After deciding on several other appointees for senior positions, Ban announced my appointment in mid-February. Diane and I said our farewells in Jakarta, spent a week in Washington signing retirement papers and reclaiming our house, and arrived in New York in time for me to start work on March 1, 2007.

As it turned out, Ban Ki-moon had a tough first couple of months at the UN. (I was still in Jakarta.) His proposals to split the overburdened DPKO into two entities (one for policy and one for logistics) and fold the Disarmament Department into the Political Department ran into fierce opposition. The Group of 77 (G-77) and the NAM (Non-Aligned Movement), groups that arguably promote the interests of smaller non-Western countries at the UN, fought the reforms on both policy and procedural grounds. DPKO predictably sought to protect its bureaucratic empire and was supported by some Europeans wary of Ban's intentions. Hovering in the background through mid-February was the question of what senior position would go to an American. France wanted to keep DPKO, the British wanted to regain DPA, and having an American run disarmament was anathema to the G-77.

Despite a bruising fight with the opposition egged on by the head of DPKO, Ban got much of what he wanted by setting up the Department of Field Support (albeit at the cost of many unnecessary new hires for DPKO that were slipped into the overall package). But his efforts to give DPA control over disarmament or some oversight over DPKO failed totally. The U.S., which had encouraged early action by Ban and had worked hard to obtain the political under-secretary-general position, proved little help in these early fights. Indeed, the Americans on this and other occasions proved to be far more adept at giving free advice to Ban than in providing political support when the going got tough. The U.S. wanted the visibility of the DPA under-secretary-generalship, but it turned out that it had no serious strategy for how to enhance the department's power or protect its interests. As the drama at the UN unfolded, I was finishing up my work in Jakarta, blissfully ignorant of and isolated from the battles in New York.

A Neglected and Demoralized Department

Soon after I reported to UN headquarters on March 1, the secretary-general called for a thorough review of UN conflict prevention efforts. He instructed me to produce a clear plan with the resources needed to allow the organization to fulfill its mandated role in an increasingly complex and difficult international environment. Several studies both from within and outside the UN had described DPA's failings as the UN's political arm, noting its resource constraints but also clearly describing how it had drifted under indifferent leadership and low morale.

The Department of Political Affairs was created in 1992 (along with the separate peacekeeping department) with a Russian diplomat, Vladimir Petrovsky, installed as the under-secretary-general. After placing several former Soviet diplomats in comfortable jobs in the department, he moved on to repeat the process at the UN office in Geneva. He was succeeded by British diplomat Marrack Goulding, who played a powerful role as virtually the number two person in the UN. From 1997 to 2005 during most of Kofi Annan's time as secretary-general, another British diplomat, Kieran Prendergast, held the position. Prendergast focused on his role as Kofi Annan's chief political adviser and DPA drifted under the growing shadow of DPKO. When Secretary-General Annan made another top UK official his deputy in the wake of the Oil-for-Food scandal, Prendergast was replaced in DPA by the Nigerian diplomat Ibrahim Gambari.

Within days of arriving in New York, I began to understand the challenge the secretary-general had described in our New Year's Day meeting. DPA was in bad shape. Its support role for several UN entities, including the Security Council, functioned adequately, and its political missions often worked fairly well; but I found the department's regional divisions in New York, which would have to form the core of the secretary-general's "preventive diplomacy" vision, to be weak and unfocused. DPA had become a deskbound, passive organization that saw itself primarily as a producer of analysis and talking points, with little focus on field work. It was hardly the action-oriented organization devoted to resolving global conflicts that Ban envisioned. DPA staff had a low self-image, as it compared itself to the Peacekeeping Department, and had deeply rooted financial, personnel, and management problems brought on by years of neglect.

I found DPA's culture and general mindset deeply invested in the status quo and averse to taking risks. It did not have the resources or the inclination to focus on what the secretary-general saw as its primary purpose—resolving critical international conflicts. As I began a series of meetings to explain the secretary-general's and my vision for the DPA, the divide between those staff members who were eager to embrace a more active and results-oriented approach and those aghast at a new direction became painfully apparent. Some people complained about putting emphasis on work in the field rather than in New York, others about the additional effort required to secure extrabudgetary funds to support our planned innovations, and still others worried about drains on their time, away from "their real job" of analysis. I even heard that it was a burden to take notes for the secretary-general's meetings with foreign visitors, a complaint I couldn't imagine a young Foreign Service Officer making. Taking notes put junior officials in the presence of the secretary-general and a foreign minister or head of state, where they could hear their issues being discussed at the highest level.

Even as the department defined its primary task as the analysis of international events and support for the secretary-general, I heard grumbling from several other senior leaders early on about the quality of DPA's political reporting. The regional officers saw their primary work as writing memos for the secretary-general about events in the countries they were following; unfortunately, these notes actually said little that was new. Anything smacking of "intelligence gathering" had long been anathema in the UN. Without a network of offices to supply them with current updates or travel funds to allow them to explore on their own, the writer's sources were often limited to newspaper articles and items on the internet. I almost choked when an American academic suggested to me that DPA should be like the State Department's Bureau of Intelligence and Research. To paraphrase the late Senator Lloyd Bentsen, "I knew INR, and DPA was no INR." What's more, given the strictures, there was no way it could become one.

Our first staff meetings included many complaints about how badly the people in DPKO were treating them, the demands of the secretary-general's office on their time, the shortage of travel money, and the general lack of respect from other parts of the UN for their work. From the first, I told my staff it was time to stop complaining and get to work. If we concentrated on the major tasks before us as laid out by the secretary-general and accomplished them, people in other departments would struggle to keep up with us. We had to stop being defensive. Morale did eventually improve, the complaints in staff meetings dropped off dramatically, and people started spending their time in the meetings reporting on accomplishments rather than venting about other departments. In time people from other parts of the UN began knocking at our door hoping to work in DPA.

Skepticism about the New American Boss

Appointing an American to head the Political Department raised major concerns among many people at the UN. Skeptics in the organization watched my actions closely, suspecting I would be a tool of U.S. policy rather than take an evenhanded approach in carrying out my duties as a UN employee. Unfortunately, acting on one's own government's behalf rather than that of the international community is all too common in New York. The comment by the previous highest-ranking American in the UN Secretariat that his loyalty remained to the United States, not the UN, still rankled in New York, since it conflicted with the UN's loyalty oath. Some of the DPA staff reportedly also feared I would emulate my Russian predecessor by packing the department with Americans, thus threatening their own jobs. Eventually, these concerns went away when they turned out to be untrue.

Ironically, the lack of a U.S. strategy on what Washington wanted from me proved a major plus in building my credibility. The State Department security people stripped me of any residual security clearances when I retired, on the grounds that I was going to be employed by an international organization. There would thus be no chance I would get anything like the weekly intelligence briefings that my British predecessors had received from their government for years. I didn't see it as much of a loss. For me, the negative optics would have outweighed the value of the briefings, because it would have looked as though I had a secret line of instruction from Washington. Fortunately, both the U.S. Mission (USUN) and the State Department gave me a wide berth, allowing me to do my job as a UN employee without Washington's interference. USUN would make an occasional démarche to me on policy issues, as would any other mission, but on sensitive requests they approached the secretary-general directly rather than put me in the middle. It thus turned out to be surprisingly easy to maintain my independence. In fact, one U.S. permanent representative told me he would have preferred to have someone from a small friendly country in the political job rather than an American, since he or she would be easier to "push around."

Given the unique reach of the United States around the world, it was inevitable that I talked with my old colleagues in the State Department when we needed support on specific issues. Their help was invaluable, but I never asked for nor received anything that could be construed as guidance on our actions in these contacts. With other countries, we tended to work through their New York missions or with regional organizations, following the same ground rules to maintain our independence. Impartiality was key for our success.

We must have gotten the balance about right. I was criticized fairly evenly by all sides on my Security Council briefings and our department's reports on the world's hot spots. Over time all the permanent representatives and their staffs in New York (including the Cubans, North Koreans, and Iranians) treated me straightforwardly as a representative of the UN and Secretary-General Ban, and not as a stooge of the United States—although I suspect some of the countries less friendly toward the U.S. thought I might be a convenient back channel to the State Department if needed.

Getting Started

Despite the early complaints about DPA's output, the people on the DPA staff were generally highly competent. They simply were not being used up to their ability, a classic recipe for low morale. Several of the younger officers and a few of the more experienced ones struck me as excellent, even brilliant; we could build on them to create the Political Department the secretary-general demanded. Most of the rest of the staff were certainly capable of becoming effective members of a reoriented department. A small amount of deadwood had to be pruned or sidelined, and I quickly reversed several of my predecessor's "tombstone promotions" to underline that promotions from now on would be based on merit, not personal ties. What the staff clearly needed—and craved—was a vision for the department and solid leadership to perform at the level they were capable of. Ban had provided the vision. We had to put it into action.

Within a couple of months, I picked a top-flight chief of staff, Karina Gerlach, who proved invaluable in carrying out our plans. Karina was a smart, no-nonsense, bureaucratically savvy UN hand from Venezuela who had worked in both the development and political sides of the UN. As Karina and I started looking at the staffing in our department, I was startled to find that we didn't know how many people actually worked for DPA, how many were in real or "borrowed" positions, or how many were temporary hires who may have been on the staff for years. Some ambassadors early on criticized me for DPA's "unfilled posts." But the positions certainly had people in them, though often in some peculiar status without the necessary personnel actions having been processed. I was also surprised at how heavily the staff was skewed toward wealthier countries—and the former Soviet Union—when the main problems we dealt with were in underdeveloped countries. We needed more people, but we also needed them to be more diverse if we were to achieve our goals.

It also became evident rather quickly that the UN personnel system—with department heads holding great power to hire, fire, and promote—was open to abuse and did not provide a sufficiently fair, effective path to ensure the best talent rose to the top. As an innocent from the highly structured U.S. Foreign Service, I was shocked to be rather obviously offered sexual favors for special consideration shortly after I arrived. I asked Karina to put out the word that promotions would be based solely on merit and to knock off other approaches. Her presumably explicit instructions put an end to such advances.

But it did not stop mission heads in New York from demanding special treatment for their nationals who wanted jobs in DPA. (These were often diplomats who were ending their cushy New York postings.) I had some unpleasant conversations with senior diplomats from countries with close ties to the United States who were insistent that I hire or promote their countrymen. There was no way I was going to be browbeaten into hiring or promoting people who did not deserve it.

I learned about the lack of coordination at the UN early on when Alex Wolf, the number two at USUN, called on me to deliver a long démarche from the State Department on Taiwan. It turned out that the secretary-general had sent a letter to Nauru (one of the countries still recognizing Taipei as the government of China) in March stating that the UN "considers Taiwan for all purposes to be an integral part of the People's Republic of China." It cited the October 1971 resolution admitting the PRC to the UN which, of course, said no such thing. The note came from the Legal Department and appeared to me to be the result either of incredibly sloppy drafting or more likely, close coordination with China. (I never received a clear answer on which it was.)

The letter's wording constituted a major concession to China that should never have gone to Ban without coordination with the Political Department. (It would be hard to imagine a more political issue.) It had been sent in early March, a few days after my arrival, but neither I nor my colleagues had seen it. Ban, who had been in office a little over two months, had presumably signed the letter as a routine restatement of past UN positions. I complained hard to the Legal Department about the lack of coordination, but the damage had already been done.

The letter put the new secretary-general in an extremely difficult position. Any effort to walk it back would have met fierce resistance from the PRC, one of Ban's key supporters and a Permanent Five member who needed to be kept on his side if he had any chance to succeed as secretary-general. The Chinese now had the precedent that they predictably used to block Taiwan journalists and officials from the UN and to toughen their position on Taiwan's involvement in any UN activities. The entire episode was a sobering early warning of the problems we faced in the Secretariat in developing coherent policy approaches.

As we were putting together our plan for transforming DPA, the restructuring of DPKO moved forward on a fast track. The General Assembly had given the reorganization a preliminary nod by late March. Ban had proclaimed the effort would not increase costs, but DPKO and the newly carved out Department of Field Support (DFS) quickly understood it was a golden opportunity to build their empires. The two departments proposed adding 332 new positions to their new structure (an increase in staff of over 50 percent). What galled me was the request for numerous new political positions in their regional divisions, which were already far more heavily staffed than DPA and duplicated our efforts. In the end they received about half of their overall request but all of the new political personnel. Despite my disgust at the DPKO maneuvering to pad their rolls, the establishment of the Department of Field Support was good news for DPA, since our political missions in the field could now draw on the same support structure (although not all the resources) peacekeeping missions had.

"Strengthening" DPA

Restructuring DPA had to be tackled immediately. After determining just how many staff we actually had on the payroll (220) and ensuring that we had the most effective people in available positions, we undertook a detailed review of what was needed to carry out the proactive role the secretary-general envisioned for the department. It was clear that DPA lacked sufficient staff to carry out our new responsibilities. (The department had received only two additional posts in recent years despite all the talk about the need for a stronger department.) To illustrate the problem, we had one part-time officer working to provide guidance and support for our mission in Somalia, while DPKO had a dozen people supposedly planning a possible peacekeeping effort there (but, in fact, working full time to ensure that it would never happen.)

We took a hard look to determine the minimum staffing required to back up our political missions, establish effective policy planning and controls, and bring functions such as our overly stretched elections assistance section up to standard. I insisted that we be able to demonstrate the need for every position and not pad the numbers. (Some members of my staff told me this was not the way things were done at the UN, pointing to the DPKO/DFS overstuffed proposal; but I argued we were trying to do things differently and our credibility was at stake.) In the end we asked for 101 new positions, a sizeable number but not out of line with Ban's effort to completely realign the purposes of the department.

To get the UN member states to take the DPA proposal seriously, we held discussions with the various groups of member states and with individual countries, seeking their input as well as their support. Getting any increases in funding at the UN requires an intensive lobbying campaign that included all (192 at that time) member states. The African Group, where DPA had the most active involvement and where my assistant Roselyn Akombe worked hard to lay out our plans, solidly backed our proposal. Some other delegations traditionally suspicious of DPA as a tool of the major powers were less enthusiastic. And some of the larger contributors didn't want to spend more money, since they had just agreed to the large increases for DPKO and DFS. We listened carefully to their complaints and suggestions, incorporating many of their ideas into our final proposal.

The secretary-general went public with his plan for "strengthening" DPA in his annual budget speech on October 25, 2007. I presented the details to the powerful budget advisory committee (known as the ACABQ) two weeks later. The proposal called for adding positions (mostly at low levels) and reorganizing DPA's regional divisions to make them more effective at understanding potential conflicts, determining how we could help, and getting efforts to quickly manage or prevent conflict on the ground. The proposal further called for the establishment of a number of additional regional offices in the field modeled on our successful West Africa office and for enhanced capacity for policy planning and mediation, as well as some badly needed administrative support. We also hoped eventually to have more flexible funding mechanisms (similar to those used by DPKO) to enable us to react swiftly to crises abroad.

The proposal was generally well received, including in Washington. Most complaints came not from DPA's traditional antagonists but from major budget contributors. Rather than attack the substance, which they claimed to support, they criticized the secretary-general for taking a "piecemeal" approach to the budget (first additions to DPKO/DFS, then to DPA) rather than making a comprehensive proposal. For U.S. mission representatives to take this line was an egregious bit of hypocrisy, since Bolton and others had urged Ban to get what changes he could underway as quickly as possible. In January the ACABQ cut the number of positions we had requested to sixty (just as my staff had predicted). And after dealing with various complaints and soliciting support from member states, we believed we had everything in place for the Fifth (Budget) Committee's approval in March.

But the expected approval did not happen. At the crucial March budget session, the U.S. representative on the committee stabbed us in the back in the early morning hours by breaking consensus on the proposal. I had not seen it coming. Top-level officials in the State Department had repeatedly assured me they were completely behind my efforts, and USUN had been generally supportive, while trying not to look like they were abandoning their demands for a tight budget. I later learned that USUN had been arguing for weeks that the United States should not support the DPA request, couching their argument in administrative terms to put off a vote on increased DPA funding until the regular December session. (They had expressed no such qualms eight months earlier on the much larger DPKO/DFS expansion.) No one in the mission had bothered to inform me that, while publicly backing our proposal, they actually opposed it. They knew I would have appealed over their heads to Secretary Rice and Under Secretary Burns, who had been fully supportive of our plans. (I am virtually certain that neither was informed that USUN planned to pull the rug out from under me in New York.) I was furious at the betrayal and sent an angry email to the department's leadership. But the damage had been done.

Nine months later, on Christmas Eve, USUN quietly joined in the consensus to approve forty-nine new posts for DPA. Their foolishness (or pettiness) cost us eleven desperately needed positions, which were given to the mostly ineffective Department of Economic and Social Affairs. U.S. duplicity also caused us nine months' delay in implementing the secretary-general's program and required us to devote long hours going over the same issues with member states to retain the support we had painstakingly developed for the proposal. It didn't help that I wasn't sure whether USUN's actions were vindictive or just plain stupid.

New Funding and Expertise

With the U.S. obstructionism on strengthening DPA and the general sluggishness of the UN budget process, it was two years before we received regular funding to help carry out the secretary-general's plan. Eventually, when the General Assembly decided in late 2008 to strengthen DPA, the new funding only covered the costs of the new staff positions. Our new allotment did not provide adequate money for travel, training, or initial start-up of new missions. It became obvious early on that we could not expect adequate funding from the regular budget. The only way we could make our vision succeed was to seek voluntary contributions, similar to the efforts of the UN specialized agencies.

We had to explain to donors how we planned to use the funding, but we also had to demonstrate that we would responsibly manage the money entrusted to us. DPA's reputation on spending voluntary contributions for specific projects was not good. After consolidating several dormant DPA trust funds into a new general purpose rapid response fund, we brought on a new staff member, Delphine Bost (using voluntary funds), to develop a professional solicitation effort. As a result of Delphine's efforts, I hosted a series of donor meetings to explain our plans and funding requirements, and several countries, notably Germany, Australia, Norway, and the UK, contributed generously to our efforts. By the end of my tenure, we received about 10 percent of the DPA budget through voluntary funding; a few years later it had risen to 40 percent. Even China contributed several hundred thousand dollars, and Russia gave some token amounts. Ironically, despite my regular pleas and Washington's continued high praise for our efforts, the United States did not contribute one cent in new voluntary funding to DPA during my time in New York.

If DPA was to carry out its new mandate from the secretary-general, it needed to increase the professionalism of its operations abroad and reorient the approach of its staff in New York. Some members of the DPA staff and several of our envoys were highly experienced people with a superb feel for events on the ground and a clear sense of what was needed to bring issues to a political resolution. The UN is also fortunate that it can draw on a wide range of former heads of state, foreign ministers, and other people with extensive experience and prestige, but they needed to be supported by strong staff and headquarters personnel with appropriate expertise and adequate resources to do their jobs.

DPA's primary resource was its people. They were capable and willing, but we had a lot of work to do if we were to be at the cutting edge of a global preventive diplomacy effort. It was imperative that we move quickly to get our corporate knowledge up to global standards and to ensure that our people were trained to use it. Our new Policy and Mediation division undertook a broad review of available information on preventive diplomacy efforts. The team (eventually led by another of my top assistants Sascha Fong) distilled the wide experience available from people across the globe from interviews and articles, the "lessons learned" reports from the UN's own negotiators, and first-hand experience to produce a series of documents ranging from "how to" manuals on running a successful negotiation to steps involved in setting up new missions. Within a few years, we had a good set of standard operating procedures in place that took much of the guesswork out of the initial stage of the process and allowed our envoys to develop a strategy and concentrate on dealing with the problem at hand, rather than reinventing the wheel.

The most innovative part of our effort was to establish (in cooperation with Norway) an in-house group of top-flight global mediation experts to serve as a kind of mediation swat team whose members could travel to hot spots around the world on short notice to add professionalism to ongoing efforts. The twelve members of this team, who were all recognized experts in their field (constitutions, natural resources, power-sharing, security arrangements, gender and inclusion issues, etc.), were normally on leave from universities or global NGOs. Like our publications, we made these experts available to support our political or peacekeeping missions, country teams, and negotiating efforts by regional organizations. Requests for their assistance usually greatly exceeded the number of team members we had available to deploy.

18
Applying the New Approach to Africa

Somalia: The World's Most Prominent Failed State

While there was strong vocal support at the UN for the secretary-general's and my efforts to take a more aggressive approach to preventing and resolving conflicts, the proof would have to come from our actions and whether we succeeded or not. We had to show we could make it work and didn't have the luxury of waiting for more personnel and reshuffling bureaucratic structures to begin the task. Circumstances and the secretary-general chose one of the most difficult challenges the UN faced—Somalia—to demonstrate we could succeed.

Three months after I arrived at the UN, I found myself in the world's most notorious "failed state," wearing a UN helmet and vest, looking through the dirty window of a South African–made armored personnel carrier (APC) at the devastation of what was once the pleasant city of Mogadishu, capital of Somalia. The landscape of destroyed buildings reminded me of the pictures of Dresden after the carpet bombing in World War II. Ruins and rubble were far more in evidence than livable buildings along the street. Our flight from Nairobi had come in low over the Indian Ocean waters teeming with sharks to avoid detection by the antiregime forces in the city, who had shot down a plane a few weeks earlier. We traveled along the one road from the airport erratically controlled by an African military force (AMISOM) to Villa Somalia (the Presidential Palace) to meet with the embattled Somali president and prime minister. After the palace call, we went to the UN compound, where a few UN humanitarian officials worked in an office vulnerable to an attack at any time. The rest of the UN country team remained in Nairobi.

The situation in Somalia was dire. Given the bad security, my trips were always kept secret until I had departed, with the understanding that at any point the head of UN security could cancel it. The leaders I called on headed a shaky, embattled government in control of little more than the Presidential Palace, the road I was on, and most of the airport. Some three million Somalis had fled abroad, and perhaps as many as a million had been internally displaced by recent fighting. One-third of Mogadishu's population had fled to the countryside. Much of the country's citizenry depended on international food aid to survive, their daily lives defined by violence and poverty. Over the previous year Somali pirates had doubled their ship seizures in waters off the country's coast, threatening vital global shipping. Foreign terrorists saw the chaotic state as a prime base for extending their global activities. Things in Somalia had been so bad for so long that world leaders shuddered at the mention of the country's name.

Putting Somalia on a path toward normalcy, long one of the UN's greatest challenges, had failed miserably. Unlike most African countries, Somalia was united by ethnicity, religion, and language; and yet it was divided by deep rivalries among its clans and subclans. After the fall of its strongman leader Siad Barre in 1991, the country disintegrated into a collection of local fiefdoms, run by warlords interested primarily in their own dominance and the profits they could extract. Somalia consistently ranked near the top of international charts for misery and poverty. After thirteen peace agreements since 1991, the current Transitional Federal Government (TFG) was the product of the UN-sponsored agreement in 2004. None of the so-called governments resulting from these agreements exerted any real control over the country.

A disastrous U.S.-led peacekeeping mission in 1992 and 1993 that was supposed to provide security for the humanitarian effort instead led to the death of thirty-four Pakistani peacekeepers. Then a few months later eighteen U.S. peacekeepers died during the infamous "Black Hawk Down" debacle, which included scenes of the bodies of American Special Forces soldiers being dragged through the streets of Mogadishu. That catastrophe led the Clinton administration to withdraw troops from UN peacekeeping missions altogether and set the stage for the UN's tragic hands-off approach to the Rwandan genocide seven months later.

In mid-2006, a coalition of Islamist organizations called the Islamic Courts Union seized Mogadishu and gained control of almost half of the country. Somalia's neighbors, the African Union, and leading global players moved to block their advance. They created an African peacekeeping force called AMISOM, which the UN Security Council endorsed in early December. Later that month Ethiopian troops and planes, with the support of its African neighbors and the United States, ousted the Islamic Courts. With their shell of a TFG government, Somalia's president and prime minister moved to Mogadishu, while the Parliament remained in Baidoa. Islamic Courts leaders then set up an opposition front in Asmara, Eritrea, called the Alliance for the Re-liberation of Somalia (ARS). The small AMISOM force of Ugandan troops in place during my visit was supposed to protect the government. Sadly, Mogadishu had reverted to its norm of open warfare over turf and money between the rival factions.

At the United Nations, the threat that terrorists tied to Al-Qaeda would set up a new base in Somalia injected a new sense of urgency into tackling Somalia's problems. The African Union and the United States saw AMISOM as a stopgap measure to be followed by a UN peacekeeping mission. DPKO, backed by France and the EU, wanted no part of a peace-enforcement mission in Somalia and opposed any efforts to set up a mission. The humanitarian side of the UN had long cut its deals with the many groups fighting in Somalia and (like the Somali war profiteers) did not welcome interference from the government. Their fraught relationship with the TFG led them to oppose any political or military actions by the UN that might disrupt their effort to feed and provide basic assistance to the desperate Somali population.

Ban wanted a political solution to the problem and sought to build a consensus in New York on the way forward. It was striking how many of the UN Permanent Representatives simply refused to engage with him on a problem that had long been put in the "too hard to do" category. I was with Ban when he asked one European ambassador what he thought the way forward on Somalia should be. The ambassador responded, "You really need to speed up the Darfur peacekeeping operation." The ambassador knew perfectly well the difference between Somalia and Sudan; he simply wanted to deflect the conversation away from Somalia.

Shortly after I arrived at the UN, a frustrated Ban convoked Under-Secretary-General for DPKO Jean-Marie Guehenno and me to discuss the way forward. Unfortunately, my small staff following Somalia (one person covering several countries) could not answer some of Ban's basic questions, and I had only a thin brief on the situation. Perhaps sympathetic but not happy, Ban called me back to his office a bit later and gave me a clear directive: "Fix Somalia." He didn't need to add that I had to fix DPA too.

As the APC bounced along the broken Mogadishu street that June day in 2007, the full weight of the Somalia problem came into focus for me. When I met with Somalia's leaders at the Villa Somalia, President Yusuf and his staff looked like cornered animals. He asked us to support his clan-based National Governance and Reconciliation Committee, which had only a modest chance to move things forward. I pressed Yusuf to ensure that the reconciliation process was inclusive and addressed the deep political and social issues dividing Somalis. I did not come away from the meeting reassured that things would improve. (The committee did eventually meet but was boycotted by the opposition in Asmara.)

My meeting with the Ugandan commander of AMISOM went somewhat better. The general came across as smart and capable; but he had very little guidance from the AU or his own president about what he was supposed to do with his troops beyond providing what security he could to TFG personnel. His small force, operating in a hostile environment and without adequate logistical or political support, was in no position to take decisive military action.

I also visited Ethiopia, Eritrea, Kenya, and Egypt on the trip to talk about Somalia with leading officials of those governments, the AU, and the League of Arab States. Everyone professed a desire to help resolve the Somalia problem (although Ethiopia and Eritrea were clearly on opposite sides), and many had their own side discussions underway. But no one had a strategy to make peace happen.

The UN operation dealing with Somalia also left a lot to be

desired. DPA's political effort, operating from Nairobi, was reactive, lethargic, and without a real plan that might lead to success. The other UN agencies dealing with Somalia seemed removed from the realities on the ground, hostile toward our efforts, and fighting among themselves. In New York, DPKO focused on one goal—staying out of Somalia—and Guehenno and I had some tough discussions as I sought to enlist his help on this priority issue of the secretary-general's. UN humanitarian leaders in New York were more civil than their colleagues in Nairobi, but I soon found out that they were as negative as DPKO about our efforts to find a political solution to Somalia's mess.

We (and the secretary-general) were obviously on our own in the UN structure. Nevertheless, I felt that if we could come up with a sensible plan and provide effective leadership, we had a reasonable opportunity to put Somalia on a better path. As I told the Security Council, hope was perhaps too strong a word to use when talking about Somalia, but I thought we had at least a fighting chance to succeed.

Newly Active UN Role

My first task was to reshape our political effort. In September, the secretary-general, on my recommendation, appointed the former foreign minister of Mauritania, ambassador to the U.S. and to Europe, and longtime UN problem solver Ahmedou Ould Abdallah as his special representative and chief of the UN Political Office in Somalia, UNPOS (the UN has the usual bureaucratic addiction to acronyms), based in Nairobi. Thoughtful, tough, wily, and well-connected internationally, Ould Abdallah proved to be a match for the cutthroat Somali political scene. His international connections also gave him the heft to deal with the many countries playing their own separate games in Somalia. And he fit my preferred approach of someone who did not need micromanaging but kept me informed and consulted on next steps. In return, he had the secretary-general's and my full support.

Ould Abdallah immediately launched into consultations with Somalis—the TFG, the opposition ARS group, other major internal actors, and the diaspora—as well as the many international players involved in Somalia. After moderates led by Sheik Sharif Sheik Ahmad took over the leadership of ARS, this group proved willing to work with Ould Abdallah and engage in discussions with the TFG. It opposed the continuing attacks on the government by Somalia's radical al-Shabaab insurgents. In December 2007, Ould Abdallah laid out to the Security Council our plans for an inclusive process, with discussions between the TFG and opposition leaders and a coherent message from the international community, to avoid the Somali habit of playing one interlocutor against another. (I encouraged the special representatives of the secretary-general, or SRSGs, who reported to DPA to brief the Security Council at regular intervals to enhance their stature in New York and abroad as well as to ensure the Council got their facts from people on the front lines.)

The special representative set out the Somalia problem in stark terms: It was neither a clan war nor an ethnic or religious conflict. "Warlords, activists, and their private militias perpetuate the chaos and violence for their own benefit. Overall, a small group drawn from various backgrounds and driven by lust for money and power is fighting to fill a power vacuum. Some do not want peace at all." He pressed Council members to abandon their "wait and see" approach and called for greater international help for Somalia, including in particular more support for AMISOM.

At a later briefing, he argued that many seemed to have "never forgiven (Somalia) for the violent activities carried out against the international community in the 1990s." This could not have been more true. One contact of mine in the State Department said he couldn't even talk to the Pentagon about Somalia. The same Black Hawk Down mentality drove DPKO's abhorrence of any peacekeeping in Somalia. Ould Abdallah spoke for the secretary-general and me as well as himself when he said a resolution was possible. And with the support of the international community, "patriotic Somalis could free themselves from the scourge of wars [and] the ghosts of the past and unite for a strong, independent and peaceful country."

The Djibouti Agreement

Ould Abdallah worked hard over several months to get talks on a political settlement started between the ARS and the TFG. He avoided the traditional format of large negotiating sessions where delegates apportioned by clan held talks in five-star European hotels. By June 2008 he had agreement from the two sides on a path for a settlement. It called for a cessation in hostilities, a request to the UN Security Council for a stabilization force of friendly countries (not including neighbors), TFG support for the withdrawal of Ethiopian troops, ARS to cut its ties with armed groups that did not support the agreement (essentially al-Shabaab), and unhindered humanitarian access. Skeptics (the *New York Times* correspondent was high on the list) treated the agreement signed in Djibouti as another in the endless succession of Somali peace deals. We knew it was far more but understood that the agreement was only the first step in a long process that would demand our engagement all along the way.

The Djibouti Agreement skillfully brokered by Ould Abdallah was essentially a deal between the moderates in the TFG led by Prime Minister Nur "Adde" Hassan Hussein and the moderates in ARS led by Sheik Sharif. President Yusuf and his supporters, including the mayor of Mogadishu and a sizeable block in Parliament, were more hardline and invested in the status quo in Somalia. They tried without success to oust the moderate prime minister. The radicals in ARS also attempted unsuccessfully to remove Sheik Sharif. Ould Abdallah kept up pressure on the two sides to follow through on their promises. These efforts produced agreements in October for a cessation of armed conflict, integration of armed forces, and the establishment of a unity government with an inclusive (and enlarged) Parliament. President Yusuf and his supporters tried and failed to slow or block progress in all these areas. Yusuf resigned on December 29, 2008, and went into exile.

As we labored to get a credible peace process underway, the situation on the ground in Somalia continued to deteriorate. Fighting across the country reached its highest levels in years. At one point, Yusuf admitted that al-Shabaab controlled most of the country. AMISOM remained seriously under strength; 850 soldiers arrived from Burundi in early 2008 to join the Ugandans, bringing the total to 2,600. Other, promised, African troops to increase the number to the planned 8,000 men simply did not materialize until much later. Attacks escalated on Ethiopian and AMISOM forces leading to tough Ethiopian reprisals. UN monitors blamed Eritrea for supporting the opposition fighters (primarily al-Shabaab), and the United States threatened Eritrea with sanctions and placement on the list of states supporting international terrorism.

UN humanitarian operations continued under horrible conditions. The TFG seized the World Food Program chief from the UN compound in November and held him for a month; Doctors Without Borders pulled out in February 2008 after three of its people were killed; and the UNICEF representative was abducted and the UNDP head killed in June. By May 2008, about half the country needed food aid as the region slipped into a major famine. And piracy was on the increase. The pessimists predicted the country would totally collapse with the planned departure of Ethiopian troops.

But by the time Yusuf resigned, the UN-sponsored talks had developed a viable plan for the transition. Two hundred members nominated by ARS and seventy business and civil society leaders would be added to Parliament to make up for the expulsion of the opposition in 2007 and Parliament would then elect a new president. Civil society and businessmen had been included from the first in Ould Abdallah's reconciliation groups, and they would play an important role in the transition. He himself, of course, was deeply involved throughout this time, and the agreements were a strong testament to his political skills. The U.S. also played an important role in the region, supporting the process from Nairobi and Djibouti.

On January 31, 2009, the newly reconstituted Parliament elected Sheik Sharif as Somalia's new president, an outcome welcomed by most Somalis. He received a warm welcome in Mogadishu a few days later (AMISOM provided his protection) and named a moderate, Omar Sharmarke, as prime minister. His government moved permanently to Mogadishu in late February. While the situation in Somalia remained bad, Somalis for the first time in almost two decades could feel some sense of hope.

AMISOM or UN Peacekeeping?

Meanwhile, in New York a debate raged over a UN peacekeeping mission to replace AMISOM. It had been clear from the start that deploying and sustaining a planned force of 8,000 soldiers exceeded the African Union's financial and logistic capabilities. The Somalis and the African Union believed they had a UN commitment to a follow-on peacekeeping operation that would absorb AMISOM. When I approached DPKO shortly after my arrival for information on where plans stood for a peacekeeping operation, the reaction was instantaneous: There would be no UN peacekeeping operation in Somalia, nor was there any interest in getting involved in anything more than giving minimal advice. (DPKO opposed "peace enforcement" missions in general, and they were having a terrible time standing up a Security Council–mandated mission in nearby Darfur, Sudan.)

The U.S., AMISOM's strongest non-African supporter, tried to force the issue repeatedly in the Security Council. France, the UK, and occasionally others backed DPKO's opposition to a UN force. At one point, DPKO convinced the secretary-general to support the idea of a multinational force led by a "strong lead country" (obviously the U.S., which had no interest in again leading an operation in Somalia). That force would not be paid out of peacekeeping funds and was exactly what AMISOM had been set up to do, but without the resources to do it. To buttress its position DPKO carried out a survey to see if countries would be willing to participate. Naturally, they got the response they were seeking and had no takers for troops. Given the differing views, our reports to the Security Council, which DPA and DPKO drafted jointly, had a split personality as the political side talked up progress and the military side emphasized chaos.

When Alain LeRoy became the DPKO under-secretary-general in June 2008, relations between DPA and DPKO greatly improved. Although his staff remained adamantly opposed to any involvement in Somalia, LeRoy was more interested in getting the job done than playing bureaucratic games. I found him to be a superb colleague. Susana Malcorra, who had taken over as the new under-secretary-general for field support three months earlier, was also far more interested in supporting the secretary-general's priorities than in pointless bureaucratic maneuvers. Both wanted to find an acceptable solution to the AMISOM puzzle, and we worked together to that end.

By late 2008, the situation in Somalia had changed dramatically, with the political process making real progress. Secretary of State Rice stepped up pressure on the Security Council by announcing publicly that the U.S. wanted a peacekeeping mission established by the end of the year. Other Council members scrambled to find a way to at least shore up AMISOM to support the improving political situation. Secretary-General Ban, with advice coming primarily from Malcorra, proposed a way out of the peacekeeping dilemma: The UN would provide logistical support for AMISOM as if it were a UN peacekeeping operation; reimbursement of salaries would come from a trust fund set up with money promised by the EU; training and equipment would continue to come from the U.S. and NATO; and securing troops and leading the force would be the responsibility of the African Union. The UN logistical support could be justified as a lead-in to a regular UN peacekeeping mission (with AMISOM troops as its core), even though it was highly unlikely UN peacekeeping would ever be approved. The Security Council unanimously agreed to this compromise in January 2009.

The compromise proved to be a brilliant solution to a problem that had been hotly debated in New York without resolution for two years. The force in Somalia was clearly what the UN refers to as a "peace-enforcement" mission, not traditional peacekeeping, and the only countries that would take on the difficult task with attendant casualties were those with a major stake in the outcome.

Malcorra and her field-support people moved quickly to create a logistics base for AMISOM. Food, fuel, field hospital, and medevacs for the wounded soon transformed the force. This new mission for the Department of Field Services (DFS) provided an opportunity to break out of the shadow of DPKO, and DFS made the most of it. Cooperation between the new department and DPA was quite close, and the combined effort worked well (far better than the "hybrid" UN-AU peacekeeping operation in Darfur). With first-class logistics in place, additional troops soon arrived. In fact, this new approach worked so well that I hoped it would serve as a model for later peace enforcement operations. But DPKO, supported as usual by France, soon came to view it as a threat to its own peacekeeping role and opposed any effort to duplicate it in other hot spots.

By March 2009, things were looking up for Somalia. The new Somali leadership was making plans for reform and reaching out to opposition groups. UN logistical support for AMSOM was assured, thousands of refugees were returning to Mogadishu, and the international community was now more engaged. The next month a UN-sponsored donors conference in Brussels generated $213 million in promised aid to Somalia. To reassure foreign donors (Somalia's dismal record of corruption was well-known), the TFG hired Price-Waterhouse to track the money to ensure it was spent as planned.

But the spoilers were gathering too. Hassan Dahir Aweys, leader of the radical arm of the ARS, returned to Mogadishu from Asmara in late April and began to rally his allies. Fighting broke out in early May with an attack on Villa Somalia, targeted assassinations of TFG officials, and open battles on the streets of Mogadishu. Al-Qaeda praised these attacks, and considerable numbers of foreign fighters joined al-Shabaab's ranks. TFG forces backed by an increasingly active AMISOM managed to blunt the onslaught, but the fighting raged for months, with a series of attacks and counterattacks.

Eritrea remained deeply involved in supporting the insurgents (it was sanctioned for its actions by the Security Council several months later). Gulf state funds and internal extortion schemes financed Al-Shabaab's assaults. I complained hard to the Qatari Permanent Representative at one point about their financing al-Shabaab through Eritrea while we were trying to strengthen the TFG. He later assured me that the funding had stopped, but I doubted this was true. In my briefings to the Security Council, I would plead for member states to strengthen their support for the TFG: "Either we help the Somali people overcome the current attempt to thwart efforts toward peace or we allow the new unity Government based on consensus and the Djibouti accords to fall to a radical armed opposition."

By early August the TFG and AMISOM had gained the upper hand. While the TFG military forces remained divided and often ineffective, AMISOM, with its troop strength up to 5,200, began to come into its own. Now with the UN logistical support, troops and commanders understood they would be paid, fed, well-equipped, and medevacked if injured. They began to take the offensive in Mogadishu against the spoilers. Over the next few months AMISOM changed from a weak, reactive force to one capable of clearing Mogadishu of rebel forces. As AMISOM proved its worth, support for a UN peacekeeping operation in Somalia disappeared in New York and at the AU, although the possibility of a UN mission in the future remained to provide a fig leaf to justify DFS's logistical support.

The secretary-general and I worked to back up Ould Abdallah's efforts in international meetings and in our contacts with the Somali leadership. We met the Somalis regularly at African Union events, Somali Contact Group meetings, and in Mogadishu and New York. To keep up the pressure for internal reconciliation, a cleaner government, distribution of humanitarian aid, and economic development, I made it a point to travel to Mogadishu when possible. (Something I could not have done for security reasons if I had been a U.S. official.) These were always hush-hush trips, with appointments made by our staff on the ground with the leaders in Villa Somalia without mentioning that I would be there. On one trip in October 2009, our airplane turned around when we were only a few miles from the Mogadishu airport. The pilot informed me that insurgents had fired mortar shells at President Sheik Sharif's airplane as it was taking off a few minutes before. Not only did it make sense to not tempt fate, but with the president gone there was no point in making the trip to Villa Somalia. I settled for a meeting with the Somali prime minister in Nairobi.

In January 2010 Ould Abdallah briefed the Security Council on improvements in Somalia. The government had not only survived a tumultuous first year, it had also established its legitimacy, was broadening its base with other factions across the country, and had begun to tackle some of Somalia's deep-seated problems in a way no other "government" had been able to do in over twenty years. The TFG still did not have control of a sizeable portion of the capital, and possibly half of the country was in rebel hands; but both its forces and AMISOM were gaining strength and preparing for a major offensive.

Ould Abdallah caught the essence of Somalia's transformation by saying that the country was moving from a "failed state" to a "fragile state." But, of course, there was still a long way to go. He noted that the international community had spent over $8 billion over the years, mostly to deal with the symptoms of Somalia's dysfunction, not with core problems. Unfortunately, only $3.5 million of the $213 million pledged in Brussels in April had made it to the TFG coffers almost a year later. This lack of financial support meant the government did not even have sufficient funds to pay salaries.

In the spring, the fractious nature of Somali politics had again come to the fore, resulting in the resignation of the speaker of Parliament and the president's firing and then the reinstating of the prime minister. The close working relationship between President Sheikh Sharif and Prime Minister Sharmarke had been critical to the progress the TFG had made in its first year. But they split over several issues, including that the constitution that was being drafted (with considerable UN assistance) for the new permanent Somali government, to be set up by August 2011. Ould Abdallah himself was caught in the crossfire for his firm backing—along with the secretary-general, the Security Council, the AU, me, and major international donors—of Sheik Sharif and his reform efforts. When Ould Abdallah tried to help the TFG and Kenya temporarily shelve their sea border dispute so that offshore oil blocks could be auctioned to provide desperately needed cash for the government, several parliamentarians accused him of giving away Somalia's claim to a 200-mile territorial sea limit. (Such a limit was untenable under the UN Law of the Sea Treaty, which specified a 12-mile limit and which Somalia had signed.) The government backed down under the criticism and abandoned any agreement with Kenya on the sea boundary.

By the time he left as the secretary-general's special representative in June 2011, Ould Abdallah had established the groundwork for transforming Somalia. Where others had failed for two decades, he had managed to get Somalia on the right path by cajoling Somali political leaders into political compromise and harnessing international financial support and pressure behind a coherent strategy to help Somalis succeed. His work was also a strong validation of Secretary-General Ban's vision that the UN could take on and help resolve some of the world's most intractable and dangerous conflicts. He was succeeded by an experienced and highly regarded Tanzanian diplomat, Augustine Mahiga.

The political turmoil in Mogadishu in the summer of 2010 over personalities and the constitution fed the cynicism of the Somali watchers in Nairobi. They had two decades of Somali governmental failures to back up their argument that our efforts would ultimately fail, and they maintained a drumbeat of news to fuel a negative narrative of events in Somalia for the world at large. Unfortunately, some UN agencies sitting comfortably in Nairobi were also complicit in adding to the negative atmosphere, because the "failed state" narrative supported their fund-raising efforts and their own sense of importance. And, of course, well embedded in the Somali dynamic was the sad reality that chaos was profitable for many, both inside and outside the country.

After a September visit, I tried to lay out a different and, I believed, more accurate sense of reality for the Somalia-watchers in Nairobi. I conceded there were many difficulties, and the challenges ahead were serious but flatly rejected the narrative that everything in Somalia was terrible and falling apart. Naturally, press reports on my comments were followed with several paragraphs of negative views from "observers" in Nairobi. I had another rough session with the UN Country Team, whose members feared we would set up a genuinely "integrated mission" for Somalia that might impinge on their independence. They were also quite unhappy with Mahiga's announcement that his office (UNPOS) would soon be moving from the comforts of Nairobi to a secure headquarters at the Mogadishu airport.

Sheik Sharif picked a Somali-American, Mohamed Abdullah Mohamed (known as Farmaajo), as the new prime minister. (Noting the number of diaspora members—usually from the U.S., the UK, or Canada—in high positions in Mogadishu, Ould Abdallah once joked that he didn't have problems with Somalis; it was the Anglo-Saxons who were giving him trouble.) Farmaajo's administration made considerable progress in increasing revenue collection, improving public services, and taking on corruption during his eight months in power. He also had some success in reducing clan conflict and strengthening regional ties to the central government. His attention to schools, health facilities, and other basic functions of government struck a responsive chord in the population and represented the sort of reform we had long urged on the TFG. The constitution-drafting process was also continuing apace. Despite being a highly popular prime minister, he was ousted in the spring as part of a deal to extend Sheik Sharif's tenure. (Years later, Farmaajo returned to Somalia to compete in the 2018 election, which he won handily. His tenure as president, however, was far less successful, and he overstayed his term. He finally left under heavy internal and international pressure.)

On my trip in July 2011, Somali leaders promised me they would focus on security, deal with the famine (which was growing worse), and finalize the constitution. When they added that they wanted to change Somalia's image from a haven for piracy, corruption, and hunger, I bluntly added "and chaotic politics." I told them we wanted to continue providing help, but the international community was fed up with their political squabbling.

While the political fights in Mogadishu were all too familiar, the security situation in the city was improving. By mid-August, pro-government forces controlled 90 percent of Mogadishu and began to assert control in other parts of the country that had long been held by the insurgents. Mogadishu, for the first time in decades, was returning to life. I was delighted to see normal activity on the streets of Mogadishu. People were again going about their daily routines, many of the ruined buildings had been rebuilt, and multicolored wares were for sale along the street where I had once seen only emptiness and rubble. The *New York Times,* which had maintained a negative, failed-state narrative on Somalia for years, reported that "the hammering sound that rings out in the mornings [in Mogadishu] is not the clatter of machine guns but the sound of actual hammers. Construction is going on everywhere—new hospitals, new homes, new shops, a six-story hotel and even sports bars (albeit serving cappuccino and fruit juice instead of beer.)" Ban made his own trip to Mogadishu in December 2011, the first visit to the city by a secretary-general in eighteen years. It would have been unthinkable for him to have gone there four years earlier, when we first discussed Somalia, but the path he had set the UN on at that time was slowly succeeding. Mahiga moved UNPOS from Nairobi to new quarters at the Mogadishu airport shortly after the secretary-general's visit.

Over the next few months, there was the usual political maneuvering in Mogadishu and occasional missed deadlines in carrying out the agreed roadmap to establish a new government. But the AU, UN, U.S., and Europe kept up pressure to set up the new Somali government by August 2012. UNPOS was at the center of this effort. When I paid my last visit to Mogadishu in March 2012, I took considerable satisfaction in how far we had come. Not only did the city appear far more prosperous than I had ever seen it, but the politicians were moving (if in fits and starts) to get the new government in place. Somalia was nowhere near a normal country yet, but things were definitely looking up.

Soon afterward, Somalia had its new constitution and a new parliament and president in place. Somalia was by no means a model democracy. The new "Federal Government of Somalia" (no longer "Transitional") was in place and obviously legitimate. With the critical support of AMISOM, the Kenyans, and the Ethiopians, the government controlled most of the country and was brokering deals to further establish its authority countrywide. Al-Shabaab was diminished but not defeated; it was still capable of carrying out terrorist bombings in Mogadishu and other cities. Its operatives had, in fact, attacked the hotel where the new president was holding his inaugural press conference. But against all odds, the "failed" Somali state had become a functioning one, with strong support from the UN and the international community.

Two of the plagues that had defined Somalia for too long—famine and piracy—had also greatly diminished. Piracy off the coast of Somalia had been a lucrative enterprise, as companies paid large ransoms to get their ships, crews, and passengers to safety. The lawlessness in Somalia allowed the pirates to act with impunity. In November 2010 there were over 438 seafarers and passengers and twenty ships being held for ransom by Somali pirates, and the number continued to grow each month. The reaction of the international community was to set up a huge "whack-a-mole" naval operation led by NATO that was estimated to cost from $1.5 billion to $2 billion a year. Given the legal difficulties involved in trying and incarcerating the pirates, a major effort was also led by the UN Legal Department to establish an international court dedicated to trying pirates.

I thought these elaborate naval and legal measures were totally misplaced. From my memories of Blackbeard stories in my youth to Thomas Jefferson's success in sending a naval expedition against the Barbary Pirates (bequeathing the line in the Marine's hymn "to the shores of Tripoli") to the drying up of piracy in the Straits of Malacca after the Aceh settlement, I was convinced that the expensive sea operations had no chance to settle the core problem of Somali piracy. I argued that the only way to effectively deal with this threat was to have the Somali (and Puntland) governments take control over the pirates' lairs. Security Council resolutions, naval armadas, and legal schemes to try pirates all had little real effect on the problem itself. If we were to be serious, we had to deal with the problem by helping the government establish control of the entire country.

Then, as if to prove our point, after Kenyan troops entered Somalia in November 2011 and made pirate lairs a major priority, the problem melted away. By May 2012 pirate seizures of ships had virtually ceased, and the big international crisis over Somali piracy vanished from the newspapers as a global problem. The self-congratulations of the ship owners and navies about their success struck me as almost comical. In fact, once again it had been demonstrated that the only way to stop pirates is to take control of their base of operations.

The most heart-wrenching problem in Somalia, however, was not the piracy but the humanitarian crises that at times had half the population dependent on food from international (primarily UN) agencies. Frequent famine conditions were mostly due to low rainfall, but the inability of the government to provide for its people was a major contributing factor. Given the severity of the crisis in Somalia, the last people I expected to oppose the secretary-general's policy to rebuild the Somali state were UN humanitarian officials. I was surprised at the hostility of the UN Country Team headquartered in Nairobi and the heads of the humanitarian agencies in New York when discussing Somalia. However, I soon discovered that, although they would never admit it even to themselves, the people most invested in the Somali failed-state status quo were those providing humanitarian aid to its desperate people.

I never doubted the dedication of the humanitarian workers to help the struggling Somali people. They had been at it for years before I arrived on the scene and had undoubtedly saved hundreds of thousands of Somali lives. To do so, of course, they often had to use means and cut corners in a corrupt, volatile society that would not stand up to normal business standards, and many of their personnel faced daily threats to their lives. Given the length of the crisis in Somalia, the corruption levels reached well beyond the usual "cost of doing business," and ties with warlords and their cronies had become far too intimate. Ultimately, it was the humanitarian workers' clients, the poor people of Somalia, who suffered.

Ould Abdallah complained to me early on that a large percentage of the food shipments by the UN's World Food Program simply disappeared when being transported by their contractors in Somalia and that much of the money from it ended up in the hands of al-Shabaab. The severity of the problem led the United States to hold up donations in late 2009 and demand a thorough review of the Somali program. The Somalia Monitoring Group issued a report concluding that about 50 percent of the WFP food had been diverted by the middlemen and sold in local markets. The companies had close ties to al-Shabaab and did indeed provide a sizeable portion of the money from these illegal sales to buy arms and support the insurgency. One of the contractors was deeply involved in various schemes to undermine the TFG. All had private militias that served as their security forces and added to the TFG's difficulties in gaining control over the country. After the disclosures, WFP was forced to revise its approach and change its distribution system to conform to the new reality of the government's growing reach and al-Shabaab's shrinking base.

Somalia today is far from being a garden spot in Africa and its political culture is fractious and its security tenuous. But it is a country much improved over the place the international community hoped to ignore when Ban Ki-moon began his term as secretary-general in 2007. Credit for the success in Somalia must be apportioned widely among the African Union, Somalia's neighbors, the Security Council, the U.S., and Europe. But the diplomacy of Ould Abdallah to bring Somalia's moderate forces into agreement and the backing of DPA and DFS were the key ingredients. A country with Somalia's problems is not going to be transformed overnight or probably even in a generation, but the changes clearly demonstrate what the UN, backed by the international community and the country's people themselves, can do to make the world a safer place.

The Eritrea-Ethiopia Border Dispute

Some of our efforts were doomed from the start, but it did not relieve us of the responsibility to try. On my first visit to Somalia in June 2007, I made stops at its neighbors, Ethiopia and Eritrea, to talk with Prime Minister Meles Zenawi and President Isaias Afwerki to discuss the conflict in Somalia. Meles's army had installed the leadership in Somalia only seven months before, and Isaias was known to be supplying the al-Shabaab rebels as a way to weaken his Ethiopian opponent, not for any ideological commitment to the Somali rebels. The two highly intelligent autocrats could be lively and charming interlocutors, as well as cunning and totally ruthless when dealing with any opposition to their rule. In addition to debating the disaster in neighboring Somalia, each wanted to talk with me about their confrontation over their shared border.

The roots of the Eritrean-Ethiopian conflict went back to the colonial era when Italy colonized Eritrea and used it as a basis for the effort to subjugate the Ethiopian empire. Emperor Haile Selassie annexed Eritrea in 1962. Meles and Isaias both left college to help found guerrilla organizations (Isaias in the late sixties, Meles after a repressive Marxist military junta called the Derg overthrew Selassie in 1974). Meles eventually became the leader of the Tigray People's Liberation Front with the aim of overthrowing the Ethiopian junta; Isaias led the Eritrean People's Liberation Front to secure Eritrean independence and overthrow the junta.

The two groups cooperated in fighting against the Derg regime and emerged victorious when the collapse of the Soviet Union ended the regime's international support. Meles became prime minister of Ethiopia in 1991; and following a UN-supervised referendum on Eritrean independence, Isaias became president of newly independent Eritrea in 1993. Relations between the two leaders soon turned sour. The two countries (both friendly to the West) waged a nasty war between May 1998 and June 2000, in which perhaps 70,000 people perished. After a long, difficult mediation effort led by former U.S. national security adviser Tony Lake, the sides agreed in 2000 to a UN peacekeeping force (the UN Mission in Ethiopia and Eritrea or UNMEE), a Temporary Security Zone 25 kilometers wide along the Eritrean side of the disputed border, and a boundary commission to define and demarcate the border between the two countries.

Both sides at first agreed to the commission's border demarcation presented in 2002, but the Ethiopian government backed away soon after. The Ethiopians did not like the idea of the line dividing villages, and most particularly the commission's surprising placement of the town of Badme in the Ethiopian province of Tigray on the Eritrean side. This riled many of Meles's fellow Tigrayan leaders and became a major issue inside the Ethiopian government. Eritrea demanded that the commission's decision be accepted without change. Ethiopia, however, found reasons to slow down the process, demanding talks on its concerns and an overall normalization of relations between the two countries. This included access to the sea, a critical issue for Ethiopia, which had become landlocked when Eritrea gained its independence.

Tensions were high between the two leaders when I had my first discussions with them in June 2007. The Boundary Commission had set a deadline for an agreement between the two sides for November 2007. If the two sides reached no agreement, the commission would go out of business at the end of the year and its boundary proposals would become final. Meanwhile, the Eritreans began sending troops back into the security zone and restricting UNMEE's ability to monitor their moves. For their part, the Ethiopians carried out major military exercises near the border. The chances for a renewed war between the two countries appeared to be growing.

In our talks both Meles and Isaias were in full charm mode, avowing their sincere interest in resolving the problems and professing a desire for the UN to help them do so. Both men were highly articulate in English, forceful, and calculating, but they struck me as more determined to best their rival than settle the dispute. They knew each other well, and it was obvious this was a very personal fight. It was also clear that both men wanted to see how they could use the new secretary-general and me to further their own long games against each other.

After hearing them out, I returned to New York for extensive discussions with my experienced assistant-secretary-general for Africa, Haile Menkerios, who had his own long history with these men. Haile had left his Harvard graduate studies in 1973 to join the fight for Eritrean independence and later served as Eritrea's first ambassador to Ethiopia, ambassador to the Organization of African Unity, and Permanent Representative to the United Nations. In 2001 he joined fourteen other longtime Eritrean leaders in signing a letter to Isaias pressing the increasingly autocratic leader to carry out promised democratic reforms. Isaias promptly arrested eleven of the signers in Eritrea (they have not been seen since), a fate Haile was spared because he was in New York. Knowing the players and the issue intimately, he provided the secretary-general and me invaluable advice on how to proceed. None of us were optimistic that Meles or Isaias would follow through on their nice words; but with the approaching November deadline and the rising tensions along the border, we felt we had no choice but to test their interest in a settlement.

I returned to Asmara and Addis Ababa in late August for further talks with the two leaders. Isaias and Meles said they were open to working-level border talks. Isaias also made positive noises about the UN peacekeeping force (which he had been strangling for months) and said an open border and normalization of relations between the two countries would be no problem once the border was demarcated. Both men waxed eloquent about the possibility of opening up trade through the Eritrean port of Assab. Meles sounded a positive note throughout but warned against the commission's plan for demarcation by coordinates rather than by placing pillars. Surprisingly, he told me that no one really cared about Badme (the key town awarded to Eritrea); it merely symbolized which side was right. Neither reacted to my floating the possibility of a meeting between the two sides at the UN General Assembly, which would open a few weeks later in New York.

With the possible window of opportunity narrowing, we put forward a last-ditch approach to both leaders that combined acceptance of the border demarcation with an announcement of normalization of relations and the possibility of a meeting between the two leaders. I intended to personally propose it to Meles at the UN General Assembly and to Isaias' chief of staff Yemane Ghebreab, who also planned to come to New York. I had a good talk with Meles, who put the usual positive spin on the Ethiopian government's position but expressed skepticism that Isaias would agree. The U.S. government refused to give Yemane a visa (relations had deteriorated badly over Eritrea's actions in Somalia), so we agreed to meet in Canada. Unfortunately, my flight to Canada to see Yemane was canceled due to severe weather, and I had to send our proposal to him by email. The secretary-general's formal meetings with the foreign ministers of the two countries in New York were predictably unproductive, since neither had been clued in by their bosses about our conversations.

The Eritreans stalled for a month and a half before responding to the substance of our proposal, which Eritrea's ambassador in New York referred to as the "notorious email." The secretary-general informed the two leaders he intended to send me back to the area for more talks. Having run out the clock, Isaias wrote the secretary-general on December 3, turning down the idea of another visit by me to the region and attaching a letter from Yemane responding negatively to my email.

I was not surprised that Isaias backed away from his earlier, more positive stance on a border settlement. Both leaders saw this as a game. Winning points over his old comrade-turned-enemy was certainly more important than satisfying the UN. Isaias found the conflict a convenient way to justify his repressive policies at home and the desperate state of the economy. With American backing, Meles had little incentive to compromise. War never seemed imminent. Normalization would have helped both economies, but it had a lower priority. The Eritreans moved quickly to kick UNMEE out of the country. It had not been effective for well over a year, but the Security Council (led by the U.S.) had been willing to let it languish rather than pulling the plug. The UN peacekeeping operation formally ended at the end of July 2008.

I also learned that diplomacy at a mile and a half above sea level has its own hazards. When Haile and I called on Meles in Addis Ababa during the January 2008 AU summit, our taxi dropped us off at the wrong entrance. We rushed a couple of blocks, hurried up three flights of stairs, and entered just at the appointed time. Meles greeted us warmly and asked me to start. I opened my mouth, but not a word came out. Instead, I was gasping for air. (It is no mystery why Ethiopian runners do so well in international marathons.) Meles laughed as he saw my predicament. After I swallowed my embarrassment and regained my voice, we had an excellent exchange.

Meles had every reason to be in a good mood. Isaias was taking the heat at the UN for trashing the mediation effort and strangling UNMEE as well as being under the threat of severe U.S. sanctions. Meles, on the other hand, had sounded reasonable throughout the process, acting as is if he wanted a solution while holding on to Badme and giving no ground in the dispute. In his game with Isaias, he had won the public competition without changing his position at all.

However, although Meles won the propaganda war that time, Isaias eventually got his way on the border. Meles died in August 2012, and a new prime minister, Abiy Ahmad (from the Omoro ethnic group), announced in 2018 that Ethiopia accepted the border commission's demarcation in full. He visited Asmara in July with appropriate statements pledging full normalization of ties between the two countries. For his settlement with Eritrea and his relaxation of repressive measures at home, Abiy received the Nobel Peace Prize later that year. He then drifted into a bitter civil war with Tigray (Meles's base). Isaias backed the Ethiopian government, joined in the fight against the Tigrayans, and pocketed the border agreement he had sought for years.

Violence in Kenya

Neither the secretary-general nor I felt it necessary for the UN to be at the forefront of every negotiation effort. We wanted results rather than pats on the back. On Sunday, December 30, 2007, I received a call from my assistant, Roselyn Akombe, that things were getting very tense in her native Kenya after the announcement that President Mwai Kibaki had been reelected despite polls showing his rival, Raila Odinga, well ahead. Both sides appeared to be encouraging the ethnic violence that left over a thousand people dead and some three hundred thousand displaced.

After I briefed the secretary-general, he began a series of phone calls to African leaders, including Ghanaian president Kufuor, then head of the African Union, to coordinate a response. Over the next couple of weeks, several African leaders, the U.S. assistant secretary for African affairs, and President Kufuor visited Nairobi but failed to break the impasse. I suggested to Ban that former secretary-general Kofi Annan might take on the mediation effort, and Ban discussed it with Kufuor. On January 10 Kufuor announced that Annan and two other African leaders would become the African Union's mediation team.

Despite our severe funding shortage, we wanted to be sure Kofi had the necessary support to launch his mission without delay. Michele Griffin, who as head of our mediation unit had drafted most of our basic papers on transforming DPA, quickly improvised a solution to the problem. She called her fellow countryman, the Irish permanent representative, and asked for a donation of a million euros. To their credit the Irish responded immediately, providing a check in two days.

We put some of our top people on an airplane to Nairobi to set up an emergency secretariat to support Annan. Their office, headed by DPA's East Africa chief, João Honwana, included UN personnel from our Nairobi office and UNDP and former aides to Annan, as well as people from the Centre for Humanitarian Dialogue. Another key player was our elections chief, Craig Jenness, who developed a plan on his flight to Nairobi that obviated the need for a drawn-out recount while people were dying on the streets. Jenness, Honwana, and later Margaret Vogt spent weeks in Nairobi. Throughout, we emphasized that the mediation effort was Annan's and the African Union's show. We were pleased to play a supporting role.

During the negotiations Ban kept in close contact with Kufuor and Annan. He visited Kenya on February 1 at a critical point in the negotiations, pressing both sides to resolve the conflict. He also worked to ensure there were no competing wannabe mediation efforts that would have allowed the main players to avoid a compromise. The U.S. and UK also kept up strong pressure for a settlement.

I briefed the Security Council, which in turn issued statements supporting Annan's efforts. After forty-one days, Annan's patient work paid off when the two sides agreed on a power-sharing structure that defused the crisis. Annan had done an excellent job, and he and the African Union received the well-deserved credit. The secretary-general and I (as well as the DPA staff) knew we had played a key role in the success, even if that fact was not in the headlines. We also proved we could move quickly in a crisis and provide the needed expertise and support to achieve a major success.

DPA Election Assistance

The Political Department also had long included an impressive elections unit that coordinated the overall UN approach to assisting countries in carrying out free and fair elections. Working closely with the United Nations Development Program, other agencies, and international NGOs, the unit led an operation second to none in providing technical advice, support, and training to countries new to elections, helping them improve the process to increase the legitimacy of those elected to high office in the eyes of their citizenry. Over half of the countries in the United Nations had requested and benefited from DPA election advice at one time or another over the years.

While a critical element in establishing the legitimacy of new governments, elections too often were seen by some to be a "magic bullet" that could stabilize conflict-ridden countries. As the Kenyan and many other cases made clear, elections by themselves were no panacea for ending internal strife. In fact, elections could exacerbate divisions in a fragile society as easily as they could heal rifts, and they all too often served as the flashpoints to reignite old conflicts. Also, unfortunately, holding good elections is no guarantee of good governance by the victors.

The head of DPA's elections division, Craig Jenness, with my strong support, used our emphasis on prevention to transform the division from one that merely dispensed technical assistance to integrating election work closely with the rest of our preventive diplomacy agenda. He refocused DPA's election efforts toward supporting a broader political strategy in a country, emphasizing the need for local political consensus on the rules of the game, a willingness to compromise, credible elections, and strong postelection follow-up. We looked for ways to ensure that elections would support a peace process in fragile, conflict-prone countries, not become the cause of a crisis. Craig's vision widened the focus of international election assistance to ensure the efforts served this broader political goal.

Guinea Pulled Back from the Brink

One crisis where the emphasis on preventive diplomacy and aggressive election advice worked particularly well was in the impoverished but resource-rich West African country of Guinea. It also served as a textbook case of international cooperation between the UN (especially our West Africa political office in Dakar), the Economic Community of West African States (ECOWAS), the African Union, the United States, France, Morocco, and Burkina Faso. Its success avoided a nasty potential internal war in yet another African country and offered the people of Guinea a democratic path forward for the first time in the country's history.

By the mid-2000s Guinea's longtime dictator, Lansana Conté, had been losing his grip on the country as his health deteriorated. Conté's appointment of a moderate prime minister, Lansana Konyaté, to deal with the country's problems in January 2007 received wide support, both locally and internationally. Konyaté had served three years as assistant-secretary-general in DPA in the nineties, as Guinea's permanent representative to the UN, and as executive secretary of ECOWAS. His struggle to decrease corruption and reorient the bureaucracy to support the needs of the Guinean people had the strong support of the UN, Guinea's neighbors, and the international community.

But it was a doomed effort. Conté refused to give up any real power, and his cronies worked to weaken the prime minister at every opportunity. Military officers and soldiers protested their low wages, reform efforts stalled, and Conté eventually fired Konyaté. The potential for bloodshed loomed large. The UN's resident coordinator in Conakry asked DPA for help.

A month earlier, the secretary-general had appointed one of Africa's most experienced diplomats, Said Djinnit, to head our Dakar-based regional office in West Africa (UNOWA). Djinnit had worked for the African Union and its predecessor for over eighteen years, most recently serving as the AU's commissioner for peace and security. We agreed his first focus should be on Guinea. Djinnit quickly developed a close cooperative relationship with two colleagues in Dakar—Mohammed Chambas, executive secretary of ECOWAS, and Ibrahima Fall, AU special representative for Guinea—to present a united front on the Guinea crisis.

When Conté's death was announced on December 23, 2008, junior officers led by Capt. Mousa Dadis Camara staged a coup. Promising to cleanse the country of corruption and hold an election in which he would not run, Camara and his co-conspirators were welcomed at first, and the civilian and military old guard gave up without a fight. However, the popularity of the junta did not last long.

Camara proved to be a bizarre and erratic leader (probably often addled by drugs), who enjoyed interrogating and tormenting suspected corrupt officials on television. His government included many incompetent military cronies incapable of carrying out the junta's promises. By the summer of 2009 the security situation had deteriorated, with elements of the military seemingly totally out of control. The Presidential Guard even beat up one of the junta's vice presidents. Most ominously, Camara brought in mercenaries from South Africa and Israel to train members of his minority ethnic group. He planned to build a militia strike force responsible only to him, a formula that in other African countries had led to all-out interethnic war.

Djinnit and his partners made several trips to Conakry to press for the promised transition to civilian rule. He also participated actively in meetings of a Guinea contact group to coordinate international efforts. And in New York we pushed the UN system as a whole to fully support these efforts.

As the months went on, the date for the elections kept slipping. Opposition forces began to regroup, and demonstrators took to Conakry's streets. After Camara announced he planned to run in the election after all, fifty thousand people gathered in a soccer stadium on September 23 to protest his plan to remain in power. The Presidential Guard attacked the demonstrators, firing their weapons indiscriminately and publicly raping numerous women caught in the chaos. Over 150 people were killed, with many more injured.

Any lingering support for the junta in Guinea quickly disappeared, and international pressure on the regime, including sanctions, became intense. To help diffuse the situation and respond to the outcry in Guinea, DPA and the UN human rights commissioner worked together to set up a UN Commission of Inquiry, made up of eminent African legal experts to determine responsibility for the massacre.

Menkerios, Djinnit, and a representative of the Human Rights Commission flew to Conakry on October 19, 2009, to obtain the regime's cooperation with the new panel. Menkerios warned Camara that the leaders could be charged by the International Criminal Court (ICC) with "crimes against humanity" for the soccer field massacre and emphasized to him and others that it was in their interest to cooperate with the panel. Cornered, Camara agreed the government would cooperate.

While the panel members were conducting their final interviews in Conakry in early December, Camara's chief of staff—responsible for the Presidential Guard and fearing he was being set up to take the fall for the massacre—shot Camara in the head at point-blank range. Seriously injured but still alive, Camara was flown to Morocco for surgery. With Camara out of Conakry, his deputy, Sekouba Konaté, took charge.

The final report of the UN panel laid out the facts of the massacre in chilling detail: 156 people killed, around 1,400 wounded, and 109 women brutally raped. It called for the referral of Camara, his chief of staff, and the head of the Presidential Guard to the ICC.

At the urging of the United States and France, Morocco had taken Camara in for treatment. The Moroccans had then sent him to Burkina Faso for President Blaise Compaoré, ECOWAS and the AU's designated mediator for Guinea, to host. Under considerable international pressure, Compaoré kept Camara in Ouagadougou rather than send him back to Conakry and encouraged him to sign an agreement that left Konaté in charge in Conakry. Djinnit worked as Compaoré's adviser throughout this process.

Guinea soon came alive politically, with twenty-four candidates, including four former prime ministers, vying for the presidency. DPA and its international partners stepped up their assistance to help the independent election commission carry off its first-ever free election. The first round of the elections made a reasonable start with the field narrowed to former prime minister Cellou Dalain Diallo and longtime opposition leader Alpha Condé. However, many complaints of irregularities arose, and the head of the elections commission was later convicted of vote tampering.

Determined to ensure that the runoff would produce a legitimate new president, our deputy elections chief, Ali Diabacte, spent almost all of the next several months camped out in the Guinean election office offering advice and assistance. There were several delays in the date for the runoff, wavering by Konaté and the elections commission, and maneuvering by various parties as they cut deals to back one of the two runoff candidates; but Diabacte and his team repeatedly pulled the commission back from questionable schemes. The secretary-general, AU, and ECOWAS, as well as the U.S. and France kept up the pressure to make sure the elections were held and the results viewed as legitimate by the Guinean people.

When the runoff finally took place in November, it was a major success. Turnout was high, and the Guinean people enthusiastically embraced this historic moment. Alpha Condé won and became president of Guinea. The country's numerous problems did not go away with a "free and fair" election, but now the country had a legitimate leader and a chance for solid progress. The outcome was a far cry from the nasty civil war that seemed inevitable a year earlier, a war that would undoubtedly have led to a billion-dollar peacekeeping effort and condemned the country to decades of continued grinding poverty. This preventive-diplomacy success, as usual, received little coverage in the world press, which is drawn more to disasters than to peace. But that did not diminish its importance for the people involved or the global community.

Several key elements made it possible. Most important was the close cooperation of the UN, AU, and ECOWAS, personified on the UN side by Said Djinnet. This cooperation on the ground was backed up in New York by a broad consensus in the Security Council, which gave us wide latitude to pursue the ultimately successful approach we used in Guinea. Equally crucial was the strong support of the United States and France, who weighed in at critical intervals with the Moroccans and Compaoré to ensure the turnover of power to Konaté that made the transition possible. Our aggressive approach in pursuing the Commission of Inquiry into the stadium massacre produced panic in the leadership, which led to the incapacitation of Camara, thus allowing the transition to take place under Konaté. Finally, the work of Diabacte and his colleagues ensured the acceptance of Condé's election.

Cooperation with Regional Organizations

The Guinea effort provided an excellent example of one of the key elements to successful conflict prevention—working with regional organizations that were themselves trying to resolve dangerous conflicts in their areas. Secretary-General Ban hosted an annual meeting of regional organizations, including the African Union, the League of Arab States, ASEAN, the OAS, SADEC (South Asia), the Shanghai Coordination Council, the CSTO (Russia + 5 neighboring states), NATO, the EU, the OSCE, and others to exchange ideas and promote greater interregional cooperation and closer coordination between these organizations and the United Nations. We offered close cooperation, training, our mediation experts, our experience, and the backing of the UN to support the efforts of these groups.

The actual level of cooperation varied widely. We worked closely with the OSCE on Kyrgyzstan, with the EU and NATO in Europe and Africa, but by far our closest partner was the African Union. Others, like ASEAN in Southeast Asia, the OAS in the Americas, and SADEC in South Asia were polite and friendly but primarily interested in keeping the UN out of their problems.

The African Union put a major effort into building its own capacity to deal with Africa's peace and security problems, and we were happy to help. The secretary-general and I felt strongly that rivalry between groups that were supposedly trying to help solve crises—private groups, individual countries, regional organizations, the United Nations, and even different parts of the UN—was a recipe for disaster. Competing peace negotiations meant that parties involved in the conflict could play one mediator off against another to advance their cause. In Somalia, Ould Abdallah spent considerable time corralling competing interventions; in Guinea, Djinnit solved this problem from the start by his close relationship to the ECOWAS and AU representatives; and in Kenya we took a low profile and were happy to let Annan, the African Union, and the Centre for Humanitarian Dialogue receive full credit. The important thing was the resolution of the conflicts, and we didn't care who did it or who got the final credit. I remained convinced that if we succeeded, people would look to DPA for leadership and help. If our advice was solid, it would likely be followed. If we were incompetent, no amount of public relations spin or self-praise would put us in the lead role.

The relationship with the African Union became increasingly close. We included them in our training courses, had joint strategy sessions to map out a way forward on various countries, and lent them our professional mediators. The people on the staff of the AU's Peace and Security Council were first-rate. While DPA was willing to cooperate with interested regional groups at all levels, we had to be careful not to offend our bosses in the Security Council. We were happy to share, but the members of the Security Council (especially the Permanent Five) would not compromise their role as the principal global body responsible for international peace and security.

Peacebuilding, Development, and Sierra Leone

The plea for our help from the UN Resident Coordinator in Guinea underlined another part of the reform strategy—getting other parts of the UN to work together to prevent conflicts. Traditionally the UN's development side, led by the United Nations Development Program (UNDP), had been extremely wary of getting involved in UN political efforts. They didn't want their resident coordinators expelled for involvement in a country's politics or their development programs "tainted" by political concerns.

But the link between political violence and development failures was indisputable. As a World Bank study put it in 2009, "A major episode of violence, unlike natural disasters or economic cycles, can wipe out an entire generation of economic progress." Preventative diplomacy not only made sense as a way to save lives and avoid the misery of war; it could also play a crucial role in international development. The old model of keeping development and politics strictly separate (what Karina called the "First Avenue Divide," as UNDP occupied quarters across First Avenue from the UN Headquarters) was no longer tenable. We needed a more collaborative approach.

Secretary-General Ban made getting the various autonomous and competitive parts of the UN system to work together one of his top goals. This included a coordinated policy toward conflict prevention and economic development. For us, this essentially meant improving ties with UNDP. UNDP managed a system of resident coordinators who let the Country Teams in most countries. The resident coordinator (RC), who also served as the lead UNDP official, was responsible to the host government and other UN agencies represented in that country. He or she was not the representative of the secretary-general and did not feel bound by his agenda. (Indeed, when Ban traveled to Saudi Arabia early in his term the resident coordinator did not even bother to welcome him at the airport or make a call on him.) The Country Teams (consisting of development and humanitarian agencies and led by the resident coordinator) were the nearest thing the United Nations had to embassies abroad. But they were set up to promote long-term development, not for dealing with political crises. They needed our help and we needed them, because they were on the ground and could see the political problems early on.

We set up regular meetings between UNDP's administrator, Helen Clark, along with the heads of DPKO and DFS, to discuss appointments and coordinate approaches in countries with political unrest. We increased the number of political officers (usually called Peace and Development Officers) in the UN country teams, paid for by extrabudgetary funds from DPA and UNDP, to provide political advice and help manage conflicts on the ground. These officers reported to both UNDP and DPA. We met regularly with resident coordinators both in the field and in New York, briefing them on our willingness to help and on the resources we had available. Although it was often something of a struggle, coordination between the political and development parts of the United Nations improved considerably over time. The dispatch of political officers to numerous country teams greatly strengthened DPA's grasp of evolving events in fragile countries.

The situation has continued to evolve. Ban later made the resident coordinators subject to approval by the secretary-general and the representative of all of the UN, and his successor, Antonio Guterres, placed the resident coordinators under the deputy secretary-general.

Since the early nineties, the complex problem of restoring countries to some semblance of normality after a civil or interstate war had been debated under the rubric of "peacebuilding"— defined as "a range of measures targeted to reduce the risk of a country lapsing or relapsing into conflict by strengthening national capacities at all levels for conflict management and to lay the foundations for sustainable peace and development." Peacebuilding turned out to be one of those issues that is far easier to discuss in the abstract than to accomplish in practice. The issues were real and not in dispute. Many countries fell back into conflict within a few years after the initial fighting was "resolved." The relapse wiped out economic progress for years to come. A top priority of the international community had to be to find a way to get policies in place that could avoid the recurrence of these wars.

The list of problems was well known. After the celebration of the end of a conflict, the population needed a sense of security, a new political structure (elections and dialogue, for instance) must be put in place, basic public services, from water to education, usually had to be constructed from scratch; refugees must be returned home; and infrastructure destroyed in the fighting needed to be rebuilt. Some rapid economic recovery was critical to absorb unemployed youth and former combatants. These were huge issues for an impoverished country, but they had to be tackled immediately somehow.

UNDP had many programs that could address some of these problems, but they tended to be long-term and not available for immediate implementation. The same was true of the World Bank and most international aid programs. The difficulty becomes obvious when we consider the billions of dollars the United States spent (mostly wasted) on "nation building" in Iraq and Afghanistan, with relatively little progress on the underlying issues. But the fact that the problems are hard and expensive does not make them go away. And then there is the problem of coordinating and concentrating those (never sufficient) international resources available to accomplish the tasks quickly enough to make the effort evident in people's lives.

The UN's approach to these problems in the 2005 World Summit was to set up a Peacebuilding Commission made up of UN permanent representatives answerable to both the Security Council and the General Assembly, a Peacebuilding Support Office (PBSO) in the Secretariat, and a Peacebuilding Fund to distribute voluntary funds for these issues. During my time at the UN, this new, unwieldly structure accomplished very little. DPA had some loose oversight over the PBSO and eventually some access to the Fund; but the new office seemed more concerned about maintaining its bureaucratic independence than working together to manage the challenges. The various committees of the Peacebuilding Commission held meetings in New York and made visits to their individual countries, and those with strong leadership and financing from their own country made some progress.

But overall, the peacebuilding apparatus seriously underperformed. Needless to say, the Fund never received anything like the amount of money necessary to have a major impact. After I left the UN, Secretary-General Ban appointed my DPA deputy,

Oscar Fernandez-Taranco, to head the PBSO. Oscar had extensive political and development experience and was an excellent choice. He focused attention and available resources on peacebuilding's essential goals. Secretary-General Guterres tightened the political/economic nexus even more by bringing Oscar and the PBSO into DPA (now renamed the Department of Political and Peacebuilding Affairs).

Sierra Leone was on the peacebuilding agenda from the first. In many ways, the country became the concept's poster child. Between 1991 and 2002, Sierra Leone had suffered one of Africa's worst civil wars, infamous for its rapes, murders, amputation of limbs, and funding by "blood diamonds." The UN-sponsored Special Court on Sierra Leone eventually sentenced Liberia's former president, Charles Taylor, to fifty years in jail for his role in the conflict, in which at least fifty thousand people were killed. ECOWAS and the UN both tried to end the tragedy with peacekeeping missions. It took a British force that freed trapped UN peacekeepers and then stayed on to defeat the rebels. Although Sierra Leone is rich in natural resources, by the end of the conflict the impoverished country came in dead last on the UN's Human Development Index and had the world's worst child mortality rate.

A large UN peacekeeping force remained in the country until 2005, followed by a smaller observer/peacekeeping force. After a successful presidential election won by opposition leader Ernest Bai Koroma, the Security Council decided to wind down the peacekeeping operation by October 1, 2008, and replace it with a DPA peacebuilding office. I asked Michael von der Schulenburg, who had been the UN deputy mission chief in Iraq, to travel to Sierra Leone to see what help the country needed most urgently and take a fresh look at how a peacebuilding mission should be structured. I emphasized that our new mission should be focused on results, not bureaucratic tradition or past practices. We needed to know what the concept should look like in practice.

Schulenburg was a smart, creative leader, experienced in political and development issues, and a driven manager focused on getting results. He came back to New York with a clear plan for a fully integrated UN effort designed to respond directly to Sierra Leone's needs. He also discovered that DPKO was rapidly dismantling its operation in Freetown, including selling office furniture, without considering the needs of the follow-on UN office. After I chatted briefly with Susana Malcorra, she made it abundantly clear to her DFS staff that they were now responsible for servicing both the outgoing and incoming missions; and the dismantling had to wait until the Security Council decided on the structure of the new office.

The secretary-general's proposal for the new UN Integrated Office for Sierra Leone (UNIPSIL) followed Schulenburg's plan. The Security Council endorsed the concept and Ban selected Schulenburg to head it. As the executive representative of the secretary-general, he was both head of the political operation and the resident coordinator leading the UN Country Team. Schulenburg developed the Joint Vision, which aligned the various UN programs to support peacebuilding and sought to the extent possible to get other international aid programs to follow suit. UNIPSIL was the most integrated effort that the UN had ever attempted to set up, both politically and economically, with benchmarked goals. The UN had experts helping Sierra Leone deal with drug trafficking, corruption, human rights, police training, decentralization, democratic institution-building, including constitutional issues and, when appropriate, elections. Joint funding was to ensure a truly integrated effort.

Schulenburg's plan was popular in Sierra Leone, New York, and major donor capitals. Long-term development was not slighted, but the clear emphasis was on those elements most critical to getting Sierra Leone back on its feet.

As if to demonstrate that the underlying problems remained, violence flared in Sierra Leone in March 2009 between supporters of the two leading political parties. When the progovernment group ransacked the opposition's headquarters and marooned twenty-two opposition members on the roof, Schulenburg rushed to the scene, climbed up to the roof, and negotiated their safe passage through the crowd. He then led the international community effort to press the two sides to stop the violence, resulting in a public process of reconciliation that established calm. Despite the government's commitment to reform, the "peace dividend" that the population expected had yet to arrive. Government efforts to rein in corruption were slow, the threat from drug traffickers to use Sierra Leone as a transit point from Latin America to Europe was deeply troubling, the situation in neighboring Guinea was deteriorating, and youth unemployment remained at a staggering level. Moving the country to a path to solving these problems in the brief time the "peacebuilding mission" was expected to exist presented huge challenges. As Schulenburg put it, we were being asked to help "accomplish a generational change in the country in five short years."

When I met with President Koroma and other officials during a June 2009 visit, I was impressed with the government's determination to carry out its reform plans and with UNIPSIL's activities in support. The often-adversarial UN agencies were working amazingly well together and voiced strong support for UNIPSIL's leadership. Schulenburg's joint strategy was going well, and I felt we were beginning to make some headway toward ensuing success in the UN's peacebuilding efforts.

However, by the fall of 2011, growing political tensions tied to the 2012 Sierra Leone election had bubbled over onto UNIPSIL. Schulenburg and his people were working to keep a level playing field for the upcoming election to ensure a fair vote; and he became more vocal about the slow effort to reduce corruption. Koroma chose to interpret Schulenburg's actions as cozying up to the opposition and complained to the secretary-general. Ban praised Schulenburg and defended his actions, but when Koroma followed up with a formal demand for Schulenburg's removal—in effect, declaring him *persona non grata*—the secretary-general had no choice but to replace him.

But Schulenburg had shown the way to meet the peacebuilding challenges. When UNIPSIL closed its operation in March 2014, just five and a half years after its establishment, by no means were all of Sierra Leone's problems solved. But the UN had fulfilled its peacebuilding goals in the delicate post-conflict stage, and the UN Country Team would continue the effort. In the end Koroma easily won reelection, and his government deserved strong praise for managing its path forward along this tricky post-conflict path. But the UN had been there at a critical period with a plan, resources, and a commitment to help. No longer was peacebuilding just a pie-in-the-sky hope; UNIPSIL and Sierra Leone proved that the UN could make the concept work.

19
Georgia, Kyrgyzstan, and Cyprus

Russia Invades Georgia

The August 2008 Russian invasion of Georgia provided a clear example of the UN's lack of influence on great power issues. There was little doubt that one of Putin's top goals beyond staying in power and regaining Russia's Great Power status was to rebuild as much as he could of the Russian Empire. Georgia was a particular thorn in Putin's side. After the Rose Revolution in 2003, Saakashvili had acted quickly to move Georgia to the Western camp. His goal was to make Georgia a member of the EU and NATO. By 2006 his government had made impressive progress in creating a vibrant democracy, reducing corruption, reforming the government and economy, and increasing its ties to the West.

Putin saw Saakashvili's actions as a direct threat to his regathering plans and set out to reverse the process. He cut off Georgian gas supplies for several months that winter. He reacted to the Georgian arrest of four GRU generals for spying by closing the border (Russia was Georgia's largest export market) and expelling some Georgians who worked in Russia. He also increased Russian ties with the breakaway Abkhazia and South Ossetia regions of Georgia. In addition to the two leaders' opposing strategic visions, the tall, outgoing, cosmopolitan Georgian leader and the diminutive, ex-KGB Russian boss held each other in total contempt.

Demonstrations in Tbilisi in November 2007 against President Saakashvili's government—which the Russians certainly encouraged—led to early elections that the president managed to win by a relatively small majority. Then, in March 2008, the

U.S. tried and failed to get allied agreement at a NATO summit to include Georgia and Ukraine in Member Action Plans (MAPs) designed to lead to NATO membership. Germany and France opposed the effort due largely to virulent Russian opposition. The NATO leaders did, however, agree to a forward-leaning statement that stated the two countries "will become members of NATO."

The Russians struck back. Within days, Putin announced Moscow would further strengthen its ties to the breakaway regions of Abkhazia and South Ossetia and send additional paratroopers and artillery to its "peacekeeping" force in Abkhazia. The Russians stopped short of supporting independence for the two regions and signed on to a UN Security Council statement in mid-April that "reaffirm[ed] the commitment of all member states to the sovereignty, independence and territorial integrity of Georgia within its recognized borders"—though they tried to use Western recognition of Kosovo's independence from Serbia as an excuse to press the Abkhaz case.

Over the next few months, Putin engaged in attacks on the Georgian leadership and increasingly provocative actions, including shooting down a Georgian drone over Abkhazia. The U.S. and European leaders reacted with press statements, but the split in NATO made it fairly obvious to the Russians that the West had no concrete plans to help the Georgians. As the Russians tried to goad Saakashvili into taking a rash action, his friends (including me, when I saw him in New York) were reduced to urging him to stay calm. These warnings later became an excuse for the U.S. administration and the Europeans for their inaction, as they sought to shift the blame to Saakashvili to cover up their failure to counter the Russians. Sadly, the West chose to ignore the fact that the Russians were the provocateurs and had troops in place to take immediate action against Georgia.

The excuse for the Russian invasion came in early August after an exchange of mortar shells and sniper fire initiated by Russian-controlled South Ossetia's forces. The South Ossetians began evacuations from their capital, Tskhinvali, and on August 6–7, 2008, carried out an attack on a nearby Georgian village. Georgia responded by sending in troops, an action the Russians, most Europeans, and some Americans labeled as Georgian rashness that caused the war. In New York the Russians immediately called for a meeting of the Security Council, which took place at 1:15 a.m. on August 8, five hours after Russian troops had entered the area. At a second Council meeting later in the day, the Georgian representative laid out details of the invasion from the Georgian point of view. By the next day, Russian planes were dropping bombs on Georgian targets.

Diane and I were en route to California for the wedding of an old friend's son when the secretary-general (who was himself out of New York) called to ask me to return to manage our response. We turned around at the Denver airport, overnighted in the passenger terminal at Chicago's O'Hare, and took the first early morning flight to New York. My briefing to the Security Council soon after our arrival on Sunday (August 10) included a call from the secretary-general for troops to "leave the zone of conflict." It had zero effect on Russian actions as did other pronouncements by President Bush, the NATO secretary-general, and European leaders.

There were more fireworks at the UN when DPKO deputy Edmond Mulet and I updated the Security Council on the situation the next day. I gave a straightforward report of the information we had on the conflict, but Russian permanent representative Vitaly Churkin accused me of giving a biased view of events. (Churkin and I knew each other from the eighties when he worked at the Russian Embassy in Washington and I was deputy on the Soviet Desk. We had a good relationship in New York, but my rendition of events did not fit the Russian version of the "facts," and he obviously felt it necessary to respond.) The meeting was further enlivened by U.S. ambassador Zal Khalilzad's revelation that Lavrov had told Secretary Rice that morning that "Saakashvili had to go"—laying bare Putin's goal all along. Zal accused the Russians of promoting regime change of a democratically elected president. It was not an easy day for Churkin. Needless to say, both exchanges from a supposedly closed session of the Council immediately made it to the press.

The fighting was over in five days. Russian forces easily defeated the Georgians, occupying cities and driving toward Tbilisi. On Wednesday, Saakashvili and the new Russian president Medvedev signed a ceasefire agreement brokered by French president Sarkozy.

The Russians, however, slow-rolled their response, advancing troops to within twenty-five miles of Tbilisi, and only ten days later carried out the bulk of the withdrawal called for in the agreement. The West pressed hard for the Russians to leave, and I argued for all sides to carry out the agreement when I briefed the Council on August 19. Churkin flatly lied, telling the Council that they were following the deal when they obviously were not. He also refused to support a French-drafted resolution that called on both sides to fulfill the ceasefire agreement and reaffirmed the territorial integrity of Georgia within internationally recognized boundaries.

Four days later, Moscow recognized the independence of Abkhazia and South Ossetia. (A handful of countries not involved later followed suit.) The EU issued a "balanced statement" on the conflict that essentially let Russia off the hook. The U.S. reportedly debated whether or not to react more forcefully against the invasion but eventually opted to limit its response to aiding Georgia's reconstruction and rebuilding its military. Except for the removal of Saakashvili, the Russians had achieved all their objectives, most notably taking NATO membership for Ukraine and Georgia off the table. European governments had conveniently decided that Saakashvili was as much to blame for the war as the Russians, and some policy makers in Washington convinced themselves of this as a cover for inaction in the waning days of the Bush administration. The newly independent states were put on notice by the Russians that they would intervene if the countries strayed too far into the Western camp, and the West had demonstrated it did not have the appetite to intervene.

The United Nations as usual was helpless when the major powers clashed. There was no way the Security Council, much less the secretary-general or the Secretariat, could enforce the principles enshrined in the UN's Charter. The October Security Council resolution on the UN mission in Abkhazia was devoid of the principles of the April resolution and merely extended the mission another six months. The EU, UN, and OSCE did work together to broker security measures for a lasting ceasefire; but months after they had promised to depart, Russian forces still held some areas that had been in Georgian hands before the war.

Saakashvili served out his term to 2013 and continued his

efforts at reform and economic development, but he then left Georgia under the threat of arrest. He moved to Brooklyn and later to Ukraine, where he had obtained Ukrainian citizenship and sought to clean up corruption in Odessa. I last saw Saakashvili on Capitol Hill in Washington where he was enthusiastically lobbying U.S. congressmen to support the Ukrainian government. He later returned to Georgia and was jailed. Putin had won. NATO and EU eastern expansion was dead, and the West signaled to all it was unwilling to stand up to Russia's bullying of its neighbors. The scene was set for Moscow's later seizure of Crimea and the far bloodier war in Ukraine.

Kyrgyzstan Boils Over

By 2010, the political and economic situation in Kyrgyzstan had deteriorated badly. President Kurmanbek Bakiyev, who had replaced Akayev, turned out to be as corrupt and prone to autocratic ways as his predecessor but without his charm or earlier pretensions of support for democracy. A southerner, Bakiyev had added to his difficulties by putting cronies into positions of authority throughout the south, in some cases replacing capable members of the Uzbek minority. In addition to a growing opposition at home, Bakiyev managed to anger the Russian leadership by reversing his decision to push the Americans out of the Manas airbase when they raised their monetary offer. After the government announced large increases in the costs of the country's basic utilities, the population's frustration boiled over into large demonstrations, which Russian media (widely watched in Kyrgyzstan) supported, along with criticism of the Bakiyev regime. The government responded to the demonstrations with repressive measures, which only made the situation worse.

I accompanied the secretary-general when he met with Bakiyev on April 3, 2010, during a swing through Central Asia. Bakiyev's body language and comments left little doubt that he felt under enormous pressure. The secretary-general as usual urged the president, both privately and publicly, to deal with corruption and the violation of human rights. I met with several Kyrgyz opposition leaders, including Rosa Otunbayeva, who exuded confidence that the Bakiyev regime's days were numbered. Three days after we left, the demonstrations turned violent, several of the opposition leaders I had met with were arrested, and a massive demonstration occurred in Bishkek. The next day, April 7, police fired on protesters in Bishkek (reportedly killing forty-seven people). The prime minister resigned, a crowd took over the Parliament building, and the opposition proclaimed the formation of an interim government headed by Otunbayeva. Bakiyev fled to his residence in the country's south.

We sent Jan Kubis, a former Slovak foreign minister, to Bishkek to mediate between the two sides. Kubis was well known in Central Asia for his role in ending the Tajik civil war as the UN secretary-general's envoy and for his later appointment as the EU's representative to Central Asia. His role was critical in defusing the crisis. As a result of these talks and intense pressure from the UN, OSCE, the EU, the U.S., and Russia, Bakiyev left the country in mid-April. But the new interim government had only a tenuous grip on power in Bishkek. The removal of Bakiyev's corrupt cronies in the south led to further tensions there between the majority Kyrgyz and minority (but usually more prosperous) Uzbek communities.

From June 11 through June 15, Kyrgyz gangs roamed the streets of Osh and Jalal-Abad in southern Kyrgyzstan, attacking Uzbeks and destroying their homes, businesses, and a university. At least 170 people were killed, and another 100,000 fled across the border to Uzbekistan. I briefed the Security Council on the tragedy on June 15, laying out the UN's efforts to get humanitarian aid to the people affected in both Kyrgyzstan and Uzbekistan. The situation became sufficiently serious that the government (surprisingly supported by the U.S.) asked for Russian peacekeepers to quell the violence. The Russians turned down the request. After four days of mayhem, the Kyrgyz military itself brought things under control.

The head of our regional Central Asian office, Miroslav Jenca, joined with OSCE and EU representatives to form a united front to help the government deal with the aftermath of the conflict. He also worked closely with the UN's Country Team in Kyrgyzstan, which was capably led but before the crisis focused solely on economic development and humanitarian aid, not politics. The "troika" arrangement played a key role in returning the country to normalcy. It worked well because no one in the West or Russia (or neighboring China for that matter) wanted a continuation of the violence, and the members of the Security Council were happy to allow the secretary-general and his staff to carry out their responsibilities without interference.

Special Political Missions

There were fifteen UN Special Political Missions in 2010. Most were country-specific, but three were regional offices. The regional offices proved their worth in the Kyrgyzstan crisis and in West Africa, enabling the UN to establish ties to local leaders and regional organizations and to develop a better understanding of the issues that might lead to conflict. They were also poised to move quickly to resolve problems before they got out of hand.

The Special Political Missions (SPMs) were growing in complexity and responsibility, but they were forced to work under rules written for UN headquarters in New York. DPKO and the UN agencies had far more flexible rules and procedures more in tune with the rapidly changing nature of the problems the UN faced abroad. We set up new missions and expanded our backstopping of older ones as money became available from voluntary contributions. In 2009 DPA launched a major effort to fix various administrative problems that plagued the political missions. Our proposal called for a new funding mechanism similar to the peacekeeping budget that would reduce the pressure on other programs in the regular budget (SPMs were taking up about 20 percent of that budget). It would also provide start-up funds for new missions and support positions in New York similar to those regularly provided for new peacekeeping missions.

We succeeded in getting a proposal to resolve these problems through the ACABQ, but it was again stalled by USUN, which recruited other P-5 members to join in opposition. (The SPM budget would have been calculated on peacekeeping rates, thus raising costs for the U.S. and its P-5 colleagues.) The proposal remained bottled up and never made it to final consideration by the Fifth (Budget) Committee. Again, the administrative people at USUN and the International Organization Affairs Bureau at the State Department felt empowered to ignore the policies of their own political leadership. Despite the Obama administration's friendlier tone toward the UN, the approach toward its American-led Political Department was the same: We like what you're doing, but don't ask for money. (To be fair, USUN did try a few years later to get a similar proposal through the budget committees, but the time had passed; and other P-5 members used the earlier U.S. arguments against the new proposal.)

The Struggle for a Cyprus Settlement

After the failure of the Annan peace plan in Cyprus in April 2004, the UN made an effort to keep the process going. It was well understood that little could be accomplished with the Papadopoulos government firmly entrenched in Cyprus's south and determined to use its seat at the EU table to isolate the Turkish Cypriots and put up roadblocks to Turkey's effort to become a member of the EU. In the north, Talat led a weak government that had come to power on the promise of negotiating a settlement, but the south had little incentive to engage in serious talks. The Europeans, who had shown zero backbone in resolving the difficulties that followed their unconditional invitation to the Greek Cypriots to enter the Union, chose to put pressure on the United Nations to take the problem off their hands. When Secretary-General Ban took over on January 1, 2007, they continued the pressure. But neither Ban nor I saw any value in an all-out push to get negotiations back on track, given the lack of interest from the Greek Cypriot side.

The situation appeared to change dramatically when Demetris Christofias was elected president of the Republic of Cyprus in February 2008. The Communist Party leader had long advocated the unification of Cyprus, and he told me in 2003 that he supported the Annan plan. However, when he later sensed the plan would be defeated, he switched sides and recommended a no vote to preserve his party's role in the Papadopoulos government. Running for president in 2008, he again argued strongly for reunification of the island. Moreover, Christofias had a longtime friendship with fellow leftist leader Talat in the north. In Turkey, the Erdogan government supported a settlement as part of its all-out push to enter the European Union. Thus, the stars seemed lined up for another serious effort to finally settle the "Cyprus problem," and the secretary-general and I decided to do all we could to help achieve that end.

Three weeks after taking office, Christofias met with Talat and the secretary-general's Special Representative to lay the groundwork for new negotiations. They agreed to set up working groups to sort out areas of agreement and disagreement and to start full-fledged negotiations under UN auspices. The also agreed to open a key crossing at Ledra Street in Nicosia that had long been a symbol of the division of Cyprus. I visited the island (along with side trips to Athens and Ankara) a few days later to assess the prospects for new talks. In my meetings with Talat and Christofias, they both affirmed their willingness to reach a comprehensive settlement and to engage in talks in good faith. The atmosphere on the island was positive and expectations high, and I told the press that we expected formal talks to begin within three months.

I reported to the Security Council in mid-April that negotiations between the two sides would "draw on a considerable body of existing work," a euphemism for the Annan Plan, and that the technical committees were making progress. But I cautioned it would take time to work through the many complicated issues. I also told the Council that the secretary-general would appoint a new high-level special envoy to engage the two sides. I had earlier recommended the former foreign minister of Australia, Alexander Downer, a man Ban knew well from their service as fellow foreign ministers and a politician who could relate to Christofias's and Talat's political needs. Not surprisingly, my call to offer him the job was leaked to the press almost immediately in Australia. He agreed and began work as the secretary-general's Special Adviser in mid-July.

The substance of the Cyprus negotiations was well known. Forty-plus years of negotiations had created about nine thousand pages of agreement in the Annan plan on a "bizonal, bicommunal federation"; but it also left a heavy residue of thousands of nitpicks, arcane arguments, and announced red lines that provided ample ammunition for opponents to make the negotiations tough and tedious even in the best of circumstances. The two leaders proclaimed their support for a united Cyprus, but no one doubted the negotiations would be difficult. And, of course, whatever was decided by Christofias and Talat would ultimately be put to referenda by the two sides and would need the backing of the international community, including Turkey, Greece, the U.S., the UK, and the EU. Even the generally supportive Russians watched closely to ensure that any settlement of the island's status did not affect their major money-laundering interests there.

The issues were complicated and politically charged. They included territorial adjustments that would shrink Northern Cyprus's territory to something closer to 20 percent of the island, in accordance with the ratio of its population in 1960; the creation of a structure for the central government and the two constituent states; compensation for confiscated property; the right of return for families who had fled forty-four years earlier; protection for the minority Turkish Cypriots (enforced by 20,000 to 30,000 Turkish troops on the island and by the 1960 Treaty of Guarantee, which gave Turkey the right to intervene); citizenship laws; exploitation of natural resources; allocation of government jobs; relationship to the EU, and so on. Finally, there was a bad mismatch in the negotiating positions of the two sides. The Greek Cypriots had all the privileges of international recognition and EU membership, which the Turkish Cypriots could only hope to attain in the talks.

The UN role was well established. It would play a classic mediation role in getting the two sides to a deal; but the Cypriots had to be in control, or it would never get approved by the voters. There could not be another attempt by the UN to "fill in the blanks."

As preparations for formal talks began, hope for the talks was high but with plenty of room for skepticism. Hardliners in both communities had all the ammunition they needed from years of talks to proclaim their leaders were "giving away" something critical, even if the concessions were minor. In New York there was a long-standing war of words over UN papers and resolutions on Cyprus, often over fairly trivial issues. When I went back to Cyprus in June to emphasize the UN's support for the process, Talat refused to have dinner with Christofias and me in the old Ledra Palace Hotel in the UN buffer zone, because he was angry over some of the wording in the latest report. (Christofias and I ended up having a pleasant dinner discussion, mostly about Cypriot tourist sites, history, and our grandchildren instead of a working session on the substance.)

When asked about the snub at a press conference the next day, I emphasized that the time for endless squabbles had passed and that the focus now should be on real progress of the two leaders to reach a settlement. In fact, I noted, we found the content of the meetings and the public statements of the two leaders extremely encouraging and suggested we needed to make the process work.

Formal talks between Christofias and Talat hosted by Downer began in the buffer zone on September 3, 2008. The atmosphere was good and the tone optimistic. Substantive talks began a week later and continued on a weekly basis. The agreed negotiating strategy was to review the broad areas under negotiation in a "first read" to determine what subjects were agreed (in the Annan Plan), talk through and better define differences, and then in later discussions get down to the give and take that would be required for a final agreement.

Downer, or in his absence the leader of the UN peacekeeping mission, Taye-Brook Zerihoun, hosted these meetings. They normally consisted of the two leaders talking tête-a-tête for an hour followed by another hour or two with Downer. They went over the whole range of topics methodically, beginning with governance and power sharing, which included the roles of the executive, legislative, judiciary, and the police. While they made some significant progress, the process was slow. The Turkish Cypriots argued that Christofias was trying to run out the clock, although, with by far the stronger hand, he may just have been trying to wring maximum concessions from Talat. The Greek Cypriots in turn contended that Talat was reaching too far, given the balance of power between the two sides.

Secretary-General Ban met separately with Christofias, Talat, and Turkish prime minister Erdogan in July (2009) and then followed up with Christofias, Erdogan, the Greek prime minister, and EU officials at the opening of the UN General Assembly in September. In all of these discussions we sought to encourage them to find solutions and listened for areas where we could help. Ban also worked the phones with all parties as needed. After a rather smooth, if slow, start, things became more intense when the two moved on to property discussions in January. There was virtually no progress on this difficult topic, and the two sides still remained far apart on the basic structure of the government.

To add to Talat's difficulties, major shortfalls in his government's budget forced him to hold early parliamentary elections in March. The opposition won, and unification skeptic and Annan Plan critic Dervis Eroglu became prime minister. In the south, turmoil in Papadopoulos's party (now a junior member of the government coalition) produced increased pressures on Christofias to take a tough approach. As the talks moved to somewhat less controversial topics—relations with the EU, confidence-building measures, and economic issues—in March and April, the atmosphere and pace of the talks improved, but the limits on their maneuvering room had become more and more evident.

After taking a year to get through their "first read," in September 2009 the two leaders began the "give and take" period, where they were supposed to develop compromises. Property, territory, and the Treaty of Guarantee (Turkey's right to intervene) would be the most contentious issues, but they still hadn't closed on how the government would operate. Agreement on economic and European Union issues seemed well within reach. Turkey gave Talat wide running room to negotiate a final settlement and had signaled it would reduce its troops on the island. But it was not willing to give up its role as the ultimate protector of Turkish Cypriot security.

Downer made the point repeatedly, in public and private, that these negotiations were all about politics, not diplomatic wins and losses, with each side posturing to retain the support of its communities. It was imperative that both have some victories to show they were protecting their side's interests. When the new phase began, Talat took an optimistic line in his private comments as well as in his public statements. Christofias was more pessimistic, blaming Turkey for Talat's tough line on some issues. Christofias also grumbled about Downer's pressure on the Greek side to be more reasonable as well as his suggestion that the time had come to remove the UN peacekeepers that had been on the island since 1974. (I agreed that it was more than time to put this "beachkeeping" force on the negotiating table.) In talks with EU officials in Brussels, the Greek Cypriot leader blamed Turkey in an obvious effort to derail Turkey's strategy to move ahead on EU accession. Opponents of Turkey's accession, including France and Germany, were happy to use the slow Cyprus negotiations as an excuse to block further progress for Turkey in the EU.

The fate of the talks depended on some demonstrable progress before the Turkish Cypriot presidential election scheduled for mid-April 2010. Talat had been elected on the promise of getting an agreement to unify Cyprus and putting the Turkish Cypriots on an equal footing with their Greek Cypriot neighbors. His opponent, Prime Minister Eroglu, had promoted independence for the north for years and opposed unification. The global financial crisis was taking a toll on Cyprus in both the north and the south, and the Greek Cypriots effectively blocked the north from sharing in the benefits of membership in the EU. Talat needed to be seen on the verge of closing a deal with his "friend" in the south to win. Unfortunately, despite seventy-one meetings between the two leaders, he had very little to show as a success.

The secretary-general visited Cyprus for three days at the end of January 2010 in an effort to breathe new life into the talks before the election and to provide an opportunity for the two sides to take steps that could be heralded as a major breakthrough. But Christofias showed no interest in demonstrating to the Turkish Cypriots that an agreement was near. Instead, the Greek Cypriots spent most of their time complaining that Ban's call on Talat in his office was a breach of protocol, despite the fact that the UN had always treated the two leaders as equals. Several Greek Cypriot political leaders announced they were boycotting Ban's reception for the two sides because of the meeting, and the atmosphere at Christofias's dinner for Ban was decidedly frosty. The Greek Cypriot treatment of Ban's visit showed that Christofias was far more interested in holding together his shaky governing coalition with Papadopoulos's old party than in promoting the unification talks by keeping his negotiating partner at the table. One more time, short-term concerns had long-term consequences. Eroglu handily won the April 18 election in the north.

Making a 180-degree turn, Eroglu now assured the world community that he intended to continue the talks with Christofias to find a solution to unify Cyprus, and the negotiations resumed in May. We knew it would be more difficult to get an agreement between Eroglu and Christofias than between Talat and Christofias, but maybe not impossible, given Turkey's interest. Nevertheless, the UN had no choice but to try.

The secretary-general convened Christofias and Eroglu in November for a trilateral discussion. It was followed by similar sessions led by the secretary-general in Geneva in January and July 2011. Lisa Buttenheim replaced Zerihoun as the UN peacekeeping mission chief and, like him, served simultaneously as Downer's deputy. She and Downer pressed hard in the intervening months. By the summer the leaders had made some progress on the governance, EU affairs, and economic questions but had made no headway on the harder topics. The talks faced regular blowups over petty issues. For example, at one of the Geneva sessions, Christofias refused to come to lunch with the secretary-general and Eroglu over some issue so small that it has long since been forgotten. In the end, I had to go to his office to calm him sufficiently so he and his entourage could join us for lunch.

In July 2011 Christofias's political position was further weakened by a large blast involving confiscated Iranian arms at a Navy base that killed the Cypriot Navy commander and twelve other people and damaged a nearby power plant. The incident became a major scandal involving governmental mishandling of the material, and an independent Cypriot inquiry later accused Christofias of "gross negligence" in the case. During the same month, Cyprus's credit rating plunged over the deteriorating condition of Cypriot banks and the economy. Then, in early August, his coalition partners pulled out of the government over his handling of the negotiations and the economy, leaving Christofias with just 19 seats in the 56-seat parliament. A weakened Christofias and a skeptical Eroglu did not bode well for success of the UN-sponsored talks.

The secretary-general convened a meeting with the leaders for the last weekend in October at the Greentree Estate on Long

Island. Downer and I led the discussions for much of the time, but the secretary-general also spent many hours there that weekend. Downer told the press the meetings had been "positive, productive, and vigorous," and Ban added that the two sides had assured him they could finalize a deal. He invited them to return to Greentree in January, when he expected the "internal aspects of the Cyprus problem to have been resolved" so they could move on to an international conference to discuss the Turkish guarantee on Turkish Cypriot security.

The leaders gathered again at Greentree on a beautiful weekend in January 2012. In contrast to the weather outside, the atmosphere inside the meeting room was depressing. As the two leaders droned on and on with arguments we had heard for years, I wondered why I was wasting time on Long Island rather than being with Diane in Washington. The two leaders obviously had no intention of sealing the deal. The discussions were tense, and the secretary-general, Downer, and I had to be on our diplomatic best behavior to avoid showing our disgust. The mood changed at a dinner the Bans hosted for the two leaders, their wives, Downer, and me in Manhattan after the talks had concluded. The tension was gone as the two leaders settled in to enjoy the social get-together. It was blindingly obvious they were happy that on their return to Cyprus they could tell everyone at home that they had had nice talks without having given anything away.

Only the UN side was disappointed with the lack of progress. I sat there thinking the two sides must feel they had successfully carried on the game through another high-profile session. I regretted we had once again played a leading role in their elaborate charade. Christofias's lack of support for Talat's reelection now made complete sense. It was easier for the Greek Cypriot leader to blame the stubborn Eroglu for the lack of success, and the status quo was preferable to the tough decisions and complicated unknowns entailed in a future united Cyprus.

Christofias did not run for a second term in the February 2013 presidential election. It was won by a pro-settlement conservative leader, Nicos Anastasiades, who had his hands full dealing with Cyprus's economic crisis. Despite an intensive effort by Downer, it took a full year before the two sides' leaders sat down together again, in February 2014, to restart the talks. By then Downer had had enough. He had spent over five and a half years on the talks with no end in sight. He would soon leave to take up the post of Australian High Commissioner in London.

During a pleasant lunch the Bans hosted for Diane and me with some old colleagues in New York on Valentine's Day (three days after the Cypriot leaders announced new formal negotiations), the secretary-general pulled me aside for a brief private chat. He told me Downer was leaving and that he was thinking of naming me as his replacement. Ban said he needed someone who was tough enough to get them to an agreement and who knew the issues. When I left the UN a year and a half earlier, I had told Ban I would be happy to help him any way I could, so I gave him a noncommittal response but had a sinking feeling. I knew Ban well enough to understand he had made up his mind.

A month later, my successor at DPA, Jeff Feltman, contacted me on Ban's behalf to see if I would take the job. Jeff added that he remembered I had told him when I left New York that I would be available if they needed help "on any issue except Cyprus." My views had not changed, and I believed it would be better to have someone as Special Adviser who was more enthusiastic and less jaded by our previous attempts. But I also remembered my promise to Ban (and George Bush's reaction in Peking to being asked to run the CIA), and after discussing it at some length with Diane, I reluctantly agreed.

The secretary-general planned to announce my appointment in July, and I had made plane reservations for a quick trip to Cyprus, to be back for a granddaughter's birthday party. Interestingly, the Greek Cypriots objected to my appointment. I had had good conversations with Anastasiades several times over the years and had sparred with his new chief negotiator, Andreas Mavroyiannis, when he headed their mission in New York. But apparently it was Christofias who objected strenuously when consulted. Whatever the reason, the Greek Cypriots knew well that I had pressed for a settlement for years and that the secretary-general intended for me to push hard to get this done. I was greatly relieved when Jeff told me about the Greek Cypriot objection. I had braced myself for listening to several years of petty bickering combined with promises that a settlement was just around the corner. Now, instead, Diane and I could get on with our retirement plans.

The secretary-general then appointed a highly qualified diplomat, former Norwegian foreign minister Espen Barth Eide, as his Special Adviser on Cyprus. I congratulated him and wished him well, briefed him on my views of the process, and sent him a flash drive with everything he could possibly want to read on the issue. I also warned him that I doubted the two sides would ever come to an agreement to unify the island. Eide immediately sought to engage but made little progress at first. Then eight months later Eroglu lost his reelection effort to Mustafa Akinci, a former mayor of Turkish Nicosia, who strongly favored unification of the island. Serious talks began in May 2015 between Anastasiades and Akinci with Eide's participation.

After another two years and seventy rounds of intensive negotiations, the two leaders, Eide, UN Secretary-General Guterres, the foreign ministers of the Guarantor Powers from the 1960 treaty—Greece, Turkey, and the UK—and an EU observer gathered in Crans Montana, Switzerland, in June 2017 to hammer out a final deal. Over ten days of extensive discussions of all outstanding issues, it appeared to the participants that a settlement could finally be near.

It didn't happen. The negotiations collapsed during a final contentious dinner and late-night negotiation. Anastasiadis and his delegation returned home even though an agreement was tantalizingly close. The UN refused to assess blame; but once again it was obvious that the fear of future unknowns outweighed the possible benefits of unification. In the south, the comfortable status quo seemed more likely to win out over the uncertainties of rebuilding a new Cyprus. Thirteen years after the Annan Plan's demise and over the course of hundreds of negotiating sessions, little had changed in the effort to unite Cyprus.

20
Promoting Democracy in Asia and Central America

A Trip to North Korea

One issue close to the secretary-general's heart was the denuclearization of North Korea. Pyongyang's effort to build the bomb and the means to deliver it posed an existential threat to the South, and Ban had been involved in negotiations with the North on this and other subjects for years. Unfortunately, more than a decade and a half of negotiations, agreements, heated controversy, and lack of implementation had done little to slow the North Korean program. On October 9, 2006, the day before the Security Council approved Ban as the next secretary-general, the North detonated its first nuclear weapon to great internal fanfare. Despite international protests, Security Council condemnations, and intense negotiations, the North continued to test and refine both its nuclear weapons and the missiles to deliver them.

With the exceptions of the Security Council and the International Atomic Energy Agency, the UN was not a significant player in the nuclear discussions. The Six-Party talks included the two Koreas, China, Japan, Russia, and the United States. Nevertheless, Ban hoped that he could use his time as secretary-general to improve the deplorable conditions for the people in the North and perhaps help resolve the peninsula's critical security problems. Our relations with North Korean diplomats in New York were professional, but not particularly substantive, although I presumed Ban's close confidant and experienced negotiator with the North Koreans, Kim Won-soo, had side discussions with them from time to time.

On the other hand, the UN humanitarian agencies were

deeply involved in providing assistance for the desperately poor, underfed North Korean population, whose situation was becoming increasingly precarious. The World Food Program (WFP) supported about 25 percent of the population, but more aid was needed. As the U.S. provided the bulk of WFP funding, there was considerable muttering among U.S. conservatives that American dollars were being used to prop up the regime. Perhaps true, but few Americans were willing to use mass starvation as a tool against the North. (An effort by USUN's deputy for management Mark Wallace—the same person who torpedoed DPA's budget request—to shut down UNDP programs in the North turned out to be based on bogus documents; but his public campaign claiming UN malfeasance fed congressional and public skepticism of the UN's role in Korea.)

There had been no high-level UN visits to the North since 2004, and Ban's early efforts to visit as secretary-general were turned aside. Pyongyang had no desire to showcase the South's stunning achievement of placing one of their own in the world's most prestigious international office. However, with the nuclear talks again stalled and the humanitarian situation worsening, Ban pressed hard for the North Koreans to receive a ranking UN official to discuss improved ties to the UN, humanitarian aid, and global issues. In early 2010 when Pyongyang was again making one of its periodic feints toward international cooperation, it agreed to a UN visit.

I led a small delegation to Pyongyang on February 9–12, 2010, accompanied by Kim Won-soo and DPA's North Korea specialist, Alexander Ilichev. We visited Seoul, Tokyo, and Beijing for meetings with their foreign ministers on the way to Pyongyang to ensure there was no misunderstanding of my intentions and to better appreciate the views of the major players. I had a conversation with the State Department, and Ilichev touched base with his former colleagues in Moscow to make certain they were on board. I explained that we wanted to reconnect with the North Koreans, since there had been no high-level contacts in six years, get a close look at the humanitarian situation, and see if there were areas where we could be useful to the overall global effort to deal with Pyongyang. I assured them we would not interfere with the six-party talks (which were stalled) and offered to carry any messages they wanted delivered. The reaction of the foreign ministers was polite, but restrained, except for Yang Jiechi, then the Chinese foreign minister, who was enthusiastic about the trip and full of advice on how to approach the North Koreans.

When we were in Pyongyang, the three officials we met—vice foreign minister, foreign minister, and Presidium president—all spoke from the same set of talking points: the DPRK faced constant threats; things were fine internally, including the food situation; they wanted a peace treaty as part of any deal in the six-party talks; and the United States was key to peace on the peninsula. They said their view of the UN was complicated by history (namely, the UN's role in the Korean War) and Security Council condemnations of their nuclear program, but they valued the organization's role in promoting development. I delivered a letter from the secretary-general to Kim Jong Il, conveyed his best wishes, underlined the interest of the international community in the nonproliferation of nuclear weapons, urged them to return to the six-party talks without preconditions, expressed hope that they could improve relations with South Korea, Japan, and the U.S., and assured them of the UN's continued interest in providing humanitarian assistance. I suspected—and indeed hoped—that Kim Won-soo had franker side conversations with North Korean officials about the UN's role.

While in the North Korean capital, we stayed in an early-fifties, Soviet-style guest house, and I was transported back thirty-five years to our family's first tour in China. (When I later described it to Diane, she asked about the color of the carpets. When I said green, she said, "At least, that's different," meaning not the red or blue we had seen so often in China.) The UN offices in Pyongyang had the same flimsy construction and shabby appearance I remembered from the diplomatic quarter in those earlier days in Beijing, and the set tours and fake scientific breakthroughs we were shown brought back some not-so-fond memories. On a short trip outside Pyongyang on a cold winter day, I saw men on bicycle carts carrying brush obviously gathered to provide heat for their homes. And, like Beijing in the seventies, the elevators in some of the trophy buildings in Pyongyang did not work because the shafts were out of alignment. When we left Beijing in 1976, North Korean economic statistics, bolstered by Soviet and Chinese aid, were actually better than China's; but the contrast between the two countries in 2010 could not have been more dramatic. North Korea had lost three decades of development.

The briefings by the hardy UN staff were sobering. (I came to have deep respect for them and other UN personnel who carried out their duties in totally alien environments.) A visit to a UN facility making fortified biscuits left no doubt just how serious the struggle against malnutrition had become. Whatever happened on the political side of our visit, it was evident that I would have to press for more food assistance on my return to New York.

When I reported on the trip to the Security Council, I was careful to emphasize the limited nature of the visit and the lack of any breakthroughs. I noted that we had managed to reestablish some higher-level contact and to convey directly to leading figures in the government the views of the international community on denuclearization and the need to return to the six-party talks. I emphasized in the briefing and a later interview with CNN's Christine Amanpour that the humanitarian problems in the North were dire, and the international community needed to help deal with the malnutrition there despite the political controversies.

While our trip fulfilled its minimum goals, it produced no discernible change in the North Korean behavior in the nuclear area or elsewhere. Indeed, a little over a month later the North Koreans sank a South Korean naval vessel, and later in the year they shelled a South Korean island. In October 2011, the UN's humanitarian chief, Valerie Amos, made a trip to Pyongyang to review UN assistance. But it was another seven and half years before my successor, Jeff Feltman, would be allowed back for a visit. Our minimal expectations for the visit unfortunately turned out to be correct. Pyongyang was not interested in engaging the UN to lower tensions on the peninsula.

Nepal Struggles to Transform

Despite Nepal's allure as a tourist mecca, its government had long been notably ineffective in addressing the needs of its people. Beginning in 1996, an insurgency led by the Maoist party resulted in major population displacements, increased misery for the people, and at least thirteen thousand deaths, mostly at the hands of the security forces. The unpopular king Gyanendra had come to power after his brother and most of the royal family were murdered by the crown prince in June 2001. When Gyanendra took over complete power in February 2005, the seven traditional Nepalese political parties and the Maoists agreed to make common cause against the monarchy. They decided on a plan to end the monarchy and hold elections for a Constituent Assembly, which would draw up a new constitution.

Key to the agreement was the Maoist promise to end the insurgency and join the democratic process. They also promised that their fighters, along with their arms, would move to cantonments awaiting final demobilization or integration into the security forces. As the demonstrations against the king grew, he conceded defeat in April 2006 and allowed the Parliament to reconvene. Parliament quickly named as prime minister the 84-year-old head of the Congress Party, GP Koirala, who had held the post multiple times in the past. His government, comprising ministers from the Seven-Party Alliance, announced a ceasefire with the Maoists, called for peace talks, and took over the levers of power from the king.

The United Nations had been working to help Nepal in this transition, encouraging the Maoists to forswear violence and enter politics. Tamrat Samuel from DPA and Ian Martin, who headed UN's human rights monitoring organization in Nepal, had engaged in extensive discussions with all sides throughout this process. When the government formally requested UN assistance in July 2006, Secretary-General Annan agreed immediately.

The country's longtime patron, India, expressed its concern about UN involvement but could not block it. For years India's leaders had sought to keep other players, especially the UN, out of South Asian issues, which it considered to be in their own sphere of influence. They were particularly wary of UN Security Council involvement, in part due to the long-standing dispute with Pakistan over Kashmir. The Indians also feared that the UN's traditional neutrality would favor the Maoists, who could outmaneuver the bickering, ineffective government coalition. Indeed, both the Indian and U.S. governments were skeptical of the political process and pressed Nepal's leaders to take a tough line with the Maoists.

Annan appointed Ian Martin as his Personal Representative for Nepal to help the parties move the peace process forward. In November the government formally requested UN assistance to monitor the combatants and their arms in the cantonments and to support the upcoming Constituent Assembly election. The government and the Maoists signed a Comprehensive Peace Agreement committing to set up an interim constitution, form an interim assembly and government, and elect a Constituent Assembly that would decide the fate of the monarchy.

The Security Council established the UN Mission in Nepal (UNMIN) in January 2007, and the new secretary-general Ban Ki-moon named Ian Martin as its leader. The mission's mandate was limited to monitoring the implementation of the agreement on arms and combatants, monitoring the ceasefire, and assisting with the Constituent Assembly elections. The Security Council welcomed the continued efforts by the UN to support the peace process but, presumably at Indian and U.S. insistence, did not mandate a political role for UNMIN.

Thus, as Ban began his duties as secretary-general, the basic structure and parameters of UN assistance to Nepal were set. Backed by DPA with support from DPKO and UNDP, Ian moved quickly to establish the new mission. Within months it had both the logistics and personnel in place to carry out its mandate.

It had been a heady year of change for Nepal, and the future looked bright despite the daunting problems ahead. The Maoists entered the interim government on April 1 and made impressive deals with the Seven-Party Alliance. But trust between the major players remained low, and the interests of the large, marginalized groups in Nepal were essentially ignored. Madheshis from the lowland Terai region carried out widespread protests, demanding they receive additional seats in the Constituent Assembly to accord with the size of their population. Some of these protests in areas with very little Nepalese police presence turned into violent conflict between Madheshi groups and Maoists. Adding to the tension, Maoist youth groups continued to run roughshod over their opponents in areas under their control.

Once in the government, the Maoists turned out to be difficult partners. The other parties spent more time arguing with them and maneuvering for advantage in the upcoming election than in tackling the country's serious problems. Conditions in the cantonment sites for Maoist soldiers, which were the government's responsibility, were poor at best; and the Maoists were dragging their feet on UNMIN's program to verify former combatants to determine who might be eligible for a payout or integration into Nepal's army. The army's role in the process and its own "democratization" remained essentially unresolved. With years of participation in peacekeeping operations, cooperation with the UN was no problem. But the army had a poor human rights record internally, and its leadership strongly opposed any effort to carry out the promised integration of Maoist soldiers into their ranks.

When I visited Nepal in August 2007 to get a better feel for the country's dynamics and review UNMIN's operation, I was pleased to see that the new mission had made considerable progress in fulfilling its mandate. Despite the conditions in the cantonments, the monitoring mission was being carried out efficiently and professionally, with the verification process well underway. Obviously not a normal peacekeeping mission, UNMIN's monitoring structure was unusual with its mixture of international retired and active-duty military personnel; but the mission under Ian Martin's leadership had been assembled quickly and was operating effectively. At the same time UNMIN worked closely with the government parties and civic groups to nurture the fractious political process. Its elections staff was deeply engaged with Nepal's elections commissioner and other international organizations to prepare for the upcoming Constituent Assembly elections.

But my talks with political leaders, from the prime minister on down, including an extended session with Maoist leader Prachanda, the nom de guerre of Pushpa Kamal Dahal, and with civic leaders and representatives of marginalized groups left little doubt that resolution of Nepal's political problems would be a long-term process at best. The frail prime minister expressed optimism to me that they would succeed but worried about both the Maoists and his coalition partners. Prachanda showed off his charm and political skills but took a tough line on the political transition ahead. He had just been criticized at a Maoist party plenum for being too accommodating to the prime minister and clearly felt he needed to shore up his position with tough rhetoric and new demands. The civic and marginalized group representatives feared that they would once again be ignored and that Nepal's future would be determined by a government that had not fulfilled past promises.

Implementing agreements would be a recurring problem of the Nepal peace process, as it proved far easier to make deals than carry them out. I pressed the political leaders on all sides to get on with the political transition and to make it inclusive and in tune with the needs of the Nepalese people.

The toughened Maoist stance evident in my discussions with Prachanda—who was demanding the immediate abolition of the monarchy as well as an overhaul of the voting procedures for the Constituent Assembly—soon brought the transition process to a halt. Continued violence by the Maoist Youth League in the countryside and the government's failure to adequately fund the cantonments added to the tensions. The Maoists withdrew their ministers from the government in September, and the Constituent Assembly elections were again delayed.

Ian's brief to the Security Council in October was downbeat. He outlined UNMIN's efforts to get the peace process back on track and suggested it might to useful to broaden the mission's mandate to include more political and security advice. The Indians strongly opposed this "mission creep" and argued in New York and elsewhere that an extension of UNMIN's mandate should remain confined to its original limited goals.

Finally, in December 2007, internal negotiations and international pressure, including a trip by former president Jimmy Carter, produced an agreement by the parties that included holding the delayed election in April, with a fairer representation formula and a commitment to an immediate proclamation of a republic by the first meeting of the Constituent Assembly. A few days later, Ian announced that the verification process had been completed. Some 19,602 former Maoist soldiers were deemed eligible to be demobilized, with a compensation package or integrated into Nepalese security forces. Several thousand of the combatants were disqualified because they were underage in 2006 or were recruited after the deadline.

The Constituent Assembly election in April 2008 was a major success for Nepal's democracy. Sixty-three percent of Nepal's eligible voters took part despite the logistical challenges, and the many international and Nepalese observers gave the process high marks. To the surprise of just about everyone, including themselves and especially the Indians, the Maoists won half of the direct contests. When combined with the proportional votes, they ended up with 38 percent of the seats in the 601-member Constituent Assembly. Koirala's Congress Party, which had been the dominant party for years, won only 19 percent of the seats and the UML, the second largest traditional party, 18 percent. The other major parties in the coalition and Madheshi parties shared the rest. Women made up a third of the Assembly delegates. Nepal's election commissioner and his staff deserve the credit for the smooth election, but DPA, UNDP, UNMIN, and other international supporters certainly played a major role in Nepal's success.

The election produced intensive debates among the leaders of the major parties in the period before the Constituent Assembly, which was scheduled to meet on May 28. At one point the bickering was sufficiently serious for the secretary-general to issue a statement calling on the parties to compromise. I telephoned the major party leaders to press them to meet their own deadline. When the Assembly met, it voted to abolish the monarchy and to establish the offices of president and vice president of the Republic of Nepal. Negotiations then turned to setting up a government that would be a coalition of the major parties, led by the Maoists.

After a couple months of maneuvering caused mainly by Koirala's effort to retain power, Prachanda was elected prime minister in August. He made trips to Beijing for the Closing Ceremony of the Olympics, to India, and to the opening of the UN General Assembly in New York. In his meeting with the secretary-general in New York, Prachanda promised to finish the peace process in Nepal, support multiparty democracy, and promote human rights. With the success of the election and the formation of a new government, we expected UNMIN would be terminated when its renewal came up in July, but the government asked for an extension. The Security Council agreed, but reduced UNMIN's size by 70 percent.

The summer and fall of 2008 should logically have been a time of celebration and self-congratulation for the steps made to put Nepal on a democratic path. Instead, it was a time of tension and frustration. The intense debates to get this far had taken their toll. The Maoists, despite now being in the lead, continued to be difficult partners for the other parties in the coalition. India and its supporters tried to undermine them at every opportunity. Koirala had become a bitter and cranky leader who took his opposition role seriously. And after a few months of putting their cronies into government positions whether qualified or not, the Maoist government looked more and more like its earlier incompetent predecessors. It did little more than former governments to improve the wellbeing of Nepal's people, and the enthusiasm Nepal's voters had shown for the new leaders dissipated quickly.

To help breathe new life into the peace process, the secretary-general visited Nepal in November. In a speech to the Constituent Assembly, he congratulated its leaders on the historic transformation underway and pointedly noted that the political changes needed to be accompanied by a social and economic transformation. We talked with all the top leaders, emphasizing that it was time for them to finish the process, agree on a constitution, and resolve the issue of the former combatants in the cantonments. The atmosphere improved somewhat, and the Constituent Assembly began its first steps toward dealing with its primary task, drafting a modern democratic constitution for the Republic of Nepal.

Then a pall descended once again over integration of Maoist forces into the Nepal Army. Prachanda demanded that Koirala's promise that five thousand of the Maoist combatants would be integrated into the army be fulfilled, and that the soldiers enter in formed units rather than being dispersed as individual soldiers throughout the ranks. Both demands were anathema to the Army chief of staff. He moved to recruit three thousand new personnel through the traditional process to compensate for attrition and to extend the terms of eight generals approaching retirement age. The Maoist defense minister refused both requests. The Cabinet tried to force the chief of staff to resign, but after being overruled by the president (from Koirala's party), Prachanda himself resigned in early May.

The Maoist-led government had lasted nine months. The Special Committee set up to manage the Maoist combatants issue was going nowhere—even the disqualified troops remained in the camps—and the effort to draft a new constitution was well behind schedule. The issues being hotly debated on the constitution reflected fundamental differences among the parties on the new state structure, the form of government, and the allocation of resources. UNMIN, now led by Karin Landgren, was extended again. Finally, in December 2009, the Maoists softened their tactics. They allowed the legislature to begin functioning again and entered into an agreement with the government and UNMIN to discharge four thousand "disqualified" soldiers from the cantonments. This was completed by early February some three years after UNMIN had been established to carry it out.

I visited Nepal in March 2010 to review plans for closing UNMIN and to again press all the country's leaders to reenergize the peace process. Tensions were high as everyone looked for someone else to blame for the lack of progress. Several members of the press and the government had picked UNMIN as the main target of their frustrations, charging it (unfairly) with being pro-Maoist and mismanaging the cantonments (a role it never had). I met with most of Nepal's leaders emphasizing the need to finish the constitution and get on with the task of removing the Maoist forces from the cantonments in line with earlier agreements. When I talked with the new Army chief of staff, he reiterated privately and then publicly the army view that integration into security forces should primarily be with police, border guards, and security guards, with only individuals joining the army who qualified under its normal requirements. India had for some time been backing the Army as the only force that could withstand the Maoists and supported the chief of staff's views. The Maoists responded that this was a matter to be decided by political leaders, not the army.

It turned out that I was probably the last foreigner to meet with the 86-year-old GP Koirala. A cameraman was present during our meeting, obviously to demonstrate to the people of Nepal that Koirala was still functioning and "out of danger" (as his doctor put it), despite his frailty. Our ten-minute conversation was positive, but more symbolic than substantive. Koirala, the man who had made the compromises that created Nepal's peace process, died ten days after the meeting.

By September 2010 it was clear to the secretary-general and me, as well as to Nepal's leaders and the Security Council, that it was time to end the mission. It had accomplished most of its limited goals, except for the integration and rehabilitation of the Maoist combatants remaining in the camps, a problem the parties did not have the political will to settle. Again, with the end of UNMIN looming, the (caretaker) government and the Maoists agreed to settle the outstanding issues by January 15, 2011, and requested that UNMIN be extended for a final time to that date. When I visited Nepal again in late fall to press the leaders to meet their deadlines, the atmosphere toward the UN and UNMIN had turned positive and my conversations pleasant. I assumed this was because the Indians and their supporters knew UNMIN would be leaving soon. The new head of the Congress Party went out of his way to assure me that they did not oppose UNMIN and appreciated the UN's help. The press mimicked this change in tone. The *Kathmandu Post* welcomed me with the best headline I received as the UN Political Department chief: "PASCOE PARLEYS PEACE." It was a welcome change, but as I later briefed the Security Council, the underlying political impasse remained.

As UNMIN finally departed in January 2011, the close working relationship it had with the UN Country Team in Nepal paid off. Most of the UN's role in implementing the demobilization process had fallen to UNICEF, UNDP, and other agencies in any case, and the experienced UN resident coordinator took over many duties of the UNMIN chief, though with a lower profile. DPA supported the effort with a small political office attached to the Country Team. While UNMIN was no more, we were determined to continue our support of the peace process.

Finally, in November 2011, the parties agreed on a plan for moving the combatants out of the cantonments. Some 10,000 of the former combatants had indicated they wanted to join the army, and 7,000 chose to leave with a stipend. Those who chose to join the army were required to meet the army's normal standards, go through extensive training, and serve in units specializing in disaster relief, industrial security, and forest and environmental duties. In the end 1,451 entered the army. Those who chose demobilization were released in early 2012, and the army took over responsibility for the Maoist combatants and weapons in April. The last task that had been assigned to UNMIN was completed five and a half-years after the mission had been established. The leading parties finally made a deal on the new Constitution three years later, in April 2015, after the severe earthquake near Kathmandu that killed some nine thousand people.

Nepal's politicians had struggled for a decade to end a civil war and establish a functioning democracy. In some ways it was an impressive effort. They ended the war, abolished an unpopular monarchy, and brought the Maoists into the political tent. But it was a difficult slog for leaders who did not trust each other's motives and two armies that had been engaged in a decade of bitter struggle. The UN helped, but we had emphasized throughout the process that this was primarily a Nepalese effort. UNMIN and the UN Country Team had succeeded—if over a much longer timeline than originally anticipated—to carry out the limited tasks mandated for them by the Security Council, and they provided considerable help on the political transition. Unfortunately, the fault lines reflected in the numerous political parties were simply too deep and the political will necessary for compromise was too weak for them to deal with Nepal's fundamental economic and social problems.

The Aftermath of Sri Lanka's Brutal Civil War

In Sri Lanka, a civil war between the government and the Liberation Tigers of Tamil Eelam (LTTE) had been ongoing since 1983. By 2005 the LTTE controlled most of the north and the east coast of the country. The minority Tamils had legitimate grievances against the Sinhalese majority, but the LTTE was a particularly nasty group. Among the first to employ suicide bombers, they killed off Tamil rivals, government officials, and Sinhalese innocents with no compunction. After 9/11 the United States named them a terrorist group and worked to help the government defeat them. Sri Lanka's powerful neighbor, India, also backed the government: its former prime minister, Rajiv Gandhi, had been assassinated in 1991 by a female LTTE suicide bomber. Negotiations brokered by Norway between the government and the LTTE led to a ceasefire agreement in 2002, but further progress toward peace was largely stymied by LTTE intransigence.

Mahinda Rajapaksa won the Sri Lankan presidential election in November 2005 by a slim margin on a platform to defeat the LTTE, an election victory ironically made possible by an LTTE call for Tamils to boycott the vote. He and his brothers, particularly his naturalized-American brother, Gotabaya, the defense minister, took a tough line in negotiations with the LTTE and began to build the Sri Lankan army into a serious fighting force. Military clashes grew in intensity in 2006; and by July 2007, the army had succeeded in driving the LTTE out of the eastern part of the country.

The battle involved brutality on both sides. The LTTE carried out assassinations and suicide bombings in the capital and elsewhere, forced civilians to remain in areas they controlled as human shields against advancing troops, and forced children to serve as soldiers. The government and its supporting militias carried out their own merciless campaign, abducting people thought to be LTTE supporters, clamping down on journalists and news outlets, holding people who managed to escape from LTTE areas in armed camps, and so on. There was little sympathy for the LTTE internationally beyond a part of the Tamil diaspora, but the government undermined its own standing by its harsh measures, which disturbed its supporters in the U.S., India, and Europe.

With the war popular among the government's base in the Sinhalese south, the Rajapaksa brothers mostly ignored international criticism, assuming that all would be forgotten when they won the war, which had wracked the country for so many years. The United Nations urged the government to stop violating the human rights of its people, lift controls on the media and NGOs attempting to help the innocent victims caught up in the conflict, and treat the refugees—"internally displaced persons," or IDPs—in accordance with international law. We also encouraged the government to keep open a search for a political solution, to avoid the high death toll of innocent civilians, made inevitable by their use by LTTE as human shields, and the often-indiscriminate government bombardment of LTTE areas. Government officials from the president on down alternated between expressing soothing assurances of promised improvements in their methods and arrogant bluster against foreign interference. But their actions remained focused on eliminating the LTTE by whatever means necessary, including bombing of innocent civilians.

In time, the government's strategy on the battlefield succeeded. By January 2009 government forces had overrun the LTTE's capital of Kilinochchi and were forcing the LTTE and the estimated 250,000 civilians they controlled into a smaller and smaller area. The government proclaimed a "No-Fire Zone" of some 5.5 square miles to protect the civilians; but when LTTE fighters moved into the zone and fired on government forces from them, the army quickly resumed its aerial and artillery bombardments in areas it had proclaimed safe. The LTTE killed civilians who sought to escape. It was obvious to all that things were only going to get worse in the endgame if the tactics of the two sides did not change.

The UN was deeply involved as the crisis unfolded. Its agencies worked to avoid starvation among the displaced population in the north and to provide adequate conditions in the government refugee camps. Since the government refused to allow other international organizations and NGOs into rebel-controlled areas, only the UN and the ICRC (International Committee of the Red Cross) and some local religious groups were on the ground. The UN resident representative, Neil Buhne, was deeply engaged as he sought to manage the UN's effort to help the increasingly desperate situation in the north. The UN under-secretary-general for humanitarian affairs, John Holmes, made several trips to Sri Lanka to visit the camps and to try to convince government leaders to change their approach. The UN's high commissioner for human rights, Louise Arbour, had made a trip in October to encourage adherence to human rights norms and increase human rights monitoring, but the government deflected her attempt to set up a monitoring mission in the country.

The secretary-general took a direct role in trying to moderate the government's tactics. He argued with Sri Lanka's leaders and issued public statements in an effort to persuade them to protect civilians, negotiate an end to the war, provide a "humanitarian pause" to let more escape, and fulfill international obligations in managing the IDP camps. Holmes briefed the Security Council on the disastrous situation in Sri Lanka in informal sessions; the Chinese and Russians refused to allow formal sessions, arguing this was an "internal" Sri Lankan issue. Ban sought an invitation for himself to make one last effort to persuade the government to stop the bombing, but the government stalled. It did agree to a trip by the secretary-general's chef du cabinet, the former Indian diplomat Vijay Nambiar, to plead for a negotiated end to the conflict. (Ban had earlier designated Nambiar as the political lead on Sri Lanka, a decision I was happy with, given my own full plate of other global problems. My staff provided him full support.)

All of these efforts came to naught. The government deflected the UN's pleas just as they had the increasingly alarmed complaints coming from the Americans, the Indians, and the Europeans.

By May 18, 2009, the war was over. LTTE leaders were dead, more than 250,000 refugees had fled and been placed in the overcrowded government IDP camps, and thousands of innocent people had been killed. The Rajapaksa brothers succeeded where other Sri Lankan governments had failed to defeat the LTTE, but the humanitarian tragedy for the trapped Tamil population that resulted from the tactics of the two sides had left a dark stain. Unfortunately, President Rajapaksa's victory speech the next day did little to signal a new political approach to bringing the Tamil community fully into the Sri Lankan fold. And his response to foreign criticism was defensive and belligerent. It set the tone for continued conflict with the international community at a time when olive branches for the Tamil community and the international audience were badly needed.

The secretary-general, accompanied by Holmes and me, arrived in Colombo late on May 22. Nambiar was already there advancing the trip. Ban's public message was straightforward: The task now before Sri Lanka was to help the IDPs and get on with national recovery, renewal, and reconciliation. The priority goals should be to bring conditions in the camps to international standards, to have people out-processed quickly so they could return home, and for the government to immediately initiate a process of dialogue, accommodation, and reconciliation.

Ban and his party toured the sprawling refugee camp at Manik Farm, where conditions were appalling; we overflew the final conflict area—physically devastated with no human activity— and met with President Rajapaksa in Kandy. In the meeting with Rajapaksa, Ban emphasized the need for a political process leading to reconciliation, better access to the camps by humanitarian workers, return of the refugees to their homes, and accountability for human rights violations. The president responded with his usual combination of reassurances and bluster but pointed to demining as a key factor in how quickly the refugees could return home. He suggested that with the help of the international community on that issue, some 80 percent of the IDPs could return home by the end of the year.

The SG agreed to help and pressed for better treatment of the Tamils and Muslims as well as for progress on the long-promised devolution of power from the central government to local communities. He urged Rajapaksa to improve the government's human rights record and carry out an accountability process for past violations. The president was noncommittal on accountability for past violations, since it was obvious to all that with the LTTE destroyed and its leadership dead, the only people to investigate would be on the government's side.

After considerable back and forth, including an intense one-on-one session between Ban and Rajapaksa, the two agreed on a Joint Statement that Nambiar had earlier negotiated. Since the Sri Lankans were infamous for putting their own spin on meetings with foreign leaders, we needed the statement to tie down the results of the meeting. In the final version, Rajapaksa praised the "close cooperation with the United Nations," a real stretch, given the tense relationship. The two sides agreed that dealing with grievances and a lasting political solution were key for the future of Sri Lanka, and Rajapaksa promised once again to get on with the much-discussed devolution of power from the central government. The most contentious parts of the statement were the secretary-general's affirmation of "the importance of the accountability process for addressing violations of international humanitarian and human rights law" and a commitment of the Sri Lankan government to address the grievances of the Tamils.

At his departure press conference, the secretary-general again emphasized it was a time for healing and equal treatment for all Sri Lankans. He concluded with the clear warning that the world would be watching Sri Lanka's performance. Ban was tough. At no point in the visit did he feed the government's sense of triumphalism; in fact, he neither privately nor publicly congratulated the government on its victory.

Rajapaksa was undoubtedly disappointed in the visit, because it was hard to spin as anything but the international community putting Sri Lanka's government on notice that the defeat of the LTTE had to be followed by positive steps that the government had heretofore been reluctant to take. Although Ban's visit received considerable international criticism (opponents argued it helped the Rajapaksa brothers), he had succeeded in setting the standard by which the government's future actions would be judged.

The government moved at a snail's pace in carrying out its commitments, and Ban concluded it was time (just before the annual General Assembly meetings in New York in September) to push the Sri Lankans to fulfill the promises they made during his visit. The international community was increasingly skeptical that the Sri Lankans would fulfill any of their commitments, given that Rajapaksa had signed on to their Joint Statement with considerable reluctance. It was also becoming clear that the army had murdered LTTE leaders even after the government had promised through Nambiar that they would be allowed to surrender. Additional evidence of the extent of human rights violations during the last months of the conflict became clearer over the summer, and Ban began to consider setting up a Panel of Experts on accountability in Sri Lanka.

The secretary-general asked me to carry a tough message to Colombo to press the government on releasing the IDPs, political reconciliation, and accountability for past human rights violations, all points that were front and center of my public and private comments during my mid-September trip. I visited a demining site and engaged government officials in Colombo. The demining effort, which I had assumed the government was using as an excuse to keep people in the camps, turned out to be better organized than I had expected, and I was somewhat relieved to see the government's effort and the extensive support from the international community. In my meeting with President Rajapaksa, he reiterated his promise to move 70–80 percent of the people out of the camps by the end of January if the demining effort continued apace. He made the usual saccharine assurances on political reconciliation and avoided any commitment on accountability for human rights violations. Our meeting was followed by the usual Sri Lankan spinning of the conversation to put the president in the best possible light.

Ban and I knew few people would be happy with our efforts. Human rights advocates and antigovernment activists, especially the Tamil diaspora, had criticized Ban's trip in May and were certain to criticize mine. Even some of the diplomats in Colombo who had become increasingly disgusted with Rajapaksa's lies were quick to disparage the effort, accusing me of being naïve in thinking the government would send the Tamil IDPs home. On the other hand, the nationalistic Sinhalese press blasted my trip as part of a U.S. plot to destabilize Sri Lanka. The latter criticism was no doubt due to the deep resentment felt by the president and his followers as the international community continued to criticize the government's rights abuses during the final stage of the war rather than focusing on its victory over the notorious LTTE.

But Ban was determined to keep up the pressure. Following my visit, he sent his advisor on the human rights of IDPs to Sri Lanka, and then John Holmes made his fourth trip in November. Our message on the IDPs was consistent: treat the people in the camps up to international standards and return them to their homes as quickly as possible. The UN pressure as well as that of major international actors, and the upcoming Sri Lankan elections had an effect. Despite the skepticism in the Colombo diplomatic circuit, half of the refugees had been released from the camps by the time of John's visit and a measure of freedom of movement had been given to those still in the camps.

There was no discernible progress on the reconciliation or accountability fronts. In January 2010 President Rajapaksa easily won a second term as president over retired General Sarath Fonseka, who led the fight against the LTTE. Fonseka was arrested two weeks later by military authorities, supposedly for engaging in political activity while still in the military. His main crime more likely was his assertion on the campaign trail that Defense Minister Gotabaya Rajapaksa had ordered the execution of surrendering LTTE leaders and soldiers despite the government's promise to Nambiar to allow them to surrender.

The secretary-general asked me to return to Sri Lanka for a visit in February, but President Rajapaksa stalled for four months. Ban by this time had had enough of Sri Lankan delays and decided to set up a Panel of Experts to review human rights violations during the final stage of the war. India, China, Russia, Japan, and, of course, the Sri Lankan government all opposed the panel. I strongly supported it and suggested a friend from Indonesian days, former attorney general and human rights advocate Marzuki Darusman, as the chair. Despite his bluster, Rajapaksa was actually quite sensitive to UN views and knew that the brunt of the criticism would fall on his government and army. Earlier action on the government's part could have avoided the need for the panel, but nothing had been heard from his own toothless group on the human rights violations since it had been set up in the fall. Rajapaksa now announced a new "Lessons Lernt [sic] and Reconciliation Commission" (LLRT) in May as his counter to the UN investigation.

Although strong internally, Rajapaksa's problems in the international community over the deaths during the last few months of the war continued to grow, and he finally accepted my visit for mid-June. He also agreed to almost simultaneous visits by U.S. and Japanese officials. During the trip, I met with Rajapaksa, his top advisers, opposition politicians, human rights leaders, newspaper editors, and members of the diplomatic corps. In my conversations, I emphasized the need for reconciliation and political solutions that genuinely addressed the grievances of minorities, freedom of the press, and independence for local and international NGOs. I also pressed for the conclusion of the IDP process—there were still sixty thousand people in the camps and another ninety thousand staying temporarily with host families—and for economic development efforts in the north. Finally, I underlined the importance of accountability for human rights violations during the war.

In response, Rajapaksa mixed some soothing answers with his usual defiance. We had made our point, and I hoped he and his brothers would take some steps to alleviate the international pressure. But I was not naïve enough to expect any major changes in the government's approach. At a press conference in Colombo (held, ironically, the same day the government put on a first anniversary victory parade), I revealed that the secretary-general would announce the formation of his Panel of Experts the next week.

The panel, composed of Marzuki Darusman from Indonesia, Yasmin Sooki from South Africa, and Steve Ratner from the U.S., was not allowed in Sri Lanka despite our repeated efforts on its behalf. The members nevertheless gathered detailed information on the events and presented their findings to Ban Ki-moon in April 2011. After giving the government time to read it, Ban released the report to the public.

The panel's conclusions were damning. Essentially accusing the government of lying about the last stage of the war, the panel concluded there were credible allegations that the government had carried out large-scale shelling in the No-Fire Zones, engaged in systematic shelling of hospitals, deprived detainees in the conflict zone of humanitarian aid, and violated the human rights of people in the camps. It also concluded that the LTTE had used civilians as human shields and hostages, killed civilians attempting to flee its control, placed its artillery near civilians, forcibly recruited children as combatants, used forced labor, and carried out suicide attacks outside the conflict zone. The panel quoted "multiple credible sources" that as many as forty thousand civilians may have been killed in the last few months of the conflict and called for investigation and accountability for all of these actions.

Responding to criticisms that the UN had withdrawn its international humanitarian workers from the conflict zone prematurely, the panel concluded that the UN had "failed to take actions that might have protected civilians" and called for it to review the organization's actions in the final stage of the conflict. It also criticized the UN for stopping the release of its estimates of civilian deaths, which could have added pressure on the government. (Humanitarian officials ended the issuance of these estimates because they had no way to verify the numbers during the final months of the conflict.) Finally, the panel complained about the Human Rights Council's resolution in May 2009 praising the Sri Lankan government for ending the war with no criticism of its actions, a failure the council rectified five years later with its own inquiry.

The secretary-general followed the recommendation and ordered a formal review of the UN's actions during the last months of the conflict. The report, issued a few months after I left New York, took a tough look at the UN's failures to protect civilians. Although the report was well-resourced, it seemed overly optimistic about what the UN could have done even in the best of circumstances, given the government's determination to eradicate the LTTE regardless of the human cost or the brutality of the methods used. It is important to remember that India, European countries, and the U.S., all of whom had far more leverage than the UN, also failed to persuade the Sri Lankan government to protect civilians. The report struck me as quite unfair to the UN team in Sri Lanka, whose members worked extremely hard under almost impossible conditions to save lives and reduce suffering.

Secretary-General Ban had used his limited powers to the maximum extent possible to persuade the government to adhere to its commitments under international law, both during and after the conflict. With a government willing to kill surrendering LTTE leaders after promising his chef de cabinet that it would give them safe passage, a Security Council unable to effectively deal with the issue, and a Human Rights Council that had praised rather than censored the government, there was only so much the UN could do. Its instinct was to focus on the humanitarian problem of helping the civilians, whether it was trying to feed them, protect them in the camps, or get them home and, like embassy staffs, had to tread lightly on criticism of the government to carry out their duties.

Harsh criticisms of the regime naturally had to come from the secretary-general, me, John Holmes, and the Human Rights Commissioner Navi Pillay, not the country team. The decision to pull out the international staff from LTTE-held territory in response to government demands nine months before the war ended on safety grounds was a classic dilemma of weighing protection for your staff against serving the people they are trying to help. A refusal to comply with the government's demand would have put our people in danger and may well have led to the UN being expelled. One recommendation in the report that I agreed with wholeheartedly was that the UN needed to improve its coordination between its political and humanitarian efforts.

Tackling Guatemala's Corruption

One of the most innovative (and successful) DPA efforts during my time at the UN was the backing we provided for the International Commission Against Impunity in Guatemala, known by its Spanish initials CICIG. With the end of its thirty-year civil war in the 1990s by a UN-brokered agreement, Guatemala had established a working democracy; but its deeply corrupt security apparatus continued to undermine progress and people's well-being. Violent crime flourished, the police, security ministries, and court system were all compromised, and vicious gangs carried out a continuous crime wave with impunity. It was estimated that 98 percent of the country's serious crimes went unpunished. People fled the country in droves for their safety and that of their children, often flooding into the United States.

The Guatemalan government, strongly pressured by civil society and international friends led by the United States, again turned to the UN for help. The first attempt to set up an independent UN tribunal to bolster Guatemala's judiciary ran afoul of Guatemalan constitutional issues, but a new agreement that left final decisions on prosecution to the country's Prosecutor General was signed with the UN in December 2006. Ratification by Guatemala's Congress proved controversial, but internal and international pressure (led by the U.S.) and the murder of three El Salvadoran legislators by Guatemalan gangs tipped the balance. The agreement was ratified in August 2007.

The secretary-general quickly named Carlos Castresana, a well-known Spanish prosecutor who crafted the international indictment of former Chilean president Pinochet, as CICIG commissioner. Castresana was deeply committed to helping the Guatemalan government and people; he had the strong backing of the incoming president, Alvaro Colom, and no qualms about maintaining a high profile to gain popular support for the effort.

DPA worked hard to provide backup for this new hybrid creation funded by outside donors. Since CICIG was not a formal UN body and did not fit into UN bureaucratic rules, it would be challenging; but we were determined to make it work. Protecting Castresana and his people always had to be a top priority, as they went after some of Guatemala's most important (and corrupt) figures in an environment where criminals routinely killed people who crossed them. In fact, I worried more about Carlos Castresana's safety than that of any other of our senior officials.

Carlos and I formally opened the CICIG office in Guatemala City in January 2008. Within a year, he and his team of over one hundred local and international prosecutors, working closely with President Colom, had replaced corrupt high-level officials in the public prosecutor's office, the Interior Ministry, police, and prison systems and opened dozens of criminal cases in cooperation with the public prosecutor's office. CICIG trained local prosecutors in modern investigative procedures and in prosecuting organized crime. Its backing energized local prosecutors to proceed against forces that had acted with impunity in the past. CICIG also convinced the Guatemalan Congress to enact reform laws and to set up special courts to take on organized crime. Castresana's open and sometimes confrontational style and the successes CICIG was having in transforming the security system made him a star with the Guatemalan public by the summer of 2009. The Commission's term was easily extended for two more years because of its popularity.

In September, Castresana led a bruising fight to block appointment to the Guatemalan Supreme Court of several people with ties to organized crime. Then in January 2010 CICIG proved the value of its new investigative techniques in a bizarre case directed at President Colom. A tape recording by a prominent Guatemalan lawyer became public, claiming that if he were killed at some point in the future, it would be at the orders of the president, who wanted to silence him. Sure enough, the lawyer was assassinated on a bike ride a few days later. The tape gained widespread distribution, and Colom's opponents demanded his ouster. After careful investigation, CICIG established that the lawyer had actually contracted for his own murder. Castresana dramatically announced the findings to the press, and CICIG's conclusions were accepted by the Guatemalan people.

CICIG's successes inevitably led to a strong backlash from ousted security personnel, business leaders who preferred the old bribery system, and conservative elements in the military. These groups carried out an intense campaign against Castresana and CICIG. When President Colom's new attorney general, whom CICIG believed to be tied to organized crime, began removing officials that had worked with the commission, Castresana publicly condemned the government for its lack of cooperation and resigned. In the firestorm that followed, Colom backed off and engineered the removal of the attorney general. But Castresana was gone.

Ban named the former Costa Rican attorney general Francisco Dall'Anese as Castresana's successor. Dall'Anese adopted a lower profile, concentrating on the prosecution of cases CICIG and the government already had underway and on reform of the security sector. Dall'Anese's successor, Ivan Velasquez, along with an aggressive Guatemalan attorney general, again focused attention on political corruption cases and forced the resignation of the president and the jailing of the vice president.

Tragically, Washington's support for CICIG evaporated under the Trump administration. When CICIG began investigating the new Guatemalan president, Jimmy Morales, and his family, Morales turned on the commission and asked Washington to back him. The Trump administration, apparently oblivious to the fact that the U.S. had been a strong supporter of CICIG as a way to stabilize Guatemala, improve its justice system and economy, and curb illegal immigration to the United States, let CICIG die with minimal protest.

By all accounts, CICIG had a dozen successful years helping Guatemala dig out from the morass its legal system had become by 2007. An extensive list of legal reforms was instituted, Guatemalan prosecutors were empowered, and their investigative procedures modernized. Over a hundred important cases were prosecuted, with more than four hundred convictions, and Guatemala's murder rate declined by half. Civil society groups in neighboring countries clambered for similar help for their weak legal systems. CICIG probably needed another decade to completely fulfill its mission, but its accomplishments during its twelve years of existence were considerable. It was a tragedy for Guatemala—and the United States—that the Trump administration let this critical innovation die.

21
The Middle East and the Arab Spring

The United States Asks for UN Help on Iraq

Iraq stood high on the list of pressing international problems when Ban Ki-moon took over as secretary-general. In response to the country's deteriorating internal security situation, the Bush administration announced its "surge" strategy, trying to reestablish security in Baghdad and Anbar Province while simultaneously looking for a way out of the mess it had created by invading Iraq in March 2003. Unlike the hands-off approach to the UN four years earlier, the administration now needed the United Nations as a partner and hoped to offload as many of its "nation-building" duties as possible to the international community.

The UN mission (UNAMI—The United Nations Assistance Mission in Iraq) had been established in August 2003 with a mandate to "play a vital role in humanitarian relief, the reconstruction of Iraq, and the restoration and establishment of national and local institutions for representative governance." Five days later a suicide bomber demolished the UN headquarters in Baghdad, killing twenty-two UN officials including Special Representative Sergio Viera de Mello. What was left of the UN operation was then reestablished in Amman, Jordan, where a reduced staff carried out their duties from a distance. At the time, the UN had a few successes in Iraq in humanitarian support and assisting the 2005 elections, but overall its impact was small. The publicity disclosing the extensive corruption in the "Oil for Food" program further tarnished the UN role.

By early 2007 UNAMI had strained relations with the Maliki government as well as with the U.S. political and military operation in Iraq. Staff morale was low, and memories were still fresh of the 2003 losses, which many UN officials blamed on the U.S. To make matters worse, in April 2007 UNAMI released a draft human rights report that both the Iraqi and U.S. governments considered inaccurate and biased toward the Sunnis in the volatile Iraqi political divide. During a March trip to Baghdad, Ban Ki-moon promised he would reorganize UNAMI and increase its involvement to help the government overcome the difficulties it faced. (Ban's trip underlined the security challenge when a rocket exploded less than a hundred yards from where he was speaking in a joint press conference with Maliki.).

I led a UN team in discussions with a delegation from Washington in late June on the possibilities for a revamped UNAMI and a new Security Council resolution to define its duties. I made it clear that we could only expand the UN's role if the U.S. and the Iraqis were willing to give us room to work. The discussions included the demarcation of provincial boundaries (a hot topic for the Kurds), planning for provincial elections, sufficient political space for the humanitarian staff to carry out their tasks, and security for our people. A couple of weeks later, I accompanied Ban to a meeting with President Bush in the White House where the UN role in Iraq was the major topic. Ban told the press afterwards that Iraq was "a problem for the whole world," and the UN was prepared to be helpful. The U.S. permanent representative Zal Khalilzad followed up with a piece in the *New York Times* praising the UN role and laying out areas for cooperation.

The reaction from many on the UN staff to increasing the UN's role in Iraq was quite negative. Resentment over the U.S. invasion of Iraq without Security Council backing, the 2003 bombing, and fears for the safety of UN personnel in Iraq's volatile situation all fed a sense among much of the staff that they didn't want to have anything to do with helping the U.S. dig out of the chaos it had created. Ban was seen by these people as kowtowing to the Americans, and the American heading DPA responsible for the Iraq mission (me) was still deeply suspect. The UN Staff Council formally opposed expansion of the UN role. Rumors abounded that several senior officials—including the peacekeeping under-secretary-general (with whom I had clashed over his political staffing expansion)—were complaining privately to anyone who would listen about Ban, me, and the American request.

But the Americans and British had lined up Security Council support for an expanded UN role, and the secretary-general was firm in backing the proposal. In August 2007 the Security Council unanimously provided UNAMI with a new mandate to help the Iraqis advance an "inclusive national dialogue and political reconciliation," help organize elections and a census, assist in demarcating internal borders, promote reintegration of Iraqis who had fled their homes, and facilitate dialogue with neighboring countries. The Security Council also instructed the mission to work with the Iraqi government to improve essential services for its people and promote economic reform.

The new mandate for UNAMI was a tall order, given the inadequacies of the Iraqi government and the unstable security situation in the country. To manage the effort, the secretary-general appointed one of the UN's most seasoned leaders with considerable experience in Iraq, the Italian-Swedish diplomat Staffan de Mistura, as his Special Representative to Iraq and head of UNAMI. We also raised the staff ceiling for the mission to just under a hundred personnel. I tried to keep expectations for the new approach modest, emphasizing that any UN success depended on the Iraqis tackling their own problems. I told a press conference at the UN General Assembly opening in September that we had no "magic formula" to make things work in Iraq, and that we could only be involved on issues to the extent the Iraqis wanted us. Clearly, the UN could not resolve problems overnight that had bedeviled the U.S. for years.

On his arrival in November, de Mistura set out to develop a wide range of contacts across the political spectrum, refocused UNAMI on settling internal boundaries, regional cooperation (many of Iraq's Sunni neighbors still had not recognized the Malaki government), and getting a new election law in place for provincial elections scheduled for October 2008. The mission also continued its work on constitutional reform, humanitarian relief (including the return of displaced people), improving the government's human rights performance, and economic development. As the security situation improved, UNAMI expanded its presence in Iraq's major cities. When I visited Iraq in April 2008, UNAMI's new approach and its improved relationship with the Iraqi government had begun to gain traction. I praised the mission's efforts in my public statements there and when I returned to the Security Council.

The new mandate, an energetic and capable Special Representative, and increased financial and personnel resources were important elements of the new UN approach, but our efforts faced the same old problems created by Iraqi political dysfunction. Things moved slowly as the various players bickered over every issue. De Mistura spent most of that summer mediating disputes over Kirkuk, which the Kurds continued to occupy to the dismay of the central government. When I visited the city, the dangerous security situation reminded me of my first visit to Mogadishu. The dispute over Kirkuk's status became the primary stumbling block to holding the October provincial election. But after protracted negotiations, de Mistura managed to produce a compromise that allowed provincial elections to go ahead in January 2009.

When the secretary-general arrived for a short visit in Baghdad a week after the election, he was impressed by what UNAMI had accomplished. It was now seen as a valuable partner by the government, and Iraq's political leaders seemed focused on how to get Iraq back on its feet. When de Mistura left his post in June, UNAMI had made considerable progress on returnees and internally displaced persons. It had managed a way forward on the Kirkuk issue, supported the successful provincial elections, and increased cooperation between Iraq and its neighbors. This was progress, but there was also a long list of unresolved issues.

Unfortunately, Iraq's internal disputes only seemed to worsen as the U.S. reduced it forces. (The last American combat troops left in August 2010.) The provincial elections were followed by nine months of political stalemate. Hard work by the UN to develop an Iraqi census came to naught as the Iraqis bickered over details. While UNAMI's efforts to mediate political disputes had some success, overall its work remained captive to Iraq's chaotic and poisonous political atmosphere.

Security remained a critical issue. Travel between the barricaded Green Zone and the U.S.-secured Baghdad airport was either by helicopter or special armored personnel carriers. U.S. military contractors provided security in the Green Zone itself, with Georgian and Fijian peacekeepers responsible for close-in protection for the UN. Georgian forces left quickly when the Russians invaded Georgia in 2008. The Fijians were a constant source of friction with the New Zealanders and Australians, who wanted to eliminate Fiji's peacekeeping role to pressure the country's increasingly authoritarian leader. No one else was willing to put its forces at risk in Baghdad; and at one point during a démarche by the New Zealand permanent representative, I said we would be happy to replace the Fijians if New Zealand would provide the replacements. Of course, that was not going to happen.

UNAMI personnel worked in the Green Zone in temporary offices and slept in containers surrounded by walls of sandbags—a man-made cave to protect them from incoming rockets. During my first visit to Baghdad, three rocket-warning sirens sounded while UNAMI was briefing me. With each siren we scrambled to put on our helmets (we had kept on our armored vests) and moved to a more protected area of the compound. A few nights earlier UNAMI's living area had been hit by rockets. Even as the security situation improved over time and Iraqi forces took over responsibility, it was difficult to convince UN agency personnel comfortably (and safely) ensconced in Amman to move to Baghdad, where they could be much more effective in helping the Iraqi government and people. Talk in New York about spending $100 million or so to build a new UN facility never received much support; but the accommodations problem was finally resolved when USAID moved its people out of its compound into the new thousand-person U.S. Embassy. The UN was happy to get their cast-off facility, especially since the Iraqis paid to renovate it. Eventually, more UN agency offices and personnel moved to Baghdad.

A serious problem the Americans left in our lap involved the MEK (Mujahedeen-e-Khalq), a cultish group of 3,200 Iranians in Iraq who opposed the Iranian government. The group had carried out attacks on U.S. personnel during the shah's regime, participated in the seizure of the U.S. embassy, and supported Saddam Hussein in the Iran-Iraq War. The U.S. and many European countries designated the MEK a terrorist group. After American forces had disarmed them, and despite opposition by legal experts, Defense Secretary Rumsfeld designated them a protected group under international law and kept them safe from the new Iraqi government. The Iraqis considered their camp an affront to its sovereignty and an unnecessary irritant in its relations with Iran. When the U.S. withdrew its protection as it left Iraq, conflicts inevitably broke out between the MEK and Iraqi security forces, leading the Maliki government to vow to evict them from their camp and from the country, by force if necessary. There was no doubt that the Iraqis intended to follow through on their threat, and the UN had to try to avoid what could become a major massacre.

I had a long discussion about how to solve this problem with Antonio Guterres, the UN High Commissioner for Refugees (and later secretary-general). While reluctant to take on dealing with the controversial MEK, he did in the end agree to help. With a way forward that included moving the MEK to a former U.S. camp near the airport, followed by UNHCR processing them for onward movement to other countries, Maliki agreed to give us some time. The group moved to the new camp ("voluntarily," of course, but the Iraqi government gave them little choice); and eventually Albania agreed to allow them to settle there. Thanks to the hard work of UNAMI and UNHCR (aided by the United States), tragedy was avoided.

The expansion and redirection of UNAMI's effort had some considerable successes and made believers out of skeptics at the UN and in Iraq. The mission established itself as a reliable and neutral player trying to help the country. It could not, however, solve the fundamental problems of security, ethnic divisions, and hatred that plagued Iraq from the days of Saddam Hussein and early U.S. mismanagement of the occupation. As Iraq continued to lurch forward, UNAMI would experience its successes and disappointments in almost equal measure.

War in Gaza

The conflict between the Israelis and Palestinians has been at the forefront of issues facing the UN Security Council and the General

Assembly since the organization's establishment in 1945. Two years later the General Assembly called for the partition of British Palestine into Jewish and Arab states, with a special international status for Jerusalem. Israel proclaimed its independence the next year as the British mandate expired, and a coalition of Palestinians and Arab states attacked the new state in an effort to destroy it. The war ended through the mediation of UN envoy Ralph Bunche, an American who received the Nobel Peace Prize for his work and then headed UN political efforts around the world in the 1950s and 1960s.

The Israeli victory gave it control of considerably more territory than foreseen in the UN plan and produced hundreds of thousands of Palestinian refugees. In 1967 the Israelis won control of additional territory, including Gaza and the West Bank. Negotiations pressed by the UN, the U.S., and others over the years produced several accommodations, but tensions remained high and an overall settlement out of reach.

To keep the issue before the Security Council, DPA was required to give monthly briefs on "The Situation in the Middle East." These briefings were mostly about Israeli-Palestinian relations and the situation in neighboring Lebanon. I had my first baptism by fire before the Council when I did the Middle East brief two weeks after arriving in New York. Predictably, my statement drew criticism from both sides. The Palestinians and their supporters argued I was not sufficiently tough in criticizing Israeli actions, and the Israelis (backed by their American supporters) said I had overemphasized the principles for a settlement set by the "Quartet," consisting of the U.S., Russia, the EU, and the UN. Both sides were trying to pressure me to make my future presentations more supportive of their views. I made it clear to the DPA staff that on this and all topics our briefings had to stick to the facts as we could best determine them without shading our views toward either side. After a couple more Security Council sessions, interested missions seemed satisfied that we were doing just that, and attempts to bully DPA eased off.

The United States played the dominant role in the Israeli-Palestinian "peace process," with the UN effort more focused on political problems on the ground. Through UNRWA (UN Relief and Works Agency), the UN also led the humanitarian effort to support almost six million Palestinian refugees, providing food, health, and education opportunities since 1949. In Gaza, which was under severe Israeli economic restrictions, the UN worked to make life tolerable for a population larger than a quarter of UN member states.

In 2007 the Bush administration had just begun a new effort led by Secretary of State Condoleezza Rice to negotiate a comprehensive agreement between the Israeli government and Palestinian leaders. The negotiations were complicated by the takeover of Gaza by the radical Hamas party. Rice's intensive negotiations during repeated visits to the region, backed on the economic side by the Quartet envoy Tony Blair, set the stage for a high-level gathering in Annapolis in November 2007. Optimism that the effort might work this time was high despite tensions on the ground. The secretary-general and I attended this and numerous other international meetings promoting the process. His new Special Representative for the Middle East Robert Serry had established himself as a serious player on the ground, and Serry and I used the monthly Council briefings to further promote the chance for peace in the region.

But then, as is the norm on this issue, events brought these promising efforts to a halt. Israeli prime minister Ehud Olmert, who favored an agreement, was indicted in July 2008 for corruption, and his would-be successor failed to form a government, leaving a weakened Olmert in place. The Bush administration, and Secretary Rice's tenure, was approaching its end, while the situation on the ground was deteriorating. Once more, hope of a deal appeared to be slipping from the international community's grasp.

In November 2008 Hamas militants resumed firing rockets into Israeli territory, despite widespread understanding that the Israeli army, the IDF, would attack if provoked. The secretary-general worked the phones hard to forestall Israeli action, talking with the Israelis and regional leaders as well as with the U.S. and others. The effort failed.

The IDF invaded Gaza in late December. For the next twenty-two days it killed 1,428 Palestinians and wounded perhaps 100,000 more; it also destroyed many of Gaza's buildings and a sizeable portion of its infrastructure in an effort to dismantle Hamas's military capabilities. Civilians by the thousands fled to UN facilities for their personal safety. It turned out they weren't even safe there, despite the clear UN markings on our buildings and our providing GPS coordinates of our facilities to the IDF. On January 6 fifty people died from Israeli shelling at an UNRWA school. The IDF's excuse that Hamas militants fired from the building was simply not true. Normally, the U.S. would have stepped in to try to calm the situation, but the Israelis had timed their attack to the last few days of the lame duck Bush administration. The French, Egyptians, and UN stepped in to fill the void.

After French president Sarkozy tried and failed to get a ceasefire, Secretary-General Ban undertook a trip to the region in an effort to stop the fighting. He first visited President Mubarak in Egypt to coordinate a pitch to get Israel to declare a unilateral ceasefire.

When we arrived in Tel Aviv on January 15, the IDF had just shelled UNRWA's headquarters and its primary warehouse in Gaza. Ban demanded, and got, an Israeli apology, and then proposed the unilateral ceasefire idea to Olmert who said he would consider it. Ban went on to meet Palestinian Authority leaders in Ramallah, then to Turkey for a meeting with President Erdogan, a Hamas supporter. The next day, January 17, while Ban was in Lebanon talking to leaders there, Olmert announced a unilateral ceasefire along the lines Ban had proposed. Olmert's main motivation was presumably to withdraw from Gaza before President Obama took office, but Ban's diplomacy gave him a way out. Ban then flew to Damascus to urge President Assad to get Hamas leaders based in Syria to announce a ceasefire of their own. The next day at an emergency meeting on the war hosted by Egypt and France in Sharm el-Sheikh, Ban announced that Hamas had agreed to the ceasefire.

The secretary-general then returned to Israel to make a planned trip to Gaza to boost the morale of UN staff working in the enclave and to observe the damage caused by the Israeli invasion. The Israelis tried to dissuade him from going, arguing that he was putting himself in danger, but Ban insisted he would go. The decision was typical of Ban's determination and personal courage.

That afternoon as we entered Gaza an unfriendly crowd greeted our convoy, beating on our cars and shouting insults. Scenes of devastation surrounded us everywhere as we drove through the enclave's streets. Piles of rubble could be seen where houses once stood. Family members who appeared to have lost everything were huddled in damaged buildings still standing precariously. There was virtually no activity in the streets.

We went immediately to the bombed UN warehouse, where hundreds of tons of supplies had been turned into charred heaps. This was material paid for by the international community and desperately needed to feed the people in Gaza. As we walked around the ruins, I saw the toll this sad sight was taking on the secretary-general's emotions. Ban had endured the destruction of part of his home town as a young boy during the Korean War, and the scenes around us were clearly bringing back those terrible memories. In the still smoldering warehouse, Ban gave a short speech to the UN employees who had put their lives on the line to help the people of Gaza. It was probably one of the toughest he had made in his life.

In its attack on the warehouse, the IDF used phosphorus shells that are hard to extinguish, produce toxic fumes, and are banned for use against civilian targets. The acrid smoke choked up all of us in the secretary-general's party. Ban's voice succumbed to the fumes as he tried to make himself heard by the gathered staff. Back in New York the next day, I had to read his report to the Security Council because he still could not speak.

In the statement Ban expressed his anguish at the devastation and deaths and demanded a full explanation of the IDF attack on the UN facilities, with those responsible held accountable. He soon established his own Board of Inquiry, led by Ian Martin, to investigate the attacks on UN facilities. The Board pinned responsibility on Israel for seven of the nine attacks on UN facilities (plus one on Hamas and another ambiguous), labeling the attack on the UNRWA facility "grossly negligent amounting to recklessness." It called for the Israelis to pay compensation. Israel predictably denounced the report, but it did pay $10.5 million in compensation to the UN for the damage inflicted to its facilities.

Rebuilding Gaza proved to be a disheartening process. Despite pleas by the secretary-general and others, the Israelis, now led by Prime Minister Netanyahu, refused entry to needed supplies. Serry worked to get permission for the passage of critical construction items virtually every day, but Israel, with cooperation from the Egyptians, allowed only a trickle to enter. Netanyahu demanded that Hamas release an Israeli soldier they had kidnapped several years earlier before he would ease the restrictions. Finally, after a prisoner swap was negotiated in October 2011 some additional supplies were allowed in to rebuild Gaza, but they still came at a painfully slow rate.

As usual, the primary public praise for the Gaza ceasefire went not to the secretary-general but to Mubarak and—especially in his own telling—to Sarkozy. Ban, however, deserved the credit, along with the Israeli government's urgent desire to get out before the U.S. inauguration. And it was Ban who got Assad to lean on Hamas to follow suit. In addition, his trip into the devastated enclave generated global sympathy that led countries to pledge funds to begin rebuilding Gaza. The basic issues of the Israeli-Palestinian conflict were not resolved, but Secretary-General Ban and the UN made a heroic effort to alleviate the suffering in this episode of the never-ending conflict.

Israel and Turkey Clash

The Gaza War seriously damaged Israel's international reputation. Probably more critical in the short run was the strategic rupture it caused in relations between two friends and powerful players in the Middle East—Israel and Turkey. When Israeli prime minister Olmert paid a visit to Ankara to discuss trade and peace efforts with the Palestinians five days before the Israeli attack on Gaza, he gave no hint that an invasion was imminent. Turkish prime minister Erdogan became incensed at having been blindsided by Olmert. At a meeting in Davos a few days after the IDF withdrew from Gaza, Erdogan and Israeli president Peres got into a major public spat over Gaza, with Erdogan storming off their shared platform. His public show of anger drew wide praise inside Turkey, where public sentiments were decidedly pro-Palestinian.

After Davos, relations between Erdogan and now prime minister Netanyahu continued to deteriorate. To circumvent the Israeli blockade of Gaza, a Turkish NGO organized a large flotilla of ships and international passengers to carry supplies to Gaza. Israel tried without success to convince the Turkish government to stop this challenge to the blockade, although Turkish officials did make some efforts to discourage it. Then, when Israeli commandos boarded one of the vessels, the *Mavi Marmara*, early in the morning of May 31, 2010, many of the activists on the ship fought back. The IDF opened fire and brought in reinforcements. Nine Turkish nationals died in the fight, and Erdogan denounced the Israeli action as "state terrorism." Meeting in emergency session, the UN Security Council called for a "prompt, impartial, credible and transparent investigation" of the incident.

The secretary-general undertook to set up a Panel of Inquiry to carry out the Security Council's mandate; but it took months of excruciating negotiations over the panel's makeup and procedures, with the Americans mostly backing Israeli reluctance before it could be formed. Finally in September Ban announced that former New Zealand prime minister Geoffrey Palmer, a legal expert on maritime issues, would chair the panel, with former Colombian president Alvaro Uribe as vice chair and Turkey and Israel each naming a panel member. The panel would base its findings on the separate investigations of the two sides, and if it could not reach agreement, the chairman and vice chairman would write their own conclusions.

Given the constraints on the panel, it was obvious from the first that its real purpose was to give the two sides a way out of the mess so they could rebuild ties, rather than to develop any new facts in the case. We were involved in the negotiations, but the Americans did most of the heavy lifting.

By June 2011 the panel had reviewed the results of the two national investigations and, after much debate, drafted some "Conclusions of the Chair." Turkey and Israel also settled on a separate agreement that would include an Israeli apology and compensation, with the elimination of any lawsuits against the Israeli commandos and a return to full bilateral relations. In early July both sides voiced public optimism that a deal would be reached. But as details of the agreement leaked out, the conservative Israeli foreign minister (and essential coalition partner for Netanyahu) Avigdor Lieberman announced that he opposed an apology, which he said would "humiliate" Israel. In the end Lieberman won over the Israeli inner cabinet.

Despite several extensions of a deadline to give the parties more time, on September 2, 2011, the secretary-general finally had no choice but to announce the "Conclusions of the Chair," which stated that the flotilla had "acted recklessly"; that despite efforts by the Turkish government to dissuade the organizers, more could have been done; that the Israeli decision to board the ship without a final warning was "excessive and unreasonable"; that the loss of life and injuries the Israelis caused were "unacceptable"; and that Israel subjected the passengers to "physical mistreatment, harassment, and intimidation" when it held them in prolonged detention after the incident. It urged an Israeli statement of regret, compensation for the deceased and injured, and resumption of full relations between the two countries (essentially, the earlier agreement that the Israelis backed away from). Israel and Turkey both criticized the conclusions, which they had been debating for months; the Turks froze military ties and expelled the Israeli ambassador; and Netanyahu announced that Israel would not apologize.

Erdogan was in an exceptionally foul mood when he attended the UN General Assembly three weeks later. At one point he and his entourage attempted to enter the Assembly Hall from the wrong level, and UN security personnel tried to direct them to the right entrance. What happened next is hotly disputed, but Erdogan claimed he had been pushed (or touched) and blew up. Minutes later the shaken Turkish ambassador (a good friend) grabbed me from the floor and pleaded for me to talk to the Turkish prime minister in a nearby room. His boss was in a rage. As I entered, Erdogan rushed over to me—we knew each other a bit from meetings over the past several years—and got right in my face, yelling that he had been insulted by the UN security people. I knew this was almost certainly not the case. Our security people were used to dealing with the world's prima donnas and their aggressive security details, and it was well known that the Turkish security people were among the worst behaved; but there was no point in trying to argue with Erdogan. I apologized for the fact that he felt disrespected, and he calmed down. The secretary-general later also apologized to Erdogan for the incident. But our security people were incensed by the behavior of Erdogan's detail and felt their officer did no wrong. (Erdogan's detail later got into nasty fights with demonstrators in Washington in 2016 and 2017 and injured nine U.S. security personnel in the 2017 incident. We were probably lucky in 2011 to get off with only my tongue lashing from Erdogan.)

Eventually, in 2013, President Obama prevailed on Netanyahu to apologize for the ship incident, and the two countries reestablished formal relations, although the close cooperation between these two powers in the Middle East was unlikely to return in the foreseeable future. It would be another nine years before the leaders of the two formerly friendly countries met in person.

The Arab Spring

When the Arab uprising dubbed the "Arab Spring" broke out in Tunisia in December 2010, we at the United Nations were as surprised as the rest of the world. The UN Development Program had produced a series of excellent reports a few years earlier that analyzed the social, economic, and demographic problems in the Middle East and North Africa and predicted a political upheaval if these issues were not addressed. These reports, with the rare notion of political consequences for economic failures, had joined other UN studies on the bookshelves and by 2010 had largely been forgotten. The protests by the relatively sophisticated and well-off Tunisian population led in mid-January to the long-term dictator Ben Ali's flight to safety and inspired similar upheavals in Egypt, Bahrain, Libya, Syria, and Yemen. The grievances in these countries and others in the region (where demonstrations were quickly suppressed) arose from the people's severe economic hardships, the wealthy elite's corruption, political repression, and a general disregard for human rights.

There was no doubt that the UN would side with the people who struggled for bedrock principles that the UN system espoused. From the first, Secretary-General Ban condemned repressive and violent measures against the demonstrators and called on the leaders in these countries to respect the human rights of their people and respond with reforms. Ban had lived through the transformation of South Korea from a military dictatorship to a democracy. Along with the rest of us, he hoped the demonstrations heralded the start of a similar process in the repressive Middle East. With Ban taking the lead, we left no doubt in public and private comments that we supported peaceful, democratic demonstrations that were demanding reforms throughout the region. We spoke out strongly against the violence perpetrated by the governments in response and sought to provide humanitarian relief to those displaced in the confrontations.

It was evident from the first that the UN would have to use all the tools available if there was any chance to help the protestors succeed. We understood the long odds against them but were determined to try our best, despite the challenges they faced. In the end, of course, statements by the UN and democratic countries proved inadequate to enable the young protestors to achieve their goals. The democratic aspirations of the people in most of the countries were not met. Instead, despite our efforts, death, violence, and political repression once again became the norm in the Middle East.

Tunisia Leads the Way. Tunisia provided the spark for the Arab Spring beginning in December 2010, and it turned out to be the only country that succeeded initially in establishing a democratic system from the turmoil. On visits to Tunis in the spring and summer, I could feel the levelheadedness and confidence of the civil society and political leaders who moved into the void when Ben Ali fled. They understood the critical role of compromise that made democratic systems work. During my first visit in March 2011, I offered to help the transition in any way we could, especially on elections planned for a Constitutional Assembly, the details of a new constitution, and development of democratic institutions.

By my next visit in July, Tunisia's leaders had made progress in dismantling the old authoritarian structures, creating new institutional and social norms to replace them, planning for an independent judiciary, preparing for the elections set for October, and creating a new constitution. In addition to their own problems, the Tunisians also had to care for the refugees from Libya who had fled from the chaos in their homeland. Tunisian leaders welcomed

UN assistance in all these areas but made it clear from the start that they would own and drive the political process themselves, a sentiment with which we heartily agreed.

All the people I talked with in Tunisia stressed the crucial importance of reviving the economy and lowering unemployment, which had been at the core of the protest. When I discussed Tunisia with EU officials in Brussels, they emphasized that they wanted the EU to take the lead in helping Tunisia, given the country's traditionally close ties to Europe and the security concerns (including refugees) posed by a chaotic Tunisia. We had worked closely with the EU on many global issues, and I was happy to let the revival of Tunisia be a European project.

Unfortunately, despite Tunisia's impressive efforts to build democratic institutions, the European program to help build the economy failed miserably. Even with a large amount of European aid, the Tunisian economy did not improve. In time the blame game and contentious politics left ordinary Tunisians with little to show for their embrace of democracy. The stalled economic progress created disillusion among the populace, which over time undermined the new democracy and put the promise of a bright future on hold. A decade later the elected government was moving back to autocracy.

Egypt. Days after Ben Ali left Tunisia in January 2011, large demonstrations against Egyptian president Mubarak began in Cairo's Tahrir Square. Under heavy pressure from the military and the international community, including his close American ally, Mubarak resigned on February 11, turning power over to an Egyptian military council. I made my first of several visits to Cairo two weeks later to take stock of the situation and offer the UN's help. The youth who had led the demonstrations were an impressive group, liberal-minded but with a vague agenda and organizational skills limited to street demonstrations.

In my meetings across the political spectrum, I was struck by how consistently the members of the old regime gave lip service to the "revolution" but clearly had no sympathy for building a truly democratic government. They included the foreign minister, whom I knew from my Moscow days and who met me in the

Foreign Ministry guarded by a tank at its entrance, and the UN's chief interlocutor, a close friend of Mubarak's wife, who had given the UN office fits for years. She later led an effort to indict Americans in Egypt who were promoting democracy. Publicly and privately, I offered UN assistance to help with the transition. When the secretary-general visited Cairo the next month, he renewed the offer.

However, the Egyptian military and the political establishment wanted very little UN involvement in the months that followed, aside from some technical electoral assistance. Some of the opposition, on the other hand, were desperate for our help. As we left a meeting at the Arab League office, a group of demonstrators mobbed our party, demanding we take action against the military. Ban and the rest of us managed to get away safely, but the situation potentially could have become very nasty.

The military council took its time in deciding how to proceed with the transition to democracy demanded by the demonstrators. I felt the best chance for a real transition would be for the military to appoint an interim civilian president—former foreign minister Amr Moussa or former IAEA chairman El Baradei were prominently mentioned as possibilities—to work out governmental and constitutional changes that would lay the basis for elections and a new government. The military, however, preferred to stall. Under strong internal and international pressure, their leaders finally moved to hold an election in November 2011 for a Parliament that would draw up a new constitution, with a presidential election set for the following spring. In these elections, the democratic forces in Egypt became bit players, as the establishment, including the military, and the Muslim Brotherhood fought to control Egypt's future. When the youth tried demonstrations once again, the military quickly suppressed them. In the end, the Muslim Brotherhood leader, Muhammed Morsi, beat the establishment candidate by a small margin and was elected president in June 2012.

As I left the UN weeks later, it was clear that the UN had had no real impact on events in Egypt. The military and political establishment were willing to sacrifice Mubarak, but they had no intention of relinquishing power. This became even more obvious a year later when the military carried out a coup against Morsi, who had managed to make himself quite unpopular in his year in office. Soon the top general, Abdul Fatah al-Sisi, became president and established a regime that was basically Mubarak 2.0, though arguably more repressive. Egypt had gone back to where it had begun, with the hopes of Tahrir Square crushed.

Security Gaps Undermine Our Libya Effort

At the UN we dealt with an odd assortment of world leaders. Some were gracious and friendly, some were arrogant bullies, and some were terrorists or unbelievably brutal to their own people. Too many seemed to feel that the ultimate task of a president or prime minister consisted of looting the country's treasury and natural resources for their own or their family's benefit. But without doubt, the most bizarre was Muammar Qadhafi of Libya, a country assembled from three separate entities in the early 1950s. Qadhafi had ruled Libya for forty-two years without building any real government structure, an intentional strategy to avoid challenges to his rule. His security forces included many foreign mercenaries; and despite Libya's great oil wealth, the country's people were generally poor and isolated from the world.

I had met Qadhafi with the secretary-general on a couple of occasions in his trademark desert tent, where we listened to his mostly incoherent ravings on the topics of the day. I had also seen him in action at a couple of Arab League meetings, where he lectured his fellow Arabs on the need to abolish their group and join the African Union and where he accused the Saudi king of being a tool of the United States. At a meeting of the African Union, he refused to take his assigned seat, moving instead to an area reserved for traditional monarchs in tribal dress while proclaiming himself the "King of African Kings." His most offensive international appearance that I witnessed occurred in 2009 at his speech to the UN General Assembly, where he rambled on for a hundred minutes instead of his allotted fifteen and ripped up a copy of the UN Charter, which he threw over his head in the direction of the deputy secretary-general and General Assembly president Ali Treki, a former Libyan foreign minister. He was an embarrassment to his colleagues, many of whom despised him; but he had been around a long time, and they mostly chose to ignore his antics. His few real supporters happily accepted his largesse, which helped keep them in power.

When demonstrations broke out in Libya against Qadhafi's erratic rule in mid-February 2011, he responded with exceptional ferocity, brutally killing demonstrators and arresting large numbers in several cities. The secretary-general spoke to Qadhafi by phone to urge him to stop the violence and enter into a dialogue with the opposition on their grievances. Qadhafi was unmoved, and Ban issued a statement condemning the killing of civilians.

Defections of Libyan officials, including the deputy Libyan ambassador to the UN, began in reaction to Qadhafi's excesses. I briefed the Security Council on February 22 on what we knew about the situation in Libya. The Council issued a Presidential Statement—which required unanimous consent—that condemned the government's use of force against civilians, demanded an end to the violence, and called on the Libyan government to meet its responsibility to protect its population. It noted a statement by the League of Arab States earlier in the day that also denounced the attacks.

Reference to the regime's "responsibility to protect" its population was important. The principle (R2P in UN shorthand) had been adopted by the 2005 World Summit at the UN General Assembly to spell out the responsibility of the international community to deal with crises such as the Rwandan genocide of 1994, which the UN failed to stop. The UN Charter focuses on conflicts between states rather than on conflicts within states, and R2P was designed to fill part of that gap. Essentially, R2P established that a country had a responsibility to protect its population from genocide, war crimes, ethnic cleansing, and crimes against humanity. It encouraged the international community to help states carry out that responsibility; but if the state failed to do its duty, charged the UN to use peaceful or coercive means (under the Charter's Article VII) to ensure that the country's citizens were protected.

Although the 2005 summit endorsed the concept of responsibility to protect, the details remained to be fleshed out. Secretary-General Ban wanted to make it an effective tool of the UN and appointed a Special Advisor to refine and develop it. The African Union also embraced the concept, as it sought to deal with tyrants who argued they could do anything they wanted to their own people because of state sovereignty.

Qadhafi responded to the international condemnation with a fiery speech, vowing to "cleanse Libya house by house" and calling the demonstrators "rats" to be exterminated. By this time, most of eastern Libya had slipped out of his government's control, and much of the military stationed there had defected to the opposition.

On February 25, the Security Council again met on Libya, with the secretary-general doing the briefing. He reported that over a thousand people had been killed, the east was under opposition control, and the streets of Tripoli were deserted. He noted reports of indiscriminate killings, arbitrary arrests, shooting of peaceful demonstrators, detention and torture of the opposition, and the use of mercenaries to suppress the demonstrations. Ban emphasized that "the first obligation of the international community is to do everything possible to ensure the immediate protection of civilians" and called for concrete Council action.

The Libyan ambassador, who had known Qadhafi since childhood and had backed the regime three days earlier, now changed his tune. He quoted Qadhafi as saying he would "burn Libya" and the country would "run with blood." He pleaded with members of the Council to "save Libya" and adopt a decisive resolution to stop the killing.

The next day, February 26, 2011, the Security Council unanimously passed Resolution 1790, which noted condemnation of the violence by the League of Arab States, the African Union, and the Organization of the Islamic Conference and cited Libya's responsibility to protect its population. It demanded an end to the violence and fulfillment of the legitimate demands of the Libyan people; referred the actions of the government to the International Criminal Court (ICC) for an investigation of possible "war crimes"; and established an arms embargo, a travel ban on Libyan leaders, and a freeze of their assets. The swift Council action only ten days after demonstrations first broke out reflected the harshness of the Libyan government's response and the condemnations by Arab, African, and Islamic organizations. It also testified to Qadhafi's unpopularity around the world.

As Qadhafi's forces attacked cities where the rebels held sway, demands intensified for the international community to act. France and Britain supported calls for a no-fly zone to keep Qadhafi from using his air force against civilians, while a major debate raged inside the Obama administration over whether to become militarily involved. President Obama himself was skeptical—hardly surprising with two other wars on his hands—and insisted that any action receive UN Security Council backing, include Arab participation, and be led by the Europeans. Russia and China were reluctant to agree to the use of force, but pressure in New York grew as it became obvious Qadhafi was preparing to attack Benghazi, Libya's second largest city. The Arab League issued a call for a no-fly zone, the Gulf Cooperation Council (GCC) and the Organization of the Islamic Conference (OIC) also pressed for action, and the African Union deplored the violence. In my statement to the Council on March 13, a Sunday, and my second Libya briefing in a week, I reminded the Council that the Libyan government's actions violated "all norms governing international behavior," international human rights and humanitarian law, and the Council's Resolution 1970 passed two weeks earlier.

The secretary-general worked the phones hard throughout this period, trying to persuade the Libyans to negotiate a peaceful solution and discussing with international leaders ways to stop the coming onslaught if Qadhafi stuck to his course. He named Abdelilah al-Khatib, a highly regarded former Jordanian foreign minister, as his Special Envoy to work for a political solution. Al-Khatib immediately traveled to Libya to talk with Qadhafi's people in Tripoli. He emphasized the importance of ending hostilities, pressed for an end to attacks on civilians, and called for implementation of the UN Security Council resolutions.

A few days after the al-Khatib appointment, the African Union set up its own panel of leaders, led by South African president Jacob Zuma, to mediate. While many African leaders shared the dislike of Qadhafi and his meddling in affairs south of the Sahara, they also had some resentment against the Arabs taking the lead on Libya, since Libya was also a member of the African Union, some of whose members had benefited from Qadhafi's large financial handouts. The AU leadership in Addis Ababa, led by Jean Ping, worked closely with us and the Arab League, but some major African countries, particularly South Africa, took a more ambivalent line.

Meanwhile, intense debates continued in New York, Washington, and Europe, including at NATO Headquarters, over whether outside military force should be used to stop a looming massacre in Benghazi, as Qadhafi moved his air force, heavy weaponry, and mercenaries into position. At a G-8 meeting in Paris on March 15, France and Britain pushed for agreement on a no-fly zone, Germany and Russia opposed it, and the U.S. took a neutral stance. But Secretary Clinton had by then decided to support the use of military force, and President Obama agreed. He then persuaded the Nigerian and South African presidents to vote for a tough resolution and Russian president Medvedev (who was working to "reset" frayed relations with the U.S.) to abstain in the Security Council vote. The Chinese, who had been less negative about a tough resolution than the Russians, also decided to abstain.

At a dramatic meeting of the Security Council on March 17, 2011, the Council agreed (ten members in favor and five abstentions) to Resolution 1973, which approved the establishment of a no-fly zone over Libya and the use of "all necessary measures" to protect Libyan civilians. R2P had come of age. After U.S. ambassador Susan Rice rounded up the South African representative at the last moment to ensure he voted for the resolution as his president had promised, all of the African countries and the Arab representative voted in favor. In addition to Russia and China, Brazil, India, and Germany abstained. (The German ambassador cringed at his instructions to break ranks with his allies in the Council, and the abstention proved quite controversial in Germany.) The Russians later claimed that NATO exceeded the mandate it had been given by the Council, but in fact the members had been thoroughly briefed about what would happen at least initially.

I left New York with the secretary-general that evening for a quick trip to Spain and then on to a March 19 meeting on Libya in Paris hosted by President Sarkozy. After rushing the meeting participants through their presentations, the French president held a press conference where, with great pride, he announced that French warplanes had begun the attack on Qadhafi's forces. American and British missile strikes had destroyed Libya's air defenses.

While I supported military action to avoid an inevitable massacre of civilians, I couldn't help but feel concern about the lack of a follow-on strategy. As Sarkozy spoke excitedly at the podium, a picture flashed through my mind of Snoopy's "Red Baron" heading off to battle. All Sarkozy needed that day was a red scarf. (The irony seemed particularly rich when Sarkozy was later charged with taking illegal campaign funds from Qadhafi for his 2007 election.)

Led largely by France and Britain with the U.S. in an uncharacteristically low-key supporting role, the NATO offensive became increasingly controversial after an attack on Qadhafi's home that killed one of his sons. A few days after the decisive Libya vote and the start of the NATO bombing campaign, Putin moved to take Middle East policymaking away from his protégé Medvedev by publicly criticizing the Security Council's resolution as "deficient and flawed," likening it to a "crusade," a standard Islamic criticism of the U.S. invasion of Iraq. Medvedev tried to counter Putin's comments, but Russian support for compromise with the West on the Arab Spring upheavals had effectively ended. The Russians, echoed by China, India, Brazil, and some African countries, engaged in a drumbeat of criticism of the operation, accusing NATO of exceeding its mandate and the air strikes of causing excessive civilian casualties.

Through the spring and summer, al-Khatib kept up an intensive schedule of talks with government representatives, with the rebels—now "united" under the National Transition Council, the NTC—and with all the regional leaders having a stake in the conflict. The secretary-general made many phone calls to support al-Khatib's effort, as I did in person at Libya Contact Group meetings, to get the two sides into negotiations that could end the conflict. But in fact, neither side had any real interest in a negotiated outcome. Qadhafi seemed encouraged by Zuma's effort to find a way out, and the NTC was confident it would win, with NATO air support and a large supply of weapons coming in from the Arab states. By late August, rebel forces gained control of Tripoli, Qadhafi's family had fled, and the war was essentially over. Qadhafi himself was hunted down and killed on October 20, 2011. The NTC celebrated its victory three days later, and NATO ended its campaign at the end of the month.

In a briefing to the Security Council back in April, a month after the war began, I reported that we had begun internal discussions on post-conflict planning to carry out the secretary-general's promise to coordinate international efforts to aid Libya after the war ended. Basically, the Libyans had to build a country from scratch, and they needed help. The secretary-general, on my recommendation, asked Ian Martin to lead a task force to assess Libya's needs and manage the planning for the UN role. Ian was a terrific choice, well grounded in what the UN could do well and what was beyond its reach. This unprecedented early effort to organize UN resources received strong Security Council backing. The British government agreed to fund our planning effort; and by the time the Qadhafi government collapsed, Ian and his team had in place a plan to support the new NTC-led government on issues of political dialogue, institution building, electoral assistance, security sector reform, and economic development.

In September the UN recognized the NTC as the legitimate government of Libya. The Security Council established a political mission to support the new government—the UN Support Mission in Libya, UNSMIL—and the secretary-general named Ian Martin to head the mission. Ian traveled immediately to Libya to coordinate UN efforts with the NTC and review the situation on the ground.

When I briefed the Security Council on our plans, I emphasized that we would work closely with the NTC and were there to support the Libyans. But I noted that the Libyans needed to develop a sense of national unity and common purpose if the effort were to succeed. Building a modern country by a coalition that had little sense of national coherence presented a daunting challenge, and the list of required UNSMIL tasks was long. Security topped the list, with stockpiles of sophisticated weaponry to be controlled—the NTC had just discovered a large cache of undeclared chemical weapons. And refugees needed to be fed, housed, and returned home. I was pleased to tell the Council that many of the mission's personnel were already in place in Libya, surely a record time for the establishment of a UN mission.

Ian and his team moved quickly to do the things the UN was good at: promoting dialogue, advising on constitutional concepts and government structures, and elections. He made it clear from the first that UNSMIL would support NTC priorities and not dictate UN solutions. We understood the critical need for the Libyans to establish some sort of national security structure and regularly briefed the Security Council about this, but we did not have the means to manage this problem ourselves or the power to pressure the Libyans to do so. The winners in the conflict included troops who had defected, unruly militias, and tribal armies and ranged from secularists to radical Islamists. There was no military establishment to take over. What was left of the regular army had melted away, and the mercenaries Qadhafi had employed fled over Libya's southern border into the volatile Sahel region. To make matters worse, countries in the region funded and armed assorted groups to support their own aims. Although the NTC included people from across Libya, its real power rested with eastern anti-Qadhafi politicians from Benghazi and held little sway over the western part of the county that included Tripoli.

Some people advocated a UN peacekeeping force for Libya, something I considered a remarkably bad idea. There was no way South Asian or other troops could keep the peace in a situation where the players were so opaque, the leadership so fractured, and guns so prevalent. Fortunately, the NTC scotched the idea of a UN force early on in the discussions. The British and French had military advisors on the ground but did not have the standing or resources to build a Libyan national army.

Washington had refused to provide weapons to the opposition forces, leaving the U.S. with little leverage in the transition to a new government. In effect, the one country that could have helped the Libyans build an effective security structure and demand a coordinated international response by Libya's leaders was AWOL. The Americans limited their involvement to looking for possible weapons of mass destruction—they found and secured some yellowcake that the Libyans had earlier declared—and buying MANPAD missiles, of which Qadhafi had purchased a large supply. The weak transitional government tried to deal with the security issues itself, a task well beyond its capability, and the UN could do little more than offer general advice.

When President Obama later said that Libya was the greatest failure of his administration, it was a failure largely caused by U.S.

inaction in the critical period before and after the NTC took over. Following the rebels' win, Obama had expected the French and British to continue their strong involvement with Libya, but they virtually disappeared after a joint victory lap by Prime Minister Cameron and President Sarkozy to Tripoli in mid-September. The failure to get the security situation under control undermined Libya's entire transition effort. To make matters worse, as the mercenaries and Qadhafi loyalists fled, they took with them large stores of modern weapons from government stocks, undermining the tenuous stability of many of the country's neighbors. This would prove to have major consequences, particularly in neighboring Mali.

By January 2012, Libyan public support for the NTC had begun to wane, as it struggled to carry out the tasks of maintaining public security, building a working government, and improving the lot of ordinary Libyans. The high hopes of the autumn faded away; the interim leaders squabbled, militias fought each other, and reprisals against people involved with the Qadhafi regime continued. There was a pervasive sense of insecurity. When I traveled to Tripoli with the secretary-general and the General Assembly president in November 2011, the airport was controlled by a tough-looking bunch of militia fighters who had taken over the area and who did not answer to the government located a few miles away. The UN mission worked hard to encourage the NTC to develop a unified approach to building a Libyan security apparatus, both army and police, but the bitter rivalries among the various armed groups and the weakness of the NTC made progress in the security mission virtually impossible.

Given the rivalries and the extreme sense of wariness of foreign control (a Qadhafi legacy), UNSMIL had to tread carefully to remain welcome. Preparations for the election of a National Assembly in July produced a major political fight between eastern and western Libya, with considerable tension and some violence leading up to the vote. Miraculously (another word for careful management by UNSMIL), the election took place on July 7 with a massive turnout of the Libyan population.

When Ian Martin gave his final brief to the Security Council several days later, at the end of his one-year assignment, he praised the election success but emphasized that the problems of security within Libya and in coordination among the international community had stalled major progress. The United Nations had much to show for its rapid and expert help, but the Libyans had not resolved the political and security problems necessary for internal cohesion. Unfortunately, their inability to build national unity resulted in their most basic fear being realized, namely, the manipulation of Libyan politics by outside forces bent on securing Libyan wealth. Weapons flowed into the already overly armed country from Russia, Turkey, Qatar, and the UAE, as each country backed its favored faction. UNSMIL soon found itself trying to mediate conflicts between various competing factions, rather than pursuing its original goal of assisting the Libyans to create a new post-Qadhafi state that could bring its people peace, security, and prosperity.

A "Reformed" Security Council

Beginning in 2011 the dynamics in the Security Council provided a window into how a "reformed" Security Council might act. Four of the leading candidates for a permanent Council seat—Brazil, India, South Africa, and Germany—were on the Security Council. The other leading candidate, Japan, had just left it. During the first couple of months after the Arab Spring revolts broke out, India, Brazil, and South Africa, joined by Colombia and Nigeria, appeared to be forming a democratic center beholden neither to the U.S. and Europe nor to Russia and China. Their speeches were filled with affirmations of support for democracy and demands that the will of the Arab peoples be respected by their governments. After Qadhafi's brutal attacks on his people began in February 2011, the Council unanimously voted to refer his case to the international Criminal Court, institute an arms embargo, freeze Libyan government funds abroad, and ban travel by its leaders.

By the second Libya resolution authorizing "all necessary means," the tone of the speeches of the Indian, Brazilian, and South African representatives had changed. Russia's ambassador Churkin began convening meetings of the amorphous BRICS group—Brazil,

Russia, India, China, and South Africa—to "coordinate positions." The Russians pushed their new narrative that NATO's actions in Libya had gone well beyond those authorized by the Council and emphasized the need to avoid similar overreach on Syria.

As I listened to the ambassadors from Brazil, India, and South Africa, the tone of the speeches changed from full-throated support for the Arab peoples and democracy to more traditional G-77 rhetoric that often parroted the Russian line. The United States and EU countries came up with no effective counter, and Colombia and Nigeria no longer had support for their positioning in a new democratic center.

The experience had to be sobering for advocates of a Security Council overhaul. The inclusion of most of the Permanent Member wannabees in the Council did not improve its work or give it more credibility. The three countries missed their opportunity to develop a democratic voice to nudge the West and Russia into action to deal with the terrible developments in the Mideast. They certainly did not help their case for a permanent seat on the Council with the U.S., France, or Britain, nor, I suspect, did they make Russia or China more eager to welcome them permanently.

The Council proved resistant to even minor changes. At the suggestion of the superb British permanent representative, Mark Lyall Grant, we instituted a monthly "horizon scanning" briefing session to get the Security Council more involved in preventing conflict rather than waiting for a full-blown crisis. The briefings that covered emerging issues of concern to DPA allowed us to get out of the Council's "agenda" straitjacket and initiate discussions of emerging problems. They were highly appreciated by most elected members, who had less information on global hot spots than the Permanent Five members.

The U.S. (for reasons they never explained) and eventually India and South Africa (who wanted to be the arbiters of disputes in their regions) tried to limit or strangle the briefings and managed to end them after I left. Despite continued praise of our efforts, the United States repeatedly demonstrated a reluctance to change anything in the Security Council or get more involved in heading off conflicts. Again, USUN passed up an opportunity to take the lead (or even support the American under-secretary-general), choosing instead its standard defensive crouch.

The Russians Block Action on Syria.

Demonstrations broke out in Syria on March 15, 2011, two days before the Security Council voted on the second Libyan resolution and four days before the NATO bombing campaign began. President Assad used what had become the standard initial reaction to such protests, promises of reform (never implemented) and repression. The situation deteriorated over the months and years that followed; as the protests spread, the government's crackdown became more brutal. Unfortunately, the UN for the most part remained a bystander, unable to help much beyond reporting on the horror and providing humanitarian assistance. Its one major political effort by Kofi Annan seemed to me to be doomed from the start.

The primary reasons for UN inaction in Syria were Russia's determination to support its most important ally in the Middle East (thus effectively guaranteeing Assad's survival) and the reluctance of the neighboring Arab states to intervene against their powerful neighbor. Putin worked to protect Russia's long-standing interests in the Mideast and avoid an outcome that would strengthen the West's role there. There would be no more support from Moscow for the "responsibility to protect," at least in countries where there was a strong Russian interest. While it had been relatively easy for the Arabs to gang up on the despised and unpredictable Qadhafi, taking on Assad was a whole different issue. In addition, the wily and effective Syrian ambassador (unlike the Libyan UN representatives who had denounced Qadhafi) proved to be a staunch defender of the regime in New York; and the Lebanese ambassador, who had been such an articulate carrier of the Arab League position on Libya, could not criticize his country's powerful neighbor. Moreover, China's leadership decided this was a good issue on which to fall into lockstep with Russia at the UN, thus building their pseudo-alliance at low cost to China.

The UN had a large presence in Syria that allowed us to have a fairly good sense of what the regime was doing. We used the reports from various UN agencies on the ground (without naming them) for my regular briefings to the Security Council. With Russian and Chinese opposition to any Council action, including presidential statements expressing concern over the violence, our tools basically consisted of attempts by the secretary-general to persuade Assad to change his approach (to which Assad usually responded with bluster and a few promises never meant to be kept); Ban's public statements of concern or condemnation; and our public briefings to the Security Council that often generated press attention. We double-checked our facts in these statements, because the Syrians consistently tried to counter the depressing (and truthful) picture we painted.

After many failed attempts in the Security Council, Britain, France, and the United States proposed a watered-down resolution in October 2011 that was designed to avoid a Russian veto. But Putin overruled his UN negotiators and called Xi Jinping asking for Chinese support. When word got out that the Chinese would also veto the resolution, a large group of Arab ambassadors surrounded the Chinese ambassador as he was entering the Security Council chamber in an effort to persuade him to abstain on the resolution. It didn't happen. The Chinese ambassador followed his instructions from Beijing, and Russia and China cast a double veto against a quite mild resolution.

Syria continued to spiral downward, and the country appeared headed toward a full-scale civil war. We gave support to an Arab League effort to end the bloodshed, but its 150-person observer mission accomplished nothing. In early February 2012, Russia and China again vetoed a Security Council resolution that backed an Arab League plan for a settlement that included Assad stepping down.

The Arab League then asked the UN to send a peacekeeping force to Syria. On February 23, 2012, the secretary-general announced that he and his Arab League counterpart had appointed former UN secretary-general Kofi Annan as a Joint Special Envoy with a mandate to stop the violence. Five days later, I told the Council that the situation was rapidly deteriorating and that "well over 7,500" people had been killed as Syrian forces carried out a series of attacks on cities that were out of the regime's control. I noted that the Syrian government had "manifestly failed to carry out its responsibility to protect its people," instead carrying out indiscriminate bombing against them. I also made the obvious point that the international community had also "failed in its duty to stop the carnage," thereby encouraging the regime in its actions.

In mid-March (a year after the Syrian uprising began), Annan released a six-point plan as a basis for a settlement of the conflict. It called on the government to address the legitimate concerns of the Syrian people, stop the fighting, and pull back from the cities where the government had concentrated its attacks. It also called for emergency delivery of humanitarian supplies and acceptance of the right of the people to peacefully demonstrate. The package had little in it for the Syrian government, and the opposition knew that Assad would not implement it even if he agreed. Predictably, Assad accepted the Annan Plan and then proceeded to ignore it.

Annan called for a 250-person UN observer contingent to monitor compliance. I thought this was a major mistake, given the Arab League's failure with a similar group. Inserting UN observers before any kind of serious agreement to implement the plan was in place totally contradicted peacekeeping's long-standing mantra of needing a "peace to keep." Putting Blue Helmets on the ground in this volatile situation was premature at best. Despite my doubts, which the secretary-general and many members of the Security Council undoubtedly shared, we had no choice but to support Annan since his was the only game in town.

Assad made nice-sounding promises to Annan but continued the fighting. By early June, the situation grew increasingly desperate, with the UN/Arab League observer force unable to slow the violence. Opposition forces ridiculed the UN's ineffectiveness and, like the government troops, ignored them. By mid-June, conditions had become so dangerous that the UN observer contingent suspended its work. Annan resigned on August 2, and the observers left shortly thereafter.

The Annan peace effort in Syria was conceived in desperation. Both Ban and Annan knew that the chance for a deal was slim given the Russian cover for Assad and the opposition's determination to oust him. The six-point plan never had a chance. The points were not a compromise reached by the two sides; they were merely a hope that outsiders could buy into. And the introduction of UN observers when the "ceasefire" was not real ensured the effort would go down as a UN failure. In the years that followed, as the situation in Syria worsened, the UN basically sat on the sidelines.

DPA Reformed, but Demands on the UN Only Grow

In late 2011, I reminded the secretary-general of his desire to have top officials in place for no more than five years, adding that it was time for me to go. I knew he needed fresh blood for his second term and wanted to replace several of his original appointees whose performance had not met his expectations. We both understood that my departure would make it easier to get others to leave. Finally, the constant travel had taken its toll (my Global Entry application listed visits to seventy-five separate countries), and Diane and I were anxious to get on with my retirement and a slower pace. I recommended that Jeff Feltman replace me, and the transition took place at the end of June 2012.

I left the United Nations with genuine satisfaction about what had been accomplished, but also knowing full well that much more needed to be done. One of my mantras with my various staffs had been that a manager should make a list of things that need to be changed early on in his tenure and then try to be sure that his successor had a different list. We partially succeeded in that goal, but Jeff's list certainly included a good number of unfinished projects from my own.

On the plus side, we did manage to carry out the vision of the secretary-general to reorient the Political Department into a proactive force for political resolution of hot conflicts in many parts of the world and to make it a stronger, more competent organization in promoting world peace. DPA's goals, work style, and global relevance had been fundamentally changed in the five years of Ban Ki-moon's first term, with its attention now focused on the prevention or resolution of conflicts. We could move quickly and professionally with a clear understanding of how to proceed and who we could partner with to help in some of the world's most vexing conflicts. Morale was high, and our envoys were better equipped, backed by more capable staffs and fully supported by the secretary-general and me. Financing DPA's efforts remained cumbersome, but the voluntary support from several European countries made the department's reorientation possible. More broadly, the prevention and resolution of conflicts through diplomacy had moved from something of a sideshow at the UN to a core focus of the organization. And we had chalked up some real successes, from Somalia to Nepal, that proved our approach could be effective.

As I tried to show in reviewing several of our efforts in various countries, we had successes, failures, and partial successes in dealing with some of the world's most intractable conflicts. Sometimes the UN could be the major factor in helping a country change course to a sustainable path of peace and development; more often we would contribute to a process that held out hope, but no guarantees, for a better future. Sometimes initial democratic successes succumbed to the temptations of elected leaders to prolong their power (and access to funds) creating new crises. We understood that regardless of the outside world's intentions, it is impossible to change a country's political culture overnight. There was a lot of truth in von Schulenburg's comment that we were trying to carry out in five years or less societal changes that normally took a generation or two. Some of the efforts were bound to be superficial, and we would probably have to continue to be involved to sustain the reforms.

And, of course, the world had not fundamentally changed. Local kleptocrats, ethnic feuds, poverty, and power grabs had not gone away. Nor had the various interests of global and regional powers as they sought to order the world to their own ends. When the major powers felt their interests threatened or regional organizations were determined to solve their own problems with no UN involvement, there was little DPA could do to help. For the first few years of my time in New York, DPA had considerable room to maneuver on conflicts where there was a general interest in avoiding or ending wars. The decline in cooperation among the Security Council's permanent members after the events of the Arab Spring, however, began to seriously restrict the space for our actions. A promising beginning in Libya was overwhelmed by the international community's indifference to the chaotic security situation post-Qadhafi, Yemen descended into civil war, and the Annan effort on Syria was stillborn.

Political agreements can go only so far in resolving conflicts. At times they must be backed by military force to be effective. Sometimes peacekeeping may be sufficient, but in cases like Somalia or Libya, much more is needed. When the international community unites to provide the military muscle, the situation can be transformed. But Libya demonstrated that no matter how comprehensive the planning and execution of a UN political solution may be, if the international community has no interest in getting the security situation under control (or makes it worse by arming competing factions), the effort will fail.

The UN can play a critical role in resolving conflicts when there is at least tacit support in the Security Council. It has credibility where others may be suspected of having an ulterior motive behind their efforts at mediation, and it has the tools that can be effective. Even if the best that can be accomplished in some situations is a flawed agreement or a band-aid that covers over a serious conflict, such outcomes can save thousands of lives and the ravages of a civil war. It is also possible the UN's role will become more critical as global tensions among the great powers continue to rise, and their maneuvering in weaker countries leads to more local conflict. Finally, it is important to remember that UN tools are products of the liberal world order—democracy, elections, human rights, and so on. If China and Russia, along with the usual crowd of autocrats, manage to change the global order that underpins these concepts, the UN's prestige and moral authority will be seriously undermined and thus its effectiveness destroyed.

22
Some Closing Thoughts

When I walked down a Bangkok street in 1967 to begin work on my first day at the American Embassy, I was fairly bursting with pride at the opportunity to serve the American people and the country that I loved. To be a U.S. Foreign Service Officer was a rare privilege for a kid from a small town in Missouri, and the sense of excitement remained with me throughout the next forty-five years. (I often thought of that old saw "If you do something you love, you'll never work a day in your life.") To be among the enormously talented and dedicated people in the Foreign Service was a rewarding experience. To serve in some of the world's most critical posts and deal with foreign diplomats seeking to uphold their own countries' interests kept it always challenging. And to share it all with my wonderful wife Diane and our family made for an extraordinarily satisfying life. Although there were difficult days dealing with people pursuing interests directly opposite to your own, diplomacy is all about meeting such challenges and advancing your own country's interests.

During my four and a half decades dealing with international issues, some of which I've tried to describe in this book, the United States has been in a unique position created by its economic prowess, its victory in World War II, its creative energy, its commitment to building a more prosperous and just world, and the foresight of some excellent leaders well advised by able assistants. Some of the results—peace in Europe, the transformation of Asia, and American prosperity—were truly monumental accomplishments of the postwar era that we now tend to take for granted. The generosity of the American people and their willingness to share with the world have also played an important part. I witnessed this firsthand with the outpouring of U.S. assistance for the people of Aceh, a part of the world about as far away as you can get from mid-America.

But our country cannot rest on past accomplishments or be tempted to withdraw from world leadership. Huge challenges lie ahead—the Chinese economic and military surge; climate change; the increased belligerency of a declining Russia; turmoil in parts of Africa; and authoritarian efforts to overturn the liberal world order that the U.S. has fostered, including through the United Nations and its agencies. Inevitably, the rising global prosperity we have promoted over past decades has caused the relative weight of the United States to decline. But with its open system, its attraction of global talent, its entrepreneurial spirit, its natural resources, and its relative though challenged political cohesion, there can be no doubt that the U.S. will have the ability to play a leading role in the world in the future. If the reports are true that the Chinese leadership concluded a decade or so ago that the U.S. was in terminal decline, then they can be added to the long line of people who have been wrong about our country. We are here to stay and will continue to prosper. That being said, however, it is obvious that we must stay involved and seriously improve our game in the years ahead. We must be clear-headed about the challenges and develop effective strategies to deal with them.

China

China will head our list of difficult foreign policy problems in the years ahead. Its rise as a major power was inevitable, given its size, the ingenuity and entrepreneurial capabilities of its people, and its adoption of the export model pursued successfully by Japan and the Asian tigers that flourished in the open trading system created by the United States. That it did not rise to its current level two or three decades earlier was solely due to Mao's costly and often brutal mismanagement of China.

While its economic progress has truly set a new world standard, China has struggled to accompany successes at home with a viable foreign policy. Its arrogant approach to its neighbors, provocative acts toward its main benefactor, the United States, tying its future to a declining and flailing Russia, and mishandling its major program for global influence—the Belt and Road initiative—have been serious missteps. It is striking how China's global image has declined at the same time that its power has grown. Increased internal pressure on the regime is inevitable, given the exhaustion of cheap labor; a declining and aging population; tightening control over its most productive entrepreneurs; increasing party management of the economy; mishandling the Covid crisis; and a state surveillance system reminiscent of the fifties and sixties that risks alienating youth who grew up in its prosperous, modern cities. The temptation for the Chinese leadership will be to hide their failures behind strident appeals to Chinese nationalism and antiforeign instincts directed primarily against the United States.

The regime obviously feels insecure about its ability to stay in power, despite its unprecedented security apparatus. The steps it has taken to bring to heel Xinjiang, where there is no chance of succession from China, and the destruction of Hong Kong's autonomy, which was a key part of its value to Beijing, demonstrate the level of paranoia of the regime's leaders. Given the history of rebellions against the Chinese state led by frustrated youth, the paranoia may be well deserved.

Solutions to the world's most pressing problems will depend on the ability of the U.S. and China, as the world's two largest economies, to work together in many areas. Climate change; global poverty; flare-ups in the world's trouble spots; air, water, and space pollution; world trade rules; global health dangers; and strategic rules of the road to avoid a nuclear confrontation. Neither we nor the Chinese can manage these issues on our own, and the world will demand that we use our combined talents to resolve them.

The United States will have to deal intelligently with this proud and powerful but seriously flawed country in the years ahead. Our policies across the board must be geared to U.S. interests, not emotions. They will need to be closely tied to our friends and allies in Asia, none of whom have any interest in returning to their historical status as vassal states of China. We also need to avoid dumb mistakes like the abandonment of the Trans-Pacific Partnership, which was designed to strengthen the ability of countries on China's periphery to ward off Chinese pressures.

We also need to make absolutely clear to the Chinese which actions it may be contemplating to enhance its regional and global position are acceptable and which are decidedly not. In many instances we will need to counter Beijing's natural instincts to bully its neighbors. Inevitably, the question of war and peace between China and the U.S. will depend in the first instance on the two sides' management of the Taiwan issue. The island's status initially as an alternate Chinese government and then as a prospering Chinese democracy under a U.S. protective shield has been a thorn in the Communist regime's side for its entire existence. The regime has also used the Taiwan issue to fan the flames of Chinese nationalism in order to shore up its internal support. In the process, Beijing's continuing threats to take the island by force, its repressive approach on the mainland, and its stifling of Hong Kong have left almost no one in Taiwan interested in becoming a part of China.

During the past 125 years, Taiwan has been under mainland control for only four extremely unpleasant years, between the end of World War II and the Communist takeover. Taiwan has been able to develop a vibrant economy and democracy, free of China's police state mentality, even as China's global reach has kept Taiwan from achieving an internationally recognized political status commensurate with its strengths at home.

Beijing's constant military pressures on Taiwan, including the 2022 replay of the 1996 missile firings, have made the island a critical test of U.S. resolve to protect China's neighbors from Beijing's bullying. If the Chinese managed to take the island either through U.S. indifference or defeat of our military efforts to support Taiwan, it would destroy the U.S. strategic position in East Asia. President Biden has been right to go beyond the usual vagueness that has been part of the dialogue ever since Kissinger's discussions with Chou En-lai, and leave no doubt in Beijing that we would fight to defend Taiwan. Given Chinese threats and capabilities, ambiguity is no longer an option.

The Russian Example

Russia's invasion of Ukraine provides a clear example of the dangers involved in sending weak or mixed signals on critical global issues. Putin's determination to revive the Russian Empire has been evident since he took power at the end of 1999. His invasion of Ukraine and the huge loss of lives is a direct result of failed U.S. and European statecraft. The stage was set by the NATO decision in March 2008 not to grant Ukraine and Georgia status that would have put them on the path to NATO membership. Putin won that debate by pressuring the Europeans.

He then moved immediately to increase the heat on the Georgians, who were arguably the better candidate for NATO admission. Putin hated Saakashvili, who was all in on moving Georgia into Europe. As the Russian pressure grew on Georgia, the U.S. and Europe did little more than warn Saakashvili not to provoke the Russian bear. Then when the Georgians reacted to a Russian provocation in South Ossetia on August 7, Russian forces—which had been poised for action on the border—immediately invaded Georgia and overwhelmed the Georgian defenders.

The European and American reaction must have convinced Putin of the brilliance of his strategy. The French negotiated a weak withdrawal agreement, the U.S. decided to limit its reaction to replenishing Georgia's military supplies. Foreign policy figures in both places consoled themselves by saying it was really Saakashvili's fault. Putin had achieved all his objectives. Georgia's entry into NATO and the EU were off the table.

In February and March 2014, following the popular Medan uprising against its pro-Russian leader, Putin moved troops into the Crimean Peninsula and annexed it as part of Russia. Again, the Western reaction was incredibly mild. After some public condemnation, they consoled themselves by saying that the peninsula was "really Russian, not Ukrainian." Amazingly, the Germans kept building the Nord Stream 2 pipeline, which would cut Ukraine out of the flow of gas from Russia while making the German economy even more vulnerable to Russian manipulation.

Looking back, it is appalling how Western leaders chose to look the other way as Putin went about implementing a policy that he had long espoused. Hopefully the shock of the Putin invasion of Ukraine and NATO's response will bring gutsier policies in the future to deal with a vengeful Russian leadership of a country in decline. Putin cannot be allowed to win again.

Better U.S. Ambassadors

As we try to avoid ineffective policies in the coming decades, it is important that we strengthen our tools. Some people, who honestly don't know what they are talking about, have written about the decline of the role of ambassadors in this new age of instant communications. In fact, it is critical that the people who represent the United States abroad not only understand what is going on in the countries or organizations they are accredited to, but they must have a keen awareness of U.S. interests, make recommendations to Washington, or carry out effective policy measures while keeping Washington informed, marshal U.S. capabilities to promote our goals, and explain American approaches to the leaders and public of the country to which they are assigned. A good ambassador doesn't spend time focused on the next dinner party. Rather, he or she actively works to shape our policy to meet the end we seek; and developing a coherent U.S. position is often much easier at the embassy than in Washington. Appointing ambassadors under our "spoils system" primarily because they were major contributors to the president's campaign is a self-inflicted wound. The president has the right to appoint ambassadors, but to reward campaign contributions is little more than selling public offices that can be quite costly to long-term U.S. interests.

The U.S. Needs an Effective UN Strategy

Another important improvement needed to meet future challenges would be to make better use of the international organizations that we worked to create. I was struck during my time at the United Nations by the defensive, ad hoc, and often purely negative approach in Washington toward the organization. Polls consistently show solid popular support for the UN among Americans, not surprising for an organization essentially created by the United States after World War II on principles near and dear to the hearts of U.S. citizens—global peace and security, human rights, and (later) economic development for the world's poorest people. The UN's strong backing for democracy, human rights, women's equality, and protection of the most vulnerable (children, refugees, and others) supports cherished American values.

But the tendency in Washington is not to praise the UN for its accomplishments but rather to ignore it, criticize the organization as anti-Israel, or decry it as a waste of money. The more jaundiced view derives from the regular failure of the Security Council to act during the Cold War (which unfortunately may again become the norm), demagogic congressional attacks in the nineties against the UN disguised as an attempt to save money, UN resolutions and speeches that often unfairly single out Israel, and occasional efforts by UN members to restrain U.S. actions on the international scene.

As I observed U.S. actions from inside the United Nations, I was surprised by how reactive and unfocused the U.S. approach appeared to be. The Americans have enormous soft power at the UN that complements its recognized great power status. It contributes about $11 billion a year (two-thirds of it voluntary) to support vital UN programs; and a large portion of UN employees are sympathetic to the U.S. as they go about their daily lives in New York. The Bush administration had a particularly negative view of the UN after it failed to gain Security Council support for the invasion of Iraq. Its disdain was demonstrated by appointing as the U.S. permanent representative an ambassador, John Bolton, who seldom passed up a chance to bash the organization to which he was assigned. The bullying mostly succeeded in undermining the support for American goals and increasing the skepticism of the UN staff and members of other missions toward U.S. proposals. Fortunately, by the time Ban Ki-moon became secretary-general on January 1, 2007, Secretary of State Rice had decided to reverse these policies and to work with Ban on reform.

Despite this change in approach, as the newly minted under-secretary-general for political affairs, I soon realized how little thinking the State Department had done on what it wanted out of the Ban era at the UN. There had been almost no thought about what I was supposed to do now that they had managed to have me appointed to head the Political Department. The advice I received in Washington before going to New York seemed to be, "Try to help Ban make the UN work better." I was pleased that no one in Washington felt they could tell me what to do in my new role, but it was obvious that Washington had no real plans. And the unwillingness to back up their words of praise for DPA with even modest amounts of money was shocking.

My assumption that things would change with the Obama administration proved wrong. During both administrations, my staff and I worked closely with the regional bureaus and the top leadership of the State Department to try to resolve conflicts around the world. But there was no evidence of a serious effort in Washington to develop a policy that set priorities and strategies toward the UN as a whole. A decade after I left the UN, the American Academy of Diplomacy (AAD) released a study arguing that the weaknesses of the State Department's approach to multilateral diplomacy were not limited to the United Nations but applied to almost all of its multilateral organizations.

[Bringing America's Multilateral Diplomacy into the 21st Century, *American Academy of Diplomacy, February 2022. (Full disclosure: I was a member of the study's Advisory Group.)*]

Representing the leading world power since World War II, the State Department had concentrated its resources on bilateral diplomacy, with little attention to the tools it had itself created to sustain a liberal global order.

The International Organizations Bureau (IO) has traditionally been one of the State Department's weaker units, with policy mostly driven by regional bureaus or other government agencies. In the case of strengthening DPA, IO and USUN apparently did not bother to ascertain the views of State's top leadership that supported our efforts, nor did USUN think it useful to fund our efforts or back the horizon-scanning sessions to explore ways to get more help from the Security Council to resolve conflicts. I strongly doubt there was ever a policy paper that essentially said, "We have secured the Political Under-Secretary-Generalship for the U.S. and here's our plan to capitalize on it." If there was such a paper, we never saw any indication that anyone tried to implement it. This sort of strategy lapse would have been virtually unthinkable in a State Department regional bureau.

The Academy of Diplomacy study emphasized the need to integrate the IO bureau more closely into policy discussions and to ensure a much broader range of the department's Foreign Service and Civil Service members to serve in multilateral organizations during their careers. My scant knowledge of the UN before I was put in charge of one of its major departments should stand as exhibit A of the department's regional specialists' lack of understanding of how multilateral organizations function. After all, I spent most of my Foreign Service career dealing with two of the Security Council's Permanent Members.

During my time at the United Nations, I came to have a much greater appreciation for the UN's worth in promoting critical values for a better world, providing humanitarian assistance on a truly massive scale, dispensing advice for political and economic improvements, and helping resolve conflicts through both diplomacy and peacekeeping. Like any large organization with almost two hundred bosses, it can be quirky, painfully bureaucratic, and occasionally in pursuit of contradictory goals. But it deserves more recognition and support than it gets from the United States. And the U.S. needs to greatly improve its game at the UN and other multilateral organizations to meet the growing global challenges from our adversaries.

Index

Abbasid Caliphate, 291
Abiy Ahmad, 413
abortion, 191–93
Abrams, Elliott, 144–45
Abu Bakar Ba'aysir, 343, 348
Abu Sayyaf Groups (ASG), 344
Abzug, Bella, 50
Aceh, Indonesia, 3, 319–41, 353, 365–67
Acheson, Dean, 69
Afghanistan, 19, 86–88, 129, 141, 166, 275–76, 273–76, 279, 282, 284–87, 289–90, 304, 318, 348, 375
African Union, 414–15, 416, 492, 493
Agency for the Rehabilitation and Reconstruction of Aceh (BRR), 337–41
Agnew, Spiro, 34, 46
AIT (American Institute on Taiwan), 30, 81, 195–197, 201–41, 245
Akayev, Askar, 281–84
Akinci, Mustafa, 445
Akombe, Roselyn, 386, 414
AKP (Peace and Justice Party), 305
Albright, Madeleine, 255, 257, 259
Aliyev, Heydar, 247–52, 304
Al-Khatib, Abdelilah, 493, 495
Allen, Richard, 87
Alliance for the Reliberation of Somalia (ARS), 393, 397
Al-Qaeda, 266, 272–76, 290, 318, 344, 393, 401
American Academy of Diplomacy (AAD), 514–15

American Foreign Corrupt Practices Act (FCPA), 211–12
American Legation, 39, 40
Ames, Aldrich, 119–20
AMISOM (African military force), 391, 393–94, 396–402, 406
Amos, Valerie, 450
amulets, 23
Amur River, 26–27
Anastasiades, Nicos, 443
Anderson, Don, 36, 41, 73, 80
Andropov, Yuri, 91, 95, 101, 103, 108, 127
An Lushan Rebellion, 291
Annan, Kofi, 297, 315, 379, 414–15, 502
Annan Plan (Cyprus), 315–16, 436–37, 439–40, 166
Annan Plan (Syria), 503
Anti–Lin Piao, Anti-Confucius movement (Pi-lin, Pi-kong), 34, 40, 46, 48, 62
Anwar Ibrahim, 255, 257–62, 267, 269
APEC summits, 177, 217, 257, 259
Arab League, 420, 489, 490, 491, 494, 502, 503
Arab Spring, 486–506
Argentina, 67
Armenia, 245–52, 271, 293, 295, 301–3, 311–12
arms control, 66, 95–96, 98, 102, 108, 129, 132, 134, 138, 142. *See also* Geneva Summit (1985); Reykjavik Summit (1986); SALT II agreement;

Strategic Defense Initiative (SDI; "Star Wars"); Washington Summit (1987)
ASEAN, 230, 255, 341, 420, 421
Asia Foundation, 203, 352
Asian Games, 172, 217
Assad, Bashar al-, 481, 503
avian influenza, 354–58
Aweys, Hassan Dahir, 401
Azerbaijan, 245–52, 302, 303–5, 311–12

Badawi, Abdullah, 260, 270
Bahrain, 486
Baker, James, 134, 173–74, 177–78, 195, 294, 296
Bakiyev, Kurmanbek, 283–84, 433–34
Bali, 318, 343
Bangkok, Thailand: Pascoe assigned as DCM, 187; Pascoe as junior diplomat in, 15–23, 507. *See also* Thailand
Ban Ki-moon, 194, *368, 369*; appointment of, 436; Gaza conflict and, 481; Kenyan violence and, 414–15; as leader of regional cooperation events, 420–21, 423; on Libya conflict, 491; Pascoe's appointment and, 373–374; Somalia conflict and, 6, 393, 408; Sri Lankan civil war and, 467, 468; UN vision by, 374–78, 404, 504
Barnett, Doak, 12, 52
Battle of Talas, 291
Beijing (Peking), China: Pascoe's work as USLO officer in, 5, 36–63; Tiananmen Square massacre, 152–60. *See also* China

Bell, Griffin, 109
Belt and Road Initiative, 291, 509
Ben Ali, Zine El Abidine , 486–88
Benghazi, Libya, 493, 494, 497
Bentsen, Lloyd, 79, 380
Berezhkov, Andy (Andrei), 98
Berry, Paul, 239
Birabhsongse Kasemsri, 18
Black Hawk Down (film), 5
Black Hawk Down incident, 5, 392–93
Blackman, Robert, 326–27
Blair, Tony, 480
Bolton, John, 373, 387, 513
Borich, Joe, 196
Bosnia, 241
Bost, Delphine, 388
Boundary Commission (Eritrea–Ethiopia), 410
Boxer Rebellion (China; 1900), 39
Bo Yang, 203
Brazil, 494–95, 499–500
Brezhnev, Leonid, 88–89, 91, 93, 95, 304
BRICS group, 499–500
bridge (game), 161–62
bridge project, 286
Brimob (Mobile Brigade), 346
Brooks, Stan, 221
Brown, Ron, 219, 226, 247
Bruce, David K. E., 38–40
Bruce, Evangeline, 38, 40
Brzezinski, Zbigniew, 12, 70–74, 77
Bulgaria, 168, 300
Bunche, Ralph, 374, 479
Burjanadze, Nino, 297, 299–300
Burkina Faso, 416, 419
Burns, Nicholas, 373, 387
Burt, Rick, 100
Burton, Bob, 11–12
Bush, Barbara, 45–46, 80, *361*
Bush, George H. W., 45–46, 56, 80,

150–51, 169, 177, 188, 220, 332, *362, 366*
Bush, Jeb, 328
Bush administration (G. H. W.): China policies of, 150–51, 173; on MFN status of China, 173, 175, 181, 191
Bush administration (G. W.): Central Asia policies of, 272–76; Mid-East peace process, 480; Indonesian tsunami aid by, 322–34; Iraq policy of, 306–11, 473, 478; Mahathir on, 269; Turkey policy of, 305–9; on UN, 513; relations with Putin, 289–90

Camara, Mousa Dadis, 417–20
Cambodia, 17, 20–21, 27, 166, 176
Camdessus, Michel, 337
Camp David Accords, 70
cancer research, 12, 14
Carlucci, Frank, 137–38
Carter, Jimmy, 175, 454
Carter administration: conventional arms policy of, 69–70; Deng's visit and, 74–81; espionage and, 109; on human rights, 66–68; Korea policy of, 69; Soviet policies of, 86
Casey, William, 87, 102, 131–32, 143–44
Cassidy & Associates, 224–25, 227
Castresana, Carlos, 469–71
CDC (Centers for Disease Control), 355
Ceaușescu, Nicolae, 167
Centre for Humanitarian Dialogue, 414, 421
Chai Tze-min, 82
Chang Chun-chiao (Zhang Chunqiao), 34

Chambas, Mohammed, 417
Chancellor, John 58
Chechnya, 296
Cheney, Dick, 290, 309
Chen Pao (Zhen Bao)/Damansky Island, 26
Chernenko, Konstantin, 127
Chernobyl, Ukraine, 302
Chiang Ching (Jiang Qing), 5, 25, 34, 53, 57, 59
Chiang Ching-kuo, 34, 203
Chiang Kai-shek, 14, 57, 201
Chiang Mai, Thailand, 22–23
Chien, Fred, 214, 224, 226, 239, 241
childhood of author, 9–11
child mortality rate, 425
China: a cultural catastrophe, 52–54; American delegations in, 50–52; economic conditions and policies in, 41–43, 149–50, 157–58, 179–85; Deng Xiaoping's visit to U.S., 74–81; earthquakes in, 57, 60, 63; Great Wall, 44, 73, 150, *360*; human rights report & "The Power of Truth" (Lewis), 170–71; MFN status of, 173, 175, 181, 217–18; normalization of relations with the U.S., 71–74; political turmoil in, 5, 34–36, 40–41, 44–45, 59–63; –Soviet relations, 89–90, 178–79; Taiwan arms sales, 188–90; tensions over Taiwan, 204–05, 214–17, 226–36; Tiananmen Square massacre and its aftermath, 149–62; U.S. Marines in, 39; Vietnam invasion by, 83. *See also* Beijing, China; Hong Kong; Taiwan

Chinese Archaeology Exhibition, 53–54
Chinese language: Pascoe's education in, 11, 13, 33; Pinyin system, 74
Chinoy, Mike, 326
Chou En-lai (Zhou Enlai), 5, 25, 27–28, 34–35, 41, 49, 57, 60–61, 510
Christofias, Demetris, 315, 436–44
Christopher, Warren, 66–68, 70, 73, 82, 198, 218, 229–30, 234, 240
Chungking Mansions, Hong Kong, 15–16
Churkin, Vitaly, 431–32, 499
CIA (Central Intelligence Agency), 13, 26, 29–30, 46, 56, 108–10, 115–21, 123, 125, 132, 143–44, 151–52, 267
CICIG (International Commission Against Impunity in Guatemala), 469–71
Clark, Helen, 423
Clark, William Jr. (State Department) 187, 190–91
Clark, William P. Jr. (NSC), 97, 102, 132, 143
Clerides, Glafcos, 314–15
Cline, Ray, 26, 30
Clinton, Bill, 332, *366*
Clinton, Hillary, *369*
Clinton administration: China policies of, 217–20; Malaysia policies of, 259–61; Taiwan and, 206, 231–35; Wood and election funding, 236–41
cloud seeding, 55, 86–87
Clubb, Edmond, 12
Colbert, Evelyn, 26
Colom, Alvaro, 469–71
Colombia, 499–500
Columbia University, 11–12

communism: collapse of, in Europe, 166–68; in Latin America, 143–45, 198. See also *names of specific countries and parties*
Communist Party Congress (China), 34, 49, 53, 180–81
Communist Party of Cyprus (AKEL), 314
Compaoré, Blaise, 419–20
Condé, Alpha, 419
Congress Party (Nepal; GP Koirala), 451, 455–58
conspiracy theories, 104–5, 254
Conté, Lansana, 416–17
Conventional Arms Talks (CAT), 69–70
CORDS (civilian advisory program, Vietnam), 15
Costa Rica, 223, 471
counterterrorism, 267–68, 343–54. *See also* terrorism
Crosher, Ken, 113–14
Crowder, Doug, 324–25, 330
Cultural Revolution (China), 5, 25, 34, 40, 41, 49, 52, 59. *See also* Mao Zedong
Cyprus, 271, 305, 313–16, 436–45
Czechoslovakia, 66, 167

Dall'Anese, Francisco, 471
Daniloff, Nick, 122–23, 134
Darusman, Marzuki, 466–67
Davitoglu, Ahmet, 306
Dean, David, 196, 236
Defense Intelligence Agency (DIA), 29, 188–89
De Mistura, Staffan, 475–76
Democratic People's Party (DPP), 203, 205, 207, 222, 325
Deng Xiaoping (Teng Hsiao-ping), *363*; as leader, 5, 34, 41,

71–72, 190–91; economic policies of, 149–50, 157–58, 179–81; meeting with U.S. congresswomen, 50–51, 61; Soviet policies of, 166–67; U.S. visit of, 74–81
Deng Yingchao, 158
Denktash, Rauf, 314–16
Derian, Patricia "Patt," 67
Dewey, John, 35
Diabacte, Ali, 419–20
Diallo, Cellou Dalain, 419
Diaoyu/Senkaku islands, 55–56, 177
disaster relief, 3–4, 319–41, 353–4, 366, 367
Djerejian, Ed, 88
Djibouti Agreement, 397–98
Djinnit, Said, 417–20
Dobrynin, Anatoly, 95–97
Dolan, Tony, 141
Doonesbury cartoon, 58–59
Downer, Alexander, 437, 439–40, 442–44
DPA (Department of Political Affairs, UN), 373–90, 399–400, 415–16, 479, 504–6. *See also* United Nations (UN)
DPKO (Department of Peacekeeping Operations, UN), 395, 399–401. *See also* United Nations (UN)

Eagleburger, Lawrence, 100, 110, 164–5, 177, 195
earthquakes: in Armenia, 302; in China, 57, 60, 63; in East Timor, 331; in Indonesia, 319, 331, 353–54, 367; in Nepal, 459
East Asian and Pacific Affairs Bureau (EAP), 30–31, 191, 193, 206, 225, 227

East Timor, 193, 317–18, 323, 331, 348
ECOWAS (Economic Community of West African States), 416–17, 421, 425
Egypt, 481, 486, 488–90
Eide, Espen Barth, 445
El Baradei, Mohamed, 489
El Salvador, 145, 198, 201
Entrapment (film), 266
Erdogan, Tayyip, 305–7, 309–12, 437, 439, 481, 483–86
Eritrea, 394, 398, 401, 409–13
Eritrean People's Liberation Front, 409
Eroglu, Dervis, 440–43, 445
espionage, 108–25
Ethiopia, 67, 73, 394, 409–13
European Union and Turkey, 310–11

Fall, Ibrahima, 417
famine, 398, 405–07. *See also* hunger and malnutrition
Fang Lizhi, 150–51, 156–57, 165, 170, 173
Fargo, Thomas, 322–23, 328–29
Fatah al-Sisi, Abdul, 490
FBI (Federal Bureau of Investigation), 109–10, 115, 117–23
Feldman, Harvey, 75, 195–96
Feltman, Jeff, 444, 450, 504
FEMA, 328
Fenwick, Millicent, 50
Fernandez-Taranco, Oscar, 425
Finland Railways, 139
500th MI, Taiwan, 29–30
Fong, Sascha, 389
food relief, 392, 398, 407–8. *See also* hunger and malnutrition
Ford, Gerald, 34, 46, 47, 57–59, 65
Ford administration, 34, 47, 195

Foreign Corrupt Practices Act (FCPA), 211
Foreign Service Examination, 13
Foreign Service Institute (FSI), 85–86, 134
France, 246, 282, 301, 311, 378, 416, 419, 430, 441, 481, 494
Frey, Bill, 325–26, *365, 367*
Fulbright exchange program, 169–70

G-77 (Group of 77), 378, 500
GAM (Free Aceh Movement), 320, 322, 326, 341
Gambari, Ibrahim, 379
Gandhi, Rajiv, 459–60
Gang of Four, 41, 63, 71
Garrison, Mark, 88
Gaseor, Kathy, 256
Gates, Robert, 144, 356
Gates, Thomas, 62
Gaza, 478–84
Geithner, Tim, 256
Gelb, Leslie, 69, 70
General Agreement on Tariffs and Trade (GATT), 183, 202–03
Geneva Summit (1985), 127–30. *See also* arms control
Georgia, 271, 293–301, 429–33, 477, 511
Gerlach, Karina, 383
Gleysteen, William, 26
Gnehm, Edward "Skip," 253
Goldfish drug case (1988), 171
golf, 208, 213–14, 223, 227, 234, 239, 240, *364*
Golkar party, 337
Goralczyk, Zdzislaw, 168
Gorbachev, Mikhail, 4, 119, 123–24, 127–47, 178–79, 245
Gore, Al, 259–60, 269
Goulding, Marrack, 379

Grant, Mark Lyall, 500
Gray, Bob, 10–11
Great Leap Forward, 42
Great Wall of China, 44, 73, 150, *360*
Greece, 271, 313–16, 438, 445
Greek Cypriots, 313–16, 436–45. *See also* Cyprus
Greek Orthodox Church, 313
Green, Marshall, 30–31
Green Zone, 476–77
Grenada, 106–8
Griffin, Michele, 414
Gromyko, Andrei, 101–03, 107, 133
Guatemala, 469–71
Guehanno, Jean-Marie, 394–95
Guinea, 416–22
Gul, Abdullah, 305–07, 312
Gulf Cooperation Council (GCC), 493
GUNMAN project, 110–11, 117
Gus Dur (Abdurrahman Wahid), 317
Guterres, Antonio, 423, 425, 445, 478
Gyanendra (king), 451

H5N1, 354–57
Habibie, B. J., 317
Haig, Alexander, 88, 95, 131, 188–89
Halloween party, 156–57
Hamas, 480–83
Hanssen, Robert, 115, 119–20
Hartman, Arthur, 93, 110, 124
Hau Pei-tsun, 204
Heckler, Margaret 50
Hecklinger, Dick, 256
Helms, Jesse, 105, 230, 257
Hersh, Seymour, 105
Hezbollah, 351
Hill, Charles, 130–31, 144

Hills, Carla, 183, 190
Hirohito (emperor), 337
Hizbut-Tahrir, 274
Hoagland, Dick, 268
Holbrooke, Richard, 68–69, 71, 73
Holdridge, John, 41
Holmes, John, 461-2, 465, 468
Hong Kong, 5, 33–37, 40–41, 171, 177, 180, 254, 356, 510. *See also* China
Honwana, João, 414
Hoover, J. Edgar, 109
Hope (US hospital ship), 331
hospital ships, 330–31
hostage crisis (Iran), 86
Howard, Edward Lee, 118
Howe, Jon, 330
Hu Yaobang, 149–50, 52
Hua Kuo-feng, 60–63
Huang, John, 239–40
Human Development Index (UN), 425
Human Rights Council (UN), 467–68
human rights policies, 66–68, 96, 142, 151, 170, 173–175, 178, 191, 198–99, 217–18, 254, 276–81, 346–47, 418, 460-61, 464, 467–8, 475
Hungary, 90, 167, 301
hunger and malnutrition, 398, 405–07, 448, 450. *See also* food relief
Hussein, Nur "Adde" Hassan, 397
Hussein, Saddam, 276, 306, 477, 478
Hu Yaobang, 149, 150, 152
hydroelectric dam, 285

ICAO (International Civil Aviation Organization), 103, 106, 196
IDF (Israeli Defense Forces), 480–83, 483–84
Ilichev, Alexander, 448
illegal immigration, 192–93, 214, 471
IMF (International Monetary Fund), 255, 337
immigration policy, 191–93
India, 451, 456, 499–500
Indonesia: 2004 tsunami in Aceh, 3–4, 319–21, 323, 331–34, 340–41, 353, *363*; avian influenza in, 354–58; counterterrorism in, 343–51; earthquakes in, 319, 353–54, *367*; governmental response to tsunami, 322–23, 336–41; NGO efforts in, 334–36; Pascoe as ambassador in, 3–4, 317–18, 357; strengthening democracy in, 351–53; U.S. disaster assistance in, 321–34
Indonesian Red Cross, 321–22, 325
influenza outbreak, 354–57
INR (Bureau of Intelligence and Research), 25–30, 380
Intermediate-range Nuclear Forces (INF) Treaty, 138–40
Internal Security Act, 266
International Civil Aviation Organization (ICAO), 103, 106, 196
International Criminal Court (ICC), 418–19, 492
International Crisis Group, 281
International Organization on Migration, 325
International Organizations Bureau (IO), 514
Iran: –Azerbaijan relations, 305; hostage crisis, 70, 86; –U.S. relations, 68
Iran-Contra affair, 143–45

Iraq, 173–75, 177, 306–12, 473–78
Ireland, 414
Isaias Afwerki, 409–13
Islam, 258, 267–68, 317
Islamic Courts Union, 393
Islamic Movement of Uzbekistan (IMU), 274, 279
Israel: –Gaza conflict, 478–83; –Hezbollah conflict, 351; –Turkey conflict, 483–86
Ivanov, Igor, 297, 299

Japanese influence in Taiwan, 215
Jaruzelski, Wojciech, 90
Jemaah Islamiyah (JI), 266, 318, 343–44, 348
Jenca, Miroslav, 434
Jenness, Craig, 414, 416
Jiang Zemin, 158–59, 163, 178, 190, 216, 226–27, 232
Johnson administration, 13, 21–22, 313–14
Jones, Beth, 271, 314
Jordan, Vernon, 239

KAL 007 (airliner) shootdown, 99–107, 194
Kalb, Marvin 58
Kalla, Yusuf, 320–22, 336–37, 339, 341
Kampelman, Max, 97
Karimov, Islam, 277, 279–81, 285, 291
Karimova, Gulnara, 280
Kazakhstan, 288–89, 291, 304
Keays, Michael, 247
Keegan, Dave, 196
Kelly, John, 144
Kennedy, Pat, 139
Kenya, 403, 414–16
Keyser, Don, 169
KGB, 92, 110, 117–19, 122

Khalilzad, Zal, 431, 474
Khan, Yahya, 27–28
Khoman, Thanat, 21
Kibaki, Mwai, 414
Kim Il-sung, 38, 69, 194
Kim Jong Il, 194, 449
Kim Won-soo, 447–49
Kirby Simon Foreign Service Trust, 223
Kissinger, Henry: Carter and, 65, 71; China policy and, 27–28, 33, 35–36, 510; China visits of, 47–48, 49, 57–59
Klar, Dick, 241
KMT (Kuomintang), 203, 207, 216, 224, 232, 239
Kocharian, Robert, 250–52, 302
Koirala, GP, 451, 455–58
Konaté, Sekouba, 418–19
Konyaté, Lansana, 416–17
Koppel, Ted, 58
Korea, 69, 193–94, 447–50
Korniyenko, Georgy, 91, 101
Koroma, Ernest Bai, 425, 427
Kuala Lumpur, Malaysia, 255, 260, 264–65. *See also* Malaysia
Kubis, Jan, 434
Kufuor, John, 41415
Kuntoro Mangkusubroto, 338–39
Kurdistan, 306
Kurds, 306, 308–10
Kuwait, 173, 175
Kyrgyzstan, 274, 275, 281–84, 291, 421, 433–35

La Grange, Missouri, 9–10
Lake, Joseph, 194–95
Lake, Tony, 236, 410
Landgren, Karin, 457
language training: Chinese, 11, 13–14, 33; Russian, 85; Thai, 16, 187

Laos, 17, 23, 31, 152
Latin America, 131, 143, 192. See also *names of specific countries*
League of Arab States. *See* Arab League
Leahy, Patrick, 121, 299, 349
Lebanon, 143, 351, 481
Le Carré, John, 116
Lee Kuan Yew, 254
Lee Teng-hui, 203–05, 214–17, 223–36, *364*
LeRoy, Alain, 399
Liberation Tigers of Tamil Eelam (LTTE), 459–69
Libya, 486, 490–501, 505–6
Lieberman, Avigdor, 484–85
Lilley, James, 36, 40, 151–53, 155, 157, 173–76
Lin Piao (Lin Biao), Marshall, 34, 40, 46, 48, 62
Li Peng, 150, 157–58, 163–64, 172–73, 178–79, 219, 232
Li Shuxian, 156
Liu Shao-chi (Liu Shaoqi), 41–42
Liu Huaqiu, 163–64, 169, 173
Liu Tai-ying, 224, 227, 239
Lonetree, Sergeant Clayton, 124, 137
Lord, Winston, 191, 197, 206, 217, 224, 228, 237, 242
Lozinsky, Vladimir, 251

Madame Chiang Kai-shek, 203
Maertens, Tom, 105
Mahathir bin Mohamad, 253–60, 262, 266, 269–70
Mahiga, Augustine, 404, 406
Makarios III, 313–14
Malacca Strait, 261, 268–69, 324, 341, 407
Malaysia: Pascoe as U.S. ambassador in, 253, 256–57, 260–70; political and economic conditions in, 253–56, 257–60, 264–66
Malcorra, Susana, 399–400, 426
Malott, John, 257
Manas Air Base, 275, 282–84, 433
Mann, Steve, 107
Mao Yuan-hsin, 51
Mao Zedong, 25, 508; economic conditions and, 41–42; illness and death of, 5, 35, 45, 57, 63; on U.S. incursion in Cambodia, 27. *See also* Cultural Revolution (China)
Mark Twain, 9, 51
Martin, Graham, 21–22
Martin, Ian, 451–52, 482, 496, 498–99
Matlock, Jack, 88, 91–92, 96
Mavi Marmara (ship), 484
McCain, John, 299
McCall, Sherrod, 35, 87–88
McDonald, Larry, 99, 105
McDonald's, 184
McFarlane, Robert "Bud," 132
MacLaine, Shirley, 52
Medvedev, Dmitry, 252, 431, 494–95
Meese, Edwin, 132, 192
Megawati Sukarnoputri, 317–19, 349
MEK (Mujahedeen-e-Khalq), 477–78
Meles Zenawi, 409–13
Menkerios, Haile, 411, 418
Meredov, Rashid, 287
MFN (Most Favored Nation) status of China, 173, 175, 182, 191, 217–19
Milam, Bill, 257
Miles, Richard, 296–97

Milton & Matilda (musk oxen), 56–57
Mink, Patsy 50
Minsk Group, 245–52
Mobil (company), 289
Mogadishu, Somalia, 391–94, 398, 401–06
Mohamed Abdullah Mohamed (Farmaajo), 404–5
Mondale, Walter, 69
Mongolia, 177, 194–95
Moose, Dick, 237
Morocco, 416, 418
Moro Islamic Liberation Front (MILF), 344
Morsi, Muhammed, 489
Moscow, Russia: 1980 Olympics in, 86; Pascoe's work in, 86–93. *See also* Russia
The Most Wanted Man in China (Fang), 156
Moussa, Amr, 489
Mt. Alto, 114–15
Mt. Merapi, 353
Mubarak, Hosni, 481, 483, 488–89
Muhammadiyah, 352
Mulet, Edmond, 431
Munir Said Thalib, 347
musk oxen, 56–57
Muslim Brotherhood, 489

Nagorno-Karabakh 245–52, 302, 304
Nahdlatul Ulama (NU), 352
NAM (Non-Aligned Movement), 378
Nambiar, Vijay, *368, 369*, 462–63
NAMRU (Naval Medical Research Unit), 324, 353, 354–57
National Defense Education Act (NDEA), 11
National Development Planning Agency, 337

Nationalist Party (Taiwan). *See* KMT (Kuomintang)
National Security Agency (NSA), 13, 110–11, 113, 115,118, 137–38
National Security Study Memoranda (NSSMs), 29–30
National Transition Council (NTC; Libya), 495–98
National War College, 94
NATO (North American Treaty Organization): desired membership in, 300–301, 430, 511; Georgia–Russia conflict and, 429–33; Libya campaign of, 495; Partnership for Peace, 273; at regional cooperation events, 420–21; –Russian relations, 289, 494; Somalian piracy and, 406; Turkey and, 306–7
Naval Medical Research Unit (NAMRU), 324, 353–54; avian influenza, 354–57
Nazarbayev, Nursultan, 288–89
Nepal, 450–505
Netanyahu, Benjamin, 482–83, 485–86
NGO disaster relief, 334–36
Nigeria, 500
9/11/2001 attacks (U.S.), 266–67, 271–72
9/11 Commission Report, 266, 267
Nine Dash Line, 56
Nitze, Paul 137
Nixon, Richard, 21, 35, 47, 61, 163–64
Nixon administration: appointees of, 46; China policy of, 26–28, 33, 154; Cyprus and, 314; NSSMs of, 29; Watergate crisis and, 34

Niyazov, Saparmurat, 286–88
N-K region. *See* Nagorno-Karabakh region, Armenia–Azerbaijan
Nobel Peace Prize, 413, 479
Nord Stream 2 pipeline, 511
North Korea (DPRK), 38, 69, 176–77, 194, 219, 243, 447–50
nuclear power, 211, 302
nuclear weapons, 4, 93, 95, 108, 129, 135–36, 194, 219, 447–50, 509

OAS (Organization of American States), 420–21
Obama, Barack, *369*
Obama administration and Libya, 493–94, 497–98
Odinga, Raila, 414
Office of Foreign Missions (OFM), 111–12
oil and gas industry: of Azerbaijan, 303–04; in China, 56; of Iraq, 308, 310, 379, 473; of Kazakhstan, 288–89, 304; of Libya, 490; of Malaysia, 254, of Russia, 511; in Somalia, 403; in South Caucasus/Central Asia, 273; in Turkmenistan, 286–88
Okinawa, 14, 55–56, 253
Oksenberg, Mike, 73, 163
Olmert, Ehud, 480–81, 483
"one child" policy and U.S. asylum, 192–93
Orange Revolution, 300–01
Organization of African Unity, 411
Organization of the Islamic Conference (OIC), 492–493
OSCE (Organization for Security and Co-operation in Europe), 246–47, 249–50, 298, 420–21, 432, 434

Ottoman Empire, 293, 301
Otunbayeva, Rosa, 434
Ould Abdallah, Ahmedou, 395–97, 402–5, 408–9, 421
Oxfam, 335

Pakistan, 27–28, 45, 168, 175, 257, 285, 392, 451
Palestinian–Israeli conflict. *See* Gaza
Palmer, Mark, 128
Panama Canal Treaty, 66, 70
pandas, 56
Papadopoulos, Tassos, 315, 436, 440
Paracel Islands, 56, 83
Park Chung-hee, 69
Parris, Mark, 128, 137
Partnership for Peace (NATO), 273
Pascoe, B. Lynn: as AIT director, 201–41; as ambassador in Indonesia, 3–4, 319–41, 345; as ambassador in Malaysia, 253, 260–70; in Carter's State Department, 65–83; China policy paper by, 242–43; as EAP staff assistant, 30–31; as EAP officer on East Asia, 187–97; early childhood of, 9–11; education of, 11–14, 94; as EUR deputy officer, 271, 272–78, 295, 301–16; Georgia work of, 293–301; Guinea work of, 416–21; as Hong Kong political officer, 33–36; as INR officer on China, 25–30; as junior diplomatic officer in Bangkok, 15–23, 507; language training of, 11, 13, 33, 85, 187, 257; as Moscow officer, 4, 86–147; as Peking USLO

officer, 36–63; pictures of, 360–69; security measures for, 345, 392; at Senior Seminar, 146; UN work of, 373–90
Pascoe, Diane, 161, 360, 362
PAS party, 258
peacebuilding, defined, 423
Peacebuilding Commission (UN), 424
Peacebuilding Support Office (PBSO) 424–25
Peace Corps, 169–70, 287, 302, 351
Pei, I. M., 78, 168
Peking. See Beijing, China
Pelton, Ronald, 118–19
Peña, Federico, 227
Pentagon, attacks and evacuation (2001), 267, 271–72
People's Republic of China (PRC). See China
Perle, Richard, 87, 137
Perot, Ross, 218
Peshmerga, 308
Petrovsky, Vladimir, 379
Philadelphia Orchestra, 34–35, 53
Philippines, 55, 68, 217, 343–44, 348
Phillips, David, 312
Pickering, Tom, 199
Pillay, Navi, 468
Ping, Jean, 493–94
Pipes, Richard, 87, 96
piracy, 268–69, 341, 398, 405–07
PKK (Kurdish independence movement), 306, 309–10, 312
Platt, Nicholas, 26, 36, 130–31, 136
Poindexter, John, 132
Poland, 90, 301
Pollution in China, 42, 172–73
Pol-Mil (Political-Military) Section, U.S. Embassy, Bangkok, 17–21

Polovchek, Walter, 99
polygraphs, 13, 132–33
Powell, Colin, 4, 137, 277, 290, 297, 299, 308–10, 319, 326, 349, 358
Powell Doctrine, 94, 276
Powers, Gary, 108
Prachanda (Pushpa Kamal Dahal), 453–56
Prendergast, Kieran, 379
Price, Ying, 210
Project Hope, 330
Project Stormfury, 55
Putin, Vladimir, 289–90, 294, 296–97, 300–01, 429–33, 495, 501–02, 511–12

Qadhafi, Muammar, 490–95, 497–98, 501
Qian Qichen, 163, 173–74, 178, 230
Quinn, Kenneth, 131

R2P (responsibility to protect) principle, 491, 494
Rahmonov, Emomali, 284–85
Rajapaksa, Gotabaya, 460–66
Rajapaksa, Mahinda, 460–66
Rakhmanin, Oleg, 89
Rather, Dan, 58
Ratner, Steve, 467
Reagan, Nancy, 95, 132, 140, 144
Reagan, Ronald, 70
Reagan administration: Soviet policies of, 87–99, 102; Taiwan policies of, 188–90; talks with Gorbachev, 4, 119, 127–47
Rees, Grover III, 192–93
Remler, Philip, 246–48, 251
Reykjavik Summit (1986), 122–23, 134–36. See also arms control
Rice, Condoleezza, 306, 349–50,

373, 377, 387, 400, 431, 480, 513
Rice, Susan, *369*, 494
Ridgeway, Roz, 137
Rieser, Tim, 349, 350
Ripley, Dillon, 56
River Elegy (film), 150
Robinson, Charles, 65
Rockefeller, Jay, 51–52, 239
Rockefeller, John D., 52
rodeo, 79–80
Rogers, William, 27, 30, 113
Romania, 28, 167, 301
Rose Revolution, 297, 300–01, 429
Rostropovich, Mstislav, 210
Roughhead, Gary, 331
Roy, Stapleton, 73, 176, 227–28, 230
Rumsfeld, Donald, 46, 275–76, 278, 284, 290, 309, 478
Rusk, Dean, 22
Russia: –China relations, 178–79, 289–92; establishment of, post–Soviet Union, 125, 179, 245; Georgia invasion by, 429–33; Georgia policy of, 294–98; Kazakhstan policy of, 288–89; Syria action by, 501–3; –U.S. future relations, 511–12; –U.S. relations of Bush/Putin, 289–92. *See also* Soviet Union
Russian language, 85, 91–92
Rwanda, 393, 491

Saakashvili, Mikhail, 297–301, 429–33, 511
SADEC (South Asia Democratic Congress), 420–21
Sakhalin Island, 99, 101, 103–4
Sakharov, Andrei, 142
SALT II agreement, 70, 73, 86, 109–10, 129. *See also* arms control

Samuel, Tamrat, 451
Sargsyan, Serzh, 252
Sarkozy, Nicolas, 431, 481, 483, 494–95, 498
Save the Children organization, 322, 325, 335
SBY. *See* Yudhoyono, Susilo Bambang (SBY)
Scali, John, 115
Schifter, Richard, 174, 178
Schrage, Barbara, 240
Schroeder, Pat, 50
Schulenburg, Michael von der, 425–27, 505
Schwartz, Adam, 338
scorpions, 184
Scowcroft, Brent, 164–66, 170, 175
SDI. *See* Strategic Defense Initiative (SDI; "Star Wars")
Selassie, Haile, 409
Senior Seminar, 145–46, 155, 199
Senkaku/Diaoyu islands, 55–56, 177
September 11, 2001, attacks (U.S.), 266–67, 271–72
Serry, Robert, 480, 482
Sestanovich, Stephen, 250
Shanghai Cooperation Organization (SCO), 291
Sharmarke, Omar, 398, 403
Sheik Sharif Sheikh Ahmad, 396–98, 403–05
Shevardnadze, Eduard, 4, 122–23, 127, 129, 133–41, 293–98
Shulman, Marshall, 12
Shultz, George, *363*; 1985 Geneva Summit and, 127–30, 134; 1986 Reykjavik Summit and, 134–36; 1987 Washington Summit, 140–43; on Daniloff, 122–23; KAL 007 tragedy and, 100–103; Pascoe's work for, 130–34; policies

on Latin America and, 143–45; Reagan/Gorbachev cooperation and, 4, 127–30; traveling with, 136–40; on U.S.–Soviet relations, 94–99
Siberian Pentecostals, 96–97
Sierra Leone, 422–27
Silver, Charles, 325
Simon, Kirby, 223
Simons, Tom, 94, 96, 100, 137, 142
Sipidan incident (2000), 267
Sloan-Kettering, 12, 14
Smith, Chris, 176
Solidarity Movement (Poland), 90
Somalia, 5–6, *368*, 391–409, 505
Somalia Monitoring Group, 408
Sooki, Yasmin, 467
Soros, George, 254, 282
South Africa, 417, 467, 494, 499–500
South Korea, 69, 106, 193–94, 204, 450, 486–87
Soviet Embassy, U.S., 62, 106–07, 114–15
Soviet Union: 1985 Geneva Summit, 108, 119, 127–30, 134, 141; 1986 Reykjavik Summit, 134–36; 1987 Washington Summit, 140–43; Afghanistan invasion by, 70, 86; –China relations, 26–27, 89–92, 151; collapse of, 125, 179, 245; Gorbachev and U.S. diplomacy with, 4, 127–47; human rights violations of, 66; *See also* Russia
Special Political Missions (SPMs), 435–36
Spellman, Gladys 50
Spelman, Doug, 224
Spier, Patsy, 350
Spratly Islands, 177
spy dust (NPPD), 116

Sri Lanka, 459–69
Sri Mulyani Indrawati, 337
Stanford Center, Taipei, Taiwan, 13
"Star Wars." *See* Strategic Defense Initiative (SDI; "Star Wars")
Status of Forces Agreement (SOFA), 17, 18, 323
Steer, Andrew, 339
Steuerle, Norma, 267
Stoessel, Walter, 27, 116
Strategic Defense Initiative (SDI; "Star Wars"), 95–96, 134–35, 138. *See also* arms control
Suharto, 317, 323, 337
Sullivan, Roger, 75
Sullivan, William, 30–31, 55
surveillance, 92, 110–11
Syria, 486, 500, 501–3, 505

Taipei American School, 208, 233
Taipei Economic and Cultural Office (TECRO), 225
Taipei Medical College, 14
Taiwan: arms sales, 188–90; –China tensions, 214–17, 223–36; as democratic nation, 202–14; economic conditions and policies in, 202–5; Taiwan Strait, 27, 189, 205, 207, 214–17, 231–36; U.S. Embassy in Taipei, 220; –U.S. relations, 81–83, 195–97, 219–20, 510. *See also* AIT (American Institute on Taiwan); China
Taiwan Relations Act, 77, 81–82, 189, 196, 223, 237
Taiwan Strait, 27, 189, 214–17, 231–36
Tajikistan, 274–75, 284–86
Talbott, Strobe, 197, 238, 241, 245, 246–48, 272, 296
Taliban, 272–76, 280, 290

Tamba, Minoru, 103–04
Tang, Nancy, 49, 59
Tangshan earthquake, 63
Tarnoff, Peter, 229–30, 241
Taylor, Charles, 425
Taylor, Jay, 34
Teng Hsiao-ping. *See* Deng Xiaoping
Ter-Petroysian, Levon, 248–51
terrorism, 266–67, 271–73, 280–81, 309, 318–19, 343–48. *See also* counterterrorism
Thailand, 15–23, 187, 254, 507
Thai language, 187
Thanksgiving, 47, 209–10
Thayer, Harry, 61, 73, 75
Tiananmen Square massacre (1989; China), 152–60
Tibet, 151, 169, 175, 177, 179, 227
Tigray, Ethiopia, 410, 413
Tigray People's Liberation Front, 409
TNI (Indonesian Army), 317, 320, 323, 326, 328, 337, 348–51
Timbie, Jim, 137
Tommy's Tours, 19–20
Tomsen, Peter, 197, 206
Trans-Caspian Pipeline, 287
Trans-Pacific Partnership, 509
Treaty of Aigun (1858), 89
Treaty of Guarantee, 438, 440
Treaty of Nerchinsk (1689), 26
Treki, Ali, 490
Trudeau, Gary, 58–59
tsunami (2004, Indonesia), 3, 319–21. 322–41. *See also* Aceh, Indonesia
Tulip Revolution, 283, 300
Tunisia, 486–88
Turkey: Cyprus settlement with, 436–45; –Israel conflict, 483–86; trading partners of, 302; –U.S relations, 303–12

Turkish-Armenian Reconciliation Commission (TARC), 312
Turkish Cypriots, 313–16, 436–45. *See also* Cyprus
Turkmenistan, 286–88
Twin Oaks, 82

Uganda, 67, 393–94
Ukraine, 430, 432–33, 511
UNAMI (UN Assistance Mission in Iraq), 473–78
UNDP (UN Development Program), 422–24
Unger, Anne, 21
Unger, Leonard, 21
UNHCR (UN High Commissioner for Refugees), 335
UNIPSIL (UN Integrated Office for Sierra Leone), 426, 427
United Nations (UN): 2005 World Summit, 375, 424, 491; Baghdad office bombing, 309; on Cyprus, 314–16; disaster relief by, 331–32, 335, 336; DPA, 373–90, 399–400, 409, 415–16, 423, 479, 504–6; DPKO, 373–87, 399–401; Human Rights Council, 467, 468; improvement of U.S. strategy with, 512–15; Iraq and, 473–78; Pascoe on UN–U.S. strategy, 512–14; Peacebuilding Commission, 424; peacekeeping mission in Somalia of, 391–405; Population Fund, 191–92; regional cooperation organizations and, 420–21; Security Council, *368*, 434–35, 490–95, 499–506; Special Political Missions, 375, 435–36
University of Kansas (KU), 11–12

Index   531

UN Law of the Sea Treaty, 403
UNMEE (UN Mission in Ethiopia and Eritrea), 410, 412
UNMIN (UN Mission in Nepal), 452–55, 457–59
UNPOS (UN Political Office in Somalia), 395, 404, 406
UNRWA (UN Relief and Works Agency), 479–81
UNSMIL (UN Support Mission in Libya), 496–99
USAID, 195, 286, 325, 328, 331, 353, 365, 367
U.S. Department of Justice, 240, 345
U.S. Embassy, Bangkok, 15–23
U.S. Embassy, Kabul, 87
U.S. Embassy, Moscow, 86–88, 96–97, 112–15
USLO (U.S. Liaison Office; China), 33, 36–63, 362
U.S. Marines, 4, 9, 13–14, 39–40, 106–07, 124, 333, 353
U.S. Mission (USUN), 242, 382, 387, 435–36, 500, 514
U.S. Navy, 4, 94, 106, 118, 125, 234, 329–30, 354, 366
USNS *Mercy*, 330–31, 367
USS *Abraham Lincoln*, 3, 323–25, 327, 329, 366, 367
USS *Bonhomme Richard*, 324, 329–330, 332–33
USS *Independence*, 234
Uzbekistan, 274–77, 278–81, 285, 434

Vance, Cyrus, 67, 70–73, 81, 195, 313–14
Vaugier, Georges, 248–49
Viera de Mello, Sergio, 249, 473
Vietnam, 17, 56, 81, 83
Vietnam War, 12, 13, 15, 19–23, 57, 68

Vogt, Margaret, 414
volcanos, 353–54
Vorobiev, Vitaly, 162

Walesa, Lech, 90
Walker, John, 118–19, 125
Wallace, Mark, 448
Wang Hung-wen (Wang Hongwen), 34
Washington Summit (1987), 140–43. *See also* arms control
Watergate crisis, 34
Watson, Thomas, 88
Webster, William, 109
Weinberger, Caspar, 87, 102, 110, 131–32
Weinberger Doctrine, 94
Westinghouse, 211
Weston, Thomas, 314–15
Wilbur, Martin, 12
Wilham, Denis, 103
Wolf, Frank, 176
Wolfowitz, Paul, 328–29, 349
Wood, Jim, 236–41, 245, 256–57
Woodcock, Leonard, 73–74
World Food Program (WFP), 408, 448
World Health Organization (WHO), 196, 355–56
World Trade Center, New York City, attacks (2001), 271–72, 274–75
World Trade Organization (WTO), 183, 202
Wu, Harry, 228

Xi Jinping, 56, 291, 502
Xinjiang, 177, 179, 227, 509

Y2K, 265–66
Yang Jiechi, 169, 176, 449
Yao Wen-yuan, 57

Yeltsin, Boris, 101, 105–6, 114–15, 139, 147, 193–94, 251
Yemane Ghebreab, 412
Yemen, 486, 505
Yogyakarta, Indonesia, 353, *367*
Young, Steve, 222
Young Turks, 301
Yudhoyono, Susilo Bambang (SBY), 318–20, 323, 332, 336–39, 341, 349–51
Yukalov, Yuri, 248, 251
Yurchenko, Vitaly, 118–19, 120

Zagoria, Don, 12
Zakharov, Gennadi, 122–123
Zerihoun, Taye-Brook, 439
Zhang Yijun, 169, 176
Zhao Ziyang, 149, 150
Zhu Rongji, 158, 179–80, 190
Zhvania, Zurab, 297, 299
Zimmerman, Warren, 93
Zuma, Jacob, 493, 495

www.ingramcontent.com/pod-product-compliance
Lightning Source LLC
Chambersburg PA
CBHW051106230426
43667CB00014B/2460